T0213701

Lecture Notes in Computer Science　　9714

Commenced Publication in 1973
Founding and Former Series Editors:
Gerhard Goos, Juris Hartmanis, and Jan van Leeuwen

Editorial Board

David Hutchison
  Lancaster University, Lancaster, UK
Takeo Kanade
  Carnegie Mellon University, Pittsburgh, PA, USA
Josef Kittler
  University of Surrey, Guildford, UK
Jon M. Kleinberg
  Cornell University, Ithaca, NY, USA
Friedemann Mattern
  ETH Zurich, Zürich, Switzerland
John C. Mitchell
  Stanford University, Stanford, CA, USA
Moni Naor
  Weizmann Institute of Science, Rehovot, Israel
C. Pandu Rangan
  Indian Institute of Technology, Madras, India
Bernhard Steffen
  TU Dortmund University, Dortmund, Germany
Demetri Terzopoulos
  University of California, Los Angeles, CA, USA
Doug Tygar
  University of California, Berkeley, CA, USA
Gerhard Weikum
  Max Planck Institute for Informatics, Saarbrücken, Germany

More information about this series at http://www.springer.com/series/7409

Ying Tan · Yuhui Shi (Eds.)

Data Mining and Big Data

First International Conference, DMBD 2016
Bali, Indonesia, June 25–30, 2016
Proceedings

 Springer

Editors
Ying Tan
Peking University
Beijing
China

Yuhui Shi
Xi'an Jiaotong-Liverpool University
Suzhou
China

ISSN 0302-9743   ISSN 1611-3349   (electronic)
Lecture Notes in Computer Science
ISBN 978-3-319-40972-6   ISBN 978-3-319-40973-3   (eBook)
DOI 10.1007/978-3-319-40973-3

Library of Congress Control Number: 2016942014

LNCS Sublibrary: SL3 – Information Systems and Applications, incl. Internet/Web, and HCI

© Springer International Publishing Switzerland 2016
This work is subject to copyright. All rights are reserved by the Publisher, whether the whole or part of the material is concerned, specifically the rights of translation, reprinting, reuse of illustrations, recitation, broadcasting, reproduction on microfilms or in any other physical way, and transmission or information storage and retrieval, electronic adaptation, computer software, or by similar or dissimilar methodology now known or hereafter developed.
The use of general descriptive names, registered names, trademarks, service marks, etc. in this publication does not imply, even in the absence of a specific statement, that such names are exempt from the relevant protective laws and regulations and therefore free for general use.
The publisher, the authors and the editors are safe to assume that the advice and information in this book are believed to be true and accurate at the date of publication. Neither the publisher nor the authors or the editors give a warranty, express or implied, with respect to the material contained herein or for any errors or omissions that may have been made.

Printed on acid-free paper

This Springer imprint is published by Springer Nature
The registered company is Springer International Publishing AG Switzerland

Preface

This volume constitutes the proceedings of the International Conference on Data Mining and Big Data (DMBD 2016), which was held in conjunction with the 7th International Conference on Swarm Intelligence (ICSI 2016), during June 25–30, 2016, at Padma Resort in Legian, Bali, Indonesia.

The theme of DMBD 2016 was "Serving Life with Data Science." Data mining refers to the activity of going through big data sets to look for relevant or pertinent information. This type of activity is a good example of the axiom "looking for a needle in a haystack." The idea is that businesses collect massive sets of data that may be homogeneous or automatically collected. Decision-makers need access to smaller, more specific pieces of data from these large sets. They use data mining to uncover the pieces of information that will inform leadership and help chart the course for a business. Big data contains a huge amount of data and information and is worth researching in depth. Big data, also known as massive data or mass data, refers to the amount of data involved that are too great to be interpreted by a human. However, the methods to process big data are ineffective. Currently, the suitable technologies include data mining, A/B testing, crowdsourcing, data fusion and integration, genetic algorithms, machine learning, natural language processing, signal processing, simulation, time series analysis, and visualization. But real or near-real-time information delivery is one of the defining characteristics of big data analytics. It is important to find new methods to enhance the effectiveness of big data. With the advent of big data analysis and intelligent computing techniques we are facing new challenges to make the information transparent and understandable efficiently. DMBD 2016 provided an excellent opportunity and an academic forum for academia and practitioners to present and discuss the latest scientific results, methods, and innovative ideas and advantages in theories, technologies, and applications in data mining, big data, and intelligent computing. The technical program covered all aspects of data mining, big data, and swarm intelligence as well as intelligent computing methods applied to all fields of computer science, signal/information processing, machine learning, data mining and knowledge discovery, robotics, big data, scheduling, game theory, parallel realization, etc.

DMBD 2016 took place at Padma Resort in Legian, Bali, Indonesia. Bali is a famous Indonesian island with the provincial capital at Denpasar. Lying between Java to the west and Lombok to the east, this island is renowned for its volcanic lakes, spectacular rice terraces, stunning tropical beaches, ancient temples, and palaces, as well as dance and elaborate religious festivals. Bali is also the largest tourist destination in the country and is renowned for his highly developed arts, including traditional and modern dance, sculpture, painting, leather, metalworking, and music. Since the late 20th century, the province has had a big rise in tourism. Bali received the Best Island Award from *Travel and Leisure* in 2010. The island of Bali won because of its attractive surroundings (both mountain and coastal areas), diverse tourist attractions, excellent international and local restaurants, and the friendliness of the local people. According to BBC Travel released in 2011, Bali is one of the world's best islands!

DMBD 2016 received 115 submissions from about 278 authors in 36 countries and regions (Algeria, Australia, Bangladesh, Brazil, Chile, China, Colombia, Egypt, France, Germany, Greece, India, Indonesia, Iraq, Ireland, Japan, Kazakhstan, Republic of Korea, Luxembourg, Malaysia, Norway, Poland, Portugal, Romania, Russian Federation, Singapore, Slovakia, South Africa, Spain, Sweden, Chinese Taiwan, Tunisia, Turkey, UK, USA, Vietnam) across six continents (Asia, Europe, North America, South America, Africa, and Oceania). Each submission was reviewed by at least two reviewers, and on average 2.8 reviewers. Based on rigorous reviews by the Program Committee members and reviewers, 57 high-quality papers were selected for publication in this proceedings volume with an acceptance rate of 49.57 %. The papers are organized in 10 cohesive sections covering all major topics of the research and development of data mining and big data and one Workshop on Computational Aspects of Pattern Recognition and Computer Vision.

As organizers of DMBD 2016, we would like to express sincere thanks to Peking University and Xian Jiaotong-Liverpool University for their sponsorship, and to Beijing Xinghui Hi-Tech Co. for its co-sponsorship as well as to the IEEE Computational Intelligence Society, World Federation on Soft Computing, and International Neural Network Society, IEEE Beijing section for their technical co-sponsorship. We would also like to thank the members of the Advisory Committee for their guidance, the members of the international Program Committee and additional reviewers for reviewing the papers, and the members of the Publications Committee for checking the accepted papers in a short period of time. We are especially grateful to the proceedings publisher Springer for publishing the proceedings in the prestigious series of *Lecture Notes in Computer Science.* Moreover, we wish to express our heartfelt appreciation to the plenary speakers, session chairs, and student helpers. In addition, there are still many more colleagues, associates, friends, and supporters who helped us in immeasurable ways; we express our sincere gratitude to them all. Last but not the least, we would like to thank all the speakers, authors, and participants for their great contributions that made DMBD 2016 successful and all the hard work worthwhile.

May 2016   Ying Tan
                                                                          Yuhui Shi

Organization

General Chairs

Ying Tan   Peking University, China
Russ Eberhart   IUPUI, USA

General Program Committee Chair

Yuhui Shi   Xi'an Jiaotong-Liverpool University, China

Technical Committee Co-chairs

Haibo He   University of Rhode Island Kingston, USA
Martin Middendorf   University of Leipzig, Germany
Xiaodong Li   RMIT University, Australia
Hideyuki Takagi   Kyushu University, Japan
Ponnuthurai Nagaratnam   Nanyang Technological University, Singapore
  Suganthan
Kay Chen Tan   National University of Singapore, Singapore

Special Sessions Co-chairs

Shi Cheng   Nottingham University Ningbo, China
Yuan Yuan   Chinese Academy of Sciences, China

Publications Co-chairs

Radu-Emil Precup   Politehnica University of Timisoara, Romania
Swagatham Das   Indian Statistical Institute, India

Plenary Session Co-chairs

Nikola Kasabov   Auckland University of Technology, New Zealand
Rachid Chelouah   EISTI, France

Tutorial Chair

Milan Tuba   University of Belgrade, Serbia

Publicity Co-chairs

Yew-Soon Ong   Nanyang Technological University, Singapore
Pramod Kumar Singh   Indian Institute of Information Technology
                              and Management, India
Eugene Semenkin   Siberian Aerospace University, Russia
Somnuk Phon-Amnuaisuk   Institut Teknologi Brunei, Brunei

Finance and Registration Co-chairs

Andreas Janecek   University of Vienna, Austria
Chao Deng   Peking University, China
Suicheng Gu   Google Corporation, USA

DMBD 2016 Program Committee

Mohd Helmy Abd Wahab   Universiti Tun Hussein Onn, Malaysia
Miltiadis Alamaniotis   Purdue University, USA
Rafael Alcala   University of Granada, Spain
Tomasz Andrysiak   UTP Bydgoszcz, Poland
Duong Tuan Anh   HoChiMinh City University of Technology, Vietnam
Carmelo J.A. Bastos Filho   University of Pernambuco, Brazil
Vladimir Bukhtoyarov   Siberian State Aerospace University, Russia
David Camacho   Universidad Autonoma de Madrid, Spain
Jinde Cao   Southeast University, China
Carlos Costa   University of Minho, Portugal
Jose Alfredo Ferreira Costa Universidade Federal do Rio Grande do Norte, Brazil
Bogusław Cyganek   AGH University of Science and Technology, Poland
Kusum Deep   Indian Institute of Technology Roorkee, India
Mingcong Deng   Tokyo University of Agriculture and Technology,
                              Japan
Pragya Dwivedi   JNU New Delhi, India
Jianwu Fang   Xi'an Institute of Optics and Precision Mechanics
                              of CAS, China
Fangyu Gai   National University of Defense Technology, China
Teresa Guarda   Isla - Superior Institute of Languages and
                              Administration of Leiria, Portugal
Cem Iyigun   Middle East Technical University, Turkey
Dariusz Jankowski   Wrocław University of Technology, Poland
Mingyan Jiang   Shandong University, China
Imed Kacem   LCOMS - Université de Lorraine, France
Kalinka Kaloyanova   University of Sofia - FMI, Bulgaria
Jong Myon Kim   School of Electrical Engineering, South Korea
Pawel Ksieniewicz   Wroclaw University of Technology, Poland
Germano Lambert-Torres   PS Solutions, Brazil
Bin Li   University of Science and Technology of China, China

Andrei Lihu	Politehnica University of Timisoara, Romania
Shu-Chiang Lin	National Taiwan University of Science and Technology, Taiwan
Bin Liu	Nanjing University of Post and Telecommunications, China
Wenlian Lu	Fudan University, China
Wenjian Luo	University of Science and Technology of China, China
Wojciech Macyna	Wroclaw University of Technology, Poland
Michalis Mavrovouniotis	De Montfort University, UK
Mohamed Arezki Mellal	M'Hamed Bougara University, Algeria
Sanaz Mostaghim	Institute IWS, Germany
Maria Muntean	1 Decembrie 1918 University of Alba Iulia, Romania
Sheak Rashed Haider Noori	Daffodil International University, Bangladesh
Benoit Otjacques	Luxembourg Institute of Science and Technology, Luxembourg
Piotr Porwik	University of Silesia, Poland
Wei Qin	Shanghai Jiao Tong University, China
Vignesh Raja	CDAC, India
Mohamed Salah Gouider	Institut Supérieur de Gestion de Tunis, Tunisia
Volkmar Schau	Friedrich Schiller University of Jena, Germany
Ivan Silva	University of São Paulo, Brazil
Pramod Kumar Singh	ABV-IIITM Gwalior, India
Hung-Min Sun	National Tsing Hua University, Taiwan
Ying Tan	Peking University, China
Christos Tjortjis	International Hellenic University, Greece
Paulo Trigo	ISEL, Portugal
Milan Tuba	University of Belgrade, Serbia
Agnieszka Turek	Warsaw University of Technology, Poland
Gai-Ge Wang	Jiangsu Normal University, China
Guoyin Wang	Chongqing University of Posts and Telecommunications, China
Lei Wang	Tongji University, China
Qi Wang	Northwestern Polytechnical University, China
Xiaoying Wang	Changshu Institute of Technology, China
Yong Wang	Zhongnan University, China
Ka-Chun Wong	City University of Hong Kong, SAR China
Michal Wozniak	Wroclaw University of Technology, Poland
Bo Xing	University of Johannesburg, South Africa
Bing Xue	Victoria University of Wellington, New Zealand
Yingjie Yang	De Montfort University, UK
Kiwon Yeom	NASA Ames Research Center, USA
Jie Zhang	Newcastle University, UK
Qieshi Zhang	Waseda University, Japan
Yujun Zheng	Zhejiang University of Technology, China

| Cui Zhihua | Complex System and Computational Intelligence Laboratory, China |
| Huiyu Zhou | Queen's University Belfast, UK |

Additional Reviewers

Andrysiak, Tomasz
Burduk, Robert
Hu, Jianqiang
Jackowski, Konrad
Jiang, Zhiyu
Koziarski, Michał
Li, Rui
Loruenser, Thomas
Shi, Xinli

Wan, Ying
Wang, Yi
Wozniak, Michal
Yakhchi, Shahpar
Yan, Shankai
Zawoad, Shams
Zhao, Yang
Zhong, Jie

Contents

Data Visualization Analysis

Privacy Policy

Social Media

Query Optimization and Processing Algorithm

Big Data

Computational Aspects of Pattern Recognition and Computer Vision

Challenges in Data Mining and Big Data

Evolutionary Computation and Big Data: Key Challenges and Future Directions

Shi Cheng[1]([✉]), Bin Liu[2], Yuhui Shi[3], Yaochu Jin[4], and Bin Li[5]

[1] School of Computer Science, Shaanxi Normal University, Xi'an, China
cheng@snnu.edu.cn
[2] School of Computer Science and Technology,
Nanjing University of Posts and Telecommunications, Nanjing, China
bins@ieee.org
[3] Department of Electrical and Electronic Engineering,
Xi'an Jiaotong-Liverpool University, Suzhou, China
yuhui.shi@xjtlu.edu.cn
[4] Department of Computing, University of Surrey, Guildford, Surrey, UK
yaochu.jin@surrey.ac.uk
[5] University of Science and Technology of China, Hefei, China
binli@ustc.edu.cn

Abstract. Over the past few years, big data analytics has received increasing attention in all most all scientific research fields. This paper discusses the synergies between big data and evolutionary computation (EC) algorithms, including swarm intelligence and evolutionary algorithms. We will discuss the combination of big data analytics and EC algorithms, such as the application of EC algorithms to solving big data analysis problems and the use of data analysis methods for designing new EC algorithms or improving the performance of EC algorithms. Based on the combination of EC algorithms and data mining techniques, we understand better the insights of data analytics, and design more efficient algorithms to solve real-world big data analytics problems. Also, the weakness and strength of EC algorithms could be analyzed via the data analytics along the optimization process, a crucial entity in EC algorithms. Key challenges and future directions in combining big data and EC algorithms are discussed.

Keywords: Big data analytics · Data science · Evolutionary algorithms · Evolutionary computation · Swarm intelligence

1 Introduction

Nowadays, big data has been attracting increasing attention from academia, industry and government [2,20,36]. Big data is defined as the dataset whose size is beyond the processing ability of traditional databases or computers. Four elements are emphasized in the definition, which are capture, storage, management, and analysis [26]. The focus of the four elements is the last stage, the big

© Springer International Publishing Switzerland 2016
Y. Tan and Y. Shi (Eds.): DMBD 2016, LNCS 9714, pp. 3–14, 2016.
DOI: 10.1007/978-3-319-40973-3_1

data analytics, which is about automatic extraction of knowledge from a large amount of data.

Big data analysis can be seen as mining or processing of massive data, thereby retrieving "useful" information from large dataset [29]. Big data analytics can be characterized by several properties, such as large volume, variety of different sources, and fast increasing speed (velocity) [26]. It is of great interest to investigate the role of evolutionary computation (EC) techniques, including evolutionary algorithms and swarm intelligence for the optimization and learning involving big data, in particular, the ability of EC techniques to solve large scale, dynamic, and sometimes multiobjective big data analytics problems.

Traditional methods for data analysis are based mainly on mathematical models and data is then collected to fit the models. With the growth of the variety of temporal data, these mathematical models may become ineffective in solving problems. The paradigm should shift from the model-driven to the data-driven approach. The data-driven approach not only focuses on predicting what is going to happen, but also concentrates on what is happening right now and how to be prepared for future events.

With the amount of data growing constantly and exponentially, the current data processing tasks are beyond the computing ability of traditional computational models. The data science, or more specifically, the big data analytics, has received more and more attention from researchers. The data are easily generated and gathered, while the volume of data is increasing very quickly. It exceeds the computational capacity of current systems to validate, analyze, visualize, store, and extract information. To analyze these massive data, there are several kinds of difficulties, such as the large volume of data, dynamical changes of data, data noise, *etc.* New and efficient algorithms should be designed to handle massive data analytics problems.

Evolutionary computation (EC) algorithms, which include swarm intelligence and evolutionary algorithms, are a set of search and optimization techniques [13,14,22]. To search a problem domain, an EC algorithm processes a population of individuals. Different from traditional single-point based algorithms such as hill-climbing algorithms, each EC algorithm is a population-based algorithm, which consists of a set of points (population of individuals). Each individual represents a potential solution to the problem being optimized. The population of individuals is expected to have high tendency to move towards better and better solution areas over iterations through cooperation and competition among themselves.

In this paper, we present the analysis of the relationship from data science to evolutionary computation algorithms, which include swarm intelligence and evolutionary algorithms. EC algorithms could be applied to optimize the data mining problems or to handle data directly. In evolutionary computation algorithms, individuals move through a solution space and search for solution(s) for the data mining task. The algorithm could be utilized to optimize the data mining problem, e.g., the parameter tuning. The EC algorithms could be directly applied to the data samples, e.g., subset data extraction. With the EC algorithms, more effective methods can be designed and utilized in massive data analytics.

In evolutionary computation algorithms, solutions are spread in the search space. Each solution can also be considered as a data point in the search space; the distribution of solutions can be utilized to reveal the landscape of a problem. Data analysis techniques have been exploited to design new swarm intelligence/evolutionary algorithms, such as brain storm optimization algorithm [30,31] and estimation of distribution algorithms [17,28].

The aim of this paper is to analyze the association between big data analytics and evolutionary computation (EC) algorithms. The possible directions of utilizing evolutionary computation algorithms on data science and applying data science methods for EC algorithms will be discussed. The remaining of the paper is organized as follows. Section 2 reviews the basic concepts of big data analytics methods. Section 3 discusses the key challenges of the combination on EC algorithms and big data analytics. Section 4 analysis the future directions of EC algorithms utilized to optimize data science methods and data analysis methods utilized to analyze EC algorithms, followed by conclusions in Sect. 5.

2   Big Data Analytics

Currently, data science or big data analytics is a popular topic in computer science and statistics. It concerns with a wide variety of data processing tasks, such as data collection, data management, data analysis, data visualization, and real-world applications.

The data science is a fusion of computer science and statistics. The statistics is the study of the collection, analysis, interpretation, presentation, and organization of data [12]. From the perspective of statistics research, the data science has the same objectives as the statistics, except that the data science emphasizes more on volume, and the variety of data. The data science is more like a synonym of big data research. From the perspective of statistics, there are two aims in data analyses [12]:

– Prediction: To predict the response/output of future input variables;
– Inference: To deduce the association among response variables and input variables.

From the perspective of computer science research, the data science is more practical. The phrase "data mining" is often used to indicate the data science tasks. The process of converting raw data into useful information, termed as knowledge discovery in databases. Data mining, which is data analysis process of knowledge discovery, attempts to discover useful information (or patterns) in large data repositories [15].

The statistics and data science both focus on the study of the extraction of knowledge from data. The main difference is that the data in data science are increasingly heterogeneous and unstructured [10].

EC algorithms, which include evolutionary algorithms and swarm intelligence, are a set of search and optimization techniques [14,22]. To search a problem domain, a swarm intelligence algorithm processes a population of individuals. Each swarm intelligence algorithm is a population-based algorithm, which consists of a set of points (individuals). Each individual represents a potential solution to the problem being optimized. The population of individuals is expected to have high tendency to move towards better and better solution areas over iterations through cooperation and competition among themselves.

3   Key Challenges

The aim of evolutionary computation and big data analytics is to combine the strengths of EC algorithms and data science techniques. It has two meanings: potential applications of evolutionary computation algorithms in the big data analytics and big data analytics techniques in enhancing evolutionary computation algorithms. With the data analytics during the optimization process, the relationship between the algorithm and problems could be revealed. The EC algorithms could be utilized to solve real-world big data analytics problems [6,7].

3.1   Data-Driven Evolutionary Computation Algorithms

In general, most of the EC algorithms share a similar framework and usually involve the following two phases [18]:

1. Generate candidate solutions (e.g., random initialization) according to a specified probabilistic distribution.
2. Update the explicit or implicit model, on the basis of the information (solutions and their fitness values) collected in the previous/current step, to guide the future search toward "better" solutions.

This framework could obtain "good enough" solutions for problems with low dimensions or simple landscape. However, with the developments of evolutionary computation techniques, problems with more complex structures and large-scale data are arising in real-world applications. To handle the new challenges of optimization problem, more efficient and adaptive algorithms should be designed. For the traditional algorithms, there are several obstacles need to overcome for this framework:

1. Not much problem specific information is used: algorithms with the same parameters and structure are used to solve different kinds of problems. The problem's information is not taken advantage of during the search process.
2. The algorithms need a balance between short and long time memory. There are two kinds of memories which are used in EC algorithms: the short time memory, e.g., the previous solutions (parent generation in genetic algorithm, previous position in particle swarm optimization algorithm) and the long time memory, e.g., the personal best position.

3. Only the fitness of objective function is used to guide the search. Normally, the individuals with the better fitness values have more possibility to reserve in next iteration, and other individuals are more likely to be abandoned during the search.

With the development of big data analytics techniques, more data could be stored and more unstructured information could be analyzed. The EC algorithms could be understood better and improved through the information analyses during the search. The paradigm in data-driven EC algorithms seems to be: collect a (massive) dataset, design an explicit or implicit model such as evolutionary algorithm or particle swarm optimization algorithm that can propagate search information from one individual to another, and finally converge to some good enough solutions until time runs out.

The meta-heuristics algorithms could be roughly divided into two categories: instance-based search and model-based search [18,37]. Most of the traditional search methods, such as simulated annealing and iterated local search, could be classified into instance-based search, which the new candidate solutions are generated using solely the current solution or the current group of solutions. For the recently meta-heuristics algorithms, such as ant colony optimization and estimation of distribution algorithms, could be classified as model-based search. In model-based search, candidate solutions are generated using an explicit or implicit model, which is updated using the information of previously solutions. The search is guided to concentrate on the regions containing high quality solutions iteration over iteration.

Figure 1 gives a framework of data-driven EC algorithms. Each candidate solution is a data sample from the search space. The model could be designed or adjusted via the data analysis on the previous solutions. The landscape or the difficulty of a problem could be obtained during the search, i.e., the problem could be understood better. With the learning process, more suitable algorithms could be designed to solve different problems, thus, the performance of optimization could be improved.

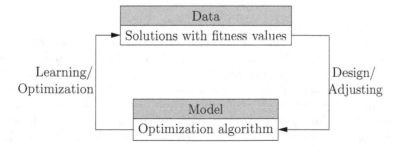

Fig. 1. A framework for data-driven evolutionary computation algorithms.

Massive information exists during the search process. For EC algorithms, there are several individuals existed at the same time, and each individual has a corresponding fitness value. The individuals are created iteration over iteration. There is also massive volume of information on the "origin" of an individual, such as that an individual was created by applying which strategy and parameters to which former individual(s). The data-driven EC algorithm is a new approach to analyze and guide the search in evolutionary algorithms/swarm intelligence. These strategies could be divided into off-line methods and online methods. An off-line method is based on the analysis of previous storage search history, such as history based topological speciation for multimodal optimization [25] or maintaining and processing submodels (MAPS) based estimation of distribution algorithm on multimodal problems [32]. While for an online method, the parameters could be adaptively changed during the different search states.

3.2   EC on Solving Data Analytics Problems

The big data analytics is a new research area of information processing, however, the problems of big data analytics have been studied in other research fields for decades under a different title. The rough association between big data analytics and evolutionary computation algorithms can be established and shown in Table 1.

Table 1. The rough association between big data analytics and evolutionary computation algorithms.

Big data analytics	Evolutionary computation algorithms
Volume	Large scale/high dimension
Variety	
Velocity	Dynamic environment
Veracity	Noise/uncertain/surrogates
Value	Fitness/objective

The characteristics of the big data analytics are summarized into several words, which are volume, variety, velocity, veracity, and value. These complexities are a collection of different research problems that existed for decades. Corresponding to the EC algorithms, the volume and the variety mean large-scale and high dimensional data; the velocity means data is rapidly changing, like an optimization problem in dynamic environment; the veracity means data is inconsistent and/or incomplete, like an optimization problem with noise or approximation; and the value is the objective of the big data analytics, like the fitness or objective function in an optimization problem.

The big data analytics is an extension of data mining techniques on a large amount of data. Data mining has been a popular academic topic in computer science and statistics for decades. The swarm intelligence and evolutionary algorithms are subfields of evolutionary computation techniques which study the collective intelligence in a group of simple individuals. Like data mining, in the evolutionary computation algorithms, useful information can be obtained from the competition and cooperation of individuals.

The key challenges of EC solving big data analytics problems could be divided into four elements: handling a large amount of data, handling high dimensional data, handling dynamical data, and multiobjective optimization. Most real world big data problems can be modeled as a large scale, dynamical, and multiobjective problems.

Handling Large Amount of Data. The big data analysis requires a fast mining on a large scale dataset, i.e., the immense amount of data should be processed in a limited time to reveal useful information. As the computing power improves, more volume of data can be processed. The more data are retrieved and processed, the better understanding of problems can be obtained.

The analytic problem can be modeled as an optimization problem. An evolutionary computation algorithm is a search process based on the previous experiences. To reveal knowledge from a large volume of data within the big data context, the search ranges of the solved problem have to be widened and even extended to the extreme.

A quick scan is critical to solve the problem with massive data sets. Evolutionary computation algorithms are techniques based on the sampling of the search space. Through the meta-heuristics rules, data samples are chosen from the massive data space. From these representative data samples, the problem structure could be obtained. Based on the evolutionary computation algorithms, we could find a "good enough" solution with a high search speed to solve the problem with a large volume of data.

A large amount of data does not necessarily mean high dimensional data, and a high volume of data can accumulate in single dimension such as high frequency data sampled by sensors with higher resolutions.

Handling High Dimensional Problems. In general, the optimization problem concerns with finding the best available solution(s) for a given problem within allowable time, and the problem may have several or numerous optimal solutions, of which many are local optimal solutions. Normally, the problem will become more difficult with the growth of the number of variables and objectives. Specially, problems with a large number of variables, e.g., more than a thousand variables, are termed as large scale problems.

Many optimization methods suffer from the "curse of dimensionality", which implies that their performance deteriorates quickly as the dimension of the search space increases [3, 11, 16, 24]. There are several reasons that cause this phenomenon.

The solution space of a problem often increases exponentially with the problem dimension and thus more efficient search strategies are required to explore all promising regions within a given time budget. An evolutionary computation algorithm is based on the interaction of a group of solutions. The promising regions or the landscape of problems are very difficult to reveal by small solution samples (compared with the number of all feasible solutions).

The characteristics of a problem may also change with the scale. The problem will become more difficult and complex when the dimension increases. Rosenbrock's function, for instance, is unimodal for two dimensional problems but becomes multimodal for higher dimensional problems. Because of such a worsening of the features of an optimization problem resulting from an increase in scale, a previously successful search strategy may no longer be capable of finding an optimal solution. Fortunately, an approximate result with a high speed may be better than an accurate result with a tardy speed. Evolutionary computation algorithms can find a good-enough solution rapidly, which is the strength of the EC algorithms in solving the big data analytics problems.

A data mining problem can be modeled as an optimization problem, and the research results of the large scale optimization problems can also be transferred to data mining problems. In evolutionary computation algorithms, many effective strategies are proposed for high dimensional optimization problems, such as problem decomposition and subcomponents cooperation [34], parameter adaptation [35], and surrogate-based fitness evaluations [21]. Especially, the particle swarm optimization or ant colony optimization algorithms can be used in the data mining to solve single objective [1] and multiobjective problems [9].

In the EC algorithms, the problem of handing a large amount of data and/or high dimensional data can be represented as large scale problems, i.e., problems with massive variables to be optimized. Based on the EC algorithms, an effective method could find good solutions for large scale problems, in terms of both the time complexity and the result accuracy.

Handling Dynamical Problems. The big data, such as the web usage data of the Internet and real time traffic information, rapidly changes over time. The analytical algorithms need to process these data swiftly. The dynamic problems are sometimes also termed as non-stationary environment [27] or uncertain environment [19] problems. The EC algorithms have been widely applied to solve both stationary and dynamical optimization problems [33].

The EC algorithms often have to deal with the optimization problems in the presence of a wide range of uncertainties. Generally, uncertainties in the problems can be divided into the following categories.

1. The fitness function or the processed data is noisy.
2. The design variables and/or the environmental parameters may change over the optimization process, and the quality of the obtained optimal solution should be robust against environmental changes or deviations from the optimal point.
3. The fitness function is approximated, such as surrogate-based fitness evaluations. The fitness function suffers from the approximation errors.
4. The optimum in the problem space may change over time. The algorithm should be able to track the optimum continuously.

5. The optimization target may change over time. The computing demands need to adjust to the dynamical environment. For example, there should be a balance between the computing efficiency and the power consumption for different computing loads.

In all these cases, additional measures must be taken so that the EC algorithms are still able to solve the dynamic problems satisfactorily [4,19].

Handling Multiobjective Problems. A general multiobjective optimization problem (MOP) or a many objective optimization problem (MaOP) can be described as a vector function **f** that maps a tuple of n parameters (decision variables) to a tuple of k objectives.

Different sources of data are integrated in the big data research, and for the majority of the big data analytics problems, more than one objective need to be satisfied at the same time. In a multiobjective optimization problem, we aim to find the set of optimal trade-off solutions known as the Pareto optimal set. Pareto optimality is defined with respect to the concept of nondominated points in the objective space. EC algorithms are particularly suitable to solve multiobjective optimization problems because they deal simultaneously with a set of possible solutions. This allows us to find an entire set of Pareto optimal set in a single run of the algorithm, instead of having to perform a series of separate runs as in the case of the traditional mathematical programming techniques [8,23]. Additionally, EC algorithms are less susceptible to the shape or continuity of the Pareto front.

4   Future Directions

The future direction is combining the strengths of EC algorithms and big data analytics to design new algorithms on the optimization or data analytics.

4.1   EC Algorithms for Big Data Problems

The big data is created in many areas in our everyday life. The big data analytics problem not only occurs in Internet data mining, but also in complex engineering or design problems [5]. The big data problem could be analyzed from the perspective of computational intelligence and meta-heuristic global optimization [36]. A real-world application could be modeled as a multiobjecitve, dynamic, large scale optimization problem. It is recognized that the EC algorithms are good ways to handle this kind of problems. Based on the utilization of EC algorithms, the real-world system will be more efficient and effective [6, 7].

4.2   Big Data Analytics for EC Algorithms

A population of individuals in EC algorithms is utilized to evolve the optimized functions or goals by cooperative and competitive interaction among individuals.

Massive information exists during the search process, such as the distribution of individuals and the fitness of each solution. To improve the search efficiency or to recognize the search state, the data generated in the optimization process should be analyzed.

The following list gives some directions on the combination of big data analytics and evolutionary computation:

1. High-dimensional and many-objective evolutionary optimization;
2. Big data driven optimization of complex engineering systems;
3. Integrative analytics of diverse, structured and unstructured data;
4. Extracting new understanding from real-time, distributed, diverse and large-scale data resources;
5. Big data visualization and visual data analytics;
6. Scalable, incremental learning and understanding of big data;
7. Scalable learning techniques for big data;
8. Big data driven optimization of complex systems;
9. Human-computer interaction and collaboration in big data;
10. Big data and cloud computing;
11. Cross-connections of big data analysis and hardware;
12. GPU-based EC algorithms;
13. Big data techniques for business intelligence, finance, healthcare, bioinformatics, intelligent transportation, smart city, smart sensor networks, cyber security and other critical application areas;
14. MapReduce implementations combined with evolutionary computation algorithms approaches.

5   Conclusions

In evolutionary computation (EC) algorithms, a population of individuals is utilized to evolve the optimized functions or goals by cooperative and competitive interaction among individuals. Massive information exists during the search process, such as the distribution of individuals and the fitness of each solution. To improve the search efficiency or to recognize the search state, the data generated in the optimization process should be analyzed.

With the amount of data growing constantly and exponentially, the data processing tasks have been beyond the computing ability of traditional computational models. To handle these massive data, i.e., deal with the big data analytics problem, more effective and efficient methods should be designed. There is no complex mathematical model in evolutionary computation algorithms. The algorithm is updated based on few iterative rules and the evaluation of solution samples. The massive data analytics may be benefited from these properties because massive data are difficult or impossible to be represented by mathematical models.

In this paper, the connection between big data analytics and evolutionary computation algorithms was discussed. The potential applications of the EC algorithms in the big data analytics and the big data analytics techniques in EC algorithms were analyzed. The big data analytics involves prediction or inference on a large amount of data. Most real world big data problems can be modeled as a large scale, dynamical, and multiobjective problems. EC algorithms study the collective behaviors in a group of individuals. With the combination of big data analytics and evolutionary computation algorithms, more rapid and effective methods can be designed to solve optimization and data analytics problem.

Acknowledgments. This work is partially supported by National Natural Science Foundation of China under Grant Numbers 60975080, 61273367, 61571238, and 61302158.

References

1. Abraham, A., Grosan, C., Ramos, V. (eds.): Swarm Intelligence in Data Mining, Studies in Computational Intelligence, vol. 34. Springer, Heidelberg (2006)
2. Alexander, F.J., Hoisie, A., Szalay, A.: Big data. Comput. Sci. Eng. **13**(6), 10–13 (2011)
3. Bellman, R.: Adaptive Control Processes: A guided Tour. Princeton University Press, Princeton (1961)
4. Bui, L.T., Michalewicz, Z., Parkinson, E., Abello, M.B.: Adaptation in dynamic environments: a case study in mission planning. IEEE Trans. Evol. Comput. **16**(2), 190–209 (2012)
5. Chai, T., Jin, Y., Sendhoff, B.: Evolutionary complex engineering optimization: opportunities and challenges. IEEE Comput. Intell. Mag. **8**(3), 12–15 (2013)
6. Cheng, S., Shi, Y., Qin, Q., Bai, R.: Swarm intelligence in big data analytics. In: Yin, H., Tang, K., Gao, Y., Klawonn, F., Lee, M., Weise, T., Li, B., Yao, X. (eds.) IDEAL 2013. LNCS, vol. 8206, pp. 417–426. Springer, Heidelberg (2013)
7. Cheng, S., Zhang, Q., Qin, Q.: Big data analytic with swarm intelligence. Ind. Manag. Data Syst. **116**(4) (2016, in press)
8. Coello, C.A.C., Lamont, G.B., Veldhuizen, D.A.V.: Evolutionary Algorithms for Solving Multi-Objective Problems. Genetic and Evolutionary Computation Series, 2nd edn. Springer, New York (2007)
9. Coello, C.A.C., Dehuri, S., Ghosh, S. (eds.): Swarm Intelligence for Multi-objective Problems in Data Mining, Studies in Computational Intelligence, vol. 242. Springer, Heidelberg (2009)
10. Dhar, V.: Data science and prediction. Commun. ACM **56**(12), 64–73 (2013)
11. Domingos, P.: A few useful things to know about machine learning. Commun. ACM **55**(10), 78–87 (2012)
12. Donoho, D.L.: 50 years of data science. Technical report, Stanford University September 2015
13. Dorigo, M., Stützle, T.: Ant Colony Optimization. MIT Press, Cambridge (2004)
14. Eberhart, R., Shi, Y.: Computational Intelligence: Concepts to Implementations. Morgan Kaufmann Publisher, San Francisco (2007)
15. Fayyad, U., Piatetsky-Shapiro, G., Smyth, P.: From data mining to knowledge discovery in databases. AI Mag. **17**(3), 37–54 (1996)
16. Hastie, T., Tibshirani, R., Friedman, J.: The Elements of Statistical Learning: Data Mining, Inference, and Prediction. Springer Series in Statistics, 2nd edn. Springer, New York (2009)

17. Hauschild, M., Pelikan, M.: An introduction and survey of estimation of distribution algorithms. Swarm Evol. Comput. **1**(3), 111–128 (2011)
18. Hu, J., Fu, M.C., Marcus, S.I.: A model reference adaptive search method for global optimization. Oper. Res. **55**(3), 549–568 (2007)
19. Jin, Y., Branke, J.: Evolutionary optimization in uncertain environments - a survey. IEEE Trans. Evol. Comput. **9**(3), 303–317 (2005)
20. Jin, Y., Hammer, B.: Computational intelligence in big data. IEEE Comput. Intell. Mag. **9**(3), 12–13 (2014)
21. Jin, Y., Sendhoff, B.: A systems approach to evolutionary multiobjective structural optimization and beyond. IEEE Comput. Intell. Mag. **4**(3), 62–76 (2009)
22. Kennedy, J., Eberhart, R., Shi, Y.: Swarm Intelligence. Morgan Kaufmann Publisher, San Francisco (2001)
23. Kim, Y.S.: Multi-objective clustering with data- and human-driven metrics. J. Comput. Inf. Syst. **51**(4), 64–73 (2011)
24. Lee, J.A., Verleysen, M.: Nonlinear Dimensionality Reduction. Information Science and Statistics. Springer, New York (2007)
25. Li, L., Tang, K.: History-based topological speciation for multimodal optimization. IEEE Trans. Evol. Comput. **19**(1), 136–150 (2015)
26. Manyika, J., Chui, M., Brown, B., Bughin, J., Dobbs, R., Roxburgh, C., Byers, A.H.: Big data: the next frontier for innovation, competition, and productivity. Technical report, McKinsey Global Institute, May 2011
27. Morrison, R.W., De Jong, K.A.: A test problem generator for non-stationary environments. In: Proceedings of the 1999 Congress on Evolutionary Computation (CEC 1999), vol. 3, pp. 2047–2053, July 1999
28. Pelikan, M., Goldberg, D.E., Lobo, F.G.: A survey of optimization by building and using probabilistic models. Comput. Optim. Appl. **21**(1), 5–20 (2002)
29. Rajaraman, A., Leskovec, J., Ullman, J.D.: Mining of Massive Datasets. Cambridge University Press, Cambridge (2012)
30. Shi, Y.: Brain storm optimization algorithm. In: Tan, Y., Shi, Y., Chai, Y., Wang, G. (eds.) ICSI 2011, Part I. LNCS, vol. 6728, pp. 303–309. Springer, Heidelberg (2011)
31. Shi, Y.: An optimization algorithm based on brainstorming process. Int. J. Swarm Intell. Res. (IJSIR) **2**(4), 35–62 (2011)
32. Yang, P., Tang, K., Lu, X.: Improving estimation of distribution algorithm on multimodal problems by detecting promising areas. IEEE Trans. Cybern. **45**(8), 1438–1449 (2015)
33. Yang, S., Li, C.: A clustering particle swarm optimizer for locating and tracking multiple optima in dynamic environments. IEEE Trans. Evol. Comput. **14**(6), 959–974 (2010)
34. Yang, Z., Tang, K., Yao, X.: Differential evolution for high-dimensional function optimization. In: Proceedings of 2007 IEEE Congress on Evolutionary Computation (CEC 2007), pp. 35231–3530. IEEE (2007)
35. Yang, Z., Tang, K., Yao, X.: Scalability of generalized adaptive differential evolution for large-scale continuous optimization. Soft. Comput. **15**(11), 2141–2155 (2011)
36. Zhou, Z.H., Chawla, N.V., Jin, Y., Williams, G.J.: Big data opportunities and challenges: discussions from data analytics perspectives. IEEE Comput. Intell. Mag. **9**(4), 62–74 (2014)
37. Zlochin, M., Birattari, M., Meuleau, N., Dorigo, M.: Model-based search for combinatorial optimization: a critical survey. Ann. Oper. Res. **131**, 373–395 (2004)

Prospects and Challenges in Online Data Mining

Experiences of Three-Year Labour Market Monitoring Project

Maxim Bakaev$^{(\boxtimes)}$ and Tatiana Avdeenko

Economic Informatics Department,
Novosibirsk State Technical University, Novosibirsk, Russia
bakaev@corp.nstu.ru, avdeenko@fb.nstu.ru

Abstract. The paper provides reflections on feasibility of online data mining (ODM) and its employment in decision-making and control. Besides reviewing existing works in different domains of Data Mining, we also report experiences from ongoing project dedicated to monitoring labour market with the aid of dedicated intelligent information system. Benefits of ODM include high efficiency, availability of data sources, potential extensiveness of datasets, timeliness and frequency of collection, good validity. Among special considerations we highlight a need for sophisticated tools, programming and maintenance efforts, hardware and network resources, multitude and diversity of data sources, disparity between real world and Internet. Finally, we describe some examples of the intelligent system application, in particular analyzing labour market data for several regions.

Keywords: Data Mining · Intelligent information systems · Big Data · Web content mining · Decision-making

1 Introduction

As the amount of data being created and copied in the world currently has the order of 10^{21} bytes, it is no wonder that many major companies and organizations seek to intensify Big Data (BD) research and application [1]. So, BD became an established field in quite a short timeframe, and a significant share of research works is already recounting the state-of-the-art in it. For example, a review of the field progress and the relevant technologies is provided in [1], while [2] looks back on the development of Data Mining (DM), which is often viewed as most essential component for successful utilization of BD. The recitation of popular DM algorithms was already done in 2007 [3], and by now they, as well as specially adapted methods (see, e.g. [4]), are widely employed for processing BD. This prompt development is in particular stimulated by the need to support decision-making, management, and control in general, which can no longer rely on traditional statistics, such as administrative registers. Among their disadvantages that are often noted, is virtually unavoidable time lag, conservatism in

© Springer International Publishing Switzerland 2016
Y. Tan and Y. Shi (Eds.): DMBD 2016, LNCS 9714, pp. 15–23, 2016.
DOI: 10.1007/978-3-319-40973-3_2

terms of measuring novel concepts and phenomena, inability to embrace rapid trends, lack of coverage of certain sectors of economy, etc. [5].

At the same time, the development of DM is not uniform per different domains, and it is said to be problem-oriented [2]. Quite a lot of progress has been made recently in medicine, where advancement of expert and intelligent systems remains a mainstream [6], and it's expected that Big Medical Data classification and analysis will be able to significantly decrease the ever-growing health care expenses in developed countries. Extensive review of milestones in the field since the beginning of the millennium can be found in [7], where principal DM approaches are listed as follows: classification, regression, clustering, association and hybrid. Overall, already in this domain the desired goals seem to be agreed upon, the data collection and structuring have been carried out for a long time, and current research is to a significant degree aimed on benchmarking and perfection of various mining methods, compared per metrics of accuracy, sensitivity, specificity, etc. [6].

Another example of a long-established field is Business Intelligence and Analytics, which lately has also been seeking to harness BD – a review of research and biblio-metric study can be found in [8]. The development in this domain made it clear that having enough data and decent processing algorithms are not sufficient, as most problems seem to arise due to ambiguous objectives and lack of clear indexes to be analyzed or monitored. Also, unlike in medicine and health care domain, major organizations in business may be reluctant to cooperate in research, to share data or agree on their common structure. We'd also like to highlight some relatively novel applications of DM, one of which is Educational DM, whose increasing popularity is understandable in the light of boom in online educational services. The author of [9], having considered 240 works in the field, notes that it is still incipient, as only a few options from DM repertory are used. Another new challenge in BD analysis is said to be the Internet of Things, with its naturally voluminous and diverse data that are considered "too big and too hard to be processed by the tools available today" [10, p. 78]. We'd also like to highlight that unless some aggregators are employed, these data should be available at innumerable nodes *(things)* accessible via online channels, which would make their collection quite arduous. Indeed, ODM, when no readily open databases or dedicated data outputs exist, should be viewed as a particular domain, due to specifics of data allocation, acquisition, structuring, etc. Currently, its most popular applications are rather "qualitative" ones, such as social networks mining, usually for e-commerce (see review in [11]), or semantic mining, for which numerous tools exist, such as described in [12]. However, for decision-making, management, control, etc., often quantitative analysis of online data is highly desirable, though it seems to receive less attention [13] – most of available works deal with merely tech-nical aspects of web mining, not enquiring how information obtained online could be used and what decisions might be improved with it.

Thus, in our paper we reflect on prospects in ODM, as well as up-to-date challenges in this field – by which we mostly consider *web content mining*, not *web structure mining* or *web usage mining* (see explanation of the distinction in [14]). In Sect. 2, we provide some theoretical considerations and review existing research works. In Sect. 3 we describe an ongoing project, intelligent system that performs collection, processing, and analysis of online data related to labour market. We provide an example of real data collected by the system and how it could be used in decision-making, control and forecasting. Overall, we would like to encourage discussion on theoretical and practical aspects of employing online data, on automation and intellectualization of this process.

2 Online Data Mining

Analyzing advantages of employing online (web) data in control and decision-making, put forward by various research works, such as [13–15], coupling them with our own practical experiences described later in the paper, we composed the following list:

- **High efficiency** in terms of labour-intensiveness, which *may* also mean lower costs. However, break-even point is highly sensitive to the number of websites, their changeability, volume and structure (if any) of collected data.
- **Open availability of data sources** – websites that voluntarily publish data to be accessed by human visitors or, in rarer cases, robots. Other factors being equal, data sources that have better coverage (that is, more data and more frequent updates) and more stable output in terms of data structure (proper HTML/XML mark-up and meaningful CSS styles) are first candidates for ODM.
- **Extensiveness of datasets**, as Internet is surely a Very Big Data source. Higher efficiency and data availability allow to dramatically increase sample size, possibly even extending the coverage to the whole population, as well as to record more attributes of studied objects. However, generalizations are to be made carefully, as information available online is only representative of online universe.
- **Timeliness and frequency**, which mean that data can be gathered in real-time and with unprecedented regularity, if the studied field calls for it. This is often helpful in studying short-lived phenomena that are common in the WWW.
- **Better validity of data** due to the removal of respondent burden (as information is gathered indirectly) and prevention of manual-processing errors. However, this is only true if suitable data are available and the scraping algorithms work correctly and accurately maintained.

As for problems and special considerations of ODM, we'd like to note the following:

- **Much more sophisticated tools**, compared to general Data Mining, are necessary to collect online data, which are prone to changeability and sometimes hard-to-get. Indeed, algorithm for scraping a particular webpage data can be created automatically, based on the page contents' analysis, with the use of the so-called wrappers technology (see the definition and detailed review in [16]) that has a potential to significantly reduce programming effort. However, it seems that currently, despite admitted advances in automated wrapper generation, human involvement is still required to maintain data extraction in the long run. Thus, the availability of open-source or free-to-use components and products such as RoadRunner or XPath, or commercial solutions such as Mozenda, Diffbot, etc. (see in [16]), doesn't fully resolve the issue.

- **More hardware and network resources** needed, even though in terms of computational complexity, the problem of structured information extraction from web pages is said to be polynomial or even linear for specific domains [17] (there are estimations that a web page contains about 5000 elements on average). The situation is more complex for Rich Internet Applications, where both all URLs **and** all application states have to be attended by a data scrapping algorithm, so that the task can be mapped to directed graph exploration problem. Still, satisfactory performing methods exist (see review in [18]), such as distributed greedy algorithm or vision-based approach (see ViDE algorithm [19]). In should be noted that Flash-based websites currently remain largely inaccessible for automated online data mining, but their number is already comparably low.
- **Incompleteness of Internet** – not all objects of the real world have "online footprint", but only those involved in some kind of online information transactions. Naturally, the existence of economic benefit for both sides is a good motivation – well-known examples of online data suitable for mining include e-commerce prices for goods and services, stock and currency markets, tickets costs and availability, real estate, labour markets, etc. [13]
- **Multitude of sources**, which leads to increased need for efforts and resources required to collect and process data, given high probability of inconsistencies between sources. If online data are scattered among many diverse websites, the number of different scraping algorithms may become too high, imposing prohibitive development, customization or maintenance costs. In certain fields it is possible to select a number of data sources that would make up satisfactory sample, but this may lead to threats in data validity.
- **Threats to data validity**, as data sources are selected without non-random sampling, but based on their data volume, technical properties, accessibility, etc.
- **No quantity can make up for understanding the goals and means** – ODM has to start with "why" and "for whom" questions (see a simple algorithm for estimating the feasibility of online data employment in [21]), unlike general DM that often seem to commence with "we have these data, what can we do with them?".

So, with the above points we tried to justify the claim that ODM is indeed a distinct field, requiring special methods, tools, and methodological considerations. The following section of our paper shows how these were reflected in a real project – intelligent system to analyze regional labour markets, – and what new lessons we could learn.

3   The Labour Market Online Monitoring Project

3.1   The Project Background

The developed software system is dedicated to supporting decision-making in labour market management by the City Hall of Novosibirsk, Russia. The system was put into operation in 2011 and currently its database contains more than 10 million records on vacancies and resumes for Novosibirsk and certain other regions (more details can be found in [20, 21]).

The data structuring data is straightforward in most cases, as web pages content fields are marked with respective id names and the implicit data model is known to us. Often it's desirable to exclude multiple copies of the same item, e.g. collected from different websites or in different time periods, from the analysis. The first step in the intelligent filtering process is generation of hash-code for the collected page, with all the variable elements, such as counters or advertisements, removed. This approach works for most of the copies and excludes them from further structuring, thus decreasing the system load. However, for more accurate filtering on the second step, structured data are used – they are merged into a string for which we also generate a hash-code for subsequent validation and comparison. The resulting productivity, even given the high volumes of data in the system, is quite satisfactory, and the filtering mechanism can work as a daemon when the system load is low in the absence of data collection or processing.

3.2   The Project Experiences

- **Feasibility may vary.** The advantages of automated online data collection are not guaranteed, and the most important factors are: (a) whether the object of analysis has a reliable "online footprint", i.e. enough of its properties are manifest online, regularly updated by an interested party, and relatively trustworthy; (b) whether the concentration is high enough, i.e. most of the information universe is represented on a handful of websites – about 10, not 1000, which would make the system maintenance nearly impossible.
- **Changeability and monitoring.** Inevitably, the structure of sites and webpages change with time, as they try to put up more data, improve interface, introduce more advanced technologies like AJAX, and so on, which significantly affects accuracy and completeness of ODM, and introduce considerable maintenance costs. While the latter seem unavoidable, the former could theoretically be aided by a monitoring sub-system, overseeing correctness of data collection. However, setting up monitoring is not a trivial problem, as only relatively simple data gathering malfunctions can be validated, but generally human programmer involvement is still required periodically.
- **This is not Big Data.** The online data collection, in most cases, seems to be of "Small Data" domain. That is, all of the accessed data can be stored and re-processed later if necessary (e.g., with more advanced algorithms or to extract more object of analysis's properties). We even store HTML code of webpages, although with certain optimization, and still our database size that after 3.5 years of the system's operation contains about 10 million records, amounts to about 120 GB.
- **Customer doesn't know what to ask for.** Decision-making based on online data is quite a novel approach, and it was confirmed in our project that management, at least on municipal level, does not fully grasp its potential. So, the customer, for whom data is collected and analyzed, cannot directly drive the development of the system.

3.3   Highlights of Labour Market Online Data Analysis

Below we provide some data from our system for selected regions (*obl.*, *krai*) of Russia (mostly based in Siberian Federal District), gathered and processed up to the end of 2014 (as the data disclosure was approved by the system's management). Table 1 contains data on average weekly numbers of vacancies and resumes (so that only unique items are considered, not repeating postings). The official data on the regions' urban population is for the 1st of January, 2015. The data for 2015 was also collected and will be analyzed and subsequently made available with the approvement by the system's management.

Table 1. Average weekly numbers of vacancies and resumes per regions, 2014.

Region	Vacancies (weekly)		Resumes (weekly)		Ratio (V/R)
	Total	Per 100,000	Total	Per 100,000	
Krasnoyarski krai	997	45.45	639	29.13	1.56
Kemerovsk. obl.	1446	61.91	1202	51.47	1.20
Novosibirsk. obl.	3204	148.55	3300	153.00	0.97
Omskaya obl.	1102	77.19	729	51.06	1.51
Tomskaya obl.	825	106.72	659	85.25	1.25
Tyumenskaya obl.	539	18.83	444	15.51	1.21

From the data presented in Table 1, we can conclude that the considered regions significantly differ in the numbers of vacancies and resumes published online. While Novosibirsk region is special, as we noted above, the Tomskaya oblast still has notable lead from the others. It indeed can be explained by higher "online mobility" of its citizens, quite a significant share of which is students. Interestingly, the ratios between vacancies and resumes are more stable, although in most of the regions there are more companies looking for staff than people looking for jobs. We are continuously monitoring this ratio, which is a good indication of the state of economy.

Table 2 presents data on average salaries that are proposed in vacancies and requested in resumes. We compare these data to the official salary statistics (which is taken for the whole year 2014) and calculate the ration between the average salaries data from the system to the official data. The official salary data for Tyumenskaya obl. is taken excluding the ones in its autonomous regions, which are rarely present online but introduce bias due to high salaries in their oil industry. Table 3 contains the salary-related information for Novosibirsk region by years. The data is shown for half-years, but official salaries are taken for the whole year, due to lack of more detailed statistics. It's interesting to note that in 2013, when the economic situation was quite stable, the ration between proposed and requested salaries (Ratio V/R) was close to 1, but how the situation changed in 2014, when the economy worsened in the fall. Prior to the decline, the requested salaries boomed (it's a well-known fact that the cost of resources increases prior to crises), but after most of the workforce experienced the economic troubles, they got ready to work for much lower salaries.

Table 2. Average monthly salaries per regions, 2014.

Region	Salary (Rubles per month)			Ratio (V/R)	Percentage of official
	Official	In vacancies	In resumes		
Krasnoyarski krai	34224	30915	25514	1.21	82.4 %
Kemerovskaya obl.	26732	30124	22938	1.31	99.2 %
Novosibirskaya obl.	27267	33110	22100	1.50	101.2 %
Omskaya obl.	26313	27350	24538	1.11	98.6 %
Tomskaya obl.	32503	27807	24809	1.12	80.9 %
Tyumenskaya obl.	34221	38865	28566	1.36	98.5 %

Table 3. Average monthly salaries for Novosibirsk region, per years.

Period (half-year)	Salary (Rubles per month)			Ratio (V/R)	Percentage of official
	Official	In vacancies	In resumes		
2012 (I)	23246	26986	22796	1.18	107.1 %
2012 (II)	23246	27151	23973	1.13	110.0 %
2013 (I)	25528	24798	23355	1.06	94.3 %
2013 (II)	25528	25370	25774	0.98	100.2 %
2014 (I)	27267	27589	30563	0.90	106.6 %
2014 (II)	27267	33110	22100	1.50	101.2 %

4 Conclusions

Nowadays, as annual growth rate in the amounts of data created and transferred in the world is estimated as 50 %, Internet is increasingly viewed as a data source, and already not only business organizations, but even understandably conservative National statistical institutes initiate projects to employ online data. It is said that BD and DM are domain-specific [2], and in such fields as health care (medical data), business intelligence, education, etc. they are on different stages of maturity. Thus we reason that ODM should be seen as a distinct field as well, having very specific considerations in terms of data collection, methodological aspects and so on.

The paper discusses certain issues in intelligent online data employment in analysis of various phenomena and supporting decision-making. Although technological problems seem to be mostly resolved [17, 18], the matter of general feasibility seems to be less explored [13]. Apparently, most promising application of automated data collection is not in replacing existing manual procedures, but in reaching new areas and achieving higher level of detail. There are decisions to be made in domains where the amount of data generated or updated daily is beyond any hand-processing, so automation and intellectualization are the only reasonable options. From our relevant experiences from a project ongoing from 2011, the intelligent information system for monitoring labor market, we in particular conclude that an important challenge in development such systems is their potential users' (that is, government agencies officials) conservatism with IT, which puts requirements generation burden on developers.

We also provide real data from the system, for selected regions of Russia and various time periods, and offer economy-related observations. Interestingly, we can conclude that capabilities of our and similar intelligent solutions so far exceed the information needs of responsible authorities, and we attempt to outline directions for securing wider acceptance of ODM methods.

Acknowledgement. This work was supported by RFBR according to the research project No. 16-37-60060 mol_a_dk.

References

1. Chen, M., Mao, S., Liu, Y.: Big data: a survey. Mob. Netw. Appl. **19**(2), 171–209 (2014)
2. Liao, S.H., Chu, P.H., Hsiao, P.Y.: Data mining techniques and applications–a decade review from 2000 to 2011. Exp. Syst. Appl. **39**(12), 11303–11311 (2012)
3. Wu, X., et al.: Top 10 algorithms in data mining. Knowl. Inf. Syst. **14**(1), 1–37 (2008)
4. Wu, X., Zhu, X., Wu, G.Q., Ding, W.: Data mining with big data. IEEE Trans. Knowl. Data Eng. **26**(1), 97–107 (2014)
5. Beręsewicz, M.: Estimating the size of the secondary real estate market based on internet data sources. Folia Oeconomica Stetinensia **14**(2), 259–269 (2014)
6. Seera, M., Lim, C.P.: A hybrid intelligent system for medical data classification. Exp. Syst. Appl. **41**(5), 2239–2249 (2014)
7. Esfandiari, N., Babavalian, M.R., Moghadam, A.M.E., Tabar, V.K.: Knowledge discovery in medicine: current issue and future trend. Exp. Syst. Appl. **41**(9), 4434–4463 (2014)
8. Chen, H., Chiang, R.H., Storey, V.C.: Business intelligence and analytics: from big data to big impact. MIS Q. **36**(4), 1165–1188 (2012)
9. Peña-Ayala, A.: Educational data mining: a survey and a data mining-based analysis of recent works. Exp. Syst. Appl. **41**(4), 1432–1462 (2014)
10. Tsai, C.W., Lai, C.F., Chiang, M.C., Yang, L.T.: Data mining for internet of things: a survey. IEEE Commun. Surv. Tutor. **16**(1), 77–97 (2014)
11. Polanco, W.: Web Mining technologies for the e-Commerce solutions in the social networks systems. A Thesis Master of Science - Information Systems, pp. 1–60. SIT, NJ (2013)
12. Milne, D., Witten, I.H.: An open-source toolkit for mining Wikipedia. Artif. Intell. **194**, 222–239 (2013)
13. Beresewicz, M.E.: On representativeness of Internet data sources for real estate market in Poland. Austrian J. Stat. **44**(2), 45–57 (2015)
14. Gök, A., Waterworth, A., Shapira, P.: Use of web mining in studying innovation. Scientometrics **102**(1), 653–671 (2015)
15. Barcaroli, G.: Internet as data source in the Istat survey on ICT in enterprises. Austrian J. Stat. **44**(2), 31–43 (2015)
16. Ferrara, E., De Meo, P., Fiumara, G., Baumgartner, R.: Web data extraction, applications and techniques: a survey. Knowl.-Based Syst. **70**, 301–323 (2014)
17. Kraychev, B., Koychev, I.: Computationally effective algorithm for information extraction and online review mining. In: Proceedings of the 2nd International Conference on Web Intelligence, Mining and Semantics, vol. 64 (2012)
18. Choudhary, S. et al.: Crawling rich internet applications: the state of the art. In: Proceedings of the 2012 Confrence of the Center for Advanced Studies on Collaborative Research, pp. 146–160 (2012)

19. Liu, W., Meng, X., Meng, W.: Vide: a vision-based approach for deep web data extraction. IEEE Trans. Know. Data Eng. **22**(3), 447–460 (2010)
20. Bakaev, M., Avdeenko, T.: Data extraction for decision-support systems application in labour market monitoring and analysis. Int. J. e-Educ. e-Bus. e-Manage. e-Lear. (IJEEEE) **4**(1), 23–27 (2014)
21. Bakaev, M., Avdeenko, T.: Intelligent information system to support decision-making based on unstructured web data. ICIC Expr. Lett. **9**(4), 1017–1023 (2015)

Data Mining Algorithms

Enhance AdaBoost Algorithm by Integrating LDA Topic Model

Fangyu Gai[1(✉)], Zhiqiang Li[2], Xinwen Jiang[1], and Hongchen Guo[2]

[1] School of Computer, National University of Defense Technology, Changsha, China
greferry@gmail.com, xinwenjiang@sina.com
[2] Network Service Center, Beijing Institude of Technology, Beijing, China
{Lizq,guohongchen}@bit.edu.cn

Abstract. AdaBoost is an ensemble method, which is considered to be one of the most influential algorithms for multi-label classification. It has been successfully applied to diverse domains for its tremendous simplicity and accurate prediction. To choose the weak hypotheses, AdaBoost has to examine the whole features individually, which will dramatically increase the computational time of classification, especially for large scale datasets. In order to tackle this problem, we a introduce Latent Dirichlet Allocation (LDA) model to improve the efficiency and effectiveness of AdaBoost by mapping word-matrix into topic-matrix. In this paper, we propose a framework integrating LDA and AdaBoost, and test it with two Chinese Language corpora. Experiments show that our method outperforms the traditional AdaBoost using BOW model.

Keywords: AdaBoost · Ensemble method · Text categorization

1 Introduction

AdaBoost is an adaptive Boosting algorithm [6] with accurate prediction and great simplicity. It has become one of the most influential ensemble methods for classification task. The core idea of AdaBoost is to generate a committee of weak hypotheses and combine them with weights. In each iteration, AdaBoost will enhance the performance depending on the accuracy of previous classifiers. Ferreira and Figueiredo [4] review the AdaBoost algorithm in details, and its variants have been exploited in diverse domains such as text categorization, face detection, remote sensing image detection, barcode recognition, and banknote number recognition [15].

AdaBoost was designed only for binary classification, while AdaBoost.MH [11] is an extension of AdaBoost to be fit for multi-class multi-label classification. In AdaBoost.MH, a "pivot term" will be selected if the term has been found harder to classified by previous classifiers in each iteration. An improved version of AdaBoost.MH, called MP-Boost, is proposed by Esuli et at. [3]. In each iteration of boosting process, MP-Boost selects several "pivod terms" and one for each category instead of one for all categories in AdaBoost.MH. This mechanism outperforms in effectiveness and efficiency.

© Springer International Publishing Switzerland 2016
Y. Tan and Y. Shi (Eds.): DMBD 2016, LNCS 9714, pp. 27–37, 2016.
DOI: 10.1007/978-3-319-40973-3_3

Both methods mentioned above have to scan the whole feature space to select the pivot term or terms, which is obviously sensitive to the number of features. For Text Categorization (TC), traditional methods utilize Vector Space Model (VSM) and Bag-of-Words (BOW) to represent the original corpus, and form a high-dimensional sparse matrix. However, it is a time consume task in case of large scale dataset. In order to accelerate the boosting process, it is necessary to use feature selection or feature extraction techniques, such as mutual information, information gain, χ^2-statistic consume etc., to reduce dimensions. However, these methods make a common assumption that the words are isolated from each other, which may cause information loss and poor classification performance.

Latent Dirichlet Allocation (LDA) [2] is a generative probabilistic topic model for collections of textual data and it has been widely used for feature reduction. LDA maps documents into a small number of "Latent Topics", and each topic is a mixture of words. LDA can reduce the feature number, but also handle ambiguity because LDA captures the semantic relation among the words in each topic.

In this paper, we propose a principle framework to integreate topic modeling with boosting process. We conduct experiments on real-world dataset, and compare our approach with the state-of-art baselines. Experimental results demonstrate the effectiveness and efficiency of proposed algorithm.

2   Related Works

Schapire and Singer [11] have proposed AdaBoost.MH, which is one of the most popular boosting algorithms for text categorization. An improved version, called MP-Boost is proposed by Esuli et al. [3]. It has better performance in multilabel text classification, due to its selecting several pivot terms for each category in each iteration. Furthermore, AdaBoost-SHAMME [16] is a natural extension of the AdaBoost algorithm to the multi-class case, instead of reducing it to multiple two-class problems. $AdaBoost_{AR}$ [8] attempts to make the weak hypotheses more efficient and the experimental results illustrate that $AdaBoost_{AR}$-based algorithm performed fast improvement of accuracy.

All mentioned approaches above focus on enhancing the performance of boosting algorithms, however, some studies such as feature selection can also improve the performance of classification task. There are a wide variety of methods, e.g., the mutual information, information gain and χ^2-statistic are to determine the most important features for classification [1]. Changki Lee proposed an information gain and divergence-based feature selection method [9], which strives to reduce redundancy between features while maintaining information gain in selecting appropriate features for text categorization. In [13], a two-staged feature selection method is used to reduce the high dimensionality of a feature space.

Instead of picking from the original set of attributes, feature extraction methods create a new and smaller set of features as a function of the original set of features [1]. LDA is a typical example and it has been applied to information retrival and TC. Morchid et al. [10] presents an architecture to distinguish the themes of

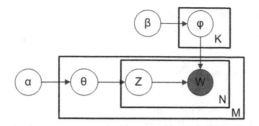

Fig. 1. Graphical model representation of LDA

conversation combining two conversation representations with SVM classification. The result of the study turns out that using a LDA-based method achieved better performance than the classical TF-IDF-Gini method. Wang et al. [14] uses LDA as a method of feature reduction and boosting strategy for classification. The weak classifiers they choose for boosting are Naïve Bayes and Support Vector Machine. But the exprerimental results only demonstrate slightly outperform than the algorithms using VSM in accuracy without considering the improvement on recall, F1-measure and other indicators.

In this paper, LDA is applied for building topic model and produces document-topic vector for learning two versions of AdaBoost algorithm, AdaBoost.MH and MP-Boost. We also illustrate how the topic number and the iteration times affect the results.

3   Methods

Our method introduces LDA to enhance AdaBoost Algorithm, which can be divided into two different parts: one is topic model part, from which we will get a document-topic distribution by using LDA, which will be treated as input into the classification part. In the classification, we will apply two different extensions of AdaBoost to accomplish classification job.

3.1   Feature Extraction by LDA

Latent Dirichlet Allocation (LDA) [2] is a generative probabilistic model for topic modeling in a collection of documents. In LDA, documents are represented as a mixture of fixed number of topics, and each topic is a multinomial distribution over words. Figure 1 illustrates the graphical model of LDA.

Here is some notations for LDA.

1. A word is the basic unit of textual data from a vocabulary, represented as $w = (1, ..., V)$.
2. A document is a sequence of N words represented as $d = (w_1, w_2, ..., w_i)$, where w_i is the ith word in the sequence.
3. A corpus is a collection of M documents represented as $D = (d_1, d_2, ..., d_m)$.

We assume that there are k latent topics, and then the ith word w_i in the document d can be represented as follows:

$$P(w_i) = \sum_{j-1}^{T} P(w_i|z_i = j)P(z_i = j) \tag{1}$$

where z_i is a latent variable which means this topic is assigned to the ith word; $P(w_i|z_i = j)$ means the probability of the word w_i belonging to topic j; $P(z_i = j)$ means the probability of the given document d belonging to topic j. the jth topic is represented as the multinomial distribution over a word vocabulary:

$$\phi_{w_i}^j = P(w_i|z_i = j) \tag{2}$$

The corpora is represented as the random mixture of the K latent topics

$$\theta_j^d = P(z_i = j) \tag{3}$$

Then the probability of the word w coming to the document d can be described as follows:

$$P(w|d) = \sum_{j=i}^{T} \phi_w^j \theta_j^d \tag{4}$$

The total probability of the model is:

$$P(\theta, \boldsymbol{z}, d|\alpha, \beta) = P(\theta|\alpha) \prod_{n=1}^{N} P(z_n|\theta)P(w_n|z_n, \beta) \tag{5}$$

where α is the parameter of the Dirichlet distribution of the topics over the documents, and β is a $K \times V$ matrix for each topic and each term where $\beta_{ij} = P(w_i = 1|z_i = 1)$.

Using Gibbs sampling algorithm, we can obtain the approximate solution of the parameters.

3.2   Classification by AdaBoost

AdaBoost [5] is one of the most influential boosting algorithms, which along with its variants have been applied to diverse domains with great success for their accurate prediction and great simplicity. In this research, we will use two extensions of AdaBoost, called AdaBoost.MH and MP-Boost to complete classification task.

AdaBoost.MH AdaBoost.MH works by iteratively building a committee of weak hypotheses of $weakclassifier$(usually decision stumps). The input to the algorithm is a training set $S = \{< d_1, C_1 >, ..., < d_i, C_i >, ..., < d_m, C_m >\}$, where $d_i \subseteq D$ is the ith document of all the m documents and $C_i \subseteq C$ is a set of categories to each of which the ith document belongs. At each iteration t, the algorithm tests the predictions of the newly generated weak hypothesis h_t and uses their results to update the weight distribution D_t, then the new weight distribution D_{t+1} along with the training samples will pass to the weak learner to build a new weak hypothesis h_{t+1}.

In the end, the output is the final hypothesis H combining a sequence of weak hypotheses $h_1, h_2, ..., h_T$ in a linear weighting way. The details of the AdaBoost.MH algorithm are showed as follows.

MP-Boost MP-Boost [3] is an improved version of AdaBoost.MH. In MP-Boost, multiple terms are selected as "pivot terms" at every iteration for each category instead of only one in AdaBoost.MH. MP-Boost basically concentrates on the form of weak hypotheses and how they are generated. The basic algorithm of AdaBoost.MH is as follows:

Algorithm 1. AdaBoost.MH algorithm

1: *Input*: A training set $S = \{< d_1, C_1 >, ..., < d_i, C_i >, ..., < d_m, C_m >\}$ where
   $C_i \subseteq C = c_1, ..., C_m$ for all $i = 1, ..., m$.
2: *Procedure*: Initiate $D_1(d_i, c_j) = \frac{1}{mn}$ for all $i = 1, ..., n$ and for all $j = 1, ..., n$.
3: **for** $t = 1, ..., T$ **do**
4:     Pass distribution D_t and training samples to the weak classifier;
5:     Get the weak hypothesis h_t from the weak learner;
6:     Choose $\alpha_t \in \mathbb{R}$;
7:     Update $D_{t+1}(d_i, c_j) = \frac{D_t(d_i, c_j) exp(-\alpha_t \phi(d_i, c_j) h_t(d_i, c_j))}{Z_t}$;
8: *Output*: A final hypotheses $H(d, c) = \sum_{t=1}^{T} h_t(d, c)$

A weak hypothesis of MP-Boost at iteration t is the union of weak hypotheses for c_j, one for each $c_j \in C$, which are defined as follows:

$$h^j(d_i) = \begin{cases} a_{0,j}, & w_{ki} = 0 \\ a_{1,j}, & w_{ki} = 1 \end{cases} \tag{6}$$

where t_k is the pivot term chosen for category c_j. At each iteration t, the algorithm for choosing a weak hypothesis $h^j(d_i)$ is as follows:

3.3   Integrating LDA with AdaBoost

In this section, we will propose a framework integrating LDA and AdaBoost. The framework can be divided into training part and test part. The input is a pre-processed(tokenization, stemming, stop words removal, normalization and segmentation for Chinese word) texual dataset for both training and test.

Algorithm 2. Choose MP-Boost weak hypothesis

1: **for** $c_1, ..., c_n,\ t_1, ..., t_r$ **do**
2:      Select $h^j_{best(k)}(t_k$ as the pivot term) which minimizes;

$$Z^j_t = \sum_{i=1}^{n} D_t(d_i, c_j)exp(-\alpha_t \phi(d_i, c_j)h^j(d_i)) \tag{7}$$

3: **for** $h^j_{best(1)}, ..., h^j_{best(r)}$ **do**
4:      Select h^j_t for which Z^j_t is minimum;
5: Across all $c_j \in C$, unite the hypotheses as h_t;

In training part, firstly we employ Gibbs Sampling method [7] for topic estimation from which we gain two useful vector as result:

- $\boldsymbol{\theta_d} < \boldsymbol{p_{t_1}}, ..., \boldsymbol{p_{t_k}} >$, for each document in D, where p_{t_i} is the probability of the ith topic in the document. Of all the documents, it is known as the document-topic distribution index θ.
- $\boldsymbol{\phi_t} < \boldsymbol{p_{w_1}}, ..., \boldsymbol{p_{w_n}} >$, for each topic, where p_{w_i} is the probability of the ith word in the vocabulary. Of all the topics, it is known as the topic-word distribution index ϕ.

After that, we will use the document-topic distribution index θ for AdaBoost learning. Before doing that, some of the topics for each document must be excluded, because the weight of them is low which will negatively affect the classification performance. The method to filter the topics is an experienced method, as followed:

Algorithm 3. Topic filter

1: *Input*: Sorted $(w_1, ..., w_k)$, where w_i is the weight of the ith topic;
2: $sum = 0$;
3: **for** $w_1, ..., w_k$ **do**
4:      $sum+ = w + i$
5:      **if** $sum > w_{mean}$ **then**
6:           $Break$
7: *output*: The rest of topic

Finally, each document will be represented as a number of topics insetead of a bag of words for learning AdaBoost.

In test part, the difference is that we need to predict the latent topics of the new documents in the test set instead of topic estimation. For prediction, LDA uses the index of topic assignments of the words and the other parameters that obtained in training part. Then the matrix of test document-topic distribution θ will be produced for the evaluation of AdaBoost.

4   Experiments

4.1   Datasets

To evaluate the performance of our architecture, we have used the Tan-CorpV1.0[1,2,3] and CompusWebCorp.

The TanCorpV1.0 is a Chinese language corpora for TC, which was collected and preprocessed by Songbo Tan et al [12]. It consists of a set of 14150 documents which belong to 12 categories. This corpora has not determine the training set and test set, so we randomly choose 10000 documents as training sets and the rest as test sets.

The CompusWebCorp is a Chinese language corpora collected by ourselves. We crawled the text contents according to the visiting web log. We employed ICTCLAS[4] for segmentation. This datasets contains 5758 documents labeled to 10 categories manually and we randomly choose two thirds of the datasets for training and the rest is for test.

4.2   Experiment Settings

All of the datasets above will be pre-processed which is the first step of any text categorization task. In text pre-processing, stop words have been removed, punctuation has been removed, numbers have been removed, all letters have been converted to lowercase, and stemming has been performed. The Information Gain feature reduction method has been used to reduce the feature dimensions.

In our experiment, we will use a free software written by Esuli, that is available online[5]. The software realised AdaBoost.MH and MP-Boost. The text representing in BOW method will be used for comparing the efficiency and effectiveness of the representation by topics with LDA. For LDA, we employed a free software called JGibbLDA, which is a Java implementation of LDA using Gibbs Sampling technique for parameter estimation and inference[6].

The estimation and prediction tasks of LDA will be conducted on training set and test set individually. The iteration numbers for estimation will be set to 2000 and 1000 for inference. For each dataset, we will run LDA seval times to create a sequence of *theta* files whose number of topics will be 100, 200, ..., 1000. After LDA process, we will exclude some topics whose weights are below the threshold. After that the features of each document will be topic indices which will be used for learning AdaBoost.MH and MP-Boost. The number of iterations given for training AdaBoost.MH and MP-Boost is 100, 200, ..., 1000.

After LDA process, we will exclude some topics whose weights are below the threshold. After that the features of each document will be topic indices which

---

[1] http://www.searchforum.org.cn/tansongbo/corpus.htm.
[2] http://web.ist.utl.pt/acardoso/datasets/.
[3] https://garnize.latin.dcc.ufmg.br/savannah/projects/cadecol.
[4] http://sewm.pku.edu.cn/QA/reference/ICTCLAS/FreeICTCLAS/.
[5] http://www.esuli.it/software/mpboost/.
[6] http://jgibblda.sourceforge.net/.

will be used for learning AdaBoost.MH and MP-Boost. The number of iterations given for training AdaBoost.MH and MP-Boost is 100, 200 ... 1000. Accuracy, precision, recall and F1 are performance measures to evaluate classification performance.

5   Results and Discussion

5.1   Results on TanCorpV1.0

As demonstrated in Fig. 2, The Accuracy(other) of AdaBoost-LDA equals to that of AdaBoost with traditional BOW representation when the topic number reaches 100, after this, AdaBoost-LDA surpasses AdaBoost-BOW. Since the AdaBoost-BOW is not influenced by the number of topics, It is a straight line in the figure. When the topic number reaches 400, AdaBoost-LDA had the best performance and it is stable afterwards.

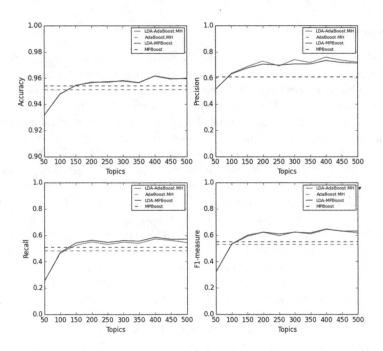

Fig. 2. The experimental results on the TanCorpV1.0 with fixed iterations

Figure 3 shows that AdaBoost-LDA converged faster than AdaBoost-BOW. The number of iterations do not affect AdaBoost-LDA very much, for it is nearly a straight line in the figure. As the iteration number increases, the performance of AdaBoost-BOW is getting slightly better, but it still has a worse performance than AdaBoost-LDA.

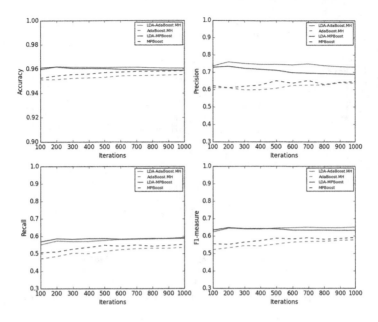

Fig. 3. The experimental results on the TanCorpV1.0 with fixed topics

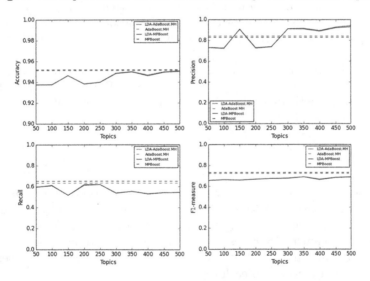

Fig. 4. The experimental results on the BITWebCorp with fixed iterations

5.2   Results on CompusWebCorp

Figure 4 illustrates the experimental results on the BITWebCorp when the iteration number is fixed. As topic number grows, the four indicators performed an increased trend during fluctuations except recall, which stayed the same or even dropped over the topic number growth. During the topic number growth,

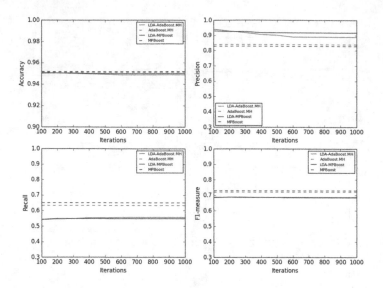

Fig. 5. The experimental results on the BITWebCorp with fixed topics

accuracy and F1-measure, gradually reach the value that AdaBoost-BOW equals to. However, the precision reaches the value of AdaBoost-BOW when the topic number equals to 300, after which the growth continues and finally stabilized around 0.9.

In Fig. 5, the lines are stable. The LDA methods value of accuracy is very close to that of BOW methods. In recall and F1-measure, BOW methods performed better than LDA methods while LDA performed better than BOW in precision at the value of around 0.9.

6   Conclusion

In this paper, we propose a framework integrating AdaBoost and LDA(Latent Dirichlet Allocations) for text categorization, which successfully improve the performance of classification using AdaBoost. By using LDA to model the documents, each document is represented as a mixture of topics, and each topic is represented as a mixture of words, from which LDA captures the semantic relation between the words in each topic.

We test our framework with two Chinese language corpora. The results of the first corpora indicate that our method outperforms traditional methods in all four indicators when the topic number is more than 100 and our framework performed faster converging than traditional methods. The second corpus is real-world data, and our method performed better in precision. Since we only tested our method on Chinese language corpora, in the future we will test it on other corpora of different languages and find out the details of how topic number influences the results.

Acknowledgments. This work is supported by the National Science Foundation of China under Grants 61272010.

References

1. Aggarwal, C.C., Zhai, C.: A survey of text classification algorithms. In: Aggarwal, C.C., Zhai, C. (eds.) Mining Text Data, pp. 163–222. Springer, Heidelberg (2012)
2. Blei, D.M., Ng, A.Y., Jordan, M.I.: Latent dirichlet allocation. J. Mach. Learn. Res. **3**, 993–1022 (2003)
3. Esuli, A., Fagni, T., Sebastiani, F.: MP-Boost: a multiple-pivot boosting algorithm and its application to text categorization. In: Crestani, F., Ferragina, P., Sanderson, M. (eds.) SPIRE 2006. LNCS, vol. 4209, pp. 1–12. Springer, Heidelberg (2006)
4. Ferreira, A.J., Figueiredo, M.A.: Boosting algorithms: a review of methods, theory, and applications. In: Zhang, C., Yunqian, M. (eds.) Ensemble Machine Learning, pp. 35–85. Springer, Heidelberg (2012)
5. Freund, Y., Schapire, R., Abe, N.: A short introduction to boosting. J. Jap. Soc. Artif. Intell. **14**(771–780), 771–780 (1999)
6. Freund, Y., Schapire, R.E.: A decision-theoretic generalization of on-line learning and an application to boosting. J. Comput. Syst. Sci. **55**(1), 119–139 (1997)
7. Geman, S., Geman, D.: Stochastic relaxation, gibbs distributions, and the bayesian restoration of images. Pattern Anal. Mach. Intell., IEEE Trans. **6**, 721–741 (1984)
8. Iwakura, T., Saitou, T., Okamoto, S.: An AdaBoost for efficient use of confidences of weak hypotheses on text categorization. In: Pham, D.-N., Park, S.-B. (eds.) PRICAI 2014. LNCS, vol. 8862, pp. 782–794. Springer, Heidelberg (2014)
9. Lee, C., Lee, G.G.: Information gain and divergence-based feature selection for machine learning-based text categorization. Inf. Process. Manage. **42**(1), 155–165 (2006)
10. Morchid, M., Dufour, R., Linares, G.: A lda-based topic classification approach from highly imperfect automatic transcriptions. In: LREC 2014 (2014)
11. Schapire, R.E., Singer, Y.: Boostexter: a boosting-based system for text categorization. Mach. Learn. **39**(2–3), 135–168 (2000)
12. Tan, S., Cheng, X., Ghanem, M.M., Wang, B., Xu, H.: A novel refinement approach for text categorization. In: Proceedings of the 14th ACM International Conference on Information and knowledge Management, pp. 469–476. ACM (2005)
13. Uğuz, H.: A two-stage feature selection method for text categorization by using information gain, principal component analysis and genetic algorithm. Knowl. Based Syst. **24**(7), 1024–1032 (2011)
14. Wang, Y., Guo, Q.: Multi-lda hybrid topic model with boosting strategy and its application in text classification. In: 2014 33rd Chinese Control Conference (CCC), pp. 4802–4806. IEEE (2014)
15. Xiong, W., Wan, Z., Bai, X., Xing, H., Zuo, H., Zhu, K., Yang, S.: Adaboost-based multi-attribute classification technology and its application. In: 76th EAGE Conference and Exhibition 2014 (2014)
16. Zhu, J., Zou, H., Rosset, S., Hastie, T.: Multi-class AdaBoost. Stat. Interface **2**(3), 349–360 (2009)

An Improved Algorithm for MicroRNA Profiling from Next Generation Sequencing Data

Salim A.[1](✉), Amjesh R.[2], and Vinod Chandra S.S.[3]

[1] College of Engineering Trivandrum, Thiruvananthapuram, Kerala, India
salim.mangad@gmail.com
[2] Department of Computational Biology and Bioinformatics,
University of Kerala, Thiruvananthapuram, Kerala, India
[3] Computer Center, University of Kerala, Thiruvananthapuram, India

Abstract. Next Generation Sequencing(NGS) is a massively parallel, low cost method capable of sequencing millions of fragments of DNA from a sample. Consequently, huge quantity of data generated and new research challenges to address storage, retrieval and processing of these bulk of data were emerged. microRNAs are non coding RNA sequences of around 18 to 24 nucleotides in length. microRNA expression profiling is a measure of relative abundance of microRNA sequences in a sample. This paper discusses algorithms for pre-processing of reads and a faster Bit Parallel Profiling (BPP) algorithm to quantify microRNAs. Experimental results shows that adapter removal has been accomplished with an accuracy of 91.2 %, a sensitivity of 89.5 % and a specificity of 89.5 %. In the case of profiling, BPP outperform an existing tool, Bowtie in terms of speed of operation.

1 Introduction

Nucleic acid sequencing is the process of finding exact order of nucleotides present in a given DNA or RNA molecule. First major endeavor in DNA sequencing was Human Genome Project. This was a 13 year long project completed in the year 2003 and method employed was Sanger sequencing. The demand for faster and cheaper alternative lead to the development of Next Generation Sequencing(NGS) [1]. NGS platforms are massively parallel, low cost and high throughput sequencing methods. The Life Technologies Ion Torrent Personal Genome Machine(PGM), Illumina: HiSeq, Roche: GS Flx+ or 454 and ABI: SOLiD are examples of NGS platforms. RNA-Seq is a NGS technique developed to analyze transcripts such as mRNAs, small RNAs and non-coding RNAs [2]. Approximately, length ranges from 400 base pairs for longer reads to 30 base pairs for shorter reads. NGS data analysis is a challenging big data analysis task as millions reads are to be pre-processed and aligned to genome or assembled to transcriptome before performing the required down stream analysis. The following sections discuss steps involved in and algorithm employed for NGS data processing.

© Springer International Publishing Switzerland 2016
Y. Tan and Y. Shi (Eds.): DMBD 2016, LNCS 9714, pp. 38–47, 2016.
DOI: 10.1007/978-3-319-40973-3_4

1.1   Pre-processing

During the library preparation, adapter sequence or fragments of adapter sequence are added to a *read*. Adapters are not part of biological sequences and needs to be removed before further processing of reads. Otherwise, it may lead to missed alignments or discarding of genuine match and finally results in wrong analysis. A sequence *read* in *fastq* format, consists of four lines- (i) sequence identifier (ii) actual sequence (iii) quality score identifier (iv) quality score. The quality score is a measure of error probability associated with each nucleotide of the sequence. The score is $Q = -10\ log_{10}e$, where e is estimated probability that a base call is wrong. A proper downstream data analysis demands to trim off the part of sequence *read* which are more probable to be wrong base call.

1.2   Sequence Mapping

Sequence mapping is the task of finding a best fit position where a *read* is to be placed in a reference sequence. This is a difficult task when the reference sequence contains millions of nucleotides. There are possibilities that *read* has multiple approximate/exact matches with the reference sequence. A number of tools have been developed in recent years for genome scale sequence mapping. Speed and accuracy are two contradicting trade-offs in the design of sequence mapping algorithms. Run time is minimum, when quality is compromised by applying limits to number of mismatches allowed and to gap lengths. The general work flow of a genome scale mapping tool starts with the indexing of reference sequence to which reads are to be aligned. Either hash table or Burrows Wheeler Transform (BWT) are the indexing techniques used in most of the tools. Hash table based indexing keeps a keyword and value pair, where keyword is k-mer generated from the reference sequence and value is the position of matched location in the reference sequence. FM Index is an index based on BWT and works with very small amount of memory. BWA [3], Bowtie [4] and SOAP [5] are examples of tools based on BWT indexing, whereas NovoAlign [6], and mrsFast [7] are tools based on Hash table.

1.3   microRNA

microRNAs belongs to the family of non-coding RNAs, very short in length and found in many eukaryotes including human. Around 1800 microRNAs have been identified in human. Studies revealed its role in wide variety of biological processes such as normal cell development, differentiation and growth control [8–10]. Precursors (pre-microRNA) of microRNAs are longer sequences and are characterized by a stable hair pin structure. During the biogenesis, sequence of around 22 nucleotide in length are separated from the pre-microRNA and form mature microRNA. Mature microRNAs binds to 3' untranslated region of mRNA, thus causing gene expression regulation. There are considerable differences in expression levels of microRNA in normal conditions and different stages of diseases [11].

1.4   microRNA Profiling

RNASeq data processing can be categorized into three types - mapping of reads into reference genome, assembling reads into partial or full length transcripts, and profiling of transcripts. microRNA expression profiling shows the degree of abundance of microRNA sequences in a given sample. There are many hurdles in proper profiling of microRNAs. Very short sequence length, lack of common start or stop sequences, very low presence in the total RNA mass make microRNA profiling to a difficult task. The sequence of operations for profiling microRNA from NGS data are preprocessing followed by sequence mapping. In preprocessing, reads are tested for adapter contamination followed by threshold tests for minimum quality and read length. Resultant reads are aligned to microRNA sequences during the mapping phase. Quantification of mature microRNAs are preferred than pre-microRNAs as the former is having active role in gene regulation. There is lack of consensus among researchers and experts for policy by which a *read* is considered as a *hit*. In a transciptome profiling experiment connected with *Colorectal Cancer*, mature microRNA sequences aligned to a *read* with a maximum of one mismatch were considered as *hit* [12]. Two or three mismatches for longer reads were allowed in other experiments [13]. There are examples of studies with a restriction that exact match between *read* and mature microRNA were made mandatory to prevent the reads mapped to paralogs of a given microRNA, and to avoid multiple ambiguous hits [14].

microRNA profiling applications using the present day tools have to perform indexing, followed by sequence mapping to generate a mapped output. This is further analyzed using other tools to quantity the exact presence of each microRNAs. Indexing is a time consuming operation, and depends on the size of reference sequence. The length of reads, especially for microRNA based studies are as low as 50 base pairs. When pre-processing steps are completed, length could further reduced and almost equivalent to that of mature microRNA sequence. When a mature microRNA sequence is acting as the reference sequence, reads can be aligned efficiently without generating an index. In this scenario, there is need for development of an alternate approach for short sequence profiling. This paper discusses, a direct parallel and faster approach for microRNA profiling from NGS data.

2   microRNA Profiling: Bit Parallel Profiling Algorithm(BPP)

We have developed a faster scheme for microRNA profiling from NGS data. Algorithm 1 shows major operations in profiling, a pre-processing of *reads* followed by sequence mapping and quantification. Initial step of preprocessing is removal of adapter/fragments of adapter sequences. Adapter removal starts by generating all overlapping sub sequences of length k from a given adapter sequence. Each $k - mer$ is scanned for an exact match with the *read* from the beginning. The scan length is limited to the maximum of length of the adapter. We used

Boyer − Moore − Horspool algorithm for exact sequence match, which rely on *bad character rule*. This rule ensures longer shifts of the pattern during the search operation. If a *k − mer* match is detected in a *read*, adapter and *read* are further aligned using Watermann Smith algorithm, keeping already matched part intact. The portion to be removed is identified as longest aligned portion with user specified threshold of mismatches that are allowed. Algorithm 3 depicts the steps in pre-processing operations. When a read completed adapter removal process, a base quality check is performed. Normally, read quality contamination is at the trailing end of *read* than initial portion. The low quality portion is trimmed when the accumulated sum of difference between the quality score and a specified threshold value falls below zero.

Algorithm 1. Bit Parallel Profiling algorithm(BPP)

$NGSdata$: **Reads in fastq format**
M : **microRNA;** k : **Number of mismatches**
procedure MIRPROFILE
    $miRP \leftarrow 0$
    while *not end of NGSdata do in parallel* **do**
        Get next read from $NGSData$ to R_i
        $R_i = RemoveAdapter(R_i, A)$
        $Rd = TrimQS(R_i, QT)$
        $match = miRQuantify(Rd, M, k)$
        if *match* **then**
            $miRP \leftarrow miRP + 1$

As both microRNA sequence and a *read* are of short length, we prefer pattern matching algorithm for quantification rather than building an index of reference sequence. We used a modified version of bit parallel approximate string matching algorithm developed by Myers, to quantify microRNAs [15]. Let $R = r_1 r_2 .... r_n$ be a read and $M = m_1 m_2 ......m_m$ be a mature microRNA sequence, and threshold value for number of mismatches that can be allowed, $k \geq 0$, then the problem of profiling can be treated as task of finding M in R with k or fewer differences. This problem can be solved with a complexity $O(mn)$ by calculating cell in a dynamic programming matrix(d.p), $C[0..m, 0..n]$ using the recurrence:

$$C[i,j] = min(C[i-1, j-1] + (0 \; if M_i = R_j, else \; 1)), C[i-1, j]+1, C[i, j-1]+1)$$

Myers modified the cost computation to an optimal level with a complexity of $O(kn/w)$, where w is the word length of the computer. The reduction in computational cost is obtained by introducing bit vectors so as to have an $O(1)$ rather than $O(m)$ computation for each column in the matrix. Both the pattern and sequence are represented as bit string. This algorithm returns set of all occurrences of given pattern in a longer sequence with k or lesser mismatches. We added constraints to the algorithm so that seed length and number of mismatches in seed region are taken into account when read hit is identified. The steps in matching process is depicted in Algorithm 2.

Algorithm 2. Algorithm to map Reads to microRNA sequences with utmost k mismatch

procedure MIRQUANTIFY($R[n]$, $M[m]$, k)   ▷ $R[n]$: a *read* of length n
    $mir = false$
    for each $c \in \Sigma$ **do** $D[c] \leftarrow 0^m$ **do**
    for $i \leftarrow 1$ to m $D[M[i]][i] = 1$ **do**
    $Pv \leftarrow 1^m$; $Mv \leftarrow 0$; $g = m$; $i \leftarrow 0'$
    while $j \leq n$ **do**
        $match \leftarrow D[R[j]]$
        $Xh \leftarrow (((match \wedge Pv) + Pv) \oplus Pv) \vee match$
        $Ph \leftarrow Mv \vee \neg(Xh \vee Pv)$
        $Mh \leftarrow Pv \wedge Xh$; $Xv \leftarrow match \vee Mv$
        $Pv \leftarrow (Mh << 1) \vee \neg(Xv \vee (Ph << 1))$
        $Mv \leftarrow (Ph << 1) \wedge Xv$; $g \leftarrow g + Ph[j] - Mh[j]$
        if $g \leq k$ **then**
            $mir = mircheck(R)$
            if mir **then**
                return $True$
        $j \leftarrow j + 1$

Algorithm 3. Algorithms to pre-process NGS reads

procedure REMOVEADAPTER($R[n]$, A)
    Generate all k-mer patterns of the adapter sequence A
    for each k-mer of A **do**
        Scan for exact match with 5' end of read
        if match **then**
            $Invoke$ $WSAlign(read, A)$
            $Trim$ $matched$ $part$ of $Sequence$
            $Exit$
procedure TRIMQS($R[n]$, $QT]$)   ▷ R - a read sequence
                                                ▷ QT - minimum quality score required
    $Lr = len(R)$ $j = 1$ $Sum = 0$
    while $Sum \geq 0$ **do**
        $Sum = Sum + Q(R[i]) - QT$
        $j = j + 1$
    if $j \geq 17$ **then**
        $Rd = Remove(R[j + 1], Lr)$; $return$ Rd
    else
        $discard$ R

2.1   Experimental Validation

Performance of the BPP algorithm has been evaluated by measuring the time required to quantify a set of microRNAs from NGS data samples. Data samples were downloaded from NCBI. These are experimental data connected with disease association of microRNAs and Hepatocellular Carcinoma (HCC) [16]. microRNA genome coordinates and sequences of microRNAs as well as for mRNAs were obtained from RefSeq [17]. Quantification of the same set of microRNAs were again computed using sequence mapping tool, Bowtie for comparison. Number of reads aligned to microRNA sequences were treated as expression level. To evaluate performance of pre-processing part the tool, we used synthesized reads of length 75 generated by ART [18] for Illumina sequencing system. A total of 5000000 reads were used and 50 % reads were added with adapter contamination. The experiments were conducted Intel(R) Xeon CPU E5-1620 v3 3.5 GHz machine.

3 Results and Discussions

Adapter removal starts with an exact string match of a possible $k - mer$ of adapter sequence. Output from the contaminated part of reads were categorized into four sets- number of reads that happens to be trimmed more, namely *Over_trim*, trimmed less namely, *Under_trim*, and *Exact_trim* and *Untrim*. Non contaminated reads were grouped into *Nc_Untrim* and *Nc_trim*. Fragments of adapter sequence of length 15 added to the beginning of 50 % reads. Table 1 shows specificity, sensitivity and accuracy of adapter removal with length of $k - mer$ chosen as 4, 6 and 8. To calculate above measures, we treated *Over_trim* and *Nc_trim* as false positives, *Under_trim* and *Untrim* as false negatives. When maximum adapter ligation was fixed at 15, Table 1 shows that the optimal value for length of k-mer is 6.

Table 1. Performance measures of adapter removal evaluated using synthesized data set (5000000 reads). 50 % of reads were contaminated with adapter residues of maximum length 15. Measures are evaluated for different k-mers, where q as 4, 6 and 8

length k-mer	Over trim	Under trim	Untrim	Exact trim	NcUn trim	NC trim	Sensitivity	Specificity	Accuracy
4	54808	75247	75114	2294831	2162968	337032	0.854	0.847	0.892
6	45309	70317	104175	2280199	2278088	221912	0.895	0.895	0.912
8	40317	62779	287950	2108954	2277700	222300	0.889	0.897	0.877

Complexity Analysis of Bit Parallel Profiling Algorithm. The backbone of proposed profiling scheme is Myers bit vector algorithm. The computational time complexity of algorithm is $O(nm/w)$ time, where w is word length of the machine. This algorithm computes values of a single column of relocatable dynamic programming matrix by $O(1)$ time using bit operations. Also, computation is independent of k, the number mismatches permitted. As the length of microRNA is around 22 nucleotides, a single word is sufficient to represent the pattern. This results in a linear time performance. Algorithm works even faster in a sub-linear manner, when parallelism is incorporated by threading the mapping process to different points in the read file.

Bowtie is a memory efficient and ultra fast sequence mapping tool. Memory efficiency and speed are attained by creating an index of the reference sequence. Index creation time will depends on length of reference sequence. Bowtie provides

Table 2. Comparison of execution time to quantify microRNAs in a NGS data sample, SRR1642970, using the proposed BPP algorithm and Bowtie sequence mapping tool. Bowtie with number of number of mismatches, v=1 and v=2 are compared

microRNAs	Execution time in seconds		
	Bit parallel profiling	Mapping by Bowtie, v=1	Mapping by Bowtie, v=2
hsa-miR-122-5p	68.05	119.73	168.48
hsa-miR-21-5p	73.57	119.34	167.31
hsa-miR-143-3p	76.2	120.51	168.48
hsa-miR-148-3p	90.09	121.68	164.58
hsa-miR-1269a	78.49	118.56	161.85
hsa-miR-183-5p	70.47	116.22	161.85
hsa-miR-10b-5p	88	118.56	164.58
hsa-miR-199a-5p	76.31	120.51	168.87
hsa-miR-30b-3p	97.01	121.68	167.31

a tool, *bowtie − build* to accomplish this task. Bowtie alignment policy can be set by either seed length (-l) and number of mismatches in seed region(-n) or total number mismatches (-v). When a sequence mapping tool such as Bowtie is used to map reads to a mature microRNA sequence, the total number of aligned *reads* can be taken as the measure its expression level [19]. Table 2 shows a comparison of execution time when Bowtie and proposed Bit Parallel Profiling (BPP) algorithm were used to quantity microRNAs in NGS data sample SRR1642970. This sample contains 10163785 reads. There is considerable difference in execution time when profiling were executed using BPP than that of Bowtie. We repeated profiling experiments with number of NGS data samples. Table 3 shows comparison of execution time to profile a microRNA hsa-miR-143-3p from

Table 3. Comparison of execution time for profiling of a single microRNA hsa-miR-143-3p using proposed BPP algorithm and Bowtie sequence mapping tool

Sample ID	Number of reads	Proposed Algorithm (BPP)	Mapping by Bowtie, v=1
SRR1642952	28,312,100	196.23	296.34
SRR1642950	20,922,731	138.34	198.78
SRR1642968	13,555,600	92.34	139.45
SRR1642966	12,934,901	87.56	134.56
SRR1642954	11,923,774	82.23	128.34
SRR1642970	10,163,737	76.21	116.22
SRR1642980	8,413,826	66.45	104.58

Table 4. Comparison of execution time to quantify longer transcripts such as mRNAs in a NGS data sample SRR1642970, using BPP algorithm and Bowtie sequence mapping tool

RNA sequences	Length	Execution time in seconds		
		Bit parallel Algorithm	Mapping by Bowtie, v=1	Mapping by Bowtie, v=2
mir-122	22	68.05	119.73	168.48
mir-122(pre-miRNA)	122	91	120.965	177.84
BTG2	684	335.21	121.225	207.74
REC	972	491.99	121.16	212.16
E2F1	2722	1157.39	121.875	234.39
RECK	4001	2094.11	122.59	239.46
APAF1	6497	2626.33	123.825	246.87

different data samples using bit parallel algorithm and Bowtie. Performance of Bowtie is not independent of number mismatches to be allowed in the mapping. Figure 1 shows an increase in execution time of Bowtie when number mismatches is varied from 0 to 3. BPP algorithm is independent of number of mismatches, hence keeps constant time with different values of mismatches. Table 4 shows execution time when the experiment is extended to longer transcripts such as mRNAs. Complexity of the BPP algorithm is linear. But Bowtie keeps execution time constant for a given value of mismatches allowed. The is attained by the index structure created by Bowtie. Figure 2 shows the same fact. It is evident that BPP performance is good only the length of reference sequence is lesser than 200 base pairs.

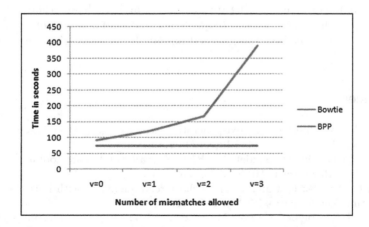

Fig. 1. Comparison in terms of execution time for microRNA profiling between BPP Algorithm and Bowtie, when number of mismatches allowed is varied from 0 to 3 (Color figure online)

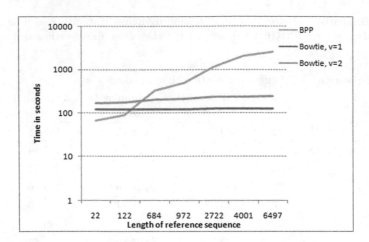

Fig. 2. Performance Comparison of Bit Parallel Profiling Algorithm with Bowtie in RNA profiling with transcripts of different lengths (Color figure online)

4 Conclusion

The developments in NGS systems resulted in generation of large quantity of genomic data. This data has to be carefully analyzed for the better understanding of the functions of any living forms. We are focusing on profiling microRNAs from these genomic data. Numerous studies reported links between alterations of microRNA and pathological conditions such as cancer, neurological diseases and cardiovascular disease. Profiling of miRNAs helps in the development of clinically useful molecular diagnostic tests. We have developed an algorithm specifically to microRNA profiling which can perform much faster and accurate than a popular sequence mapping tool Bowtie. Further, this method is a direct profiling approach results in absolute quantification, and hence no other profiling tools need to be applied on the mapped output from sequencing tools such as Bowtie.

References

1. Grada, A., Weinbrecht, K.: Next-generation sequencing: methodology and application. Soc. Invest. Dermatol. **133**(8), e11 (2013)
2. Wang, Z., Gerstein, M., Snyder, M.: RNA-Seq: a revolutionary tool for transcriptomics. Nat. Rev. Genet. **10**, 57–63 (2009)
3. Li, H., Durbin, R.: Fast and accurate short read alignment with burrows wheeler transform. Bioinformatics **25**(14), 1754–1760 (2009)
4. Langmead, B., Trapnell, C., Pop, M., Salzberg, S.L.: Ultrafast and memory-efficient alignment of short DNA sequences to the human genome. Genome Biol. **10**, r25 (2009)
5. Li, R., Li, Y., Kristiansen, K., Wang, J.: SOAP: short oligonucleotide alignment program. Bioinformatics **24**(5), 713–714 (2008)

6. Miller, J.R., Koren, S., Sutton, G.: SOAP: short oligonucleotide alignment program. Genomics **95**(6), 315–326 (2010)
7. Hach, F., Sarrafi, I., Hormozdiari, F., Alkan, C., Eichler, E.E., Sahinalp, S.C.: Mrsfast-ultra: a compact, snp-aware mapper for high performance sequencing applications. Nucleic Acid Res. **42**, W494–500 (2014)
8. Li, Y., Kowdley, K.V.: MicroRNAs in common human diseases. Genomics Proteomics Bioinf. **10**, 246–253 (2012)
9. Reshmi, G., Vinod Chandra, S.S., Mohan Babu, V.J., Babu, P.S.S., Santhi, W.S., Ramachandran, S., Lakshmi, S., Nair, A.S., Pillai, M.R.: Identification and analysis of novel microRNAs from fragile sites of human cervical cancer: computational and experimental approach. Genomics **97**(6), 333–340 (2011)
10. Salim, A., Vinod Chandra, S.S.: Computational prediction of microRNAs and their targets. J. Proteomics Bioinform. **7**(7), 193–202 (2014)
11. Landi, M.T., Zhao, Y., Rotunno, M., Koshiol, J., Liu, H., Bergen, A.W., Rubagotti, M., Goldstein, A.M., Linnoila, I., Marincola, F.M., Tucker, M.A., Bertazzi, P.A., Pesatori, A.C., Caporaso, N.E., McShane, L.M., Wang, E.: MicroRNA expression differentiates histology and predicts survival of lung cancer. Clin. Cancer Res. **16**(2), 430–441 (2010)
12. Schee, K., Lorenz, S., Worren, M.M., Günther, C.-C., Holden, M., Hovig, E., Fodstad, Ø., Meza-Zepeda, L.A., Flatmark, K.: Deep sequencing the microRNA transcriptome in colorectal cancer. PLoS ONE **8**(6), e66165 (2013)
13. Schulte, J.H., Marschall, T., Martin, M., Rosenstiel, P., Mestdagh, P., Schlierf, S., Thor, T., Vandesompele, J., Eggert, A., Schreiber, S., Rahmann, S., Schramm, A.: Deep sequencing reveals differential expression of microRNAs in favorable versus unfavorable neuroblastoma. Nucleic Acids Res. **38**(17), 5919–5928 (2010)
14. Chang, H.T., Li, S.C., Ho, M.R., Pan, H.W., Ger, L.P., Hu, L.Y., Yu, S.Y., Li, W.H., Tsai, K.W.: Comprehensive analysis of microRNAs in breast cancer. BMC Genomics **13**(6), S18 (2012)
15. Horspool, R.N.: Practical fast searching in strings. Softw. Pract. Experience **10**(6), 501–506 (1980)
16. Wojcicka, A., Swierniak, M., Kornasiewicz, O., Gierlikowski, W., Maciag, M., Kolanowska, M., Kotlarek, M., Gornicka, B., Koperski, L., Niewinski, G., Krawczyk, M., Jazdzewski, K.: Next generation sequencing reveals microRNA isoforms in liver cirrhosis and hepatocellular carcinoma. Int. J. Biochem. Cell Biol. **53**, 208–217 (2014)
17. Tatusova, T., Ciufo, S., Fedorov, B., O'Neill, K., Tolstoy, I.: Refseq microbial genomes database: new representation and annotation strategy. Nucleic Acids Res. **42**, D553–D559 (2014)
18. Huang, W., Li, L., Myers, J.R., Marth, G.T.: Art: a next-generation sequencing read simulator. Bioinformatics **28**(4), 593–594 (2012)
19. Eminaga, S., Christodoulou, D.C., Vigneault, F., Church, G.M., Seidman, J.G.: Quantification of microRNA expression with next-generation sequencing. In: Current Protocols in Molecular Biology, Chapter 4, Unit-4.17 (2013)

Utilising the Cross Industry Standard Process for Data Mining to Reduce Uncertainty in the Measurement and Verification of Energy Savings

Colm V. Gallagher$^{(\boxtimes)}$, Ken Bruton, and Dominic T.J. O'Sullivan

Intelligent Efficiency Research Group, University College Cork, Cork, Ireland
c.v.gallagher@umail.ucc.ie

Abstract. This paper investigates the application of Data Mining (DM) to predict baseline energy consumption for the improvement of energy savings estimation accuracy in Measurement and Verification (M&V). M&V is a requirement of a certified energy management system (EnMS). A critical stage of the M&V process is the normalisation of data post Energy Conservation Measure (ECM) to pre-ECM conditions. Traditional M&V approaches utilise simplistic modelling techniques, which dilute the power of the available data. DM enables the true power of the available energy data to be harnessed with complex modelling techniques. The methodology proposed incorporates DM into the M&V process to improve prediction accuracy. The application of multi-variate regression and artificial neural networks to predict compressed air energy consumption in a manufacturing facility is presented. Predictions made using DM were consistently more accurate than those found using traditional approaches when the training period was greater than two months.

Keywords: Measurement and Verification · Data mining · Energy efficiency · Baseline energy modelling

1 Introduction

The European Union has issued the Energy Efficiency Directive (2012/27/EU) to ensure member states shift to a more energy efficient economy [1]. The effective implementation of the Directive relies heavily on the cumulative effect of energy savings across a number of projects. An example of this is the Energy Efficiency Obligation Scheme (EEOS) in Ireland, which is being implemented pursuant to Article 7 of the Directive [2]. Ireland has chosen to use the EEOS as a mechanism to ensure targets set out in the Directive are achieved. The scheme obligates energy distributors and retail energy sales companies to achieve energy efficiency improvement targets based on their market share. This structure requires the aggregated savings of multiple individual projects to reach these targets. Over or under estimation of savings in individual cases can lead to national targets not being met, therefore failing to achieve the overall objective of the Directive.

© Springer International Publishing Switzerland 2016
Y. Tan and Y. Shi (Eds.): DMBD 2016, LNCS 9714, pp. 48–58, 2016.
DOI: 10.1007/978-3-319-40973-3_5

In the energy efficiency sector, Measurement and Verification (M&V) is the process of quantifying energy savings delivered by an Energy Conservation Measure (ECM). M&V is a requirement of a certified Energy Management System (EnMS). The Efficiency Valuation Organization publish standardised M&V guidelines entitled the International Performance Measurement and Verification Protocol (IPMVP). IPMVP is a framework of definitions and broad approaches for M&V. In addition to this, ASHRAE publish Guideline 14P, which provides detail on implementing M&V plans. Both guidance documents require metering to estimate energy savings.

There are two periods of analysis in the M&V of energy savings: the pre-ECM period and the post-ECM period. In most cases, real data is available for the pre-ECM period and post-ECM period (measured energy). To quantify the savings achieved, the energy consumption post-ECM must be compared to what the consumption would be had the ECM not been implemented. This is known as the adjusted baseline. This requires the baseline energy consumption in the pre-ECM period to be modelled and used to quantify the adjusted baseline in the post-ECM period by normalising post-ECM consumption to pre-ECM conditions. Figure 1 contains a graphical representation of this calculation process. Hence, M&V is not an exact science as there is always a margin of error in predicting energy consumption [3].

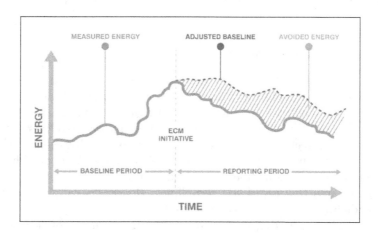

Fig. 1. Overview of measurement and verification savings calculation [4] (Color figure online)

The normalisation of the adjusted baseline to an acceptable degree of certainty is a critical step in M&V. The methods most commonly used to predict the adjusted baseline are reviewed in Sect. 2.3. This study proposes an alternative M&V methodology that utilises data mining (DM) to harness the power of the energy data available. DM is being utilised as a mechanism to progress M&V of energy savings towards more accurate and reliable results. This is possible as

DM enables efficient processing of the data and prediction of the adjusted baseline, hence maximising the potential power of the available data.

2 Related Work

2.1 Data Mining in Energy Engineering Applications

Continual improvement and development is a vital component in the success of an EnMS. This requirement is being satisfied through the use of DM to support and implement these systems. DM has successfully been used to define, develop and implement an EnMS. Velázquez et al. utilised a DM approach to identify key performance indicators and subsequently energy consumption models [5].

Energy consumption has also been predicted through the use of DM with a view to allowing for more informed decision making. This was achieved by extracting information from unstructured data sources, processing the data and presenting it in a manner that maximises its use to the decision maker [6]. If patterns in energy consumption are not obvious, DM has been shown to be the most effective mean of capturing consumption trends in the case of efficiently maintaining buildings [7]. Also, in a study which applied DM techniques to optimise building heating, ventilation and air-conditioning performance, DM has been shown to accurately model the operation of buildings, when supplied with sufficient data [8].

2.2 Modelling Energy Consumption

In engineering, the ability to predict electrical loads in an accurate manner is a valuable tool in demand side management. A DM approach using unsupervised learning has been taken in M&V to estimate baseline load for demand response in a smart grid [9]. The self-organizing map and K-means clustering were the modelling techniques applied. The results of which were compared to the accuracy of day matching methods, which is a simplistic approach to predicting energy consumption. Root mean square error was reduced by 15–22% on average through the use of DM techniques. Hence, the suitability of more complex modelling algorithms was vindicated [9].

The use of soft computing models to improve the accuracy of electrical load forecasting has also been investigated. Neuro-fuzzy systems have been proven to perform better than artificial neural networks and statistical forecasting based on Box-Jenkins ARIMA model [10]. Electrical load forecasting for smart grids analyse data across a larger project boundary than a typical M&V case. M&V of energy savings generally focuses on a smaller project boundary which in some cases is as large as an entire facility, while in other cases it can be as small as only covering a single piece of equipment. Hence, the application of DM techniques, such as those mentioned, to M&V of smaller scale electrical loads should be investigated.

2.3 Baseline Modelling in M&V at Present

Modelling techniques that are commonly used in industry include linear regression, day matching and change-point regression models. Walter et al. stated that a limitation of methods used for predicting baseline energy is the inadequate quantification of uncertainty in baseline energy consumption predictions. The importance of uncertainty estimation is highlighted as being essential for weighing the risks of investing in ECM [11]. Reviews of the possible modelling techniques have been carried out. One such study compares five models which include change point models, monthly degree-day models, and hourly regression models. This presented a general statistical methodology to evaluate baseline model performance. The study showed that results generated using 6-months pre-ECM data, i.e. training data, may be just as accurate as those that use a 12-month training period [12]. Crowe et al. investigated using baseline regression models for individual homes to move towards an automated M&V approach using interval data. The results were found to offer a promising first step in the process, while recommendations were made to develop more a robust M&V methodology [13].

This paper assesses the suitability of using DM to provide this robustness in M&V. The need to progress the methods used to quantify the adjusted baseline in M&V projects has been highlighted. As the methods used at present are rigid in nature, they tend to generalise the variables affecting energy consumption. DM is proposed to progress this aspect of M&V through the use of complex modelling techniques that are capable of capturing the trends of energy consumption. The case study presented reviews the application of data mining for energy consumption prediction in a biomedical manufacturing facility. Each stage of the data mining process is detailed within the context of the case study.

3 Application of CRISP-DM for Purposes of M&V: A Case Study in a Manufacturing Facility

The CRoss Industry Standard Process for Data Mining (CRISP-DM) was identified as a method to further standardise the M&V methodology and enable more accurate estimation of energy savings. A case study was carried out to assess the viability of the methodology proposed in this paper. Figure 2 outlines the procedure applied. Rapidminer Studio (v7.0.001) was the software used to implement the CRISP-DM [14].

3.1 Business Understanding

A biomedical manufacturing facility was chosen as a case study to assess the feasibility of the application of DM to aid M&V. A quality understanding of the business under analysis was essential to interpret the results at the modelling and evaluation stages of the process. This was achieved by carrying out

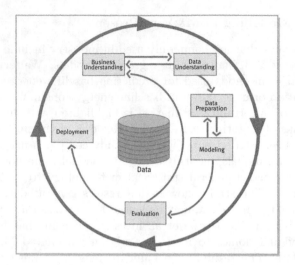

Fig. 2. Phases of the CRISP-DM reference model [15]

a process walk-through, studying process flow diagrams, and piping and instrumentation diagrams. A knowledge of the systems within the boundary of analysis was acquired from this process and any additional issues were discussed with the facility's engineering team. The boundary of the analysis was the electrical energy consumption across the entire manufacturing facility.

3.2   Data Understanding

The data understanding phase of the CRISP-DM reference model was completed through investigation into the information technology infrastructure at the facility. An understanding of the flow of energy consumption data and the databases in which it was stored was gained. This enabled the data preparation stage detailed in Sect. 3.3 to be carried out in an efficient manner with all pre-processing completed using as little resources as possible. The objective of streamlining the M&V process was considered at each stage of the study.

3.3   Data Preparation

Energy consumption data is often difficult to compute due to the nature of the metering. Cumulative meters are generally used for electrical energy and as a result, pre-processing must be completed on the outputted data. In the case under investigation, this was completed prior to being output to the user. However, despite this pre-cleansing of the data, outliers remained in the data set as the pre-cleansing process did not remove all anomalies. Therefore, the data preparation stage was utilised to remove any remaining outliers in the data set delivered to the user. Figure 3 illustrates the steps undertaken to prepare the data for the modelling stage.

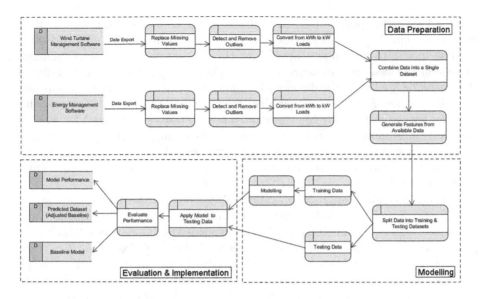

Fig. 3. Application of CRISP-DM in case study

Two data sources were used to gather the data required for a complete analysis of the electrical energy consumers on-site: energy management software and wind turbine management software. The electrical energy consumed on-site is measured by cumulative kilowatt-hour (kWh) meters. Pre-processing of this data involved detecting outliers caused by meter errors and converting the data from kWh to average electrical loads in kilowatts (kW). The second step was required in order to analyse all data in the same format and units. The individual datasets were then joined together and forwarded to the modelling stage described in Sect. 3.4.

The use of data mining methods to pre-process the data reduced the resources required to clean the dataset into a useful form. Without the use of these DM techniques, the detection of anomalies can be a manual, time-intensive process. The process developed in the software environment can be applied to any data export from the systems within the analysis boundary. Hence, future projects can utilise this resource, further streamlining the M&V process.

3.4 Modelling

The dataset output from the data preparation stage was in a clean and functional format as a result of the data cleansing performed. For the purposes of this case study, the compressed air load was the chosen quantity to be modelled, as it was the most appropriate variable to highlight the power of the available energy data. When the load was analysed at a high-level, there was no clear and obvious correlation to other significant energy users on-site. The other significant energy users were more predictable due to scheduling of equipment and the presence of standard operating procedures. An electrical meter measured the total electrical energy consumed by the compressed air generation system in 15-min intervals.

The modelling techniques applied to the dataset were multivariate linear regression and feed-forward neural networks. Following a review of the techniques that could be applied to the dataset, these were found to be the most appropriate for this analysis. A total of 11 variables were available to be used to construct a model for compressed air consumption. These variables accounted for 44 % of electricity consumption across the facility. The modelling process was developed within the software environment and the variables utilised to build each model were chosen automatically by the software based on significance to the attribute being predicted.

A traditional M&V approach was also considered for the purposes of evaluating the effectiveness of the techniques proposed. This approach consisted of single variable linear regression modelling. For M&V purposes, this is an approach that most practitioners are familiar with through the use of Microsoft Excel [16]. A correlation matrix was generated to assess which variable in the dataset had the greatest influence on the compressed air load, the quantity to be predicted. The electricity consumed by production related equipment had the highest correlation coefficient with a value of 0.902, hence this was chosen to be used as the input variable for developing the single variable regression model for compressed air consumption. Figure 3 illustrates the modelling process carried out.

Following initial modelling using the techniques described above, the results were evaluated. As per the CRISP-DM methodology, the data understanding stage was revisited within the context of the modelling process. The process of constructing the models was then refined to ensure the knowledge contained in the dataset was accurately represented and the power of this knowledge was maximised. This was achieved by choosing modelling parameters, such as tolerance levels and learning rates, in a heuristic manner. For the feed-forward neural network, this process identified a learning rate of 0.3 and a total of three layers as the most appropriate for the data under analysis. Similarly, the minimum tolerance used to construct the linear regression models was chosen as 0.05.

3.5 Evaluation

The models developed in Sect. 3.4 were applied to a new dataset containing energy consumption knowledge for a time period outside that with which the models were constructed. This independent dataset was used for cross validation of the models. Relative error was the metric used to evaluate the performance of each model. The modelling technique that resulted in the lowest relative error was deemed as the most appropriate for the given data set. The equation for N data points is as follows:

$$Mean\ Relative\ Error = \frac{1}{N} \sum_{i=1}^{N} \frac{pred(i) - real(i)}{real(i)}. \tag{1}$$

Table 1 contains the relative error of each model in predicting the compressed air load during the testing period. The training period duration was varied to assess the affect that this had on model performance. It was found that the single variable regression model is the most appropriate modelling technique in cases where the training data available is less than 62 days, as this technique minimised the relative error. For greater training periods, the multivariate linear regression model and feed-forward neural network performance improved greatly and surpassed that of the single variable regression model.

Table 1. Relative error in predictions from each model.

Training period	Testing period	Single variable linear regression	Multivariate linear regression	Feed-forward neural network
31 Days	28 Days	40.4 %	64.32 %	46.81 %
62 Days	28 Days	37.18 %	38.18 %	58.26 %
92 Days	28 Days	29.92 %	22.09 %	23.09 %
111 Days	28 Days	28.67 %	21.49 %	28.16 %
139 Days	28 Days	26.84 %	19.87 %	21.6 %

Multi-variate linear regression performed with the lowest relative error for the longest training period. As energy data is largely affected by the outdoor air temperature, historical data over a 12-month period is usually used for analysis. This ensures a wide range of operating conditions are contained within the data. A full cycle of a facility's operation is also required to capture all levels of energy consumption. The manufacturing facility in this study operates continuous processes so a full cycle of operation is not as defined as that of a batch process. Hence, a default value of 12-months of data would suffice. However, approximately 6-months of data that was fit for use was available at the time of this analysis.

Taking the prediction accuracy of the models developed across the range of training periods, multi-variate linear regression was the most appropriate technique for modelling the baseline compressed air energy consumption in this case. Figure 4 illustrates a sample of the prediction accuracy of this leading performing model, developed using 139 days of training data. The decrease in compressed air load on February 6 is as a result of reduced plant operations on weekends. The performance gap between the traditional modelling technique and multi-variate linear regression was approximately constant at 7 % for training periods greater than 92 days. A longer period of analysis must be considered to investigate this relationship further.

3.6 Deployment

Deployment of the models generated would consist of predicting the adjusted baseline in the post-ECM period. This would then be compared with metered

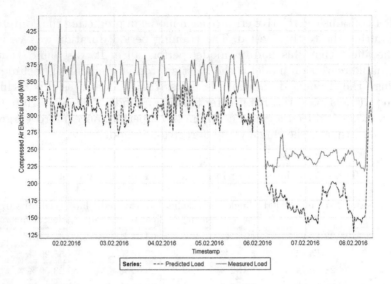

Fig. 4. Sample of prediction performance of multi-variate linear regression model (Color figure online)

data to identify the savings made. For an M&V project, the largest training dataset would be used in order to capture the widest range of production levels possible. Hence, given that the models constructed using a DM approach were more accurate than those constructed using a traditional modelling approach, deployment in an M&V application would improve the performance of the energy savings estimation.

4 Conclusions

The prediction of compressed air electricity consumption in a large biomedical manufacturing facility was chosen to apply and review the proposed methodology. Multi-variate linear regression models and feed-forward neural networks were constructed using a variety of training periods. Single variable linear regression was also performed as it is a common approach used in M&V. Cross-validation of all models found that the traditional approach was more appropriate when the training period was two months or less. Training periods longer than this resulted in the models developed using a DM approach performing with improvements in relative error of approximately 7 %. The data mining process was found to improve the prediction accuracy, therefore reduce the uncertainty in energy savings estimation for M&V purposes. More detailed analysis using a calendar year of training data should be performed to further substantiate the findings of this case study. The use of DM to improve performance and reduce the resources required for M&V was presented with promising results for this case study. One can broaden the scope of this analysis across a variety of M&V applications to advance the research into the subject area.

5   Future Work

The research presented in this paper is part of a wider study which has a primary objective to move towards automating the process of M&V. The results of the CRISP-DM included in this paper form an initial evaluation of the potential and effectiveness of DM in these circumstances. Future research will consist of broadening the scope of the analysis presented in this paper through the use of larger datasets, alternative case studies and more complex baseline modelling techniques.

Acknowledgements. The authors would like to acknowledge the financial support of the Science Foundation Ireland MaREI Centre and the NTR Foundation.

References

1. European Parliament: Directive 2012/27/EU of the European Parliament and of the Council of 25 October 2012 on energy efficiency (2012)
2. Sustainable Energy Authority of Ireland: Energy efficiency obligation scheme. Technical report (2014)
3. Drive, B., Afb, T.: Measurement & Verification handbook. Technical report (1998)
4. C^3 Resources. http://www.c3resources.co.uk
5. Velázquez, D., González-Falcón, R., Pérez-Lombard, L., Marina Gallego, L., Monedero, I., Biscarri, F.: Development of an energy management system for a naphtha reforming plant: a data mining approach. Energy Convers. Manag. **67**, 217–225 (2013)
6. Peral, J., Ferrández, A., Tardío, R., Maté, A., de Gregorio, E.: Energy consumption prediction by using an integrated multidimensional modeling approach and data mining techniques with Big Data. In: Indulska, M., Purao, S. (eds.) ER Workshops 2014. LNCS, vol. 8823, pp. 45–54. Springer, Heidelberg (2014)
7. Gao, Y., Tumwesigye, E., Cahill, B., Menzel, K.: Using data mining in optimisation of building energy consumption and thermal comfort management. In: Kou, G., Peng, Y., Franz, I.S., Chen, Y., Tateyama, T. (eds.) SEDM 2010, pp. 434–439. IEEE Xplore (2010)
8. Ahmed, A., Korres, N.E., Ploennigs, J., Elhadi, H., Menzel, K.: Mining building performance data for energy-efficient operation. Adv. Eng. Inform. **25**, 341–354 (2011)
9. Park, S., Ryu, S., Choi, Y., Kim, H.: A framework for baseline load estimation in demand response: data mining approach. In: IEEE SmartGridComm 2014, pp. 638–643. IEEE Xplore (2014)
10. Abraham, A., Nath, B.: A neuro-fuzzy approach for modelling electricity demand in Victoria. Appl. Soft Comput. **1**, 127–138 (2001)
11. Walter, T., Price, P.N., Sohn, M.D.: Uncertainty estimation improves energy measurement and verification procedures. Appl. Energy **130**, 230–236 (2014)
12. Granderson, J., Price, P.N.: Evaluation of the predictive accuracy of five whole-building baseline models. Technical report, Lawrence Berkeley National Laboratory (2012)
13. Crowe, E., Reed, A., Kramer, H., Kemper, E., Hinkle, M.: Baseline energy modeling approach for residential M&V applications. Technical report, Northwest Energy Efficiency Alliance (2015)

14. RapidMiner Studio 7. https://rapidminer.com/products/studio
15. The Modeling Agency. https://the-modeling-agency.com/crisp-dm.pdf
16. Bonneville Power Administration: Regression for M&V: reference guide. Technical report, May 2012

Implementing Majority Voting Rule to Classify Corporate Value Based on Environmental Efforts

Ratna Hidayati$^{(\boxtimes)}$, Katsutoshi Kanamori, Ling Feng,
and Hayato Ohwada

Department of Industrial Administration, Faculty of Science and Technology,
Tokyo University of Science, 2641 Yamazaki, Noda-shi
Chiba-ken 278-8510, Japan
7415623@ed.tus.ac.jp, {katsu,ohwada}@rs.tus.ac.jp,
fengl@rs.noda.tus.ac.jp

Abstract. The Japanese understanding of corporate social responsibility (CSR) is linked with the country's history of industrial pollution. As a result, the top area Japanese companies are addressing is the environment. This study aims to classify the corporate value of Japanese companies calculated by the Ohlson model based on environmental efforts using several classification techniques. The corporate value is divided into high, medium, and low. Since the classification leads to imbalanced classes, five classification techniques (Gradient Boosting, Decision Tree, Support Vector Machine (SVM), and K-Nearest Neighbor (KNN)) were chosen to deal with this problem. KNN, with the lowest accuracy (0.68), was found predict smaller classes better than the others. To improve its accuracy, a majority voting rule is implemented in this study. In the voting rule, three classifiers (KNN, Random Forest, and Decision Tree) are combined. The accuracy for the combination of the three classifiers is 0.71. However, this study found that the impact on biodiversity is the most important variable among Japanese companies. This indicates that recent efforts to differentiate corporate value among Japanese companies based on environmental efforts arises from their understanding of the impact of business activities on biodiversity.

Keywords: Corporate value · Ohlson model · Environmental efforts · Classifier techniques · Majority voting rule

1 Introduction

Nowadays, various stakeholders such as customers, shareholders, financial institutions, governments, and civil society organizations consider corporate social responsibility (CSR) to be an essential part of business practices. CSR is important and has become a fundamental market force affecting long-term financial viability and success. In Japan, the concept of CSR has been widely discussed in recent years as an innovative business dimension. CSR has become an indispensable element of Japanese corporate management. Domestically, many companies are undertaking efforts in the areas of the

© Springer International Publishing Switzerland 2016
Y. Tan and Y. Shi (Eds.): DMBD 2016, LNCS 9714, pp. 59–66, 2016.
DOI: 10.1007/978-3-319-40973-3_6

environment, human rights, and women's advancement. Overseas, the top area they are addressing is the environment as well [1]. At the same time, the Japanese government is also developing systems to facilitate more environmentally friendly business and a recycling economy that better balances the environment and economics. According to this issue, it is clear that the strength of Japanese corporations in doing CSR activities stems from the environmental aspects.

This study aims to classify corporate values calculated by the Ohlson model based on environmental efforts using several classifier methods. We choose some common classifiers to deal with the nature of our data. The Ohlson model is used to estimate an income based on expected profits. Using the Ohlson model, we wanted to explore the relation of environmental efforts and corporate value from a long-term perspective, since many previous studies only focused on the relation of CSR and financial performance such as ROA or ROE from a short-term perspective.

The paper proceeds as follows. The following section provides an overview of environmental efforts by Japanese companies. Section 3 describes how the data in this paper were collected and the methodology that was used in this study. Section 4 discusses the study's findings. The paper ends with the recommendations and limitations of the study in light of the given topic.

2   Environmental Efforts by Japanese Companies

In Japanese companies, the relationship between CSR and corporate competitiveness in the area of the environment is relatively easy to understand. For instance, efforts to reduce environmental burdens often lead to greater efficiency and lower costs. The market for environmentally friendly products or services is also growing [2]. The environmental efforts of CSR are linked with the history of industrial pollution in Japan. High economic growth in postwar Japan resulted in massive environmental pollution during the 1960s and 1970s, known as the kōgai incident [3].

Many Japanese companies put the environment high on their agendas. They have endeavored to promote environmental awareness and ecologically sound corporate management, and to create a recycling society [4]. Many Japanese companies have become sensitive to pollution and its risks and have implemented environmental corporate management tools for daily business conduct. They have begun to realize that environmentally benign management can improve their competitiveness [5]. A growing share of firms also has begun to consider investing in environmentally friendly products and processes as a strategic move rather than as a cost [6]. With its several benefits, the number of companies that have implemented environmental management standard ISO 14001 is high in Japan [7].

Japan has experienced a large number of corporate scandals, most of them related to industrial pollution or environmental destruction resulting from their business activities. Hence, many Japanese companies have reported on their environmental performance for years, such as publishing information concerning their environmental policies, mainly out of accountability considerations or as part of their risk management. Another study concluded that developments such as the ISO standard were larger drivers for the implementing CSR policies than pressures from society [8]. In Japan, the association of CSR with compliance and philanthropic activities is very strong. That is why Japanese companies are less likely to discuss issues that were of no importance in the traditional corporate system [9]. Consequently, CSR inside or outside Japan is mainly focused on environmental aspects rather than employment and human rights issues [10].

3   Data and Methodology

Based on the history of Japanese companies dealing with environmental issues, we selected 12 attributes from the Toyo Keizai database in 2015. The attributes involve the presence of an environmental department, an environmental officer, an environmental report, environmental accounting, an environmental audit, an environmental management system (ISO14001), planning for reduction of CO_2 emissions, green purchasing efforts, the possibility of pollution, environment-related laws and regulations, and climate change initiatives, along with the impact on biodiversity. All of these attributes are categorical. For instance, regarding the environmental department attribute, companies are asked about the presence or absence of an environmental measures department. The answers are 1 for a full-time department, 2 for concurrent department, 3 for none, 4 for other, and 0 for no answer.

Originally, we had data on more than 1000 companies from Toyo Keizai. However, to calculate corporate values by the Ohlson model, we need financial information from the NikkeiNEEDS_CD-ROM (Nikkei Economic Electronic Databank System) also in 2015. Unfortunately, not all companies provide their financial data. In the end, we obtained values for only 260 companies. The highest value is 1766976, and the lowest value is -51160.2. We clustered these values using simple k-means and the elbow method to determine the optimal number of clusters for k-means clustering. We found the k in k-means clustering is 3. Then, k-means provide results from 260 samples, with a low value of 205, a medium value of 39, and a high value of 16. Hence, we utilized certain classifiers that can deal with these data or categorical data. In machine learning, common classifiers for dealing with categorical data include Gradient Boosting, Decision Tree, Support Vector Machine, Random Forest, and K-Nearest Neighbors. We tried all of these classifiers to find out which classifier would give the best result.

4   Result

4.1   Classifier Accuracy

The data are imbalanced, so we used a stratified k-fold to evaluate the performance of each classifier. Stratification is the process of re-arranging the data to ensure that each fold is a good representative of the whole.

According to Table 1, the highest accuracy is obtained by SVM, Gradient Boosting or Random Forest, Decision Tree, and KNN, respectively. However, looking at the accuracy information is not enough to make a decision. Classification accuracy is just the starting point. The accuracy is the number of correct predictions divided by the total

Table 1. Accuracy for each classifier

Classifiers	Accuracy
Gradient Boosting	0.75
Decision Tree	0.74
Support Vector Machine (SVM)	0.79
Random Forest	0.75
K Nearest Neighbor (KNN)	0.68

number of predictions and multiplied by 100 to turn it into a percentage. Next we will take a look at Table 2, the classification report for each classifier.

Precision is the number of positive predictions divided by the total number of positive class values predicted. Recall is the number of positive predictions divided by the number of positive class values in the data test. The F1 score conveys the balance between precision and recall. Table 2 indicates that all classifiers give good classification reports for predicting class 0. However, only Decision Tree, Random Forest, and KNN can predict class 1.

Table 2. Classification report

Precision					Recall					F1 Score				
GB	DT	SVM	RF	KNN	GB	DT	SVM	RF	KNN	GB	DT	SVM	RF	KNN
0.8	0.8	0.79	0.8	0.83	0.96	0.94	1	0.96	0.83	0.87	0.86	0.88	0.87	0.83
0	0.21	0	0.18	0.17	0	0.08	0	0.05	0.23	0	0.11	0	0.08	0.2
0	0	0	0	0	0	0	0	0	0	0	0	0	0	0
0.63	0.67	0.62	0.66	0.68	0.75	0.75	0.79	0.77	0.69	0.69	0.7	0.7	0.7	0.68

Next, we consider the confusion matrix for each classifier, a clean and unambiguous way to present the prediction results of a classifier. The diagonal cells show where the true class and predicted class match. The higher the diagonal values of the confusion matrix the better, indicating many correct predictions.

Based on Table 3, we can see that the best confusion matrix for predicting small classes is obtained from KNN, followed by Random Forest, Decision Tree, and Gradient Boosting. Gradient Boosting is better for predicting class 0 than the Decision Tree and Random Forest confusion matrices. However, Decision Tree and Random Forest are better for predicting class 1. Moreover, KNN is the only classifier that predicted class 2, though only one is correct.

Table 3. Confusion matrix

Classifier / label	GB			DT			SVM			RF			KNN		
0	196	6	3	186	17	2	205	0	0	194	6	5	175	30	0
1	33	1	5	34	3	2	39	0	0	34	4	1	32	7	0
2	13	3	0	13	3	0	16	0	0	12	4	0	8	7	1

4.2   Majority Voting Rule/Ensemble Classifier

When the class distribution is unbalanced, accuracy is considered a poor indicator as it gives high scores to models that just predict the most frequent class. Sometimes a classifier with the lowest accuracy can give a better result. The majority voting rule is a technique for improving classifier accuracy. It is considered one of the simplest and most intuitive methods for combining classifier methods [11]. There are two common methods, hard and soft voting. In hard voting, the majority rule of the predictions by the classifiers is taken. For example, among three classifiers, if two classifiers predict the sample as class 0, we will classify the sample as class 0. If weights are provided, the classifier multiplies the occurrence of a class by this weight. In soft voting, a weight parameter is provided to assign a specific weight to each classifier. We collect the predicted class probabilities for each classifier, multiply them by the classifier weight, and then take the average.

The problem with an ensemble or combination of classifiers is how to pick the right classifiers. In this study, we provide some steps to choose which classifier can best deal with imbalanced classes (Fig. 1).

Fig. 1. Steps for combining classifiers

We begin by evaluating the performance of classifiers using stratified k-folds. The classification report in this study shows that all classifiers are able to predict class 0. However, only Decision Tree, Random Forest, and KNN can predict class 1. In this step, we consider those three classifiers. Decision Tree, Random Forest, and KNN. Looking at the classification report is not enough, since we still do not know which classifier can predict the smallest class or class 2. From the confusion matrix, we found that KNN is the only classifier that can predict class 2. At this point, we conclude that KNN is the best classifier to predict the smallest class, although its accuracy is the lowest. To improve its accuracy, we will combine KNN with Random Forest and Decision Tree. Random Forest and Decision Tree are chosen because of their performance, as demonstrated in the classification report and confusion matrix.

Table 4 shows that both hard and soft voting can increase the accuracy of the classifier. However, we still do not know which one is better. The goal of combining classifiers is not only to increase the accuracy, but also to increase the ability to predict the smallest class. To understand which ensemble is better for predicting the smallest class, we test the ability of both of the ensembles to predict a sample in class 2. This process is important mainly because the goal is to improve the ability of KNN to predict the smallest class. In addition, in the soft voting rule, a different combination of

Table 4. Majority voting rule

Classifiers	Accuracy	Hard voting	Soft voting
KNN	0.67	0.67	0.67
Random Forest	0.76	0.76	0.76
Decision Tree	0.72	0.72	0.72
Ensemble		0.74	0.71

weights can give the same accuracy. We thus need to test a combination of weights to know which combination is best to predict the smallest class. The results are provided in Figs. 2 and 3.

Figures 3 and 4 show the differences between the hard voting and soft voting results in predicting a sample from class 2. The accuracy of hard voting is better than that of soft voting. However, when it comes to predicting the smallest class, soft voting can predict the sample as class 2, and hard voting cannot. In this step, we conclude that combining KNN, Random Forest, and Decision Tree with soft voting is the best method to improve the accuracy of classification of corporate values based on environmental efforts among Japanese companies. The accuracy is 0.71 and the weights are given as 6 for KNN and 2 for Random Forest and Decision Tree. If we are not satisfied with the result, in step 5 we can return to step 2 to eliminate or add classifiers.

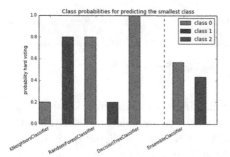

Fig. 2. Hard voting (Color figure online)   **Fig. 3.** Soft voting (Color figure online)

4.3 Variable Importance

In this step, we measure the importance of the various variables in the environmental efforts. Our main purpose in measuring variable importance is to consider pairs of variables that contain similar information, since our study is performing classification, not regression or predictions of corporate values. We want to know which variables can differentiate Japanese companies based on their environmental efforts. The following figure shows the importance values for all attributes.

According to Fig. 4, the impact on biodiversity is the only variable that scored 100. In contrast, the audit variable obtains an importance score of nearly zero, indicating that this variable never appears as either a primary or a surrogate splitter and that eliminating it from the data set should make no difference to the results. However, the fact

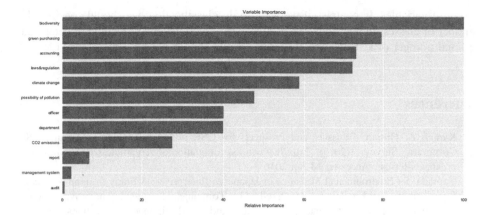

Fig. 4. Variable importance

that a variable has high importance does not mean that it should always be included in the final model. Some variables have high importance because they are overly specific and therefore act more like identifiers.

5 Conclusions and Further Research

Accuracy in classification techniques can be misleading. Sometimes it may be desirable to select a model with a lower accuracy because it has a greater predictive power in the current situation. This problem usually comes when there is a large class imbalance. Having imbalanced data is common. Most classification data sets do not have an exactly equal number of instances in each class, but a small difference often does not matter. Classification accuracy alone therefore cannot be trusted to select a well-performing model. By using the classification report and the confusion matrix we can determine which classifier is best. In this study, we provide a procedure for combining classifiers using a majority voting rule.

Our study only focused on the environmental aspects of CSR in Japanese companies. In this study, we found that the most important variable is the impact on biodiversity. For this variable, companies are asked about their ability to understand the impact of their activities on biodiversity. In conclusion, the distinguishing characteristic among Japanese companies in doing CSR activities based on environmental aspects is their understanding about the impact on biodiversity of their business activities. For further research, we would like to explore the relation between CSR and corporate value from other dimensions, such as corporate governance, human resource utilization, and social performance. Moreover, since CSR has many dimensions, we would like to investigate all dimensions of the CSR activities and their relation to corporate value. It is not impossible to do so with machine learning, but we should consider choosing techniques that are appropriate given the nature of our data and the purpose of our study, namely doing either classification or regression. If we want to do regression, we should consider the linear and nonlinear relationships between predictors and response variables. In contrast, if we want to do classification, we should consider the number of classes. In this study, we used k-means with the elbow method to determine optimal number of k. However, clustering results should not be generalized [12].

References

1. Kamei, Z., Hirano, T.: Issues and Prospects for CSR in Japan Analysis of Japan's CSR Corporate Survey. (2015) http://www.tokyofoundation.org/en/articles/2015/issues-and-prospects-for-csr. Accessed 18 Jan 2016
2. Yamada, S.: Environmental Measures in Japaneses Enterprises: A Study from an Aspect of Socialisation for Employees. In: Szell, G., Tominaga, K. (eds.) The environmental challenges for japan and germany: intercultural and interdisciplinary perspectives, pp. 297–322. Peter Lang, Frankfurt/Main (2004)
3. Yamada, S.: Corporate social responsibility in Japan. Focused on environmental communication. In: Gyorgy Szell (ed.): Corporate Social Responsibility in the EU & Japan, pp. 341–358. Frankfurt/Main: Peter Lang (2006)
4. Nippon, K.: Japan 2025: Envisioning a Vibrant, Attractive Nation in the Twenty-first Century. Nippon Keidanren, Tokyo (2003)
5. Nakao, Y., Amano, A., Matsumura, K., Genba, K., Nakano, M.: Relationship between environmental performance and financial performance: an empirical analysis of japanese corporations. Bus. Strategy Environ. 16(2), 106–118 (2006)
6. Tanabe, T.: Kankyō CSR-ron ni arata-na shiten o [a new perspective for environmental CSR theory]. Econ. Rev. Fujitsu Res. Inst. 9(1), 114–115 (2005)
7. Hanada, M.: The trend of environmental reports in Japan: a consideration from the viewpoint of corporate social responsibility. Osaka Sangyo Univ. J. Hum. Environ. Stud. 3, 21–44 (2004)
8. Goo Research: Kankyō hōkokusho hakkō kigyō no ishiki chōsa [Awareness survey of companies issuing environmental reports] (2002). Online poll undertaken in November 2001. http://research.goo.ne.jp/database/data/000046/. Accessed 19 Dec 2015
9. Anjō, T.: CSR keiei to koyō rōdō [CSR management, employment and labor]. Jpn. J. Labour Stud. 46(9), 33–44 (2004)
10. Tanimoto, K., Suzuki, K.: Corporate social responsibility in Japan: analyzing the participating companies. In: Global Reporting Initiative (= European Institute of Japanese Studies Working Paper; 208). Stockholm: European Institute of Japanese Studies (2005)
11. Kuncheva, L.I.: Combining Pattern Classifiers: Methods and Algorithms. Wiley InterScience, Chichester (2004)
12. Madhulatha, T.S.: An overview on clustering methods. IOSR J. Eng. II(4), 719–725 (2012)

Model Proposal of Knowledge Management for Technology Based Companies

Jorge Leonardo Puentes Morantes[⊠], Nancy Yurani Ortiz Guevara[⊠],
and José Ignacio Rodriguez Molano[⊠]

Universidad Distrital Francisco José de Caldas, Bogotá, Colombia
jorgelpmorantes@hotmail.es, nyortizg@gmail.com,
jirodriguez@udistrital.edu.co

Abstract. This article focuses on knowledge management for knowledge intensive companies (technology based companies), where despite being its biggest resource (intangible capital), does not exist mechanisms allowing to quantify and support the improvement and growth at the company obtained through the KM. It was made a count of technology-based companies (TBCs), of process of knowledge management worldwide current, from which are obtained important pillars to finally presents and develops a proposal KM model for TBC's.

Keywords: Knowledge management · Intangible capital · Technology based companies · Tacit and explicit knowledge · Measurement · Continuous improvement

1 Introduction

In the XXI century, the companies which are not able to adapt to a constantly changing environment are destined to disappear in the time, whereby the knowledge and its management take an important role inside the organizations relegating other aspects in its importance, leaving the man as the essential part of an organization and their knowledge as differentiators intangible asset within the mechanics of the organization.

The technology based companies by their side, they have been found themselves immersed in this environment, generating waste of time and money on constant and repetitive training in specific processes and specialized in the development of their missionary activities, as well as in the transmission of specific knowledge within all their areas. Keeping in mind this perception of the current business environment and their needs, it presents a Knowledge management model applicable to technology based companies (TBCs) with the structure and tools needed to implement, besides this model could be used as guide for the future development of similar models applied to TBCs.

2 Characterization of Technology Based Companies

Within the research was made the characterization of Technology Based Companies. Those companies fulfill the following main characteristics:

© Springer International Publishing Switzerland 2016
Y. Tan and Y. Shi (Eds.): DMBD 2016, LNCS 9714, pp. 67–74, 2016.
DOI: 10.1007/978-3-319-40973-3_7

- Are SMEs with intensive knowledge and immersed in high-tech sectors, based on the intensity grade of R&D+I [1].
- These companies produces innovator goods and services, compromised with its design, development and production, through the systematic application of technical and scientific knowledge [2, 3].
- These companies have mostly an academic beginning as innovative business ideas, which are linked to collaborators such as business incubators, research centers, science parks, universities and others who from its birth have given support and infrastructure. It works by projects [4].

3   Characterization of the Main Models of Knowledge Management

Although the literature subscribe to several authors the beginnings of modern knowledge management, this can be assigned to Peter Senge in the 90s with his book "The Fifth Discipline", giving a holistic view of the company and the way how this can become a smart organization. From this time, begins the development of different approaches that through the years have been generating KM models with different perspectives and focused on different areas. Its presented a summary of the KM models with their main contributions and characteristics for KM (Table 1).

It was not found specific characteristics based or applied for technology based companies, the most are generalists tools that superficially cover the structure and needs of the company, therefore have been extracted from all models common features that help the implementation of the KM in TBCs as follows:

- The Common structure to implement the organizational KM is follow by the next steps: Analysis of the existing Knowledge within the company – New knowledge acquisition for the company – Knowledge structuring for the company use – Communication of the new knowledge to the collaborators and establishment of knowledge within the company. The Nonaka and Takeuchi model [12] strengthens this structure through knowledge flow explained in their model.
- Application of tools for KM: Maps and other tools to know the knowledge gap for the knowledge inventory within the company; the knowledge databases are powerful and necessary tools in Knowledge Management for traceability of knowledge within the company, avoiding rework or loss of important knowledge; and the generation of knowledge measuring tools for continuous improvement in the company considering the knowledge management as a cyclical process.

4   Proposal for Knowledge Management Model for Technology Based Companies

Taking into account the referential research performed, it is proposed a KM model for TBCs oriented to adapt and focus the resources and procedures of existing KM and the relational structure between the knowledge of the companies, employees and its

Table 1. Relevant characteristics of the Knowledge Management main models. (Source: Own development based on the different authors named)

Model	Main settings
Nonaka and Takeuchi [5, 12]	Tacit and explicit knowledge division
	Implementation of organizational conditions (intention, autonomy, fluctuation, redundancy, and variety). And application of the knowledge cycle through Socialization, Externalization, combination and internalization
Wiig [6]	Application of Check - Conceptualize - Reflect -Act for the development of the KM cycle
	Propose a Knowledge inventory and improvement actions.
CIBIT Model [5]	Organization Knowledge Management through three steps: Focus, organize, Perform
Garcia-Tapial [7]	Implementation of a more specific structure for the KM through the process of identification - Creation -Storing - Structuring - Distribution -Maintenance - Accounting
	Establish the requirements for KM measurement indicators
Karagabi Model [8]	Handle three main steps: An intervention methodology, a KM models library, and a knowledge base to save the experience gained through the model application
	Specific Application Filtering and cataloging within the process of inventory of Knowledge
	Dissemination of knowledge and information acquired
Delgado and Montes [9]	Focus on companies which works on projects applying the model of Nonaka and Takeuchi and the integrated projects management.
	Systemic KM approach through the cycle: Identification - Acquisition and development of knowledge - knowledge retention - Knowledge distribution and sharing
	Handling specific cataloging for the knowledge retention
Triana et al. [10]	Propose the application of a model of excellence (EFQM) in KM
	Approaching to the use of information and communication technology
	Management and interaction with Stakeholders
	Assessment of the relevance of the KM in the company to continuous improvements
Florez Gonzales [3]	Using specific tools for defining KM strategies
	Definition of knowledge gaps - organizational knowledge gaps
	Using indicators for KM measuring
Gomez [11]	Handling and proximity to Stakeholders
	Applying learned lessons as an important source of organizational knowledge

mission to gain a competitive advantage. The Km model includes three (3) main parts: the core, development and the periphery, as shown in Fig. 1.

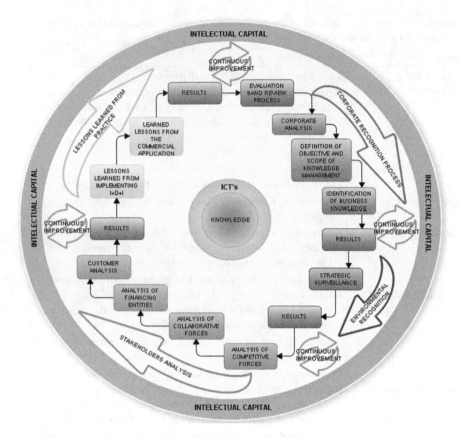

Fig. 1. Knowledge management model for technology based companies (TBCs) (Source: Own development (Authors)).

The "core" refers to the factors which must have the TBC to apply the KM model proposed. In this case, the TBC must have some kind of relevant knowledge to the development of their missionary activities, and must have the interest and desire to manage and improve their activities and products/services. Also the TBC should have a minimum infrastructure in information technology and communication as a base to store, share and disseminate the results of the different model [13].

"Development", refers to the main structure of the model. This section is divided into five (5) core processes which are shown and explained later:

✓ Business Recognition.   ✓ Lessons Learned by Practice
✓ Environment Recognition   ✓ Continuous Improvement
✓ Stakeholder analysis

These components are grouped into what are known as intellectual capital (periphery), which is composed by: Human Capital, Strategic capital, and Relational Capital [11]. Through this section the TBC could generate and manage an atmosphere of openness and welfare, making this an attribute of its context, could perceive greater initiative and participation of employees, which they will act consistent with its own objectives and own powers, and in line with the organization objectives [14]. Then exposed the five (5) model processes:

As follows, just for further search and applications.

4.1 Corporate Recognition Process

Its contains the next steps which includes the main aspects to get the corporate target recognition.

- Corporate analysis.
- Definition of objective and scope for Knowledge Management.
- Identification of business knowledge.

4.2 Environmental Recognition Process

This process consists in the application of sub processing about the identification of relevant information for the project environment through Strategic Surveillance Subprocess. Its design was based on the GTC 186 [15] oriented to the management of R&D+I and management surveillance system.

4.3 Stakeholders Analysis

This process was designed to collect, analyze, storage and select the most relevant Stakeholders information for the TBC according to the needs and scopes, this process contains elements from Krick, Forstater, Monaghan, & Sillampää, [16] and David [17].

4.4 Lessons Learned from Practice

It is the knowledge acquired during a project or task that shows how they should be addressed in the future events of the project or task, in order to improve future performance [18]. The main phases are:

- Lessons learned from implementing R&D+i.
- Lessons learned from the commercial application.

4.5 Continuous Improvement Process

This process consists of different types of sub-process that allows the TBC's share, communicate and disseminate the results of each process, in addition to assessing compliance indicators. The sub-process are:

- Diffusion and communication of results.
- The assessment and review processes.

5 Proposed Model Validation

The KM model for TBC's validation was performed by experts judgments oriented to the individual aggregation, which is, to obtain information from each expert without they have any kind of contact, link or relationship [19]. The expert judgments are taken as three different points of view: The company (TBC's) view; The stakeholders view with the participation of technology development and research centers, and the transfer of research results office of Bogotá, and finally the academic view, with the participation of la teachers specialized in the theme from different universities from Bogotá.

First, the specific knowledge level for each expert was evaluated in the research topic. A survey to know the expert competence coefficient (K), where every experts obtained a K bigger than 0,8 points and less or equal than 1, indicating a high level of influence from all sources.

Each of the experts made a trial using the KM model executable, examined the model and the attached tools giving a different scores for each of the model steps, evaluating different topics for each phase. The conclusion for the validation results was favorable from the three perspectives.

6 Concluding Remarks and Future Work

The model of Knowledge Management for Technology-Based companies was designed with respect to the identified TBC's process which starts with an idea, contextualizes, develops and applies it to market. It also has a close relationship with the processes of creation, identification, collection, analysis, storage, dissemination and communication of knowledge of the TBC.

It is important to point out and clarify that there must be elements at the core and the periphery, i.e., business skills that wish to maintain and protect technological infrastructure in terms of information and communication and intellectual capital of the TBC for the implementation of the model.

The model of knowledge management for TBC's can be established as a first step towards innovation processes with the company to achieve the kind of innovation that aspire, given the applicability of the model and the possibility of orientation towards product innovation, process, marketing and/or organization, depending on the strategy of the TBC.

The time for the implementation of the model within the company are directly dependent on the variables mentioned at the top, among them, the experience and expertise of those responsible for the implementation of the model and the prioritization the enterprise gives to knowledge management respect to other projects.

References

1. March, I., Mora, R.: Creación de empresas de base tecnológica: factores de éxito y fracaso. Revista de contabilidad y dirección, no. 5, pp. 97–120. Asociación Catalana de Contabilidad y Dirección, ACCID (2007)
2. Briones, A.J., Garcia, J.C.: Estrategias para industrias con base tecnológica: aspectos significativos en la creación de empresas innovadoras de base tecnológica, vol. 20, pp. 131–148. FISEC-Estrategias - Fac. Ciencias Soc. la Univ. Nac. Lomas Zamor (2008) .
3. Florez González, S.V.: La Gestión Del Conocimiento Como Herramienta Para La Innovación En Una Empresa De Base Tecnológica. Instituto Politécnico Nacional De México (2011)
4. Merritt, H.: Las empresas mexicanas de base tecnológica y sus capacidades de innovación: una propuesta metodológica. Trayectorias **14**(33–34), 27–50 (2011)
5. Agencia Nacional De Infrastructura: Guia Para La Gestión Del Conocimiento. http://ani.gov.co/sites/default/files/u233/8_guia_para_la_gestion_del_conocimiento_ani.pdf. Accessed 19 Apr 2015
6. Arís, E.P.: La gestión tecnológica del conocimiento. EDITUM (2007)
7. García-Tapial, J.: Gestión del conocimiento y empresa Una aproximación a la realidad española. EOI (2002)
8. Capote, J., Llanten, C.J., Pardo, C., Collazos, C.: Knowledge management in a software process improvement program in micro, small and medium-sized enterprises: KMSPI Model. Rev. Fac. Ing. Antioquia 223–235 (2009)
9. Delgado, R., Montes de Oca, R.: Modelo de Gestión del Conocimiento organizacional para Empresas que trabajan por Proyectos, vol. 5 (2011)
10. Triana, J., Medina, V., Rodriguez, J.I.: Modelo para fortalecer el rol de las PYMES en el emprendimiento de Bogotá D.C., vol. 17, pp. 131–147. Rev. Científica Cienc. e Ing. la Univ. Dist., Bogotá (2012)
11. Gomez, J: Modelo conceptual de Gestión del conocimiento, en un Sistema de Incubadoras de Empresas de Base Tecnológica (2011)
12. Nonaka, I., Takeuchi, H.: The Knowledge-Creating Company: How Japanese Companies Create the Dynamics of Innovation. Oxford University Press, New York (1995)
13. Fernández Marcial, V.: Gestión del conocimiento versus gestión de la información. Investig. Bibl. **20**(41), 44–62 (2006)
14. Acosta Prado, J.C., Longo-Somoza, M., Fischer, A.L.: Capacidades dinámicas y gestión del conocimiento en nuevas empresas de base tecnológica. Cuadernos de Administración **26** (47), 35–62 (2013)
15. Instituto Colombiano de Normas Tecnicas y Certificación (ICONTEC): GTC 186 - Gestión de la investigación, desarrollo e innovación (I+D+i). Gestión de la I+D+i: sistema de vigilancia (v). p. 21 (2009)
16. Krick, T., Forstater, M., Monaghan, P., Sillampää, M.: De las palabras a la acción. El compromiso con los stakeholders. Manual para la práctica de las relaciones con los grupos de interés. AccountAbility, p. 135 (2006)

17. David, F.R.: Conceptos de Administración Estratégic*a*. Pearson Educación, México (2013)
18. Project Management Institute, Guía de los Fundamentos Para la Dirección de Proyectos (Guía del PMBOK®). Quinta Edi. Project Management Institute (2013)
19. Cabero-Almenara, J., Osuna, J.: La utilización del juicio de experto para la evaluación de TIC: el coeficiente de competencia experta. Bordón. Rev. Pedagog. (2013)

Frequent Itemset Mining

Oracle and Vertica for Frequent Itemset Mining

Hristo Kyurkchiev and Kalinka Kaloyanova(⊠)

Faculty of Mathematics and Informatics, Sofia University,
5 James Bourchier Blvd, 1164 Sofia, Bulgaria
{hkyurkchiev, kkaloyanova}@fmi.uni-sofia.bg

Abstract. In the last few years, organizations have become much more interested in using data to create value. Big Data, however, presents new challenges to the extraction of knowledge using traditional Data Mining methods. In this paper we focus on a concrete implementation of association rules generation. The proposed algorithm is specialized for four datasets and its performance for different support thresholds is measured. This is done for two Database Management Systems (DBMS) – a traditional row-oriented DMBS in the face of Oracle and a column-oriented DBMS represented by Vertica. The results indicate the suitability of these DBMSs as tools for association rules generation.

Keywords: Big data · Data mining · Association rules · Apriori algorithm

1 Introduction

Data mining concerns the processing of data with the primary purpose of finding interesting patterns and trends. The methods used to explore the data vary significantly and include associative rules, classification, clustering, etc. all of which are being widely discussed in literature [7, 18].

Today, Big Data urges the use of more extensive data mining techniques due to the big data volumes as well as the variety of information content and dynamic data behavior [1, 12, 19]. This combined with the ever growing desire to mine the data directly in the transactional database [4, 8] presents new challenges to the traditional relational database management systems (DBMS).

In this paper we study the performance of two popular DBMS – Oracle and Vertica – for association rule mining. The paper is organized as follows:

In Sect. 2 some background information on the different data mining methods is provided together with reasoning on why association rules were chosen for this study. It continues by describing the Apriori algorithm for frequent itemsets discovery and the concrete implementation, which was used in the tests. Section 3 outlines the setup and characteristics of the employed environment. It also features information on the datasets used. The performance results of using the SQL implementation of the Apriori algorithm in both Oracle and Vertica are presented, analyzed and discussed in Sect. 4. In the last section conclusions and directions for future research are given.

© Springer International Publishing Switzerland 2016
Y. Tan and Y. Shi (Eds.): DMBD 2016, LNCS 9714, pp. 77–85, 2016.
DOI: 10.1007/978-3-319-40973-3_8

2   Background

Data Mining (DM) incorporates methods and techniques from several areas – statistics, machine learning, artificial intelligence, etc. The most common ways to mine data to discover the underlying patterns and structure are [7]:

- **Association rule analysis** – enables the discovery of interesting and frequent relations in large databases that concern the co-occurrences of different elements. The method is mainly used for market-basket analysis for direct marketing, sales promotions, and for discovering business trends.
- **Clustering analysis** – used to understand the differences and the similarities within the data. During the process datasets where the objects are grouped based on their similarity are identified.
- **Classification analysis** – a systematic approach for obtaining important and relevant information about data and metadata. It helps to identify to which of a set of categories a specific type of data belongs.
- **Regression analysis** – defines the dependency between variables. Using this method different levels of customer satisfaction can be presented for analyzing customer loyalty.
- **Other** – DM techniques like text mining, time series analysis, sequence analysis, etc. are also widely used in recent years due to the challenges, which Big Data introduced [19].

Association rule analysis was selected as the method to be researched because of its popularity and relatively simple implementation in SQL [5, 15].

An association rule can be defined as follows:

Given a set of transactions, where each transaction is a set of items, an association rule is an implication A -> B, where both A and B are sets of items.
In database terms, it can be translated to a condition similar to: if a transaction T contains the items in A, there is a high probability that T also contains the items in B. A is called the *antecedent* of the rule and B – its *consequent*.

Three other basic characteristics of association rules are [10, 13, 18]:

- High support – the number of transactions in which the itemsets are present;
- High confidence – the probability of finding itemsets A where itemsets B are present;
- Interest confidence – the probability of finding A and B in the same transaction is significantly higher/lower than fining B in a random transaction.

Usually it is enough to concentrate on the high support, as for example in the discrete case the probabilities (confidence and interest) can easily be computed based on the counts already used for verifying the support threshold.

There are numerous algorithms available for the computation of association rules. Most of them, however, only find the frequent itemsets with another step required to define the actual association rules afterwards. The most popular of these are:

- **APRIORI** [2], which counts the transactions in order to find frequent itemsets and then derives association rules from them. It calculates rules that express probabilistic relationships between items in frequent itemsets. For example, a rule derived from frequent itemsets containing A, B, and C might state that if A and B are included in a transaction, then C is likely to also be included in it.
- The **ECLAT** [17, 18] algorithm finds frequent itemsets with equivalence classes, depth-first search and set intersection instead of counting.
- **FP-growth** [9] (from frequent pattern) is a two pass algorithm, which counts occurrence of items in the dataset and stores them to a 'header table' in the first pass. Then, in the second pass, it builds an FP-tree by inserting instances.

For our experiments we have selected APRIORI because of its simplicity and straight forward implementation in the SQL language used by the selected DBMSs [5, 6, 14, 15]. A generalization of it for the *i-th* frequent itemsets' computation looks like:

```
INSERT INTO Fi
SELECT Ci.item1_id, …, Ci.itemi_id, COUNT(*)
FROM candidatesi Ci, dataset D1, …, dataset Di
WHERE Ci.item1_id = D1.item_id AND … AND Ci.itemi_id = Di.item_id AND
      D1.transaction_id = D2.transaction_id AND … AND Di-1.transaction_id = Di.transaction_id
GROUP BY Ci.item1_id, …, Ci.itemi_id
HAVING COUNT(*) > <threshold>;
```

3   Test Environment

Having chosen the algorithm, we concentrated on the setup by selecting components typical for modest modern server machines and the most commonly used versions of the DBMSs. The main purpose of this selection being to compare the performance of the two DBMSs in conditions as close to those in a live environment as possible. This was also the reason for our choice of four datasets and three support thresholds.

3.1   Hardware and Software

In order for the comparison to be valid the same hardware was used in all tests.

Hardware setup. The DBMSs were run as virtual machines on VMWare Fusion running CentOS 7, each equipped with 2 CPU cores (2.3 GHz each), 8 GB of RAM and 50 GB of storage.

Database setup. No specific tweaks have been done on each database to improve performance, except the ones, which are implicit or completely trivial:

- For Oracle, Oracle 11 g EE with no indices.
- HP Vertica Community Edition 7.0.2 was used as the Vertica instance with the compulsory super projection on each table.

3.2   Database Schemas and Datasets

To check the performance in different setups we selected four datasets from the Frequent Itemset Mining Dataset Repository [20]:

- Mushrooms – data for several thousand mushroom species and their features;
- Retail market – market basket data from an anonymous Belgian retail store;
- T10I4D100K – data generated by the IBM Almaden Quest research group;
- PUMSB – census data from PUMS (Public Use Microdata Sample).

Some statistics for the datasets sorted by size is shown in Table 1.

Table 1. Properties of the datasets used in the experiment

Set name	Items	Transactions	Total rows	Avg. items per transaction	Std. dev. items per transaction
Mushrooms	119	8124	186852	23	0
Retail market	16470	88163	908576	10.31	8.16
T10I4D100K	870	100000	1010228	10.10	3.67
PUMSB	2113	49046	3629404	74	0

The different parameters of the datasets allowed for testing the performance in various scenarios. The 0 for standard deviation above is natural as each transaction in these datasets has a fixed number of items in it.

In order for the experiments to be performed all datasets were converted into binary relations with the following structure:

- Transaction_id – number;
- Item_id – number.

3.3   Benchmarking and Measurement Approach

To perform the tests, we chose to construct the frequent itemsets of length 3 or less for three different support thresholds – 100, 200 and 400. This decision was dictated by hardware and time constraints. Generalizations of the used algorithm to create higher length frequent itemsets are easily achievable, however, performing these would have required significantly more resources.

4   Experiments

In Tables 2, 3, 4 and 5 one can see the number of different frequent itemsets and candidate frequent itemsets for each of the support thresholds and for each of the datasets used. In them, F_i stands for the number of frequent itemsets with length i and C_i means the candidate frequent itemsets with length i.

Table 2. Mushrooms number of sets

FIM	Support 100	Support 200	Support 400
F1	90	83	73
C2	36045	3403	2628
F2	2657	1791	1333
C3	60629	32249	19800
F3	25323	17594	10645

Table 3. Retail market number of sets

FIM	Support 100	Support 200	Support 400
F1	1838	803	273
C2	1688203	322003	37128
F2	2754	887	283
C3	1018889	113289	10628
F3	1452	408	117

Table 4. T10I4D100K number of sets

FIM	Support 100	Support 200	Support 400
F1	797	741	629
C2	317206	274170	197506
F2	8734	3840	757
C3	155304	29892	1828
F3	7067	3248	375

Table 5. PUMSB number of sets

FIM	Support 100	Support 200	Support 400
F1	768	567	405
C2	294528	160461	81810
F2	59997	40152	26583
C3	7743015	3774176	1875416
F3	n/a	n/a	n/a

In Table 5 indicates that the result could not be calculated with the tested setup by neither Oracle, nor Vertica. The reason being the insufficient RAM and the need to spill the result on the hard drive, which in the case of the PUMSB dataset also proved to be insufficient. This high memory requirement is a known issue with the Apriori algorithm as noted by [10]. In addition, except for the Mushrooms and the Support 400 test for T10I4D100K, all other F3 tests for Vertica failed and were stopped manually after running for 12+ h. No errors were generated by the DBMS and all system resource usage remained normal throughout the tests.

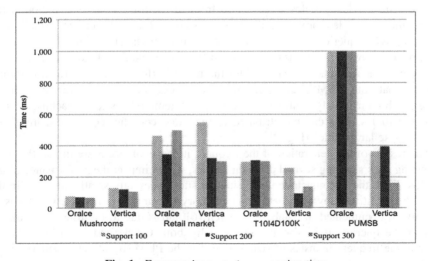

Fig. 1. Frequent itemsets 1 - generation time

The results of the tests are available in the charts below. In them, we have not included the time for the generation of the candidate frequent itemsets as it was negligible compared to the one for the generation of the actual frequent itemsets.

Both DBMSs are obviously handling the task of generating the frequent itemsets of size 1 quite well with response times of up to 1 s. Vertica is performing slightly better with the benefits getting more pronounced as the datasets get larger, reaching more than 5-fold performance gain compared to Oracle. This is not surprising taking into account previous research [11] and the fact that generating frequent itemsets of size 1 involves simple aggregate queries without any joins (Fig. 1).

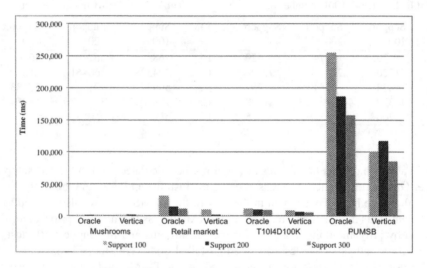

Fig. 2. Frequent itemsets 2 - generation time

The same tendency holds true for the frequent itemsets of size 2, although the performance gain is less pronounced – Vertica is about 2 times faster here. This is a bit surprising as the queries in this case involve both an insert and a join. Based on the actual results, however, one has to conclude that the computations take precedence over these operations and this is the reason for the better performance of Vertica. It should be noted that both DBMSs are performing the generation of the frequent itemsets of size 2 much more slowly than that of the frequent itemsets of size 1, reaching 41 min compared to 1 s. This can be attributed to the more complicated queries, involving joins of quite large tables (Fig. 2).

The results of the generation of the frequent itemsets of size 3 are in fact the most interesting ones showing several different factors, which impact the performance of the DBMSs. First, they demonstrate that to handle such seemingly small datasets – in the range of several megabytes, much larger memory resources are necessary. This is of course well documented in database research [6] and is due to the usage of multiple joins in the queries. It is also the reason why both Oracle and Vertica could not compute the frequent itemsets of size 3 at all for the PUMSB dataset. Furthermore, it

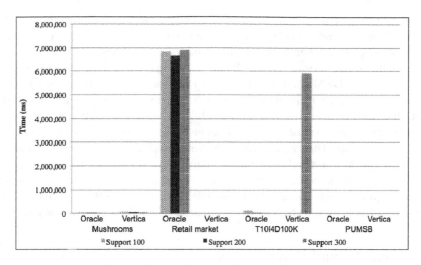

Fig. 3. Frequent itemsets 3 - generation time

can be seen that although the retail market data has a little less number of rows than the T10I4D100K dataset, the fact that it has approximately 20 times more different items degrades the performance of Oracle significantly – with 400 or 20 ^ 2 times. This is most likely due to the use of the item_id in the join condition of two joins in the query to build the frequent itemsets of size 3 as well as the significantly larger size of the candidates' itemsets for the retail market dataset as compared to the T10I4D100K dataset. At last, Vertica shows significant performance degradation with most of the tests for the larger datasets not being able to finish within 12 h. This can be attributed to the growing number of joins used in the queries, which are Vertica's Achilles' heel.

A summary of the results can be seen on Fig. 4. For it each query was assigned a cost in the principle similar to the one used in the query optimizer [6], i.e. the product of the

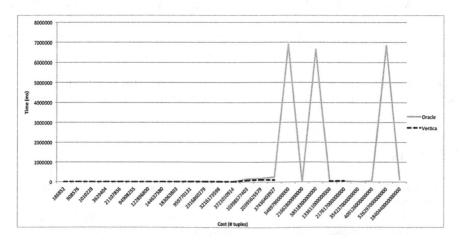

Fig. 4. Summary of the results – generation time versus join cost

tuples in the relations in the join, divided by the product of the number of unique values in each attribute that appears at least twice in the join condition. This graph confirms our previous findings that when both DBMSs produce results they are very close with Vertica slightly outperforming Oracle. It also shows that when the cost estimate of the query is high both DBMS fail to perform the necessary queries. There are, however, some inconsistencies, which suggest that such cost measure may not be enough to validate the findings, as the results for some higher cost queries are much better than those for some lower cost queries – the peaks in the line of Oracle. These peaks are for the retail market data. Thus we can conclude that the combination of higher number of transactions and higher number of unique items has a direct effect on performance. Unfortunately, such properties have a high likelihood to appear in real-life conditions. This puts into question whether the tested DBMSs and the SQL implementation of Apriori are a viable option for performing efficient calculations on such datasets.

5   Conclusions and Future Work

In this paper we presented the performance results of an SQL implementation of the Apriori algorithm. The experiments with two Oracle and Vertica demonstrate the behavior of this implementation over several datasets of different sizes and domains.

The results are promising. The applied algorithm performs well in real time when smaller size frequent itemsets are computed regardless of the size of the dataset and the DBMS, although Vertica has a slight advantage over Oracle. There is a significant degradation in the performance of both DBMSs when higher volume itemsets are generated. With the increase in the amount of data to be processed both Oracle and Vertica begin to struggle and fail to complete some of the tests. Thus, there is no clear recommendation on which of them is better – Vertica is usually faster when it can handle the load, however, Oracle is more reliable and succeeded to fulfill more tests.

There are several directions for future work. First, the performance of the SQL Apriori algorithm which we used could be compared to the ones implemented in some popular DM tools, e.g. RapidMiner, WEKA, R, etc. [3]. Second, new types of DBMSs could be tested e.g. array databases [16] which promise to offer fast performance for data analytics. Finally, tuning the method based on the findings so far will increase its suitability and value for association rules discovery.

Acknowledgments. This work is partially supported by Sofia University SRF/2016 under contract "Big data: analysis and management of data and projects" and FMI – Sofia University.

References

1. Adhikary, D., Roy, S.: Issues in Quantitative Association Rule Mining: A Big Data Perspective. ICT for Sustainable Development, India (2015)
2. Agrawal, R., Srikant, R.: Fast algorithms for mining association rules. In: Proceedings of 20th VLDB Conference, Santiago, Chile, vol. 42 (1994)

3. Al-khoder, A., Harmouch, H.: Evaluating four of the most popular open source and free data mining tools. Int. J. Acad. Sci. Res. **3**(1), 13–23 (2015)
4. Brice, B., Alexander, W.: Finding interesting things in lots of data. In: 23rd Hawaii International Conference on System Sciences (1990)
5. Danubianu, M., et al.: Mining association rules inside a relational database–a case study. In: 6th ICCGI, pp. 14–19 (2011)
6. Garcia-Molina, H., et al.: Database Systems: The Complete Book. Pearson Prentice Hall, Upper Saddle River (2009)
7. Han, J., et al.: Data Mining: Concepts and Techniques. Elsevier, San Francisco (2012)
8. Han, J., et al.: Knowledge discovery in databases: an attribute-oriented approach. In: Proceedings of the 18th VLDB Conference, Vancouver, British Columbia, Canada, pp. 547–559 (1992)
9. Han, J., et al.: Mining frequent patterns without candidate generation. In: Proceedings of the 2000 ACM SIGMOD International Conference on Management of Data, SIGMOD 2000, pp. 1–12 (2000)
10. Khurana, N., Datta, R.K.: Pruning large data sets for finding association rule in cloud: CBPA (Count Based Pruning Algorithm). Int. J. Softw. Web Sci. **5**, 118–122 (2013)
11. Kyurkchiev, H., Kaloyanova, K.: Performance Study of Analytical Queries of Oracle and Vertica. In: Proceedings of the 7th ISGT International Conference. pp. 127–139, Sofia (2013)
12. Moens, S., et al.: Frequent itemset mining for big data. In: Proceedings of 2013 IEEE International Conference on Big Data, vol. 1, pp. 111–118 (2013)
13. Piatetsky-Shapiro, G.: Discovery, analysis, and presentation of strong rules. In: Piatetsky-Shapiro, G., Frawley, W.J. (eds.) Knowledge Discovery in Databases, pp. 229–248. MIT Press, Cambridge (1991)
14. Psaila, G., Torino, P.: SQL-like operator for mining. In: Proceedings of 22nd VLDB Conference, Mumbai (Bombay), India, pp. 122–133 (1996)
15. Shiby, T., Sarawagi, S.: Mining generalized association rules and sequential patterns using SQL queries. In: Conference on Knowledge Discovery and Data Mining, pp. 344–348 (1998)
16. Woodie, A.: Array Databases: The Next Big Thing in Data Analytics? http://www.datanami. com/2014/04/09/array_databases_the_next_big_thing_in_data_analytics_/
17. Zaki, M.J.: Scalable algorithms for association mining. IEEE Trans. Knowl. Data Eng. **12** (3), 372–390 (2000)
18. Zhao, Y.: R and Data Mining: Examples and Case Studies. Elsevier, San Francisco (2013)
19. Zikopoulos, P., et al.: Understanding Big Data. McGraw-Hill, San Francisco (2012)
20. Frequent Itemset Mining Dataset Repository. http://fimi.ua.ac.be/data/

Reconstructing Positive Surveys from Negative Surveys with Background Knowledge

Dongdong Zhao[1,2], Wenjian Luo[1,2(✉)], and Lihua Yue[1,2]

[1] School of Computer Science and Technology,
University of Science and Technology of China, Hefei 230027, Anhui, China
zdd@mail.ustc.edu.cn, {wjluo,llyue}@ustc.edu.cn
[2] Anhui Province Key Laboratory of Software Engineering in Computing
and Communication, University of Science and Technology of China,
Hefei 230027, Anhui, China

Abstract. Negative Survey is a promising technique for collecting sensitive data. Using the negative survey, useful aggregate information could be estimated, while protecting personal privacy. Previous work mainly focuses on improving the general model of the negative survey without considering background knowledge. However, in real-world applications, data analysts usually have some background knowledge on the surveys. Therefore, in this paper, for the first time, we study the usage of background knowledge in negative surveys, and propose a method for accurately reconstructing positive surveys with background knowledge. Moreover, we propose a method for evaluating the dependable level of the positive survey reconstructed with background knowledge. Experimental results show that more reasonable and accurate positive surveys could be obtained using our methods.

Keywords: Privacy protection · Sensitive data collection · Negative survey · Background knowledge

1 Introduction

Nowadays, along with the rapid development of network techniques, an increasing amount of information is flowing across the network. Meanwhile, more and more sensitive data have been disclosed. Consequently, techniques for protecting data privacy have been widely studied in recent years. The negative representation of information, which was inspired by the negative selection mechanism in Biological Immune Systems, is an emerging technique for protecting data privacy [1, 2]. In order to collect sensitive data while protecting personal privacy, Esponda [3, 4] proposed a strategy for administering surveys based on the negative representation of information, and it is called negative survey.

In traditional surveys, participants are asked to choose a category (or an answer) that they belong to (this category is called positive category). Traditional surveys are called positive surveys in this paper. In negative surveys, participants are asked to choose a category that they do NOT belong to (this category is called negative category). The number of categories in a negative survey should be larger than 2, and thus only part of information related to the truth is provided by a participant. Therefore, when the survey involves sensitive questions, the privacy of participants could be

© Springer International Publishing Switzerland 2016
Y. Tan and Y. Shi (Eds.): DMBD 2016, LNCS 9714, pp. 86–99, 2016.
DOI: 10.1007/978-3-319-40973-3_9

protected. Based on the negative survey, some aggregate information about the overall distribution could be estimated, e.g. the expected population proportion of each category in the corresponding positive survey.

So far, some work about the negative survey has been done. In 2006, Esponda [3] proposed the uniform negative survey, in which the participants are requested to select each negative category with an equal probability. He also proposed a method (called NStoPS) for estimating the population distributions in positive surveys from the negative surveys (called estimating or reconstructing positive surveys from negative surveys, for simplicity). Afterwards, Xie et al. [5] proposed the Gaussian negative survey, in which the probabilities that a participant selects negative categories follow the Gaussian distribution. They also used the Gaussian negative survey to collect aggregate spatial data and answer range aggregate queries. In 2007, Horey and his colleagues [6] applied the negative survey to anonymous data collection in sensor networks and showed that the negative survey could be effectively used to classify traffic behaviors under reasonable traffic scenarios. Groat and his colleagues [7, 8] proposed the multidimensional negative surveys, which could produce aggregated models and knowledge for participatory sensing applications. They showed that their algorithms can protect data privacy and be employed in a computation efficient manner. In 2012, Horey et al. [9] applied the negative survey to location privacy protection and proposed a negative quad tree. They showed that their method is accurate and efficient enough for some real-world scenarios. Then, Bao et al. [10] pointed out that previous methods for estimating positive surveys from negative surveys could produce negative values which are unreasonable, and they proposed two effective methods (called NStoPS-I and NStoPS-II) for estimating more reasonable positive surveys. Recently, Bao et al. [11] proposed the first method for calculating the dependable level of the negative survey, and this method enables data analysts to evaluate the quality of the estimated results. Based on the negative survey, Du et al. [12] proposed a model for privacy preserving data publication, which is called negative data publication. In [13], an efficient method based on the Differential Evolutionary (DE) was proposed for searching the optimal negative surveys.

Previous work mainly focuses on the models of the negative survey without considering background knowledge; however, data analysts usually have some prior knowledge on the surveys in real-world applications. Therefore, in this paper, for the first time, we study how to use the background knowledge in negative surveys. Overall, our contributions are listed as follows.

(1) We propose a method (called NStoPS-BK) for reconstructing positive surveys from negative surveys with background knowledge.
(2) We propose a method for estimating the dependable level of the reconstructed positive survey with background knowledge.
(3) We carry out several experiments, and show that more reasonable and accurate results could be obtained using our method.

2 Preliminaries

In this section, the general negative survey is introduced. In a positive survey, the question is designed to directly ask participants which category they belong to [3, 4], e.g.

Q: In last year, you got sick ___ times.

(A) 0   (B) 1-2   (C) 3-5   (D) 6-10   (E) more than 10

In the negative survey, the question is designed to ask participants which category they do NOT belong to [3, 4], e.g.

Q: In last year, you did NOT get sick ___ times.

(A) 0   (B) 1-2   (C) 3-5   (D) 6-10   (E) more than 10

Typically, in the negative survey, participants are asked to select one category (as the negative category) with a certain probability. Assume there is only one question in the negative survey for simplicity. The number of categories in the negative survey is c, and the number of participants is n. The results obtained from the negative survey are $r = (r_1, r_2, ..., r_c)$, where r_i denotes the number of participants who select category i as his negative category [4]. Our goal is to estimate the results of the positive survey, i.e. $t = (t_1, t_2, ..., t_c)$. Assume the probability that a participant, who actually belongs to category i, selects category j as the negative category is q_{ij}. Then, the expected relation between r and t is $r = tQ$, where Q is [4, 10]:

$$Q = \begin{bmatrix} 0 & q_{12} & \cdots & q_{1c} \\ q_{21} & 0 & \cdots & q_{2c} \\ \cdots & \cdots & \cdots & \cdots \\ q_{c1} & q_{c2} & \cdots & 0 \end{bmatrix}, \sum_{j=1}^{c} q_{ij} = 1, \; q_{ii} = 0, \; i = 1 \ldots c.$$

If Q is nonsingular, the expectation of t is [4, 10]:

$$\hat{t} = E[t] = rQ^{-1}. \tag{1}$$

Typically, if the uniform negative survey is employed, we have $q_{ij} = 1/(c-1)$ when $i \neq j$, and

$$\hat{t}_i = n - (c-1)r_i. \tag{2}$$

The uniform negative survey is the most widely used model, and it does not need extra devices for negative selection. Especially, because the negative category is selected by the participant, the corresponding positive category is not disclosed at the first beginning of data collection. Therefore, we mainly focus on the uniform negative survey in this paper.

3   Motivations

In real-world surveys, data analysts usually have some background knowledge. For example, we want to monitor the status of diseases in regions around a hospital, and conduct negative surveys to obtain useful aggregate information while protecting privacy of participants. Obviously, the usage of negative surveys could encourage people to participate in this survey because they do not need to worry about disclosure of privacy. The negative surveys could contain a question like the one mentioned in Sect. 2. It is proper to assume that we have some prior knowledge, e.g. we know the number of people who actually got sick more than 10 times is larger than the value obtained directly from the treatment data in the hospital. The positive surveys reconstructed from negative surveys should be consistent with this background knowledge.

For another example, in a positive survey of user experience of a product, the question is:

Q: You think the quality of this product is:

(A) very good   (B) fair   (C) poor   (D) very poor

In the negative survey, the question is:

Q: You do NOT think the quality of this product is:

(A) very good   (B) fair   (C) poor   (D) very poor

It is reasonable to assume that we have some background knowledge about this negative survey. Typically, we know most of the regulars have good experience of this product, and they would select A in positive surveys. Therefore, if the negative survey is conducted instead of the positive survey, this background knowledge could be used in reconstructing positive surveys.

The usage of background knowledge could enhance the accuracy of reconstructed positive surveys and prevent producing unreasonable results. For example, assume 100 regulars have participated in the negative survey. If this background knowledge is not used, the reconstructed number of participants who actually belong to A could be considerably less than 100, and obviously this is unreasonable. If the background knowledge is used, the reconstructed positive surveys will be at least consistent with this background knowledge. Therefore, because data analysts usually have some background knowledge in many real-world applications, it is very important to study the reconstruction of positive surveys from negative surveys with background knowledge.

4 Reconstructing Positive Surveys with Background Knowledge

First, we formally model the background knowledge in negative surveys in Subsect. 4.1. Then we investigate the reconstruction of positive surveys from negative surveys with background knowledge in Subsect. 4.2.

4.1 Modeling Background Knowledge

In many situations, the background knowledge could be modeled as limits on the value ranges of the positive survey results, and we have:

$$r = tQ, \quad \sum_{i=1}^{c} r_i = n, \ r_i \geq 0, \quad \sum_{i=1}^{c} t_i = n, \ l_i \leq t_i \leq u_i. \tag{3}$$

In above model, l_i and u_i are known positive integers in $[0, n]$. We have the background knowledge that the number of participants that belong to category i ($1 \leq i \leq c$) in the positive survey is not less than l_i and not larger than u_i.

For the first example, according to the treatment data in a hospital, assume we have known that at least 30 people got sick more than 10 times in last year. If these people have participated in the negative survey, we have the background knowledge that $t_5 \geq 30$, i.e. $l_5 = 30$. On the other hand, we know that most people averagely got sick no more than 10 times per year. Therefore, t_5 must be smaller than $n/2$, i.e. $u_5 = n/2$. In the second example mentioned in Sect. 3, the background knowledge is: 100 regulars have participated in the negative survey. If every regular is assumed to rate option A as positive category, this background knowledge can be formalized as $100 \leq t_1 \leq n$, i.e. $l_1 = 100$, $u_1 = n$ (labeled the option A, B, C, D as category 1, 2, 3, 4, respectively).

4.2 Reconstructing Positive Surveys

In this subsection, a method called NStoPS-BK is proposed for reconstructing positive surveys from uniform negative surveys with background knowledge, and its pseudo code is given as Algorithm 1.

Algorithm 1: NStoPS-BK
Input: Results of a negative survey $r = (r_1, ..., r_c)$, number of participants n.
Background knowledge $BK = [l, u] = ([l_1, u_1], ..., [l_c, u_c])$.
Output: Reconstructed results of the positive survey $t = (t_1, ..., t_c)$.
1. $t_i \leftarrow n-(c-1)r_i$ $(i=1...n)$
2. $n_1 \leftarrow n$
3.   **do**
4. $isRemoved \leftarrow$ **false**
5. $n_2 \leftarrow n_1$
6.   **for** $i \leftarrow 1$ **to** c
7.   **if** category i is not removed
8.   **if** $t_i < l_i$
9. $t_i^* \leftarrow t_i, t_i \leftarrow l_i$
10.   remove category i: $isRemoved \leftarrow$ **true**
11. $n_1 \leftarrow n_1 - l_i, n_2 \leftarrow n_2 - t_i^*$
12.   **else if** $t_i > u_i$
13. $t_i^* \leftarrow t_i, t_i \leftarrow u_i$
14.   remove category i: $isRemoved \leftarrow$ **true**
15. $n_1 \leftarrow n_1 - u_i, n_2 \leftarrow n_2 - t_i^*$
16.   **for** $i \leftarrow 1$ **to** c
17.   **if** category i is not removed and $n_2 \neq 0$
18. $t_i \leftarrow t_i \times n_1/n_2$ // scale t_i
19.   **while** $(isRemoved =$ **true**$)$
20.   **return** $t = (t_1, ..., t_c)$

In NStoPS-BK, (2) is used to estimate the positive survey from a uniform negative survey first. Then, if the estimated positive survey results violate the background knowledge (i.e. they do not locate in the intervals in **BK**), they are adjusted to reasonable values. If the result t_i ($1 \leq i \leq c$) is less than the lower bound l_i, t_i is adjusted to l_i. If t_i is more than the upper bound u_i, t_i is adjusted to u_i. After t_i is adjusted, category i will be removed. Assume the number of participants is n before removing category i. After category i is removed, the current number of participants that belong to remaining categories is $n_2 = n - t_i^*$. However, the number of participants that belong to remaining categories is actually expected to be $n_1 = n - l_i$ or $n - u_i$. Therefore, after the positive survey results of all categories are checked, if some categories are removed, the results of remaining categories should be scaled by n_1/n_2. Above procedure will be conducted iteratively until no unreasonable results are produced (that is, no categories will be removed). Note that NStoPS-BK is somewhat similar to NStoPS-II [10], however, NStoPS-BK could handle more general violations to background knowledge (in fact, negative values in [10] can also be regarded as a part of background knowledge).

5 Calculating Dependable Level Using Background Knowledge

In this section, the dependable level of the positive survey that is reconstructed from a uniform negative survey with background knowledge, is calculated using the Bayes' theorem.

Usually, we need to assess the reconstructed result of one positive category independently, and thus its dependable level needs to be calculated. For example, if we want to know whether the reconstructed result of the number of participants who got sick more than 10 times in last year is dependable, we need to calculate the dependable level of the reconstructed result of category 5.

Given the results r of a uniform negative survey, the positive survey results can be reconstructed. Assume the confidence interval of the reconstructed result of category i is denoted as $d_i = [\hat{t}_i - \varepsilon_i, \hat{t}_i + \varepsilon_i]$, where $2\varepsilon_i$ is the length of the confidence interval. Typically, ε_i can be the precision that is set based on requirements. Therefore, the dependable level for d_i can be calculated as follow.

$$1 - \alpha = \sum_{t_i = \hat{t}_i - \varepsilon_i}^{\hat{t}_i + \varepsilon_i} P(t_i | r_i), \tag{4}$$

where $P(t_i|r_i)$ denotes the probability that the number of participants that belong to category i in the positive survey is t_i when the number of participants that select category i in the corresponding negative survey is given as r_i.

According to Bayes' theorem, we have:

$$P(t_i | r_i) = \frac{P(r_i | t_i) P(t_i)}{\sum_{t_i'=0}^{n} P(r_i | t_i') P(t_i')}. \tag{5}$$

According to the background knowledge, we have:

$$P(t_i) = \begin{cases} \frac{1}{u_i - l_i + 1}, & l_i \leq t_i \leq u_i \\ 0, & otherwise \end{cases}, \tag{6}$$

where $P(t_i)$ denotes the prior probability that t_i participants select category i in the positive survey. Note that "$P(t_i) = 1/(u_i - l_i + 1)$ when $l_i \leq t_i \leq u_i$" is based on the Bayes' assumption because we have no extra prior knowledge about t_i. Given t_i, $P(r_i|t_i)$ denotes the posterior probability that r_i participants select category i in the corresponding negative survey. According to the uniform negative survey, we have:

$$P(r_i|t_i) = \binom{n - t_i}{r_i} \times \left(\frac{1}{c - 1}\right)^{r_i} \times \left(\frac{c - 2}{c - 1}\right)^{n - t_i - r_i}. \tag{7}$$

By substituting (5), (6), (7) to (4), the dependable level for d_i is:

$$1 - \alpha = \sum_{t_i = \hat{t}_i - \varepsilon_i}^{\hat{t}_i + \varepsilon_i} \frac{\binom{n - t_i}{r_i} \times \left(\frac{1}{c - 1}\right)^{r_i} \times \left(\frac{c - 2}{c - 1}\right)^{n - t_i - r_i} P(t_i)}{\sum_{t'_i = l_i}^{u_i} \binom{n - t'_i}{r_i} \times \left(\frac{1}{c - 1}\right)^{r_i} \times \left(\frac{c - 2}{c - 1}\right)^{n - t'_i - r_i} \times \frac{1}{u_i - l_i + 1}}.$$

It can be further simplified as follow.

$$1 - \alpha = \sum_{t_i = \hat{t}_i - \varepsilon_i}^{\hat{t}_i + \varepsilon_i} \frac{\binom{n - t_i}{r_i} \times \left(\frac{c - 1}{c - 2}\right)^{t_i} P(t_i)}{\sum_{t'_i = l_i}^{u_i} \binom{n - t'_i}{r_i} \times \left(\frac{c - 1}{c - 2}\right)^{t'_i} \times \frac{1}{u_i - l_i + 1}}. \tag{8}$$

6   Experiments

In this section, first, we carry out several experiments on reconstructing positive surveys from uniform negative surveys with background knowledge. Then, we carry out several experiments on calculating the dependable level of the positive survey results that are reconstructed by NStoPS-BK using background knowledge.

6.1   Experiments on Reconstructing Positive Surveys

In order to investigate the influence of background knowledge on reconstructed positive survey results, several experiments are carried out. The total number of participants is $n = 500$. The number of categories is $c = 5$. The background knowledge is given in Table 1. First, similar to [6, 10], the original positive survey results t are sampled with four different distributions (as shown in Table 1), i.e. uniform distribution, normal distribution, exponential distribution and log-normal distribution. The parameter settings for these distributions are shown in Table 2. The original positive survey should also satisfy the background knowledge $[l, u]$. Based on t, we simulate the uniform negative survey, and obtain its results $r = (r_1...r_c)$ (as shown in Table 1). Then, based on the NStoPS-BK, we obtain the reconstructed positive survey results $\hat{t} = (\hat{t}_1...\hat{t}_c)$ using both r and the background knowledge. Finally, the results $\hat{t}$ are compared with the results reconstructed by NStoPS [3, 4, 10] and NStoPS-II [10], which do not use the background knowledge.

Table 1. Background knowledge and results of original positive surveys and negative surveys

Distribution	Background knowledge	Positive survey	Negative survey
Uniform	([0,100], [0,500], [0,500], [100,500], [0,500])	(99, 89, 103, 109, 100)	(95, 96, 108, 114, 87)
Normal	([0,20], [0,500], [250,500], [0,500], [0,10])	(10, 102, 290, 96, 2)	(143, 106, 55, 98, 98)
Log-normal	([0,10], [200,500], [200,500], [0,50], [0,10])	(5, 269, 205, 19, 2)	(122, 50, 96, 103, 129)
Exponential	([250,500], [0,200], [0,100], [0,20], [0,10])	(317, 130, 38, 10, 5)	(53, 100, 114, 133, 100)

Table 2. Distribution parameter settings

Distribution	Parameters
Uniform	$U(1, 5)$
Normal	$N(3, 2/3)$
Log-normal	$Log\text{-}N(0.9, 0.2)$
Exponential	$E(1.0)$

Figure 1 shows the positive survey results reconstructed by NStoPS, NStoPS-II and NStoPS-BK as well as the original positive surveys. Obviously, compared to NStoPS, NStoPS-II can eliminate unreasonable negative values. However, some results produced by NStoPS-II conflict with the background knowledge, e.g. $\hat{t}_1 = 120 > u_1, \hat{t}_4 = 44 < l_4$ in Fig. 1(a). For all the four distributions, NStoPS-BK can produce more reasonable results, which satisfy the background knowledge, than NStoPS and NStoPS-II.

On the other hand, with the same parameter settings (the positive survey results and background knowledge are set according to Table 1), we carry out above experiments 1000 times independently, and calculate the average error of reconstructed positive survey results. Assume the reconstructed positive survey results are $\hat{t}$, the error is calculated as follow [14]

$$error = \frac{1}{n}\sqrt{\sum_{i=1}^{c}(\hat{t}_i - t_i)^2}. \tag{9}$$

The experimental results are shown in Table 3. Obviously, for all the four distributions, the accuracy of reconstructed positive survey results could be improved by using the background knowledge and the NStoPS-BK.

6.2 Experiments on Calculating the Dependable Level

In order to investigate the influence of the background knowledge on the dependable level of the reconstructed positive survey results, several experiments on calculating the

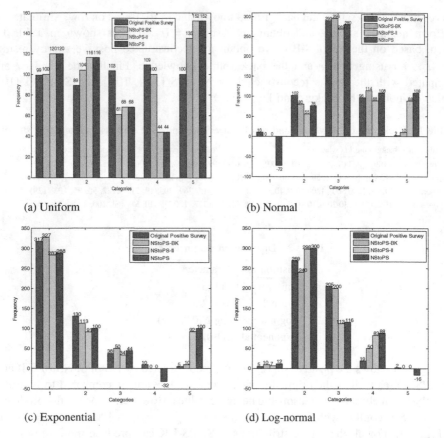

(a) Uniform

(b) Normal

(c) Exponential

(d) Log-normal

Fig. 1. The positive survey results reconstructed by NStoPS [3, 4, 10], NStoPS-II [10] and NStoPS-BK (Color figure online)

Table 3. Average error of positive survey results reconstructed by different methods

Distribution	Uniform	Normal	Log-normal	Exponential
NStoPS	0.145536	0.142783	0.144949	0.145078
NStoPS-II	0.144717	0.114871	0.097850	0.107853
NStoPS-BK	**0.126373**	**0.094054**	**0.061160**	**0.090846**

dependable level of the results that are reconstructed by NStoPS-BK are carried out in this subsection.

Assume the positive survey result of category i (reconstructed by NStoPS-BK) is $\hat{t}_i$. If $t'_i = n - (c-1)r_i$ violates the background knowledge, NStoPS-BK will produce $\hat{t}_i = low_i$ or up_i, and the confidence interval is assumed to be $d_i = [low_i, low_i + 2e_i]$ or $[up_i - 2e_i, up_i]$ (because NStoPS-BK will not produce a $\hat{t}_i$ that is less than low_i or larger than up_i); otherwise, the confidence interval is assumed to be $d_i = [\hat{t}_i - e_i, \hat{t}_i + e_i]$ (as that in Sect. 5). We will calculate the confidence level for d_i in the experiments.

We use *Bias_Length* to denote the level that t_i' violates the background knowledge $[l_i, u_i]$, i.e.

$$Bias\_Length = \begin{cases} low_i - t_i', & t_i' < low_i \\ 0, & low_i \le t_i' \le up_i \\ t_i' - up_i & t_i' > up_i \end{cases} \tag{10}$$

That is to say, when *Bias_Length* is larger, the estimated t_i' by (2) is more conflicted with the known background knowledge. We will demonstrate the curves of the dependable level for d_i when *Bias_Length* varies.

First, r_i is set as 20, 40, 60, 80 and 100, respectively. The number of categories is $c = 5$ and the number of participants is $n = 500$. Next, we vary low_i from $t_i' + 1$ to $n - l_{bk}$ (i.e. the *Bias_Length* from low_i varies from 1 to $n - l_{bk} - t_i'$), and set $up_i = low_i + l_{bk}$ where l_{bk} is set as 40. Finally, we compute the dependable level for d_i according to (8) where $\varepsilon_i = n/100$.

As shown in Fig. 2(a) (only results with *Bias_Length* $\le$ 300 are presented), the dependable level for d_i increases (until to the maximum value) with the *Bias_Length* from low_i. It indicates that when the expected positive survey result t_i' is more conflicted with the background knowledge, the usage of background knowledge will be more important, and the NStoPS-BK will be more effective.

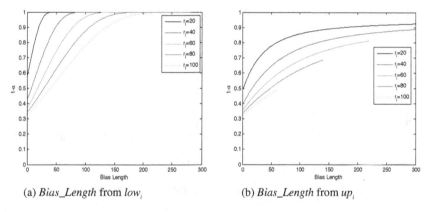

(a) *Bias_Length* from low_i (b) *Bias_Length* from up_i

Fig. 2. The influence of the *Bias_Length* and r_i on the dependable level for d_i (Color figure online)

On the other hand, we also calculate the dependable level for d_i with the *Bias_Length* from up_i varying from 1 to $t_i' - l_{bk}$, i.e., up_i varies from l_{bk} to $t_i' - 1$ ($low_i = up_i - l_{bk}$), where l_{bk} is set as 40. Figure 2(b) demonstrates that the dependable level for d_i increases with the *Bias_Length* from up_i (only results with *Bias_Length* $\le$ 300 are presented). Moreover, the dependable level for d_i increases more quickly when r_i is smaller.

Furthermore, we investigate the influence of l_{bk}, c, ε_i and n on the dependable level for d_i. In these experiments, the default parameter settings are $n = 500$, $c = 5$, $l_{bk} = 40$,

$\varepsilon_i = n/100$, $r_i = n/c$ and *Bias_Length* from *low$_i$* is $n/50$. Figure 3(a) shows the dependable level for d_i with l_{bk} varying from 0 to 200. The dependable level for d_i keeps 1 when $l_{bk} \in [0, 10]$, because the dependable interval length ($2\varepsilon_i = 10$) is not smaller than l_{bk}. Then the dependable level for d_i quickly decreases with l_{bk} in [10, 60] and seems to be relatively stable after $l_{bk} > 80$. Figure 3(b) shows that the dependable level for d_i decreases with the number of categories c. Figure 3(c) demonstrates that the dependable level for d_i increases with ε_i until to 1.0. It is also shown in Fig. 3(d) that the dependable level for d_i increases with n, where l_{bk} is set as $n/20$ in this experiment.

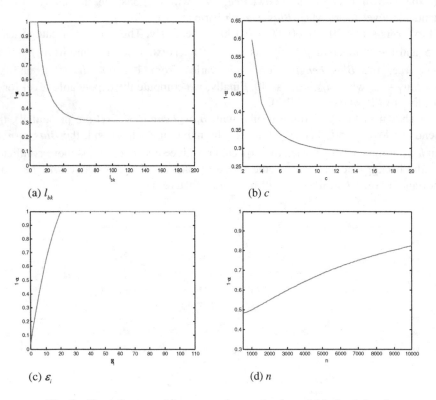

(a) l_{bk} (b) c

(c) ε_i (d) n

Fig. 3. The influence of l_{bk}, c, ε_i and n on the dependable level for d_i

7 Discussion

In some applications, the quality of the whole positive survey results also needs to be evaluated, and thus the dependable level of the whole positive survey results reconstructed from a negative survey with background knowledge needs to be calculated. According to the negative survey, different categories are not independent from each other when calculating the dependable level, so it needs to be further investigated.

Noted that, in [11], the dependable level of the whole positive survey results for the uniform negative survey without background knowledge has been studied. Based on

[11], when using background knowledge, the dependable level of the whole positive survey results can be calculated as follow.

$$1 - \alpha = \sum_{t=\hat{i}-\varepsilon, t \in S}^{\hat{i}+\varepsilon} P(t|r), \tag{11}$$

where $P(t|r)$ denotes the probability that the distribution of participants in the positive survey is t when the distribution of participants in the corresponding negative survey is given as r. $S = \{t | \forall i = 1 \ldots c, \ l_i \le t_i \le u_i, \ \sum_{i=1}^{c} t_i = n\}$, and $\varepsilon = \{\varepsilon_1 \ldots \varepsilon_c\}$. The $P(t|r)$ can be calculated by:

$$P(t|r) = \frac{P(r|t)P(t)}{\sum_{\hat{t} \in S} P(r|\hat{t})P(\hat{t})}, \tag{12}$$

where $P(t)$ denotes the prior probability that the distribution of participants in the positive survey is t, and we assume:

$$P(t) = \begin{cases} \frac{1}{|S|}, & t \in S \\ 0, & otherwise \end{cases}. \tag{13}$$

The $P(r|t)$ denotes the probability that the distribution of participants in the negative survey is r when the distribution of participants in the corresponding positive survey is given as t. The $P(r|t)$ can be calculated by the method in [11] (in its Subsect. 3.1). Finally, we obtain that:

$$1 - \alpha = \sum_{t=\hat{i}-\varepsilon, t \in S}^{\hat{i}+\varepsilon} \frac{\sum_{\forall k \in S_1 \cap S_3} \prod_{i=1}^{c} \frac{t_i!}{\prod_{j=1}^{c} k_{ij}!} P(t)}{\sum_{\hat{t} \in S} \sum_{\forall k \in S_2 \cap S_3} \prod_{i=1}^{c} \frac{\hat{t}_i!}{\prod_{j=1}^{c} k_{ij}!} P(\hat{t})}, \tag{14}$$

where $k = \{k_{ij} | \forall i, j \in [1, c]\}$, and:

$$S_1 = \left\{ k | \forall i, j \in [1, c], 0 \le k_{ij} \le t_i, k_{ii} = 0, \sum_{j=1}^{c} k_{ij} = t_i \right\},$$

$$S_2 = \left\{ k | \forall i, j \in [1, c], 0 \le k_{ij} \le \hat{t}_i, k_{ii} = 0, \sum_{j=1}^{c} k_{ij} = \hat{t}_i \right\},$$

$$S_3 = \left\{ k | \forall i, j \in [1, c], 0 \le k_{ij} \le r_j, k_{ii} = 0, \sum_{i=1}^{c} k_{ij} = r_j \right\}.$$

8 Conclusions and Future Work

As data analysts usually have some background knowledge in real-world applications, we study how to use background knowledge in accurately reconstructing positive surveys from negative surveys. First, we propose a method (called NStoPS-BK) for reconstructing positive surveys from the uniform negative surveys with background knowledge. Then, based on the background knowledge, we propose a method for calculating the dependable level of the reconstructed result of a category. The experimental results show that the usage of background knowledge could prevent producing unreasonable results and improve the accuracy of the reconstructed positive survey results. Moreover, we also discuss the dependable level of the whole positive survey results reconstructed from a uniform negative survey with background knowledge.

In future work, we will try to improve the efficiency of calculating the dependable level of the whole reconstructed positive survey results. Besides the uniform negative survey, using background knowledge in some other types of negative surveys will be studied as well.

Acknowledgements. This work is partly supported by National Natural Science Foundation of China (No. 61175045).

References

1. Esponda, F., Ackley, E.S., Helman, P., Jia, H., Forrest, S.: Protecting data privacy through hard-to-reverse negative databases. Int. J. Inf. Secur. **6**, 403–415 (2007)
2. Esponda, F.: Everything that is not important: negative databases. IEEE Comput. Intell. Mag. **3**, 60–63 (2008)
3. Esponda, F.: Negative surveys (2006). arXiv:math/0608176
4. Esponda, F., Guerrero, V.M.: Surveys with negative questions for sensitive items. Stat. Probab. Lett. **79**, 2456–2461 (2009)
5. Xie, H., Kulik, L., Tanin, E.: Privacy-aware collection of aggregate spatial data. Data Knowl. Eng. **70**, 576–595 (2011)
6. Horey, J., Groat, M., Forrest, S., Esponda, F.: Anonymous data collection in sensor networks. In: The Fourth Annual International Conference on Mobile and Ubiquitous Systems: Computing, Networking and Services, Philadelphia, USA, pp. 1–8 (2007)
7. Groat, M.M., Edwards, B., Horey, J., Wenbo, H., Forrest, S.: Enhancing privacy in participatory sensing applications with multidimensional data. In: The 2012 IEEE International Conference on Pervasive Computing and Communications (PerCom 2012), Lugano, pp. 144–152 (2012)
8. Groat, M.M., Edwards, B., Horey, J., He, W., Forrest, S.: Application and analysis of multidimensional negative surveys in participatory sensing applications. Pervasive Mob. Comput. **9**, 372–391 (2013)
9. Horey, J., Forrest, S., Groat, M.M.: Reconstructing spatial distributions from anonymized locations. In: The 2012 IEEE 28th International Conference on Data Engineering Workshops (ICDEW), Arlington, VA, pp. 243–250 (2012)
10. Bao, Y., Luo, W., Zhang, X.: Estimating positive surveys from negative surveys. Stat. Probab. Lett. **83**, 551–558 (2013)
11. Bao, Y., Luo, W., Lu, Y.: On the dependable level of the negative survey. Stat. Probab. Lett. **89**, 31–40 (2014)
12. Du, X., Luo, W., Zhao, D.: Negative publication of data. Int. J. Immune Comput. **2**, 1–14 (2014)

13. Lu, Y., Luo, W., Zhao, D.: Fast searching optimal negative surveys. In: Proceedings of the 2014 International Conference of Information and Network Security (ICINS 2014), Beijing, China, pp. 172–180 (2014)
14. Bao, Y.: Research on some problems of negative survey. Master's thesis, Department of Computer Science and Technology, University of Science and Technology of China (2013) (in Chinese)

Spatial Data Mining

Application of the Spatial Data Mining Methodology and Gamification for the Optimisation of Solving the Transport Issues of the "Varsovian Mordor"

Robert Olszewski[✉] and Agnieszka Turek[✉]

Faculty of Geodesy and Cartography,
Warsaw University of Technology, Warsaw, Poland
{r.olszewski, a.turek}@gik.pw.edu.pl

Abstract. The objective of the paper was to develop a specialised knowledge base using data mining methods, as the basis for and expert, decision making support system, created for the needs of development of action against negative spatial phenomena, which occur within the biggest office district of the capital of Poland. After collecting representative answers to a questionnaire from responders, who are professionally involved with this area, the authors "enriched the data" with commonly accessible spatial information and analysed the resulting dataset using artificial, regression and classification neural networks, CART decision trees and created fuzzy inference systems. Inference rules, developed with the use of the knowledge base and a limited amount of accessible information allow to specify highly probable types of social problems important for particular employees of this district. Using data mining techniques, the authors transformed collected data into information and knowledge, diagnosing main infrastructural and spatial problems in "Varsovian Mordor". Generalisation of inference rules, developed as a result of knowledge acquisition allowed the authors to propose unique, social gamification techniques, precisely dedicated for particular groups of inhabitants and employees of "the Mordor".

Keywords: Spatial data mining · Gamification · Geoinformation society · Artificial neural networks (ANN) · CART · Fuzzy inference systems (FIS) · Knowledge discovery · Smart city

1 Introduction

As Manuel Castels pointed out in "The Information Age" [1], "the paradox of the great civilization change consists in the fact that we have practically unlimited access to information and data and yet we are nearly unable to use it in any way". Thus, knowledge acquisition based on available information (including spatial information) is essential in the era when economic value is not generated in factories any more, but is produced by mass media and IT and telecommunication networks instead. Industrialism has given way to informationism, and the industrial society has been replaced by network society.

© Springer International Publishing Switzerland 2016
Y. Tan and Y. Shi (Eds.): DMBD 2016, LNCS 9714, pp. 103–114, 2016.
DOI: 10.1007/978-3-319-40973-3_10

The process of social digitalisation is based not only on the creation of a physical broadband network infrastructure, but also on unlimited access to data (also spatial data), and first of all, on education related to the ability to convert source information into useful knowledge. The so-called DIKW Pyramid (data-to-information-to-knowledge-to-wisdom transformation), proposed in the 1970's, may constitute a useful analogy for the development of geoinformation infrastructure.

In his work "A whole new mind" [2], Daniel H. Pink noticed that we are living in a period of civilizational transition, moving from the Information Age to the Conceptual Age. In the period dominated by agrarian culture (Agricultural Age), development resulted from innovations in agriculture, while in the Industrial Age it required the improvement of tools and machinery, and in the Information Age – gathering of data. Currently, what is indispensable is the ability to process the available information, and to use the obtained knowledge [3].

One of the most interesting social phenomena that have emerged as a result of the development of geoinformational technologies is crowdsourcing. The essence of "working in the hive" is the division of complex tasks into elementary factors and entrusting a large (usually unidentified) group of voluntaries with the performance of the task. Therefore, crowdsourcing is a way of solving problems and generating information by means of connecting people around a common idea.

Social activity connected with crowdsourcing may be used in many ways. The application of modern geoinformation technologies may be used not only for the effective gathering of source data about existing objects (such as the Open Street Map created spontaneously by millions of users), but also to obtain spatial knowledge about phenomena and processes – both physical and social ones. Transforming "raw" data into useful information is particularly important for the development of modern urban agglomerations that aspire to be "smart cities". The key factor for this process is the development of appropriate geoinformational technologies enabling social participation. However, this requires not only the use of sophisticated high-tech tools, but also persuading local communities to use them widely. In the opinion of the authors of this study, the impulse that triggers social energy and releases the creative potential of inhabitants is gamification. The use of this approach will permit not only collecting enormous sets of data, but also processing them and developing models of optimal use and development of space.

According to Homa Bahrani in "Super-flexibility: Toolkit for Dynamic Adaptation" [4], the changes occuring in the modern post-industrial world are stimulated by five transformational trends: innovation, digitization, collaboration, globalization, and ability to act – execution. Therefore, it is crucial not only to notice the tendencies shaping the world's information society and striving to actively participate in the transformation process defined at a global scale, but also to be able to consistently implement the adopted objectives. One of the concepts constituting a perfect example of both digitisation and innovation, and in particular collaboration, is the application of the idea and tools related to gamification for the activation of local community. The process of social (geo)participation initiated this way may be used both for the purposes of creating a vision of smart city, and (in a longer perspective) for the development of (geo)information society.

1.1 Geoinformation Society

Over the last decade, the supply of spatial data has grown by two orders of magnitude. Users are "flooded" with data of various quality, originating from various sources. However, "raw" data do not directly create new added value. As Clive Humby points out, "Data is the new oil. Models are the new gold". Just like oil requires refining to produce gasoline, plastic, or gum, data collected in a database require processing to obtain useful information, and, in turn, to transform it into knowledge about the surrounding space.

The globalisation process re-defines the way in which we perceive both social-cultural and economic relations. It also contributes to the evolution of information society based on technological knowledge and common access to information. The objective set by the information society is to provide every member of the society with the possibility to create, obtain, use, and share information and knowledge [5]. In modern post-industrial states, this objective is achieved by means of applying information and communication technologies (ICT). The technological expansion that stimulates the development of information society also indirectly fosters the development of civic society, which contributes to the democratisation of the decision-making processes [3]. The feedback loop between the development of democracy (civic society) and the technological revolution (information society) is particularly noticeable in the area of geoinformation. According to the EU Directorate General for Information Society, more than 50 % of the economic value of public information in the EU is generated by geoinformation. On the other hand, according to the estimations of the US Federal Geographical Data Committee, approximately 80 % of public data contain a spatial component. This means that we are witnessing the process of emergence of geoinformation society, which "widely uses information obtained by means of generally available services of the geoinformation infrastructure" (Geomatic Lexicon of Polish Association for Spatial Information (PASI)).

Thus, one may notice an interesting parallel between the development of technology and the emergence of (geo)information society and the formation of the open society (as defined in 1945 by Karl Popper) that is able to discuss all important facts from the political and economic life, and to adopt various points of view as well as to adapt new ideas, both external ones and those generated by the society itself. The development and popularisation of the Internet, mobile devices and, geoinformation technologies, including spatial data, make it easier than ever before. Moreover, this refers to all citizens, not just selected social groups. The inevitable situation where we, as users of the Internet and mobile devices, are becoming (whether consciously or not) suppliers of spatially localised information, forces us to ask about the possibilities to use the growing popularity of the crowdsourcing and VGI (Volunteered Geographic Information) ideas [6]. In the opinion of the authors, the activity of inhabitants of developing smart cities may be used in the social participation process for the purposes of co-creation of spatial development plans by the local community.

2 Test Area

Służewiec is a part of the Warsaw district of Mokotów, located on the left bank of the Vistula River, in the south-west part of Warsaw. Pursuant to the governmental decision of 1951, an industrial centre with an area of approximately 260 hectares was created here. It was characterised by low-rise buildings. Approximately 60 industrial investments and a housing complex for 26,000 inhabitants were designed. Production plants dealing with electronic equipment (Unitra Unima), semiconductors (Tewa), capacitors (Elwa), Radio Ceramic Production Plants, and Lift Production Plants (Zremb) started their operations in the area.

After 1989, the system transformation took place in the Polish economy. Significant changes in the system of the Polish economy involved the transformation from the planned economic system (rejection of the centrally planned state) to the market economy (adoption of the strategy aiming at creation of liberal free-market economy). As a result of the restructuring of the economy and intensive technological, property, and organisational changes, the process of liquidation of large industrial plants was initiated in the majority of industrial sectors. Instead, high office buildings offering an increasing number of workplaces were constructed. The previously existing housing districts became neglected.

In Western Europe, office districts were developed also outside direct centres of cities (e.g. Canary Wharf in London, La Défense in Paris). Their development was based on a specifically designed district layout - the transport network was designed first. Only then developers were allowed to start their investments. The development of Służewiec in Warsaw, however, was highly dynamic, and the local infrastructure still cannot keep up with the development of office buildings. After the fall of the industrial sector, the area of Służewiec Przemysłowy was highly attractive for developers due to the presence of all utilities and relatively low prices. Investors, however, did not pay much attention to the infrastructure when purchasing land parcels. They did not invest in restaurants, coffee shops, or places of cultural activities. As early as in 2002, a big shopping mall was constructed. It quickly began to function as a parking place for employees of the surrounding companies. Moreover, in Poland, the lack of involvement of local communities in the creation of their own surroundings is observed [7]. This problem particularly results from low social awareness of spatial planning issues, poor information policies related to participation or disclosing planning documents to the public, the form and course of social consultations, or the form of planning studies, which are often unclear for the inhabitants.

All of the above changes led to the development of a group of skyscrapers on previously industrial land. The area was recognised as unfriendly for people, "a ghetto for employees", and called "the Mordor of Warsaw", as a reference to the place of accumulation of evil forces in books by J.R.R. Tolkien. This part of the city was transformed from a neglected area in the suburbs into a business area of Warsaw. The number of office buildings located close to the Domaniewska Street equals to the total number of office buildings in Poznań, Kraków, and Łódź. Approximately 1.2 million sq. m. of modern office space was created within the last fifteen years. This equals to approximately 27 % of the total office space in Warsaw. It is the largest concentration of foreign corporations in the capital of Poland. According to various estimations, approximately 80–100 thousand employees commute every day to the area, while only 4 thousand inhabitants live there. In terms of public transportation, the area is one of the worst planned areas in the city. As a result, it features a high concentration of difficult transportation issues of Warsaw. Not enough space at tramway stops is provided in rush hours. It takes around one hour to travel several hundred metres along the main street. Not enough parking space is available. The number of parking places in office buildings is not sufficient, and they are usually occupied by members of higher managerial personnel. Also the new section of the SKM (the fast city train), constructed for Euro 2012, does not meet the requirements. Trains are overcrowded, they are often recalled, and the station - PKP Służewiec – is hardly accessible. The underground is located close to the Domaniewska Street. No transfer points or bus connections exist, however, between the underground and the Służewiec area. Służewiec is located between the city bypass and express roads. The main roads lead to the city centre, however, and provide no connections between city districts.

Traffic jams and overcrowded means of public transport make living in the office area close to the Domaniewska Street unbearable. Although new office buildings are still being constructed in the area (particularly due to rental fees lower than in the Warsaw centre), some companies are already moving to other places in Warsaw, such as the Wola district, providing better transportation solutions, including connections with the 2nd underground line. The characteristic feature of the office district is that it becomes completely empty after 7 p.m. on Fridays.

2.1   The Questionnaire on the "Warsaw Mordor".

In order to identify the main issues, and to collect opinions of arriving individuals concerning possible improvements in spatial planning, a short questionnaire addressed to employees of the "Mordor area" (as it is commonly called) was developed. The questionnaire was made accessible by social media (Facebook), and it was directly distributed in e-mails as a link to the Google form.

The questionnaire was constructed in such a way that data of responders are collected first (gender, age, place of residence, education level, current profession, period of residence in Warsaw); followed by their opinions concerning the current status of land management and existing issues. The questions concerned the level of importance of possibilities of commuting by car and by public transport, the insufficient number of restaurant facilities and pubs, the insufficient number of shops and places of cultural activities, public utilities, and green areas. The questionnaire also concerned potential interest in purchasing or renting an apartment close to the analysed office area. Answers were formulated according to the 10-level scale (an unimportant issue - a highly important issue). An open question concerned other issues noticed within the analysed area. Specification of addresses of companies employing the responders allowed to spatially locate the answers, and to draw additional conclusions concerning the analysed area.

The questionnaire was available for a period of three days; 122 individual answers from 69 men (57 %) and 53 women (43 %) were obtained. The majority of responders were young persons, at the beginning of their professional careers, at the age between 24 and 31. Almost 93 % of them are highly educated individuals. The majority of them are connected with the IT sector (broadly defined). Every fourth respondent (31 individuals) lives close to the place of work (the district of Mokotów), 12 % of responders travel to work from outside Warsaw. 40 individuals were born in Warsaw, 56 are people from outside the city, and the remaining individuals (about 10 %) refused to answer this question.

The "raw" data collected in the questionnaire were "enriched" by assigning appropriate spatial location and classification of acquired answers. Official topographic data (the state register of borders), made accessible by the Geodetic and Cartographic Documentation Centre, was used to georeference particular data records. Spatial information was also used to complement the resulting database with:

- *the average travel time* of a responder to the "Mordor" area by public transport, and the *distance* between the place of residence and the place of work. Each questionnaire contained information concerning the place of residence (part of Warsaw or a place outside Warsaw). The use of a navigation application (Jak.Dojade) permitted the determination of the estimated time of travel from a specified location to the centre of Służewiec Przemysłowy during rush hours. Google Maps services permitted the determination of the approximate road distance from the place of residence to "Mordor",
- *the accessibility of public transport* (in particular the underground and the fast city train). Distances between bus and tram stations, as well as the fast city train and the underground stations were determined using the database of topographic objects and spatial locations of places of residence of particular responders. Due to high difficulties in operations of city buses in the Służewiec area, the accessibility to the train transport was distinguished as a separate information category,
- *proximity to green areas*. For all of the address points located within the "Mordor" area, distances to the closest parks were determined. Information concerning surrounding areas, divided into lawns, concrete/asphalt, hardened grounds, were assigned to particular objects using the database of topographic objects.

Data from the questionnaire were also classified according to different criteria; for example, based on information on the place of birth, respondents were assigned to one of the following categories: born in Warsaw, strangers and individuals who did not decide to disclose this information. The importance of particular issues was also determined as a result of the analysis of histograms of distribution of responders' answers. Due to transportation difficulties, dominant in open questions, the issues of Służewiec were dichotomically reclassified, and the categories "transport" (almost 64 % of answers) and "other" were distinguished.

2.2 Analysis of Data Using *Spatial Data Mining* Tools

As stated in the introduction, acquisition of the questionnaire data, connection with spatial locations, and initial enrichment with topographic information is the first stage of the knowledge acquisition. The process of transforming the "raw" data to useful information can be implemented in many ways. The authors decided to apply the broadly defined computational intelligence (CI) methods and exploration spatial data mining). According to Poole, Mackworth and Goebel [8], computational intelligence is "the study of behaviour of intelligent agents", and concluding is equivalent to symbolic manipulations (computations). The group of algorithms of computational intelligence consists of, among others, fuzzy inference systems (FIS), artificial neural networks [9–11], rough sets, and decision trees.

Applying the theory of rough sets to reduce the problem of dimensionality, the authors selected key predicators (explaining variables) for several issues of regression and classification nature, and developed and trained neural networks modelling such processes:

1. The regression ANN network for explanation of the dependant variable "significance of travel by car". In the scope of the research works, several dozens of neural networks of MLS, RBF, and GRNN types were tested with different numbers of hidden layers and neurones in the input layer, which corresponds to a different number of considered factors. Division into "teaching" and "validating" sets (in the proportion 70 % to 30 %) was applied in the process of teaching, testing the effectiveness of several diversified ANN teaching algorithms. Eventually, the MLP type network was selected as the neural network allowing for the correct explanation of the respondents' answers. It considered 9 independent variables: education, being a native-born/stranger Varsovian, number of years spent in Warsaw, time of possible travel by public transport (in minutes), distance between the place of work and the transport station, and the distance to the underground station.

2. The regression ANN network for the explanation of the dependant variable "significance of travel by public transport". Similarly to the case of the above network, several dozens of networks with different architecture and levels of complexity were analysed. In the scope of the performed works, the key role was played by searching for a minimum subset of decision attributes (predicators) which would allow for explaining the process with sufficient accuracy, at the appropriate level of generalisation. The selected network considers the following features as independent variables: gender, age, education, being a native-born/stranger Varsovian, number of years spent in Warsaw, and distance from the underground and the train.

3. The regression ANN network for the explanation of the dependant variable "significance of lack of green areas". After the implementation of works similar to the above described operations, and after testing several dozens of ANN networks, it was determined that the following predicators are of key importance for the explanation of the respondents' opinions: education, access by car, access by public transport, time of access by public transport, distance from public transport.

4. The classification network for the explanation of the dichotomic division of distinguished social issues in "Mordor": transportation and others. The research works performed for a set of several dozens of networks with diversified architecture proved that the use of the following variables is recommended for satisfactory explanation of the classification: gender, age, being a native-born/stranger Varsovian, number of years spent in Warsaw, significance of access by car, significance

of access by public transport, time of access by public transport (in minutes), distance from the place of residence (in km).

The performed research works proved that the MLP type network (Fig. 1) of four initial variables: gender, being a native-born/stranger Varsovian, number of years spent in Warsaw, and time of access by public transport, permits obtaining the classification correctness coefficient equal to 0.79. The RBF type network (Fig. 2 - left) of five initial variables: gender, being a native-born/stranger Varsovian, number of years spent in Warsaw, time of access by public transport, and distance from the place of residence, permits obtaining the classification correctness coefficient equal to 0.81, and the RBF type network (Fig. 2 - right) of only three initial variables: gender, number of years spent in Warsaw, and time of access by public transport – 0.76. This means that by using several easy to obtain parameters it is possible to correctly forecast the significance of problems related to transport for approximately 80 % of individuals.

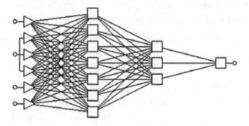

Fig. 1. The MLP type network of four initial variables: gender, being a native-born/stranger Varsovian, the number of years spent in Warsaw and the time of access by the public transport.

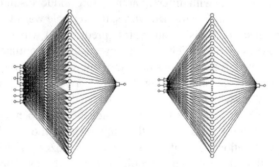

Fig. 2. On the left: The RBF type network of five initial variables: gender, being a native-born/stranger Varsovian, the number of years spent in Warsaw, the time of access by the public transport and the distance from the place of living. On the right: The RBF type network of three initial variables: gender, the number of years spent in Warsaw and the time of access by the public transport

The analysis of many types of neural networks permitted developing a prototype expert classification system bale to identify – with the high probability – important social or transport issues experienced by employees in the "Mordor" area, based on several easily accessible decision variables characterising such individuals. The use of the ANN, trained in this way for classification of thousands of employees of the Warsaw office district, will allow for the development of a series of proposals concerning solutions to key issues of the Służewiec area, and for dedicating an appropriate scheme for a precisely defined social group. The disadvantage of this solution is the "black box" nature of the ANN developed by the authors – it allows for obtaining correct solutions (reliable classification of multi-feature objects), but it does not explain the significance of the influence of particular factors on the decision making process. Aiming at the development of a prototype expert system allowing for the generation of the knowledge base, and explaining relations between variables, the authors analysed the same classification problem using another approach, employing the CART type decision tree. This allowed for the acquisition of decision rules in an open form.

Classification trees are applied for the determination of the membership of cases or objects in classes of the quality variable explained based on measurements of one or more explaining variables. The priority of the analysis based on classification trees is to forecast or to explain answers (reaction) which are hidden in the qualitative dependant variable. The basic advantages of the CART method include:

- use of any combination of continuous and range variables;
- co-operation with data sets of the complex structure;
- insensibility to the presence of untypical observations;
- use of the same variables in different parts of the tree, allowing for the detection of the context of relations [12].

The obtained results (Fig. 3) prove that transport is the main problem for individuals whose distance to a stop exceeds 250 m (leaf No. 3 of the tree), or those who have stayed in Warsaw shorter than 4.5 years (leaf No. 10). Other problems are considered as key problems by individuals who have lived in Warsaw shorter than

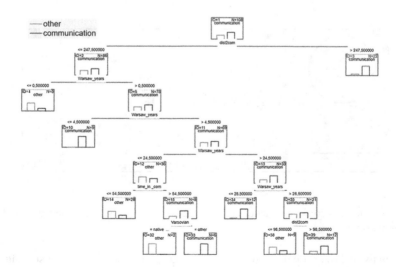

Fig. 3. Classification and Regression Tree for four explanatory variables (Color figure online).

six months (leaf No. 4), or who spend less than 54 min in public transport, and individuals who have lived in Warsaw shorter than 25 years (leaf No. 14). The analysis of answers presented by native-born Varsovians (leaf No. 32) and strangers (leaf No. 33) is also interesting. Although all of them spend much time in public transport, transport problems are NOT the key issues for native-born Varsovians. Strangers consider such problems as key problems. Extraction of the "rules" defined this way is of fundamental importance for the development of proposals of solutions to defined problems, dedicated for a particular group of the society.

Interesting results were also obtained for the analysis of questionnaire data using a relatively simple methodology of spatial statistics (determination of correlations in the so-called circular moving window with a radius of 250 m). This permitted visualising interesting relations (Fig. 4). For individuals declaring the possibility to travel by car as an important issue, proximity to green areas is less important (Fig. 4) than for individuals travelling by public transport (Fig. 4). In the case of both of the groups, the influence of locations of their offices in the neighbourhood of city parks is observed (parks are marked as green in Fig. 4).

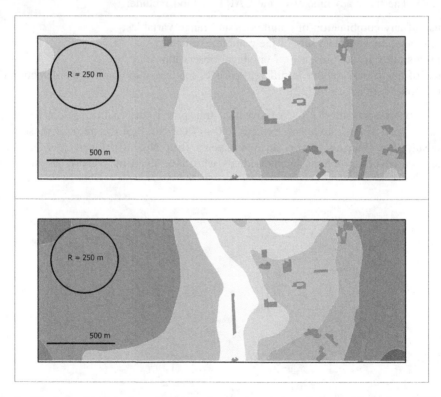

Fig. 4. The determination of correlations in the circular moving window, of the radius of 250 m. (Color figure online)

The analytical diagram defined this way, using spatial statistics, is the starting point for the development the knowledge base utilising fuzzy logics, and including if-then decision rules. The following problem can be used as an example: *if a person USUALLY travels to work by public transport and works QUITE FAR from the closest park, the lack of green areas is an IMPORTANT problem for such a person.* The use of appropriately selected linguistic variables and membership functions allows for correct parametrisation of terms such as: *quite far, usually* etc. Similarly to a set of rules based on the CART analysis, the obtained results are the basis for the development of solutions to the problems of problems, precisely selected for a particular group of society members.

3   Conclusion - Gamification as a Tool for Solving Social Problems of the "Mordor"

The performed analyses, observed trends, the developed knowledge base, and extracted rules allowed for the identification of key social issues of Służewiec Przemysłowy, and for the selection of the optimum methods of solutions. Because from the perspective of correct operations of this part of Warsaw, the key issue is related to transport, the authors proposed applying gamification techniques to solve this problem.

Results obtained for the data mining approach allowed for proposing two various gamification techniques for particular groups of users of the space (considering features such as age, education, or current profession). The authors assume that a gamification scheme, adopted to specified demands, can support the solution of transport problems of this part of Warsaw. However, it will not substitute infrastructural investments which should be implemented by the city. Gamification stresses the role of humans in a given process. The gamification idea also assumes to be successful only if its participants declare their voluntary participation in the programme. A system of scores for meeting specified goals highly motivates employees and encourages them to change their behaviour and habits. For example, in order to solve the problems of traffic jams in Służewiec Przemysłowy, employers may assign additional points to employees who decide to travel to work on bicycles. Employees who use bicycles can expect special bonuses every time they travel by bicycle. A mobile application specifically designed for different users (considering their age, distances of travel) helps rank kilometres and numbers of travels. Employees compete, and winners are rewarded. Another approach also utilising the gamification technique (and dedicated for older individuals travelling farther), promotes commuting with the use of HOV (high-occupancy vehicles). Those travelling by car every day can get special bonuses for collecting passengers – from the same as well as from other companies located in Służewiec. The system of scores, similar to "loyalty programmes" used by fuel concerns, would allow for rewarding the most pro-social individuals. "Team classification" and dynamically changing ranking of companies whose employees use the HOV formula may also be important. Developing a mobile application allowing for the implementation of such gamification, and promoting deeper social relations, would allow for collecting additional information concerning issues and preferences of individuals involved in the "Mordor" area. This would contribute to the optimisation of the proposed solutions.

New generation geoinformation portals and gamification tools will allow us not only to collect data and transform them into useful information. They will also enable us to acquire spatial knowledge, and to use it to get to know the surrounding space, and to transform it in a rational way. Remembering the words by Einstein: "Imagination is more important than knowledge. For knowledge is limited to all we now know and understand, while imagination embraces the entire world, and all there ever will be to know and understand", we may believe that imagination is the only limit for the geoinformation society in the era of creating smart cities.

In the opinion of the authors of this study, gamification can be the impulse triggering social energy and releasing the creative potential of inhabitants. Gamification means the "application of game mechanics, aesthetics and thinking in game categories in order to increase human involvement, motivate people to act, promote learning and practice problem-solving". The use of this approach will permit not only collecting enormous sets of data, but also processing them and developing models of optimal use and development of space. The performed analysis are based on several attributes, which are relatively easy to obtain. Confirmation of the study can be based on the analysis of the responses of thousands of users.

References

1. Castels, M.: Mobile Communication and Society: A Global Perspective. MIT Press, Cambridge (2006)
2. Pink, D.: A Whole New Mind: Why Right-Brainers Will Rule the Future. Penguin Group, New York (2005)
3. Buczek, A., Olszewski, R.: Rola bazy danych obiektów topograficznych w tworzeniu infrastruktury wiedzy przestrzennej. In: Olszewski, R., Gotlib, D. (eds.) Rola bazy danych obiektów topograficznych w tworzeniu infrastruktury informacji przestrzennej w Polsce, pp. 307–317. Główny Urząd Geodezji i Kartografii, Warszawa (2013)
4. Bahrani, H., Evans, S.: Super-Flexibility for Knowledge Enterprises: A Toolkit for Dynamic Adaptation. Springer, Heidelberg (2010)
5. Gaździcki, J.: Repository of Geomatics, digital library of PASI (2003). http://www.ptip.org.pl/
6. Goodchild, M.F.: Citizens as sensors: the world of volunteered geography. GeoJournal 69(4), 211–221 (2007)
7. Szlachetko, J.: Consultation-based forms of social participation in spatial planning (2014). http://www.im.edu.pl/
8. Poole, D., Mackworth, A., Goebel, R.: Computational Intelligence. A Logical Approach. Oxford University Press, New York (1998)
9. Tadeusiewicz, R.: Elementarne wprowadzenie do sieci neuronowych z przykładowymi programami. Akademicka Oficyna Wydawnicza, Warszawa (1998)
10. Fausett, L.: Fundamentals of Neural Networks. Prentice Hall, New York (1994)
11. Olszewski, R.: Kartograficzne modelowanie rzeźby terenu metodami inteligencji obliczeniowej, Prace Naukowe - Geodezja, z. 46, Oficyna Wydawnicza Politechniki Warszawskiej, Warszawa (2009)
12. Breiman, L., Friedman, J.H., Olshen, R.A., Stone, C.J.: Classification and Regression Trees. Chapman & Hall, Wadsworth Inc., New York (1984)

A Geo-Social Data Model for Moving Objects

Hengcai Zhang[1,2], Feng Lu[1,2(✉)], and Jie Chen[1,2]

[1] State Key Lab of Resources and Environmental Information System,
Institute of Geographic Sciences and Natural Resources Research,
Chinese Academy of Sciences, Beijing 100101, China
{zhanghc,luf,chenj}@lreis.ac.cn
[2] Fujian Collaborative Innovation Center for Big Data
Applications in Governments, Fuzhou 350003, China

Abstract. In this paper, we combine moving-object database and social network systems and present a novel data model called $\underline{G}$eo-$\underline{S}$ocial-$\underline{M}$oving (GSM) that enables the unified management of trajectories, underlying geographical space and social relationships for massive moving objects. A bulk of *data types* and corresponding *operators* are also proposed to facilitate geo-social queries on moving objects.

Keywords: Moving objects · Social relationships · Data model · Geo-social

1 Introduction

There is currently a wide diffusion of mobile devices equipped with positioning technologies including Global Positioning System (*GPS*), cellular triangulation, and WiFi, to name a few. Therefore, online location-based services (*LBSs*) and location-based social networks (*LBSNs*), such as *Facebook, Twitter, Foursquare, Gowalla,* and *Brightkite*, have increased the generation of geo-social data [10,13]. Compared with traditional movement data with spatial-temporal characteristics, such as *GPS* points $<time, longitude, latitude>$, these datasets involve more dimensions. For example, in *LBSs* and *LBSNs*, users are associated with geo-locations through check-ins made by mobile devices and have many online social relationships such as *friendships* and *fellowships* [11]. Geo-social data are useful for next-generation *LBSs* and online recommender services, and belong to a new data source for human mobility research. *e.g.*, the analysis of the effect of geographic distance on a social structure [15] and investigation of the connection between social ties and correlated activity [3,19].

With the availability of such data, more and more real-world applications require ad-hoc data management technologies for the data, leading to a rise in new study challenges and opportunities in the data management community [3]. For instance, when we visit a shopping mall, a mobile device might highlight those friends who had checked in there, or tell us the nearest restaurants that have been visited by our friends.

© Springer International Publishing Switzerland 2016
Y. Tan and Y. Shi (Eds.): DMBD 2016, LNCS 9714, pp. 115–122, 2016.
DOI: 10.1007/978-3-319-40973-3_11

Over the past few years, there has been much research on spatial-temporal database modeling issues in the fields of geographical information systems (*GISs*) and moving-object databases (*MODs*) [7]. These works have focused on different needs, such as data modelling, indexing, and querying. However, current *MOD* approaches do not provide appropriate solutions for the manipulation of geo-social data.

Recently, the fact that many applications rely on trajectories with additional information, such as human activities (*e.g.*, shopping, having lunch, and relaxing), events, behaviours or transport modes, has shifted the research focus from raw trajectories to semantic trajectories. Although relationships can be modelled as one kind of semantic information, the research results obtained for the semantic model are not well adapted to it. That is because many studies, such as those on *CONSTAnt* [2], symbolic trajectories, annotations [12] and ontology, model semantic information as labels that link to specific points, segments or whole trajectories. In particular, these semantics are represented as dynamic attributes that denote attributes as functions of time.

Graph database systems such as *Flockdb*, *Giraph*, and *Neo4J* are undoubtedly suitable for representing social relationships. However, they cannot be directly applied to store trajectories because of the lack of an abstraction level and upper logical data model [1]. In respect to the above mentioned research, there is a paucity of literature regarding an integrated approach to modelling and querying geo-social data. Although *Pelekis* and co-workers presented a novel graph-based model that uses a dynamic graph to represent semantic mobility timelines [13], related issues of modelling social relationships have not been addressed.

In this paper, we extend the *MOD* to support social relationships and present a composite graph-based data model, called **G**eo-**S**ocial-**M**oving (***GSM***), to integrate spatial, temporal and relational dimensions when representing geo-social data at abstract and logical levels. A bulk of *data types* and *operators* including *interception, extension, projection* and *multi-dimensional projection* are then provided.

The remainder of the paper is organised as follows. Section 2 summarizes related research work. Section 3 introduces the novel geo-social data model and elaborates on the basic concepts. Section 4 defines the user-defined *datatypes* and corresponding *operators*. Finally, Sect. 5 concludes the paper and suggests future work.

2   Related Work

Early related studies on data models for moving objects focused on the representation of raw trajectories that consist of a temporal sequence of the positions of moving objects [13,16]. For example, the moving objects spatio-temporal (*MOST*) data model allowed the management of the current position of moving objects, and the prediction of future movement based on an important concept of the dynamic attribute that values change over time according to a given function of time [17,20]. Discrete data models mapped trajectories into discrete and simple segments [5,6]. A discrete spatialtemporal-trajectory-based moving object database (*DSTTMOD*) that models trajectories as a function curve in three-dimensional space was developed. It represents trajectories as a set of points, trajectory segments or a function $f(x)$ of time. However, semantic information of trajectories such as stay points, objects' behaviour, contextual annotations or social relationships mentioned in our study was neglected [12]. Those data models for raw trajectories did not embrace different underlying environments such as *free space* [12], *networks* [7,14], and *indoor* [8].

Recently, many additional information from the application context is considered in the modelling process. For example, the trajectories of a person can be interpreted as the sequences of points of interest such as a library, shopping mall, office building or museum. Hence, the research trends shift from raw trajectories to semantic trajectories [2]. A semantic trajectory can be defined as a trajectory enhanced with annotations such as activity, instant speed, transport mode and one or several complementary segmentations [12,18]. Among them, social relationships between moving objects are one of the important types of semantic information and need to be considered by the data management community, especially with respect to the trends of prevalent online social networks or location-based social networks [11]. This has provided the research motivation for this paper.

3   Modelling Geo-Social Data

3.1   Geographical Graph

Consider that objects often move around common *POIs* in free space, the proposed geographical graph adopts the Voronoi diagram as the underlying framework for subdivision. A Voronoi diagram is an effective decomposition of a space according to the position of set points [9]. For each *POI*, there is a Voronoi region containing all points closer to this *POI* than to any other. The formal definition of a Voronoi region is

$$V(p_i) = \{q | \forall q \in P, d(q, p_i) \le d(q, p_j), i \ne j, p_i, p_j \in P, j = 1, 2, \ldots, n\}. \quad (1)$$

where $V(p_i)$ is a Voronoi region, P is a set of *POIs*, n is the number of location records, q is an arbitrary point in space, and $d(q, p_j)$ is a distance function.

A geographical graph can be regarded as a collection of nodes and edges based on the space subdivision using a Voronoi diagram. Nodes denote a set of Voronoi regions. Edges connect two Voronoi regions. The presented data model employs an *OGC* (Open Geospatial Consortium)-compliant nine-intersection model that presents a comprehensive definition of topological relationships between spatial objects in two-dimensional space. Spatial relationships include disjoint, touching, overlapping, covering and containing relationships [4].

3.2   Social Graph

Modelling social relationships between moving objects with graphs is taken for granted, where nodes correspond to a set of moving objects and edges correspond to a set of social relationships. The attributes of nodes could be static; e.g., a name or type. The attributes of edges could be property fields representing a feature of social relationships in physical or cyber space.

3.3 Movement Graph

Movement graphs are designed to model the trajectories of moving objects. In our model, an objects trajectory is split into trajectory segments using a Voronoi diagram as described by a geographical graph. Each segment is represented as a single graph node. The complete trajectory is modelled as a set of nodes. A set of edges is then generated to associate these nodes sequentially.

4   Data Types and Operators

4.1   Data Types

With the concepts defined in Sect. 3, this section gives a formal definition of graphs involved in the GSM model and provides data types G_{geo}, G_{social}, and G_{move} to represent geographical space, social relationships and movement trajectories, respectively.

Definition 1 (*geographical graph* structure). A geographical graph structure G_{geo} is defined as a pair of nodes (Voronoi regions) and edges (spatial relations between Voronoi regions):

$$G_{geo} = (G_{vertexs}, G_{edges}). \tag{2}$$

Here, $G_{vertexs}$ is a subset of Voronoi regions VR that corresponds to the geographical space:

$$G_{vertexs} = (vr_1, vr_2, \ldots, vr_n), vr_i \in VR. \tag{3}$$

$$vr = (rid, geom, area, poi). \tag{4}$$

where rid is the identification of a Voronoi region, $geom$ is the geometry of the Voronoi region, $area$ is the whole area of the Voronoi region, and poi denotes the POIs contained in the Voronoi region.

G_{edges} is a set of spatial relationships between Voronoi regions. In this paper, topological relationships are used to define as

$$G_{edges} = (disjoint, meet, equal, inside, converedby, contains, covers, overlap). \tag{5}$$

Any position in this Voronoi region vr can then be defined as g_{pos}:

$$g_{pos} = (rid, lat, lon). \tag{6}$$

where rid is the identification of a Voronoi region and lat and lon are the latitude and longitude of the position.

Definition 2 (*social graph* structure). A social graph structure is used to model the social relations between moving objects:

$$G_{social} = (S_{vertexs}, S_{edges}).\tag{7}$$

Here, $S_{vertexs}$ denotes moving objects and S_{edges} denotes the social relations between two moving objects:

$$S_{vertexs} = (mo_1, mo_2, \ldots, mo_n).\tag{8}$$

$$mo = (mid, name, param).\tag{9}$$

where *mid* and *name* are the identification and name of a moving object. *param* refers to other attributes of the object;

$$S_{edges} = (rel_1, rel_2, \ldots, rel_m), rel_i \in (relation_{physical}, relation_{cyber}).\tag{10}$$

There are two kinds of social relations $relation_{physical}$ and $relation_{cyber}$ between objects, including *colleagues*, *kindredrelationships* or *friendships* for $relation_{physical}$, and *followership*, *interest group* or *fan relationships* for $relation_{cyber}$.

Definition 3 (*movement graph* structure). A movement graph structure is defined to represent the trajectories of moving objects:

$$G_{move} = (M_{vertexs}, M_{edges}).\tag{11}$$

Here, $M_{vertexs}$ is a set of trajectory segments *tseg* (sometimes called the sub-trajectory) of an object in Voronoi region *vr*:

$$M_{vertexs} = (tseg_1, tseg_2, \ldots, tseg_n).\tag{12}$$

$$tseg = ((mo, vr), (t_i, g_{pos}^i, v_i)_{i=1}^m).\tag{13}$$

where t denotes the time of location points and m denotes the count of location points;

$$M_{edges} = (next, prev, link_{mo}, link_{geo}).\tag{14}$$

There are four different relations in M_{edges}. Among them, *next* and *prev* are used to represent the ordinal relations between trajectory segments. $link_{mo}$ and $link_{geo}$ are used to point to the moving objects and geographical regions related to a defined trajectory segment.

A moving objects trajectory can be modelled as a set of trajectory segments:

$$trajectory = (mo, (tseg_p, tseg_{p+1}, \ldots, tseg_q)).\tag{15}$$

4.2 Operators

Definition 4 $select(G, C)$. The *select* operator receives the query condition and the specific graph layer of the GSM model, and returns all graph nodes or edges that meet the condition. Depending on the hierarchical graph layers, it is written as $select(G_{geo}, C)$, $select(G_{social}, C)$, or $select(G_{move}, C)$ for queries on a geographical graph, social graph, and movement graph respectively, where C is the query condition.

For example, to find graph nodes with the name David over a social graph, the query expression is written as

$$select(G_{social}, name = {}'David'). \tag{16}$$

To find nodes with areas larger than $10,000 \, \text{m}^2$ over a geographical graph, the query is written as

$$select(G_{geo}, area > 10000 \, \text{m}^2). \tag{17}$$

Over movement graphs, aggregate operations can be executed. For example, sum_{dist} sums the distance of trajectory segments and sum_{time} sums a moving objects activity time in a specific Voronoi region. A query that finds all trajectory segments of a moving object longer than $10 \, \text{Km}$ is written as

$$select(G_{move}, sum\_dist > 10 \, \text{km}). \tag{18}$$

The *select* operator can also be applied on graph edges. For instance, the query of all pairs of moving objects that have working relationships over a social graph can be written as

$$select(G_{social}, e\_rel = working). \tag{19}$$

Definition 5 $expand(N, d)$. The *expand* operator belongs to graph traversal operators, where $N \subseteq (G_{vertexs}, S_{vertexs}, M_{vertexs})$. It receives a bulk of nodes and distance parameters, and returns a set of adjacent nodes that satisfy the traversal number d.

Definition 6 $cross(G_f, G_t, t)$. The *cross* operator projects the graph G_f to another graph layer G_t at time t, where $G_f, G_t \subseteq (G_{geo}, G_{social}, G_{traj})$. For example, $cross(G_{social}, G_{geo}, t)$ can project a social graph layer to a geographical layer, so as to find all the moving objects that move around the special space regions at time t or in the time period t. $cross(G_{social}, G_{move}, t)$ can project a social graph layer to a movement graph layer. $cross(G_{geo}, G_{move}, t)$ can find all trajectories of a moving object in a certain geographical region.

Supposing that we want to find Davids trajectories or locations in a specific time interval, the query can be expressed as

$$cross(select(G_{social}, name = {}'David'), G_{geo}, s_{time}, e_{time}). \tag{20}$$

$$cross(select(G_{social}, name = {}'David'), G_{move}, s_{time}, e_{time}). \tag{21}$$

Definition 7 $multicross_{G_t}(G_{f1}, G_{f2}, T)$. The operator *multicross* can project both the graphs G_{f1} and G_{f2} to graph G_t at time T. When $G_t \subseteq G_{move}$ and $G_{f1} \subseteq G_{social}$, $G_{f2} \subseteq G_{geo}$, $multicross_{G_{move}}(G_{social}, G_{geo}, T)$ can find objects movements that simultaneously meet the conditions G_{social} and G_{geo}. That is, given a set of moving objects and a set of geographical regions, this operator returns all these objects trajectories to these specified regions. Similarly, $multicross_{G_{social}}(G_{geo}, G_{move}, T)$ can find all moving objects with trajectories passing through the given set of geographical regions during time T. $multicross_{G_{geo}}(G_{social}, G_{move}, time)$ can find the set of geographical regions where the given set of moving objects has gone through.

For example, supposing that we want to retrieve Davids trajectories in the geographical region vr_1 during time t, the query can be written as

$$multicross_{G_{move}}(select(G_{social}, name = 'David'), select(G_{geo}, rid = 'vr_1', t). \tag{22}$$

5   Conclusion

This paper presented a composite-graph-based data model for the integrated representation of *trajectories, social relationships* and *geographical space* for moving objects in free space, to tackle management challenges related to the explosive growth of geo-social data. A bulk of user-defined *data types* and corresponding *operators* were proposed to facilitate geo-social queries on the moving objects. The proposed GSM model is a step forward in the data modelling of moving objects in that it considers social relationships and large-scale geographical spaces, even indoor spaces.

Further work will involve the development of a corresponding index structure and various query algorithms, and the distributed implementation of a data model using a large-scale graph commutating processing framework such as *Pregel* or *Bulk Synchronous Parallel*.

Acknowledgments. This research was supported by the National Natural Science Foundation of China (Grant No. 41401460, 41271408) and the Key Research Program of the Chinese Academy of Sciences (Grant No. ZDRW-ZS-2016-6-3). And we also thank the anonymous referees for their helpful comments and suggestions.

References

1. Angles, R., Gutierrez, C.: Survey of graph database models. ACM Comput. Surv. (CSUR) **40**(1), 1–10 (2008)
2. Bogorny, V., Renso, C., Aquino, A.R., Lucca Siqueira, F., Alvares, L.O.: CONSTAnT-a conceptual data model for semantic trajectories of moving objects. Trans. GIS **18**(1), 66–88 (2014)
3. Crandall, D.J., Backstrom, L., Cosley, D., Suri, S., Huttenlocher, D., Kleinberg, J.: Inferring social ties from geographic coincidences. Proc. Natl. Acad. Sci. **107**(52), 22436–22441 (2010)
4. Egenhofer, M.J., Franzosa, R.D.: Point-set topological spatial relations. Int. J. Geogr. Inf. Syst. **5**, 161–174 (1991)

5. Forlizzi, L., Gting, R.H., Nardelli, E., Schneider, M.: A data model and data structures for moving objects databases. ACM SIGMOD **29**(2), 319–330 (2000)
6. Guting, R.H., Bhlen, M.H., Erwig, M., Jensen, C.S., Lorentzos, N.A., Schneider, M., Vazirgiannis, M.: A foundation for representing and querying moving objects. ACM Trans. Database Syst. (TODS) **25**, 1–42 (2000)
7. Guting, R.H., Ding, Z.: Modeling and querying moving objects in networks. VLDB J. **15**(2), 165–190 (2006)
8. Jensen, C.S., Lu, H., Yang, B.: Indoor - a new data management frontier. IEEE Data Eng. Bull **33**, 12–17 (2010)
9. Kolahdouzan, M., Shahabi, C.: Voronoi-based k nearest neighbor search for spatial network databases. In: Proceedings of the Thirtieth International Conference on Very Large Data Bases, VLDB Endowment, vol. 30, pp. 840–851 (2004)
10. Long, J.A., Nelson, T.A.: A review of quantitative methods for movement data. Int. J. Geogr. Inf. Sci. **27**, 292–318 (2013)
11. Mokbel, M.F., Sarwat, M.: Mobility and social networking: a data management perspective. Proc. VLDB Endow. **6**, 1196–1197 (2013)
12. Parent, C., Spaccapietra, S., Renso, C., Andrienko, G., Bogorny, V., Damiani, M.L., Macedo, J., Pelekis, N., Theoderidis, Y., Yan, Z.: Semantic trajectories modeling and analysis. ACM Comput. Surv. **45**(4), 39–76 (2013)
13. Pelekis, N., Theodoridis, Y., Janssens, D.: On the management and analysis of our lifesteps. ACM SIGKDD Explor. Newsl. **15**, 23–32 (2014)
14. Sandu Popa, I.: Modeling. University of Versailles-Saint-Quentin, Querying and Indexing Moving Objects with Sensors on Road Networks (2010)
15. Scellato, S., Noulas, A., Mascolo, C.: Exploiting place features in link prediction on location-based social networks. In: Proceedings of the 17th ACM SIGKDD International Conference on Knowledge Discovery and Data Mining, pp. 1046–1054 (2011)
16. Schneider, M.: Moving Objects in Databases and GIS: State-of-the-Art and Open Problems. In: Navratil, G. (ed.) Research Trends in Geographic Information Science, pp. 169–187. Springer, Heidelberg (2009)
17. Sistla, A.P., Wolfson, O., Chamberlain, S., Dao, S.: Modeling and querying moving objects. In: International Conference on Data Engineering (ICDE), pp. 422–422 (1997)
18. Spaccapietra, S., Parent, C.: Adding meaning to your steps (keynote paper). In: Jeusfeld, M., Delcambre, L., Ling, T.-W. (eds.) ER 2011. LNCS, vol. 6998, pp. 13–31. Springer, Heidelberg (2011)
19. Tang, W., Zhuang, H., Tang, J.: Learning to infer social ties in large networks. In: Gunopulos, D., Hofmann, T., Malerba, D., Vazirgiannis, M. (eds.) ECML PKDD 2011, Part III. LNCS, vol. 6913, pp. 381–397. Springer, Heidelberg (2011)
20. Wolfson, O., Chamberlain, S., Kalpakis, K., Yesha, Y.: Modeling moving objects for location based services. In: König-Ries, B., Makki, K., Makki, S.A.M., Pissinou, N., Scheuermann, P. (eds.) IMWS 2001. LNCS, vol. 2538, pp. 46–58. Springer, Heidelberg (2002)

Optimization on Arrangement of Precaution Areas Serving for Ships' Routeing in the Taiwan Strait Based on Massive AIS Data

Jinhai Chen[1,2(✉)], Feng Lu[2,3], Mingxiao Li[2], Pengfei Huang[1],
Xiliang Liu[2,3], and Qiang Mei[1]

[1] Navigation College, Jimei University, Xiamen 361021, China
{jhchen,pfhuang,qmei}@jmu.edu.cn
[2] LREIS, Institute of Geographic Sciences and Natural Resources Research,
CAS, Beijing 100101, China
{luf,limx,liuxl}@lreis.ac.cn
[3] Fujian Collaborative Innovation Center for Big Data Applications in
Governments, Fuzhou 350003, China

Abstract. The Taiwan Strait is the gateway used by ships of almost every kind on passage to and from nearly all the important ports in Northeast Asia. To minimize the possibility of collisions between crossing and through traffic, Precaution Areas (PAs) were laid out to remind mariners where the crossing and encountering situations may occur in the strait. Recent advances in telemetry technology help to collect ships movement data more efficiently and accurately. These advances would be useful for delineating Principal Fairways (PFs) in the crowded strait-corridor. Based on ship trajectory observations of transit-passage and cross-strait transits, cumulative activity patterns are characterized in the form of probability density. Bringing the layer of popular direct cross-strait lanes to the iso-surface of PFs, all conflict areas were extracted as PAs of the Ships Routing System Plan in Taiwan Strait. For direct cross-strait transportations, by linking the centers of PAs in the strait with the official pass points outside the western Taiwan harbors, this paper recommends the applicable direct cross-strait routes to reduce the risk of conflicts in the strait.

Keywords: Geostream data mining · Ships' routeing · Taiwan strait

1 Introduction

This paper is concerned with optimizing Precautionary Areas (PAs) serving for Ships' Routeing (hereafter cited as Routeing) exemplified by the intense traffic in the Taiwan Strait; and it would be as well first to be clear about what we mean by the relevant terms. Here **Routeing** involves vessels being channeled by more or less mandatory means into traffic lanes so as to reduce risks of casualties [1]. Since the first modern **Traffic Separation Scheme** (TSS) was adopted by International Maritime Organization (IMO) in 1967, most of the basic concepts of routeing (i.e. traffic separation at sea) have been proved and greatly extended [2, 3]; and IMO has released a specific

© Springer International Publishing Switzerland 2016
Y. Tan and Y. Shi (Eds.): DMBD 2016, LNCS 9714, pp. 123–133, 2016.
DOI: 10.1007/978-3-319-40973-3_12

guidance (hereafter cited as the IMO Guidance) on the methodology of routeing and the various criteria currently used in planning routeing systems in 2003 [4], given in accordance with IMO Resolution A.572(14) titled *General Provisions on Ships' Routeing* in 1985 [5]. The provisions is aimed at standardizing the design, development, charted presentation and use of routeing measures adopted by IMO; and they state that a **routeing system** includes PAs, TSSs, traffic lane, deep-water routes, recommended tracks, two-way routes, areas to be avoided, inshore traffic zones, roundabout and such; a **PA** is a an area within defined limits where ships must navigate with particular caution [4]; a **Traffic Lane** is an area within defined limits where one–way traffic is established; and a **TSS** is to ease the congestion and lessen the likelihood of end-on encounters by separating opposing streams of traffic, and somehow spacing out the meeting points or areas between the Traffic Lanes. TSSs are pre-eminent in various routeing measures because they alone have been subject to regulation under and encouraged by international conventions [1].

In the existing literature related to traffic at sea, there are various excellent reviews on detailed history of routeing [2] or traffic regulation [1]. Especially the IMO Guidance has proposed a credible philosophy to make the discipline inherent in routeing acceptable to seamen [4]. Because Routeing is intended to alleviate **particular hazardous circumstances** on concerned area. A basic need therefore exists for realistic data on traffic flow, in the light of where are precautionary labelling of hazardous to be chosen as PA. Since 2006, most of ocean-going ships have been required to carry an Automatic Identification System (AIS), which broadcasts a vessel's position, identity and voyage information at variable refresh rates. Such advances in ship tracking and telemetry technology help to collect the movement tracks more efficiently and accurately. The ship tracks have increased tremendously, and these advances have been accompanied by new methods for routeing planning [6]. In recent years, any coastal states built terrestrial AIS networks to monitor vessel traffic [7]. Because open oceans cannot be covered using only shore-based AIS stations, satellite-based AIS receivers were developed to pick up messages in the open ocean [8]. AIS data have become a valuable decision support element in maritime traffic management. This allows ship traffic patterns to be recognized by learning strategies without any priori information [7].

This paper presents a distinct solution that have been developed by the authors over the last 3 years. Some aspects to this work have been previously published [6, 9], whereas the rest is novel and is presented here for the first time. What makes this collection unique is that the different solutions are based on the same AIS data feed provided by the MOT of China Mainland. The broad scope of the problems assessed should give the reader a sense of the value and benefit of applying visualization techniques and analytical algorithms using ships' tracking data. As a direct result of this approach, marine domain experts are able to use their knowledge during analysis, leading to deeper understanding of the data, higher trust in the obtained results. We therefore hope to demo the benefits of geo-visualization for design and development of routeing system.

2   Concerned Area

The Taiwan Strait is bounded by Taiwan, mainland China, the South China Sea and the East China Sea on its east, west, south and north, respectively (Fig. 1). About 350 km in length, 180 km in average width and 60 m in average depth, the strait connects two largest marginal seas in the western Pacific [10]. Traffic through the Taiwan Strait carries all the cargoes essential to everyday life in the Far East Region of the world, including many of a hazardous or pollution nature. The Taiwan Strait is not the most congested stretch of narrow water in the world but it is the gateway used by ships of almost every kind on passage to and from nearly all the important ports in Northeast Asia [9]. This scene is complicated, in season, by large numbers of fishing vessels attracted by the rich fishing grounds in the Strait [11, 12]. Although direct links via waterway transport between two sides of the Taiwan Strait were once suspended from 1949 [13], the cross-strait Direct Shipping Links (DSLs) has been established since the Cross-strait Sea Transport (CST) agreement was signed in 2008 [13]. With the opening of 63 ports in mainland China and 11 ports in Taiwan, The Strait is crossed by large numbers of carriers whose presence adds s to the complexity of the situation confronting through traffic [13]. It brings some accident-prone segments of the strait and in such a case some Precautionary Areas (PAs) can be instituted so as to emphasize the need for particular caution in navigation.

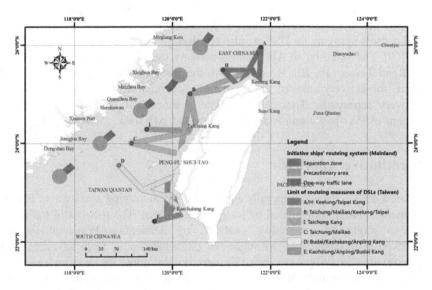

Fig. 1. The initiative routeing measures serving for main through streams of traffic in the Taiwan Strait issued by the mainland China and their formal counterparts serving for crossing traffic issued by Taiwan (Color figure online)

In order to alleviate particular hazards in conflict-prone segments of the strait, the maritime administrations (i.e. Ministry of Transportation, hereafter cited as the MOT) from two sides of the Strait are responsible to create routing systems (including PAs) to separate vessels, control crossing and meeting situations. On one hand, since 2008 the MOT of Taiwan has released routeing measures of DSLs in the government gazettes [14], which has required all vessel carriers applying for DST should navigate via the promulgated points (see Point A–E in Fig. 1) for entering and exiting the prearranged docking ports (i.e. Keelung, Taipei, Taichung, Anping, Mailiao, Kaohsiung Harbor etc.) [15]. As shown in Fig. 1, there are sufficient routing measures to keep CST in good order at Eastern Taiwan Strait. On the other hand, since 2011 the MOT of China Mainland (hereafter cited as the mainland) has issued comprehensive plans of national ships' routeing system [16] and put forward initiative routeing measures for transit passages through the strait-highway [17, 18]. The conceptual design of five TSSs (see No. 1-5 TSSs in Fig. 1) and corresponding Precautionary Areas (see No. 1-5 PAs in Fig. 1) were developed in the initiative strait-highway. Unfortunately, for China coast seaway system network, the strait-highway is still the only one whose ships' routeing system in has not been enforced.

The problem of introducing any system of routeing in the Strait is how to achieve effective control at an international level with drawing up hard and fast rules or imposing restrictions that might well, in view the impossibility of policing vast ocean areas, prove nugatory [5]. To solve this problem, cross-strait cooperation should be enhanced for providing safe passage for ships cross and through the Strait without unduly restricting their legitimate rights and practices. Thus two sides of the strait should consider various factors, including the existing traffic pattern, aids to navigation, hydrographic surveys and nautical charts of the strait [4]. For the case in Taiwan Strait, all vessel carriers applying for DST are also required to carry an AIS in the government gazettes [19]. The shore-based AIS Stations network established along the coast of the mainland and Taiwan [6, 20]. However, both the initiative routeing measures for the strait were subjectively selected based on ordinary practices of semen and are not quantitatively repeatable. Thus we formulate a numerical method for optimizing arrangement of PAs based on historical shore-based AIS data.

3   Quantitative Approach

As discussed above, PAs are generally established in converging areas where freedom of movement of shipping inhibited by restricted sea-room. The patterns of traffic flow within PAs might be quantitative analyzed by delineating Principall Fairways (PFs) derived from cumulative streamlines of clustered routes. Such advances in the spatial correlation analysis of involves PFs help to gain more precise knowledge about concerned PAs. In the light of where are the boundary and utilisation distribution of PFs, the authors have developed a cross-disciplinary application of ecological methods found in habitat use of wild animal [6, 9]. A PF perceived in the authors is a concept that attempts to provide basic information about cumulative activity patterns for vessels group in a strait and serve as the basis of quantifying space-use patterns. PFs boundaries could be intersected with bathymetric-cover maps in a GIS to identify which corridors are used by seagoing merchant vessels over the course of their tracking period.

The authors made used of the same AIS dataset covering western Taiwan Strait provided by MOT of Mainland, who owns a terrestrial AIS network. The navigation traffic data collected by MOT of Mainland were used to illustrate the PFs extraction as described in the previous publication of the authors [6]. There were 35,500 route objects of main through traffic generated from 7,528 vessels over a period of 12 months (Oct 2011–Sep 2012) using the ship route extraction method [7]; and the same dataset witnessed 7,126 route objects of cross-strait linking major ports of Fujian and Taiwan.

Following the proposed quantitative space-use approach of delineating PFs [7], the authors has gained deep understandings about the sea-room utilization distribution of main through and cross traffic in the Taiwan Strait (see Fig. 2). When coupled with existing routeing system plan, PFs boundaries might be useful to identify gaps between existing plan of TSSs and cumulative activity patterns for ships group derived from real AIS tracks. As shown on Fig. 2, existing plan of routeing system issued by MOT of China Mainland involves inshore recommended tracks, PAs and TSSs in the western strait. Some gaps might play a role in giving valuable guidelines and advise of further refined routeing in the Strait.

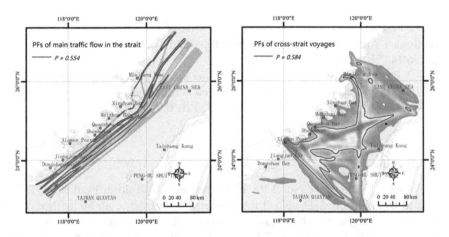

Fig. 2. PFs in the Taiwan Strait: (a) main through traffic and (b) the cross traffic

4   Optimization Schemes

4.1   Calibrating *PAs*

As shown in Fig. 3, there are two step to west to refine the centres of PAs: To begin with the common turning point in Taiwan Strait can be identify by the axis lines of PFs; Finally, combine the space use of cross traffic with the axis lines of PFs. The centre of PAs on the axis lines of PFs would be obtained. The following is the update version of No. 2 and No. 3 *Precautionary Area* (PA):

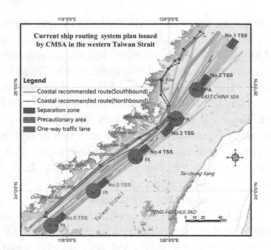

Fig. 3. The extracted PFs of main through traffic coupled with Current ships' routeing system plan issued by MOT of China Mainland in western strait

i. No. 2 Precautionary Area: On the northern side of *Dongyi Island*, the No. 2 Precautionary Area is bounded by a circle with a radius of 9 nautical miles, centred at 25°56′14″ N, 120°23′19″ E.

ii. No. 3 Precautionary Area (Adjacent to *Niushan Island*):On the eastern side of *Niushan Island*, the No. 2 Precautionary Area is bounded by a circle with a radius of 9 nautical miles, centred at 25°23′12″ N, 120°0′9″ E.

4.2   Adjusting the TSSs

For the current NCSRP, the No. 2 PA is intersected to the north by the No. 2 TSS adjacent to *Dongyi Island*. The No. 3 PA is intersected to the south by the No. 3 TSS adjacent to *Niushan Island*. Thus, the adjustments of the No. 2 and No. 3 PAs affect the corresponding TSS. The improved TSS should reflect that the common turning point for open sea shipping is close to *Wuqiu Light*. Our solution is to add a turn segment in the No. 4 TSS adjacent to *Wuqiu Island*. By adjusting the No. 3 PA, the location of the corresponding TSS (No. 3) is shifted to the north. The improved open sea TSS is shown in the right side of Fig. 4.

5   Evaluating and Discussion

A tendency reflected in the case of TSSs to bases treat provisions or approval of individual schemes on inadequate analysis or on analysis based on an unrepresentative model to react to crises rather than to plan in advance, and to fail to coordinate different regulations.

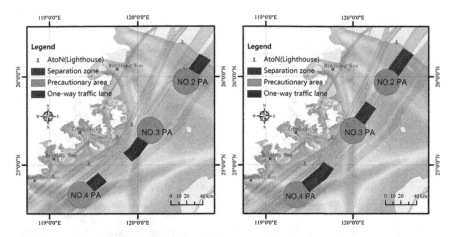

Fig. 4.   Original and optimal design of precautionary area in western Taiwan Straitl

5.1   Evaluating the Optimized Routeing System Planning

Because the plan and layout of PA is an important issue in the routing system planning in the Taiwan Strait, PA assessment is selected as a quantification demo to perceive the advantages given by the optimized routing system. A basic nautical hypothesis is that there should be multi-strand traffic flows from different direction converging in PA to a certain degree. Cumulative frequencies of ship-ship crossing encounter within PA is a straightforward indicator to evaluate the rationality of routeing system planning. However, have found significant uncertainty in the definition of vessel encounter. In light of this, we select the distribution of the *distance* from each route object to the centre of PA as assessment indicator. For briefly discussing, all the PAs noted in this paper is bounded by a circle with a radius of 9 nautical miles (NM).

The following is performance comparison between the PAs in existing routeing system and those in optimized routeing system. Two class of routes objects' *distance distribution* to involved PAs are visualized in the form of histogram with fitted kernel density curve (the bandwidth is 0.3 nautical miles for the case of Taiwan Strait).

5.2   No. 2 Precautionary Area (PA)

i. Routes objects of cross traffic

As shown in the left column of Fig. 5, compared with No. 2 PA in the existing routeing system planning depicted in the top row, No. 2 PA in the optimized routeing system planning embraces more cross-strait routes and witness a significant increase of 35 %, morewhile the mean distance from involved cross-strait routes to No. 2 PA in the optimized routeing system is reduced by 5 %. Thus from the perspective of cross-strait traffic flow, there is a distinct advantages of No. 2 PA in the optimized routeing system planning.

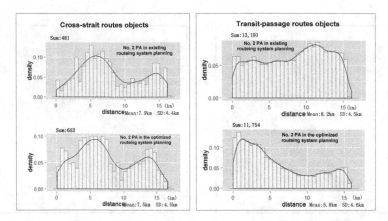

Fig. 5. Comparison of distance distribution of routes objects which passage No. 2 PA (nearby is Dongyin Island): The top row shows the case of No. 2 PA in the existing and the bottom row shows the case of optimized routeing system planning; Left column shows the performance of cross-strait traffic flow and Right column shows the performance of transit-passage.

ii. Transit-passage routes objects

As shown in the right column of Fig. 5, compared with No. 2 PA in the existing routeing system planning depicted in the top row, No. 2 PA in the optimized routeing system planning embraces less transit-passage routes(a decrease of 11 %), however the mean distance from involved transit-passage to No. 2 PA in the optimized routeing system witness a significant reduction of 29 %. The curve in the bottom row likes a monotone decreasing function under the condition of *2 km < distance < 10 km*. It indicates that the optimized PA is well fit the PFs of transit-passage. Thus from the perspective of Transit-passage traffic flow, there is credible advantages of No. 2 PA in the optimized routeing system planning.

5.3   No. 3 Precautionary Area (PA)

i. Cross-strait routes objects

As shown in the left column of Fig. 6, compared with No. 3 PA in the existing routeing system planning depicted in the top row, No. 3 PA in the optimized routeing system planning embraces more cross-strait routes and witness a increase of 12 %, morewhile there is a significant reduction (decrease 22 %) for the mean distance from involved cross-strait routes to No. 3 PA in the optimized routeing system. The curve in the bottom row is similar as a monotone decreasing function under the condition of *distance > 3 km*. It indicates that the optimized PA is well fit the PFs of Cross-strait routes. Thus from the perspective of cross-strait traffic flow, there is a distinct advantages of No. 3 PA in the optimized routeing system planning.

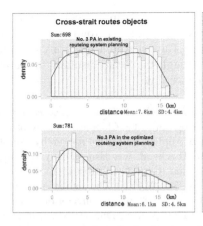
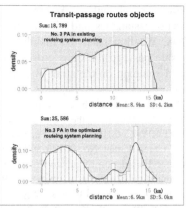

Fig. 6. Comparison of distance distribution of routes objects which passage No. 3 PA (nearby is Niushan Island): The top row shows the case of No. 2 PA in the existing and the bottom row shows the case of optimized routeing system planning; Left column shows the performance of cross-strait traffic flow and Right column shows the performance of transit-passage.

ii. Transit-passage routes objects

As shown in the right column of Fig. 6, compared with No. 3 PA in the existing routeing system planning depicted in the top row, No. 3 PA in the optimized routeing system planning embraces more transit-passage routes and witness a significant increase of 36 %, morewhile there is a significant reduction for the mean distance from involved transit-passage to No.3 PA in the optimized routeing system witness a significant reduction of 22 %. There is a distinct advantages of No. 3 PA in the optimized routeing system planning. It is worth noting that the curve in the bottom row shows a double peaking pattern, especially the steeper peek happens under the condition of distance = 14 km. The reason lies in the waterway on the west side of Niushan Light is a typical neckbottle with crowded traffic in the Strait.

As discussed by the above, compared with the existing routing system planning, the layouts of No. 2 and No. 3 PAs adopted by the optimized routing system are more suitable for the PFs extracted by real traffic observation data. Eventual this optimized routing system planning will help captains to forecast where is the potential converging place, so as to avoid ship-ship collision.

6 Conclusions

Understanding and quantifying groups of ship (human) behaviours in marine environments is a challenging task. Our studies on PAs arrangement is intended to alleviate particular hazardous circumstances on concerned area. The novelty of our method is that it reflects the spatial correlation of through and cross traffic, and provides a repeatable, quantitative approach that enables statistical testing of the effects of routeing measures of PAs. To demonstrate the applicability of the proposed method, we constructed test cases in the study area, in which the outcomes were obtained using a GIS spatiotemporal analysis. We reviewed existing data from the Taiwan Strait and offer descriptive statistics and visualisations of an optimised routing system for the China MSA. We hope that the mainland and Taiwan would reach a consensus on providing safe passage for ships cross and through the Strait, resulting in the implementation of routeing on the strait at some future time.

Acknowledgments. This study was supported by the National Nature Science Foundation of China (Grant No. 41501490), the Key Research Program of the Chinese Academy of Science (Grant No. ZDRW-ZS-2016-6-3) and Fundamental Applied Research Program by Ministry of Transport of China (Grant No. 2013329815290). This work was also partially supported by Natural Science Foundation of Fujian Province, China (Grant No. 2015J01166) and Scientific Research Foundation of Jimei University (Grant No. ZC2014005). The authors are grateful for their financial support. Special thanks are given to Sir. Lu Xiang, the director of Xiamen Navigation Aids Department of Donghai Navigation Safety Administration (DNSA), in providing ships movement tracks.

References

1. Plant, G.: International traffic separation schemes in the new law of the sea. Mar. Policy **9**, 134–147 (1985)
2. Beattie, J.H.: Routing at Sea 1857–1977. J. Navig. **31**, 167–202 (1978)
3. Paton, J.: Ships' routeing present status and future trends. Int. Hydrogr. Rev. **LX**, 113–123 (1983)
4. IMO: MSC/Circ.1060: Guidance Note on the Preparation of Proposals on Ships' Routeing Systems and Ship Reporting Systems IMO (2003)
5. IMO: Res. A.572(14): General provisions on ships' routeing (1985)
6. Chen, J., Lu, F., Peng, G.: A quantitative approach for delineating principal fairways of ship passages through a strait. Ocean Eng. **103**, 188–197 (2015)
7. Pallotta, G., Vespe, M., Bryan, K.: Vessel pattern knowledge discovery from AIS data: a framework for anomaly detection and route prediction. Entropy-Switz. **15**, 2218–2245 (2013)
8. Skauen, A.N.: Quantifying the tracking capability of space-based AIS systems. Adv. Space Res. **57**, 527–542 (2016)
9. Chen, J., Lu, F., Peng, G.: Analysis on the spatial distribution characteristics of maritime traffic profile in western taiwan strait. IOP Conf. Ser. Earth Environ. Sci. **18**, 012111 (2014)
10. Huh, C.-A., Chen, W., Hsu, F.-H., Su, C.-C., Chiu, J.-K., Lin, S., Liu, C.-S., Huang, B.-J.: Modern (<100 years) sedimentation in the Taiwan Strait: rates and source-to-sink pathways elucidated from radionuclides and particle size distribution. Cont. Shelf Res. **31**, 47–63 (2011)
11. Hu, W., Ye, G., Lu, Z., Du, J., Chen, M., Chou, L.M., Yang, S.: Study on fish life history traits and variation in the Taiwan Strait and its adjacent waters. Acta Oceanol. Sin. **34**, 45–54 (2015)
12. Tseng, H.-S., Ou, C.-H.: Taiwan and China: A unique fisheries relationship. Mar. Policy **34**, 1156–1162 (2010)
13. Yang, S.-H., Chung, C.-C.: Direct shipping across the Taiwan Strait: flag selections and policy issues. Marit. Policy Manag. **40**, 534–558 (2013)

14. CNMOO: The Limit of Routing Measures of "Taiwan, Mainland Direct Cross-Strait Shipping Links" (No. 184). Naval Meteorologic & Oceanographic Office of Taiwan (2008)
15. Chen, C.-W., Lee, C.-C., Tseng, C.-P., Chen, C.-H.: Application of GIS for the determination of hazard hotspots after direct transportation linkages between Taiwan and China. Nat. Hazards **66**, 191–228 (2013)
16. Li, S., Zhou, J., Zhang, Y.: Research of vessel traffic safety in ship routeing precautionary areas based on navigational traffic conflict technique. J. Navig. **68**, 589–601 (2015)
17. Xu, F., Chen, P.: Cross-strait cooperation on search and rescue in the Taiwan Strait and its implication for the South China Sea (Chap. 12). In: Wu, S., Zou, K. (eds.) Securing the Safety of Navigation in East Asia, pp. 233–243. Chandos Publishing, Cambridge (2013)
18. CMSA: The General Planning of China Coastal Ships Routeing (No. 388 Official Document). In: Mainland, M.o.C. (ed.) vol. 2011 (2011)
19. MOTC: Regulations Governing the Approval and Administration of Direct Cross-Strait Sea Transport Between the Taiwan Area and the Mainland Area. In: R.O.C, M.o.T.a.C.M.o. (ed.) (2008)
20. Chang, S.J., Hsu, G.Y., Yang, J.A., Chen, K.N., Chiu, Y.F., Chang, F.T.: Vessel traffic analysis for maritime intelligent transportation system. In: 2010 IEEE 71st Vehicular Technology Conference. IEEE, New York (2010)

Prediction

Bulk Price Forecasting Using Spark over NSE Data Set

Vijay Krishna Menon[1(✉)], Nithin Chekravarthi Vasireddy[2],
Sai Aswin Jami[2], Viswa Teja Naveen Pedamallu[2],
Varsha Sureshkumar[3], and K.P. Soman[1]

[1] Center for Computational Engineering and Networking (CEN),
Amrita School of Engineering, Amrita Vishwa Vidyapeetham,
Amrita University, Coimbatore, India
m_vijaykrishna@cb.amrita.edu, kp_soman@amrita.edu
[2] Department of Computer Science and Engineering,
Amrita School of Engineering, Amrita Vishwa Vidyapeetham,
Amrita University, Coimbatore, India
nithinchekravarthi.biit@gmail.com,
winash1994@gmail.com, tejanaveen1994@gmail.com
[3] Amrita School of Business, Amrita Vishwa Vidyapeetham,
Amrita University, Coimbatore, India
s_varsha@cb.amrita.edu

Abstract. Financial forecasting is a widely applied area, making use of statistical prediction using ARMA, ARIMA, ARCH and GARCH models on stock prices. Such data have unpredictable trends and non-stationary property which makes even the best long term predictions grossly inaccurate. The problem is countered by keeping the prediction shorter. These methods are based on time series models like auto regressions and moving averages, which require computationally costly recurring parameter estimations. When the data size becomes considerable, we need Big Data tools and techniques, which do not work well with time series computations. In this paper we discuss such a finance domain problem on the Indian National Stock Exchange (NSE) data for a period of one year. Our main objective is to device a light weight prediction for the bulk of companies with fair accuracy, useful enough for algorithmic trading. We present a minimal discussion on these classical models followed by our Spark RDD based implementation of the proposed fast forecast model and some results we have obtained.

Keywords: Big data · Spark · Scala · Streaming · RDD · NSE · ARMA · ARIMA · ARCH · GARCH · Financial forecasting · Econometrics

1 Introduction

Financial data consists of tick by tick stock prices for all enlisted company trades in the stock market. Even though very interesting models have been proposed by eminent econometrists and machine learners [1, 2], in reality especially in the Indian market scenario, very few dynamic advances has happened in forecast prediction models and

© Springer International Publishing Switzerland 2016
Y. Tan and Y. Shi (Eds.): DMBD 2016, LNCS 9714, pp. 137–146, 2016.
DOI: 10.1007/978-3-319-40973-3_13

volatility analysis. The classical ARMA based models are still in use and do effective forecasting for majority of the highly traded stocks. Among the most appealing of the recent contributions in this front are the works on deep neural nets for forecast prediction [3], the variational mode decomposition on carbon prices and subsequent forecasting using Spike Neural Nets [4] and the convex optimization techniques for time series models [5]. While we believe these methods will eventually catch up and replace traditional Time Series approaches, we have refrained from using such cutting edge models for the sheer sake of simplicity of computations and parameter estimations. Our focus rather is on how we can handle this massive data at the finest resolution possible. This will be the work that entails in this paper.

The National Stock Exchange of India (NSE) is one among the two stock markets in India, where our data is sourced from. The data is available as a series of nested archives packed over monthly sub directories and daily transactions in 'pipe' separated flat files. Individual transactions contain an id; running sequential index giving the order of the transaction. This value is followed by the stock name, share category, timestamp in 'hh:mm:ss' format string, the price as a decimal floating point value and then the volume: number of stocks bought in that particular trade. The trades are tick by tick which means we have at least 30–40 transaction per second and sometimes even more. Since the data has no day stamp, it was exceedingly difficult to manage it in bulk of transaction strings alone. It was necessary to try different assortments, so that we can get usable comparable data at the same time without losing information as to which day it happened. The day stamp is important if we are to use some well-known effects such as 'the day of the week' effect [6] in our analysis.

There are about 150 million transactions recorded on average per month starting from 1st July 2014 till 30th June 2015, which has 244 working days, grossing around 1.8 billion transactions for the entire period. The exploded size of the whole data is over 87 GiBs.

1.1 Data Processing and Transformations

To forecast and analyse such massive data, it was necessary to reorganise the data. Data cleaning and augmenting process we have done include the following:

1. Stock-wise splitting.
2. Day tagging.
3. Second-wise amalgamation.
4. Minute-wise amalgamation.
5. Nifty tagging over Second-wise amalgamated data.

The stock-wise splitting posed a special challenge and was the most time-consuming of all. The process iterates over each day for 244 days and tries to filter individual stock transactions out for all 1721 companies know to have traded. The response is expected to be quite slow as this need to be done over 2 nested for-loops one iterating on day files and the other over companies, as nested RDDs or RDD operations are not supported, which means this cannot be done entirely parallel. The process recorded two to three hours per file which took a little over 26 days to complete. The segregation helped us to do more localised analysis which we shall not discuss here and will be tabled for another publication.

The day wise tagging, as mentioned before was a very crucial step to do volatility analysis and certain causal relations of interest. This process again iterates day wise, tagging every transaction with the day stamp extracted from the current file name. We initially ran the process on Hadoop cluster and found it to be too slow. So it was migrated to the Spark environment which completed the process in less than 2 h and 40 min. The resultant data expanded to 98 GiBs; a mere 12 GiBs increase in size but can speed up a lot of processes. We used this transformed data set for all the tasks we discuss here.

Other kind of subtle analysis like causality tests and media announcement responses requires data at lower resolution. This was realised with 2 types of amalgamation processes. One process reduces all transactions of a stock on a day for any given second to a single entry that takes the second wise closing price (price of the last trade in that second, selected by finding the biggest id over the whole second). This was also necessary for tagging transaction with the appropriate nifty indices which were also amalgamated per second. Further on we found we need to compress data even smaller if we are to see and understand patterns over it. A different process was written to output the minute-wise amalgam of the day tagged set mentioned above, so as to see the bigger picture.

1.2   Cluster Framework

We use an Apache Spark cluster with Hadoop Distributed File System (HDFS) to store and disperse data; detailed configuration is given in Table 1. Spark is a new revolution in Big Data computing as it can do pure in-memory data manipulations especially in iterative jobs which require housing initial and intermediate data sets for multiple map-reduce tasks. This trivialises the map-reduce paradigm, so that we can design complex computational systems without framework level concerns and data redundancy delays.

Table 1. Cluster configuration and hardware specifications. The environment is an Apache Spark cluster in spark standalone mode, with HDFS support, running with 4 machines.

Configuration	Virtualized Cluster	Real Hardware
Worker Nodes	8 Executer Nodes	4 Nodes (Ubuntu 14.04 LTS)
Processor Cores	16 Cores/Node	8 Cores/Node (Core i7)
Memory	96 GBs visible	32 GB/Node (DDR3)
Java	64-bit Hotspot	64-bit Hotspot
Disk	6.1 TB DFS	2 TB/Node
File System	HDFS (replication-2)	EXT4FS

Spark's basic computational element is a distributed data structure called Resilient Distributed Dataset (RDD), which manipulates key-value pairs. RDD are immutable making them resilient to data loss and inconsistencies as well as fault tolerant without duplicating data, unlike Hadoop. Fault in one of the partitions is fixed by recreating the affected partition from a lineage graph called an RDD DAG. RDDs also manage memory efficiently, creating disk spills where ever physical space is lacking; it will never affect the program by throwing an '*OutOfMemoryError*'. Furthermore since RDDs are created from lineages, they are designed to do lazy evaluation which gives an opportunity to optimize the computation as the entire transformations are stacked up and data processing (computations) is triggered only on an action call. Spark is capable of truly high performance data processing over even huge datasets such as the one we are to use [7].

Over RDDs, Spark comes packed with all vital data processing libraries such as machine learning, stream and graph processing along with an SQL like query engine all compatible with cotemporary big data warehouse tools such as *Hive* and *HBase*. Spark streaming is particularly powerful as it interfaces with all popular data broker protocols such as *Kafka, Flume, MQTT, Twitter* etc. These interfaces support windowing of the data over continues streams. Spark's stream receiver is a *DStream* object that has almost all transformation capabilities of RDDs. The easiest way to see this is as a *DStream* being a queue of RDDs polled at regular intervals and operated on.

Our proposed forecasting works on streaming. We validate our model on the static data we have, by artificially streaming it and using the *SocketTextStream* object to collect the data. The data is mapped to proper key-value structure and indexed before it can be shoved to a time series RDD and computations applied on it.

2   Classical and Contemporary Forecast Models

Interest in the conditional forecast of volatility emerged largely from [8] which showed ARCH (Auto regressive conditional heteroscedasticity) model, a prediction from previous values of time series data by considering the lag required. The accuracy in predicting the future stock returns using GARCH were previously examined by [9] for NIKKIE stock data, the study showed the accuracy in predicting the average stock prices of NIKKIE with different lags. In this study, the data considered is day ending price.

Moving Averages are calculated in [10] using four methods Durbin's Method (DM), Inverse Covariance Method (ICM), Covariance Recursion Method (VRM), Vocariance Espirit Method (VEM). Using these methods, they are checking whether zeroes lie near the unit circle or not. The methods are compared to Non Linear Least Square (NLS) estimation and concluded to be 100 times faster than it. They also state that VRM is the only satisfactory method. Further when zeroes are closer to unit circle for fixed value of 'm' then VRM or VEM are best methods. DM fairs well for higher value of m. Parameter estimation of ICM is lower than VRM.

From [11], the model is applied on Amman Stock Exchange general daily index data samples for a week. They have tested the stationarity of the sequence using unit root tests and found it to be non-stationary. They took the first difference and used ARIMA (p, 1, q) for each values of p and q, however, it failed to predict for the next week.

There have been many who proposed prediction on a finer scale. Such predictions have to be quick and easy to compute, at the same time giving a good idea of the immediate future trends, with nominal errors. It is better to go into more basic predictive models such as AR and MV.

2.1   Autoregressive (AR) Process

Autoregressive models are models in which the value of a variable in one period is related to its values in previous periods. AR(p) indicates an autoregressive process with p lags is, or of order p. An AR(p) process is modelled as follows:

$$Y_t = \mu + \sum_{i=1}^{p} Y_{t-i}\, \alpha_i + \varepsilon_t \tag{1}$$

where Y_t is a linear combination of its p previous values and an error term ϵ_t. The coefficients are estimated from known data by method of least squares. Apart from these parameters the lag value p is also an unknown quantity and is estimated by multiple trials and an application of the either the Akaike's or Bayesian Information Criterion [10].

2.2   Moving Average (MA) and Simple Exponential Smoothing

Moving average (MA) model account for the possibility of a relationship between a variable and a residual from previous periods. MA (q) indicates a moving average process with q lags:

$$Y_t = \mu + \sum_{i=1}^{q-1} \varepsilon_{t-i}\theta_i + \varepsilon_t \tag{2}$$

where all θ's are the parameters to be estimated. Now applying least square method on this will not work as it yields a system of nonlinear equations in θ even if we consider an MA(1) process. Alternative methods were cited in the previous section which are much faster and more efficient; yet these methods have extensive dependencies and are difficult to accurately implement and test in time. Exponential smoothing reduces this problem to some extend and proposes a single fractional parameter that reduces with preceding lag.

The true idea of using an MA(1) model is that it can be seen as a pure AR process of infinite order [12]. Coupling both AR and MA processes will complement the predictive nature of both the models.

2.3   Autoregressive Moving Averages (ARMA) and Other Derivatives

Autoregressive moving averages model combines both p Autoregressive and q moving average processes terms of respective orders, as suggested, and is indicated by ARMA (p, q)

$$Y_t = \mu + \sum_{i=1}^{q-1} \varepsilon_{t-i}\theta_i + \varepsilon_t + \sum_{i=1}^{p} Y_{t-i}\alpha_i \tag{3}$$

ARMA(p, q) requires the data to be stationary; a stationary process has a mean and variance that do not change over time and the process does not have trends. As the stock prices are not stationary, to make the data stationary, traditionally we consider the returns of the prices, called first difference

$$R_t = \ln(Y_t/Y_{t-1}) \quad \text{or} \quad R_t = (Y_t - Y_{t-1})/Y_{t-1} \tag{4}$$

Autoregressive integrated moving averages (ARIMA) model denotes an ARMA model with returns as the dependent variable. So the model is the same ARMA but predicts the return value R_t. Since this model predicts first order differences it will be termed as ARIMA(p, 1, q)

$$R_t = \mu + \sum_{i=1}^{q-1} \varepsilon_{t-i}\theta_i + \varepsilon_t + \sum_{i=1}^{p} Y_{t-i}\alpha_i \tag{5}$$

Heteroscedasticity is the variability of a variable being unequal across the range of values of the second variable that predicts it. Considering this variation one can formulate the error terms in ARIMA as yet an AR(q) process with an error term V_t follows.

$$\varepsilon_t^2 = \omega + \sum_{i=1}^{q} \beta_i \varepsilon_{t-i} + V_t \quad \text{and} \quad V_t = \varepsilon_t^2 - \sigma_t^2 \tag{6}$$

Here, ϵ is the ARIMA residual and σ is the forecasted variance. This is called the Autoregressive conditional heteroscedasticity (ARCH) model. A more generalised version of the same can be conjured where the conditional variance is predicted directly as a non-linear forecast of the residuals.

$$\sigma_t^2 = \omega + \sum_{i=1}^{q} \theta_i \varepsilon_{t-i}^2 + \sum_{j=1}^{p} \beta \sigma_{t-j}^2 \tag{7}$$

This is Generalised ARCH or commonly called as GARCH. The requirement for such extended predictors is mainly due, when the series has non stationary variation and shows a lot of trend with in the predicting period.

3 Fast Forecast Model and Implementation

We have chosen a basic ARMA type predictor for our forecast. As mentioned in most ARMA literature we have deliberated on, the lag for each constituent AR or MA is to be decided by making several fits and by applying AIC or BIC [10]. This incurs considerable computation for any fast prediction to be delayed. Since we work with fine resolution data (minute-wise amalgamated). We assume the data to be of similar nature for all the companies, based on the premise that it is created from a singular process. In order to understand the appropriate model and its lag to fit our cause we ran several controlled tests on the data using the standard 'forecast' module in R language. We used many samples from different companies and ran the 'auto-arima' model on it. The suggestions for almost all where coherent and was either ARIMA(2, 1, 1) or ARIMA(2, 1, 2).

Our second most crucial assumption was that over considerably smaller window samples, the price data itself is stationary and can directly withstand an ARMA model without the need to compute the first differences. We reached this conclusion by observing several data samples. This result can be empirically proved. The advantage of this were many folds as it saved us the extra burden of three time intensive data transformations, which we shall discuss in detail soon. Eventually we conjured our essentially linear model as follows:

$$Y_t = \beta_0 Y_{t-1} + \beta_1 Y_{t-2} + \varepsilon_t \text{ and } Y_t = \alpha_0 + \alpha_1 \varepsilon_t \tag{8}$$

where the former is the AR(2) estimator and the latter is the MA(1) estimator. Even though MA(2) was recommended after the R experimental fitting, we had two reasons to revert to this model; the model might over fit as MAs have more history quotient; the parameter estimation becomes exponentially more complex. Please note that the AR model lacks any constant as we saw the AR fits quite well with the origin orientation rather than with a constant. The MA on the other hand has got a tendency to magnify subtle disturbances so a controlling constant can be adjusted to impart a cut on these hyper fluctuations.

The estimation of parameters is done using a double least square approach, one for the AR and the other for the MA. Due to fear of over fitting again we have carefully separated the estimations. Once the AR parameters are found, we generate the predictions on the same window to estimate real errors. These errors are further fitted against the real values to generate the MV parameters. This method is quick and clean compared to sophisticated MV estimators such as MLE, ICM and VRM based methods discussed above. The separate estimation is suggested by Robert Nau form Duke University [12].

3.1   Implementation

The implementation is a pseudo stream Spark application. The values are read in bulk for all the stocks which are streamed at window of 5000 trades per second using *SocketTextStream*. The receiver is partitioned in to 'n' other filter streams that filter for specific companies. Once this is done, the values are sorted on timestamp and then indexed using a 'zip with index' mapping and then reverse mapping it, so we can use this as a key value. This is important as time series data is order sensitive and require to hold the sequencing. We devised a simple skewing trick to eliminate the infamous time series dependency problem in map-reduce application. We employ a skewing of data so that we can couple all the required lags for any datum in the RDD. This is the savings we achieved by not opting ARIMA model, that would require 2 rounds of this operation, one for the real price series and then again for the returns series. Once this is done we can directly map the values to compute models and estimate parameters. We truly like to elaborate on this but it will shift the focus of our forecasting problem so we will hold it for a later publication. Figure 1 illustrates our basic data transformations and streams. It merits mentioning about the time-series RDD library brought out by Cloudera which we shall use in future. For this particular problem we found it to be a bit heavy weight as the RDD duplicates all lags for the entire window. Furthermore it requires data to be handled with Data Frames which might again increase not just memory but also computational overhead. Hence it was advisable to refrain from such use full technology on the sheer basis of faster computation.

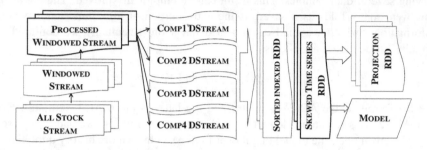

Fig. 1. Data flow chart showing important transformations with in our system. The RDD transformations are general to all streams and usually is done on a 'for-each' basis.

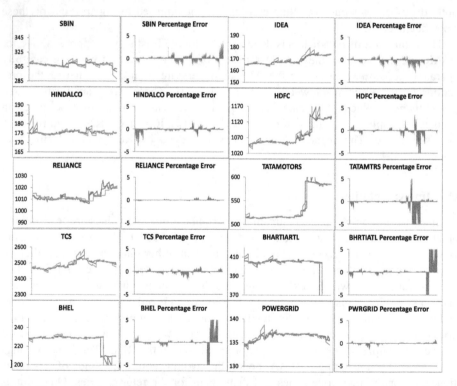

Fig. 2. These plots show case the predictions we have done on various sectors. The predictions have a RMSPE of less than 4 % in most cases. Some stock splits cause the prediction in those windows to be erratic at worst. Most stock splits are observed over banking stocks. This problem can only be solved if this can be announced prior to the prediction where a splitting bias can be considered. In reality however the splits are announce well in advance. Since we considered no such announcements, we simply omitted the windows that failed due to a stock split. Above, one such split can be seen with BHARTIARTL where the price dropped instantly

Table 2. Here we report some observations of our complete experiment. Prediction was made for 20 highly traded (found by sorting) stocks over a window (W) of 50 min sliding (S) by 25 min and over 20 such runs (R). The root mean square percentage error was calculated for each stock over this 20 window sliding (500 values). Some stocks have stock splits in between windows, which were omitted in the error calculation as this will create a new trend line and prediction will be grossly wrong. The time per prediction is computed over 20 runs.

Stock	W-S-R	RMSPE	Time (ms)	Remarks
HINDALCO	50-25-20	1.103374	58	Low priced commodity
HCLTECH	50-25-20	3.536248	75	Moderate priced techno
RELIANCE	50-25-20	0.293011	76	Moderate priced retail
MARUTI	50-25-20	3.315542	101	High priced automotive
INFY	50-25-20	1.990972	73	High priced techno
ITC	50-25-20	4.966947	105	Low priced retail
ICICIBANK	50-25-20	3.073277	95	Moderate priced banking
TCS	50-25-20	0.685945	107	High priced techno
HDFC	50-25-20	1.835524	128	Moderate priced banking
ONGC	50-25-20	0.869672	83	Low priced petroleum
TATAMOTORS	50-25-20	4.317752	102	Low priced auto with split
YESBANK	50-25-20	3.260518	73	Low priced bank with split
BHARTIARTL	50-25-20	4.552875	83	Low priced telecom
BHEL	50-25-20	3.550686	79	Low priced commodity
LT	50-25-20	3.738453	99	Moderate priced infrastructure
AXISBANK	50-25-18	0.519407	80	Moderate-low bank with split
SUNPHARMA	50-25-19	3.429886	104	Low priced pharmaceuticals
IDEA	50-25-19	1.041839	58	Very low priced telecom
SBIN	50-25-18	1.21876	97	Moderate-low bank with split
POWERGRID	50-25-20	0.425548	78	Very low priced energy

Our forecast works by building an ARMA(2, 1) model over a specified window size and then forecasting for time beyond the window using the same. We were able to successfully predict up to the 25th minute over a window of size 50. This by and far up to our knowledge, is the *first time it is being done on Indian NSE data*. But our original promise was to predict simultaneously for multiple companies, which we believe we were able to deliver. We could predict simultaneously for 20 companies in less 2 min disregarding all streaming delays. Our model will correct the predictions by the minute if only it had real time minute–wise stream data. Regarding widow size, we have empirically concluded that a size of 50 for high price stocks and 30/20 for low priced ones with a sliding interval of 25 and 15/10 respectively.

4 Results and Conclusion

We present plots on samples over multiple (twenty) window runs of some selected stocks in Fig. 2. We have validated these predictions by also plotting the percentage error on each case. The main stocks that were projected are HCLTECH, TCS,

HINDALCO, SBIN, BHARTIARTL IDEA, HDFC, RELIANCE, BHEL and POW-
ERGRID. These constitute major players from various industries. Our prediction works
well for all of them despite stock splits in some cases. Another Insight we have gained
is that AR predictions are positive at best while ARMA has an exaggeration trend. So if
the prediction is a rise, then the AR value will better quantise that and if it's a fall then
we can bank on the ARMA forecast value.

Table 2 gives the predictions on twenty stocks and their related root mean squared
percentage errors (RMSPE). All the experimental code and result is available at https://
github.com/vijaykrishnamenon/nse-forecast. Our research is fully reproducible.

References

1. Merh, N., Saxena, V.P., Pardasani, K.R.: Next day stock market forecasting: an application
   of ANN and ARIMA. IUP J. Appl. Finan. **17**(1), 70–85 (2011)
2. Pai, P.F., Lin, C.S.: A hybrid ARIMA and support vector machines model in stock price
   forecasting. Omega **33**(6), 497–505 (2005)
3. Vengertsev, D.: Deep learning architecture for univariate time series forecasting. Technical
   report, Stanford University (2014)
4. Sun, G., et al.: A carbon price forecasting model based on variational mode decomposition
   and spiking neural networks. Energies. **9**(1), 54 (2016)
5. Chrétien, S.,Wei, T., Al-Sarray, B.A.H.: Joint estimation and model order selection for one
   dimensional ARMA models via convex optimization: a nuclear norm penalization approach.
   arXiv preprint arXiv:1508.01681 (2015)
6. Chen, Y., Lai, K.K., Du, J.: Modeling and forecasting Hang Seng Index Volatility with
   day-of-week effect, spillover effect based on ARIMA and HAR. Eurasian Econ. Rev. **4**(2),
   113–132 (2014)
7. Zaharia, M., Chowdhury, M., Das, T., Dave, A., Ma, J., McCauley, M., Franklin, M.J.,
   Shenker, S., Stoica, I.: Resilient distributed datasets: a fault-tolerant abstraction for
   in-memory cluster computing. In: 9th USENIX Conference on Networked Systems Design
   and Implementation (NSDI 2012). USENIX Association, Berkeley (2012)
8. Engle, R.F.: Autoregressive conditional Heteroscedasticity with estimates of Variance of
   United Kingdom inflation. Econometrica **50**, 987–1007 (1982)
9. Kita, E., Zuo, Y., Harada, M., Mizuno, T.: Application of Bayesian Network to stock price
   prediction. Artif. Intell. Res. **1**(2), 171–184 (2012)
10. Sandgren, N., Stoica, P.: On moving average parameter estimation. In: 20th European Signal
    Processing Conference (EUSIPCO), Bucharest, Romania, pp. 2348–2351 (2012)
11. Al-Shiab, M.: The predictability of the amman stock exchange using univariate
    autoregressive integrated moving average (ARIMA) model. J. Econ. Adm. Sci. **22**(2), 17–
    35 (2006)
12. Nau, R.: Fuqua School of Business, Duke University. http://people.duke.edu/~rnau/
    Mathematical_structure_of_ARIMA_models–Robert_Nau.pdf

Prediction and Survival Analysis of Patients After Liver Transplantation Using RBF Networks

C.G. Raji[1](✉) and S.S. Vinod Chandra[2]

[1] Department of Computer Science and Engineering,
Manonmaniam Sundaranar University, Tirunelveli, Tamil Nadu, India
rajicg80@gmail.com
[2] Computer Center, University of Kerala, Thiruvananthapuram, Kerala, India
vinod@keralauniversity.ac.in

Abstract. Prognostic models are becoming useful in assessing the severity of illness and survival analysis in medical domain. Based on the studies, we realized that the current models used in liver transplantation prognosis seems to be less accurate. In this paper, we propose a highly improved model for predicting three month post liver transplantation survival. We performed experiments on the United Nations Organ Sharing dataset, with a 10-fold cross-validation. An accuracy of 86.95 % was observed when Radial Basis Function Artificial Neural Network model was used. Other similar methods were compared with the proposed one based on the prediction accuracy. A survival analysis study for a span of 13 years was also done by comparing with MELD an actual dataset. The reported results indicate that the proposed model is suitable for long term survival analysis after liver transplantation.

Keywords: Liver transplantation · Survival prediction · Radial Basis Function network · Artificial Neural Networks · Survival analysis

1 Introduction

Liver Transplantation (LT) is considered as the viable treatment for the end stage liver disease for the past several decades. In transplantation, the physicians are regularly forced to decide which patients will get priority for limited resources. The medical experts decided the priority of allocating resources according to the disease severity of patient in liver transplantation. The medical experts judge the outcome of LT based on the Model for End Stage Liver Disease (MELD) score [5]. As it follows sickest first policy, the patients in the top in waiting list will get the liver first during LT [5]. Even though there are so many difficulties with MELD score, doctors still depend upon that for the LT survival prediction due to the lack of advancement in the scoring systems. The low survival rate is due to the inappropriate selection of parameters and scoring system. Current techniques are incapable to predict the most accurate post-transplant after LT.

© Springer International Publishing Switzerland 2016
Y. Tan and Y. Shi (Eds.): DMBD 2016, LNCS 9714, pp. 147–155, 2016.
DOI: 10.1007/978-3-319-40973-3_14

The continuous exploration of high accuracy models resulted in the introduction of precise models such as Artificial Neural Networks (ANN). ANN can overcome the local optimum and performs a superior role in solving complex nonlinear problems than the traditional linear methods [15]. We proposed an accurate allocation and prediction ANN model to predict the short term and long term survival of patients after LT. The Radial Basis Function (RBF) networks can act as decision-making tools which could predict the three-month mortality of patients after LT [1].

2   Related Research

Forecasting the short term and long term surgical outcome in term of patient survival depends upon the appropriate donor-recipient matching. Researchers introduced various conventional methods and ANN models used for the survival prediction of LT. Doyle et al. conducted a study for finding out the graft failure in liver patient using logistic regression analysis [3]. But they failed to show the survival accuracy after LT due to the lack of large dataset [3]. In the same year the same group of researchers proposed a ten feed forward back propagation neural network to solve the nonlinearity among variables and survival prediction after LT [2]. They also failed to deliver the survival accuracy with the lack of full set of data [2]. Based on a time series sequence of clinical data, Paramanto et al. conducted a study with recurrent neural networks using time series sequence of medical data in 2001 [8]. They used Back Propagation Through Time (BPTT) algorithm and achieved a better survival rate with 6-fold cross validation [8]. In 2006, Cuccheti et al. proposed a Multilayer Perceptron (MLP) ANN for the survival prediction andproved that ANN is superior to MELD [6]. Marsh et al. introduced a three layer feed forward fully connected ANN in 2007 [7]. Zhang et al. performed a study for the comparison between MELD and Sequential Organ Failure Assessment (SOFA) scores. They used a MLP model for liver patients with Benign End-Stage Liver Diseases (BESLD) [14]. In 2013, Cruz-Ramirez et al. introduced a Radial Basis Function (RBF) network model using multi objective evolutionary algorithm (MPENSGA2) to address the liver allocation and survival prediction [1]. The researchers achieved an Area Under Curve (AUC) of 0.5659 [3]. In 2015, Khosravi et al. proposed a three layer MLP network for the five year survival prediction and found that ANN networks performed better than logistic regression models [6]. Due to the capability to perform nonlinear and parallel processing tasks, fault tolerant capability, long term memory and collective output, ANN models are superior to logistic regression models [4].

3   Materials and Methods

3.1   Dataset Description

For the purpose of training the prognosis models, we used the United Nations Organ Sharing (UNOS) dataset. It consists of 65535 liver transplantation related patient records from 1st October 1987 to 5th June 2015. The survival prediction attribute in the dataset is a MELD score, which was introduced in the year 2002 and thus the records before 2002 were excluded from our experiments. The Pediatric End Stage Liver Disease (PELD) records were also excluded from the study. After data pre-processing, we selected a total of 383 liver patient records with 27 input attributes [12]. A detailed description of the dataset attributes can be obtained from the data collection forms available at https://www.transplantpro. org/technology/data-collection-forms/. Out of three parameters in the MELD score, INR replaces Prothrombin Time (PT) and was measured with respect to the appropriate ISI of the local PT test system.

$$INR = \frac{Patient's\ PT}{MNPT}. \tag{1}$$

where MNPT in Eq. 1 is determined as the geometric mean of PT of at least 20 adult normal subjects in both sexes. The MELD score is determined by the formula,

$$M = 9.6 \times log_e(X) + 3.8 \times log_e(Y) + 11.2 \times log_e(INR) + 6.4 \times C. \tag{2}$$

where X and Y are the amounts(mg/dl) of creatinine and bilrubine respectively and C is given as

$$C = \begin{cases} 0\ if \text{ alcoholic or cholestatic liver disease} \\ 1 \quad \text{otherwise.} \end{cases} \tag{3}$$

Medical experts get judgment of survival of patients after LT is according to MELD score [9]. The MELD score > 15 shows the best survival of patients. If MELD score > 25, the patient survival is complicated and poor survival will get with MELD score > 40 [9]. All the above input clinical attributes were given to the RBF model and trained the data according to the attributes. The output generated from the model is a binary output that represents the graft status (GSTATUS). A value of GSTATUS $= 0$ shows the graft survived and GSTATUS $=1$ shows the graft failed.

4 Experimental Design

4.1 Long Term Survival Analysis Based on RBF

The 27 input attributes were given to the normalized Gaussian Radial Basis Function network. Let neuron in the hidden layer, j represents a radial basis function which measures the distance between input vector x_i and center of basis function c_j. We have used the commonly used Gaussian function,

$$\varphi_j(x_i) = exp[(-\|x_i - c_j\|^2)/\sigma_j^2]. \tag{4}$$

We made survival analysis in terms of number of years, each patient surviving after LT in the dataset using JMP software. The survival analysis includes two parts: (1) Calculate the survival probability (2) Survival data modeling. In order to find out the survival probability at any particular time can be calculated using the formula,

$$S_t = \frac{(\#patients\ living\ at\ the\ start) - (\#patients\ died)}{(\#patients\ living\ at\ the\ start)}. \tag{5}$$

Thus the survival probabilities at all-time intervals preceding that time were multiplied for the estimation of total survival probability from the start time until the specified time interval. For survival data modeling, a RBF ANN was used.

4.2   Long Term Survival Analysis Based in MELD Score

Most of the medical experts predict the survival of patients after LT based on MELD score. In order to compare the accuracy of our model, we evaluated long term survival analysis of LT patients with MELD score. In the analysis with MELD, we found mortality percentage of LT patients using the formula,

$$Mortality(\%) = \frac{(exp(-4.3 + 0.16 * MELD) * 100)}{(1 + exp(-4.3 + 0.16 * MELD))}. \tag{6}$$

The survival was represented as binary value 1 and 0. The survival 0 represents the patient survived if Mortality $\% < 50$. The patients are not survived with Mortality $\% > 50$ was represented as survival 1. The binary attribute, GRF_STAT represents the actual survival data of LT patients in the dataset. The long term survival analysis was done by comparing the GRF_STAT and the computed binary meld score for every followup period.

5   Results

The ranking of parameters need to be done according to their features and score [13]. The dataset consists of 27 input attributes were ranked successfully according to their features and score which is appropriate for visualization and classification dataset using WEKA software [12]. Based on the ranking, we could determine that all the parameters used for the survival of LT patients were having equal importance. All the donor parameters, recipient parameters and transplantation parameters were ranked and we reached the best survival prediction with the inclusion of all these parameters.

The input-output parameters, activation function in the hidden layer, training algorithm and conditions for performing the task are the main requirements of a RBF model. By choosing the appropriate parameters and model, we could achieve an accuracy of 86.95 %. By using the RBF model, we achieved the sensitivity 86.1 % and specificity 87.1 %. The Mean Absolute Error and Root Mean Squared error values obtained are 0.1647 and 0.3018. The Relative Absolute Error value obtained is 34.51 % and Root Relative Squared Error value obtained is 661.76 %. The results are obtained with 27 input parameters trained by a RBF model is shown in Table 1.

Table 1. Evaluation of RBF model

	Output Prediction Based on	Values Obtained		Output Prediction Based on	Values Obtained
Performance Measures	Sensitivity%	86.1	Prediction Error Measures	MAE	0.1647
	Specificity%	87.1		RMSE	0.3018
	Accuracy%	86.95		RAE%	34.51
Time taken in seconds		0.06		RRSE%	61.76

MAE: Mean Absolute Error, RMSE: Root Mean Squared Error, RAE: Relative Absolute Error, RRSE: Root Relative Squared Error, RBF: Radial Basis Function

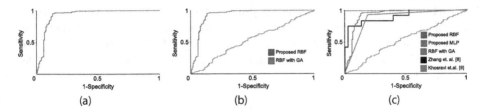

Fig. 1. (a) ROC curve of RBF model for three month survival prediction of liver patients after LT (b) ROC curve of three month survival prediction with existing RBF and (c) ROC curve of three month survival prediction with existing ANN models (Color figure online).

The AUC obtained from the ROC curve is 0.928. The graph shows that RBF model can be used for three month survival prediction of patients after liver transplantation.

5.1   Result Comparison for Three Month Survival Prediction

M-Cruz et al. proposed a RBF with Genetic Algorithm (GA) to find out the three month survival rate of LT patients [3]. They achieved 0.5659 AUC with RBF using GA for the survival prediction of LT patients. We compared the proposed RBF model with existing RBF using GA. We achieved 0.928 AUC for the three month survival prediction of LT patients. The comparison of RBF model with existing RBF is shown in Fig. 1. Zhang et al. proposed a Multilayer Perceptron (MLP) ANN for the three month survival prediction of LT patients [1]. With the training of dataset, the authors could achieve 89.70 % accuracy using MLP model. They got the sensitivity 91.30 % and Specificity 88.60 % while training with stepwise forward selection algorithm [1]. Khosravi et al. conducted a survival prediction by excluding the re transplantation data and achieved an accuracy of 91.00 % [6]. They got 78.30 % sensitivity and 80.60 % specificity while training the data [6]. M-Cruz et al. achieved the AUC 0.5659 while training the data using RBF with GA [3]. We also conducted three month survival prediction of LT patients with MLP using the same dataset and got the accuracy 99.74 % [10]. By the comparison made with existing ANN models, we can come the assumption that rather than RBF, MLP is better for the three month survival prediction of patients after LT [11].

5.2 Evaluating RBF for Long Term Survival Analysis

We experimented the survival analysis of each year separately using the follow up information which we found out from the dataset and thus we got fourteen datasets including six months. We trained the fourteen datasets and noted the performance measures of all the datasets separately. The performance measures include Accuracy, Sensitivity and Specificity of the different datasets are noted. We also noted the performance error measures such as MAE, RRSE, RMSE and RAE while training the dataset using proposed RBF model. For the long term survival analysis, the performance measures obtained while training the RBF model is as shown in the Table 3. The ROC graph of the fourteen datasets were drawn separately and AUC of each and every graph was noted and plotted as shown in the Fig. 2.

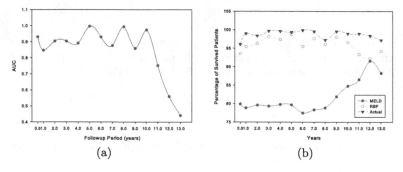

(a)   (b)

Fig. 2. (a) Performance of RBF model with respect to number of years of survival (b) Representation of RBF model with Actual survival data and MELD survival data in terms of accuracy

5.3 Performance Comparison of Models Used in Survival Analysis

The actual number of LT patients survived was obtained from the given dataset. While analyzing the survival for six months, 97 mismatches found between MELD data and actual data (Table 2).

For the first year data, 71 mismatches were found. 65 mismatches, 55 mismatches, 52 mismatches, 47 mismatches, 49 mismatches, 44 mismatches, 37 mismatches, 31 mismatches, 19 mismatches, 11 mismatches, 6 mismatches, and 5 mismatches were found in the second year, third year, fourth year, fifth year, sixth year, seventh year, eighth year, ninth year, 10th year, 11th year, 12th year and 13th year in between MELD survival data and actual survival data. The comparison of RBF model with MELD and Actual survival data prediction is as shown in Table 3 and Fig. 2(b).

Table 2. Prediction results for the proposed method

Evaluation measures	RBF Based Prediction	Number of years/Values Obtained												
		0.5	1	2	3	4	5	6	7	8	9	10	11	12	13
Performance Measures	Sensitivity%	98.89	99.05	98.29	1	1	99.57	1	1	95.21	98.66	99.15	0	1	1
	Specificity%	35.71	20	0	0	0	0	0	0	0	0	0	1	0	0
	Accuracy%	93.51	95.4	96.33	98.14	97.34	98.71	95.48	97.61	96.1	97.99	96.58	93.3	92.21	94.14
Prediction Error	MAE	0.0437	0.021	0.0386	0.0189	0.008	0.0133	0.0096	0.0096	0.0585	0.0362	0.0267	0.0227	0.0318	0.0535
	RMSE	0.1842	0.141	0.1821	0.1362	0.0627	0.113	0.0722	0.0703	0.2318	0.1858	0.1575	0.1064	0.1361	0.1757
	RAE	59.03	62.15	90.63	72.79	66.92	61.39	67.09	63.79	143.13	79.58	64.54	67.27	63.66	64.28
	RRSE	97.33	114.44	129.85	129.23	100.29	121.89	105.01	99.82	174.99	132.75	121.78	99.69	103.59	101.27
Time taken in seconds		0.08	0.13	0.11	0.05	0.08	0.03	0.06	0.03	0.04	0.09	0.08	0.02	0.02	0.01

MAE: Mean Absolute Error, RMSE: Root Mean Squared Error, RAE: Relative Absolute Error, RRSE: Root Relative Squared Error, RBF: Radial Basis Function

Table 3. Comparison of model accuracy.

% of survival data/ Years	0.5	1	2	3	4	5	6	7	8	9	10	11	12	13
MELD	79. 89	78.86	79.59	79.32	79.77	79.65	77.46	78. 33	78.86	81.88	84.75	86.5	91.53	88.24
RBF	93.51	95.4	96.33	98.14	97.34	98.71	95.48	97.61	96.1	97.99	96.58	93.35	92.21	94.14
Actual	96. 03	98.94	98.35	99.64	99.61	99.35	99.84	99. 51	97.22	99.52	98.92	98.89	98.33	97.14

MELD: Model for End stage Liver Disease, RBF: Radial Basis Function

5.4 Comparision of Survival Analysis with Existing Approaches

Researchers made an attempt to forecast the long term survival analysis of LT patients with different datasets. Zhang et al. made two year survival prediction and Khosravi et. al. made five years of survival prediction of LT patients. But we could predict thirteen years with six months survival accuracy of patients after liver Transplantation. By achieving high accuracy than the existing studies, we could assume that RBF model is suitable for long term survival prediction as shown in Table 4.

5.5 Discussions

The study done by Zhang et al. used two donor attributes and ten recipient attributes for the survival prediction. Khosravi et al. predicted the survival of LT patients with transplantation data only. But we included both transplantation data as well as retransplantation data. We could achieve a higher accuracy of survival for LT patients by selecting the proper model and attributes. Clinicians depend upon MELD score for survival prediction of LT patients. But the creatinine level may vary with gender. So inaccurate results may get with MELD score after LT. We trained the dataset using RBF model and performed the prediction of three month survival and thirteen years survival after LT. We compared the above two works to ensure the accuracy of the model. With MELD score we found out the accuracy of 79.11 %. While using RBF for the survival prediction, we achieved a survival accuracy of 86.95 %. We compared the performance measures, error measures and training time of RBF model and MLP models. It

Table 4. Liver transplantation survival probability analysis for the period of 6 months to 13 year with existing studies

Survival Probability % | Years	0.5	1	2	3	4	5	6	7	8	9	10	11	12	13
Our dataset	95	96	92	90	94	90	92	95	88	85	79	74	67	55
Dataset Zhang et al.	-	91	88	-	-	-	-	-	-	-	-	-	-	-
Dataset Khosravi et al.	-	90	89	85	84	83	-	-	-	-	-	-	-	-

can be noted that when comparing the accuracy for three month (short-term) survival prediction, RBF model is having less accuracy than MLP models. We also performed the survival analysis for six months to thirteen years using RBF model and RBF models proved to be superior in survival prediction.

6   Conclusion

We have done a thorough analysis on the suitability of RBF networks in LT prognosis. Our proposed model was able to predict with an accuracy of 86.95 % against the 79.167 % accuracy obtained from MELD based prediction. Based on the results, we arrived at an assumption that MLP is better for short term survival prediction of LT. A survival analysis for different followup periods was done and a comparison with MELD and actual dataset was done. We also computed the survival probabilities of liver patients from 6 months to 13 years and compared it with existing research. By proposing RBF ANN, we could achieve high accuracy results by a proper selection of dataset and prediction model. Based on the reported results, we conclude that the prognosis model based on RBF performed in a superior fashion when compared to prior models used in LT prognosis.

Ethical Approval and Consent. The data were collected based on OPTN data as on 5th June 2015. This work was supported in part by Health Resources and Services Administration contract 234-2005-370011C. The content is the responsibility of the authors alone and does not necessarily reflect the views or policies of the Department of Health and Human Services, nor does the mention of trade names, commercial products, or organizations imply endorsement by the U.S. Government.

Acknowledgments. We would like to express our sincere thanks to Dr. ArunKumar M.L, MS, MCh, MRCS Ed, PDF (HPB), SreeGokulam Medical College & Research Foundation, Thiruvananthapuram, India for his valuable technical support including comments and suggestions to improve the quality of the work.

References

1. Cruz-Ramírez, M., Hervás-Martínez, C., Fernandez, J.C., Briceno, J., De La Mata, M.: Predicting patient survival after liver transplantation using evolutionary multi-objective artificial neural networks. Artif. Intell. Med. **58**(1), 37–49 (2013)
2. Doyle, H.R., Dvorchik, I., Mitchell, S., Marino, I.R., Ebert, F.H., McMichael, J., Fung, J.J.: Predicting outcomes after liver transplantation. A connectionist approach. Ann. Surg. **219**(4), 408 (1994)
3. Doyle, H.R., Marino, I.R., Jabbour, N., Zetti, G., McMichael, J., Mitchell, S., Fung, J., Starzl, T.E.: Early death or retransplantation in adults after orthotopic liver transplantation: can outcome be predicted? Transplantation **57**(7), 1028 (1994)
4. Hareendran, A., Chandra, V.: Artificial Intelligence and Machine Learning. PHI Learning Pvt. Ltd., Delhi (2014)
5. Kamath, P.S., Wiesner, R.H., Malinchoc, M., Kremers, W., Therneau, T.M., Kosberg, C.L., D'Amico, G., Dickson, E.R., Kim, W.: A model to predict survival in patients with end-stage liver disease. Hepatology **33**(2), 464–470 (2001)
6. Khosravi, B., Pourahmad, S., Bahreini, A., Nikeghbalian, S., Mehrdad, G.: Five years survival of patients after liver transplantation and its effective factors by neural network and cox poroportional hazard regression models. Hepatitis Mon. **15**(9), e25164 (2015)
7. Marsh, J.W., Dvorchik, I., Subotin, M., Balan, V., Rakela, J., Popechitelev, E., Subbotin, V., Casavilla, A., Carr, B.I., Fung, J.J., et al.: The prediction of risk of recurrence and time to recurrence of hepatocellular carcinoma after orthotopic liver transplantation: a pilot study. Hepatology **26**(2), 444–450 (1997)
8. Parmanto, B., Doyle, H., et al.: Recurrent neural networks for predicting outcomes after liver transplantation: representing temporal sequence of clinical observations. Methods Arch. **40**(5), 386–391 (2001)
9. Poller, L.: International normalized ratios (INR): the first 20 years. J. Thromb. Haemost. **2**(6), 849–860 (2004)
10. Raji, C.G., Vinod Chandra, S.S.: Artificial neural networks in prediction of patient survival after liver transplantation. J. Health Med. Inform. **7**, 215–240 (2016)
11. Raji, C.G., Vinod Chandra, S.S. : Graft survival prediction in liver transplantation using artificial neural network models. J. Comput. Sci. (2016)
12. Raji, C.G., Vinod Chandra, S.S.: Predicting the survival of graft following liver transplantation using a nonlinear model. J. Pub. Health, May 2016. Springer. ISSN: 2198-1833
13. Vinod Chandra, S.S., Reshmi, G.: A pre-microRNA classifier by structural and thermodynamic motifs. In: World Congress on Nature and Biologically Inspired Computing, NaBIC 2009, pp. 78–83. IEEE (2009)
14. Zhang, M., Yin, F., Chen, B., Li, Y.P., Yan, L.N., Wen, T.F., Li, B.: Pretransplant prediction of posttransplant survival for liver recipients with benign end-stage liver diseases: a nonlinear model. PloS One **7**(3), e31256 (2012)
15. Vinod Chandra, S.S., Girijadevi, R., Nair, A.S., Pillai, S.S., Pillai, R.M.: MTar: a computational microRNA target prediction architecture for human transcriptome. BMC Bioinformatics, **10**(S:1), 1–9 (2010). ISSN 1471-2105

Link Prediction by Utilizing Correlations Between Link Types and Path Types in Heterogeneous Information Networks

Hyun Ji Jeong, Kim Taeyeon, and Myoung Ho Kim[✉]

Korea Advanced Institue of Science and Technology,
373-1, Kusung-Dong, Yusung-Gu, Daejon 305-701, South Korea
{hjjung, tykim, mhkim}@dbserver.kaist.ac.kr

Abstract. Link prediction is a key technique in various applications such as prediction of existence of relationship in biological network. Most existing works focus the link prediction on homogeneous information networks. However, most applications in the real world require heterogeneous information networks that are multiple types of nodes and links. The heterogeneous information network has complex correlation between a type of link and a type of path, which is an important clue for link prediction. In this paper, we propose a method of link prediction in the heterogeneous information network that takes a type correlation into account. We introduce the Local Relatedness Measure (LRM) that indicates possibility of existence of a link between different types of nodes. The correlation between a link type and path type, called TypeCorr is formulated to quantitatively capture the correlation between them. We perform the link prediction based on a supervised learning method, by using features obtained by combining TypeCorr together with other relevant properties. Our experiments show that the proposed method improves accuracy of the link prediction on a real world network.

Keywords: Heterogeneous information network · Link prediction · Supervised learning

1 Introduction

Link prediction is to discover relationships between two objects. It has received much attention because of the high level of demand regarding the discovery of new relationships in various applications (e.g. biological networks, social networks, etc.). For example, in biological networks, we can determine the target protein of a certain disease by using link prediction. Related works have studied the link prediction in homogeneous networks with single types of nodes and single types of links. However, most real-world networks are modelled as heterogeneous information networks that consist of multiple types of nodes and multiple types of links. In the example network shown in Fig. 1, there are various types of nodes, such as gene, disease, and pathway nodes.

One of the important features in heterogeneous information networks is that the types of paths and the links are correlated thus affect each other. Suppose, in Fig. 1,

© Springer International Publishing Switzerland 2016
Y. Tan and Y. Shi (Eds.): DMBD 2016, LNCS 9714, pp. 156–164, 2016.
DOI: 10.1007/978-3-319-40973-3_15

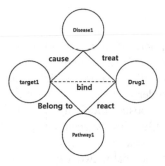

Fig. 1. Example for correlation between paths and a link

that there is a network containing three types of nodes; gene, disease, and drug, which are interconnected through three types of links; cause, treat, and bind. The semantic meaning of the link "Target1-bind-Drug1" indicates that a Drug1 binds Target1. The path "Target1-cause-Disease1-treat-Drug1" implies that Target1 causes Disease1 and that Drug1 treats Disease1. Note that the existence possibility of the link "Target1-bind-Drug1" is increased with the path "Target1-cause-Disease1-treat-Drug1" than without it. The reason why the presence of this path becomes a significant clue for the link prediction of the link is that Drug1 should bind Target1 in order to treat Disease1 in the real world. That is, the "bind" link should come before the "treat" link. Moreover, each path type has a different degree of correlation with links in a heterogeneous information network. We consider, for instance, that there are two path types, "Target-cause-Disease-treat-Drug" and "Target-belongs-to-Pathway-react-Drug. The "Target-belongs to-Pathway-react-Drug" implies that there is a target protein involved in a Pathway, and some Drug affects the Pathway. Under the situation, existence of the possibility of bind-type links is most likely higher in the "Target-cause-Disease-treat-Drug" path types than in the "Target-belongs to-Pathway-react-Drug." Since the bind link between a drug and a target should precede before treating a disease caused by a target. However, the drug can bind any protein in a pathway. The link of bind type between the target node and the drug node of the link to be predicted is not essential. Therefore, coping with this situation, we propose an appropriate type of correlation measure which represents the degree of the correlation between each path type and link type.

In this paper, we develop a method of the link prediction in the heterogeneous information networks which considers the correlations between the type of path and the type of link. Additionally, topological features between input nodes are considered. The remainder of this paper is organized as follows. First, we introduce the background concepts associated with link prediction and heterogeneous information networks. Next, we propose the link prediction score in Sect. 3. We show the experimental results in Sect. 4 and review related works in Sect. 5. In Sect. 6, we conclude our study.

2 Preliminaries

A heterogeneous information network is a network which contains multiple types of nodes and multiple types of links. Link prediction refers to the prediction of the potential existence of the possibility of a link, which is currently not in heterogeneous information network G. In order to search for the predictive function, we apply a supervised learning method. Choosing the features of supervised learning is a significant issue that considerably influences the accuracy of the link prediction process. We propose a link prediction score as a feature in Sect. 3.

In this paper, we use the biological network constructed by Lee et al. [1]. The total number of nodes is 74,848, and the average degree of the nodes is approximately 27.09. Table 1 lists the main symbols used in the paper. A schema for the data is described in Fig. 2.

Table 1. Notations

Symbol	Definition and Description
$PathType_i$	a type of a path
$LinkType_i$	a type of a link
$CycleType_{LinkTypei, PathTypej}$	a type of a cycle, i.e., a sequence of nodes $(v_1, v_2,..., v_k, v_1)$ where $v_1, v_2,..., v_k$ is a path of $PathType_j$ and (v_k, v_1) is a link of $LinkType_i$. That is, it is the type of a cycle that consists of a sequence of edges of a path $(v_1, v_2,..., v_k)$ of $PathType_j$ together with a link (v_k, v_1) of LinkType

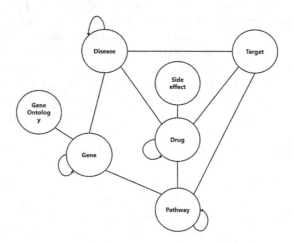

Fig. 2. Schema for target biological network

In Fig. 1, the link type of a link where the source node is Target 1 and the target node is Drug 1 is the "bind" $LinkType_{Target1, Drug1}$. There is a path between Target 1 and Drug 1 of which the $PathType_{Target1, Drug1}$ is [cause, treat]. CycleType $LinkType\_Target1, Drug1, PathType\_Target1,Drug1$ is (cause, treat, bind).

3   Proposed Method

Most conventional works on the link predictions in the heterogeneous information networks focus on the topological features of these networks and do not consider the meaning of the link type or the correlation between the link type and the path types. However, as noted above, the presence of certain paths affects considerably the existence of the possibility of a link in this type of network. Coping with this problem, we propose a link prediction score which reflects the type correlation between a link and the paths.

In the link prediction score, for predicting the existence of a link of $LinkType_i$ between two nodes s and t, we attempt to utilize how closely $LinkType_i$ is related with various path types that start from s and end in t.

Consider the following Table 2 for $LinkType_i$ and $PathType_j$.

Table 2. Relationship with CycleType, LinkType and PathType

$CycleType_{LinkTypej,\ PathTypej}$	$LinkType_i$	$PathType_j$
$cycle_1$	1	1
$cycle_2$	1	0
$cycle_3$	0	1
...	...	...
$cycle_k$	0	1

Each element in the first column denotes a cycle of $CycleType_{LinkTypei,\ PathTypej}$, i.e., a cycle consisting of a certain link l of a $linkType_i$ and a certain path p of $PathType_j$. These cycles may or may not actually exist in graph G. The 2nd and 3rd columns denote binary feature vectors of $LinkType_i$ and $PathType_j$. In each row the values of the 2nd and the 3rd columns are determined as follows:

(i)   There are 1's in both 2nd and 3rd columns if the cycle in the first column exists in graph G. That is, for each existing cycle of $CycleType_{LinkTypei,\ PathTypej}$ in G, we have a row with 1's in both 2nd and 3rd columns.

(ii) There are 1 in the 2nd column and 0 in the 3rd column if a link l of $LinkType_i$ is in G but the corresponding cycle in the first column (i.e., a cycle consisting of link l with a certain path p of $PathType_j$) does not exist in G. That is, for each link l of $LinkType_i$ that is not part of any cycle of $CycleType_{LinkTypej,\ PathTypej}$, we have a row with 1 in the 2nd column and 0 in the 3rd column.

(iii) There are 0 in the 2nd column and 1 in the 3rd column if a path p of $PathType_j$ exists in G but the corresponding cycle (i.e., a cycle consisting of path p with a certain link l of $LinkType_i$) does not exist in G. That is, for each path p of $PathType_j$ that is not part of any cycle of $CycleType_{LinkTypej,\ PathTypej}$, we have a row with 0 in the 2nd column and 1 in the 3rd column.

In Table 3 below, A, B and C denote numbers of rows that have 1 and 1, 1 and 0, and 0 and 1 in the 2nd and the 3rd columns in Table 2, respectively.

Table 3. A notation of relationships between Link Type and Path Type

LinkType$_i$	PathType$_j$	#of rows
1	1	A
1	0	B
0	1	C

A measure representing the degree of an association between LinkType$_i$ and PathType$_j$ called TypeCorr(LinkType$_i$, PathType$_j$), which is based on the Jaccard Similarity, is defined as follows.

$$TypeCorr(LinkType_i, PathType_j) = A/(A + B + C) \qquad (1)$$

A toy example for the computation of the type correlation using a network is depicted in Fig. 3. When the type of link to be predicted is the 'bind' type and the path type of the target path is [cause, treat], the value of A is 3, the value of B is 2, and the value of C is 5. Thus, TypeCorr(bind, [cause,treat]) becomes 3/(3 + 2 + 5) = 0.3. In another example in which the type of link to be predicted is the 'bind' type and the path type of the target path is [react, belong to], the A is 1, the C value is 2, and the B value is 1. Hence, TypeCorr(bind, [react,belong to]) is (1)/(1 + 2 + 1) = 0.25.

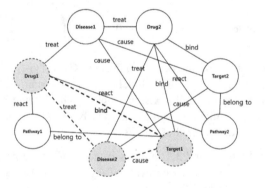

Fig. 3. Toy example of a link prediction score

Next, we designed the local relatedness measure LRM$_{PathTypej}$(s,t), which captures the topological features between a source node s and a target node. The topological features represent structural information in a graph. LRM$_{PathTypej}$(s,t), calculated for each path type, is also based on the degree of connectivity between nodes s and t. Specifically, when more paths between two nodes exist, the existence of the probability of a link between the two nodes becomes more likely.

LRM$_{PathTypej}$(s,t) is defined as shown below.

$$LRM_{PathTypei}(s,t) = |Pathset_{PathTypei}(s,t)| \qquad (2)$$

Here, s is the source node, t is the target node, and x is the path type. Pathset$_{pathTypej}$(s,t) denotes a set of paths between s and t of which the path type is x.

At this stage, we finally define the link prediction score $LPS_{LinkTypei, PathTypej}(s,t)$ used to predict the links of link type i between nodes s and t based on the correlations with the paths of path type x.

$$LPS_{LinkTypei,PathTypej}(s,t) = TypeCorr\left(LinkType_i, PathType_j\right) * LRM_{PathTypej}(s,t) \quad (3)$$

In this formula, $TypeCorr(LinkType_i, PathType_j)$ is the weight of $LRM_{PathTypej}(s,t)$. In order to achieve a high score, there are many paths, and the path type of the paths is significantly correlated with the type of target link.

Previous works have argued that a supervised learning approach promotes the accuracy of link predictions. Hence, we also perform link predictions based on supervised learning. Our algorithm undertakes link prediction for each link type. A classifier for supervised learning is the widely used support vector machine (SVM). It is trained using Gaussian kernels. The class labels for training instances indicate whether a link exists in an input graph or not; this value is either +1 or -1. For each pair of nodes, each feature vector is created based on the LPS.

4   Experiments

We test our method on the biological network constructed by Lee et al. [1] as mentioned in Sect. 2.1. The link prediction is performed for each link type and accuracy is also measured for each link type. We use the LibSVM [3] to implement a supervised learning of our method and the related method, and tests are conducted based on 10-fold-crossvalidation. A comparative study is the Heterogeneous Collectively Link Prediction (HCLP) proposed by [2], which also collectively predicts links of various types in the heterogeneous information network.

Four metrics such as accuracy, precision, recall and F-score are used to measure a performance. The reason why we check the performance in terms of four metrics, the accuracy has a limitation when there are so many true negatives in the result. A numerator of the accuracy metric is a sum of true positives and true negatives so the value of accuracy can be a high value when one of two values is high. In other words, although there are no any true positives, the accuracy can be high if there are so many truc negatives. To compensate for this, we also use the F-score to measure the performance.

In this section, we compare accuracy of our method and the HCLP. Experiments are conducted on 12 link types. One of important feature in our data is that it has a much larger node pairs without a link than those with a link. The imbalance of data causes underfitting so we use the undersampling that is a technique of machine learning to adjust the class distribution of a data set. For the undersampling setting, we sample the non-links as the same size of the links and drop remainder of the non-links for training data. On the other hand, the test data is just random sampled.

The result of our work and the HCLP using the undersampling is described in Tables 4 and 5. Both our work and the HCLP have good accuracy over 0.9, however, we cannot have confidence in the accuracy value because the accuracy measure can be high if there are so many true negatives as mentioned before. Our test data is imbalance so there are many true negatives. Hence, we evaluate our method and the HCLP using the F-score. An average F-score of our method is 0.270944 which has not a great performance, however, it is outperformed than results the HCLP. The average F-score of the HCLP is 0.0431 and its recall is seriously not good.

Table 4. Experiment result for undersampling

	Accuracy	F	Precision	Recall
target-pathway	0.979992	0.194077	0.111194	0.762262
target-disease	0.972504	0.10762	0.0608061	0.467701
pathway-pathway	0.999051	0.0144404	0.0722892	0.0080214
disease-disease	0.999865	0.526316	0.380711	0.852273
drug_target	0.989465	0.465473	0.316629	0.878399
drug-disease	0.953193	0.116599	0.0627246	0.826378
drug-side_effect	0.714622	0.305931	0.182144	0.954884
drug-pathway	0.960454	0.530589	0.363288	0.983516
gene-gene_ontology	0.992996	0.0118554	0.0146843	0.0994036
pathway-gene	0.973968	0.368729	0.244665	0.748041
gene-disease	0.996405	0.1657	0.134666	0.21532
gene-gene	0.960558	0.443993	0.641623	0.33944

Table 5. Experiment result of related work with undersampling

	Accuracy	F	Precision	Recall
target-pathway	0.9948	0	0	0
target-disease	0.0037	0.0072	0.9992	0.0036
pathway-pathway	0.895	0.0009	0.1027	0.0005
disease-disease	0.7995	0.0301	0.2861	0.0175
drug_target	0.954	0.0315	0.1435	0.0177
drug-disease	0.9152	0.0304	0.3553	0.0159
drug-side_effect	0.0658	0.1236	1	0.0658
drug-pathway	0.9231	0.1781	0.3666	0.1176
gene-gene_ontology	0.4009	0.0051	0.6	0.0025
pathway-gene	0.0102	0.0201	1	0.0102
gene-disease	0.498	0.0028	0.503	0.0016
gene-gene	0.5371	0.0877	0.4804	0.0482

The reason why pathway-pathway and gene-gene ontology have a lower F-score is that they have star shaped networks. Our algorithm is not appropriate to start shaped network so features for the star shaped network will be added in our future works.

5   Related Works

The link prediction in the heterogeneous information network relatively recently receives attention. Several works applying a meta-path approach were proposed. The meta-path concept is proposed in [4], which is a sequence of the link type, i.e. a type of a path. A research [5] generalizes some traditional topological features to be able to apply to the heterogeneous information network. B.Cao [2] proposes a method that collectively predict the links in the heterogeneous information network. This work allows of similarity measurement between nodes with different types. There are some works for the link prediction in the heterogeneous information network, however, they still have some limitation. Although [2] collectively predicts the link in the heterogeneous information network, it does not reflect that there is a difference in influence of each path type on existence possibility of the links.

6   Conclusion

Link prediction receives much attention to analysis graphs in various domains. However, there is not much researches in the heterogeneous information networks although applications in the real world require the heterogeneous information networks. Moreover, many existing works of link prediction in the heterogeneous information networks do not consider complex correlation between link types and path types. In this paper, the method of link prediction in the heterogeneous information network is proposed. To capture a degree of the correlation between the path type and the link type, we propose the TypeCorr measure. The LRM reflects the topological features between the source node and the target node. We further design the Link Prediction Score (LPS), for which the TypeCorr is a weight for the LRM. Finally, the link prediction is performed based on the supervised learning method.

Experiments show that our method is more appropriate to the link prediction in the heterogeneous information network than the related work. In the future, we plan to investigate reduce the computing time of the type correlation. The type correlation is currently computed for the entire network so it takes a little longer. Hence, we continue researches to improve it.

Acknowledgments. This work was supported by the Bio-Synergy Research Project (2013M3A9C4078137) of the MSIP (Ministry of Science, ICT and Future Planning), Korea, through the NRF, and by the MSIP, Korea under the ITRC support program (IITP-2016-H8501-16-1013) supervised by the IITP.

References

1. Lee, K., Lee, S., Jeon, M., Choi, J., Kang, J.: Drug-drug interaction analysis using heterogeneous biological information network. In: IEEE International Conference on Bioinformatics and Biomedicine
2. Cao, B., Kong, X., Yu, P.S.: Collective prediction of multiple types of links in heterogeneous information networks. In: ICDM (2014)

3. Hang, C.-C., Lin, C.-J.: LIBSVM: a library for support vector machines. ACM Trans. Intell. Syst Technol.
4. Sun, Y., Han, J., Yan, X., Yu, P.S., Wu, T.: Pathsim: meta path-based top-k similarity search in heterogeneous information networks. In: VLDB 2011 (2011)
5. Sun, Y., Barber, R., Gupta, M., Aggarwal, C.C., Han, J.: Co-author relationship prediction in heterogeneous bibliographic networks. In: Advances in Social Networks Analysis and Mining (ASONAM) (2011)

Advanced Predictive Methods of Artificial Intelligence in Intelligent Transport Systems

Viliam Lendel[(⊠)], Lucia Pancikova, and Lukas Falat

Faculty of Management Science and Informatics,
University of Zilina, Univerzitna 8215/1, 010 26 Zilina, Slovakia
{Viliam.Lendel, Lucia.Pancikova,
Lukas.Falat}@fri.uniza.sk

Abstract. Today, more and more, researchers have been trying to apply artificial intelligence (AI) into the area of transport. Using these methods, they try to solve difficult and complex transport problems and improve the efficiency, safety, and environmental-compatibility of transport systems. The main goal of this paper is to present how artificial intelligence can be applied in the area of traffic and transport with less time and money. The paper itself deals with the application of artificial intelligence method (i.e. support vector regression) for time series forecasting in terms of intelligent transport systems.

Keywords: Artificial intelligence · Support vector machines · Support vector regression · Intelligent transport system · Statistical methods · Open source · R

1 Introduction

Today, traffic engineers face challenges of increasing complexity of transport systems. Their main aim is to ensure safe, efficient and reliable transportation while minimizing its negative impact on the environment. Traffic engineers have to solve several problems. These problems are connected with unreliability and poor road safety; then there are capacity problems, environmental pollution and wasted energy. The transport systems are complex systems which involve many different components and participants who have different and often contrary objectives. Transport problems exhibit features that allow application of methods and tools of artificial intelligence. First, they include both quantitative and qualitative data. Transport systems can often be very difficult to be simulated using the traditional approach, mainly because of interactions between different elements of the transport system. In the transport problems one often has to solve difficult optimisation problems that cannot be fully met by using traditional mathematical programming methods.

Artificial intelligence (AI) provides a wide range of tools and methods for a solution of transport problems. Methods and tools of artificial intelligence are primarily used to predict the behaviour of transport systems, transport optimisation problems in control systems and clustering, also in the transport planning process, decision making and pattern recognition [1].

The goal of this paper is to create an SVR prediction model for transport data; we find the optimal kernel function as well as type of regression best suited for such data.

© Springer International Publishing Switzerland 2016
Y. Tan and Y. Shi (Eds.): DMBD 2016, LNCS 9714, pp. 165–174, 2016.
DOI: 10.1007/978-3-319-40973-3_16

Authors perform application and optimization of AI techniques called SVR using Open Source software R in the area of transport management system with affiliation to further research. Our approach is novel in using means of artificial intelligence, i.e. support vector regression into transport problems (instead of using standard methods). Article also discusses the applications of selected methods of artificial intelligence and "traditional" statistical methods for time series modelling.

The paper is divided into 5 parts. The first chapter introduces predictive modelling and forecasting of time series, it also deals with the most common methods and models used for modelling time series such as Box-Jenkins ARIMA models, GARCH models as well as modern artificial intelligence methods and models. The second part discusses the theory of Support vector machines, it deals with describing the basic theory of the SVM regression which is the default model for our prediction model. The fourth chapter defines the experiment. It described the data we used to test our prediction model, it deals the software we use for our experiments and it describes our performed experiments in details. Finally, chapter five summarizes the paper.

2 Predictive Modelling in Intelligent Transport Systems

There exists various approaches how to predict processes in intelligent transport systems. Models based on quantitative approach use historical data of the observed variable to interpret a system and predictions, on which the managers make their decisions, are made by precise mathematical and statistical models what is the undeniable advantage of this approach. The major models used for time series modelling are statistical models. Even though statistical time series forecasting started in the 1960s, the breakthrough came with publishing a study by [2] where authors integrated all the knowledge about autoregressive and moving average models. From that time ARIMA models have been very popular in time series modelling for long time as [3] showed that these models provided better results than other models used in that time. Some of the most used statistical methods in predictive modelling suitable for time series (taking into account the possibility of application in R) are exponential modelling [4–7], Kalman filtering [8], Box and Jenkins [2] ARIMA, SARIMA (seasonal autoregressive integrated moving average) models, ARCH, GARCH (generalized autoregressive conditionally heteroscedastic models) [9–11] or other types of autoregressive conditionally heteroscedastic models and spectral analysis.

In addition to "traditional" methods of statistical predictive modelling the means of machine learning (neural networks, support vector machines, hybrid models, etc.) are currently being developed and implemented in various fields, transport systems not excluding. In recent years, artificial intelligence (AI) has attracted bigger attention of researchers in many different branches from signal processing, pattern recognition, travel time estimations [12], rail vehicle system [13] or time series forecasting [14].

As for transport, methods of artificial intelligence are used massively [15]. AI models based on nonlinear predictions are used for predicting traffic demand, or predicting the deterioration of transport, infrastructure, as a function of traffic, construction, or environmental factors. Optimisation problems in transport are also calculated using AI, e.g. designing an optimal transit network for a given community, developing an optimal shipping policy for a company, developing an optimal work plan for maintaining a pavement network, and developing an optimal timing plan for a group of traffic signals. Methods of clustering are used for identification of specific classes of drivers based on driver behaviour. Pattern recognition or classification are used for example in automatic incident detection, image processing for traffic data collection and for identifying cracks in pavements or bridge structures.

AI is inspired by biological process, generally learning from previous experience. Main tasks for artificial intelligence methods are based on learning from experimental data (including learning from patterns) and transferring human knowledge into analytical models [16]. There exist many AI methods used nowadays. One of the first machine learning techniques were artificial neural networks (ANN). As ANN was a universal approximator, it was believed that these models could perform tasks like pattern recognition, classification or predictions [17, 18]. In recent years scientists try to incorporate other factors in order to increase the accuracy of neural networks, such as Evolving RBF neural networks in which genetic algorithms are implemented [19]. Even though today neural networks are not in the center of attention, their era has not finished yet. Some people talk about massive renaissance of neural networks [20] – thanks to publications about deep neural networks [21].

However, in recent years, the flagship of artificial intelligence is considered to be support vector machines (SVM) [22, 23]. In majority of studies the SVM outperforms artificial neural networks [24]. It is due to many reasons; one of them is that SVM are able to find and reach global minimum. SVM are studied in order to increase their properties. For example, Cao and Tay [25, 26] deals with more effective technique for forecasting using self-organizing maps (SOM). Moreover, the Support Vector Machine has wide application in classification tasks, as well as in predictions (SV regression). From a theoretical point of view SVM regression is the main competitor of ANN in forecasting continuous function [27] – mainly due to the fact that finding global minimum is guaranteed. The fact of finding just local minimum is the reason why many scientists prefer SVM to ANN [28].

In contrast with ANN or SVM, non-autonomous systems are the second group used in AI today. Non-autonomous systems such as Bayes networks, kernel methods or hidden Markov models are used if one wants to interpret the system.

Except for this, some researchers focus on hybrid models, i.e. models where the final model is created as a combination of two or more independent models. There exists combinations of neural networks and econometrics models – e.g. combination of ANN and ARIMA [29, 30] or combination of HMM and GARCH models [31]. Also, there exists hybrid models based on SVM and genetic algorithms [32, 33] or SVM used with SOM maps in time series forecasting [34].

3   Support Vector Regression

Support Vector Machines (SVM), which are based on statistical theory, are machine learning models developed by Vapnik [21]. From that time, they have become one of the most used algorithms in the area of machine learning. The SVM method was firstly used for linear classification. This basic SVM classifier, which is similar to logistic regression, realizes the algorithm that is searching for such a linear model which is the best linear classifier. Such linear model is also known as hyper plane with maximal margin (maximal margin classifier) as it has maximal margin from the nearest points in training set. The results of SVM is the construction of hyper plane where the points of training set are linearly separable and the distance of nearest points is maximized. Points from the training set which have the nearest distance to hyper plane are called support vectors. All other points from training set are irrelevant for defining marginal vectors. Except for classification tasks SVM can be successfully used for prognostics purposes in the form of Support Vector Regression (SVR) [22], f. ex. in forecasting financial time series [25–27]. The principles in SVR are the same as principles for SVM classification. We will now illustrate the searching for optimal regression hyper plane for linear regression (the principle for nonlinear regression is analogical).

Let D be a training set $D = \{(x_i, y_i)\}$ such that $x_i \in R^p$, $y_i \in R^1$, i = 1,... N where y_i is the output of the system with continuous values. Unlike classification, where the task is to searching for maximal margin hyper plane, task of SVM in regression type is searching for optimal range to regression function, which is called the approximation error of the regression function and can be understood as the measure of errors of the regression, where the regression error e is defined as the difference between the observed value y_i and the output from SVM regression. For evaluation of the quality of the regression function a range with a range ε is established under and above the regression line (i.e. the analogy with hyper plane in SVM classification). ε is the range of small errors (ε-residuals), and these errors in the phase of approximation are ignored as there is an assumption that there is no perfect approximator. On contrary, large errors which are over this range are expected to eliminate. The purpose of SVM regression to search for linear/nonlinear regression hyper plane. In defining SVM regression we come out from minimizing the risk function and norm w

$$\min_{w,b,\xi}\{\frac{1}{2}||w||^2 + R_{emp}\} \tag{1}$$

subject to

$$y_i - w^T x_i - b \leq \varepsilon \qquad w^T x_i + b - y_i \leq \varepsilon \tag{2}$$

where R_{emp} is the risk function defined as

$$R_{emp} = \frac{1}{n}\sum_{i=1}^{n} |y_i - f(x, w)|_\varepsilon \tag{3}$$

whereby $|y_i - f(x, w)|_\varepsilon$ is an ε-ignoring loss function defined as $|y_i - f(x, w)|_\varepsilon = 0$ if $|y_i - f(x, w)|_\varepsilon \leq \varepsilon$ or $|y_i - f(x, w)|_\varepsilon = |y - f(x, w)| - \varepsilon$. The function (1) can be expressed as

$$\min_{w,b,\xi \geq 0, \xi^* \geq 0}\{\frac{1}{2}||w||^2 + C\sum_{i=1}^{n} \xi_i + \xi_i^*\} \tag{4}$$

subject to

$$y_i - w^T x_i - b \leq \varepsilon + \xi_i \tag{5}$$

$$w^T x_i + b - y_i \leq \varepsilon + \xi_i^* \tag{6}$$

where ξ_i, ξ_i^* are free-range constants which are penalized similarly as at soft margin principle by selected value of constant C. By increasing C, larger errors are penalized ξ_i, ξ_i^* what is the consequence of lowering the approximation error. However, this can be accomplished by increasing the norm of weight vector w; however by increasing the norm w the good optimization as well as the model accuracy is not guaranteed [35]. The second option of influencing the accuracy of the model is the selection of the width range through ε. When resolving (4) we come out from Lagrange function what leads to the solving the problem of quadratic programming, i.e.

$$\max_{\alpha_i, \alpha_i^*} -\frac{1}{2} \sum_{i,j=1}^{n} (\alpha_i - \alpha_i^*)(\alpha_j - \alpha_j^*) x_i^T x_j - \varepsilon \sum_{i=1}^{n} (\alpha_i - \alpha_i^*) + \sum_{i=1}^{n} y_i(\alpha_i - \alpha_i^*) \tag{7}$$

subject to

$$\alpha^T y = 0 \tag{8}$$

$$0 \leq \alpha \leq Cf \tag{9}$$

After calculating α_i, α_i^* we get the vector of parameters and parameter b as

$$b = \frac{1}{n} \sum_{i=1}^{n} (y_i - x_i^T w) \tag{10}$$

which are afterwards substituted into the hyper plane regression function

$$f(x, w, b) = w^T x + b = \sum_{i=1}^{n} w_i x_i + b \tag{11}$$

4 Experiment

We used several daily time series for our experiments, in which we showed applicability of machine learning modelling approaches. The selected series is the daily data of financial profits in personal transport of selected economical subject. The tested data had seasonability of 5. The number of data was 825, however after modification (removing season part, time dependence, etc.) the length was shortened.

At first, the focus was on identifying seasons. After that we applied predictive methods applicable for this seasonal data. In order to compare the predictive accuracy of selected machine learning method (SVR) with the state of art methods, we implemented also statistical methods into our experiments.

In first experiment we applied predictive models applicable for data with significant season part. We applied Box Jenkins SARIMA models and Holt-Winters exponential smoothing (applicable for data with season part). Moreover, we also made experiments after removing season part from the data. Therefore, in the second experiment we applied classical Box-Jenkins models, non-seasonable exponential smoothing. For choosing best model we performed various procedures, i.e. periodogram, autocorrelation function, partial autocorrelation function, analysis of season indices and graphical representations. The correctness of modelling were checked using testing statistical significance of parameters as well as the whole model and using verification of residuals. Prediction abilities of all stated models were then compared with machine learning approach (SVR).

As for SVM, regarding wide possibilities of combination of factors, kernel function, training and validation set as well as intervals of parameters, SVM seems to be a good alternative to standard statistical models. Tables 1, 2 and 3 compares standard statistical models with SVR model with different parameters (including data with and without season part).

Table 1. Seasonal data – statistical modelling.

Model	Estimated parameters	RMSE
Holt- winter exp. smoothing	$\alpha = 0.14; \beta = 0.11; \gamma = 0.02$	4.93358
SARIMA(0,0,0,)(0,1,1), period 5	SMA(1) = 0.988	4.51469
SARIMA(0,0,0)(2,0,1) period 5, with const.	SAR(1) = 0.883; SAR(2) = 0.117; SMA (1) = 0.823; MEAN = 55.615	4.68496

Table 2. Non-seasonal data – statistical modelling.

Model	Estimated parameters	RMSE
Brown quadratic exp. smoothing	$\alpha = 0,4451$	1.65010
ARIMA(1,5) with constant	AR(1) = 0.610; MA(1) = −0.392; MA(2) = −0.390; MA (3) = 0.394; MA(4) = −0.404; MA(5) = 0.590; MEAN = 55.234	0.90435

Table 3. SV regression.

Seasonal data		Seasonally adjusted data	
Kernel function linear	RMSE = 6.13843	Kernel function linear	RMSE = 1.22457
Optimization "cost", "epsilon"	RMSE = 6.12733	Optimization "cost", "epsilon"	RMSE = 1.2239

For our experiments, we chose the R software. The detailed instructions how to use R for statistical modelling in stated in [36]. In order to create a SVR (Support Vector

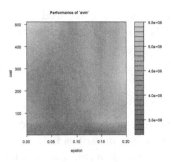

Fig. 1. Optimization of SVM [own experiments]

Regression) model [37–39] with open source R, we need the package e1071 [40, 41]. SVM function was used to train a support vector machine. It can be used to carry out general regression and classification (of nu and epsilon-type), as well as density-estimation. The standard setting of SVM is not sufficient in many cases, however, we can optimize parameters ("epsilon, cost") and make optimization of the model, such as by choosing kernel functions, defining the training and test set. In our SVM experiments we trained a lot of models with different parameters and then chose the best one. Code example to base tuning of SVM (Fig. 1) for selected data is:

```
tuneResult <-tune(svm, data~time,
+ ranges=list(epsilon=seq(0,0.2,0.01),cost=2^(2:9))
+ )
print(tuneResult)
Parameter tuning of 'svm`:
- sampling method: 10-fold cross validation
- best parameters: epsilon cost     0.13   16
- best performance: 327587561
plot(tuneResult)
```

The model is in darker region is the better one, i.e. the RMSE is closer to zero in these regions. Optimization can be also realized in other way. Our team together with student Martin Slavik implemented our own optimization of SVM in R where the optimal combination of parameter of "costs" a "epsilon" is calculated.

```
rmses2 = matrix(nrow= length(costs), ncol= length(epsilon))
> for(i  in 1:length(epsilon)){
+      for(j  in 1:length(costs)){
+          model = svm(V1~V2, data= felix.1,  type="eps-
regression",
+
kernel="linear",cost=costs[j],epsilon=epsilon[i])
+          predictions=predict(model, felix.1)
+          rmses2[j,i]=sqrt(mean((felix.1$V1-predictions)^2)) }}
```

The comparison of selected models was realized using Akaike information criteria and root mean square error (RMSE). The Table 1 illustrates selected models with their RMSE error.

5 Conclusion

In conclusion, we found out that artificial intelligence has its important place in intelligent transport systems. It is used in various fields of transport, especially in traffic management systems, incident management, travel information systems, transport management centres and models. The intelligent transport systems can organise and manage transport systems in such way that they can be used as efficiently and economically as possible. The implementation of appropriate prognostic methods and planning models allows to determine the planned value of supply and demand by evaluation of time series trend introducing the possible solution to reach stable and long-time results of region and transport enterprise activities and also the application of intelligent transport systems. AI techniques have a lot to offer to the field of transport. The versatility of the tools and their performance are well suited for the complexity and variety of transport systems. AI holds promise for a wide range of transport problems, which have been previously approached using other mathematical frameworks. In transport modelling, they are relatively young, but they have been already implemented for a wide range of problems such as forecasting, traffic control, pattern recognition and optimisation.

Acknowledgments. This paper was partially supported by the Slovak scientific grant VEGA 1/0942/14 Dynamic modelling and soft techniques in predicting economic variables and the Slovak scientific grant VEGA 1/0363/14 Innovation management – processes, strategy and performance.

References

1. Štencl, M., Lendel, V.: Application of selected artificial intelligence methods in terms of transport and intelligent transport systems. Periodica Polytech. Transp. Eng. **40**(1), 11–16 (2012)
2. Box, G.E.P., Jenkins, G.M.: Time Series Analysis: Forecasting and Control, San Francisco. Holden-Day, CA (1976)
3. Bollershev, T.: Generalized autoregressive conditional heteroskedasticity. J. Econometrics **31**, 307–327 (1986)
4. Brown, R.G.: Statistical Forecasting for Inventory Control. McGraw-Hill, New York (1959)
5. Brown, R.G.: Smoothing Forecasting and Prediction of Discrete Time Series. Prentice-Hall, Englewood Cliffs (1963)
6. Holt, CH.C.: Forecasting trends and seasonal by exponentially weighted averages. Office of Naval Research Memorandum 52. Reprinted in Holt, C.C. (2004). Forecasting trends and seasonal by exponentially weighted averages. Int. J. Forecast. 20(1), 5–10 (1957)
7. Winters, P.R.: Forecasting sales by exponentially weighted moving averages. Manag. Sci. **6**(3), 324–342 (1960)

8. Kalman, R.E.: A new approach to linear filtering and prediction problems. Trans. ASME – J. Basic Eng. **82D**, 35–45 (1960)
9. Engle, R.F.: Autoregressive conditional heteroskedasticity with estimates of the variance of United Kingdom inflation. Econometrica **50**(4), 987–1008 (1982)
10. Nelson, D.B.: Conditional heteroskedasticity in asset returns: a new approach. Econometrica **59**, 347–370 (1991)
11. Ding, Z., Granger, C.W.J., Engle, R.F.: A long memory property of stock market returns and a new model. J. Empirical Finan. **1**, 83–106 (1993)
12. Wosyka, J., Pribyl, P.: Decision trees as a tool for real-time travel time estimation on highways. Communications **15**(2A), 11–17 (2013)
13. Dizo, J., Blatnicky, M., Skocilasova, B.: Computational modelling of the rail vehicle multibody system including flexible bodies. Communications **15**(3), 31–36 (2015)
14. Smith, K., Gupta, J.: Neural Networks in Business: Techniques and Application. IRM Press, Hershey (2002). ISBN 1-931777-79-9
15. Sadek, A.W.: Artificial intelligence applications in transportation. In: Artificial Intelligence in Transportation, Transportation Research Circular E-C113 (2007)
16. Kecman, V.: Learning and soft computing: support vector machines, neural networks, and fuzzy logic models. In: A Bradford Book. The MIT Press, Cambridge (2001)
17. Anderson, J.A., Rosenfeld, E.: A collection of articles summarizing the state-of-the-art as of 1988. In: Neurocomputing: Foundations of Research. MIT Press, Cambridge (1988)
18. Hertz, J., Krogh, A., Palmer, R.G.: Introduction to the Theory of Neural Computation. Westview Press, Boulder (1991)
19. Rivas, V.M., et al.: Evolving RBF neural networks for time-series forecasting with EvRBF. Inf. Sci. **165**, 207–220 (2014)
20. Schmidhuber, J.: Invited Lecture at Google Talk 2007. California, USA (2007)
21. Hinton, G.E., Osindero, S., Teh, Y.: A fast learning algorithm for deep belief nets. Neural Comput. **18**, 1527–1554 (2006)
22. Vapnik, V.: The Nature of Statistical Learning Theory. Springer, New York (1995). ISBN 0-387-94559-8
23. Vapnik, V.N., Golovich, S., Smola, A.: Support vector method for function approximation, regression estimation and signal processing. In: Mozer, M., et al. (eds.) Advances in Neural Information Processing Systems 9, pp. 281–287. MIT Press, Cambridge (1997)
24. Kim, K.: Financial time series forecasting using support vector machines. Neurocomputing **55**, 307–319 (2003)
25. Cao, L.J., Tay, F.E.H.: Support vector machine with adaptive parameters in financial time series forecasting. IEEE Trans. Neural Netw. **14**(6), 1506–1518 (2003)
26. Cao, L.J., Tay, F.E.H.: Financial forecasting using support vector machines. Neural Comput. Appl. **10**, 184–192 (2001)
27. Cao, D.Z., Pang., S.-L., Bai, Y.-H.: Forecasting exchange rate using support vector machines. In: Proceedings of the Fourth International Conference on Machine Learning and Cybernetics, Guangzhou (2005)
28. Shawe-Taylor, J., Cristianini, N.: Kernel Methods for Pattern Analysis. Cambridge University Press, Cambridge (2004)
29. Bábel, J.: Porovnanie umelých neurónových sietí s modelmi ARCH-GARCH na ekonomických časových radoch. Dizertation thesis, Faculty of Management Science and Informatics, UNIZA (2011)
30. Falát, L.: Hybrid neural networks as a new approach in time series forecasting. AD ALTA: J. Interdiscip. Res. **2**, 134–137 (2011)

31. Zhuang, X.-F., Chan, L.-W.: Volatility forecasts in financial time series with HMM-GARCH models. In: Yang, Z.R., Yin, H., Everson, R.M. (eds.) IDEAL 2004. LNCS, vol. 3177, pp. 807–812. Springer, Heidelberg (2004)

32. Choudhry, R., Garg, K.: A hybrid machine learning system for stock market forecasting. In: World Academy of Science, Engineering and Technology, p. 39 (2008)

33. Hong, W., Pai, P., Yang, S., Theng, R.: Highway traffic forecasting by support vector regression model with tabu search algorithms. In: Proceedings of International Joint Conference on Neural Networks, pp. 1617–1621 (2006)

34. Cao, L., Tay, E.H.F.: Modified support vector machines in financial time series forecasting. Neurocomputing **48**, 847–861 (2001)

35. Marček, M.: Viacnásobná štatistická analýza dát a modely časových radov v ekonómii, Silesian University, Opava, p. 242 (2009). ISBN 978-80-7248-513-0

36. Crawley, J.M.: The R Book. Wiley, Hoboken (2007). ISBN 13: 978-0-470-51024-7

37. Smola, A.J., Scholkopf, B.A.: Tutorial on support vector regression. In: Statistics and Computing, vol. 14, pp. 199–222. Kluwer Academic Publishers, Berlin (2004)

38. SVM Tutorial. http://www.svm-tutorial.com/2014/10/support-vector-regression-r/

39. Support Vector Machines (SVM) Fundamentals Part-I. https://panthimanshu17.wordpress.com/2013/07/28/svm-fundamentals-part-1/

40. Chin-Chung, CH., Chih-Jen, L.: LIBSVM: A Library for Support Vector Machines. http://www.csie.ntu.edu.tw/~cjlin/papers/libsvm.pdf

41. Misc Functions of the Department of Statistics (e1071), TU Wien. http://cran.r-project.org/web/packages/e1071/e1071.pdf

Range Prediction Models for E-Vehicles in Urban Freight Logistics Based on Machine Learning

Johannes Kretzschmar[✉], Kai Gebhardt, Christoph Theiß,
and Volkmar Schau

Department of Computer Science, Friedrich Schiller University,
Ernst-Abbe-Platz 2, Jena, Germany
{johannes.kretzschmar,kai.gebhardt,christoph.theiss,
volkmar.schau}@uni-jena.de

Abstract. In this paper, we want to present an ICT architecture with a range prediction component, which sets up on machine learning algorithms based on consumption data. By this, the range component and therefore ICT system adapts to new vehicles and environmental conditions on runtime and distinguishes itself by low customization and maintenance costs.

Keywords: Electric mobility · Range prediction · Clustering

1 Introduction

In the last years, there is an enormous shift towards drive concepts based on renewable energies happening in the automotive industry. The use of electric driven (EV) or plug-in hybrid vehicles (PHV) becomes more and more necessary due to economical and ecological demands. The foreseeable limitations of oil production enforce an early rethinking and adapting to alternate energy resources or even the benefits of relying on energy mixes. Especially in urban areas, it is desirable to overcome today's fine dust and carbon dioxide pollution as well as increasing the overall quality of living in cities by noise reduction.

Although the acceptance of such vehicles is rather low in individual as well as commercial traffic. There are quite known technological flaws like large, expensive and heavy energy storages with a relatively low capacity and no proper battery-changing systems which results in long lasting charging time. In addition, there is still the need of an adequate charging infrastructure to put aside concerns using these type of vehicles. Developing new technologies, establishing a pervasive infrastructure and agreeing on a common industry standards will eventually take time and cost resources.

But especially in commercial use a cost efficient use of EVs can be achieved even today, by providing an information and communication technology (ICT), which facilitates full exploitation of an EV fleet. In the next chapter we like to

© Springer International Publishing Switzerland 2016
Y. Tan and Y. Shi (Eds.): DMBD 2016, LNCS 9714, pp. 175–184, 2016.
DOI: 10.1007/978-3-319-40973-3_17

introduce such a ICT in the context of urban logistics. In the following paper we present and evaluate a machine learning based range prediction model, which is a necessary core component of such an ICT system.

2   ICT Architecture for Electrified Urban Logistics

Simple the paradigm of using ICTs to transform life and working environments in communities or cities is widely discussed under the topic "Smart Cities" over the last years. [3] Our research project Smart City Logistik (SCL) [8] approaches this field in the context of logistics. Urban logistics especially features processes with multiple endpoints, short distances and often time critical constraints. Our main objective is to develop and implement an ICT reference architecture to enable these freight processes by EVs. In comparison and extension to commercial products used nowadays, we clearly focus on the challenges caused by electro mobility such as limited range of vehicles or required pauses due charging cycles. Furthermore our approach handles temporal and spatial environmental traffic restrictions, which are becoming quite popular in german urban communities over the last years. The SCL ICT acts eventually as a connective link between warehouse management, dispatching, customers and drivers and ensure information about tour processing as well as freight state.

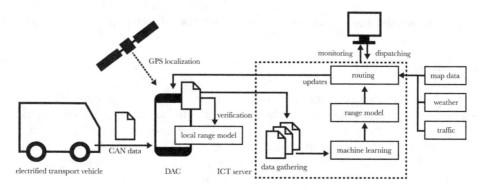

Fig. 1. The SCL architecture regarding the use and adaption of the range prediction model.

The SCL system derives the current state from data fully automatically gathered from the drivers, respectively the delivery vehicles on runtime, as illustrated in Fig. 1. A telematic in-car-unit collects data continuously from the controller area network (CAN) interface in each vehicle. These information are sent via in-car wifi to the driver assistance client (DAC), which tags them with the actual GPS data. These data allow an comprehensive monitoring of the current process for different stakeholders. In addition, these data are the basis for the adaptation and specification of the range prediction model. In the next chapter, we will introduce a sample of methods and approaches to gain such a model.

3 Related Work

The most obvious approach, a construction of a physical vehicle model requires comprehensive knowledge about the vehicle itself and the actual influences in the application area. As shown in [9] such a physical model includes the characteristics of a vehicle, a model for the energy storage as well as energy consumption. Rogge et al. presented in [7] a Matlab model for the Mitsubishi iMiev, a vehicle we used for data gathering and evaluation, too. The main difficulty of these models is the combination of energy storage and vehicle models. There are multiple factors, which influence the capacity and energy loss of an electric energy storage, like temperature or number and type of previous charging cycles. Providing mathematical models of energy storages is still a challenge and result in complex models like shown in [10]. Therefore it is also very common to usesimple machine learning methods, to predict the behaviour and capacity of electric energy storages [4].

The approach of a mathematical model in a simulation environment is not suitable in our research project, because of the lack of knowledge, degrees of freedom in the vehicle configuration or a fast changing composition of the vehicle fleet. Besides there may be a need of an offline range prediction on the DAC without the SCL server and contemporary smartphones do not have the computing power for comprehensive vehicle simulation. Therefore, we are tackling the range model problem by using machine learning methods. Ondruska et al. presented a similar hybrid approach in [6], based on a physical model combined with markov decision processes. But this approach still relies on very detailed knowledge about a specific vehicle, we can not assume as given in SCL. A straight data mining approach is presented by Ferreira in [5]. This method is based on Naive Bayes classifiers but uses only a very abstract discrete classification of influence factors.

Literature research showed, that there is no approach fulfilling every requirement of the SCL application field. But we found comprehensive and valuable information regarding the influential factors to energy consumption in the context of electro mobility. Conradi et al. [1] categorized these factors into environmental (traffic, weather and road characteristics), driver (acceleration, velocity, weight) and car (physical properties, battery) specific influences. These classes are the basis for the parameters in our learn data, which are used for configuration and adoption the range model.

4 Range Prediction Model Training

The range prediction model calculates if a given tour is achievable. The tour is specified by a predetermined route among customers and the vehicle state, especially the current charge status. An energy consumption is calculated by splitting the route into route segments and add up the consumption of every segment. The underlying idea is to segment in a way, which ensures that every parameter like speed, acceleration and gradient is assumed constant. This enables the normalization and comparability of segments as composite vectors. To gain adequate consumption values for every segment, we use the CAN data as described in Sect. 2. These data contain performance values with further information like velocity and the state of secondary consumers (f.e. air conditioning). They are tagged with a timestamp and a GPS position, which enables us to associate a gradient. On server side, these data is enhanced with information from the database, like the cargo weight for example. This means, we can transform the vehicle data into substantial segment vectors, just like used by the range model input as illustrated in Fig. 2(a) and (b). We developed and tested different methods to gain a precise consumption assumption from these measured segments, which are presented in the following section.

4.1   Interval Group Analysis

Our assumption is, that the energy loss of segments with similar properties are approximately equal. For specifying a segment consumption correlation, we need to find similar segment vectors. In our first method, we divide the range of every vector dimension over the whole data set into intervals as illustrated in Fig. 2(c). Now we have divided the vector space into different groups with similar segment vectors, as shown in Fig. 3(a). Then the inner group segments get averaged and the consumption value divided by the length to normalize the group vectors. At the end, the algorithms offers a table which can be used to look up an approximate consumption value by associating the group for an input segment vector.

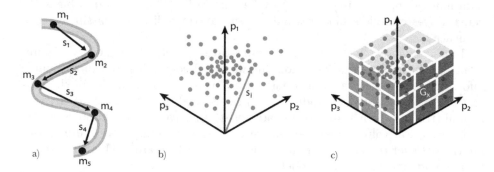

Fig. 2. (a) The generation of segments based measure points while driving a route (b) the vector space of segments (c) the vector space divided into interval groups

We implemented this method in the programming language R on basis of Mitsubishi iMiev data logged via the CAN-bus. The field test included 40 tours with about 60 Km per tour and provided 240304 measure points. After eliminating runaways, we were left with 156387 learn data segments. On this data we tested the interval grouping approach against an average across ungrouped

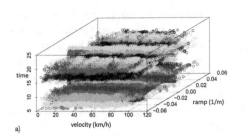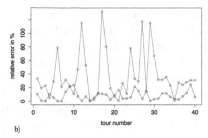

a) b)

Fig. 3. (a) Visualisation of generated groups (b) the averaged relative error of raw data compared to interval groups

raw data by cross validation. This means, we used 39 tours as learn data to validate the remaining tour. The results are shown in Fig. 3(b), with a relative error about predicted and measured consumption value. The averaged raw data lead to an expectable inapplicable result with an average relative error of 37.6 %. However, the presented interval grouping algorithm reduces the relative error to an average of 8,5 %, which is already acceptable and comparable to different approaches presented in Sect. 3.

4.2 Parameter Functions

Despite the good results of the simple clustering algorithm, Fig. 3(b) evinces a relative error ranging from 3 % to 20 % in isolated cases, suggesting there is still potential for optimisation. In this approach, segments with similar properties are approximated with the same consumption value. This inherits an obvious source of error we want to eliminate by implement parameter specific functions for every group.

These parameter functions describe the influence of a parameter on the consumption value, and offer the possibility to refine the former constant value. To

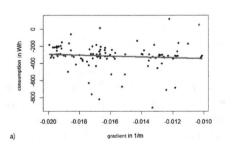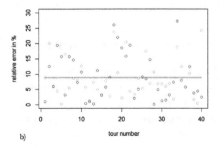

a) b)

Fig. 4. (a) Example of a regression function within a specific group, (b) the impact of using the parameter function method on interval groups compared to the interval groups method

retrieve such a function in a specific group, there have to be multiple inner-group coordinate systems with an ordinate for every property and a corresponding consumption abscissa. For every property a parameter function can then be produced by regression. Figure 4(a) shows generated parameter function for the gradient by linear regression. In this approach, the former look up table is enhanced by adding the parameter function to every group and parameter. The consumption value of a segment vector results from the according group with corrections by the function for every parameter.

We tested this method on the same data as in Sect. 4.1. As shown in Fig. 4(b), the average relative error can slightly be reduced from 8.5 % to 8 % by linear regression. The improvement seems to be insignificant, but this method has advantages in case of large interval choices. Large intervals lead to a lower demand of memory space for the look-up table at the expense of accuracy but parameter functions potentially hold up the granularity and fine adjustment.

4.3   Clustering

The group building algorithm in the previous two methods is pretty straight forward implemented. Boundaries and breaking points of the intervals are either equidistant or manually chosen. This basic approach gives us margin in testing and evaluating the influence on the results, but obviously may not be optimal chosen. Until now, there may occur overfilled or empty groups. On one hand, too many segments in a group can decrease the information content, where on another consumption values have to be estimated in empty groups. We expected a much better distribution of groups, if the boundaries are derived depending on the actual value distribution of properties. Therefore, we rebuild the grouping algorithm based on common comprehensive machine learning methods, like the x-means algorithm [2]. This algorithm finds cluster centres for every parameter and sets interval boundaries in between these.

By applying x-means clustering to the group building on our test data to the first method from Sect. 4.1, the average relative error could be reduced from 8.5 % to 6.9 %. This shows, that focused group building is very important and substantial for winning reliable consumption data.

4.4   Evaluation with Synthetical Data

Within the SCL project, we perform extensive human centred acceptance tests to evaluate the usability and functionality of the ICT, especially the DAC. Due to the fact, that logistic processes are very time critical and susceptible, we can not try out pre-versions in a field test. Therefore we built a software simulator environment which communicates with a DAC and ICT demo. For testing the data flow functionality the simulator generates consumption data, based on a simple mathematical model. This model is based on artificial segment vectors and calculates forces acting on a vehicle with realistic properties. Besides the acceptance tests running, the simulator also generates synthetical consumption data based on either artificial scenarios, or routes generated from real map and height data.

We produced consumption data for 400 tracks on the basis of the same course driven for the data generation described in Sect. 4.1. Using these artificial data as input for the grouping and clustering algorithms described above, we got a reduced average relative error ranging between 2 % and 4 %, which is an improvement. We assume, that the originally variation in the relative error can be attributed to measurement errors within the vehicle electronics and during GPS localization, as well as the time delay while tagging the data or time intervals between measuring points.

4.5   Data Refinement

To minimize the relative error further we are currently focussing our work on preprocessing the measured vehicle data. Every method described above is based on the assumption, that the vehicle drives directly from one measure point to the next one and behaves constant in between. But a closer look at the data shows, that even very similar segment vectors contain significantly deviant consumption values. This suggests, that the actual requirements to the vehicle differ from that assumption, as well as that the overall assumption is overestimated. Because of the learning data based on the shortest distance between two measure points, the probably higher requirements lead to higher associated consumption which is falsely used in later range predictions. Therefore, we need to refine the measured data with the help of map data to reconstruct the actually driven route and relate the consumption to it.

The refining data process can be subdivided in thee parts. First there has to be a relocation of the measured GPS signal to a road element as illustrated in Fig. 5(a). GPS measurements inherit immanent deviations due to signal outage in wooded environments or signal reflections in urban areas for example. We use hereby a orthogonal projection to the nearest road element(s). In a second step, we reconstruct the covered road elements to gain a new sequence of segments as shown in Fig. 5(b). Usually this is the shortest path between two relocated GPS signals and can be calculated by a route searching algorithm. If a relocation in the first step is ambiguous, due two-lanc roads or a close meshed road network for example, the algorithm tests different variations.

The third and last step is the most comprehensive and actual state of work in our research project. Our goal is to subdivide the former large segment into multiple small segments, which emulate the actually driven route and redistribute the overall consumption value on this new gained segments. The actual behaviour can partially reconstructed by assumptions about velocities and accelerations in context to the map material which often holds information about averages. The individual driver characteristics and standing periods are a big problem. As illustrated in Fig. 5(c) and (d) the final resegmentation and value distribution can vary strongly depending on the assumed behaviour of the driver. A ecologically conscious driver would accelerate and break slowly to save or even recuperate

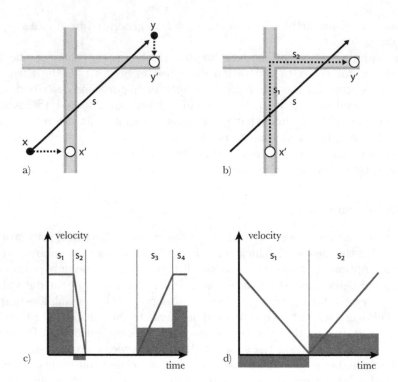

Fig. 5. (a) Relocation of GPS measure points x and y with orthogonal projection to the nearest road element, (b) routing for gaining new segments s_i, compared to former segment based on measurements, (c) possible segment refinement resulting energy consumption profile based on the assumption of an aggressive driver (d) possible segment refinement and resulting energy consumption profile based on the assumption of an ecological aware driver

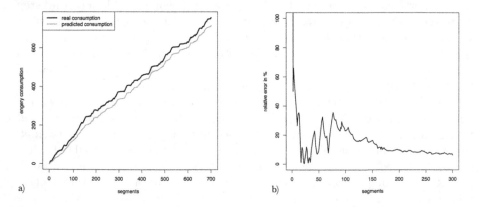

Fig. 6. (a) A predicted energy loss over route segments compared to the real data consumption values (b) the change of relative error rates while learning from measured segments

energy, where a aggressive driver always breaks and accelerates as fast as possible. The ambiguity is mostly caused by possible waiting or standing times, which are not reconstructible from the data. Therefore, we need to determine and integrate the characteristics of the driver. Until now, we try to classify segments in relation to their plausibility and use unambiguous ones for retrieval of the acceleration characteristics. Our method by now is very much dependent to the available data, due there are only rare segments, which are suitable for learning the driver characteristics. We hope to solve this problem in an upcoming field test.

5   Conclusion and Future Work

In this paper, we presented an approach to implement a range prediction model based on machine learning into an ICT structure enabling the use of electric vehicles in urban logistics. We introduced and evaluated different methods which were developed and integrated for fully automatically adapt a range model on basis of real measured consumption data on runtime. Our methods are able to reproduce consumption levels of learned real data sets with an relative error ranging from 5 % to 10 %, which is acceptable and compares to existing approaches like [6] with an average of 8 %. As shown in Fig. 6(a) our model can predict the energy loss of a electric vehicle in a reliable way. Besides, the clustering method establishes an steady converging error value as illustrated in Fig. 6(b). By this, we established a lightweight, easy to adapt model, which excludes recurring modelling effort.

Our main focus right now is the refinement of measured data to reduce the relative error in the consumption model until the first field test in spring 2016. We expect to reduce the prediction error significantly and even try out other learning methods like feed forward artificial neural networks, which failed until now due to the noisy data. We also try to implement parts of the range prediction model as heuristic into the routing algorithm to optimize route finding for electric vehicles. Lastly, we want to split up the energy consumption and storage model, which are implicit combined right now. Related work has shown, that electric energy storages have very complex characteristics which might infer with the consumption model. Our idea is to automatically adapt a storage model like in [4] in combination to the methods presented in this paper.

References

1. Conradi, P., Bouteiller, P., Hanßen, S.: Dynamic cruising range prediction for electric vehicles. In: Meyer, G., Valldorf, J. (eds.) Advanced Microsystems for Automotive Applications 2011. VDI-Buch, pp. 269–277. Springer, Heidelberg (2011)
2. Moore, A., Pelleg, Dan.: X-means: extending k-means with efficient estimation of the number of clusters. In: Proceedings of the Seventeenth International Conference on Machine Learning, pp. 727–734. Morgan Kaufmann, San Francisco (2000)
3. Deakin, M., AI Waer, H.: From intelligent to smart cities. Intell. Buildings Int. **3**(3), 140–152 (2011)

4. Jiani, D., Liu, Z., Wang, Y.: State of charge estimation for li-ion battery based on model from extreme learning machine. Control Eng. Pract. **26**, 11–19 (2014)
5. Ferreira, J.C., Monteiro, V.D.F., Afonso, J.L.: Data mining approach for range prediction of electric vehicle (2012)
6. Ondruska, P., Posner, I.: The route not taken: driver-centric estimation of electric vehicle range. In: Proceedings of the 24th International Conference on Automated Planning and Scheduling (ICAPS), Portsmouth, NH, USA, June 2014
7. Rogge, M., Rothgang, S., Sauer, D.U.: Operating strategies for a range extender used in battery electric vehicles. In: Vehicle Power and Propulsion Conference (VPPC), pp. 1–5. IEEE, October 2013
8. Schau, V., Rossak, W., Hempel, H., Spathe, S.: Smart City Logistik erfurt (SCL): ICT-support for managing fully electric vehicles in the domain of inner city freight traffic. In: 2015 International Conference on Industrial Engineering and Operations Management (IEOM), pp. 1–8. IEEE (2015)
9. Schreiber, V., Wodtke, A., Augsburg, K.: Range prediction of electric vehicles. In: Shaping the Future by Engineering: Proceedings; 58th IWK, Ilmenau Scientific Colloquium, Technische Universitat Ilmenau, 8–12 September 2014
10. Seaman, A., Dao, T.-S., McPhee, J.: A survey of mathematics-based equivalent-circuit and electrochemical battery models for hybrid and electric vehicle simulation. J. Power Sources **256**, 410–423 (2014)

Feature Selection

Partitioning Based N-Gram Feature Selection for Malware Classification

Weiwei Hu and Ying Tan[✉]

Key Laboratory of Machine Perception (MOE),
Department of Machine Intelligence,
School of Electronics Engineering and Computer Science,
Peking University, Beijing 100871, China
{weiwei.hu,ytan}@pku.edu.cn

Abstract. Byte level N-Gram is one of the most used feature extraction algorithms for malware classification because of its good performance and robustness. However, the N-Gram feature selection for a large dataset consumes huge time and space resources due to the large amount of different N-Grams. This paper proposes a partitioning based algorithm for large scale feature selection which efficiently resolves the original problem into in-memory solutions without heavy IO load. The partitioning process adopts an efficient implementation to convert the original interactional dataset to unrelated data partitions. Such data independence enables the effectiveness of the in-memory solutions and the parallelism on different partitions. The proposed algorithm was implemented on Apache Spark, and experimental results show that it is able to select features in a very short period of time which is nearly three times faster than the comparison MapReduce approach.

Keywords: Malware classification · Feature selection · Data partitioning · Apache Spark

1 Introduction

With the rapid popularization of the Internet, malware has become the main threat to computer security. Hundreds of millions of new malware samples are created every year [2]. How to detect and classify such a large amount of new malware has become a challenging issue in computer security.

Many researchers have proposed to use machine learning to detect and classify new malware in recent years. The malware detection task trains a classifier such as support vector machine [12] and random forest [6] to classify executable files into benign or malware, while the malware classification task uses a classifier to classify executable files into families. It can be seen that malware detection is just a special case of malware classification. Therefore, we just use the term malware classification to refer to both tasks hereinafter.

The machine learning based malware classification approaches proposed so far mainly differ on the way to extract malware features. Schultz et al. [9] proposed to use DLLs, APIs, strings and byte sequences as malware features. Kolter

© Springer International Publishing Switzerland 2016
Y. Tan and Y. Shi (Eds.): DMBD 2016, LNCS 9714, pp. 187–195, 2016.
DOI: 10.1007/978-3-319-40973-3_18

et al. [4,5] selected a certain number of byte level N-Grams using information gain [17] to construct malware features. Tabish et al. [13] divided binary files into blocks and calculated 13 statistical features on each block. Each block was classified as a normal block or a potentially malicious block, and the correlation module was used to combine the classification results of different blocks from a single binary file. Shafiq et al. [10, 11] regarded the key fields of the PE structure [7] as features.

Among the proposed feature extraction algorithms, N-Gram shows good experimental performance and is more robust than other algorithms. Therefore, there are many derived feature extraction algorithms from N-Gram. Wang et al. proposed the immune concentration of N-Grams to construct a low dimensional feature [15, 16]. Zhang et al. used the class-wise information gain to select malicious N-Grams to detect infected executables [18].

The value N for N-Gram is usually set to 4, which is able to keep a balance between final classification performance and the robustness. A smaller N will decrease the classification performance heavily while a larger N can be easily obfuscated by the insertion of irrelevant machine instructions.

However, the feature selection of N-Gram is very expensive in real world applications. Most feature selection algorithms need to count the numbers of N-Grams in all classes, while there are a huge number of different N-Grams when the dataset is large. The main memory of an ordinary computer usually does not have enough space to store the variable (e.g. a hash map which stores the counts of all N-Grams for each class) used to collect the counts. Kolter et al. [4] adopted a disk-based implementation to handle this problem but they said that their implementation was very slow.

This paper proposes a partitioning based N-Gram feature selection algorithm which divided the huge number of N-Grams into several partitions and uses an in-memory implementation to select the most informative features.

We will introduce the N-Gram feature selection algorithm in Sect. 2 and explain the proposed partitioning based algorithm in Sect. 3. Sections 4 and 5 will give the experimental results and the conclusion respectively.

2   N-Gram Feature Selection for Malware Classification

In the feature selection process of malware classification, each executable sample is broken into N-Grams using an overlapping sliding window of N bytes. The window slides from the beginning of a binary file to the end with a step of one byte. At each step the binary content in the window is regarded as an N-Gram feature. Duplicated N-Grams in a sample will be removed.

After generating N-Grams for all of the samples in the training set a feature selection metric score is calculated for each unique N-Gram and the top K N-Grams with the largest metric scores will be selected as the final features, where K is a pre-specified variable.

Information gain is the most used feature selection metric, which is defined as Formula 1 [5].

$$IG\left(f\right) = \sum_{v_f \in \{0,1\}} \sum_{c \in C} P\left(v_f, c\right) \frac{P\left(v_f, c\right)}{P\left(v_f\right) P\left(c\right)} . \tag{1}$$

In this formula f represents the feature and v_f represents the feature value. $v_f = 0$ means the feature f is not in a sample, while $v_f = 1$ means the feature f appears in a file sample. C is the set of all classes. $P\left(v_f, c\right)$ is the probability that the class of a sample is c and its feature value for f is v_f. $P\left(v_f\right)$ represents the probability that a sample's feature value for f is v_f and $P\left(c\right)$ represents the probability that a sample's class is c.

Formula 1 needs to calculate three probabilities (i.e. $P\left(v_f, c\right)$, $P\left(v_f\right)$ and $P\left(c\right)$) in advance. $P\left(c\right)$ can be easily obtained by calculating the fraction of samples with class c in the training set. If we have calculated $P\left(v_f, c\right)$, $P\left(v_f\right)$ can be derived as the sum of $P\left(v_f, c\right)$ over all classes, as shown in Formula 2.

$$P\left(v_f\right) = \sum_{c \in C} P\left(v_f, c\right). \tag{2}$$

The remaining work is to calculate $P\left(v_f, c\right)$. We can obviously get Formula 3.

$$P\left(v_f = 0, c\right) + P\left(v_f = 1, c\right) = P\left(v_f, c\right). \tag{3}$$

Therefore we only need to calculate $P\left(v_f = 1, c\right)$ first and then derive $P\left(v_f = 0, c\right)$ using Formula 4.

$$P\left(v_f = 0, c\right) = P\left(v_f, c\right) - P\left(v_f = 1, c\right). \tag{4}$$

$P\left(v_f = 1, c\right)$ can be calculated using Formula 5.

$$P\left(v_f = 1, c\right) = \frac{T\left(v_f = 1, c\right)}{T}. \tag{5}$$

T in Formula 5 is the total number of samples in the training set and $T\left(v_f = 1, c\right)$ is the number of samples in the training set whose feature values for f are all 1 and classes are all c.

When applied to N-Gram feature selection for malware classification, $T\left(v_f = 1, c\right)$ can be written as $T\left(g, c\right)$, which represents the number of an N-Gram g in class c, provided that the duplicated N-Grams in a single executable file are removed.

However, the number of possible N-Grams is exponential to the length of N-Gram N. For example when $N = 4$ there will be 2^{32} (i.e. about 4.3 billion) possible N-Grams. For a large training set a large fraction of the possible N-Grams will appear. If there are 100 classes and we use a 32-bit integer to store the number of an N-Gram, we will need at most 1.6 TB space to store the numbers, even not including the additional space used by the data structure (e.g. a hash table) to store and organize the N-Grams, which could be in the same order of magnitude as the space used by the numbers.

When traversing the training set to calculate $T\left(g, c\right)$, the whole variable that stores $T\left(g, c\right)$ for all of the N-Grams and all of the classes should be kept in main memory because the variable will be accessed frequently and randomly, while an ordinary computer with a limited memory size is not able to store such a large variable in main memory.

To handle this problem, Kolter et al. [4] claimed that they implemented a disk-based approach which consumed a great deal of time and space, but they didn't give the detailed description of their implementation.

A straightforward solution is to split the training set into small subsets and calculate the numbers of N-Grams for each subset. The result for each subset is written to a file on the disk. After all the subsets are traversed the files for different subsets are merged into a single one. This solution is workable but it needs a lot of IO operations which are very inefficient.

Another possible solution is to use MapReduce [3,8] which is designed for distributed systems. Most MapReduce tutorials begin with a word count example, while calculating the number of N-Grams is just a special case of the word count problem; we need to take count of N-Grams for all of the classes. However, the shuffle operation of MapReduce is very time-consuming which will heavily decrease the time efficiency of feature selection.

In the next section we will propose an efficient N-Gram feature selection algorithm based on partitioning.

3   Partitioning Based N-Gram Feature Selection

The process of partitioning based N-Gram feature selection is shown in Algorithm 1.

Algorithm 1. Partitioning Based N-Gram Feature Selection

Input: the training set.
Input: K: the number of N-Gram features to be selected.
Output: K N-Gram features with the largest information gains.
1: Determine the number of partitions P according to the training data size and the main memory size available in a computer.
2: Create P lists which are stored in the external memory, namely $L_0, L_1, ..., L_{P-1}$.
3: **for all** executable sample in the training set **do**
4:     $c = the\ class\ of\ the\ sample$
5:     **for all** unique N-Gram g generated from the sample **do**
6:         $L_{hash(g)\%P}.add(< g, c >)$.
7:     **end for**
8: **end for**
9: the feature set $F = \varnothing$
10: **for all** $i \in \{0, 1, ..., P-1\}$ **do**
11:     Use an in-memory feature selection algorithm to select top K features from L_i.
12:     Add the selected N-Gram features to F.
13: **end for**
14: **return** the top K features in the set F.

First of all, the number of partitions should be determined so that each partition can be processed using an in-memory algorithm. Let the total size of the training data be S and the main memory size available be M. The average data size of each partition is S/P.

The actual memory occupied by the in-memory algorithm used below is approximatively proportional to the size of data in a partition. Let the proportionality coefficient be λ. Then we have $\lambda * S/P \leq M$, that is $P \geq \lambda * S/M$.

The coefficient λ depends on the programming language and the data structure used in the program. We need to estimate its value according to the detailed implementation. If λ is underestimated, there may be not enough main memory space for the program and the program may crash. Therefore, we should select a slightly large value for λ.

Then, P lists are created to store the temporary data. The temporary data is also too large to be stored in main memory. Therefore, the data are actually stored in external memory such as the disk. A cached implementation of the list in external memory will significantly reduce the amount of IO operations. When adding data to the list, the new data are stored into a buffer in main memory first. Once the buffer is full all the data in it will be written to external memory and the buffer is set to empty again.

Next, each executable file in the training set is broken into N-Grams and duplicated N-Grams in a file are removed. For each N-Gram a hash function is calculated based on its binary content. The remainder of Euclidean division of the hash value and P determines which list the N-Gram goes to. The pair of the N-Gram and the class of the executable file is added to the list.

For the cached implementation of the list in external memory, a smaller P will consume less cache space for all the lists in main memory. From the above analysis we know that the condition for selecting P is $P \geq \lambda * S/M$. Therefore, we can just choose $P = \lambda * S/M$.

This partitioning process will make the same N-Gram across the whole training set to be partitioned into the same list. Therefore, the information gain of the N-Gram can be calculated within the list.

After that, for each list an in-memory feature selection algorithm is used to select top N-Grams. The numbers of all N-Grams in the list is counted for each class and the information gains are calculated using Formulas 1-5. The K N-Grams with largest information gain is selected. The P lists produce $P * K$ N-Grams in total.

Finally, the top K N-Grams are selected from the $P * K$ N-Grams.

The time complexity of Algorithm 1 is proportional to the size of training data. The partitioning process reads the whole training set linearly and writes the pairs of N-Grams and the classes to external memory. We estimate the total size of data in external memory here without considering the data compression and indexing. For $N = 4$, after removing duplicated N-Grams the number of N-Grams will reduced to about one half according to our experiment. Therefore, the external memory space occupied by the contents of N-Grams is about 2 (i.e. $4 * 0.5$) times larger than the training data size. If the number of classes is not larger than 128 we can use one byte to store the class value for each N-Gram, and the external memory space occupied by the classes of N-Grams will be about the same as the training data size. If the number of classes is between 129 and 65536 the class value will need two bytes and the external space will be about 2 times larger than the training data size. Therefore, the total size of data in external memory is about 3 or 4 times larger than the training data size, depending on the number of classes. The in-memory feature selection algorithm will read the data from external memory again to calculate information gain. In conclusion the data size of IO operations is about 7 or 9 times larger than the training data size. Such amount of IO operations is acceptable in the real world application.

Algorithm 1 can be easily parallelized in a very efficient approach. The most time-consuming processes of Algorithm 1 are partitioning N-Grams from all files into different lists and calculating information gain for each list. The partitioning process for each file is independent, and the calculations of information gain for different lists are also independent. Therefore, these two processes can both be distributed to different CPU cores or even different computers.

4   Experiments

The proposed algorithm was implemented on Apache Spark [1] using Python. Apache Spark has a built-in data partitioning routine which makes the proposed algorithm very easy to be implemented. What's more, Apache Spark can distribute the computation tasks to different CPU cores and different computers, enabling the parallelization of the proposed algorithm automatically.

We used two workers for the Apache Spark cluster, each with one CPU core and 5 GB memory.

The dataset we used contains 11058 executables, including 5563 benign files and 5495 malicious files from the VX Heaven virus collection [14]. The total size of the dataset is 5.50 GB. We did a two-class malware detection task on this dataset.

When selecting the number of partitions using the formula $P = \lambda * S/M$, λ was estimated as about 100. At last we chose 100 as the number of partitions.

We also implemented a comparison algorithm based on the famous word count example using MapReduce given in the Apache Spark website[1], which is shown as follows:

```
counts = text_file.flatMap(lambda line: line.split("␣")) \
            .map(lambda word: (word, 1)) \
            .reduceByKey(lambda a, b: a + b)
```

The function of this piece code is to calculate the numbers of all words from a given text file. Each line of the file is mapped to several words and the same word will be reduced to get the count. We extend this algorithm to calculate the number of N-Grams for all of the classes and then calculate the information gains.

---

[1] http://spark.apache.org/examples.html.

Shafiq et al. [11] used the N-Gram feature as a comparison algorithm of their proposed PE-Miner. In their article they claimed they had developed an optimized implementation of N-Gram which is more efficient. We also took their implementation as one of our comparison algorithms.

The time consumption of different implementations is shown in Table 1.

Table 1. Feature selection time for partitioning based algorithm, MapReduce based extended word count algorithm and the implementation of Shafiq et al.

Algorithm	#Samples	Hardware and platform	Time
Partitioning	11058	3.0 GHz+3.3 GHz, Spark, Python	3.4 h
MapReduce	11058	3.0 GHz+3.3 GHz, Spark, Python	10.1 h
Shafiq et al.	2895	2.19 GHz, C++, STL	25.3 h

As we can see in the table, partitioning based algorithm is almost three times faster than MapReduce based algorithm. MapReduce needs to shuffle the huge amount of N-Grams, while shuffle is very expensive.

Both partitioning based algorithm and MapReduce based algorithm have two stages in the Spark jobs. The time consumption of each task for the two algorithms is shown in Fig. 1.

For partitioning based algorithm, stage 1 partitions the N-Grams, while stage 2 counts the N-Grams and calculates information gain to select top N-Grams. The two stages takes 1.6 h and 1.8 h respectively. The most expensive operation of the two stages is IO, and the IO data sizes of the two stages are close. Therefore, the time consumptions of this two stages are close. The calculation of information involve some expensive logarithm operations in stage 2, so that the time consumption of stage 2 is slightly higher than that of stage 1.

For MapReduce based extended word count algorithm, stage 1 uses MapReduce to obtain the numbers of N-Grams in each class while stage 2 maps the counts of an N-Gram in all the classes to information gain. Stage 1 takes 6.8 h which is twice as the whole time consumption of partitioning based algorithm. The most expensive operation of stage 1 is shuffle. We can see that shuffle will

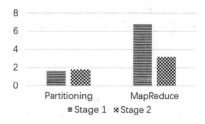

Fig. 1. The time (in hour) of different stages for partitioning based algorithm and MapReduce based extended word count algorithm

significantly decline the time efficiency of the whole algorithm. Stage 2 of this algorithm takes 3.2 h while stage 2 of partitioning based algorithm only takes 1.8 h. The superiority of partitioning based algorithm is achieved by using the concentrative in-memory feature selection for the whole partition.

The last row of Table 1 gives the estimated result of Shafiq et al.'s implementation. They used many categories of executables in their experiments. The average number of executables in each category is 2895. They reported that the average feature selection time for a file of their implementation is 31.5 s. Therefore, we estimated that the total feature selection time for 2895 files is 25.3 h.

The size of dataset used by partitioning based algorithm is almost 4 times larger than that used by Shafiq et al. We used two CPU cores and the CPUs' frequencies are higher than theirs. Besides, they adopted a faster C++ implementation. We can estimate that our computation capability is about 4 times stronger than theirs. Considering the dataset size and the computation capability, the numeric difference between the time consumption of Shafiq et al.'s implementation and the partitioning based algorithm in Table 1 is able to roughly reflect the difference between the time efficiencies of the two algorithms. Shafiq et al.'s implementation took more than one day to select features, while partitioning based algorithm only took 3.4 h, which is more than 7 times faster.

5   Conclusions

Byte level N-Gram is a well-known feature extraction algorithm for malware classification which is able to extract relevant features for malware and is very robust. However, the feature selection of N-Gram suffers from heavy time and space load because the large number of features generally cannot be stored in main memory. This paper proposed a partitioning based approach to accelerate the feature selection process. The proposed approach divides N-Gram features into independent partitions and uses the in-memory feature selection algorithm for each partition. Experimental results showed that the partitioning based algorithm is very efficient and is superior to a MapReduce based implementation and the optimized implementation by Shafiq et al.

Acknowledgments. This work was supported by the Natural Science Foundation of China (NSFC) under grant no. 61375119 and the Beijing Natural Science Foundation under grant no. 4162029, and partially supported by National Key Basic Research Development Plan (973 Plan) Project of China under grant no. 2015CB352302.

References

1. Apache: Apache spark (2016). http://spark.apache.org/
2. AV-TEST: Malware statistics & trends report (2016). http://www.av-test.org/en/statistics/malware/
3. Dean, J., Ghemawat, S.: Mapreduce: simplified data processing on large clusters. Commun. ACM **51**(1), 107–113 (2008)

4. Kolter, J.Z., Maloof, M.A.: Learning to detect and classify malicious executables in the wild. J. Mach. Learn. Res. **7**, 2721–2744 (2006)
5. Kolter, J.Z., Maloof, M.A.: Learning to detect malicious executables in the wild. In: Proceedings of the Tenth ACM SIGKDD International Conference on Knowledge Discovery and Data Mining, pp. 470–478. ACM (2004)
6. Liaw, A., Wiener, M.: Classification and regression by randomforest. R News **2**(3), 18–22 (2002)
7. Pietrek, M.: Peering inside the pe: A tour of the win32 portable executable file format (1994). https://msdn.microsoft.com/en-us/library/ms809762.aspx
8. Rajaraman, A., Ullman, J.D.: Mining of Massive Datasets, vol. 1. Cambridge University Press, Cambridge (2012)
9. Schultz, M.G., Eskin, E., Zadok, E., Stolfo, S.J.: Data mining methods for detection of new malicious executables. In: 2001 IEEE Symposium on Security and Privacy. Proceedings, S&P 2001, pp. 38–49. IEEE (2001)
10. Shafiq, M.Z., Tabish, S.M., Mirza, F., Farooq, M.: A framework for efficient mining of structural information to detect zero-day malicious portable executables. Technical report. Citeseer (2009)
11. Shafiq, M.Z., Tabish, S.M., Mirza, F., Farooq, M.: PE-Miner: mining structural information to detect malicious executables in realtime. In: Kirda, E., Jha, S., Balzarotti, D. (eds.) RAID 2009. LNCS, vol. 5758, pp. 121–141. Springer, Heidelberg (2009)
12. Suykens, J.A., Vandewalle, J.: Least squares support vector machine classifiers. Neural Process. Lett. **9**(3), 293–300 (1999)
13. Tabish, S.M., Shafiq, M.Z., Farooq, M.: Malware detection using statistical analysis of byte-level file content. In: Proceedings of the ACM SIGKDD Workshop on CyberSecurity and Intelligence Informatics, pp. 23–31. ACM (2009)
14. VX-Heaven: Virus collection (vx heaven) (2016). https://vxheaven.org/vl.php
15. Wang, W., Zhang, P., Tan, Y., He, X.: Animmune local concentration based virus detection approach. J. Zhejiang Univ. Sci. C **12**(6), 443–454 (2011)
16. Wang, W., Zhang, P., Tan, Y.: An immune concentration based virus detection approach using particle swarm optimization. In: Tan, Y., Shi, Y., Tan, K.C. (eds.) ICSI 2010, Part I. LNCS, vol. 6145, pp. 347–354. Springer, Heidelberg (2010)
17. Yang, Y., Pedersen, J.O.: A comparative study on feature selection in text categorization. In: ICML, vol. 97, pp. 412–420 (1997)
18. Zhang, P., Tan, Y.: Class-wise information gain. In: 2013 International Conference on Information Science and Technology (ICIST), pp. 972–978. IEEE (2013)

A Supervised Biclustering Optimization Model for Feature Selection in Biomedical Dataset Classification

Saziye Deniz Oguz Arikan[✉] and Cem Iyigun

Industrial Engineering, Middle East Technical University, Ankara, Turkey
saziyeden@gmail.com, iyigun@metu.edu.tr

Abstract. Biclustering groups samples and features simultaneously in the given set of data. When biclusters are obtained from the data, clusters of samples and clusters of features that determine the partitioning of samples into the underlying clusters are also obtained. We focus on a supervised biclustering problem leading to unsupervised feature selection. We formulate this problem as an optimization model which aims to maximize classification accuracy by selecting a small subset of features. We solve the model with exact and inexact solution methods based on optimization techniques. Microarray cancer datasets are used to experiment our approach.

Keywords: Biclustering · Feature selection · Classification · Optimization · Microarray

1 Introduction

In biological and biomedical research, biclustering has a critical importance, especially in DNA microarray data analysis. A typical microarray data contains gene expression values of several samples that may be in one of the two or more conditions. These conditions can be disease conditions such as tumor. Purpose of the biclustering problem is to group the samples and the features simultaneously in the given data. It is an unsupervised method which means that the class information is not known a priori, and hence, the groups (or classes) are discovered from the data, if they exist. Importance of biclustering compared to traditional clustering approaches is that biclustering does not only identify disease conditions but also obtains subsets of genes (features) that are responsible for identifying those disease conditions. Hence, these subsets of genes serve as markers for these disease conditions. Furthermore, selecting small number of features is critical in bioinformatics, especially in microarray based cancer prediction (see, [15,16]). If an algorithm selects many genes, this might limit the interpretability of the classifiers. The lack of interpretability may prevent the acceptance of such diagnostic tools [15,16].

In supervised biclustering, the class information of samples or features is known a priori. Busygin et al. in [2] introduced the consistent biclustering criteria to locate non-overlapping biclusters in data. This is a supervised method,

© Springer International Publishing Switzerland 2016
Y. Tan and Y. Shi (Eds.): DMBD 2016, LNCS 9714, pp. 196–204, 2016.
DOI: 10.1007/978-3-319-40973-3_19

since the authors use class labels of the samples in developing the model. For this problem, a mathematical model of supervised consistent biclustering was presented under the biclustering consistency conditions, and its objective function is to maximize the number of selected features. Their model is a nonlinear 0-1 integer model, and it has been shown to be NP-hard (see [7]). By applying a linearization approach, it can be reformulated as a linear mixed 0-1 programming problem. In order to solve this problem, linearization approach has been applied by Busygin et al. in [2], and different heuristic algorithms have been proposed in [2,10].

The focus of this paper is supervised biclustering leading to unsupervised feature selection. We work on particular datasets in which the number of features is much larger than the number of samples. We propose an alternative approach to supervised biclustering. In proposed approach, our aim is to obtain the maximum separation among the sample classes using a certain measure while simultaneously determining the classes of the selected features. In other words, we select features that maximize the separation of the samples projected on the space of those features. We formulate this approach as an optimization model which aims to maximize classification accuracy by selecting a small subset of features that mainly create (or cause) the separation. We solve the model with exact and heuristic solution methods based on optimization techniques. Microarray cancer datasets are used to experiment our approach.

The rest of this paper is organized as follow. In Sect. 2, we introduce the mathematical formulation of the proposed approach and solution methods. Section 3 presents the datasets and the experimental results. Section 4 summarizes this paper by providing its main conclusions.

2   Mathematical Formulation

For the problem of selecting the features that maximize the separation of the samples projected on the space of those features, a nonlinear mixed 0-1 integer model is introduced. We solve the model over a training data. Class labels of samples in the training data are used in the model. A small subset of selected features and class labels of these selected features are obtained as the output. These selected features are then used to predict class labels of samples in test data. Proposed nonlinear mixed 0-1 integer model is as follows.

Sets

M set of features, N set of samples, K set of classes, N_r set of samples that belong to class r, for all $r \in K$.

Parameters

A training data matrix. Each element of the matrix a_{ij} corresponds to the expression of the ith feature in the jth sample, for all $i \in M$ and $j \in N$

Decision Variables

$$f_{ir} = \begin{cases} 1 \text{ if the } i^{th} \text{ feature is assigned to class } r \\ 0 \text{ otherwise} \end{cases}, \text{ for all } i \in M \text{ and } r \in K$$

α class separation variable.

Model (P):

$$\max \alpha \tag{1}$$

$$\text{s.t.} \quad \frac{\sum_{i \in M} a_{ij} f_{i\hat{r}}}{\sum_{i \in M} f_{i\hat{r}}} \geq \alpha + \frac{\sum_{i \in M} a_{ij} f_{ir}}{\sum_{i \in M} f_{ir}}, \quad \forall \hat{r}, r \in K, \hat{r} \neq r, j \in N_{\hat{r}}, \tag{2}$$

$$\sum_{r \in K} f_{ir} \leq 1, \qquad \forall i \in M, \tag{3}$$

$$f_{ir} \in \{0, 1\}, \qquad \forall i \in M, r \in K. \tag{4}$$

$$\alpha \geq 0 \tag{5}$$

Decision variable α measures the separation of the classes defined by the samples. Objective function in Model (P) maximizes the separation between the classes. This separation is based on maximizing the minimum difference between the average feature expression values of all class pairs across all samples. In constraint (2), if sample j belongs to class $\hat{r}$, average expression value of sample j features that are assigned to class $\hat{r}$ must be greater than the average expression values of sample j features that are assigned to other classes. Constraint (3) guarantees that each feature is assigned to at most one class.

2.1   Linearization of Model (P)

Model (P) can be reformulated as a linear mixed 0-1 programming problem by applying a linearization approach. Model (P) can then be solved using standard linear mixed integer programming solvers. The following proposition in [17] can be utilized to linearize Model (P).

Proposition 1. *A polynomial mixed 0-1 term $z = xy$, where x is a 0-1 variable, and y is a nonnegative variable with upper bound $\mathcal{M}$, can be represented by the following linear inequalities: (1) $y - z \leq \mathcal{M} - \mathcal{M}x$, (2) $z \leq y$, (3) $z \leq \mathcal{M}x$, and (4) $z \geq 0$.*

By using Proposition 1, we introduce new variables for Model (P).

$$z_{ir} = \frac{f_{ir}}{\sum_{i \in M} f_{ir}}, \quad i \in M \; r \in K, \text{ and } c_r = \frac{1}{\sum_{i \in M} f_{ir}}, \quad r \in K$$

By substituting these variables, we can replace nonlinear mixed 0-1 inequalities (2), with the linear-mixed 0-1 constraint sets. The resulting model (named as P-L) is given below.

Model (P-L):

$$\max \alpha \tag{6}$$

$$\text{s.t.} \sum_{i \in M} a_{ij} z_{i\hat{r}} \geq \alpha + \sum_{i \in M} a_{ij} z_{ir}, \qquad \forall \hat{r}, r \in K, \hat{r} \neq r, j \in N_{\hat{r}}, \tag{7}$$

$$c_r - z_{ir} \leq 1 - f_{ir}, \qquad \forall i \in M, r \in K, \tag{8}$$

$$z_{ir} \leq f_{ir}, \qquad \forall i \in M, r \in K, \tag{9}$$

$$z_{ir} \leq c_r, \qquad \forall i \in M, r \in K, \tag{10}$$

$$\sum_{i \in M} z_{ir} = 1, \qquad \forall r \in K, \tag{11}$$

$$\sum_{r \in K} f_{ir} \leq 1, \qquad \forall i \in M, \tag{12}$$

$$f_{ir} \in \{0, 1\}, \ z_{ir} \geq 0 \qquad \forall i \in M, r \in K \tag{13}$$

$$c_r \geq 0, \qquad \forall r \in K. \tag{14}$$

$$\alpha \geq 0 \tag{15}$$

Constraints (8), (9), (10) and (11) of Model (P-L) guarantee that positive values of selected z_{ir} variables are equal to each other which is also equal to the value of c_r, and their summation is equal to 1.

2.2   Heuristic for Model (P-L)

Model (P-L) may suffer from intractability when dealing with large problems. As a consequence, we next introduce a heuristic approach for Model (P-L). The idea of proposed heuristic (PH) is to find a good subset of features that contains the set of selected features in the optimal solution of Model (P-L). Once such a subset of features is obtained, the optimal solution can be found by solving Model (P-L) over these selected features. The following model called (P-H) is solved iteratively to find the reduced feasible region. In particular, Model (P-H) is solved iteratively for different values of $\mathbb{M}$ (positive parameter) until reaching threshold value γ which is defined as $z_{r\_ratio} = z_r^= / z_r^+ = \gamma$, where z_r^+ is the number of z_{ir} variables that take positive values, and $z_r^=$ is the number of z_{ir}

Model (P-H):

$$\max \alpha - \mathbb{M} \sum_{r \in K} c_r \tag{16}$$

$$\text{s.t.} \sum_{i \in M} a_{ij} z_{i\hat{r}} \geq \alpha + \sum_{i \in M} a_{ij} z_{ir}, \qquad \forall \hat{r}, r \in K, \hat{r} \neq r, j \in N_{\hat{r}}, \tag{17}$$

$$z_{ir} \leq c_r, \qquad \forall i \in M, r \in K, \tag{18}$$

$$\sum_{i \in M} z_{ir} = 1, \qquad \forall r \in K, \tag{19}$$

$$z_{ir} \geq 0 \qquad\qquad \forall i \in M, r \in K \qquad\qquad (20)$$

$$c_r \geq 0, \qquad\qquad \forall i \in M, r \in K. \qquad\qquad (21)$$

$$\alpha \geq 0 \qquad\qquad\qquad\qquad\qquad (22)$$

variables that take equal positive values. Values of z_r^+ and $z_r^=$ are obtained from the solution of Model (P-H) for a certain value of $\mathbb{M}$, where we always have $z_r^+ \geq z_r^=$.

3   Experimental Study

We test Model (P-L) and the proposed heuristic (PH), and compare the results on 8 publicly available microarray cancer datasets. Information about the datasets is presented in Table 1. All datasets in Table 1 have 2 classes. Further information of datasets can be found in the corresponding references. For comparison of (PH) and Model (P-L), we randomly partition each dataset in Table 1 into training and test sets by using 2-fold cross validation (CV). Furthermore, in order to test the accuracy of (PH) for the classification of datasets, we use 5-fold CV. We run 5-fold CV five times, each with a different random arrangement.

In order to express the performance of (PH) with respect to Model (P-L), we define the gap as follows. Let $\alpha^{(P-L)}$ be the best objective function value of Model (P-L) with matrix $\mathbf{A}$ obtained within 30000 s (approximately 8 h), and $\alpha^{(PH)}$ be the optimal objective value of Model (P-L) with reduced matrix $\mathcal{A}$ which is obtained by (PH). Then, gap is defined as follow.

$$Gap = \frac{\alpha^{(P-L)} - \alpha^{(PH)}}{\alpha^{(P-L)}} \times 100$$

3.1   Comparison of Model (P-L) and Proposed Heuristic

Results of the comparison between Proposed Heuristic (PH) and Model (P-L) are given in Table 2 for Fold 1 and Fold 2. In Table 2, eight out of 16 instances

Table 1. Microarray gene expression datasets.

Dataset tissue name (Ref.)	Total nb. of genes	Total nb. of samples	Samples per class	Classes
Blood-A ([1])	12582	72	24–48	ALL, MLL
Breast-Colon ([3])	22283	104	62–42	B, C
Leukemia ([5])	7129	72	47–25	ALL, AML
Lung ([6])	12533	181	31–150	MPM, AD
Colon ([8])	22883	37	8–29	Serrated CRC, conventional CRC
Brain ([11])	7129	34	25–9	CMD, DMD
Blood-S ([12])	7129	77	58–19	DLBCL, FL
Prostate ([13])	12600	102	50–52	N, PR

are solved to optimality with Model (P-L) within a time limit of 30000 s. These instances are indicated by an asterisk in the first column. In terms of solution quality, in five out of these eight instances, (PH) managed to find the optimal solution. Model (P-L) could not to reach the optimal solutions for the remaining eight instances within 30000 s. Best integer solutions for seven of them (except for Prostate data) are given in the sixth column. The average (maximum) optimality gap of those solutions is 0.41 % (1.2 %). In four of these instances, (PH) reached the best integer solution of (P-L). Finally, Prostate (Fold 2) instance became intractable in terms of memory with Model(P-L), while (PH) managed to find the solution in 6233.16 s.

Table 2. Comparison between (PH) and Model (P-L) on 8 microarray datasets

Datasets	Nb. of selected genes		Solution time (s)		Best obj. func. value (α)		Gap (%)
	(P-L)	(PH)	(P-L)	(PH)	(P-L)	(PH)	
Fold 1							
Blood-A*	15	16	22326.44	204.61	7609.22	7598.67	0.14
Breast-Colon	19	23	time limit	434.19	277.27	277.66	-0.14
Leukemia*	25	27	13439.07	110.69	3320.45	3283.08	1.13
Lung	16	16	time limit	86.88	1133.38	1133.38	0.00
Colon*	15	15	23407.11	338.16	988.27	988.27	0.00
Brain*	12	12	7413.36	13.64	3243.50	3243.50	0.00
Blood-S*	16	16	21553.25	35.11	3237.30	3237.30	0.00
Prostate*	14	14	20374.14	101.84	150.00	150.00	0.00
Fold 2							
Blood-A	14	14	time limit	61.40	9112.38	9112.38	0.00
Breast-Colon	16	16	time limit	323.24	277.29	276.78	0.18
Leukemia*	21	21	4078.57	42.71	3413.00	3413.00	0.00
Lung	16	16	time limit	57.89	1131.66	1131.66	0.00
Colon	16	16	time limit	84.79	988.50	988.50	0.00
Brain*	15	13	16740.72	31.93	1763.44	1755.95	0.42
Blood-S	18	25	time limit	1161.56	2777.78	2771.63	0.22
Prostate	NA	30	NA	6233.16	NA	87.13	NA

The overall running time of (PH) is 582.61 s on the average. Therefore, (PH) manages to keep the problem size in reasonable limits and reduces the solution time significantly. Furthermore, it still provides good solutions with an overall average (maximum) gap of 0.13 % (1.13 %) with respect to the solution of Model (P-L) obtained within 30000 s. In two instances, Breast-Colon (Fold 1) and Prostate (Fold 2), it outperforms Model (P-L) both in terms of solution time and solution quality.

3.2 Comparison of the Proposed Heuristic and Other Methods

Classification accuracy for each dataset with the proposed heuristic is given in Table 3. We compare the accuracy performance of (PH) with the accuracy performance of other methods reported in papers [4,9,14] for each dataset (see Table 3). There are four well-known classification methods, Naive Bayes (NB), k-Nearest Neighbor (k-NN), Support Vector Machines (SVM) and Random Forests (RF) other than (PH) in Table 3. In [14], no feature pre-selection method was applied on datasets. In [9], the authors did not apply pre-selection method on datasets for the results in Table 3. In [4], the authors selected 100 genes by various feature selection methods (t-test, ANOVA, and etc.). Then, SVM and RF are applied on these subsets of 100 genes. We have taken one of the best accuracy performances which is given by t-test. According to accuracy results given in Table 3, (PH) outperforms k-NN, SVM and RF reported in [9] in all cases (Leukemia, Lung, and Colon). (PH) outperforms all methods reported in [4,9,14] in one case (Lung). For Blood-A dataset, we have not found any classification accuracy result for two-class comparison. This dataset also has three classes, so all results in the literature are given for three classes of this dataset. In fact, Model (P) can be applied to multi-class problems. However, we have only focused on two-class problem in this study.

Table 3. Classification performance of proposed heuristic (PH) for 5 replications of 5-fold CV.

Datasets	Proposed Heuristic		Results in [14]			Results in [9]			Results in [4]	
	Avg. nb. of selected genes	Accuracy (%)	NB	k-NN	SVM	k-NN	SVM	RF	SVM	RF
Blood-A	17.61	96.67	NA	NA	NA	NA	NA	NA	NA	NA
Breast-Colon	18.55	94.23	NA	NA	NA	NA	NA	NA	**98.50**	96.00
Leukemia	22.56	96.39	100	84.7	98.6	89.10	86.90	95.10	97.30	98.30
Lung	20.80	**100.00**	97.8	98.3	99.5	99.95	97.60	99.70	98.80	98.30
Colon	21.68	**90.81**	NA	NA	NA	89.70	78.60	79.55	NA	NA
Brain	16.36	78.24	**82.4**	76.5	**82.4**	NA	NA	NA	NA	NA
Blood-S	18.30	92.08	80.5	84.4	**97.40**	NA	NA	NA	NA	NA
Prostate	22.43	89.85	62.8	76.5	**91.2**	NA	NA	NA	NA	NA

Overall, (PH) consistently provides a good accuracy performance with respect to the compared methods. Overall average accuracy of (PH) is 92.28 % with a standard deviation of 6.17 %. The greatest difference between the accuracy obtained by (PH) with the best reported accuracy is 5.32 %. We would like to note that these accuracy results of PH are obtained by using a much smaller set of selected genes compared to other well-known methods.

4   Conclusion

In this paper, we have proposed an alternative approach to supervised biclustering that aims to obtain a maximum separation among the sample classes using small set of features and simultaneously to determine the classes of the selected features. Problem is modeled as a nonlinear 0-1 integer model. The model has been linearized. For solving the linearized model, a heuristic approach has also been proposed. Both linearized mathematical model and heuristic approach were tested on several microarray datasets and their performance were compared with other methods. The experimental results are reported.

References

1. Armstrong, S.A., Staunton, J.E., Silverman, L.B., Pieters, R., de Boer, M.L., Minden, M.D., Sallan, S.E., Lander, E.S., Golub, T.R., Korsmeyer, S.J.: MLL translocations specify a distinct gene expression profile that distinguishes a unique leukemia. Nat. Genet. **30**(1), 41–47 (2002)
2. Busygin, S., Prokopyev, O.A., Pardalos, P.M.: Feature selection for consistent biclustering via fractional 0-1 programming. J. Comb. Optim. **10**(1), 7–21 (2005)
3. Chowdary, D., Lathrop, J., Skelton, J., Curtin, K., Briggs, T., Zhang, Y., Yu, J., Wang, Y., Mazumder, A.: Prognostic gene expression signatures can be measured in tissues collected in RNAlater preservative. J. Mol. Diagn. **8**(1), 31–39 (2006)
4. Drotar, P., Gazda, J., Smekal, Z.: An experimental comparison of feature selection methods on two-class biomedical datasets. Comput. Biol. Med. **66**, 1–10 (2015)
5. Golub, T.R., Slonim, D.K., Tamayo, P., Huard, C., Gaasenbeek, M., Mesirov, J.P., Coller, H., Loh, M.L., Downing, J.R., Caligiuri, M.A.: Molecular classification of cancer: class discovery and class prediction by gene expression monitoring. Science **286**(5439), 531–537 (1999)
6. Gordon, G.J.G., et al.: Translation of microarray data into clinically relevant cancer diagnostic tests using gene expression ratios in lung cancer and mesothelioma. Cancer Res. **62**(17), 4963–4967 (2002)
7. Kundakcioglu, O.E., Pardalos, P.M.: The complexity of feature selection for consistent biclustering. In: Butenko, S., Pardalos, P.M., Chaovalitwongse, W.A. (eds.) Clustering Challenges in Biological Networks. World Scientific Publishing (2009)
8. Laiho, P., Kokko, A., Vanharanta, S., Salovaara, R., Sammalkorpi, H., Järvinen, H., Mecklin, J.P., Karttunen, T.J., Tuppurainen, K., Davalos, V., Schwartz, S., Arango, D., Mäkinen, M.J., Aaltonen, L.A.: Serrated carcinomas form a subclass of colorectal cancer with distinct molecular basis. Oncogene **26**(2), 312–320 (2007)
9. Mahmoud, O., Harrison, A., Perperoglou, A., Gul, A., Khan, Z., Metodiev, M.V., Lausen, B.: A feature selection method for classification within functional genomics experiments based on the proportional overlapping score. BMC Bioinform. **15**(1), 1–20 (2014)
10. Nahapatyan, A., Busygin, S., Pardalos, P.M.: An improved heuristics for consistent biclustering problems. In: Mondaini, R.P., Pardalos, P.M. (eds.) Mathematical Modelling of Biosystems. Applied Optimization, vol. 102, pp. 185–198. Springer, Heidelberg (2008)
11. Pomeroy, S.L., et al.: Prediction of central nervous system embryonal tumour outcome based on gene expression. Nature **415**, 436–442 (2002)
12. Shipp, M.A., et al.: Diffuse large B-cell lymphoma outcome prediction by gene expression profiling and supervised machine learning. Nat. Med. **8**, 68–74 (2002)
13. Singh, D., et al.: Gene expression correlates of clinical prostate cancer behavior. Cancer Cell **1**(2), 203–209 (2002)
14. Tan, A.C., Naiman, D.Q., Xu, L., Winslow, R.L., Geman, D.: Simple decision rules for classifying human cancers from gene expression profiles. Bioinformatics **21**, 3896–3904 (2005)
15. Wang, X., Gotoh, O.: Accurate molecular classification of cancer using simple rules. BMC Med. Genomics **2**(64), 1–23 (2009)

16. Wang, X., Simon, R.: Microarray-based cancer prediction using single genes. BMC Bioinform. **12**(391), 1–9 (2011)
17. Wu, T.: A note on a global approach for general 0-1 fractional programming. Eur. J. Oper. Res. **101**(1), 220–223 (1997)

Term Space Partition Based Ensemble Feature Construction for Spam Detection

Guyue Mi[1,2], Yang Gao[1,2], and Ying Tan[1,2(✉)]

[1] Key Laboratory of Machine Perception (MOE),
Peking University, Beijing 100871, China
[2] Department of Machine Intelligence,
School of Electronics Engineering and Computer Science,
Peking University, Beijing 100871, China
{gymi,gaoyang0115,ytan}@pku.edu.cn

Abstract. This paper proposes an ensemble feature construction method for spam detection by using the term space partition (TSP) approach, which aims to establish a mechanism to make terms play more sufficient and rational roles by dividing the original term space and constructing discriminative features on distinct subspaces. The ensemble features are constructed by taking both global and local features of emails into account in feature perspective, where variable-length sliding window technique is adopted. Experiments conducted on five benchmark corpora suggest that the ensemble feature construction method far outperforms not only the traditional and most widely used bag-of-words model, but also the heuristic and state-of-the-art immune concentration based feature construction approaches. Compared to the original TSP approach, the ensemble method achieves better performance and robustness, providing an alternative mechanism of reliability for different application scenarios.

Keywords: Term space partition (TSP) · Ensemble term space partition (ETSP) · Feature construction · Spam detection · Text categorization

1 Introduction

Email has been an important communication tool in our daily life. However, high volumes of spam emails severely affect the normal communication, waste resources and productivity, and threat computer security and user privacy, resulting in serious economic and social problems [1]. According to Symantec Internet Security Threat Report [2], the overall spam rate of the whole email traffic all over the world in 2015 is 53 %. Meanwhile, email remains an effective medium for cybercriminals, since one out of every 220 emails contains mailware. Statistics from Cyren Cyber Threat Report [3] also reveal that the average amount of spam sent per day in 2015 is up to 51.8 billion. Thus, taking measures to solve the spam problem is necessary and urgent.

© Springer International Publishing Switzerland 2016
Y. Tan and Y. Shi (Eds.): DMBD 2016, LNCS 9714, pp. 205–216, 2016.
DOI: 10.1007/978-3-319-40973-3_20

Machine learning based intelligent detection methods give promising performance in solving the spam problem, which can be seen as a typical binary categorization task. Machine learning techniques have been widely applied in spam classification, such as naive bayes [4–7], support vector machine [8–11], decision tree and boosting [12,13], k nearest neighbor [14–16], random forest [17,18], artificial neural network [19–22], deep learning [23,24] and so on. Besides classification technique, feature construction approach also plays an important role in spam detection, by transforming email samples into feature vectors for further utilization by machine learning methods. Feature construction approach determines the space distribution of email samples, affecting the establishment of classification model and detection performance. Effective feature construction approach could construct distinct and distinguishable features, resulting in different space distribution characteristics of different classes of email samples and complexity reduction of email classification. Research on email feature construction approaches has been focused in recent years.

In our previous work, a term space partition (TSP) based feature construction approach for spam detection [25] is proposed by taking inspiration from the distribution characteristics of terms with respect to feature selection metrics and the defined class tendency. Term ratio and term density are constructed on corresponding subspaces achieved by dividing the original term space and compose the feature vector. In this paper, we further propose an ensemble TSP (ETSP) based feature construction method for spam detection by taking both global and local features of emails into account in feature perspective. Variable-length sliding window technique is adopted for constructing local features. We conducted experiments on five benchmark corpora PU1, PU2, PU3, PUA and Enron to investigate performance of the proposed method. Accuracy and F_1 measure are selected as the main criteria in analyzing and discussing the results.

The rest of this paper is organized as follows: Sect. 2 introduces the TSP based feature construction approach. The proposed ETSP method is presented in Sect. 3. Section 4 gives the experimental results. Finally, we conclude the paper in Sect. 5.

2   Term Space Partition Based Feature Construction Approach

The TSP approach aims to establish a mechanism to make the terms play more sufficient and rational roles in spam detection by dividing the original term space into subspaces and designing corresponding feature construction strategy on each subspace, so as to improve the performance and efficiency of spam detection.

Since the feature selection metrics could give terms reasonable and effective goodness evaluation, the TSP approach first performs a vertical partition of the original term space to obtain the dominant term subspace and general term subspace according to the distribution characteristics of terms with respect to feature selection metrics. Dominant terms are given high and discriminative scores by feature selection metrics and considered to lead the categorization results. Though large amount of general terms congregate in a narrow range of the term space with similar low scores and each of them is less informative, they could contribute to spam detection integrally. The vertical partition could be performed by defining a threshold θ_{dg} with respect to the corresponding feature selection metrics employed, as shown in Eq. 1.

$$\theta_{dg} = \frac{1}{r}(\tau_{max} - \tau_{min}) + \tau_{min} \tag{1}$$

where τ_{max} and τ_{min} depict the highest and lowest evaluation of terms in the training set respectively, and variable r controls the restriction level of dominant terms. Term t_i with $\tau(t_i) \geq \theta_{dg}$ is considered as dominant term, and general term otherwise.

To construct discriminative features, a transverse partition is then performed to further divide each of the above subspaces into spam term subspace and ham term subspace according to the defined term class tendency. Term class tendency refers the tendency of a term occurring in emails of a certain class, defined as Eq. 2.

$$tendency(t_i) = P(t_i|c_h) - P(t_i|c_s) \tag{2}$$

where $P(t_i|c_h)$ is the probability of t_i's occurrence, given the email is ham, and $P(t_i|c_s)$ is the probability of t_i's occurrence, given the email is spam. Spam terms are terms that occur more frequently in spam than in ham with negative tendency, and ham terms occur more frequently in ham than in spam with positive tendency. When performing the transverse partition to separate spam terms and ham terms, terms with $tendency(t_i) = 0$ are considered useless and discarded.

In this case, the original term space is decomposed into four independent and non-overlapping subspaces, namely spam-dominant, ham-dominant, spam-general and ham-general subspaces. To construct discriminative and effective feature vectors of emails, term ratio and term density are defined on dominant terms and general terms respectively to make the terms play sufficient and rational roles in spam detection. Term ratio indicates the percentage of dominant terms that occur in the current email, emphasizing the absolute ratio of dominant terms. In this way, the contributions to spam detection from dominant terms are strengthened and not influenced by other terms. While term density represents the percentage of terms in the current email that are general terms, focusing on the relative proportion of terms in the current email that are general terms. The effect on spam detection from general terms is weakened and so is the affect from possible noisy terms. Equations 3 to 6 describe the definitions of spam term ratio, ham term ratio, spam term density and ham term density respectively.

$$TR_s = \frac{n_{sd}}{N_{sd}} \tag{3}$$

where n_{sd} is the number of distinct terms in the current email which are also contained in spam-dominant term space TS_{sd}, and N_{sd} is the total number of distinct terms in TS_{sd}.

$$TR_h = \frac{n_{hd}}{N_{hd}} \tag{4}$$

where n_{hd} is the number of distinct terms in the current email which are also contained in ham-dominant term space TS_{hd}, and N_{hd} is the total number of distinct terms in TS_{hd}.

$$TD_s = \frac{n_{sg}}{N_e} \tag{5}$$

where n_{sg} is the number of distinct terms in the current email which are also contained in spam-general term space TS_{sg}, and N_e is the total number of distinct terms in the current email.

$$TD_h = \frac{n_{hg}}{N_e} \tag{6}$$

where n_{hg} is the number of distinct terms in the current email which are also contained in ham-general term space TS_{hg}. The feature vector is achieved by combining the defined features, i.e. $v = <TR_s, TR_h, TD_s, TD_h>$.

3 Ensemble Feature Construction Using Term Space Partition Approach

3.1 Global and Local Features

For spam detection, feature construction approaches decide the spatial distribution of email samples. Effective feature construction approaches could construct distinguishable features of emails to make the spatial distribution of spam emails apparently different from that of legitimate emails. In the TSP approach, each email sample is transformed into an individual 4-dimensional feature vector, by calculating distribution characteristics of terms in the email on the four independent and non-overlapping subspaces of terms respectively. In other words, this feature vector reflects the term distribution characteristics of the whole email in the four different subspaces of terms, which could be called global features, for each dimension of the feature vector is related to and calculated from the whole email. Global features describe the overall characteristics of each email sample. In most cases, the global features constructed by the TSP approach could successfully characterize the differences between spam emails and legitimate emails. While it should also be noted that, for some specific email samples with particularly different term distribution characteristics in some local areas of the emails, the global features constructed by the TSP approach would make the distinctive features diluted and could not well reflect the differences.

In order to solve this problem, we adopt the sliding window technique to define local areas on the whole email and further extract local features of the email by constructing TSP features on each local area. The local features and global features are combined together to form the ensemble feature vector.

3.2 Construction of Local Features

Local features are constructed on local areas of samples. In the ETSP method, the sliding window is adopted to define local areas of emails. In this case, TSP

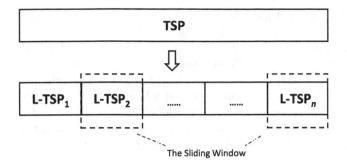

Fig. 1. Construction of local TSP feature with sliding window

features constructed on each local area could reflect independent term distribution features of each local area in the four different subspaces.

As shown in Fig. 1, independent local TSP (L-TSP) feature vector is calculated on each individual local area of the email, other than constructing global TSP feature vector on the whole email. Variable-length sliding windows are adopted to guarantee obtaining feature vectors with the same dimensionality to facilitate further use in the classification phase, for the size of email samples varies greatly. For a specific email with N_t terms, the length of corresponding sliding window utilized is defined as $\frac{N_t}{n}$, where n is constant for different email samples. To obtain independent and non-overlapping local areas, the window slides with a step of length of itself, which is $\frac{N_t}{n}$, from the beginning to the end of the email. In this case, each email is divided into n independent and non-overlapping local areas, and n individual L-TSP feature vectors are obtained. Hence, n is a core parameter during this process, determining both the granularity of local areas and dimensionality of the final feature vectors.

3.3   TSP Based Ensemble Feature Construction

Algorithm 1. Ensemble Feature Vector Construction

1: construct TSP feature vector on the given sample
2:
3: move a sliding window of $\frac{N_t}{n}$ terms over the given sample with a step of $\frac{N_t}{n}$ terms
4:
5: **for** each position i of the sliding window **do**
6:    construct TSP feature vector on the current local area
7: **end for**
8:
9: combine the achieved feature vectors together to form the final feature vector

---

Global features and local features tend to characterize samples from different perspectives, where global features describe the overall characteristics of each sample, while local features presents the local details. Global features and local features should play different but necessary roles in depicting and classifying samples. Therefore, ensemble feature vectors of emails are constructed by calculating TSP features on both the whole email and its local areas, as presented by Algorithm 1. Finally, the global feature vector and the local feature vectors are combined together to form the feature vector of the sample, i.e. $v = < TSP, L - TSP_1, L - TSP_2, \ldots, L - TSP_n >$.

4   Experiments

4.1   Experimental Setup

Experiments were conducted on PU1, PU2, PU3, PUA [26] and Enron-Spam [27], which are all benchmark corpora widely used for effectiveness evaluation in spam detection. Support vector machine (SVM) was employed as classifier in the experiments. WEKA toolkit [28] and LIBSVM [29] were utilized for implementation of SVM. 10-fold cross validation was utilized on PU corpora and 6-fold cross validation on Enron-Spam according to the number of parts each of the corpora has been already divided into. Accuracy and F_1 measure [30] are the main evaluation criteria, as they can reflect the overall performance of spam filtering.

4.2   Investigation of Parameters

Experiments have been conducted on PU1 to investigate the parameters of the ETSP approach by utilizing 10-fold cross validation. Besides the term selection parameter p and partition threshold parameter r in the TSP approach [25], the ETSP method has got an external parameter n, which determines the granularity of local areas those an sample is divided into and further the dimensionality of the corresponding feature vectors. Small n brings coarse-grained local areas and further low dimensionality of feature vectors, which may cause dilution of local features and could not describe the local details well. While large n may lead to incomplete and inaccurate representation of local features due to the meticulous partition of local areas, making the process of extracting local features meaningless.

Figure 2 shows the performance of ETSP under varied n, where information gain is selected as the representative feature selection metric. As is shown, the ETSP method achieves better performance with relatively smaller ns, and performs the best when $n = 2$ happens in the parameter investigation experiments, which meets our expectation well. For the specific problem of spam detection, the vast majority of email samples in the communication traffic are of relatively small lengths, no matter spam or legitimate emails, but with distinctive local characteristics of term distribution, especially spam.

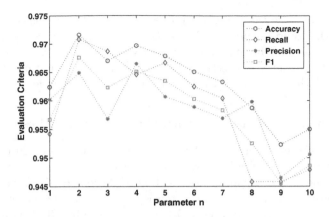

Fig. 2. Performance of ETSP under varied n

4.3 Performance with Different Feature Selection Metrics

In the TSP approach, vertical partition of the original term space is performed according to term evaluation given by feature selection metrics. Selection of appropriate feature selection metrics is also crucial to performance of the ETSP method. We selected document frequency (DF) and information gain (IG) as representatives of unsupervised and supervised feature selection metrics respectively to conduct verification experiments, which are widely used and perform well in spam detection and other text categorization issues [31].

Table 1. Performance of ETSP with different feature selection metrics

Corpus	Feature sel.	Precision (%)	Recall (%)	Accuracy (%)	F_1 (%)
PU1	DF	96.33	97.29	97.16	96.77
	IG	97.28	96.67	**97.34**	**96.95**
PU2	DF	93.95	89.29	**96.62**	**91.29**
	IG	93.87	84.29	95.63	88.23
PU3	DF	96.66	95.66	96.59	96.12
	IG	96.54	97.47	**97.29**	**96.97**
PUA	DF	96.50	96.67	**96.49**	**96.52**
	IG	96.58	94.91	95.70	95.67
Enron-Spam	DF	94.97	98.35	**97.32**	**96.57**
	IG	94.25	98.29	97.02	96.18

Performance of ETSP with respect to DF and IG on five benchmark corpora PU1, PU2, PU3, PUA and Enron-Spam is shown in Table 1. As the experimental results reveal, the ETSP method performs quite well with both DF and

IG, showing good adaptability with different kinds of feature selection metrics. Meanwhile, DF could outperform IG with ETSP as feature construction approach in more cases of the experiments, indicating that the transverse partition of the original term space is effective to make use of the information of term-class associations, as the supervised feature selection metrics provide.

4.4 Performance Comparison with Current Approaches

Experiments were conducted on PU1, PU2, PU3, PUA and Enron-Spam to verify the effectiveness of ETSP by comparing the performance with current approaches. The selected approaches are Bag-of-Words (BoW) [30], concentration based feature construction (CFC) approach [21,32], local concentration (LC) based feature construction approach [9,33] and the original TSP approach [25]. Tables 2, 3, 4, 5 and 6 shows the performance of each feature construction approach in spam detection when incorporated with SVM.

Among the selected approaches, BoW is a traditional and one of the most widely used feature construction approach in spam detection, while CFC and LC are heuristic and state-of-the-art approaches by taking inspiration from biological immune system. LC-FL and LC-VL utilize different local areas definition strategies. As we can see, ETSP far outperforms not only BoW, but also CFC and LC, in terms of both accuracy and F_1 measure. This strongly verifies the effectiveness of ETSP as a feature construction method in spam detection.

Table 2. Performance comparison of ETSP with current approaches on PU1

Approach	Precision (%)	Recall (%)	Accuracy (%)	F_1 (%)
BoW	93.96	95.63	95.32	94.79
CFC	94.97	95.00	95.60	94.99
LC-FL	95.12	96.88	96.42	95.99
LC-VL	95.48	96.04	96.24	95.72
TSP	96.90	96.67	97.16	96.74
ETSP	96.49	97.08	**97.34**	**96.95**

Table 3. Performance comparison of ETSP with current approaches on PU2

Approach	Precision (%)	Recall (%)	Accuracy (%)	F_1 (%)
BoW	88.71	79.29	93.66	83.74
CFC	95.12	76.43	94.37	84.76
LC-FL	90.86	82.86	94.79	86.67
LC-VL	92.06	86.43	95.63	88.65
TSP	94.09	83.57	95.63	88.12
ETSP	93.95	89.29	**96.62**	**91.29**

Table 4. Performance comparison of ETSP with current approaches on PU3

Approach	Precision (%)	Recall (%)	Accuracy (%)	F_1 (%)
BoW	96.48	94.67	96.08	95.57
CFC	96.24	94.95	96.05	95.59
LC-FL	95.99	95.33	96.13	95.66
LC-VL	95.64	95.77	96.15	95.67
TSP	96.37	97.09	97.05	96.69
ETSP	96.54	97.47	**97.29**	**96.97**

Table 5. Performance comparison of ETSP with current approaches on PUA

Approach	Precision (%)	Recall (%)	Accuracy (%)	F_1 (%)
BoW	92.83	93.33	92.89	93.08
CFC	96.03	93.86	94.82	94.93
LC-FL	96.01	94.74	95.26	95.37
LC-VL	95.60	94.56	94.91	94.94
TSP	95.91	96.49	96.05	96.11
ETSP	96.50	96.67	**96.49**	**96.52**

Table 6. Performance comparison of ETSP with current approaches on Enron-Spam

Approach	Precision (%)	Recall (%)	Accuracy (%)	F_1 (%)
BoW	90.88	98.87	95.13	94.62
CFC	91.48	97.81	95.62	94.39
LC-FL	94.07	98.00	96.79	95.94
LC-VL	92.44	97.81	96.02	94.94
TSP	94.29	98.21	97.02	96.14
ETSP	94.97	98.35	**97.32**	**96.57**

Compared with the original TSP, ETSP achieves not only better but also more balanced performance on different corpora in the experiments. This demonstrates that taking both global and local features into account in feature perspective could bring both better performance and better robustness. It is worth mentioning that ETSP could perform better than TSP mainly on some specific email samples with particularly different term distribution characteristics in some local areas of the emails. Thus, the performance improvement of ETSP approach compared with TSP approach could not be dramatically. The ETSP approach could be an alternative implementation strategy of TSP with better robustness.

In the experiments, we conducted parameter investigation on a small corpus and applied the selected group of parameter values on all the benchmark corpora with different sizes and email sample length distributions utilized for performance verification. From the experimental results, the ETSP method possess good parameter generalization ability and this further endows it with adaptivity in real world applications.

5 Conclusions

In this paper, a term space partition based ensemble feature construction method for spam detection was proposed by taking both global and local features into account in feature perspective. The experiments have shown: (1) utilization of sliding window successfully constructs local features of email samples; (2) the ETSP method cooperates well with different kinds of feature selection metrics and shows good parameter generalization ability, endowing it with flexible applicability in real world; (3) the ETSP method shows better performance and robustness by taking both global and local features into account during spam detection.

Acknowlegements. This work was supported by the Natural Science Foundation of China (NSFC) under grant no. 61375119 and the Beijing Natural Science Foundation under grant no. 4162029, and partially supported by National Key Basic Research Development Plan (973 Plan) Project of China under grant no. 2015CB352302.

References

1. Research, F.: Spam, spammers, and spam control: a white paper by ferris research. Technical report (2009)
2. Corporation, S.: Internet security threat report. Technical report (2016)
3. Cyren: Cyber threat report. Technical report (2016)
4. Sahami, M., Dumais, S., Heckerman, D., Horvitz, E.: A Bayesian approach to filtering junk e-mail. In: Learning for Text Categorization: Papers from the 1998 Workshop, vol. 62. AAAI Technical Report WS-98-05 98–105, Madison (1998)
5. Almeida, T., Almeida, J., Yamakami, A.: Spam filtering: how the dimensionality reduction affects the accuracy of naive bayes classifiers. J. Internet Serv. Appl. **1**(3), 183–200 (2011)
6. Zhong, Z., Li, K.: Speed up statistical spam filter by approximation. IEEE Trans. Comput. **60**(1), 120–134 (2011)
7. Trivedi, S.K., Dey, S.: Interaction between feature subset selection techniques and machine learning classifiers for detecting unsolicited emails. ACM SIGAPP Appl. Comput. Rev. **14**(1), 53–61 (2014)
8. Drucker, H., Wu, D., Vapnik, V.: Support vector machines for spam categorization. IEEE Trans. Neural Netw. **10**(5), 1048–1054 (1999)
9. Zhu, Y., Tan, Y.: A local-concentration-based feature extraction approach for spam filtering. IEEE Trans. Inf. Forensics Secur. **6**(2), 486–497 (2011)
10. Duan, L., Tsang, I.W., Xu, D.: Domain transfer multiple kernel learning. IEEE Trans. Pattern Anal. Mach. Intell. **34**(3), 465–479 (2012)
11. Li, C., Liu, M.: An ontology enhanced parallel SVM for scalable spam filter training. Neurocomputing **108**, 45–57 (2013)

12. Carreras, X., Marquez, L.: Boosting trees for anti-spam email filtering. Arxiv preprint cs/0109015 (2001)
13. DeBarr, D., Wechsler, H.: Spam detection using random boost. Pattern Recogn. Lett. **33**(10), 1237–1244 (2012)
14. Androutsopoulos, I., Paliouras, G., Karkaletsis, V., Sakkis, G., Spyropoulos, C., Stamatopoulos, P.: Learning to filter spam e-mail: a comparison of a naive Bayesian and a memory-based approach. Arxiv preprint cs/0009009 (2000)
15. Sakkis, G., Androutsopoulos, I., Paliouras, G., Karkaletsis, V., Spyropoulos, C., Stamatopoulos, P.: A memory-based approach to anti-spam filtering for mailing lists. Inf. Retr. **6**(1), 49–73 (2003)
16. Jiang, S., Pang, G., Wu, M., Kuang, L.: An improved k-nearest-neighbor algorithm for text categorization. Expert Syst. Appl. **39**(1), 1503–1509 (2012)
17. Koprinska, I., Poon, J., Clark, J., Chan, J.: Learning to classify e-mail. Inf. Sci. **177**(10), 2167–2187 (2007)
18. Amin, R., Ryan, J., van Dorp, J.R.: Detecting targeted malicious email. IEEE Secur. Priv. **10**(3), 64–71 (2012)
19. Clark, J., Koprinska, I., Poon, J.: A neural network based approach to automated e-mail classification. In: Proceedings. IEEE/WIC International Conference on Web Intelligence, 2003, WI 2003, pp. 702–705. IEEE (2003)
20. Wu, C.: Behavior-based spam detection using a hybrid method of rule-based techniques and neural networks. Expert Syst. Appl. **36**(3), 4321–4330 (2009)
21. Ruan, G., Tan, Y.: A three layer back-propagation neural network for spam detection using artificial immune concentration. Soft Comput. Fusion Found. Methodol. Appl. **14**(2), 139–150 (2010)
22. Li, C.H., Huang, J.X.: Spam filtering using semantic similarity approach and adaptive BPNN. Neurocomputing **92**, 88–97 (2012)
23. Mi, G., Gao, Y., Tan, Y.: Apply stacked auto-encoder to spam detection. In: Tan, Y., Shi, Y., Buarque, F., Gelbukh, A., Das, S., Engelbrecht, A. (eds.) ICSI-CCI 2015. LNCS, vol. 9141, pp. 3–15. Springer, Heidelberg (2015)
24. Gao, Y., Mi, G., Tan, Y.: Variable length concentration based feature construction method for spam detection. In: 2015 International Joint Conference on Neural Networks (IJCNN), pp. 1–7. IEEE (2015)
25. Mi, G., Zhang, P., Tan, Y.: Feature construction approach for email categorization based on term space partition. In: The 2013 International Joint Conference on Neural Networks (IJCNN), pp. 1–8. IEEE (2013)
26. Androutsopoulos, I., Paliouras, G., Michelakis, E.: Learning to filter unsolicited commercial e-mail. DEMOKRITOS, National Center for Scientific Research (2004)
27. Metsis, V., Androutsopoulos, I., Paliouras, G.: Spam filtering with naive bayes-which naive bayes. In: Third Conference on Email and Anti-spam (CEAS), vol. 17, pp. 28–69 (2006)
28. Hall, M., Frank, E., Holmes, G., Pfahringer, B., Reutemann, P., Witten, I.: The weka data mining software: an update. ACM SIGKDD Explor. Newsl. **11**(1), 10–18 (2009)
29. Chang, C., Lin, C.: LIBSVM: a library for support vector machines. ACM Trans. Intell. Syst. Technol. (TIST) **2**(3), 27 (2011)
30. Guzella, T., Caminhas, W.: A review of machine learning approaches to spam filtering. Expert Syst. Appl. **36**(7), 10206–10222 (2009)
31. Yang, Y., Pedersen, J.: A comparative study on feature selection in text categorization. In: Machine Learning-International Workshop Then Conference, pp. 412–420. Morgan Kaufmann Publishers, Inc. (1997)

32. Tan, Y., Deng, C., Ruan, G.: Concentration based feature construction approach for spam detection. In: International Joint Conference on Neural Networks, 2009, IJCNN 2009, pp. 3088–3093. IEEE (2009)
33. Zhu, Y., Tan, Y.: Extracting discriminative information from e-mail for spam detection inspired by immune system. In: 2010 IEEE Congress on Evolutionary Computation (CEC), pp. 1–7. IEEE (2010)

Information Extraction

Term Extraction from German Computer Science Textbooks

Kevin Möhlmann and Jörn Syrbe[✉]

Department of Computing Science, Carl von Ossietzky University of Oldenburg,
Ammerländer Heerstr. 114-118, 26129 Oldenburg, Germany
{kevin.moehlmann,joern.syrbe}@uni-oldenburg.de
https://www.uni-oldenburg.de/en/

Abstract. It is widely accepted that it is important to use a proper Computer Science terminology to communicate with other computer scientists. To learn Computer Science concepts students also need to speak about topics in school meaningfully. This article reports a method to identify German Computer Science terms for teaching from a set of German textbooks and web pages. It identifies future work to create a suitable German Computer Science Education terminology.

Keywords: Computer Science Education · Terminology · Text mining · Term extraction · Reference analysis

1   Introduction

During everyday school life students use different terminologies. Each school subject uses a characteristic terminology. These characteristic terms are used in spoken and written language. Computer Science Education (CSE) classes are no exception, students "need specific terms to communicate about topics of our science in class and also outside in everyday life" [1]. The most national school curricular claim that students need to use a proper human language/terminology for learning Computer Science (CS) concepts. Without an understanding of CS terms students are hardly able to adapt CS concepts in action (cf. [3]).

In 2015 Diethelm and Goschler reflected on the meaning of terminology in CS classes and explained the importance of language skills (cf. [1]). They formulated different general questions related to CSE and its terminology. Above other, they formulated the following question:

"What is a suitable set of terms and definitions for CS teaching for introducing and applying a certain concept in CS classes?" [1]

At first sight national CSE curricular and CS dictionaries are helpful to identify potential topics or terms, but their content is very heterogeneous and may not help us to define CSE terms. This depends, for instance, on different school-based competence definitions, school types, age groups and educational

© Springer International Publishing Switzerland 2016
Y. Tan and Y. Shi (Eds.): DMBD 2016, LNCS 9714, pp. 219–226, 2016.
DOI: 10.1007/978-3-319-40973-3_21

regulations. The example of Germany demonstrates the complexity of educational frameworks: Each German federal state (there are 16 federal states in Germany) has more or less, but at least one CSE curriculum. Each of these curricular describes competences or CS skills but they do not describe school content/terms in detail, define them or describe the requirements of language in class (cf. [1]).

Another source of terms are different CS dictionaries. They are editorial and contain CS terms and definitions, but in general they are not approved for CS teaching. To create a suitable dictionary, as introduced by Kim and Cavedon (cf. [4]), by using terms from different web pages like `wikipedia.org` we may not achieve terms for CS teaching.

To create a German CSE terminology we apply a difference analysis to identify terms from a text corpus. The initial corpus consists of 40 German textbooks and content from 10 German CSE web pages (cf. http://www.uni-oldenburg.de/informatik/ddi/personen/dipl-inform-joern-syrbe/korpus/).

These textbooks are made available from the German publishers: Herdt-Verlag, DUDEN PAETEC Verlag, Oldenborg Schulbuch Verlag and Ernst-Klett-Verlag.

Our method to extract technical terms is described in Sect. 2. An evaluation of our first results is presented in Sect. 3. We will then discuss our findings in Sect. 4 and will finish with an outlook in Sect. 5 to find a suitable set of German CSE terms.

2 Methods

For the purpose of detecting technical terms in a text corpus we apply a method called "difference analysis". This method compares two text corpora in order to determine the words which occur at a significantly higher frequency in one of these corpora. The text corpus, in which we want to detect technical terms, consists of a number of school texts about computer science. We call this corpus the analysis corpus. Since this corpus consists of texts about computer science we are looking for technical terms in the field of computer science. The second text corpus, which we compare against the analysis corpus, is composed of thousands of newspaper articles and is supposed to be general-language. This corpus is called the reference corpus.

The method is based on the underlying assumption that technical terms occur more frequently in technical texts than in common language texts. Since not all words which occur more frequently in technical texts than in the general language are necessarily technical, we speak of potential technical terms. The efficacy of the difference analysis for detecting technical terms is measured as the ratio of the number of actual technical terms to the number of all words which occur more frequently in our analysis corpus than in our reference corpus.

Our approach is based on the description of the difference analysis in [2]. For the Performing of the difference analysis it is necessary to determine the frequency of occurrence for each word of the analysis corpus in both corpora. Each word is then classified into one of four classes as follows:

1. Words which occur relatively less frequently in the analysis corpus than in the reference corpus.
2. Words which occur approximately the same number in both corpora.
3. Words which occur relatively more frequently in the analysis corpus than in the reference corpus.
4. Words which occur in the analysis, but not in the reference corpus.

The classes 3 and 4 are relevant for the detection of technical terms. Whereas no further steps are needed for words of class 4, we need to define a threshold for words of class 3. This threshold specifies the border between words of class 2 and class 3. It defines when a word belongs to the resulting set of potential technical terms. In order to get this resulting set, we have to compare a word of the analysis corpus with the same of the reference corpus. We accomplish that by determining the ratio between this word and the word which occurs most frequently in the text corpus. More precisely, we determine for each word a certain value, which is called the "frequency category". The frequency category of a word w is calculated by the following formula:

$$FC(w) = \lfloor log_2 \frac{|w_{max}|}{|w|} \rfloor. \tag{1}$$

In this formula $|w|$ stands for the frequency of occurrence of the word w. $|w_{max}|$ is the frequency of occurrence of the most frequent word of the text corpus. For each word of the analysis corpus which occurs also in the reference corpus we calculate the above formula twice, once for the analysis corpus and once for the reference corpus. The resulting frequency category is an integer starting with 0. A low value of the frequency category of a word w indicates that the w occurs frequently in the text corpus.

To determine if a word w with the frequency category $FC_{ana}(w)$ of the analysis corpus and the frequency category $FC_{ref}(w)$ of the reference corpus belongs to the resulting set of the potential technical terms we now just need to define a threshold. This threshold is a factor f. A word belongs to the resulting set if for the threshold the following applies:

$$FC_{ana}(w) \cdot f <= FC_{ref}(w). \tag{2}$$

The threshold has to be greater than zero. Otherwise every word of the analysis corpus belongs to the resulting set. This threshold is the only variable that affects the ratio of technical terms to non-technical terms in the difference analysis.

3 Results

We had an analysis corpus with a size of 1,627,382 words and a reference corpus with a size of 131,195,951 words. We conducted the difference analysis for different values of the threshold f. For increasing values of the threshold we expected a decreasing number of potential technical terms which were identified by the difference analysis. Actually we obtained the following results (Table 1):

Table 1. Potential technical words

Threshold f	Number of potential technical words
2	32,410
4	31,945
8	31,942
16	31,942
32	31,942

As shown in the table a value larger than eight always results in the same number of identified potential technical words. This is because all of these 31,942 words just occur in the analysis corpus. They are therefor words of the class 4 and belong independently of their frequency categories to the resulting set.

Since we are looking for technical terms we are interested in the resulting set which has the highest ratio of the number of technical terms to the total number of all words of the set. Therefor we examine the resulting set more closely which we obtained with a threshold of eight or greater.

To gain the ratio of technical terms to to all words of the resulting set we determine for a collection of 100 random words whether they are technical or not. We consider a word to be technical in the field of computer science if this word has a specific meaning within computer science. In the collection obtained with a threshold of eight we found 46 technical terms. Hence, approximately 46 % of the words can be regarded as technical terms. But this ratio can be increased with the following steps.

Lower Bound for the Frequency of Occurrence

Of the 31,942 words of the resulting set 17,363 words occur only once in the analysis corpus. The unique occurrence of a word can often be explained with spelling mistakes. Therefor we reduce the resulting set of the potential technical terms by every word which occurs only once in the analysis corpus. The new set consists of 14,579 words. Again we determine the ratio of technical terms to all words with a random selection of 100 words. Now we have 50 technical terms so that 50 % of the words of the resulting set can be regarded as technical. This is just an improvement by four percentage points. It is obvious that this heuristic not only removes non-technical terms but also actual technical terms. However, we apply this heuristic because we aim for a high proportion of technical terms.

No Punctuation Characters and Digits

Many words of the resulting set are not proper words. We find URLs, file names and parts of source code, which we sometimes can easily identify by the full-stop operator. To remove these non-technical terms we ban all words which include digits or punctuation characters. The only punctuation character we allow is the hyphen. With this approach we reduce the set by 833 words to 13,746 words while the ratio of technical terms to all words increases by seven percentage points to 57 %. Compared to the lower bound we achieved with this method a bigger growth in the ratio of technical terms to all words by a less decrease of the total number of words in the resulting set.

List of Verbs

Stop words and other general-language words are supposed to occur approximately the same proportion in both corpora. Thus, these words are classified into class 2 and will not be included into the resulting set. Some verbs however occur in the resulting set because they are used in the analysis corpus, but not in the reference corpus. In order to remove these verbs from the resulting set we assembled a list of all German verbs and their inflections by means of the website http://www.verbformen.de/. With this list we are able to reduce the resulting set again. The number of potential technical terms decreases by 288 words from 13,746 to 13,458. But the ratio of technical terms to all words increases by two percentage points to 59 %.

As shown in Fig. 1 the improvements cause a change in the ratio of technical terms to all words and also in the number of words in the resulting set. The ratio of technical terms to all words raises by 13 % percentage points, while concurrently the number of words in the resulting set decreases from 31,942 to 13,458. This means that the number of words reduces by almost 58 %. In Fig. 1 the steps 1 to 4 refer to the resulting sets which we gained by execution of the difference analysis, by applying a lower bound for the frequency of occurrence, by removing all words with punctuation characters or digits and by removing all verbs from the resulting set.

A selection of potential CS terms we identified are presented in Table 2.

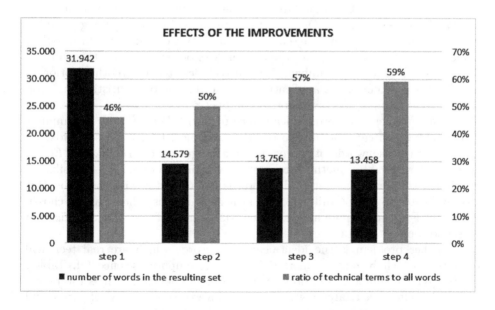

Fig. 1. Effects of the improvements

Table 2. Selection of potential German CSE terms

$F(w)$	German	English translation
725	Klassendiagramm	Class diagram
524	Datentyp	Data type
488	OOP	Abbr.: object oriented programming
440	Attributwerte	Attribute value
435	Konstruktor	Constructor
417	Bezeichner	Identifier
382	Struktogramm	Structure chart
341	Primärschlüssel	Primary key
333	SELECT	Select
341	Datenelement	Data element
246	Fremdschüssel	Foreign key
241	Anforderungsdefinition	Requirements definition
148	Schl	Schl
126	DBMS	DBMS
125	PROLOG	Prolog
120	Ampel	Traffic light

Left Problems

Table 2 demonstrates that some problems still need to get solved to get a better quality of the resulting set. One problem, that remains, are spelling mistakes that occur more often than once (cf. Table 2 *Schl*). We can manage this problem by increasing the lower bound for the frequency of occurrence. But this will also result in a loss of a great number of actual technical terms. Another option to manage this problem is the application of a normalization heuristics based on stemming algorithms, which we motivate in Sect. 5.

Another problem are words which belong to the field of expertise of computer science, but which can not be considered as technical terms. These words, for example, can be keywords of a programming language (cf. Table 2 *SELECT*), identifiers for variables, methods or pseudo code instructions. It is possible to remove the keywords by a list of all keywords like we did it with the verbs. But it is impossible to have a full list of all identifiers because these can be chosen arbitrarily. For that, a more advanced heuristic is needed (e.g. the identification of pseudo code with regular expressions).

A further problem is the identification of words which are real technical terms, but which belong to another field than computer science (cf. Table 2 *Ampel*). With a simple comparison of the words frequencies, as it is the procedure of the difference analysis, we can not remove these terms. A solution could be a clustering of words [2] or the inspection of the words co-occurrences [2] to determine the affinity to one or another field of expertise. It is also worth mentioning that even with a small threshold factor many technical terms which are used in the analysis corpus do not get into the resulting set. These terms also occur in the reference corpus frequently. Also we have to underline the fact that the most words of the resulting set occur in different inflections, like singular or plural forms. Hence we have to consider how we can remove redundant words.

4   Conclusion

With the difference analysis it is possible to detect technical terms in a text corpus. But the resulting set of words contains too many words which are not technical. Without improvements roughly every second word is not a technical term. We were able to increase the ratio of technical terms to all words of this set by applying various heuristics. But this increase has been at the expense of words which are actually technical. Especially a lower bound for the frequency of occurrence reduces the number of words and technical terms in the resulting set significantly. In order to minimize the amount of unintentionally removed technical terms it is, therefor, necessary to increase the frequency of occurrence of each technical term. This can only be achieved by extending the analysis corpus.

But also the reference corpus is too small although it is more than 80 times larger than the analysis corpus. All words of the resulting set which we obtained with a threshold of eight or greater just occurred in the analysis corpus. To compare the frequency of occurrence of a technical term with its frequency of occurrence in the common language it is required that the term also occurs in the reference corpus, which is used in the difference analysis. Only this way we get a meaningful result. Otherwise the technical term belongs independently of its frequency category to the resulting set of potential technical terms. So, with a much bigger reference corpus we expect also for threshold factors larger than eight a decreasing number of words in the resulting set. This would allow us to specifies a stricter threshold.

Despite all applied heuristics 41 % of the words of the resulting set are not technical. To reduce this percentage further improvements are necessary. Also we need to find a solution for finding technical terms which were not identified by the difference analysis.

5   Outlook

With the lower bound for the frequency of occurrence of a word we not just remove spelling mistakes, but also a lot of actual technical terms. This is because many technical terms only occur very rarely or they occur in different inflections. A Solution, proposed in [5], could be the inflectional stemming. This method has the goal to eliminate variations of one and the same word. An inflected word is supposed to be mapped on its uninflected version. This would result in higher frequencies of all words which occur in the text corpus more than in one inflection.

For detecting technical terms we have to look for nouns, because verbs or adjectives rarely represent a technical term. Another method that is proposed in [5] is the part-of-speech tagging. This method allows to recognize nouns or other word classes. Thus, it allows us in both text corpora to reduce the number of words to nouns before we even start with the difference analysis. A reliable part-of-speech tagging would render unnecessary lists of words, like the verbs list we used in Sect. 3, and it would reject even more words which can not be technical.

Big problems are also caused by code fragments which are used in texts of the analysis corpus. These fragments contain identifiers of variables and methods which, after all improvements, still can be found frequently in the resulting set of potential technical terms. To remove these identifiers from the resulting set we could need an approach that is able of identifying and eliminating code fragments from given texts. Such an approach could exploit the fact that all programming languages follow a strict syntax. A heuristic that is able to detect parts of code would remove these from all texts of the analysis corpus before we actually assemble the corpus.

In this article we applied a known technique to extract terms from a corpus of German textbooks. With this technique and some further heuristics we received a set of terms from German CSE textbooks. This set of terms can be considered as a starting point to create an appropriate dictionary for CSE terminology. Now we need to improve the method by additional techniques.

References

1. Diethelm, I., Goschler, J.: Questions on spoken language and terminology for teaching computer science. In: ITiCSE 2015, Vilnius (2015)
2. Heyer, G., Quasthoff, U., Wittig, T.: Text Mining: Wissensrohstoff Text: Konzepte, Algorithmen, Ergebnisse. W3L GmbH, Herdecke (2012). Second reprint edition
3. Holmboe, C.: Conceptualization and labelling as cognitive challenges for students of data modelling. Comput. Sci. Educ. **15**(2), 143–161 (2005). http://dx.doi.org/10.1080/08993400500150796
4. Kim, S.N., Cavedon, L.: Classify domain-specific terms using a dictionary. In: Proceedings of the ALTA (2011)
5. Weiss, S.M., Indurkhya, N., Zhang, T.: Fundamentals of Predictive Text Mining, 1st edn, pp. 13–39. Springer, London (2010)

An FW-DTSS Based Approach for News Page Information Extraction

Leiming Ma and Zhengyou Xia$^{(\boxtimes)}$

College of Computer Science and Technology,
Nanjing University of Aeronautics and Astronautics, Nanjing 211106, China
Mlm19910311@163.com, xiazhengyou@nuaa.edu.cn

Abstract. Automatically identifying and extracting main text from a news page becomes a critical task in many web content analysis applications with the explosive growth of News information. However, body contents are usually covered by presentation elements, such as dynamic flashing logos, navigational menus and a multitude of ad blocks. In this paper, we have proposed a function word (FW) based approach which involves the concept of DOM tree structure similarity (DTSS). Function words are the word that have no real meaning but semantic or functional meaning. Experiment statistics show that function words emerge a lot in main text, while they don't appear or appear just once or twice in presentation elements. Our approach involves three separate stages. Stage 1 is learning stages. In stage 2, the number of function words in each paragraph is counted and then the paragraph having the most function words is chosen to be the sample. In stage 3, all body paragraphs are extracted according to their similarity with the sample paragraph in DOM tree structure. Experiments results on real world data show that the FW-DTSS based approach is excellent in efficiency and accuracy, compared with that of statistics-based and Vision-based approaches.

Keywords: News information extraction · Function word · DOM tree · DOM tree structure similarity

1 Introduction

With the advance of News information online as well as the blooming of Internet, Internet turns into the most widely information source. Then traditional News reading model has changed, and it is the first choice to more and more people reading News on the internet. In the work of Gibson et al. [1], they estimate that layout presentation elements constitute 40 % to 50 % of all internet content and this volume has been increasing approximately 6 % yearly. In recent years, large numbers of researches have addressed this problem and many important researches have been put forward. Differentiated by their scopes, these works can be categorized into three methods, which are DOM (Document Object Model) based, vision-based and statistics based:

(a) DOM-based segmentation approaches [2–4] need construct the DOM tree structure from the HTML source of the news page and then do extraction operation. The news page needs firstly to be transferred to normalized XHTML and built to a

© Springer International Publishing Switzerland 2016
Y. Tan and Y. Shi (Eds.): DMBD 2016, LNCS 9714, pp. 227–234, 2016.
DOI: 10.1007/978-3-319-40973-3_22

DOM tree. Thus target contents are fetched by HTML tags. However, Such DOM tree processing tasks are time-consuming and is not suitable for explosive news sources.

(b) Vision-based page segmentation (VIPS) [5–7] is an approach based on the characteristics of human vision. It firstly extracts all the suitable nodes from the DOM tree. After that, it makes full use of page layout features such as font, color and size to find the separators, which denotes the horizontal or vertical lines in a web page that visually do not cross any node. However, large amounts of computations are needed in this kind of algorithm to analyze the web page, besides, the algorithm has inherent dependence on the data sources.

(c) Statistics-based segmentation approaches [8] don't concentrate on detailed structure of news pages but aim to extract main text from large chunks of HTML code through large training sets. It uses statistics methods to save time, but such methods doesn't keep accuracy.

In this paper, An FW-DTSS based approach is designed that integrates the concepts of DOM tree structure similarity (DTSS) with the function words' characteristic of a news page. Our approach is based on a practical observation that function words emerge a lot in main text while don't appear or appear just once or twice in presentation elements. Chinese lexicon are mainly divided into two categories which are function and content words. Function words are the word that have no real meaning but semantic or functional meaning that include adverb, preposition, conjunction, auxiliary word, interjection and mimetic word [9, 10]. According to our statistical results, function words usually appear with high probability in the body contents. In this paper, sample paragraphs of news pages should firstly be fetched. After that, all the target paragraphs would be fetched based on the fact that all the body paragraphs share similar DOM tree structures.

2 FW-DTSS Based Approach

The FW-DTSS based approach we propose in this paper can extract target texts higher efficiency and better accuracy. The main tasks are (1) to extract the sample paragraph by counting for the number of function words occurred in every paragraph; (2) to extract all body paragraphs according to their similarity in DOM tree structure.

2.1 Code Preprocessing

In today's information storage and retrieval applications, the growth in presentation elements increases difficulty in extracting relevant content. For example, tokens, phrases, extraction results, those presentation elements need to be removed, as shown below:

(1) Get the text between the pair of <BODY> tags;
(2) Delete all blank lines and redundant white-spaces;
(3) Delete HTML tags listed in Table 1 from the paper of Bu et al. [18], because the contents between which are always noise information.

Table 1. Some useless tags in HTML source files

Useless HTML tags
\<head\>,\<script\>,\<noscript\>,\<style\>,\<meta\>,\<!--\>,\<param\>,\<button\>,\<select\>,\<opt group\>,\<option\>,\<label\>,\<textarea\>,\<fieldset\>,\<legend\>,\<input\>,\<image\>,\<map\>, \<area\>,\<form\>,\<iframe\>,\<embed\>,\<object\>,\<link\>

(4) All HTML tags must be nested and matched, that is, they must be the structure like \<A\>...\<B\>...\</B\>...\</A\>.
(5) Read one line from top to bottom of HTML source, and add \<text\> before text information, and add \</text\> finally when all text information is read.
(6) Replace all tags between \<text\> and \</text\> with " ".

After the above steps, we obtain normalized web page HTML source with less noise information. For convenience, we regard all texts including very short one between \<text\> and \</text\> as paragraphs.

2.2 Feature Extraction

Main texts of a News page are usually divided into several long and short paragraphs where many function words appears frequently, while function words appears in short presentation elements in a low probability. To prove our assumption, we performs a statistical analysis that precision, recall and F-measure of the paragraphs having at least i function words which belongs to body paragraphs on 10000 News pages including Sina news, Xinhua net, CCTV news and so on based on function words table in Table 2 from Quan et al. [11], and the results are in Fig. 1.

In Fig. 1, precision of the paragraphs, which have at least 3 function words, belonging to body paragraphs is 99.23 %, and the more function words a paragraph has, the higher precision it is a body paragraph according to the figure. Recall of the paragraphs, which have at least 3 function words, belonging to body paragraphs is 98.02 %, that is, 9802 ones in these 10000 news pages have paragraphs including at least 3 function words. We did an another experiment to prove our assumption further. We firstly fetched the paragraphs having the largest number of function words in these 10000 news pages. And the probability of these paragraphs belonging to body paragraphs is 99.84 %. Thus we can draw the conclusion that the paragraph having the largest number of function words has a high possibility to be body paragraph.

3 Experiment and Analysis

3.1 Crossover-Randomized Experiment

We chose 10 mainstream news sites including Sina news, Xinhua net, CCTV news and so on, then we random fetched 1000 news pages in each site. To ensure the experiment

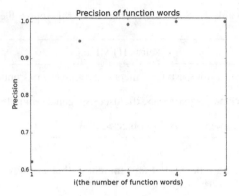

(a) Precision of function words

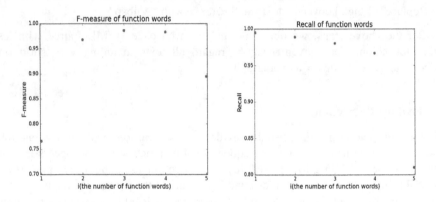

(b) Recall of function words;　(c) F-measure of function words

Fig. 1. Precision, recall and F-measure of the paragraphs having at least i function words

Table 2. Experiment results on 5 test news sites

	Fenghuang	Chinanews	Cankaoxiaoxi	Zhonghua	Yangshi
Precision	100%	100%	100%	100%	100%
Recall	100%	100%	96.2%	100%	100%
F-measure	100%	100%	98.1%	100%	100%

randomness, training set consists of 5000 news page from 5 mainstream news sites, while test set consists of 5000 news page from the other 5 mainstream news sites. Specifically, there are two stages here. Stage 1 is from step 1 to step 5. Stage 2 is in step 6, which exchange the training and test sets and carry out all steps above again.

- Step 1: To all the 5000 training sets extracted already, preprocess the codes according to Sect. 3.1. Then record the normalized web page HTML sources and label them from 1 to 5000 to make sure that every page is independent.

- Step 2: To every normalized news page in the training set, read the HTML source codes row by row, and record all the chains from root <html> to leaf <text>. The record is shown in Fig. 2, all 5000 pages are recorded like this.

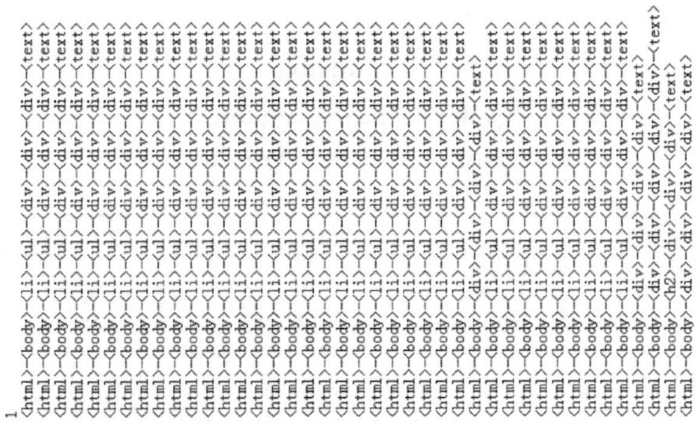

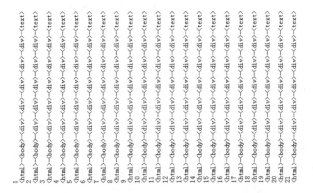

Fig. 2. Root-to leaf chains of training set

- Step 3: Calculate the number of function words between <text> and </text>, the paragraph with the largest number of function words is chosen to be the sample paragraph. Record the root-to-leaf chain of the sample paragraph. The chains of sample paragraph record are shown in Fig. 3, all chains of sample paragraphs in 5000 pages are recorded like this.

Fig. 3. Root-to-leaf chains of sample paragraphs

- Step 4: To all paragraphs of every news page in training set, calculate their indexes of DOM tree structure similarity with sample paragraph according to formula 1. The threshold is then selected so that the news page information extraction in this training set is optimal. Corresponding results are shown in Fig. 4 when different thresholds are set. We can see from the figure, it is optimal when the threshold is set

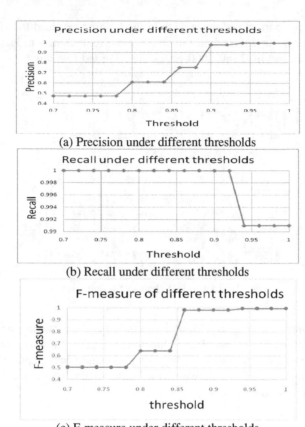

(a) Precision under different thresholds

(b) Recall under different thresholds

(c) F-measure under different thresholds

Fig. 4. Experiment result of 5000 test sets

to be 0.95 as F-measure is the highest. The corresponding precision, recall and F-measure of 5000 test sets are 100 %, 99.3 % and 99.6 %

- Step 5: According to the threshold set in step 4, experiment on 5000 test set is done to and the result on different news sites is shown in Table 3. And the precision, recall and F-measure of total 5000 test sets are 100 %, 99.3 % and 99.6 % when the threshold is 0.94. From the results we can draw a conclusion that the FW-DTSS method is excellent in efficiency and accuracy.

Table 3. Experiment results on 5 test news sites

	Sina	Xinhua	Sohu	Tengxun	Hao123
Precision	97.3%	100%	100%	100%	100%
Recall	100%	100%	100%	94.3%	100%
F-measure	98.6%	100%	100%	97.1%	100%

– Step 6: To ensure accuracy and randomness, exchange training sets and test set and carry out all steps above, the result is shown in Fig. 5 and Table 3. And the precision, recall and F-measure of total 5000 exchanged test sets are 99.2 %, 99.1 % and 99.1 % when the threshold is 0.95. From the results we can draw a conclusion that the FW-DTSS method is excellent in efficiency and accuracy.

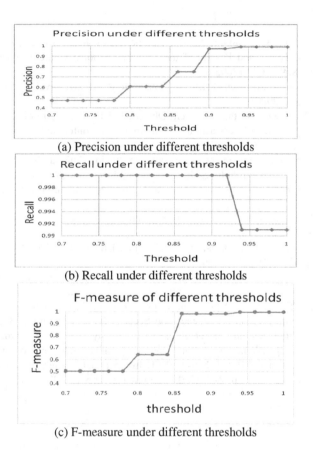

(a) Precision under different thresholds

(b) Recall under different thresholds

(c) F-measure under different thresholds

Fig. 5. Experiment result of 5000 exchanged test sets

4   Conclusion

In this paper we have proposed an FW-DTSS based approach to extract the main text content from web pages, which involves the following two steps: (1) to fetch the sample paragraph by counting for function words occurred in every paragraph. (2) To fetch the all body paragraphs according to their similarity in DOM tree structure. In order to complete the steps, our experiment has three Stages. Stage 1 is learning stage, where the original HTML source needs necessary preprocessing and function words' features in main text are extracted. In Stage 2, similar preprocessing is performed on testing sets, after that, the paragraph which has most function words is chosen to be the sample paragraph. In Stage 3, all the paragraphs' feature in DOM tree structure are extracted, according to which all body paragraphs are fetched and they are the target main texts of News pages.

References

1. Gibson, D., Punera, K., Tomkins, A.: The volume and evolution of web page templates. In: Special Interest Tracks and Posters of the 14th International Conference on World Wide Web, pp. 830–839. ACM (2005)
2. World Wide Web Consortium: Document Object Model (DOM) Level 2 Specification. W3C Recommendation (2000)
3. Chakrabarti, S.: Integrating the Document Object Model with hyperlinks for enhanced topic distillation and information extraction. In: International Conference on World Wide Web, WWW 2001, pp. 211–220 (2001)
4. Koch, P.P.: The document object model: an introduction. Digital Web Magazine (2001). http://www.digital-web.com/articles/the_document_object_model/
5. Li, D.: Visual communication and design performance research for webpage. Henan University (2009)
6. Deng, C., Yu, S., Wen, J.: VIPS: A Vision-based Page segmentation. Microsoft Technical Report, MSR-TR-203-79 (2003)
7. He, Z., Gu, J., Yang, J.: Information extraction of BBS posting based on vision feature. Comput. Appl. **29**, 171–174 (2009)
8. Alexjc: The easy way to extract useful text from arbitrary HTML (2007). http://ai-depot.com/articles/the-easy-way-to-extractuseful-text-fromarbitrary-html/
9. Zhang, J., Ya, T.: A study of the identification of authorship for Chinese texts. In: IEEE International Conference on Intelligence and Security Informatics, pp. 263–264 (2008)
10. Ding, J.: Existential state and presentation of Chinese style. Rhetoric Learn. **3**, 1–6 (2006)
11. Quan, S., Zhan, B., Zheng, Y: Authentication of online authorship or article based on hypothesis testing model. In: The 14th IEEE International Conference on Computational Science and Engineering, pp. 3–8. IEEE Computer Society (2011)

A Linear Regression Approach to Multi-criteria Recommender System

Tanisha Jhalani[1], Vibhor Kant[1(✉)], and Pragya Dwivedi[2]

[1] The LNMIIT, Jaipur 302031, India
tanishajhalani75@gmail.com, vibhor.kant@gmail.com
[2] MNNIT Allahbad, Allahbad 211004, India
pragya.dwijnu@gmail.com

Abstract. Recommender system (RS) is a web personalization tool for recommending appropriate items to users based on their preferences from a large set of available items. Collaborative filtering (CF) is the most popular technique for recommending items based on the preferences of similar users. Most of the CF based RSs work only on the overall rating of the items, however, the overall rating is not a good representative of user preferences for an item. Our work in this paper, is an attempt towards incorporating of various criteria ratings into CF i.e., multi-criteria CF, for enhancing its accuracy through multi-linear regression. We suggest the use of multi-linear regression for determining the weights of individual criterion and computing the overall ratings of each item. Experimental results reveal that the proposed approach outperforms the classical approaches.

Keywords: Recommender systems · Collaborative filtering · Multi-criteria decision making · Linear regression

1 Introduction

During last decade, information is expanding tremendously. Instead of helping the users, this great amount of information caused the problem of information overload. To handle this explosive growth of information, a personalization tool is needed that can assist a user to get the valid and appropriate information. Recommender system (RS) is one of the most successful personalization tools that guides a user to select an appropriate item from a large set of alternatives [1,2].

Generally, recommender system employs three major filtering techniques, namely, collaborative filtering (CF), content-based filtering (CBF) and hybrid filtering (HF). Among these techniques, collaborative filtering is widely used in the recommender system. Most of the existing RSs are based on the single criterion collaborative filtering [3,4], In a single criterion CF, only overall rating of item is considered, but the overall rating of an item depends on the different criteria. So instead of considering only single criterion, multiple criteria are should be used in multi-criteria CF [3,5]. In heuristic approaches of MCCF, all criteria have same priorities, but this is not an optimal scenario because different users have different priorities on various criteria, so in [3,9], it was suggested

© Springer International Publishing Switzerland 2016
Y. Tan and Y. Shi (Eds.): DMBD 2016, LNCS 9714, pp. 235–243, 2016.
DOI: 10.1007/978-3-319-40973-3_23

that weights on these criteria can be computed using either some machine learning techniques or any appropriate statistical techniques. Based on the above discussion, the contributions of our paper can be summarized as follows:

- First of all, we propose the use of multi linear regression approach for deriving the individual weight for each criterion.
- Second, we aggregate similarities and ratings for different criteria using these weights.
- Third, we perform rigorous experiments, on very popular and large Yahoo movie dataset by varying the number of users and compare our approach with various benchmark algorithms for single criterion and multi-criteria CF.

The rest of this paper is organized as follows: Sect. 2 describes background related to MCCF and multi linear regression. In Sect. 3, we have discussed proposed approach. Section 4 shows experimental evaluation of our proposed approach. Finally, last Section provides some concluding remarks.

2   Background and Related Work

This section briefly describes collaborative filtering for multi-criteria and multi linear regression.

2.1   Multi-criteria Recommender System

In multi-criteria RS, user rates various criteria of an item. The complete process of multi-criteria CF can be summarized into the following three phases:

- **Phase 1 (Similarity computation):** In this phase, first multi-criteria data set is divided into k single criterion datasets (where k is the number of criteria) and then similarities are computed for each criterion separately using some similarity measures like Pearson correlation and cosine similarity [3]. Now, overall similarity is computed using any aggregation function [10,11] which is expressed as follows :

$$Sim_{aggregate}(u, u') = \sum_{c=0}^{k} w_c sim_c(u, u') \tag{1}$$

where, w_c is the weight of each criterion. In the above equation, if weights are same for all criteria, like $w_1 = w_2 = w_3 = ... = w_k$ then aggregation function is similar to the average of similarities [3]. But this technique is not appropriate for aggregation because weights may be different for each criterion and it is a challenge to find these weights. Therefore, we use multi linear regression for computing these weights for various criterion.
- **Phase 2 (Neighborhood generation):** After computing similarities between active user and remaining users, neighborhood set is formed as a collection of similar users either using nearest neighbor approach (Top N users) or threshold based approach.

– **Phase 3 (Prediction of unknown rating):** In this phase, unknown rating is predicted for each criterion separately using following prediction function [7,12]:

$$r_{u,i}^p = \frac{1}{\sum_{u' \in U_t} |Sim(u, u')|} \sum_{u' \in U_t} Sim(u, u') \times r_{u',i} \qquad (2)$$

Now, these ratings are aggregated and overall rating is predicted for the users [12,13].

2.2 Multi Linear Regression

Linear regression is a statistical technique for finding the relationship between a dependent variable Y and independent variable X [14,15]. If independent variable is one then it is called simple linear regression and in case of more than one independent variables it is known as multi linear regression. Multi linear regression can be represented as follows:

$$Y = w_0 + w_1 x_1 + w_2 x_2 + ... + w_k x_k \qquad (3)$$

where, Y is called as dependent variables and $x_1, x_2, ..., x_k$ are independent variables. $w_0, w_1, w_2, ..., w_k$ are the weight parameters corresponding to independent variables which are computed on the basis of some observations. In proposed approach, multi linear regression is used to find the weights for different criteria.

3 Proposed Recommendation Approach

This section describes the proposed multi-criteria recommender system utilizing the concept of multi linear regression. Multi linear regression is used to aggregate the similarities and to find the overall ratings by using weights for each criterion. Before presenting our proposed approach, we discuss about the inputs required for our system. For multi-criteria RS, Let $U = \{u_1, u_2, u_3, ..., u_n\}$ be the set of n users , $I = \{i_1, i_2, i_3, ..., i_m\}$ is the set of m items. and $C = \{c_1, c_2, c_3, ..., c_k\}$ is the set of k criteria. The rating vectors for user u to item i is represented as $R(u, i) = (r_{u,i}^0, r_{u,i}^1, r_{u,i}^2, ..., r_{u,i}^k)$, which consists of an overall rating $r_{u,i}^0$, and k multi-criteria ratings $r_{u,i}^1, r_{u,i}^2, ..., r_{u,i}^k$. Our proposed system has following three phases:

Phase 1: Multi-linear regression based similarity computation
Phase 2: Neighborhood generation
Phase 3: Multi-linear regression approach to prediction

– **Phase 1. Multi-linear regression based similarity computation:**
In proposed multi-criteria RS, following two steps are required for similarity computation.

- **Step 1 (Similarity computation for each criterion):** In this step, multi-criteria ratings are divided into k single criteria ratings and then similarities are estimated between user u and u' is computed as follows:

$$sim^c(u, u') = \frac{\sum_{i \in I}(r^c_{u,i} - \bar{r}^c_u)(r^c_{u',i} - \bar{r}^c_{u'})}{\sqrt{\sum_{i \in I}(r^c_{u,i} - \bar{r}^c_u)^2}\sqrt{\sum_{i \in I}(r^c_{u',i} - \bar{r}'^c_u)^2}} \quad (4)$$

where c represents the different criteria, i.e., $c = \{1, 2, 3, ..., k\}$.

- **Step 2 (Aggregation of similarities):** In this step, overall similarity is computed using following equation:

$$sim(u, u') = w_0 + \sum_{c \in \{1,...,k\}} w_c sim^c(u, u') \quad (5)$$

where, $sim^c(u, u')$ is the similarity between user u and $u' \in U$ for criteria $c \in \{1, ..., k\}$, w_c is the weight parameter for criteria $c \in \{1, ..., k\}$ and w_0 is the error term.

Using multi-linear regression, weight parameters are estimated on the basis of previously rated item by users which is called training data. Table 1 represents the training data.

Table 1. Presentation of training data

S.No.	C_1	C_2	...	C_k	C_0
1	$r_{1,1}$	$r_{2,1}$		$r_{k,1}$	$r_{0,1}$
2	$r_{1,2}$	$r_{2,2}$		$r_{k,2}$	$r_{0,2}$
.	.	.		.	.
.	.	.		.	.
n	$r_{1,n}$	$r_{2,n}$		$r_{k,n}$	$r_{0,n}$
Total	$\sum_i r_{1,i}$	$\sum_i r_{2,i}$		$\sum_i r_{k,i}$	$\sum_i r_{0,i}$

where, $C_1, C_2, ..., C_k$ are different single criteria ratings and C_0 is the overall rating. $r_{k,i}$ is the rating of ith; $i \in \{1, 2, ..., n\}$ training data for criteria k. Based on the training data weight values are derived using following equation in matrix form [5]:

$$\begin{bmatrix} w_1 \\ \vdots \\ w_k \end{bmatrix} = \begin{bmatrix} \sum_i u^2_{1,i} & \cdots & \sum_i u_{1,i}u_{k,i} \\ \vdots & \ddots & \vdots \\ \sum_i u_{1,i}u_{k,i} & \cdots & \sum_i u^2_{k,i} \end{bmatrix}^{-1} \begin{bmatrix} \sum_i u_{1,i}v_i \\ \vdots \\ \sum_i u_{k,i}v_i \end{bmatrix} \quad (6)$$

where,

$$\sum_{i \in \{1,...,n\}} u_{j,i}u_{k,i} = \sum_{i \in \{1,...,n\}} r_{j,i}r_{k,i} - \frac{\sum_{i \in \{1,...,n\}} r_{j,i} \sum_{i \in \{1,...,n\}} r_{k,i}}{n} \quad (7)$$

$$\sum_{i\in\{1,...,n\}} u_{j,i}v_i = \sum_{i\in\{1,...,n\}} r_{j,i}r_{0,i} - \frac{\sum_{i\in\{1,...,n\}} r_{j,i} \sum_{i\in\{1,...,n\}} r_{0,i}}{n} \quad (8)$$

here, n is total number of samples in training data and $j \in \{1, 2, ..., k\}$. w_0 is called the error term which is computed as follows.

$$w_0 = \bar{r_0} - w_1\bar{r_1} - w_2\bar{r_2} - ... - w_k\bar{r_k} \quad (9)$$

By applying these weight values in Eq. (5) overall similarity is calculated.
- **Phase 2. Neighborhood generation:**
  This phase is similar to the phase 2 of MCCF.
- **Phase 3. Multi linear regression approach to prediction:**
  In this phase, we predict the overall rating using Eq. (2). In this equation, the overall rating of an item given by these nearest neighbors is utilized. The important task in this phase is to compute the overall rating of an item through its criteria ratings. We have employed again a linear regression approach to aggregate the criteria ratings. The aggregation function for this task is expressed as follows:

$$r(u, u') = w_0 + \sum_{c\in\{1,...,k\}} w_c r_c \quad (10)$$

where, r_c represents the rating for criteria $c \in \{1, ..., k\}$, w_c is the weight parameter for criteria $c \in \{1, ..., k\}$ and w_0 is the error term. these weights are calculates using Eq. (6) and then we compute overall rating. After finding overall rating, we have used Eq. (2) for predicting unknown rating to an active user. Finally, we have recommended highly some predicted items to users.

4 Experiments and Results

We performed various experiments to analyze the effectiveness of the proposed multi-criteria recommender system using Yahoo movie dataset, which consists of 6078 users and 976 items. Each item has five different criteria from which four are individual features and fifth is the overall rating. For experiments, 10 fold cross-validation mechanism is used. In each fold, 60 % data of each user is considered as training data and 40 % data is used as test data. Training data is used to learn the system and test data is used to analyze the performance of the system. In order to evaluate the performance of our proposed system, we have used mean absolute error (MAE), coverage, recall and f-measure as evaluation metrices:

To demonstrate the feasibility and effectiveness of proposed system we have compared our results with the following approaches:

- Single criterion CF (SCCF)
- Multi-criteria collaborative filtering using average similarity and ratings (MCCF-A)

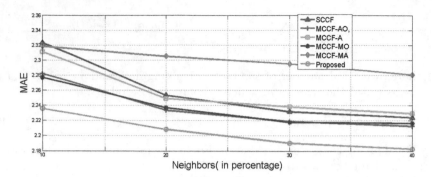

Fig. 1. MAE comparison on different number of neighbors

Table 2. Performance comparison via MAE, coverage, recall, f-measure

	MAE	Coverage	Recall	F-measure
SCCF	2.2406	0.9989	0.8477	0.8377
MCCF-AO	2.2367	0.9989	0.8483	0.8386
MCCF-A	2.2191	0.9989	0.8811	0.8452
MCCF-MO	2.2434	0.9990	0.8458	0.8367
MCCF-A	2.2227	0.9990	0.8786	0.8440
Proposed	2.1995	0.9990	0.9108	0.8500

Table 3. Performance comparison of the proposed approach with other approach for different number of users

Performance Measures	Y_1000	Y_2000	Y_3000	Y_4000	Y_5000	Y_6078
SCCF	MAE	2.3819	2.2.2803	2.2939	2.2539	2.2343	2.2406
	F-Measure	0.8132	0.8280	0.88271	0.8370	0.8403	0.8377
MCCF-AO	MAE	2.3861	2.2952	2.2982	2.2466	2.2390	2.2367
	F-Measure	0.8120	0.8291	0.8283	0.8369	0.8405	0.8386
MCCF-A	MAE	2.2396	2.2596	2.2692	2.2217	2.2164	2.22191
	F-Measure	0.8165	0.8344	0.8354	0.8450	0.8455	0.8452
MCCF-MO	MAE	2.3842	2.2927	2.2934	2.2506	2.2387	2.2434
	F-Measure	0.8088	0.8267	0.8290	0.8354	0.8404	0.8367
MCCF-MA	MAE	2.3521	2.2622	2.2586	2.2293	2.2183	2.2227
	F-Measure	0.8137	0.8336	0.8364	0.8447	0.8454	0.8440
Proposed	MAE	2.2212	2.2352	2.1987	2.1731	2.2030	2.1995
	F-Measure	0.8457	0.8394	0.8435	0.8509	0.8484	0.8500

- Multi-criteria collaborative filtering using average similarity &overall rating (MCCF-AO)
- Multi-criteria collaborative filtering using minimum similarity &average rating (MCCF-MA)
- Multi-criteria collaborative filtering using minimum similarity &overall rating (MCCF-MO).

4.1   Experiment 1

In this experiment, we calculate the predictive and classification accuracy of proposed approach via MAE, coverage, recall and f-measure. Table 2. presents results for these measures by taking 30 % most similar user as neighbors and shows that our proposed approach outperformed in terms these measure. Figs. 1 and 2, show the results for different percentages of users (10 %, 20 %, 30 % and 40 %) on MAE and f-measure. It reveals that proposed approach has minimum MAE and maximum f-measure.

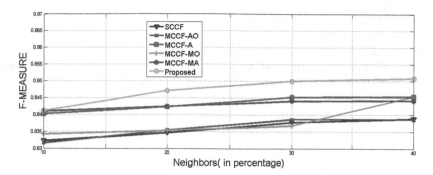

Fig. 2. F-measure comparison on different number of neighbors

4.2   Experiment 2

This experiment reflects the scalability of proposed approach. For this experiments we choose six different subsets of Yahoo movie dataset, called Y_1000, Y_2000, Y_3000, Y_4000, Y_5000, Y_6078. Table 3. depicts the effectiveness of proposed approach under varying number of participating users. Fig. 3 depicts the results of F-measure for different scheme on different subset of dataset.

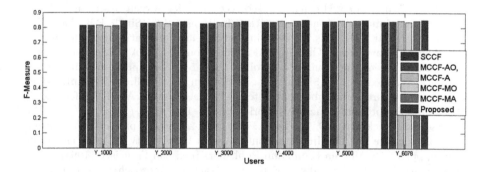

Fig. 3. F-measure comparison for different users (Color figure online)

5   Conclusion

In this work, we have presented linear regression based multi-criteria recommender system (MCRS) where linear regression is used to aggregate similarity components on various criteria and to compute overall rating. Generally different users have different priorities on various criteria where they evaluate these criteria based on their perceptions. The aggregation of similarities based on each criterion is quite challenging task in the area of MCRS because the used weights in aggregation task are not optimal. We have used linear regression approach to compute these weights optimally. Experimental results on a popular Yahoo dataset demonstrated that the adoption of linear regression approach in MCRS has produced quality recommendation and established that our proposed approach outperformed other heuristic approaches.

In our future work, we are planning to handle uncertainty associated with user preferences using fuzzy sets [16] and we will explore some new methods for dealing with correlation based similarity problems.

References

1. Adomavicius, G., Tuzhilin, A.: Toward the next generation of recommender systems: a survey of the state-of-the-art and possible extensions. IEEE Trans. Knowl. Data Engg. **17**(6), 734–749 (2005)
2. Bobadilla, J., Ortega, F., Hernando, A., Gutirrez, A.: Recommender systems survey. Knowl. Based Syst. **46**, 109–132 (2013)
3. Adomavicius, G., Kwon, Y.: New recommendation techniques for multicriteria rating systems. IEEE Int. Syst. **22**(3), 48–55 (2007)
4. Soboroff, I., Nicholas, C.: Combining Content and Collaboration in Text Filtering. In: International Joint Conference on Artificial Intelligence, pp. 86–92 (1999)
5. Balabanovi, M., Shoham, Y.: Fab: content-based collaborative recommendation. ACM Comm. **40**(3), 66–72 (1997)
6. Kant, V.: A user-oriented content based recommender system based on reclusive methods and interactive genetic algorithm. In: Bansal, J.C., Singh, P.K., Deep, K., Pant, M., Nagar, A.K. (eds.) Proceedings of Seventh International Conference on Bio-Inspired Computing: Theories and Applications (BIC-TA 2012). Advances in Intelligent Systems and Computing, vol. 201, pp. 543–554. Springer, India (2013)
7. Resnick, P., Iacovou, N., Suchak, M., Bergstrom, P., Riedl, J.: GroupLens: an open architecture for collaborative filtering of netnews. In: ACM Conference on Computer Supported Cooperative Work, pp. 175–186. ACM (1994)
8. Breese, J.S., Heckerman, D., Kadie, C.: Empirical analysis of predictive algorithms for collaborative filtering. In: 14th Conference on Uncertainty in Artificial Intelligence, pp. 43–52. Morgan Kaufmann Publishers Inc., San Francisco (1998)
9. Al-Shamri, M.Y.H., Bharadwaj, K.K.: Fuzzy-genetic approach to recommender systems based on a novel hybrid user model. Expert Syst. Appl. **35**(3), 1386–1399 (2008)
10. Delgado, J., Ishii, N.: Memory-based weighted majority prediction. In: SIGIR Workshop on Recommender System. Citeseer (1999)
11. Jannach, D., Karakaya, Z., Gedikli, F.: Accuracy improvements for multi-criteria recommender systems. In: 13th ACM Conference on Electronic Commerce, pp. 674–689. ACM (2012)
12. Winarko, E., Hartati, S., Wardoyo, R.: Improving the prediction accuracy of multi-criteria collaborative filtering by combination algorithms. Int. J. Adv. Comput. Sci. App. **52**(4), 52–58 (2014)
13. Bilge, A., Kaleli, C.: A multi-criteria item-based collaborative filtering framework. In: 11th International Joint Conference on Computer Science and Software Engineering, pp. 18–22. IEEE (2014)
14. Agarwal, B., L.: Basic Statistics. New Age International (2006)

15. Kutner, M.H.: Applied Linear Statistical Models, vol. 4. Irwin, Chicago (1996)
16. Kant, V., Bharadwaj, K.: Integrating collaborative and reclusive methods for effective recommendations: a fuzzy bayesian approach. Int. J. Int. Syst. **28**(11), 1099–1123 (2013)

Classification

Classification of Power Quality Disturbances Using Forest Algorithm

Fábbio Borges[1], Ivan Silva[1(✉)], Ricardo Fernandes[2],
and Lucas Moraes[1]

[1] Department of Electrical and Computer Engineering, University of São Paulo,
USP/EESC/SEL, CP 359, São Carlos 13566-590, Brazil
{fabbioborges,insilva}@sc.usp.br
[2] Department of Electrical Engineering, Federal University of São Carlos,
UFSCar/DEE, São Carlos 13565-905, Brazil
ricardo.asf@ufscar.br

Abstract. This paper presents a methodology for the classification of disorders related to the area of Power Quality. Therefore, we used the Random Forest algorithm, which corresponds to an effective data mining technique, especially when dealing with large amounts of data. This algorithm uses a set of classifiers based on decision trees. In this sense, the performance of the proposed methodology was evaluated in a comparative way between the Random Forest and the type J48 Decision Tree. For this analysis to be possible, synthetic electrical signals were generated, where these disturbances were modeled through parametric equations. After the performance analysis, it was observed that the results were promising, since the Random Forest algorithm provides the best performance.

Keywords: Random forest · Decision trees · Pattern classification · Feature extraction · Power quality

1 Introduction

Disturbances related to the area of Power Quality (PQ) are characterized by changing the waveforms of sinusoidal voltage and current, which can affect the operation of certain equipment [1]. Among these disturbances, there are sags, swells, interruption, harmonic distortion and oscillatory transients. Such disturbances are becoming a problem for both the power utilities as well as consumers, making it necessary to eliminate or mitigate the cause of their occurrences in order to ensure good power quality.

Thus, the detection and classification of disturbances is a primary task so that measures to control and mitigate disturbances can be adopted. However, this is no easy task, because the identification of these disturbances often requires the analysis of a large amount of data measured by equipment installed on the network, besides the fact that many of the disturbances have similar features.

In this context, it is desirable to employ data mining tools, because they can identify these PQ disturbances in a fast and automated manner. Additionally, it is desirable that

© Springer International Publishing Switzerland 2016
Y. Tan and Y. Shi (Eds.): DMBD 2016, LNCS 9714, pp. 247–252, 2016.
DOI: 10.1007/978-3-319-40973-3_24

these tools are able to analyze a large volume of data and to recognize a pattern in the data in order to relate it to a possible disturbance.

The area of disturbance detection and classification has been the subject of several studies in recent years [2]. These studies utilize techniques to extract relevant signal characteristics. They reduce the dimensionality of the input data and remove redundant features of the original vector.

The extracted features are then used as inputs to a method of pattern classification responsible for relating an input vector with a disturbance. Among the most used methods, we highlight Fuzzy Logic, Artificial Neural Network and Support Vector Machine (SVM).

Following the above context, this work proposes the Random Forest (RF) algorithm with the interest to hold a review/classification for a database composed of waveforms that contain power quality disturbances. Random forest was developed by Leo Breiman [3] and it fits many classification trees to a data set and then combines the prediction from all the correlated trees. Each tree depends on the value of a separately sampled random vector.

During the feature extraction step, time calculations on time domain that have low computational effort are used.

Following, the feature vector is used as input to the RF so that the final response is defined by the class that has the highest number of outputs, that is, by the account of the outputs presented by each of the decision trees that compose the algorithm. Finally, the classification results are obtained and compared with the response of a Decision Tree (DT) that uses the training algorithm J48.

2   Database Composed of Synthetic Signals

The objective of the database modeling is to store the maximum number of signals with different characteristics of the disturbances. These signs will be used to test the proposed methodology. In this work, the occurrence of the following disturbances was considered: voltage sags, swells, flickers, harmonic distortion, voltage interruptions, oscillatory transients, voltage sags in conjunction with harmonic distortion and swells together with harmonic distortions. A database was created consisting of windows obtained for synthetically modeled disturbances, based on mathematical models proposed in [4].

Therefore, the windows that make up the database were derived from 100 case studies for each disturbance, and each of the disturbances has a total of 10 cycles at nominal frequency of 60 Hz and sampled rate of 128 points per cycle.

This windowing occurs through the shifting of the data window (which is the size of one cycle of the signal) in steps of 1 point until it covers the entire length of the signal.

The result of the process is the construction of a database comprised of approximately: 14864 sag windows, 12671 swell windows, 19706 flicker windows, 34084 harmonic distortion windows, 13277 harmonic distortion with windows, 12769 harmonic distortion with swell windows, 10366 interruption windows and 5836 transient windows.

3 Feature Extraction from Windowed Signals

As soon as a disturbance is detected, the classification step is activated, which uses a stage of extraction of features combined to a decision tree. Thus, a set of 11 features is extracted with the purpose of reducing the dimension of data and, hence, minimizing the computational effort.

This set consists of the following features: standard deviation, entropy, Rényi entropy, Shannon entropy, mean deviation, Kurtosis, RMS value, crest factor, the balance between the maximum and minimum amplitude and peak value.

Thus, for each d_j data, a C_k vector is extracted, where j represents the index of each element contained in the window and that varies in the range $\{1 \rightarrow N\}$, N is the size of the window, and k represents each characteristic in the range $\{1 \rightarrow 11\}$.

4 Random Forest

Random Forest corresponds to a collection of combined Decision Tree $\{h_k(x,T_k)\}$, with $k = 1,2,\ldots,L$, where L is number of the tree, T_k is the training set built at random and identically distributed, and h_k represents the tree created from the vector T_k that is responsible for producing an output x.

Decision Trees are tools that use divide-and-conquer strategies as a form of learning by induction [5], the main advantage of which is the creation of compact, highly readable structures, so that its results are easily understood. Thus, this tool uses a tree representation, which helps in pattern classification in data sets, being hierarchically structured in a set of interconnected nodes.

The internal nodes of which test an input attribute/feature in relation to a decision constant and, in this way, determine what will be the next descending node.

So the nodes considered to be leaves classify the instances that reach them according to the associated label. Therefore, knowledge in a decision tree is represented by each node which, when tested, engages in the search for a derived node until it reaches a leaf node [5].

The induction process of a tree can be done manually. However, when there is a large amount of data, this process becomes exhaustive, and therefore an automatic induction approach may be used, which is normally based on supervised learning. Thus, the algorithm proceeds to determine the nodes and leaves of the tree working from a set of training data with its respective desired output values.

Other tools such as the Gabor Transform [6], the Phase Space Transform [7, 8] and the Hilbert Transform [9] were also used within the ambit of Power Quality disturbances. In the case of the Gabor Transform, it can be said that among its advantages are a good time-frequency resolution and a good signal/noise ratio, however, its computational complexity is directly proportional to the signal sampling rate. The Phase Space Transform of signals, despite the good results shown in the literature, presents poorer answers when signals are influenced by noise. As for the Hilbert Transform, in [9], the authors used it together with empirical mode decomposition to decompose the signal into simple oscillatory components in order to perform preprocessing; however, this transform requires that the start and end of the signal have an amplitude equal to zero.

Based on the surveys of the literature mentioned above, it is evident that a good deal of the transforms present some disadvantageous aspect in relation to their application in the extraction of features of Power Quality disturbances. Thus, for applications in Smart Meters, the Fast Fourier Transform presents itself as a more efficient alternative, even by the fact that it has been widely employed for applications in embedded hardware [10–12].

In addition to these features related to the transforms, it was noted that many of the studies do not report accurately the size of the data window that is analyzed at each interval of preprocessing of the signal or else they undertake the analysis using a large data window (around 10 cycles), which is an uncommon procedure for applications in Smart Meters.

Thus, classification methods that use windows with sizes less than or equal to one cycle are more suitable for embedding in hardware, even though this approach makes the problem of classification more complex due to the reduction in the amount of information present in the window when compared to windows containing many cycles.

The trees that make up the Random Forest are built randomly selecting m (value fixed for all nodes) attributes in each node of the tree, where the best attribute is chosen to divide the node. The vector used for training each tree is obtained using random selection of the instances. Thus, to determine the class of an instance, all of the trees indicate an output, where the most voted is selected as the final result.

Thus, the classification error depends on the strength of individual trees of the forest and the correlation between any two trees in the forest.

5 Experimental Results

In problems that aim for pattern classification, the extraction of features is extremely important since it seeks to reduce the dimensionality of the data that are synthesized in the form of a feature vector, preserving and highlighting the useful information from the original data. Thus, the computational effort required by the classifier can be minimized, and therefore can be a facilitating agent for methods to be embedded in hardware [13].

As previously mentioned, the Decision Trees (DT) and the Random Forest (RF) were trained and validated using a set of data consisting of the windows of signals acquired from the database.

Therefore, the training set is composed of 70 % of the windows and the test/validation set corresponds to the 30 % of the remaining windows. The random forest is formed by 10 decision trees and the number of attributes selected in each node is equal to 4. This made it possible to obtain and evaluate the success rate for each disturbance, as well as the average accuracy of classifiers. The comparison of the classification results is presented in Table 1.

Through the results presented in Table 1 it is found that the performance of the two used classifiers is satisfactory, however, it can be seen that the approach based on Random Forest presents better results when compared with the approach based on type J48 Decision Trees.

Table 1. Results obtained for synthetic signals.

Power quality disturbances	DT	RFs
Voltage sags	83.0 %	99.4 %
Voltage swells	94.4 %	99.9 %
Flickers	97.9 %	99.9 %
Harmonic distortions	96.9 %	99.6 %
Voltage sags with harmonic distortions	78.9 %	98.5 %
Voltage swells with harmonic distortions	88.8 %	98.9 %
Voltage interruptions	89.4 %	99.3 %
Oscillatory transients	87.5 %	99.2 %
Mean precision	**89.6 %**	**99.3 %**

The RF had a precision 10 % higher than the DT. Additionally, the proposed algorithm can identify large part of the disturbances with accuracy greater than 99 %.

Since the results obtained during the validation step were quite satisfactory, it was then possible to subject the classifiers to the test step, where the feature extraction step and the classifiers were embedded in the smart meter. Thus, laboratory tests were conducted to evaluate the effectiveness of the proposed method, in which a programmable source from the Doble Engineering manufacturer (model F6150) was used to deliver the input signals to the smart meter. It should be noted that the smart meter's data acquisition is handled by means of Hall effect transducers and, sequentially, the signal from the transducers is constrained to a range appropriate to the analog digital converter of the ARM microcontroller (model Cortex M4).

6 Conclusions

The paper presents a performance comparison between type J48 Decision Trees and the Random Forest algorithm for classification of power quality disturbances. According to the results, we note that the worst performances were obtained for windows containing combinations of voltage sags with harmonic distortion and swells with harmonic distortion (respectively, 98.5 % and 98.9 %).

It should be noted that this methodology was designed compactly, mainly so that it could be embedded in smart meters. Thus, there was the need for a detailed study regarding the features extracted so that its computational efficiency could be guaranteed. Therefore, in general, the results may be considered satisfactory for electric power systems.

Acknowledgement. The authors gratefully acknowledge the financial support for the development of this research provided by FAPESP (Process 2011/17610-0 and 2013/16778-0).

References

1. Dugan, R.C., McGranagham, M.F., Santoso, S., Beaty, H.W.: Electrical Power Systems Quality, 3rd edn. McGraw-Hill Education, New York (2002)
2. Granados-Lieberman, D., Romero-Troncoso, R.J., Osornio-Rios, R.A., Garcia-Perez, A., Cabal-Yepez, E.: Techniques and methodologies for power quality analysis and disturbances classification in power systems: a review. IET Gener. Transm. Distrib. 5(4), 519–529 (2011)
3. Breiman, L.: Random forests. Mach. Learn. 45(1), 5–32 (2001)
4. Erişti, H., Uçar, A., Demir, Y.: Wavelet-based feature extraction and selection for classification of power system disturbances using support vector machines. Electr. Power Syst. Res. 80, 743–752 (2010)
5. Witten, I.H., Frank, E.: Data Mining: Practical Machine Learning Tools and Techniques. Morgan Kaufmann, San Francisco (2005)
6. Soo-Hwan, C., Jang, G., Kwon, S.: time-frequency analysis of power-quality disturbances via the gabor-wigner transform. IEEE Trans. Power Deliv. 25(1), 494–499 (2010)
7. Ji, T.Y., Wu, Q.H., Jiang, L., Tang, W.H.: disturbance detection, location and classification in phase space. IET Gener. Transm. Distrib. 5(2), 257–265 (2011)
8. Pires, V.F., Amaral, T.G., Martins, J.F.: power quality disturbances classification using the 3-D space representation and PCA based neuro-fuzzy approach. Expert Syst. Appl. 38(9), 11911–11917 (2011)
9. Biswal, B., Biswal, M., Mishra, S., Jalaja, R.: automatic classification of power quality events using balanced neural tree. IEEE Trans. Indus. Electron. 61(1), 521–530 (2014)
10. Cabal-Yepez, E., Garcia-Ramirez, A.G., Romero-Troncoso, R.J., Garcia-Perez, A., Osornio-Rios, R.A.: reconfigurable monitoring system for time-frequency analysis on industrial equipment through STFT and DWT. IEEE Trans. Indus. Inform. 9(2), 760–771 (2013)
11. McKeown, S., Woods, R.: Power efficient, FPGA implementations of transform algorithms for radar-based digital receiver applications. IEEE Trans. Indus. Inform. 9(3), 1591–1600 (2013)
12. Jimenez, O., Lucia, O., Barragan, L.A., Navarro, D., Artigas, J.I., Urriza, I.: FPGA-based test-bench for resonant inverter load characterization. IEEE Trans. Indus. Inform. 9(3), 1645–1654 (2013)
13. Uyar, M., Yildirim, S., Gencoglu, M.T.: An expert system based on S-transform and neural network for automatic classification of power quality disturbances. Expert Syst. Appl. 36(3), 5962–5975 (2009)

A Sequential k-Nearest Neighbor Classification Approach for Data-Driven Fault Diagnosis Using Distance- and Density-Based Affinity Measures

Myeongsu Kang[1], Gopala Krishnan Ramaswami[2],
Melinda Hodkiewicz[3], Edward Cripps[4], Jong-Myon Kim[5],
and Michael Pecht[1(✉)]

[1] Center for Advanced Life Cycle Engineering (CALCE),
University of Maryland, College Park, MD, USA
{mskang, pecht}@calce.umd.edu
[2] Department of Physics, National University of Singapore,
Singapore, Singapore
phyrgk@nus.edu.sg
[3] School of Mechanical and Chemical Engineering,
University of Western Australia, Crawley, WA, Australia
milinda.hodkiewicz@uwa.edu.au
[4] School of Mathematics and Statistics,
University of Western Australia, Crawley, WA, Australia
edward.cripps@uwa.edu.au
[5] Department of IT Convergence, University of Ulsan, Ulsan, South Korea
Jmkim07@ulsan.ac.kr

Abstract. Machine learning techniques are indispensable in today's data-driven fault diagnosis methodolgoies. Among many machine techniques, k-nearest neighbor (k-NN) is one of the most widely used for fault diagnosis due to its simplicity, effectiveness, and computational efficiency. However, the lack of a density-based affinity measure in the conventional k-NN algorithm can decrease the classification accuracy. To address this issue, a sequential k-NN classification methodology using distance- and density-based affinity measures in a sequential manner is introduced for classification.

Keywords: Data-driven fault diagnosis · Density-based affinity measure · k-Nearest neighbor · Machine learning

1 Introduction

There is an ever-increasing demand for reliability and safety of industrial systems. To address this issue, model-based condition monitoring and fault diagnosis approaches using physical and mathematical knowledge of industrial systems have been developed [1–4]. These model-based methodologies have been successfully applied for a number of industrial systems. However, as industrial systems have become more complex, it has become impractical to establish model-based methods for them due to the need for

© Springer International Publishing Switzerland 2016
Y. Tan and Y. Shi (Eds.): DMBD 2016, LNCS 9714, pp. 253–261, 2016.
DOI: 10.1007/978-3-319-40973-3_25

complicated a priori knowledge of process models derived from first principles [5]. Fortunately, the rapid development of data acquisition, data mining, and machine learning techniques has led to an efficient alternative way for industrial systems' condition monitoring and fault diagnosis [6].

In general, today's data-driven fault diagnosis methodologies involve machine learning (especially supervised machine learning) techniques to preemptively detect and identify potential faults in industrial systems. Among support vector machines [7], artificial neural networks [8], decision trees [9], and k-nearest neighbors (k-NN) [10], a k-NN algorithm is appealing to many who engage in fault diagnosis due to its relative simplicity and effectiveness. For classification, the conventional k-NN algorithm using a similarity-weighted decision rule first measures the degree of affinity (or similarity) between a test sample and its neighbors (in a training set) that may belong to various classes. Then it finds k nearest neighbors based on affinity measures. Finally, it assigns the test sample to the class most common among its k nearest neighbors [11]. In general, this k-NN algorithm suffers from a problem when the density of the training set is uneven. That is, it may decrease the classification accuracy if the sequence of the first k nearest neighbors is only considered but the density of the training set is not properly considered [12].

Figure 1 depicts why a proper density measure is needed in k-NN. Assume that a red-circle test sample must belong to the orange-square class. Under the distance-based k-NN classification scheme (e.g., $k = 3$ in Fig. 1), the test sample will possibly be classified into the blue-triangle class because its common nearest neighbors belong to the blue-triangle class. That is, two of three common nearest neighbors are in the blue-triangle class, whereas the other common nearest neighbor is in the orange-square class in Fig. 1. However, if the density of the red-circle test sample is appropriately considered, the test sample can be partitioned into the orange-square class. More specifically, if the density of the test sample is measured under the assumption that the test sample is in the blue-triangle class and the orange-square class, respectively, and is compared with the density of each sample in each class, the test sample will definitely have a chance to be assigned to the orange-square class. This is mainly because the density of the test sample towards the orange-square class is close to the density of each sample in the orange-square class, whereas the density of the test sample to the blue-triangle class is not very close to that of each sample in the blue-triangle class. Accordingly, this paper introduces a sequential k-NN classification method to combine the advantages of distance- and density-based affinity measures.

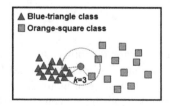

Fig. 1. Necessity of a proper density-based affinity measure in the conventional distance-based k-NN classification method.

The rest of this paper is organized as follows. Section 2 presents a density-based affinity measure used for *k*-NN. Section 3 verifies the efficacy of the presented sequential *k*-NN classification methodology that employs distance- and density-based affinity measures for bearing fault diagnosis. Section 4 presents the conclusions.

2 A Density-Based Affinity Measure Used for *k*-NN

To measure the density of a given sample s, the ratio of its and its neighbor's local reachability densities is used [13]. The first step in calculating the density is to compute the kth nearest Euclidean distance between the sample and its k neighbors, denoted as k-dist(s). Then, the reachability distance (also regarded as the 'actual distance') of the sample s with regard to a sample t is computed in the next step, which is defined as follows:

$$r\text{-dist}(s,t) = \max(k\text{-dist}(s), \text{dist}(s,t)), \tag{1}$$

where r-dist(s,t) is the reachability distance between the two samples s and t, and dist (s,t) is the Euclidean distance. Figure 2 illustrates the concept of reachability distance. If a sample t_1 is far away from a sample s, the reachability distance between these two samples is simply the Euclidean distance. On the other hand, if they are closely agglomerated (see t_2 in Fig. 2), the reachability distance between the two is considered as the k-dist(s).

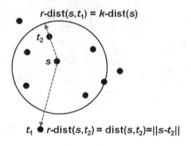

Fig. 2. Concept of reachability distance between the two samples, where $k = 7$.

The third step is to calculate a local reachability density of the sample s (i.e., lrd(s)), defined as the inverse of the average reachability distance of the sample s based on its M nearest neighbors. The mathematical form of lrd(s) is expressed as follows:

$$\text{lrd}(s) = \frac{M}{\displaystyle\sum_{t \in Neighbors} r\text{-dist}(s,t)}, \tag{2}$$

where *Neighbors* is a set of M nearest neighbors of the sample s. Finally, the degree of the density-based affinity of the sample s (i.e., *d*-affinity(s)) is computed as follows:

$$d\text{-affinity}(s) = \frac{1}{M} \sum_{t \in Neighbors} \frac{\mathrm{lrd}(s)}{\mathrm{lrd}(t)}. \tag{3}$$

That is, since the density of the sample s is defined as the average of ratios of its local reachability density to its neighbor's local reachability density in (3), d-affinity (s) will be small if the sample s is closely agglomerated with its M nearest neighbors.

3　Application: Data-Driven Bearing Fault Diagnosis

In this study, a data-driven bearing fault diagnosis application was used to verify the efficacy of the sequential k-NN classification method. To do this, a machinery fault simulator was used, as depicted in Fig. 3. The fault simulator consisted of a three-phase induction motor, a gearbox (reduction ratio of 1.52:1), cylindrical roller bearings (FAG NJ206-E-TVP2), and adjustable blades. Additionally, three different defective bearings were used: a bearing with a crack on its inner race (BCI), a bearing with a crack on its outer race (BCO), and a bearing with a crack on its roller (BCR). The crack length, width, and depth were 3 mm, 0.35 mm, and 0.3 mm, respectively. In this study, a defect-free bearing (DFB) was used for reference as well.

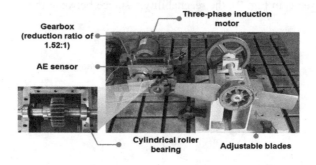

Fig. 3. Screenshot of the machinery fault simulator.

Since low-speed bearing fault diagnosis is challenging [14], signals were recorded from defect-free and defective bearings rotating at 350 RPM. To capture the dynamic behavior of low-speed bearings, a general-purpose wideband acoustic emission sensor was used and installed at the top of the non-drive-end bearing housing (see Fig. 3).

3.1　Feature Vector Configuration

Due to the fact that statistical parameters from the time and frequency domains are well corroborated by intelligent fault diagnosis schemes [15], they are used to configure a feature vector in this study. Tables 1 and 2 summarize these parameters computed from the given AE signal, $x(n)$.

Table 1. Summary of time-domain statistical parameters

Parameter	Equation	Parameter	Equation
Root-mean-square (RMS, f_1)	$f_1 = \sqrt{\frac{1}{N}\sum_{n=1}^{N} x(n)^2}$	Crest factor (f_6)	$f_6 = \frac{\max(\lvert x(n)\rvert)}{\text{RMS}}$
Square root of the amplitude (SRA, f_2)	$f_2 = \left(\frac{1}{N}\sum_{n=1}^{N}\sqrt{\lvert x(n)\rvert}\right)^2$	Impulse factor (f_7)	$f_7 = \frac{\max(\lvert x(n)\rvert)}{\frac{1}{N}\sum_{n=1}^{N}\lvert x(n)\rvert}$
Skewness (f_3)	$f_3 = \frac{1}{N}\sum_{n=1}^{N}\left(\frac{x(n)-\bar{x}}{\sigma}\right)^3$	Margin factor (f_8)	$f_8 = \frac{\max(\lvert x(n)\rvert)}{\text{SRA}}$
Kurtosis (f_4)	$f_4 = \frac{1}{N}\sum_{n=1}^{N}\left(\frac{x(n)-\bar{x}}{\sigma}\right)^4$	Shape factor (f_9)	$f_9 = \frac{\text{RMS}}{\frac{1}{N}\sum_{n=1}^{N}\lvert x(n)\rvert}$
Peak-to-peak (f_5)	$f_5 = \max(x(n)) - \min(x(n))$	Kurtosis factor (f_{10})	$f_{10} = \frac{\text{Kurtosis}}{\left(\frac{1}{N}\sum_{n=1}^{N}x(n)^2\right)^2}$

where N is the total number of data samples in the given AE signal, $x(n)$, and $\bar{x}$ and σ are the mean and the standard deviation of $x(n)$, respectively.

Table 2. Summary of frequency-domain statistical parameters

Parameter	Equation	Parameter	Equation
Frequency center (FC, f_{11})	$f_{11} = \frac{1}{N_f}\sum_{f=1}^{N_f} F(f)$	Root variance frequency (f_{13})	$f_{13} = \sqrt{\frac{1}{N_f}\sum_{f=1}^{N_f}(F(f) - \text{FC})^2}$
RMS frequency (f_{12})	$f_{12} = \sqrt{\frac{1}{N_f}\sum_{f=1}^{N_f} F(f)^2}$		

where $F(f)$ is the magnitude response of the fast Fourier transform of $x(n)$, and N_f is the total number of frequency bins.

3.2 Experimental Results

As briefly stated in Sect. 1, the sequential *k*-NN classification methodology is used to identify defect-free and defective bearings. That is, probable classes of a test sample are first determined based on the distance-based affinity measure; if *k* nearest neighbors of the test sample belong to the same class (i.e., a single class), then the test sample will be labeled as a member of that class. However, in the case that *k* nearest neighbors of the test sample belong to more than one class, the output of the distance-based *k*-NN classification method will be discarded. Instead, the density-based affinity measure determines to which class the test sample belongs.

Figure 4(a) compares classification results between the conventional and the sequential *k*-NN algorithms, where *k* is experimentally set to 7 for the purpose of comparison. As shown in Fig. 4(a), although a test sample should belong to BCI, it is actually classified as BCO. This is due to the fact that the common nearest neighbors of the test sample (i.e., four of seven nearest neighbors) are BCOs, as the distance-based affinity measure is used. On the other hand, the sequential k-NN algorithm outputs a vector $\{y_1, y_2, ..., y_i\}$ for the test sample because k nearest neighbors of the test sample are not in the same class, where y_i indicates the density of the test sample towards class i (i.e., $i = 1, 2, ..., N_{classes}$). Then, the test sample is assigned to the class yielding the minimum sum of absolute differences between y_i and the density of each sample in class i. In Fig. 4(b), the developed sequential k-NN ultimately yields a vector $\{y_1 = 4.979, y_2 = 3.192\}$ since the number of classes is two (i.e., BCI and BCO). Then, the test sample is discriminated as BCI because the sum of absolute differences between y_2 and the density of each sample in class 2 (i.e., BCI) is smaller than that for class 1 (i.e., BCO). As a consequence, the developed sequential k-NN method can correctly classify the test sample. Moreover, an optimal subset (f_2 and f_{13} in Fig. 4) of the 13 statistical parameters (see Tables 1 and 2) was used for bearing fault diagnosis. Specifically, this optimal set was determined by the minimal ratio of the intra-class compactness to the inter-class separability. The mathematical definition of the compactness and the separability is given in [16].

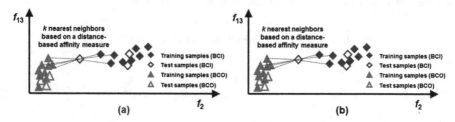

Fig. 4. Classification results for BCI and BCO under (a) the conventional k-NN classification scheme and (b) the presented sequential k-NN classification scheme.

To show classification performance, classification accuracy, denoted as CA, is computed as follows:

$$CA = \frac{\sum_{i=1}^{N_{classes}} N^i_{truepositives}}{N_{tsamples}} \times 100\ (\%),\qquad(4)$$

where $N_{tsamples}$ is the total number of samples used to test conventional and sequential k-NN classification methods, respectively; $N_{classes}$ is the number of classes considered in this paper; and $N^i_{truepositives}$ is the number of samples in class i that are correctly classified as class i. In general, CA is a metric used to understand the overall classification performance. Furthermore, to evaluate diagnostic performance for each bearing condition (i.e., defect-free and defective bearings), sensitivity is obtained as follows:

$$\text{Sensitivity} = \frac{N_{\text{truepositives}}^{i}}{N_{\text{truepositives}}^{i} + N_{\text{falsenegatives}}^{i}} \times 100\ (\%), \qquad (5)$$

where $N_{\text{falsenegatives}}^{i}$ is the number of samples in class i that are not correctly classified as class i. Table 3 briefly presents the classification performance for conventional and sequential k-NN classification methods. As expected, the developed classification scheme outperforms the conventional k-NN approach, yielding an average classification accuracy of 97.25%.

Table 3. Comparison of sensitivities and classification accuracies for conventional and sequential k-NN classification methods (unit: %)

		Sensitivity				CA
		BCI	BCO	BCR	DFB	
$k = 3$	Conventional k-NN	99	95	100	98	98
	Sequential k-NN	99	95	100	98	98
$k = 5$	Conventional k-NN	73	80	98	89	85
	Sequential k-NN	96	92	100	100	97
$k = 7$	Conventional k-NN	97	92	96	99	96
	Sequential k-NN	98	92	99	99	97
$k = 9$	Conventional k-NN	71	85	92	88	84
	Sequential k-NN	98	94	98	98	97

An interesting observation that can be made from Table 3 is that the presented classification approach is particularly effective for identifying BCI and BCO compared to the conventional k-NN classification method. In general, as the AE signals are captured for BCI and BCO, signal attenuation occurs more slowly due to the shorter distance between the AE sensor and the source (i.e., the location of a defective element of a bearing) than for BCR. That is, the densities of the statistical parameters (i.e., f_2 and f_{13}) computed in relatively high-energy AE signals (due to less signal attenuation) can be more uneven for BCI and BCO rather than for BCR. Accordingly, as stated in Sect. 1, the conventional k-NN classification method considering the first k nearest neighbors in uneven samples yields lower average classification accuracies of 85% and 88% for BCI and BCO, respectively, than the presented sequential k-NN classification methodology, which yielded average classification accuracies of 97.75% and 93.25% for BCI and BCO, respectively. Additionally, although the choice of k values in k-NN significantly influences classification performance, the sequential k-NN methodology is very effective for achieving high classification accuracy.

4   Conclusions

To improve the conventional k-NN classification method used in data-driven diagnostics, a sequential k-NN classification scheme was presented in this study, which combined the advantages of distance- and density-based affinity measures. To validate the efficacy of this sequential k-NN method, a bearing fault diagnosis application, which identifies a DFB and three defective bearings (i.e., BCI, BCO, and BCR), was used. Experimental results indicated that the presented method achieved classification performance improvements of up to 13% over the conventional k-NN approach in terms of classification accuracy. This was mainly because the density-based affinity measure in sequential k-NN was capable of dealing with the uneven training set.

Acknowledgements. This research was supported by the over 100 CALCE members of the CALCE Consortium and also by the National Natural Science Foundation of China (NSFC) under grant number 71420107023.

References

1. Campos-Delgado, D.U., Espinoza-Trejo, D.R.: An observer-based diagnosis scheme for single and simultaneous open-switch faults in induction motor drives. IEEE Trans. Ind. Electron. **58**(2), 671–679 (2011)
2. Huang, S., Tan, K.K., Lee, T.H.: Fault diagnosis and fault-tolerant control in linear drives using the Kalman filter. IEEE Trans. Ind. Electron. **59**(11), 4285–4292 (2012)
3. Gritli, Y., Zarri, L., Rossi, C., Filippetti, F., Capolino, G., Casadei, D.: Advanced diagnosis of electrical faults in wound-rotor induction machines. IEEE Trans. Ind. Electron. **60**(9), 4012–4024 (2013)
4. Seshadrinath, J., Singh, B., Panigrahi, B.K.: Vibration analysis based interturn fault diagnosis in induction machines. IEEE Trans. Ind. Informat. **10**(1), 340–350 (2014)
5. Yin, S., Li, X., Gao, H., Kaynak, O.: Data-based techniques focused on modern industry: an overview. IEEE Trans. Ind. Electron. **62**(1), 657–667 (2015)
6. Dai, X., Gao, Z.: From model, signal to knowledge: a data-driven perspective of fault detection and diagnosis. IEEE Trans. Ind. Informat. **9**(4), 2226–2238 (2013)
7. Jegadeeshwaran, R., Sugumaran, V.: Fault diagnosis of automobile hydraulic brake system using statistical features and support vector machines. Mech. Syst. Signal Process. **52–53**, 436–446 (2015)
8. Shao, M., Zhu, X.-J., Cao, H.-F., Shen, H.-F.: An artificial neural network ensemble method for fault diagnosis of proton exchange membrane fuel cell system. Energy **67**, 268–275 (2014)
9. Muralidharan, V., Sugumaran, V.: Feature extraction using wavelets and classification through decision tree algorithm for fault diagnosis of mono-block centrifugal pump. Measurement **46**, 353–359 (2013)
10. Hevi-Seok, L.: An Improved kNN learning based korean test classifier with heuristic information. In: 9th International Conference on Neural Information Processing, Singapore, pp. 732–735 (2002)
11. Shang, W., Huang, H.-K., Zhu, H., Lin, Y., Wang, Z., Qu, Y.: An improved kNN algorithm – fuzzy kNN. In: Hao, Y., Liu, J., Wang, Y.-P., Cheung, Y.-m., Yin, H., Jiao, L., Ma, J., Jiao, Y.-C. (eds.) CIS 2005. LNCS (LNAI), vol. 3801, pp. 741–746. Springer, Heidelberg (2005)
12. Seshadrinath, J., Singh, B., Panigrahi, B.K.: Investigation of vibration signatures for multiple fault diagnosis in variable frequency drives using complex wavelets. IEEE Trans. Power Electron. **29**(2), 936–945 (2014)

13. Breunig, M. M., Kriegel, H. –P., Ng, R. T., Sander, J.: LOF: identifying density-based local outliers. In: 2000 ACM SIGMOD International Conference on Management of Data, Dallas, TX, USA, pp. 93–104 (2000)
14. Kang, M., Kim, J., Kim, J.-M., Tan, A.C.C., Kim, E.Y., Choi, B.-K.: Reliable fault diagnosis for low-speed bearings using individually trained support vector machines with kernel discriminative feature analysis. IEEE Trans. Power Electron. **30**(5), 2786–2797 (2015)
15. Xia, Z., Xia, S., Wan, L., Cai, S.: Spectral regression based fault feature extraction for bearing accelerometer sensor signals. Sensors **12**, 13694–13719 (2012)
16. Islam, R., Khan, S. A., Kim, J.-M.: Discriminant feature distribution analysis-based hybrid feature selection for online bearing fault diagnosis in induction motors. J. Sens. 1–16 (2016). Article ID 7145715

A Hybrid Model Combining SOMs with SVRs for Patent Quality Analysis and Classification

Pei-Chann Chang[1,2(✉)], Jheng-Long Wu[2,3], Cheng-Chin Tsao[2], and Chin-Yuan Fan[4]

[1] Software School, Nanchang University, Nanchang, Jiangxi, China
[2] Innovation Center for Big Data and Digital Convergence and Department of Information Management,
Yuan Ze University, Taoyuan, Taiwan
iepchang@saturn.yzu.edu.tw
[3] Institute of Information Science, Academia Sinica, Taipei, Taiwan
[4] Science & Technology Policy Research and Information Center,
National Applied Research Laboratories, Taipei, Taiwan

Abstract. Traditional researchers and analyzers have fixated on developing sundry patent quality indicators only, but these indicators do not have further prognosticating power on incipient patent applications or publications. Therefore, the data mining (DM) approaches are employed in this paper to identify and to classify the new patent's quality in time. An automatic patent quality analysis and classification system, namely SOM-KPCA-SVM, is developed according to patent quality indicators and characteristics, respectively. First, the model will cluster patents published before into different quality groups according to the patent quality indicators and defines group quality type instead of via experts. Then, the support vector machine (SVM) is used to build up the patent quality classification model. The proposed SOM-KPCA-SVM is applied to classify patent quality automatically in patent data of the thin film solar cell. Experimental results show that our proposed system can capture the analysis effectively compared with traditional manpower approach.

Keywords: Patent analysis · Patent quality · Data clustering · Patent quality classification · Machine learning

1 Introduction

Currently, there are various tools that are being utilized by organizations for analyzing patents. However, an important issue of patent analysis is patent quality analysis. The high-quality patent information can ensure success for business decision-making process or product development [1, 2]. This study reviewed the patent analysis approaches that can understand patent status like patent quality, novelty, litigation, trends and so on [3]. However, traditional patent analysis requires spending much time, cost and manpower. The potential patents for high quality determining approach need have shortened analysis at times. In general, the analysis approaches are statistical analysis or indicators computation. Recently, the clustering method is widely applied to cluster patent according to patent characteristics for patent trend [4]. The methods with

© Springer International Publishing Switzerland 2016
Y. Tan and Y. Shi (Eds.): DMBD 2016, LNCS 9714, pp. 262–269, 2016.
DOI: 10.1007/978-3-319-40973-3_26

statistical analysis can help analysts to understand patent situation or trend of this time, but if we want to know the potential quality of a newly applied patent, it doesn't provide effective rules or solutions to determination. The future patent evaluation is a key issue when a new patent is applied or published because patent has been producing impact on the industry according to the past industrial development such as patent litigation, specifically high-tech or information.

The patent officers approve a large amount of patents each year and current patent systems face a serious problem of evaluating these patents' qualities. Traditional researchers and analyzers have focused on developing various patent quality indicators. The patent indicators are collected from patent corpuses, including the number of patent citations and the number of International Patent Classifications (IPC). The primary patent quality indicators [5–7] are related to investment, maintenance, and litigation, which form a basis for assessing patent. But, these indicators do not have further predicting power on a new patent application or publication. Though the value can be estimated manually or by experts studying about the actual quality decisions, this is slow and expensive. In this study, we introduce an automatic analysis and classification system of patent quality named SOM-KPCA-SVM, which represents the quality in which the application will be classified.

2 Literature Reviews

The patent analysis is a set of techniques and visual tools that analyze the trend and patterns of technology innovation in a specific domain based on statistics of patents. The analysis objects on patent include [8–10]: (1) patent count analysis, it is counting the quantity of patents, including the technology life cycle chart and the patent quantity comparison chart; (2) country analysis, it is comparing the patents of various countries in a specific technology domain; (3) assignee analysis, it is comparing detailed data on R&D, citation ratio, cross-citation, event charts, ranking chart, and competitors; (4) citation rate analysis, it is comparing the number of citation made by other patents during its valid period; and (5) International Patent Classification (IPC) analysis, it is including IPC patent activity chart and no. of IPC patent companies. There are various tools utilized by organizations for analyzing patents. These tools are capable of performing wide range of tasks, such as forecasting future technological trends, detecting patent infringement and determining patent quality. Moreover, patent analysis tools can free patent experts from the laborious tasks of analyzing the patent documents manually and determining the quality of patents. The tools assist organizations in making decisions of whether or not to invest in manufacturing of the new products by analyzing the quality of the filed patents [2]. This eventually may result in imprecise recommendation of patents. The authors [11] proposed a patent portfolio value analysis that uses the leverage page patent information for strategic technology planning. They used five directions of patent quality such as claim, citation, market coverage, strategic relevance and economic relevance to analyze patent portfolio value. The study [12] used renewal data to estimate the value of U.S. patents. In their analysis results, they mentioned that the ratio of U.S. patent value to R&D is only about 3 % but these had a high value in terms of litigation.

Usually the patent quality indicators are related to investment, maintenance, litigation and patent claims. The quality is used to evaluate the potential patents for a business or government policy [13, 14]. For example, one kind of indicator of patent quality is legal status (LS), which means the technology's potential. In this movement, the competitors may litigate a claim in this patent. Therefore, the quality indicators can respond to the future value for business intelligence.

3   Proposed Method

This study proposed an automatically patent quality classification system that integrated system combining three approaches including self-organizing maps, kernel principal component analysis and support vector machine, namely SOM-KPCA-SVM. This quality classification system has two stages to implement: the stage one is patent analysis and quality definition, and stage two is a patent quality classification model building as shown in Fig. 1. Our proposed system is developed as follows:

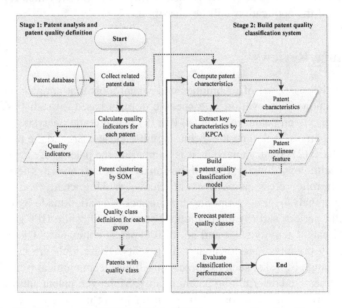

Fig. 1. The framework of SOM-KPCA-SVM patent quality classification system.

Stage 1: Patent Analysis and Patent Quality Definition. In this stage, we must know the current trend of patent quality from past years. Therefore, we need to analyze the phenomenon of patent quality based on patent quality indicators and cluster them into different kinds of quality groups. Next, we will define which patent has which quality type according to SOM clustering analysis. The details of quality analysis and patent quality definition are following:

Stage 1.1: Patent Data Collection, Quality Indicators Calculation and Patent Characteristics Computation. This patent data in a specific industry will be collected from patent database such as WebPat, PatBase, Google Patent Search, Thomson Innovation, patent office of country and so on. These patent offices can provide all the patent documents. The patent service organization can provide other information such as legal status. Therefore, our patent data includes characteristics of the patent document and quality indicators from additional information. The quality indicators and characteristics will normalized using the Min-Max method.

Stage 1.2: Patent Quality Analysis Using SOM Approach Based on Quality Indicators. The patent clustering is adopted the SOM approach, identify patent quality and explore hidden patterns among these patents. According to this algorithm, these patents will be split to several groups (clusters) in order to cluster a similar quality patents based on quality indicators. Therefore, we use SOM clustering method based on quality indicators to analyze and cluster patents. The analysis process continues until all input vectors are processed.

Stage 1.3: Patent Quality Definition for Groups. The SOM is used to cluster patents into several groups according to patent quality indicators. Each group has a specific difference compared to the other. Therefore, we define different quality type for each group such as high, middle and low in 3 clusters. The average quality on each group $Quality(group_g)$ based on normalized quality indicators is calculated as in Eq. (1).

$$Quality(group_g) = \frac{1}{m \times n} \sum_{i=1, i \in group_g}^{m} \sum_{j=1}^{n} q_{ij} \qquad (1)$$

Where q_{ij} denotes value of quality of the jth quality indicator of ith patent in g^{th} group. The m and n denote number of patent in a group and number of quality indicators, respectively.

Stage 2: Build Patent Quality Classification System. In this stage, the task of patent quality prediction is predicting quality potentiality on new patent application. There are two steps in extracting key characteristics of a patent document and building an SVM-based quality classification system according to patent characteristics. However, the quality indicators cannot be used directly in variables of classification system because the quality indicators are calculated at patent publication afterwards. The new patent application that its volume of quality indicators may very less or empty, in commonly, new patent application or published has some potential but its event is not appear in this time. Therefore, we only use the characteristics from patent document such as count of claim, priority date and so on.

Stage 2.1: Key Patent Characteristic Extraction by KPCA. All patents will separate into two datasets, which are training and testing data. The characteristics of a patent document in training dataset are used to compute mean centering for kernel, eigenvalues and eigenvectors.

Stage 2.2: Build a Patent Quality Classification Model by SVM. The input vector of SVM training use new nonlinear feature space $Training(tr^k)$ by KPCA and the output vector of quality classes is given by SOM with quality indicators.

Stage 2.3: Forecast Patent Quality for New Sample of Testing Data. The trained model of SVM classifier will be used to classify the new sample of testing data $Testing(ts^k)$ for patent quality classification.

Stage 2.4: Evaluation of Patent Quality Classification Performance. To evaluate the performance of the trained model of SVM classifier, the classification results will be collected in the confusion matrix. The confusion matrix is for each quality class i, the TP_i denotes the correct classification into quality class i, the TN denotes the correct classification into non quality class i, the FN_i denotes incorrect classification into quality class i, the FP_i denotes incorrect classification into non quality class i.

4 Experimental Results

In this section, we have designed a series of testing for evaluating our proposed methodology as SOM-KPCA-SVM. There are three parameters for experiments, first one, the scale of data on time has three different period datasets which are five years, ten years and forty years; second one, the amount of quality groups has three types which are three quality groups, five quality groups and seven quality groups; finally, the number of feature extraction has four percentages which are 25 %, 50 %, 75 % and 100 %.

4.1 Patent Dataset and Statistical Analysis

In this patent data, we collected 18,747 patents in last 40 years from Thomson Innovation[1] database. These patents are related to "Thin film solar cell" technical field and search on title, abstract, claim and description. In this study, we want to analyze the trends of different time scales, so there are three datasets as follows:

(1) The patent applications in last 5 years (2009–2013, 5YD), (2) The patent applications in last 10 years (2004–2013, 10YD), (3) The patent applications in last 40 years (1974–2013, 40YD).

Moreover, the variables of patent data are of two type including patent quality indicators (PQI), which are calculated from the additional information and another one is patent document characteristics (PDC) from patent document.

4.2 Result on Patent Quality Analysis

In this patent analysis, the result of quality analysis of past patent development is obtained by SOM clustering computation. To decide the right number of groups, the

---

[1] The Thomson Innovation is proved the fully patent data from around the world, http://info.thomsoninnovation.com/.

rule of thumb is that the smaller the groups are; the lager the quality differences are. Of course, the number of patents is also an important factor in deciding number of groups. To properly cluster the patent data, in this study, we designed different quality groups, i.e., three, five and seven. In addition, we will look into the patents within each group and check with the quality indicators of each patent to ensure the consistence of the clustering. There are three different amounts of clustering such as 3 quality groups (3QG), 5 quality groups (5QG) and 7 quality groups (7QG).

Figures 2, 3, and 4 shows the distribution of patent applications in 3QG, 5QG and 7QG, respectively. The results show that all G1 have lowest quality on different datasets with different groups are most number of patent applications. The highest quality groups such as G3 in 3QG, G5 in 5QG and G7 in 7QG which only the G7 and G 5 have less number of patent applications. The reason is usually higher quality patent only relatively few patents, especially in the number of groups rising.

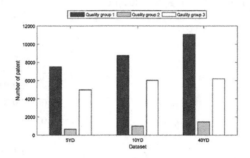

Fig. 2. Distribution of patent applications in 3 quality groups

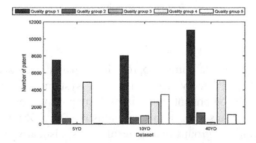

Fig. 3. Distribution of patent application in 5 quality groups

4.3   Performance Evaluation of the Proposed Approach

In this paper, the automatic analysis and classification system of patent quality are evaluated and the classification results are collected in the confusion matrix. Therefore, we use accuracy (ACC) as the measurement of the system performance. The performance (%) on different nonlinear features by Gaussian kernel as shown in Table 1.

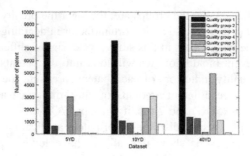

Fig. 4. Distribution of patent applications in 7 quality groups

Table 1. The performance (%) on different nonlinear features by Gaussian kernel

Amount of group	KPCA feature	5YD	10YD	40YD
3QG	25 %	65.78	65.36	64.79
	50 %	79.75	81.67	81.59
	75 %	82.52	82.83	82.32
	100 %	82.1	82.21	82.35
5QG	25 %	65.72	61.45	62.81
	50 %	79.24	72.06	79.86
	75 %	82.27	71.63	80.2
	100 %	81.7	72	80.12
7QG	25 %	62.53	61.57	61.88
	50 %	73.59	71.38	77.97
	75 %	74.32	70.87	77.97
	100 %	73.42	71.24	77.8

5   Conclusions

This study proposed three data mining approaches to patent analysis and patent quality forecasting. The SOM-KPCA-SVM patent quality system combined self-organizing maps, kernel principal component analysis and support vector machine to classify patent quality of a thin film solar cell in solar industry. The SOM has successful cluster patent into different quality groups and its result has statistically significant difference in the quality indicators between the quality groups. The KPCA has effectively transformed a nonlinear feature space from characteristics of a patent document and it can improve classification performance. The SVM has built a powerful classification model for patent quality problem. Therefore, our proposed SOM-KPCA-SVM automatic patent quality classification system has improved analysis time, cost and manpower by traditional patent analysis approaches. Thus, SOM-KPCA-SVM system can take a short time to determine patent quality.

References

1. Trappey, A.J.C., Trappey, C.V., Wu, C.Y., Lin, C.L.: A patent quality analysis for innovative technology and product development. Adv. Eng. Inform. **26**(1), 26–34 (2012)
2. Trappey, A.J.C., Trappey, C.V., Wu, C.Y., Fan, C.Y., Lin, Y.L.: Intelligent patent recommendation system for Innovative design collaboration. J. Netw. Comput. Appl. **36**(6), 1441–1450 (2013)
3. Abbas, A., Zhang, L., Khan, S.U.: A literature review on the state-of-the-art in patent analysis. World Pat. Inf. **37**, 3–13 (2014)
4. Dereli, T., Durmuşoğlu, A.: Classifying technology patents to identify trends: applying a fuzzy-based clustering approach in the Turkish textile industry. Technol. Soc. **31**(3), 263–272 (2009)
5. Narin, F.: Patent bibliometrics. Scientometrics **30**(1), 147–155 (1994)
6. Narin, F., Hamilton, K., Olivastro, D.: The increasing linkage between US technology and public science. Res. Policy **26**, 317–330 (1997)
7. Allison, J.R., Lemley, M.A., Moore, K.A., Trunkey, R.D.: Valuable patents. Georgetown Law J. **92**, 435–479 (2004)
8. Yu, W.D., Lo, S.S.: Patent analysis-based fuzzy inference system for technological strategy planning. Autom. Constr. **18**, 770–776 (2009)
9. Ju, S.S., Lai, M.F., Fan, C.Y.: Using patent analysis to analyze the technological developments of virtualization. Procedia Soc. Behav. Sci. **57**, 146–154 (2012)
10. Brügmann, S., Bouayad-Agha, N., Burga, A., Carrascosa, S.: Towards content-oriented patent document processing: intelligent patent analysis and summarization. World Pat. Inf. **40**, 30–42 (2015)
11. Grimaldi, M., Cricelli, L., Giovanni, M.D., Rogo, F.: The patent portfolio value analysis: a new framework to leverage patent information for strategic technology planning. Technol. Forecast. Soc. Change **94**, 286–302 (2015)
12. Bessen, J.: The value of U.S. patents by owner and patent characteristics. Res. Policy **37**, 932–945 (2008)
13. Nair, S.S., Mathew, M., Nag, D.: Dynamics between patent latent variables and patent price. Technovation **31**, 648–654 (2011)
14. Saint-Georges, M.D., Potterie, B.P.: A quality index for patent systems. Res. Policy **42**, 704–719 (2013)

Mining Best Strategy for Multi-view Classification

Jing Peng[1]([✉]) and Alex J. Aved[2]

[1] Computer Science Department, Montclair State University,
Montclair, NJ 07043, USA
jing.peng@montclair.edu
[2] Information Directorate AFRL/RIED, Rome, NY 13441, USA
alexander.aved@us.af.mil

Abstract. In multi-view classification, the goal is to find a strategy for choosing the most consistent views for a given task. A strategy is a probability distribution over views. A strategy can be considered as advice given to an algorithm. There can be several strategies, each allocating a different probability mass to a view at different times. In this paper, we propose an algorithm for mining these strategies in such a way that its trust in a view for classification comes close to that of the best strategy. As a result, the most consistent views contribute to multi-view classification. Finally, we provide experimental results to demonstrate the effectiveness of the proposed algorithm.

1 Introduction

In classification, it is useful to develop techniques that take input from multiple views for classification. Most of these algorithms, however, are focused on either view consistency (agreement among the views) [1], or view diversity (complementary views) [10]. In this paper, a multi-view classifier is given a set of strategies for selecting views. A strategy is simply a probability distribution over the views. Each strategy allocates a different probability mass to a view at different times. The goal is to mine these strategies so that the classifier's trust in each view for classification comes close to that of the best strategy.

We introduce a probabilistic boosting algorithm for achieving the above goal. We also provide experimental results using simulated and real examples to demonstrate the efficacy of the proposed algorithm.

2 Related Work

A class of multi-view learning algorithms has been investigated such as SVM-2K [6], multi-view learning [8], and Bayesian co-training [11], among others. The idea is to perform not only within-view regularization but also between-view regularization. This is motivated by the idea that the generalization error can be bounded by the disagreement between classifiers along independent views [5]. This results in co-training where a view with large variance contributes less to the overall loss. We derive a similar technique in a Bayesian framework.

© Springer International Publishing Switzerland 2016
Y. Tan and Y. Shi (Eds.): DMBD 2016, LNCS 9714, pp. 270–275, 2016.
DOI: 10.1007/978-3-319-40973-3_27

3 Probabilistic Boosting

We now describe our proposed algorithm for mining strategies for multi-view classification. We are given a set of training examples: $S = \{(\mathbf{x}_i, y_i)\}_{i=1}^n$, and M disjoint features for each example $\mathbf{x}_i = \{x_i^1, \cdots, x_i^M\}$, where $x_i^j \in \Re^{q_j}$, and $y_i \in \mathcal{Y} = \{-1, +1\}$. Each member x_i^j is known as a *view* of example $\mathbf{x}_i$. Assume that examples $(\mathbf{x}_i, y_i)$ are drawn randomly and independently according to a fixed but unknown probability distribution over $\mathcal{X} \times \mathcal{Y}$, and $\mathcal{X} \subseteq \Re^q$, where $q = \sum_{j=1}^M q_j$. In the proposed technique, a view is selected probabilistically.

We define the following reward function for view j

$$r_t(j) = 1 - \sqrt{1 - \beta_{t,j}^2}. \tag{1}$$

Here $\beta_{t,j}$ is the edge of the jth view at time t. The edge plays an important role in bounding training errors.

We now present the proposed probabilistic booting algorithm, called Prob-Boost, shown in Algorithm 1. u_t represents a probability distribution over strategies, and $\boldsymbol{\pi}^i$ denotes a strategy. When i_t is selected, estimated reward $\hat{r}_{i_t}$ for the view is set to $r_{i_t}(i)/p_{i_t}(t)$. This choice compensates the reward of views that are unlikely to be chosen.

Algorithm 1. ProbBoost

Input: $\gamma \in (0, 1]$, $S = \{(\mathbf{x}_i, y_i)\}_{i=1}^n$.
Initialize: $u_1(i) = 1$ for $i = 1, \cdots, N$ and $w_1(i) = \frac{1}{n}$, $i = 1, \cdots, n$.
For $t = 1$ **to** T

1. Obtain $\boldsymbol{\pi}_t^1, \cdots, \boldsymbol{\pi}_t^N$, and set $U_t = \sum_{j=1}^N u_t(j)$.
2. For $j = 1, \cdots, M$

$$p_t(j) = (1 - \gamma) \sum_{i=1}^N \frac{u_t(i)\pi_t^i(j)}{U_t} + \frac{\gamma}{M}$$

3. Choose view i_t according to $p_t(1), \cdots, p_t(M)$.
4. Compute base classifier $h_t^{i_t}$ using distribution $\mathbf{w}_t$.
5. Compute edge $\beta_t(i_t)$, and let $\alpha_t = \frac{1}{2} \ln(\frac{1+\beta_t(i_t)}{1-\beta_t(i_t)})$.
6. Compute $r_t(i_t)$ according to (1)
7. For $j = 1, \cdots, M$

$$\hat{r}_t(j) = \begin{cases} r_t(j)/p_t(j) & \text{if } j = i_t; \\ 0 & \text{otherwise.} \end{cases}$$

8. For $i = 1, \cdots, N$

$$\hat{z}_t(i) = \boldsymbol{\pi}_t^i \cdot \hat{\mathbf{r}}_t \quad \text{and} \quad u_{t+1}(i) = u_t(i)e^{\gamma \hat{z}_t(i)/M}$$

9. Update $w_{t+1}(i) = \frac{w_t(i)}{Z_t} \times e^{-\alpha_t y_i h_t^{i+t}(x_i^{i_t})}$, where Z_t is a normalization factor.

Output: $H(\mathbf{x}) = sign(\sum_{t=1}^T \alpha_t h_t^*(x^*))$

The main steps of ProbBoost are shown in Algorithm 1. Note the probability distribution for choosing views is a mixture (weighted by γ) of the uniform distribution ($\frac{1}{M}$) and the weighted average of strategies $\boldsymbol{\pi}^i$ (with weight $u_t(i)$). This provides ProbBoost with an opportunity to examine potential views that may prove to be useful, which ensures diversity.

Input to ProbBoost is the set of n training examples from all M views. The algorithm produces as output a classifier that combines data from all the views. We can state the following convergence result of the proposed algorithm.

Theorem 1. *Let $V = \{V_1, \cdots, V_M\}$ be a set of M views. Suppose that there exists a view $V_{i+} \in V$ and a constant $0 < \rho <= 1$ such that for any distribution over the training data, the base learner returns a weak classifier from view V_{i+} (or simply i^+) with edge $\beta_{i+} \geq \rho$. Then, with probability at least $1 - \delta$ and for any set of N strategies that includes the uniform strategy and the strategy whose distribution is concentrated on V_{i+}, the training error of ProbBoost will become zero in time at most*

$$T = \max\left(\left(\frac{4C}{\rho^2}\right)^3, \frac{4\log n}{\rho^2}\right). \tag{2}$$

Here $C = 4.62(M\log\frac{N}{\delta})^{1/3}$, and $\gamma = \min\left\{1, \left(\frac{M\log\frac{N}{\delta}}{((e-1)/2)^2 g}\right)^{1/3}\right\}$.

The proof is along the lines of the proof of Theorem 1 in [2].

The time bound involves both M, the number of views, and ρ, the quality that the views can provide. A large M requires more trials to explore the views so that the best view(s) can be exploited. When the views can not provide sufficient separation of the classes, ρ must be lowered, resulting in reduced edges (hence small asymptotic margins). This in turn demands a large number of trials to construct enough base classifiers so that the final classifier can be a strong one. In practice, a trade-off between the competing goals has to be made.

We note that ProbBoost is a boosting algorithm that mines a multi-view classification strategy that comes close to the best strategy. Thus, it should output a classifier H with zero training error after $T = O(\log n)$ iterations, as long as there exists a strategy whose distribution is concentrated on view V_{i+}. Several boosting algorithms meet this condition [9].

4 Experiments

4.1 Methods

We have carried out empirical study evaluating the performance of the proposed algorithms along with some competing methods.

1. **ProbBoost**–The proposed algorithm for mining the best strategy from a pool of strategies (Algorithm 1). In this experiment, the set of strategies includes the inverse variance strategy, where the strategy allocates probability mass to

a view inversely proportional to the view's variance, and the uniform strategy. For the inverse variance strategy, the consensus function is simply true training labels. f_j, the classifier along the jth view, is estimated by applying the base learner to the view.

2. **AdaBoost**–AdaBoost is applied to the concatenation of all the views.
3. **SVMs**–Support Vector Machines with the Gaussian kernel are applied to the concatenation of all the views [4].
4. **MVK**–The multi-view kernel learning algorithm proposed in [8], where the objective involves both within and between view regularization[1]. We obtained Matlab code from github.com/lorisbaz/Multiview-learning.

All the boosting type algorithms employ a decision tree learner to build base classifiers. Compared to other base learners such as Naive Bayes, decision trees are known to better exploit features, resulting in a better baseline. The number of base classifiers is set to 100. For ProbBoost, we set γ to 0.3, as suggested in [2]. For kernel techniques such as SVMs and MVK, ten-fold cross-validation was used for model selection (kernel width and soft margin constraint).

4.2   Data Sets

The following binary data sets are used to evaluate the performance of the competing methods.

BioMetrics Data: The *BioMetrics* dataset is a publicly available WVU multimodal dataset [3]. The dataset consists of fingerprint, iris, palmprint, hand geometry and voice modalities from subjects of different age, gender and ethnicity as described in [3]. The dataset is difficult because many examples are low quality due to blur, occlusion and sensor noise.

Out of these, we chose iris and fingerprint modalities (views) for evaluating the proposed algorithms, where each subject has sufficient examples in both views. Also, the evaluation was done on randomly selected 5 pairs of subjects (binary classification) having samples in both views. These 5 pairs are labeled as *BioM1* (Iris: 36&27. Fingerprint: 61&49) *BioM2* (Iris: 30&27. Fingerprint: 62&46), *BioM3* (Iris: 30&29. Fingerprint: 61&60), *BioM4* (Iris: 28&28. Fingerprint: 61&46), and *BioM5* (Iris: 27&28. Fingerprint: 61&60).

Each iris image is first segmented into 25×240 templates, which are then convolved a log-Gabor filter at a single scale to form a 6000×1 feature vector [7]. For fingerprints, ridge and bifurcation features are computed to form a feature vector of size 7241×1.

CiteSeer Data: The *CiteSeer* data consist of 3,312 documents or papers that are grouped into six classes. Each document has three natural views: (1) Text view–title and abstract of the paper; (2) Inbound reference or link view; and (3) Outbound reference or link view. For this experiment, Artificial Intelligence (668 examples) and Machine Learning (701 examples) classes are used.

---

[1] We chose MVK over SVM-2K because SVM-2K is inherently a two-view learning algorithm.

4.3   Experimental Results

For all the experiments reported here, we randomly split the data into 60 % as training and remaining 40 % as testing. This process is repeated 30 times and the average results are reported. All features are normalized to have zero mean and unit variance. Test data are similarly normalized using corresponding training mean and variance.

Table 1 shows the average accuracy over 30 runs on the eight datasets by the competing methods. The last row shows the overall average performance across the tasks. The bold faces indicate that results are significantly different from non-bold faces at the 5 % significance level. ProbBoost achieved the best performance on the problems we have experimented with. SVMs performed the worst, followed by MVK. AdaBoost is in between.

One procedural parameter, $\gamma = 0.3$, input to ProbBoost (Algorithm 1) was fixed throughout the experiments without expensive cross-validation to determine their values. In contrast, the performance registered by the kernel methods (SVMs and MVK) involved costly cross-validation to choose procedural parameters. This again shows the advantage of the proposed technique.

Table 1. Average accuracy of the methods.

	ProbBoost	SVMs	AdaBoost	MVK
BioM1	**0.84**	0.59	0.81	0.67
BioM2	**0.91**	0.52	0.87	0.66
BioM3	**0.81**	0.59	0.76	0.65
BioM4	**0.91**	0.81	**0.89**	0.71
BioM5	**0.77**	0.61	0.68	0.62
CiteSeer	**0.85**	0.81	**0.85**	**0.84**
Ave	0.85	0.66	0.81	0.69

5   Summary

We have developed the ProbBoost algorithm for mining the best strategy for multi-view classification. We have established the convergence of the proposed algorithm with high probability. The experimental results show that the proposed ProbBoost algorithm performs very competitively in several real world problems we have experimented with. Our future work includes investigating different strategies for robust multi-view classification.

References

1. Brefeld, U., Buscher, C., Scheffer, T.: Multi-view hidden Markov perceptrons. In: Proceedings of GI Workshop
2. Busa-Fekete, R., Kegl, B.: Fast boosting using adversarial bandits. In: Proceedings of International Conference on Machine Learning (2010)
3. Crihalmeanu, S., Ross, A., Schukers, S., Hornak, L.: A protocol for multibiometric data acquisition, storage and dissemination. In: Technical report, WVU, Lane Department of Computer Science and Electrical Engineering (2007)
4. Cristianini, N., Shawe-Taylor, J.: An Introduction to Support Vector Machines and Other Kernel-based Learning Methods. Cambridge University Press, Cambridge (2000)
5. Dasgupta, S., Littman, M., McAllester, D.: PAC generalization bounds for co-training. In: Dietterich, T.G., Becker, S., Ghahramani, Z. (eds.) Advances in Neural Information Processing Systems, vol. 14, pp. 375–382. The MIT Press, Cambridge (2002)
6. Farquhar, J., Hardoon, D., Meng, H., Shawe-Taylor, J., Szedmak, S.: Two View Learning: SVM-2K Theory and Practice. Advances in Neural Information Processing Systems, vol. 18, pp. 355–362. MIT Press, Cambridge (2005)
7. Masek, L., Kovesi, P.: MATLAB source code for biometric identification system based on iris patterns. Technical report, The University of Western Australia (2003)
8. Minh, H., Bazzani, L., Murino, V.: A unifying framework for vector-valued manifold regularization and multi-view learning, pp. 100–108 (2013)
9. Schapire, R.E., Singer, Y.: Improved boosting algorithms using confidence rated predictions. Mach. Learn. 3(37), 297–336 (1999)
10. Wang, W., Zhou, Z.-H.: Analyzing co-training style algorithms. In: Kok, J.N., Koronacki, J., Lopez de Mantaras, R., Matwin, S., Mladenič, D., Skowron, A. (eds.) ECML 2007. LNCS (LNAI), vol. 4701, pp. 454–465. Springer, Heidelberg (2007)
11. Yu, S., Krishnapuram, B., Rosales, R., Rao, R.: Bayesian co-training. J. Mach. Learn. Res. 12, 2649–2680 (2011)

Anomaly Pattern and Diagnosis

Detecting Variable Length Anomaly
Patterns in Time Series Data

Ngo Duy Khanh Vy$^{(\boxtimes)}$ and Duong Tuan Anh

Faculty of Computer Science and Engineering,
Ho Chi Minh City University of Technology, Ho Chi Minh City, Vietnam
dtanh@cse.hcmut.edu.vn

Abstract. The anomaly detection algorithm, developed by Leng et al. (2008), can detect anomaly patterns of variable lengths in time series. This method consists of two stages: the first is segmenting time series; the next is calculating anomaly factor of each pattern and then judging whether a pattern is anomaly or not based on its anomaly factor. Since the lengths of patterns can be different from each other, this algorithm uses Dynamic Time Warping (DTW) as distance measure between the patterns. Due to DTW, the algorithm leads to high computational complexity. In this paper, to improve the above mentioned algorithm, we apply homothetic transformation to convert every pair of patterns of different lengths into the same length so that we can easily calculate Euclidean distance between them. This modification accelerates the anomaly detection algorithm remarkably and makes it workable on large time series.

Keywords: Time series · Anomaly detection · Segmentation · Anomaly factor

1 Introduction

Anomaly detection is a challenging topic, mainly because we need to obtain the lengths of anomaly patterns before detecting them. There has been an extensive study on time series anomaly detection in the literature. Some popular algorithms for time series anomaly detection include window-based methods such as brute-force and HOT SAX by Keogh et al. (2005) [4] and WAT by Bu et al. (2007) [2]; a method based on neural-network by Oliveira et al. (2004) [8]; a method based on segmentation and Finite State Automata by Salvador and Chan (2005) [10]; a method based on time series segmentation and anomaly scores by Leng et al. (2008) [6]; and a method based on Piecewise Aggregate Approximation bit representation and clustering by Li et al. (2013) [7]. Most of these above-mentioned algorithms for time series anomaly detection [2, 4, 7, 8] require the user to specify the length of anomaly pattern as an input parameter, but this length is often unknown.

Among these algorithms, the method proposed by Leng et al. [6] is the first one in the literature that can detect anomaly patterns of variable lengths in time series and hence does not require the length of the anomaly pattern as a parameter supplied by user. This method consists of two stages. The first is segmenting time series using a quadratic regression model. The next is discovering all the anomaly patterns by calculating anomaly factor of each pattern and then judging whether a pattern is anomaly

© Springer International Publishing Switzerland 2016
Y. Tan and Y. Shi (Eds.): DMBD 2016, LNCS 9714, pp. 279–287, 2016.
DOI: 10.1007/978-3-319-40973-3_28

or not based on its anomaly factor. Since in this algorithm, the lengths of patterns can be different from each other, Leng et al. suggested that Dynamic Time Warping (DTW) distance [1] should be used to calculate the distances between the patterns in this algorithm. Due to this suggestion, the algorithm proposed by Leng et al. becomes a very complicated algorithm with high computational complexity and is not suitable to work on large time series.

In this work, to improve the algorithm proposed by Leng et al., we apply homothetic transformation to convert every pair of patterns of different lengths into the same length so that we can easily calculate Euclidean distance between them. In addition, we reduce the number of distance calculations in building the distance matrix by constraining the possible alignments between each pair of patterns. These two modifications bring out a remarkable improvement for the original anomaly detection algorithm in time efficiency while maintaining the same detection accuracy. Besides, we try to apply in our proposed anomaly detection algorithm another method of time series segmentation which is based on important extreme points instead of quadratic regression model.

Experimental results on eight real world time series datasets demonstrate the effectiveness and efficiency of our proposed methods in detecting anomaly patterns of variable lengths in time series.

2 Background

2.1 Some Definitions

A time series $T = t_1, t_2, ..., t_m$ is an ordered set of m real values measured at equal intervals. Given a time series T of length m, a subsequence C is a sampling of length $n < m$ of contiguous positions from T, i.e., $C = t_p, t_{p+1}, ..., t_{p+n-1}$, for $1 \leq p \leq m-n+1$. Sometimes, C is denoted as (s_p, e_{p+n-1}), where $s_p = t_p$ and $e_{p+n-1} = t_{p+n-1}$.

Definition 1. *Distance function*: $Dist(C, M)$ is a positive value used to measure the difference between two time series C and M, based on some measure method.

Definition 2. *k-distance of a pattern*: Given a positive integer k, a pattern set D and a pattern $P \in D$, the k-distance of P, denoted as k-$dist(P)$, is defined as the distance between P and a pattern $Q \in D$ such that.

(i)   For at least k patterns $Q' \in D$ it holds that $Dist(D, Q') \leq Dist(D, Q)$.
(ii) For at most k-1 patterns $Q' \in D\backslash\{Q\}$ it holds that $Dist(D, Q') < Dist(D, Q)$.

Definition 3. *Non-Self Match*: Given a time series T, its two subsequences P of length n starting at position p and Q starting at position q, we say that Q is a non-self-match to P, if $Dist(P, Q) \geq e$ or $|p - q| \geq n$, where e is a given value of distance threshold.

Definition 4. *Anomaly factor*: For any pattern set D and a pattern $P \in D$, k-$dist$ (D) denotes all k-$dist$ of patterns, anomaly factor of pattern P defined as the ratio of k-$dist(P)$ to $median(k$-$dist(D))$.

Definition 5. *Anomaly Pattern*: Given any pattern set D, a pattern $P \in D$, P is anomaly only if its anomaly factor is larger than a, where a is the threshold of anomaly pattern.

2.2 Detecting Variable Length Anomaly Patterns in Time Series Based on Segmentation and Anomaly Factors

Leng et al. [6] proposed the algorithm for detecting anomaly patterns in time series. This algorithm consists of two phases: segmenting time series and detecting anomaly patterns based on anomaly factors.

Leng et al. used quadratic regression model to segment time series. Regression function is defined as $f(t) = \beta_0 + \beta_1 t + \beta_2 t^2$, where the t values, the values of time domain are real values. The segmentation algorithm searches for a segment $S = t_p, \ldots, t_{p+m+1}$ of a given time series T, starts at t_p and end at t_{p+m-1}, such that the sum of squared errors, is less than ε_1, where $f(t) = \beta_0 + \beta_1 t + \beta_2 t^2$ and ε_1 is a threshold specified by the user. We can extract all the patterns in the time series T by applying repeatedly this search procedure.

The segmentation procedure is described as follows.

1. Let $s_1 = 1$ denote the start position of the first segment, l denote the initial length of each segment, $m = s_1$ and then update this segment, the updating procedure is as follows. Calculate the values of β_0, $\beta_1 t$, and β_2 and the sum of squared errors:

$$SSE = \sum_{i=p}^{p+l-1} (f(i) - t_i)^2 \tag{1}$$

2. If $SSE < \varepsilon_1$ let $l = l + 1$, go to step 1, else goto step 3.
3. Let (s_1, e_1) denote this segment, e_1 denotes the end position of this segment and $e_1 = l - 1$.
4. Let $i = 1$, if $Dist((s_1, e_1), (s_1 + i, e_1 + i)) \leq \varepsilon_2$, increment i by 1, calculate it, repeat this procedure until $Dist((s_1, e_1), (s_1 + i, e_1 + i)) > \varepsilon_2$ or $i > (e_1 - s_1)$, let $s_2 = e_1 + i$, the s_2 is the start position of the next segment.
5. Let $m = s_2$, calculate e_2 using the steps 1-3, and then obtain the second segment (s_2, e_2).
6. Calculate s_j using the step 4, let $m = s_j$, calculate the value of e_j using the steps $1 - 3$, and then obtain the j-th segment (s_j, e_j).
7. Repeat the above procedure until the end position of the segment is n

Notice that the segmentation procedure uses Dynamic Time Warping (DTW) as distance measure for the patterns and Step 4 aims to eliminate the trivial matches. The parameter ε_1 determines the length of each segment. The parameter ε_2 (called *non-self match threshold*) helps in removing trivial matches and hence it has impact on the number of extracted segments.

The procedure for Anomaly Pattern Detection is described as follows.

1. Find the maximum value, l_{max} and minimum value l_{min} of the lengths of all extracted segments.
2. Calculate the distance matrix $D = (d_{ij})_{m \times m}$ of segments:

$$d_{ij} = \min_{l_{min} \leq l \leq l_{max}} Dist((s_i, e_i), (s_j, s_j + l)) \tag{2}$$

where $1 \leq i, j \leq m$ and $i \neq j$.

3. Compute k-distance of each segments based on the distance matrix, let $k\text{-}dist$ (D) denote the set of all these distances.
4. Calculate median($k\text{-}dist(D)$)
5. Calculate anomaly factor of each segment, and determine whether each segment is an anomaly pattern or not basing on the anomaly factor threshold a.
6. Given two anomaly patterns (s_i, e_i) and (s_j, e_j), if they are overlapped, merge them into one pattern.

Notice that in Step 2, we need to compute $(l_{max} - l_{min} + 1)$ DTW distances when calculating the DTW distance between (s_i, e_i) and (s_j, e_j), and the algorithm selects the minimum value of them as the real DTW distance of (s_i, e_i) and (s_j, e_j). Step 6 helps to merge two anomaly patterns if they are overlapped and this can weaken the influence of ε_1 if the value of ε_1 is smaller than its real value.

3   The Proposed Algorithms

The main idea of our method for detecting anomaly patterns of variable lengths in time series is to apply homothetic transformation to convert each pair of patterns of different lengths into the same length so that we can easily calculate Euclidean distances between them rather than using computationally complicated DTW distance. We call our proposed method VL_QR|HT (Variable Length anomaly pattern detection based on Quadratic Regression and Homothety).

3.1   Homothetic Transformation

Homothety is a transformation in affine space. Given a point O and a value $k \neq 0$. A homothety with center O and ratio k transforms the point M to the point M' such that $\overrightarrow{OM'} = k \times \overrightarrow{OM}$

Homothety can transform a time series T of length n ($T = \{y_1, y_2, ..., y_n\}$) to time series T' of length n' by performing the following steps. First, compute $Y\_MAX = MAX$ $(y_1, ..., y_n)$, $Y\_MIN = MIN(y_1, ...,y_n)$. Second, set the center I of homothety with the coordinates $X\_C = n/2$, $Y\_C = (Y\_MAX + Y\_MIN)/2$. Next, perform the homothety with the center I and the ratio n'/n.

To compute Euclidean distance of two time series, first we check their lengths. If the two lengths are similar, we can compute their distance right away. Otherwise, we apply homothety to convert them to the same length and then compute their Euclidean distance. Here we select the average length of the two time series as the length to which we convert the two time series using homothety.

Besides, we note that two 'similar' subsequences will not be recognized where a vertical difference exists between them. To make the Euclidean distance calculation in the anomaly pattern detection algorithm able to handle not only uniform scaling but also shifting transformation along vertical axis, we modify our Euclidean distance by using Modified Euclidean Distance as a method of negating the differences caused through vertical axis offsets. Details of Modified Euclidean Distance are given in our previous work; interested reader can refer to [11].

3.2 Reducing the Number of Distance Calculations in Building the Distance Matrix

In the procedure for detecting anomaly patterns of variable lengths proposed by Leng et al. [6], to compute the distance between two patterns (s_i, e_i) and (s_j, e_j), we need to compute $(l_{max} - l_{min} + 1)$ times of distance calculations, where l_{min} and l_{max} are the maximum and minimum length of all the patterns extracted from the original time series (see Eq. 2 in Subsect. 2.2). When l_{max} is much larger than l_{min}, the algorithm has to perform so many distance calculations in order to determine the real distance between two patterns and this might bring out the pathological cases in which a very short segment can match with a very long segment.

In order to reduce the number of distance calculations as well as to prevent pathological alignments between two patterns, in our proposed algorithm, we modify Eq. 2 by adding the parameter r and replace l_{max} and l_{min} with l_{upper} and l_{lower} respectively. The lower bound l_{lower} and the upper bound l_{upper} are defined by:

$$l_{upper} = \lfloor l_{avg}(1 + r) \rfloor \tag{3}$$

$$l_{lower} = \lfloor l_{avg}(1 - r) \rfloor \tag{4}$$

where l_{avg} is the average length of all the segments extracted from the original time series. Now, the formula to compute the distance between two patterns i and j is:

$$d_{ij} = \min_{l_{lower} \leq l \leq l_{upper}} Dist((s_i, e_i), (s_j, s_j + l)) \tag{5}$$

By the parameter r, we limit how far the length of the pattern j may differ from the average length of all the extracted patterns. The parameter r (called *length difference width*) should be chosen in order that the difference between l_{upper} and l_{lower} is not high while still maintaining the accuracy of the algorithm. Through experiment, we find out that r should vary in the range 0.05 to 0.25.

3.3　Other Issue: Using Some Alternative Segmentation Method

Using the same framework of VL_QR|HT, we can develop another anomaly detection algorithm by replacing the segmentation method based on quadratic regression with another time series segmentation method. The other segmentation method we selected here is based on the concepts of Important Extreme Points, proposed by Pratt and Fink [9]. This time series segmentation consists of two following steps. First, we extract all important extreme points of the time series T. The result of this step is a sequence of extreme points $EP = (ep_1, ep_2, ..., ep_l)$. Secondly, we compute all the candidate patterns iteratively. A candidate pattern $CP_i(T)$, $i = 1, 2,..., l - 2$ is the subsequence of T that is bounded by extreme points ep_i and ep_{i+2}. Candidate patterns are subsequences that may have different lengths. To be able to calculate distance between them, we bring them to the average length by using homothety.

After segmentation stage, we calculate anomaly factor for each candidate pattern in the same way as in VL_QR|HT. We call this anomaly detection algorithm VL_EP|HT (Variable Length anomaly pattern detection based on Extreme Points and Homothety). Note that in identifying important extreme points of a time series, we need the parameter R, called *compression rate*, which is greater than one and an increase of R leads to selection of fewer important extreme points [9]. To set a lower bound for the length of all extracted subsequences, we introduce the parameter *min_length*, the minimum time lag between two adjacent important extreme points. When a candidate pattern is extracted, its length must be greater than or equal to 2*min_length.

4　Experimental Evaluation

We implemented all four algorithms: VL_QR|DTW (the original algorithm proposed by Leng et al.), VL_QR|HT, VL_EP|HT and HOT SAX. The first experiment aims to compare VL_QR|HT to original VL_QR|DTW in terms of time efficiency. The second experiment aims to compare VL_QR|HT and VL_EP|HT to HOT SAX in terms of time efficiency and anomaly detection accuracy.

Our experiments were conducted over the datasets from the UCR Time Series Data Mining Archive for discord discovery [5]. There are 8 datasets used in these experiments. The datasets are from different areas (finance, medicine, manufacturing, science). The names and lengths of the eight datasets are: ECG108 (17500 points), ECG308 (1300 points), ERP (5000 points), Memory (6875 points), Power_Italy (7000 points), Power_Dutch (9000 points), Stock20 (5000 points) and TEK1 (5000 points).

For each dataset, we have to set the required parameters for each of the three algorithms: VL_QR|HT, VL_EP|HT and HOT SAX. For VL_QR|HT, the parameters are regression error threshold ε_1, non-self match threshold ε_2, anomaly factor threshold a and the length difference width r. For VL_EP|HT, the parameters are compression rate R, the minimum length of extracted subsequence *min_length*, anomaly factor a and the length difference width r. For HOT SAX, the parameters are the discord length n and the length of PAA segment *PAA_size*. The values of parameters in the three algorithms for some datasets are shown in Table 1.

Table 1. Parameter values in the three algorithms for each dataset

Datasets	VL_QR| HT	VL_EP| HT	HOT SAX
ECG108	ε_1= 5.0, ε_2 = 0.3, a = 3.5, r = 0.1	R = 1.04, min_lenth = 50, a = 4, r = 0.1	n = 600, PAA_size = 60
ERP	ε_1 = 3.0, ε_2 = 1.0, a = 3.0, r = 0.15	R = 1.42, min_lenth = 10, a = 3.5, r = 0.1	n = 100, PAA_size = 10
Memory	ε_1= 8.0, ε_2 = 0.1, a = 2.2, r = 0.1	R = 1.1, min_lenth = 40, a = 1.6, r = 0.1	n = 100, PAA_size = 20
Power_ Italy	ε_1 = 100000, ε_2 = 100, a = 2.5, r = 0.1	R = 1.8, min_lenth = 20, a = 3.0, r = 0.1	n = 300, PAA_size = 30

4.1 Experiment 1: Comparing VL_QR |HT to VL_QR |DTW

This experiment aims to compare the efficiency of our proposed algorithm, VL_QR| HT to that of the algorithm proposed by Leng et al. (VL_QR|DTW). Over 8 datasets, we found out that the anomaly pattern detected by VL_QR|HT is exactly the same as the one detected by VL_QR|DTW. Table 2 shows the run times (in seconds) of the two algorithms over 8 datasets. Since VL_QR|DTW performs extremely slowly, we have to limit the lengths of the eight datasets to less than 3000 data points. Besides, to accelerate the DTW distance calculation, we employed a multithreading method, proposed by Huy in 2015 [3], in computing this distance.

Table 2. Run times (in seconds) of VL_QR|HT and VL_QR|DTW over eight datasets

Dataset	VL_QR|HT	VL_QR|DTW
ECG 108 (1000 points)	1	14
ECG 308 (1300 points)	1	11
ERP (1000 points)	1	5
Memory (1000 points)	1	4
Power_ Italy (3000 points)	6	200
Power_Dutch (3000 points)	1	24
Stock20 (3000 points)	2	194
TEK16 (2000 points)	1	81

The experimental results in Table 2 demonstrate that with all the datasets, the VL_QR|HT is remarkably faster than VL_QR|DTW while brings out the same accuracy. The speedup of our proposed algorithm over to the original algorithm by Leng et al. varies from 4 (dataset Memory) to 97 times (dataset Stock20) and in average is about 33.6.

4.2 Experiment 2: Comparing VL_QR|HT and VL_EP|HT to HOT SAX

In the second experiment we compare VL_QR|HT and VL_EP|HT to HOT SAX in terms of time efficiency and anomaly detection accuracy. The HOT SAX [4] is used as the baseline algorithm in this experiment. The HOT SAX is selected for comparison since it is the most cited algorithm for detecting time series discords up to date and has been applied in many applications.

In order to compare with HOT SAX which always brings out the top-anomaly pattern in a time series, in this experiment, we set the parameter k in k-*distance* for patterns to 1 for both VL_QR|HT and VL_EP|HT.

Over 8 datasets, we found out that the anomaly pattern detected by VL_QR|HT or VL_EP|HT is exactly the same as the one detected by HOT SAX.

Additionally, we measured the execution times of the three algorithms over 8 datasets. From the experimental results we can see that:

- VL_QR|HT and VL_EP|HT perform remarkably faster that HOT SAX in all the tested datasets.
- The speedup of VL_QR|HT over HOT SAX varies from 8 to 302 times and is about 71.9 times in average. The speedup of VL_EP|HT over HOT SAX varies from 6 to 94 times and is about 27.8 times in average.
- The run time of VL_QR|HT is always lower than that of VL_EP|HT over all the datasets.

5 Conclusions

We have introduced the two proposed algorithms which are improved variants of the method for variable length anomaly pattern detection in time series proposed by Leng et al. [6]. These two algorithms, called VL_QR|HT and VL_EP|HT, hinge on using homothetic transformation to convert each pair of patterns of different lengths into the same length so that we can easily calculate Euclidean distances between them. This modification that avoids using DTW distance brings out a remarkable improvement for the original algorithm in time efficiency without compromising anomaly detection accuracy.

References

1. Berndt, D., Clifford, J.: Finding patterns in time series: a dynamic programming approach. J. Adv. Knowl. Discov. Data Min. 229–248. AAA/MIT Press, Menlo Park (1996)
2. Bu, Y., Leung, T.W., Fu, A., Keogh, E., Pei, J., Meshkin, S.: WAT: finding top-K discords in time series database. In: Proceedings of the 2007 SIAM International Conference on Data Mining (SDM'07), Minneapolis, MN, USA, 26–28 April 2007
3. Huy, V.T.: Anytime k-medoids clustering of time series under dynamic time warping using an approximation technique. Master Thesis, Faculty of Computer Science and Engineering, Ho Chi Minh City University of Technology, Vietnam (2015)

4. Keogh, E., Lin, J., Fu, A.: HOT SAX: efficiently finding the most unusual time series subsequence. In: Proceedings of 5th ICDM, Houston, Texas, vol. 226–233 (2005)
5. Keogh. E.: www.cs.ucr.edu/~eamonn/discords/. Accessed 24 Jan 2015
6. Leng, M., Chen, X., Li, L.: Variable length methods for detecting anomaly patterns in time series. In: International Symposium on Computational Intelligence and Design (ISCID'08), vol. 2 (2008)
7. Li, G., Braysy, O., Jiang, L., Wu, Z., Wang, Y.: Finding time series discord based on bit representation clustering. Knowl.-Based Syst. **52**, 243–254 (2013)
8. Oliveira, A.L.I., Neto, F. B.L. Meira, S.R.L.: A method based on RBF-DAA neural network for improving Novelty detection in time series. In: Proceedings of 17th International FLAIRS Conference. AAAI Press, Miami Beach (2004)
9. Pratt, K.B., Fink, E.: Search for patterns in compressed time series. Int. J. Image Graph. **2**(1), 89–106 (2002)
10. Salvador, S., Chan, P.: Learning states and rules for time series anomaly detection. Appl. Intell. **23**(3), 241–255 (2005)
11. Truong, C.D., Tin, H.N., Anh, D.T.: Combining motif information and neural network for time series prediction. Int. J. Bus. Intell. Data Min. **7**(4), 318–339 (2012)

Bigger Data Is Better for Molecular Diagnosis Tests Based on Decision Trees

Alexandru G. Floares[1]([⊠]), George A. Calin[2], and Florin B. Manolache[3]

[1] SAIA - Solutions of Artificial Intelligence Applications, OncoPredict,
Cluj-Napoca, Transilvania, Romania
alexandru.floares@saia-institute.org, alexandru.floares@oncopredict.com
[2] University of Texas MD Anderson Cancer Center, Houston, TX, USA
gcalin@mdanderson.org
[3] Carnegie Mellon University, Pittsburgh, PA, USA
florin@andrew.cmu.edu

Abstract. Most molecular diagnosis tests are based on small studies with about twenty patients, and use classical statistics. The prevailing conception is that such studies can indeed yield accurate tests with just one or two predictors, especially when using informative molecules like microRNA in cancer diagnosis. We investigated the relationship between accuracy, the number of microRNA predictors, and the sample size of the dataset used in developing cancer diagnosis tests. The generalization capability of the tests was also investigated. One of the largest existing free breast cancer dataset was used in a binary classification (cancer versus normal) using C5 and CART decision trees. The results show that diagnosis tests with a good compromise between accuracy and the number of predictors (related to costs) can be obtained with C5 or CART on a sample size of more than 100 patients. These tests generalize well.

1 Introduction

Development of cancer diagnosis, prognosis, and response to treatment tests using high-throughput molecular data is an important but difficult biomedical problem. Most of the existing cancer tests are based on small studies (around twenty patients), and use classical statistical methods. This impacts test accuracy on new patients who were not used for the development of the test. There are many small studies in the literature reporting a reasonably good test accuracy (e.g. greater than 80 %) with a very small number of predictors, even one or two of them. Despite the fact that the biomedical problem is the same and the patient cohorts look similar, the proposed molecular predictors are different from one test to another. These studies are considered contradictory and confusing for the biomedical community. Small studies are usually justified by the cost of molecular determinations, but these costs are constantly decreasing, becoming quite affordable nowadays. Thus, we believe that the true reason for small studies is the prevailing conception of the biomedical community that they are indeed capable of leading to good cancer tests.

© Springer International Publishing Switzerland 2016
Y. Tan and Y. Shi (Eds.): DMBD 2016, LNCS 9714, pp. 288–295, 2016.
DOI: 10.1007/978-3-319-40973-3_29

In our opinion, cancer tests should be based on predictive genes embedded in a machine learning classifier, not on differentially expressed genes. Thus, studies investigating the relationships between differentially expressed genes, sample size, and statistical power [1–3] are not directly related to ours. Similar relationships were investigated in [4] for differentially expressed and predictive genes, but for a much smaller dataset of 120 patients instead of 865 used in our study. Thus, our results can be considered to better reflect the true relationships between accuracy, sample size, and number of predictors used in the test. Moreover, we fitted power functions to these relationships, which allow estimations of sample size and number of predictors for a desired accuracy level. The much larger dataset allows us to also explore the generalization capability of the small sample classifiers.

We are using one of the largest collections of microRNA (miRNA or miR) cancer determinations from The Cancer Genome Atlas consortium (TCGA) (http://cancergenome.nih.gov/). The connection of miRNA to human cancer was first revealed by George Calin and Carlo Croce in 2002 [5]. We have chosen miRNAs because they are more informative for cancer diagnosis than other molecular determinations available in the TCGA data. Being regulatory molecules and being causally related to cancer, miRNAs are important biomarker candidates for diagnosis test development. We focused on breast cancer because this is the largest dataset of the collection, and the most frequent type of cancer in women.

Studies with various sample sizes were simulated, starting from the size of typical small studies (around 20 patients) and ending with the full dataset size. To check the generalization capability of the diagnosis tests, especially of those based on small sample sizes, we also validated the models on all the data not used for training and testing. Stratified sampling was used to preserve the class proportions of the original dataset. The diagnosis tests were developed using the decision tree (DT) algorithms C5 [6] and Classification and Regression Trees (CART) [7]. Decision trees were chosen because they have a series of advantages (Sect. 2.2), making them one of the best choices for molecular tests [8]. We deliberately chose simple and transparent modeling algorithms, to be useful for the biomedical community which is less inclined to dive into advanced techniques like ensemble methods, boosted C5 [9], and Random Forests hyperparameter optimization [10]. However, these are on our to do list. While C5 is one of the most powerful and popular DT in other fields, it is not frequently used in biomedical informatics. We investigated the evolution of accuracy and number of predictors with sample size. The generalization capability of the predictive models was also investigated, being especially interesting for evaluating models based on small sample sizes.

2 The Proposed Methodology

For building the models, a preprocessing step was first necessary to clean and normalize the data as explained in Sect. 2.1. Then, the data was split into training, testing, and validation sets, and the appropriate algorithms were applied as discussed in Sect. 2.2.

2.1   Datasets and Preprocessing

The original datasets were generated by The Cancer Genome Atlas consortium. They consist of next generation sequencing microRNA determinations in nine types of cancer, and apparently normal adjacent tissues. The molecular determinations were performed on an Illumina HiSeq 2000 platform. There are two freely available datasets, one for cancer and one for normal tissue, integrated from individual studies stored on the Synapse site (https://www.synapse.org/; accessing code: syn1695324). The total number of cancer probes is 2770 and the normal set contains 316 probes, summing up to 3086 samples, which is considered a Big Data set in the field.

To perform any binary classification, e.g. certain cancer type versus normal, these two datasets should be integrated. First, the common miRNAs subset must be identified. The Cancer set has 1071 miRNAs and the Normal set has 1046 miRNAs, with 1046 miRNAs in common. Without entering into preprocessing details, it is important to mention that, after eliminating the miRNAs with all values zero and with many NaNs (Not a Number or not available) values, there are just 644 miRNAs left. We selected the invasive breast carcinoma subset (549 patients) and the normal subset (316 probes), totaling 865 cases. This is one of the few existing biomedical high-throughput datasets with more cases (865) than variables (644). As a consequence, the risk of overfitting is alleviated, and the credibility or the statistical power of the results is increased. The dataset was log_2 transformed and standardized with mean zero and standard deviation one.

2.2   Classification Problems and Algorithms

As most of the small studies are based on about twenty patients, we created random stratified subsets of the original datasets using *createDataPartition* function from *caret* R package. Stratification is important because if it is omitted, some small datasets could entirely miss one of the two classes. Small studies are supposed to contain distinct but also similar patients. Thus, we allowed for possible overlap between datasets. The computationally intensive experiments benefit from the capability of parallel computing in the *caret* R package. The BRCA and N dataset is increased from 22 cases to the full set of 865 cases in steps of 9. Each dataset was partitioned into a 75 % training and 25 % test set, and the accuracy was reported on the test set.

To estimate the generalization capability of the predictive models, the remaining cases were used as a validation set. Obviously, this is more relevant for models with small sample size where the validation set is much larger than the training and testing sets taken together. The accuracy on the training, testing, and validation data sets were compared.

Three-fold cross-validation on the training set was repeated 100 times, to mimic 100 studies with various numbers of patients, and the test accuracy was estimated using Receiver Operating Characteristic (ROC) area under the curve (AUC) metric. The variation of ROC AUC and the number of predictors with sample size was statistically and graphically explored. When the number of predictors varied with the sample size, this variation was explored as well. Also, we performed curve fitting to the accuracy versus sample size and predictor data, to gain more insight into these dependencies. The MATLAB R2015b (MathWorks, Inc., Natick, United States) Curve Fitting Toolbox was used for testing various techniques available. The best fit was obtained with a power formula of the form $ax^b + c$.

The advantages of decision trees (DT), especially useful for the biomedical community, are the following:

- Implicitly perform feature selection.
- Discover nonlinear relationships and interactions.
- Require relatively little effort from users for data preparation:
    - they do not need variable scaling;
    - they can deal with a reasonable amount of missing values;
    - they are not affected by outliers.
- Easy to interpret and explain.
- Can generate rules helping experts to formalize their knowledge.

For each sample size, we developed 100 C5 decision trees and CART models respectively. The difference in the relevant miRNAs predictors for each model was investigated. Then, their average ROC AUC and the average number of predictors were estimated. To avoid overfitting, especially for the small sample datasets, cross-validation was performed only on the training set, and a test set was left out; the error on the test set was reported. To further estimate the generalization capability, the remaining cases were used as a validation set. For both classification algorithms default parameter settings were used. Ensemble methods and hyperparameter optimization are on our to do list.

For C5, the R package *C50* combined with *caret* were used, with the following settings: $CF = 0.25$, $minCases = 2$. Usually, the first parameter (related to pruning intensity) does not influence the accuracy significantly. The second parameter specifies the minimum number of cases for a terminal node, and its increase improves the generalization capability of the model but can decrease the performance. For CART, the R package *rpart* together with *caret* were used, setting the complexity parameter which penalizes the tree complexity regarding the number of variables to $cp = 0.2$.

3 Results and Discussions

This section analyzes the results we obtain by trying different algorithms on different sample sizes.

C5 decision tree ROC AUC has a minimum of 0.8523, a mean of 0.9646, and a maximum of 0.9873. Figure 1 shows that the C5 decision tree ROC AUC increases with the sample size of the datasets. The increase is more pronounced for small data sizes and slows down for bigger data sizes. From the available techniques included in MATLAB Curve Fitting Toolbox, *power* gives the best results.

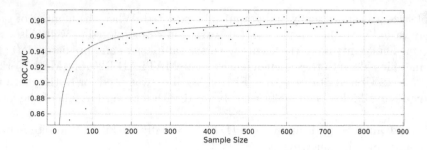

Fig. 1. The C5 decision tree ROC AUC versus the sample size of the datasets: results and fitted *power* curve.

It fits a function of the form $ax^b + c$, where x represents the sample size, and the coefficients (with 95 % confidence bounds) are: $a = -0.5636(-0.7332, -0.3939)$, $b = -0.5461(-0.6466, -0.4456)$, and $c = 0.9931(0.9865, 0.9997)$. Goodness of fit was measured with summed squared error, $SSE = 0.001883$, $R-square = 0.968$, Adjusted $R-square = 0.9674$, and root mean squared error, $RMSE = 0.004452$. If one considers an AUC of 0.95 a good accuracy for a diagnosis test using C5 decision trees, the power function shows that a sample size of about 100 patients could be considered reasonable. However, the accuracy continues to increase with the sample size even beyond the value of the full study (865). This shows that in this case bigger data improves the predictive power.

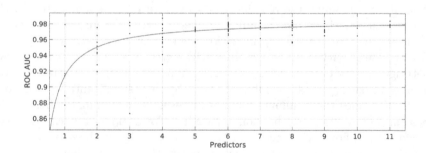

Fig. 2. The ROC AUC of C5 decision tree versus the number of miRNAs predictors: results and fitted *power* curve.

Figure 2 shows the increase of the C5 decision tree ROC AUC with the number of miRNAs predictors. The number of predictors varies between 1 and 11, with a rounded mean of 6. Again, the best fitting results were given by the *power* algorithm from MATLAB Curve Fitting Toolbox. It fits a function of the form $ax^b + c$, where x represents the sample size, and the coefficients (with 95 % confidence bounds) are: $a = -0.07035(-0.07597, -0.06473)$, $b = -1.053(-1.278, -0.8282)$, and $c = 0.9845(0.9795, 0.9895)$. Goodness of fit was measured with summed squared error,

$SSE = 0.002932$, $R - square = 0.9502$, Adjusted $R - square = 0.9492$, and root mean squared error, $RMSE = 0.005555$.

If we consider an AUC of 0.95 as a good accuracy for a diagnosis test, this can be achieved even with two predictors. The accuracy on the validation set is similar with that on the test set. This is a good estimate of the generalization capability of miRNA diagnosis tests based on about 100 cases and two predictors.

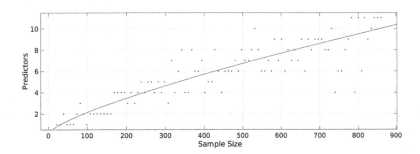

Fig. 3. The number of predictors of the C5 decision tree versus the sample size: results and fitted power curve.

Figure 3 shows the increase in the number of miRNAs predictors with the sample size of the datasets. The best-fitted curve was done with the *power* algorithm from the Curve Fitting MATLAB Toolbox. It fits a function of the form $ax^b + c$, where x represents the sample size, and the coefficients (with 95 % confidence bounds) are: $a = 0.06151(-0.05961, 0.1826)$, $b = 0.7511(0.4774, 1.025)$, and $c = 0.1754(-1.499, 1.85)$. Goodness of fit was measured with summed squared error, $SSE = 147.1$, $R - square = 0.8037$, Adjusted $R - square = 0.7995$, and root mean squared error, $RMSE = 1.244$. The fit is not as good as the previous two cases, but the fitting accuracy is not the main point of this exploratory analysis. It is just the general trend of these dependencies that matters, and this is better seen by inspecting the fitted curves. An important observation here is that the number of miRNAs predictors is still increasing after the sample size reached the maximum available cases in the original dataset.

For CART, the ROC AUC has a minimum of 0.5000, a mean of 0.9408, and a maximum of 0.9819. Comparing with the accuracy of the C5 decision tree - minimum 0.8523, mean 0.9646, maximum 0.9873 - we can see that C5 performed better. This is more significant for the minimum value, but less significant for the mean and the maximum value. As the minimum value corresponds to small studies, we conclude that C5 decision trees are better performers for such cases.

Figure 4 shows the CART ROC AUC dependence on the sample size. Data is fit with a power function of the form $ax^b + c$, where the coefficients (with 95 % confidence bounds) are: $a = -1078(-1363, -792.5)$, $b = -2.514(-2.598, -2.431)$, and $c = 0.954(0.9531, 0.955)$. The goodness of fit is measured by: $SSE = 0.00189$, $R - square = 0.9933$, Adjusted $R - square = 0.9932$, and $RMSE = 0.00446$.

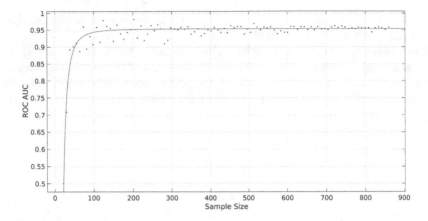

Fig. 4. The ROC AUC of CART versus the sample size: results and fitted power curve.

An interesting fact is that all CART models have the same number of predictors (six), no matter what the value of the sample size is. However, the miRNAs predictors are different for different models, with some overlaps. It is remarkable to note that CART accuracy is almost constant for samples larger than about 100 patients. Moreover, a reasonable accuracy of 0.95 is reached around the same sample size as C5 decision trees. Thus, if CART or C5 decision trees are used, a good accuracy can be obtained with about 100 patients. This is about five times more than the usual size of small studies, but also five times less than our full breast cancer dataset. C5 benefits more than CART from bigger data size, its accuracy increasing even beyond the full dataset sample size. The difference in the discovered relevant miRNAs decreases with the sample size for both C5 and CART, becoming negligible beyond 100 cases.

4   Conclusions

Most existing molecular diagnosis tests are based on small studies and classical statistics. Decision trees are more powerful but still simple and can lead to accurate, transparent, robust, and affordable diagnosis tests. Their accuracy and number of predictors depend on the sample size of the study. The common belief that small studies with about twenty patients can yield accurate diagnosis tests with one or two molecular predictors is not well founded. Diagnosis tests with a good compromise between accuracy and the number of predictors (related to costs) can be developed using decision trees and a patient cohort of about 100 cases. However, the generalization capability of diagnosis tests based on sample size between 20 and 100 is reasonably good, on the expense of lower accuracy. To our best knowledge, this is the first time when such a large scale analysis is presented, and the results offer important hints for developing accurate, robust, and affordable molecular diagnosis tests.

Acknowledgments. This work was supported by the research grants UEFISCDI PN-II-PT-PCCA-2013-4-1959 INTELCOR and UEFISCDI PN-II-PT-PCCA-2011-3.1-1221 IntelUro, financed by Romanian Ministry of Education and Scientific Research.

References

1. Jung, S.H.: Sample size for FDR-control in microarray data analysis. Bioinformatics **21**(14), 3097–3104 (2005)
2. Jung, S.H., Young, S.S.: Power and sample size calculation for microarray studies. J. Biopharm. Stat. **22**(1), 30–42 (2012)
3. Jung, S.H., Bang, H., Young, S.S.: Sample size calculation for multiple testing in microarray data analysis. Biostatistics **6**(1), 157–169 (2005)
4. Stretch, C., Khan, S., Asgarian, N., Eisner, R., Vaisipour, S., Damaraju, S., et al.: Effects of sample size on differential gene expression, rank order and prediction accuracy of a gene signature. PLoS ONE **8**(6), e65380 (2013)
5. Calin, G.A., Dumitru, C.D., Shimizu, M., Bichi, R., Zupo, S., Noch, E., Aldler, H., Rattan, S., Keating, M., Rai, K., et al.: Frequent deletions and down-regulation of microRNA genes mir15 and mir16 at 13q14 in chronic lymphocytic leukemia. Proc. Natl. Acad. Sci. USA **99**, 15524–15529 (2002)
6. Quinlan, J.R.: C4.5: Programs for Machine Learning. Kluwer Academic Publishers, Boston (1993)
7. Breiman, L., Friedman, J.H., Olshen, R.A., Stone, C.J.: Classification and Regression Trees. CRC Press, New York (1984)
8. Floares, A.G., Birlutiu, A.: Decision tree models for developing molecular classifiers for cancer diagnosis. In: Proceedings of the 2012 International Joint Conference on Neural Networks (IJCNN), pp. 1–7 (2012)
9. Schapire, R.E., Freund, Y.: Boosting: Foundations and Algorithms. MIT press, Cambridge (2012)
10. Breiman, L.: Random forests. Mach. Learn. **45**, 5–32 (2001)

Waiting Time Screening in Diagnostic Medical Imaging – A Case-Based View

Marisa Esteves[1], Henrique Vicente[2,3], Sabino Gomes[1],
António Abelha[3], M. Filipe Santos[4], José Machado[3], João Neves[5],
and José Neves[3(✉)]

[1] Departamento de Informática, Universidade do Minho, Braga, Portugal
marisa.araujo.esteves@gmail.com,
sabinogomes.antonio@gmail.com
[2] Departamento de Química, Escola de Ciências e Tecnologia,
Universidade de Évora, Évora, Portugal
hvicente@uevora.pt
[3] Centro Algoritmi, Universidade do Minho, Braga, Portugal
{abelha,jmac,jneves}@di.uminho.pt
[4] Centro Algoritmi, Universidade do Minho, Guimarães, Portugal
mfs@dsi.uminho.pt
[5] Drs. Nicolas & Asp, Dubai, United Arab Emirates
joaocpneves@gmail.com

Abstract. Due to the high standards expected from diagnostic medical imaging, the analysis of information regarding waiting lists via different information systems is of utmost importance. Such analysis, on the one hand, may improve the diagnostic quality and, on the other hand, may lead to the reduction of waiting times, with the concomitant increase of the quality of services and the reduction of the inherent financial costs. Hence, the purpose of this study is to assess the waiting time in the delivery of diagnostic medical imaging services, like computed tomography and magnetic resonance imaging. Thereby, this work is focused on the development of a decision support system to assess waiting times in diagnostic medical imaging with recourse to operational data of selected attributes extracted from distinct information systems. The computational framework is built on top of a Logic Programming Case-base Reasoning approach to Knowledge Representation and Reasoning that caters for the handling of incomplete, unknown, or even self-contradictory information.

Keywords: Waiting time · Diagnostic medical imaging · Knowledge representation and reasoning · Logic programming · Case-based reasoning · Similarity analysis

1 Introduction

The complex organization of the majority of health care systems across the world has lead to the fragmentation of care services, increasing the challenges on the communication among facilities. The advances in technology are rapidly enhancing the capacity of communication and integration of information coming from multiple sources and/or services, being the Imagiology ones, without any doubt, one of them.

© Springer International Publishing Switzerland 2016
Y. Tan and Y. Shi (Eds.): DMBD 2016, LNCS 9714, pp. 296–308, 2016.
DOI: 10.1007/978-3-319-40973-3_30

Imagiology is one of the most important medical specialties and may be summarily defined as the branch of medicine, which uses imaging to diagnose and treat diseases seen within the body [1]. Under this context a variety of imaging techniques may be used to diagnose or to treat diseases, such as X-ray radiography, UltraSound (US), Computed Tomography (CT), Magnetic Resonance Imaging (MRI), Positron Emission Tomography (PET), Nuclear Medicine (NM), among others. Thus, a big amount of data deriving from different information systems, such as the Radiology Information System (RIS), Picture Archiving and Communication System (PACS), and Electronic Patient Record (EPR), is being collected in each diagnostic medical imaging service [1, 2].

One of the most critical issues regarding diagnostic medical services is the waiting times in the delivery of diagnostic medical imaging like CT and MRI examinations [2]. These modalities are normally associated with greater waiting times, which must be undoubtedly improved. Indeed, the standards expected from diagnostic medical imaging services are high and the analysis of information regarding waiting lists via different information systems, such as RIS and PACS, is of the utmost importance. Thus, the operational data extracted from the clinical information systems should be processed, aiming to generate relevant indicators in order to reduce the waiting times [3]. Several factors are involved in the assessment of waiting times in the delivery of diagnostic medical imaging examinations, such as the modality, type, priority and ordering specialty. In addition, the patient gender and age also influence waiting times, although gender should be, possibly, the weakest predictor in such analysis. The establishment, its correspondent status (i.e., public, private, semi-private) and region are other features that may certainly affect waiting lists and consequently the waiting times associated to a given request [3].

Solving problems related to the screening of waiting times in the delivery of diagnostic medical imaging services requires a proactive strategy, able to take into account all these factors. In this work, the estimation of the waiting time will be emphasized, under a Case Based Reasoning (CBR) approach to problem solving [4, 5]. Indeed, CBR provides the ability of solving new problems by reusing knowledge acquired from past experiences, i.e., CBR is used especially when similar cases have similar terms and solutions, even when they have different backgrounds [6]. Thereby, this work is focused on the development of a decision support system to assess waiting times in the delivery of diagnostic medical imaging services like CT and MRI, in diagnostic medical imaging facilities.

2   Knowledge Representation and Reasoning

The Logic Programming (LP) approach to problem solving has been used in areas like the ones related to knowledge representation and reasoning, either in terms as Model Theory [7, 8], or Proof Theory [9, 10]. In present work the proof theoretical approach is followed, leading to an extension to LP. Indeed, an Extended Logic Program is a finite set of clauses, in the form:

$$\{$$

$$p \leftarrow p_1, \cdots, p_n, not\ q_1, \cdots, not\ q_m$$

$$?\ (p_1, \cdots, p_n, not\ q_1, \cdots, not\ q_m)\ (n, m \geq 0)$$

$$exception_{p_1}$$

$$\cdots$$

$$exception_{p_j}\ (0 \leq j \leq k),\ being\ k\ an\ integer\ number$$

$$\}:: scoring_{value}$$

where "?" is a domain atom denoting falsity, the p_i, q_j, and p are classical ground literals, i.e., either positive atoms or atoms preceded by the classical negation sign ¬ [9]. Under this formalism, every program is associated with a set of abducibles [7, 8], given here in the form of exceptions to the extensions of the predicates that make the program. The term $scoring_{value}$ stands for the relative weight of the extension of a specific *predicate* with respect to the extensions of the peers ones that make the overall program.

In order to evaluate the knowledge that can be associated to a logic program, an assessment of the *Quality-of-Information (QoI)*, given by a truth-value in the interval 0, ..., 1, that stems from the extensions of the predicates that make a program, inclusive in dynamic environments, is set [11, 12]. Thus, $QoI_i = 1$ when the information is *known (positive)* or *false (negative)* and $QoI_i = 0$ if the information is unknown. Finally for situations where the extension of $predicate_i$ is unknown but can be taken from a set of terms, $QoI_i \in [0, 1]$. Thus, for those situations, the QoI is given by:

$$QoI_i = 1/Card \tag{1}$$

where *Card* denotes the cardinality of the *abducibles* set for i, if the *abducibles* set is disjoint. If the *abducibles* set is not disjoint, the clause's set is given by $C_1^{Card} + \cdots + C_{Card}^{Card}$, under which the QoI evaluation takes the form:

$$QoI_{i_{1 \leq i \leq Card}} = 1/C_1^{Card}, \cdots, 1/C_{Card}^{Card} \tag{2}$$

where C_{Card}^{Card} is a card-combination subset, with *Card* elements. As an example, let us consider the logic program given by:

$\{$

$\neg\, a_1\left((QoI_{x_1}, DoC_{x_1}),\; (QoI_{y_1}, DoC_{y_1}),\; (QoI_{z_1}, DoC_{z_1})\right)$

$\leftarrow not\; a_1\left((QoI_{x_1}, DoC_{x_1}),\; (QoI_{y_1}, DoC_{y_1}),\; (QoI_{z_1}, DoC_{z_1})\right)$

$a_1\underbrace{\left((QoI_{15}, DoC_{15}),\; (QoI_{[8,12]}, DoC_{[8,12]}),\; (QoI_{\perp}, DoC_{\perp})\right)}_{attribute's\; values} :: QoI :: DoC$

$\underbrace{[0,25] \qquad\qquad [4,24] \qquad\qquad [1,32]}_{attribute's\; domains}$

$exception_{a_1}\left((QoI_{[1,4]}, DoC_{[1,4]}),\; (QoI_{\perp}, DoC_{\perp}),\; (QoI_{15}, Doc_{15})\right) :: QoI :: DoC$

$exception_{a_1}\left((QoI_{\perp}, DoC_{\perp}),\, (QoI_{20}, Doc_{20}),\, (QoI_{[2,21]}, DoC_{[2,21]})\right) :: QoI :: DoC$

$exception_{a_1}\left((QoI_{25}, DoC_{25}),\, (QoI_{[9,24]}, Doc_{[9,24]}),\, (QoI_{\perp}, DoC_{\perp})\right) :: QoI :: DoC$

$\}:: 1$ *(once the universe of discourse is set in terms of the extension of only one predicate)*

where $\perp$ denotes a null value of the type unknown. It is now possible to split the abducible or exception set into the admissible clauses or terms and evaluate their QoI_i. A pictorial view of this process is given below (Fig. 1), as a pie chart.

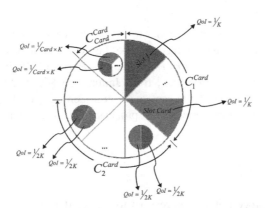

Fig. 1. QoI's values for the abducible set of clauses referred to above, where the clauses cardinality set, K, is given by the expression $C_1^{Card} + C_2^{Card} + \cdots + C_{Card}^{Card}$

The objective is to build a quantification process of QoI and measure one's Degree of Confidence (DoC) that the argument values or attributes of the terms that make the extension of a given predicate with relation to their domains, fit into a given interval [13]. The DoC is evaluated as it is illustrated in Fig. 2, i.e., $DoC = \sqrt{1 - \Delta l^2}$, where Δl stands for the argument interval length, which was set in the interval [0, 1]. Thus, the

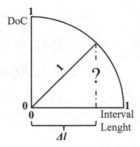

Fig. 2. Degree of confidence evaluation

universe of discourse is engendered according to the information presented in the extensions of such predicates, according to productions of the type:

$$predicate_i - \bigcup_{1 \leq j \leq m} clause_j((QoI_{x_1}, DoC_{x_1}), \cdots, (QoI_{x_n}, DoC_{x_n})) :: QoI_i :: DoC_i$$

$$(3)$$

where $\cup$ and m stand, respectively, for *set union* and the *cardinality* of the extension of *predicate_i*. DoC_i stands for itself [13].

3 Methods

Aiming at developing a predictive model to assess the waiting time for an exam sent from a diagnostic medical imaging facility. The data was acquired from the *Diagnostic Imaging Department* (*DID*) *of Centro Hospitalar do Porto* (*CHP*), in Oporto, Portugal, during the first trimester of 2015 (i.e., from January to March 2015). The personal information was removed in order to protect the confidentiality of the patients involved. Indeed, this section specifies, briefly, the process of data set creation and how it is processed.

3.1 Case Study

To feed the CBR process it was necessary to gather data from several sources and organize it. In the present study the information was organized at a *star schema*, which consists of a collection of tables that are logically related to each other [14]. To obtain it was necessary to go through a set of phases, where in the former one it is analyzed the patients' data in order to select the relevant information for the problem at hand, i.e., the development of a predictive model to estimate the waiting time in diagnostic medical imaging. Based on literature [3] and taking into account the opinions of the professionals of DID, the parameters chosen to estimate the waiting time was grouped in three categories, i.e., related with the ordering, associated to the patient and related with the healthcare facilities. The variables chosen are presented in Fig. 3. The next step had into account the dimensions that would be needed to define these parameters on the fact table. This table consists of numeric values (IDs) and foreign keys to dimensional data where the descriptive information is kept. Finally, information from several sources was collected, transformed according the fact and dimension table and loaded to fact table. Thus, a database was developed according the dimensional model with recourse to *Oracle SQL Developer* in order to collect data that stems from different information systems that are currently used by the Diagnostic Imaging Department of *Centro Hospitalar do Porto*, including RIS and PACS.

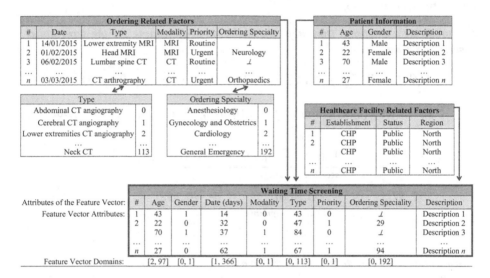

Fig. 3. A fragment of the knowledge base for waiting time screening in diagnostic medical imaging

3.2   Data Processing

After having obtained the data it is possible to build up a knowledge database given in terms of the extensions of the relations depicted in Fig. 3, which stand for a situation where one has to estimate the waiting time of an exam sent from a diagnostic medical imaging facility. Under this scenario some incomplete and/or default data is present (for instance, the *ordering specialty* in case 1 is unknown, and symbolized as $\perp$).

The columns *Gender, Modality* and *Priority* of *Waiting Time Screening* table are populated with 0 (zero) or one (1) denoting, respectively, *Female/Male, MRI/CT* and *Routine/Urgent*.

Once the data was acquired from the same healthcare facility, the healthcare facility related factors were not considered in the present study. Thus, applying the reduction algorithm presented in [13], to the fields that make the knowledge base for *Waiting Time Screening* (Fig. 3), excluding of such a process the *Description* one, and looking to the *DoCs* values obtained as described in [13], it is possible to set the arguments of the predicate *waiting time* (*wt*) referred to below, which extensions denote the objective function with respect to the problem under analysis:

$$wt : Age, G_{ender}, Date, Mod_{ality}, T_{ype}, Prio_{rity}, O_{rdering}S_{pecialty} \rightarrow \{0,1\} \qquad (4)$$

where 0 (zero) and 1 (one) denote, respectively, the truth values *false* and *true*.

Exemplifying the application of the algorithm presented in [13], to a term (request) that presents feature vector ($Age = 62$, $G_{ender} = 0$, $Date = [23, 28]$, $Mod_{ality} = 1$, $T_{ype} = 69$, $Prio_{rity} = 0$, $O_{rdering}$ $S_{pecialty} = \perp$), and applying the procedure referred to above, one may get:

Begin (DoCs evaluation),

The predicate's extension that maps the Universe-of-Discourse for the term under observation is set ←

$\{ \ \neg wt \ \left((QoI_{Age}, DoC_{Age}), \ ..., \ (QoI_{Date}, DoC_{Date}), \ \cdots, (QoI_{OS}, DoC_{OS}) \right)$

$\leftarrow not \ wt \ \left((QoI_{Age}, DoC_{Age}), \ ..., \ (QoI_{Date}, DoC_{Date}), \ \cdots, (QoI_{OS}, DoC_{OS}) \right)$

$\underbrace{wt \left((1_{62}, DoC_{62}), \ \cdots, \ (1_{[23,28]}, DoC_{[23,28]}), \ \cdots, (1_{\perp}, DoC_{\perp}) \right)}_{\text{attribute's values}} :: 1 :: DoC$

$\underbrace{[2, 97] \quad \cdots \quad [1, 366] \quad \cdots \quad [0, 192]}_{\text{attribute's domains}}$

$\} :: 1$

The attribute's values ranges are rewritten ←

$\{ \ \neg wt \ \left((QoI_{Age}, DoC_{Age}), \ ..., \ (QoI_{Date}, DoC_{Date}), \ \cdots, (QoI_{OS}, DoC_{OS}) \right)$

$\leftarrow not \ wt \ \left((QoI_{Age}, DoC_{Age}), \ ..., \ (QoI_{Date}, DoC_{Date}), \ \cdots, (QoI_{OS}, DoC_{OS}) \right)$

$\underbrace{wt \left((1_{[62,62]}, DoC_{[62,62]}), \cdots, \ (1_{[23, 28]}, DoC_{[23, 28]}), \cdots, (1_{\perp[0,192]}, DoC_{[0,192]}) \right)}_{\text{attribute's values ranges}} :: 1$

$:: DoC$

$\underbrace{[2, 97] \quad \cdots \quad [1, 366] \quad \cdots \quad [0, 192]}_{\text{attribute's domains}}$

$\} :: 1$

The attribute's boundaries are set to the interval [0, 1] ←

$\{ \ \neg wt \left((QoI_{Age}, DoC_{Age}), \ ..., \ (QoI_{Date}, DoC_{Date}), \ \cdots, (QoI_{OS}, DoC_{OS}) \right)$

$\quad\quad \leftarrow not \ wt \left((QoI_{Age}, DoC_{Age}), \ ..., \ (QoI_{Date}, DoC_{Date}), \ \cdots, (QoI_{OS}, DoC_{OS}) \right)$

$\quad\quad wt \left(\underbrace{(1_{[0.63,0.63]}, DoC_{[0.63,0.63]}), \cdots, (1_{[0.06,0.08]}, DoC_{[0.06,0.08]}), \cdots, (1_{[0,1]}, DoC_{[0,1]})}_{attribute's\ values\ ranges\ once\ normalized} \right)$

$\quad\quad\quad\quad\quad\quad\quad\quad\quad\quad\quad\quad\quad\quad\quad\quad\quad\quad\quad\quad :: 1 :: DoC$

$\quad\quad\quad \underbrace{[0,1] \quad\quad\quad \cdots \quad\quad\quad [0,1] \quad\quad\quad \cdots \quad\quad\quad [0,1]}_{attribute's\ domains\ once\ normalized}$

$\} :: 1$

The DoC's values are evaluated ←

$\{ \ \neg wt \left((QoI_{Age}, DoC_{Age}), \ ..., \ (QoI_{Date}, DoC_{Date}), \ \cdots, (QoI_{OS}, DoC_{OS}) \right)$

$\quad\quad \leftarrow not \ wt \left((QoI_{Age}, DoC_{Age}), \ ..., \ (QoI_{Date}, DoC_{Date}), \ \cdots, (QoI_{OS}, DoC_{OS}) \right)$

$\quad wt(\underbrace{(1, 1), \quad \cdots, \quad (1, 0.999), \quad \cdots, \quad (1, 0)}_{\substack{attribute's\ quality-of-information \\ and\ respective\ confidence\ values}}) :: 1 :: 0.857$

$\quad\quad \underbrace{[0.63, 0.63] \quad \cdots \quad [0.06, 0.08] \quad \cdots \quad [0,1]}_{attribute's\ values\ ranges\ once\ normalized}$

$\quad\quad\quad \underbrace{[0,1] \quad\quad\quad\quad [0,1] \quad\quad\quad\quad [0,1]}_{attribute's\ domains\ once\ normalized}$

$\} :: 1$

End.

Under this approach, it is now possible to represent the case repository in a graphic form, showing each case in the Cartesian plane in terms of its *QoI* and *DoC* (see Fig. 5 in Sect. 4). Thus, the data can be presented in two different forms, one that is comprehensible to the user and the other in a way that speeds the retrieve process.

4   Case-Based Reasoning

CBR methodology for problem solving stands for an act of finding and justifying the solution to a given problem based on the consideration of past ones, by reprocessing and/or adapting their data and/or knowledge [4, 5]. The cases are stored in a Case Base, and those cases that are similar or close to a new one are used in the problem solving process.

The typical CBR cycle presents the mechanism that should be followed to have a consistent model. The first stage comprises an initial description of the problem. The new case is defined and it is used to retrieve one or more cases from the repository. At this point it is important to identify the characteristics of the new problem and retrieve cases with a higher degree of similarity to it. Thereafter, a solution for the problem emerges, on the Reuse phase, based on the combination of the new case with the retrieved case. The suggested solution is reused, i.e., adapted to the new case, becoming a Solved Case [4, 5]. However, when adapting the solution it is crucial to have feedback from the user, since automatic adaptation in existing systems is almost impossible. This is the Revise stage, in which the suggested solution is tested by the user, allowing its correction, adaptation and/or modification, originating the test repaired case that sets the solution to the new problem. The test repaired case must be correctly tested to ensure that the solution is indeed correct. Thus, one is faced with an iterative process, since the solution must be tested and adapted while the result of applying it is unsatisfying. During the Retain (or Learning) stage the case is learned and the knowledge base is updated with the new case [4, 5]. Despite promising results, the existent CBR systems are neither complete nor adaptable enough for all domains. In some cases, the user is required to follow the similarity method defined by the system, even if it does not fit their needs [5, 15]. Furthermore, the existent CBR systems have limitations related to the capability of dealing with unknown, incomplete or self-contradictory information [5, 15].

Unlike other problem solving methodologies, namely those that use Decision Trees or Artificial Neural Networks, relatively little work is done offline. Undeniably, in almost all the situations, the work is performed at query time. The main difference between this new approach and the typical CBR one relies on the fact that not only all the cases have their arguments set in the interval 0, ..., 1, but it also allows for the handling of incomplete, unknown, or even self-contradictory data or knowledge [15]. The typical CBR cycle was changed in order to include a normalization phase aiming to enhance the retrieve process (Fig. 4). Thus, the case base will be given in terms of triples that follow the pattern:

$$Case = \{ <Raw_{case}, Normalized_{case}, Description_{case} > \} \tag{5}$$

where Raw_{case} and $Normalized_{case}$ stand for themselves, and $Description_{case}$ is made on a set of production rules or even in free text, which will be analyzed using string similarity algorithms.

In presence of a new case, the system is able to retrieve all cases that meet such a structure and optimize such a population, i.e., it considers the attributes DoC's value of each case or of their optimized counterparts when analysing similarities among them. Thus, under the occurrence of a new case, the goal is to find analogous cases in the knowledge base. Having this in mind, the algorithm given in [13] is applied to the new case, with feature vector ($Age = \bot$, $Gender = 1$, $Date = 45$, $Mod_{ality} = \bot$, $Type = 23$, $Prio_{rity} = 1$, $O_{rdering} \, S_{pecialty} = 152$), leading to:

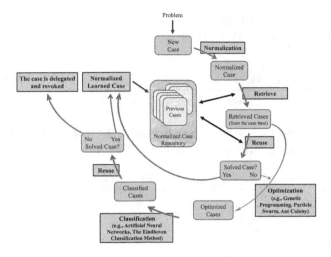

Fig. 4. An extended view of the CBR cycle [15]

$$\underbrace{wt_{new}((1,0),(1,1),(1,1),(1,0),(1,1),(1,1),(1,1))}_{new\ case} :: 1 :: 0.714 \qquad (6)$$

Now, the *new case* may be visualized on the Cartesian plane, and by using data mining techniques, like clustering, one may identify the clusters that intermingle with the new one (epitomized as a square in Fig. 5). The *new case* is compared with every retrieved case from the cluster using a similarity function *sim*, given in terms of the average of the modulus of the arithmetic difference between the arguments of each case of the selected cluster and those of the *new case* (once *Description* stands for free text, its analysis is excluded at this stage). Thus, one may get:

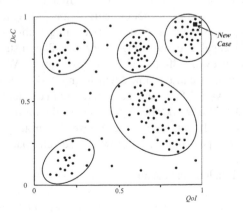

Fig. 5. A case's set split into clusters

$$wt_1((1,1),(1,1),(1,0.98),(1,1),(1,1),(1,1),(1,1)) \ :: \ 1 \ :: \ 0.997$$
$$wt_2((1,1),(1,1),(1,1),(1,1),(1,1),(1,1),(1,0.87)) \ :: \ 1 \ :: \ 0.981$$
$$\vdots \qquad\qquad\qquad\qquad\qquad\qquad\qquad (7)$$
$$\underbrace{wt_j((1,0.95),(1,1),(1,1),(1,1),(1,1),(1,1),(1,0)) \ :: \ 1 \ :: \ 0.850}_{\text{normalized cases from retrieved cluster}}$$

Assuming that every attribute has equal weight, the dissimilarity between wt_{new}^{DoC} and the wt_1^{DoC}, i.e., $wt_{new \to 1}^{DoC}$, may be computed as follows:

$$wt_{new \to 1}^{Doc} = \frac{\|0-1\| + \|1-1\| + \|1-0.98\| + \|0-1\| + \|1-1\| + \|1-1\| + \|1-1\|}{7}$$
$$= 0.288$$
$$\qquad\qquad\qquad\qquad\qquad\qquad\qquad\qquad\qquad (8)$$

Thus, the similarity for $wt_{new \to 1}^{DoC}$ is $1 - 0.288 = 0.712$. Regarding QoI the procedure is similar, returning $wt_{new \to 1}^{QoI} = 1$. With these values we are able to get a global similarity measure, i.e.,

$$wt_{new \to 1}^{QoI,DoC} = \frac{1 + 0.712}{2} = 0.856 \qquad\qquad (9)$$

These procedures should be applied to the remaining cases on the retrieved cluster in order to obtain the most similar ones, which may stand for possible solutions to the problem.

5 Conclusions

This work starts with the development of an intelligent system to assess the waiting time in the delivery of diagnostic medical imaging services, like computed tomography and magnetic resonance imaging, centred on a formal framework based on Logic Programming for Knowledge Representation, complemented with a CBR approach to computing. The knowledge representation and reasoning techniques presented above are very versatile and capable of covering every possible instance, by considering incomplete, unknown, or even self-contradictory information. With this approach the retrieval stage was optimized and the time spent in this task was shortened in 28.9 % and the overall accuracy was 86.8 %, when compared with existent systems. Moreover, the approach followed in this work allows the user to define the cases weight of the cases' attributes on the fly, letting the user to choose the strategy he/she prefers. This feature gives the user the possibility to narrow the search space for similar cases at runtime.

Future work should include data acquired from several healthcare facilities (public, semi-public and private), and from different regions of Portugal. Different string similarity strategies will be considered and implemented, once *Descriptions* will be given in terms of logical *formulae,* being therefore subject to proof. Furthermore, it is also mandatory to specify and to implement an independent CBR system to automatically choose which strategy is the most reliable, considering the problem's specifity.

Acknowledgments. This work has been supported by COMPETE: POCI-01-0145-FEDER-007043 and FCT – Fundação para a Ciência e Tecnologia within the Project Scope: UID/CEC/00319/2013.

References

1. Nuti, S., Vainieri, M.: Managing waiting times in diagnostic medical imaging. BMJ Open **2**, e001255 (2012)
2. McEnery, K.W.: Radiology information systems and electronic medical records. In: IT Reference Guide for the Practicing Radiologist, American College of Radiology, USA, pp. 1–14 (2013)
3. Fotiadou, A.: Choosing and visualizing waiting time indicators in diagnostic medical imaging department for different purposes and audiences. Master's thesis in Health Informatics, Karolinska Institutet, Sweden (2013)
4. Aamodt, A., Plaza, E.: Case-based reasoning: foundational issues, methodological variations, and system approaches. AI Commun. **7**, 39–59 (1994)
5. Richter, M.M., Weber, R.O.: Case-Based Reasoning: A Textbook. Springer, Berlin (2013)
6. Balke, T., Novais, P., Andrade, F., Eymann, T.: From real-world regulations to concrete norms for software agents – a case-based reasoning approach. In: Poblet, M., Schild, U., Zeleznikow, J. (eds.) Proceedings of the Workshop on Legal and Negotiation Decision Support Systems (LDSS 2009), pp. 13–28. Huygens Editorial, Barcelona (2009)
7. Denecker, M., Kakas, A.C.: Abduction in logic programming. In: Kakas, A.C., Sadri, F. (eds.) Computational Logic: Logic Programming and Beyond: Essays in Honour of Robert A. Kowalski. LNCS (LNAI), vol. 2407, pp. 402–436. Springer, Heidelberg (2002)
8. Pereira, L.M., Anh, H.T.: Evolution prospection. In: Nakamatsu, K., Phillips-Wren, G., Jain, L.C., Howlett, R.J. (eds.) New Advances in Intelligent Decision Technologies: Results of the First KES International Symposium IDT 2009. SCI, vol. 199, pp. 51–63. Springer, Heidelberg (2009)
9. Neves, J.: A logic interpreter to handle time and negation in logic databases. In: Muller, R., Pottmyer, J. (eds.) Proceedings of the 1984 Annual Conference of the ACM on the 5th Generation Challenge, pp. 50–54. Association for Computing Machinery, New York (1984)
10. Neves, J., Machado, J., Analide, C., Abelha, A., Brito, L.: The halt condition in genetic programming. In: Neves, J., Santos, M.F., Machado, J.M. (eds.) EPIA 2007. LNCS (LNAI), vol. 4874, pp. 160–169. Springer, Heidelberg (2007)
11. Machado, J., Abelha, A., Novais, P., Neves, J., Neves, J.: Quality of service in healthcare units. In: Bertelle, C., Ayesh, A. (eds.) Proceedings of the ESM 2008, pp. 291–298. Eurosis – ETI Publication, Ghent (2008)
12. Lucas, P.: Quality checking of medical guidelines through logical abduction. In: Coenen, F., Preece, A., Mackintosh, A. (eds.) Proceedings of AI-2003 (Research and Developments in Intelligent Systems XX), pp. 309–321. Springer, London (2003)

13. Fernandes, F., Vicente, H., Abelha, A., Machado, J., Novais, P., Neves, J.: Artificial neural networks in diabetes control. In: Proceedings of the 2015 Science and Information Conference (SAI 2015), pp. 362–370, IEEE Edition (2015)
14. O'Neil, P., O'Neil, B., Chen, X.: Star Schema Benchmark. Revision 3, 5 June 2009. http://www.cs.umb.edu/~poneil/StarSchemaB.pdf
15. Neves, J., Vicente, H.: Quantum Approach to Case-Based Reasoning (In preparation)

Data Visualization Analysis

Digital Particle Image Analysis

Real-Time Data Analytics:
An Algorithmic Perspective

Sarwar Jahan Morshed[1]([⊠]), Juwel Rana[1,2], and Marcelo Milrad[1]

[1] Department of Media Technology, Linnaeus University, Växjö, Sweden
{Sarwar.Morshed,Juwel.Rana,Marcelo.Milrad}@lnu.se
[2] Telenor Group, Oslo, Norway
Juwel.Rana@telenor.com

Abstract. Massive amount of data sets are continuously generated from a wide variety of digital services and infrastructures. Examples of those are machine/system logs, retail transaction logs, traffic tracing data and diverse social data coming from different social networks and mobile interactions. Currently, the New York stock exchange produces 1 TB data per day, Google processes 700 PB of data per month and Facebook hosts 10 billion photos taking 1 PB of storage just to mention some cases. Turning these streaming data flow into actionable real-time insights is not a trivial task. The usage of data in real-time can change different aspects of the business logic of any corporation including real time decision making, resource optimization, and so on. In this paper, we present an analysis of different aspects related to real-time data analytics from an algorithmic perspective. Thus, one of the goals of this paper is to identify some new problems in this domain and to gain new insights in order to share the outcomes of our efforts and these challenges with the research community working on real-time data analytics algorithms.

Keywords: Big data · Real-time data analytics · Machine learning algorithms · Large-scale stream data processing

1 Introduction

One of the current challenges for today's businesses is not only to understand who the customers are but also to gain a better understanding related to the users' contextual information including their location, real-time actions and patterns of communication. Large volume of data sets are continuously generated from online communication, emails, video and audio sharing images, user clicks, log data, posts in social media, search queries, user health records, social networking interactions, scientific information, sensor data and mobile phones and their applications. All these different pieces of data add new dimensions to customer related information, thus creating new challenges for business and organizations in relation to how to take benefits of these data. But Big Data by itself does not have any value until it is organized, processed and visualized in ways that help to resolve some vital business challenges. Using Big Data in real time involves access to powerful analytics techniques and methods that include both software tools and the required expertise to use them. In this respect, real time services are very significant for customer centric care in order to prevent churn and to form loyal

© Springer International Publishing Switzerland 2016
Y. Tan and Y. Shi (Eds.): DMBD 2016, LNCS 9714, pp. 311–320, 2016.
DOI: 10.1007/978-3-319-40973-3_31

customers within a particular market. Real-time information can be used for churn prediction as it may provide necessary feedback in real time for avoiding churn. In real time data analytics, there are many factors such as low latency data ingestion, fast data aggregation, flexible data filtering, clustering data stream, data exploration, and data visualization that effect overall performance [1, 2]. All of these factors need to be addressed in different phases of real-time data analytics using different algorithms. Thus, in order to explore this issue, we have identified the following research question:

How do the different algorithms perform real-time stream data processing and what are the most salient advantages and drawbacks of those?

However, most of the data analytics frameworks and algorithms are introduced initially for batch processing. It is not sufficient to deal with real time streaming data processing using these batch-processing algorithms. Some studies for improving the real-time data analytics tools and frameworks have been presented in [1–3]. In one of our recent papers [4], we have also discussed different frameworks in term of tools and technologies for real time analytics. Thus, for complementing those efforts, the focus of this paper on those aspects related to real time data analytics algorithms.

The building blocks for real time data analytics are *data collection, data analysis, and response access* [1–3]. Different kinds of algorithms are required to carry out the different processes performed in these building blocks. To the best of our knowledge, few are the studies that illustrate and classify the different algorithms used on the building blocks of real-time data analytics. In this paper, we illustrate and discuss the different stream data algorithms used in these building blocks.

The rest of the paper is organized as follows. The motivation and problems in real-time data analytics were stated in Sect. 1. The algorithms used in the different building blocks of real-time data analytics are discussed, analysed, and illustrated in Sect. 2. Hence, attributes and limitations can be understood for further improvement of the real-time data analytics algorithms from this section. A discussion about the different approaches and the associated challenges is the focus of Sect. 3. Section 4 presents the conclusion of this paper.

2 Analysis of Real-Time Data Analytics Algorithms

Real-time data analytics is a combined process consisting of other sub-processes performed at different stages during the data analysis. Multiple data analytics algorithms are required for executing these sub-processes. Figure 1 above shows the building blocks and corresponding processes of real-time data analytics phases [1–3]. In the following sub-sections, different algorithms used in these building blocks will be presented and discussed.

2.1 In Real-Time Data Collection

Real-time data collection is the first building block of real-time data analytics as described in Fig. 1. In this block, we have identified three different processes such as stream data filtering, data anonymization, and data correlation.

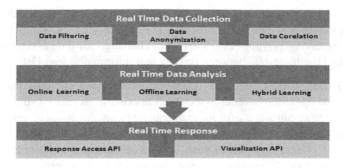

Fig. 1. Building blocks of real-time data analytics

Stream Data Filtering. Filtering stream data is one of the important processes in real-time data analytics, since huge volume of stream data often may not be required for all kind of data analysis. Moreover, storing and processing data in a cloud environment (such as AWS of Google) is price-sensitive. Besides, identifying the inseparable part of data, collected from different sources at different points in time is a challenging issue. Algorithms for stream data filtering can be grouped as follows:

Load shedding in Data Streams: Load shedding adjusts the changes required by stream data receiver by discarding some of the unprocessed data to reduce system load [5]. Therefore, load-shedding algorithms should have the ability to tune the time and the positions in the query for performing load shedding efficiently. A load-shedding algorithm is presented in [5] considering optimal timestamp and placement of load shed.

Sliding Window for Data Stream processing: A sliding window is used for extracting features from a time series sequence and adds those features into an index structure to improve query efficiency. This type of data extraction model can be complicated as time efficient feature mining is required for individual streaming event. Incremental feature extraction method is introduced to leverage this complication [6].

Data Anonymization. Privacy and security of data are often one of the main concerns of the users for many systems. Users of these real-time data analytic systems can be either the organization's employee or its customers. Since these real-time data analytics would be involved with the user's public and private data, there should be proper specifications, as well as methods to address this concern of privacy and security of individual data, data sources, services, etc. In this regard, data in real-time data analytics should be anonymized. But there is a dilemma related to data anonymization. For example, how should this data be anonymized and at what extent is a central question. For proper data anonymization, both data and the source of data should be considered while preserving the identity of the data for future use [7].

In real-time data analytics, this dilemma is one of the key research problems. For instance, a frequent Facebook user may not disclose his/her identity while he/she is using Facebook authentication for accessing another service/s. On the other hand, the service provider needs the user behaviour, location, and frequency of access for that particular service. Therefore, it is a challenging issue to preserve the quality and merit of the data while anonymization [8]. Usually, different methods such as suppression, generalization, perturbation, and permutation are used for developing the anonymization algorithms by transforming the original data into another form [7]. For instance, K-anonymity can also be used for preserving privacy [29]. Thus main challenge for data anonymizing algorithms is to find the trade-offs between privacy and information loss [29].

Data Correlation. *Data correlation (also refers as* joining streams*)* from different sources is a basic operation in order to relate information from various stream data. Join processing in data streams is useful for many applications, for instance sensor network where stream data from different sources are needed to connect with each other. There are a couple of joining approaches such as max-subset measure, age based model, frequency based model, towards general stochastic models, etc. However, more adaptive processing approaches are required for joining stream in order to deal with the changes and fluctuations occurred in the stream data [9]. In most of the cases of real time data analytics, it is required to keep track and analyse the pattern over time in real-time data analytic [9]. Several other studies such as [10–12] have presented different methods for change detection of data stream. Identifying the significant changes in data streams is one of the primary tasks of real-time data analytics. The main methods in this category are those of data visualizing the modification in the stream data and identifying data dissolution and shifting [13].

Like time stamp there are several other issues such as the source of data, data integrity, and identification of similar event data from different sources, etc. are to be considered as well. For instance, how much time the real-time data analytics should wait for associating different sources of data, since most real-time data analytic work using the one-pass analytic approach.

2.2   In Stream Data Analysis

Referring back to the second building block, this sub-section describes the data analysis algorithms for stream data. For real time stream data processing, algorithms require to be very dynamic and robust in nature to deal with these diversified data. Researchers have been working for the last few decades to improve the data analysis algorithms in order to adjust with the increasing amount of data by speeding up processors following Moore's Law[1].

However, data analysis algorithms in real time deal with different problems such as classifying, clustering, pattern mining, creating decision tree, etc. [2]. The classification problem is one of the fundamental areas of study for data analysis in machine learning and data mining. Classification techniques illustrates the set of supervised learning methods in which a set of dependable variables have to be predicted based on another set of input features [14]. For supervised learning (in which data is completely labelled for presenting to the machine learning algorithm), there are two distinguishing models such as classification and regression. Classification deals with the categorical attributes as dependent variables while regression deals with the numerical attributes considering

---

[1] Moore's law is the declaration that throughout the history of computing hardware, the amount of transistors in an integrated circuit duplicates itself after each consecutive two years.

its output. Model building and model testing are two phases of the classification. To solve classification problems, several algorithms such as decision trees, rule based methods and neural networks are used [15]. Since data is needed to pass multiple times as input, these algorithms are used for classifying the static data sets. On the other hand, in real time stream data processing, the entire data set is required in one pass. Therefore, dealing with the large volume of stream data for classification is quite difficult and still a challenge to resolve.

Frequent pattern mining for streaming data is carried out in data analysis phase. The problem of frequent pattern mining in data streaming is first identified and presented in [16]. Later, it has been identified that frequent items sent might be found in the sliding window or the entire data stream [17]. Several numbers of proposals [18–20] have been presented in the last decades for pattern mining or matching. But these algorithms require consistent dataset with two or more pass constraint. Considering all stream processing tasks, there are three issues to identify the frequent patterns [16]. First of all, an exponential number of patterns are required to search in the objective space in frequent pattern mining. The dataset that contains the samples of frequent pattern can also be large. Therefore, space cost for pattern answering set is significant in a streaming environment. Hence, memory efficiency of the algorithms should be very high [16].

Secondly, frequent pattern mining depends on the functionalities of pruning infrequent patterns while generating the frequent patterns. The process of generating patterns by pruning infrequent patterns is computationally expensive. Besides, adjusting high velocity stream data is also difficult for memory constraint [16]. Therefore, level of acceptability of mining result varies from user to user. Additionally, pattern mining algorithm should offer the flexibility to the user for selecting the threshold point for pattern mining result [16]. In this case, clustering, decision tree algorithms can be applied in data analysis phase.

Online Learning Algorithms. Online learning algorithms deal with the problem to make decisions instantly using the real-time data or in combination with historical data. Online learning algorithms and their relevant criteria have been reviewed in [21, 22]. These papers stated that online learning methods are involved with machine learning and pattern recognition algorithms. Further, online learning algorithms have been classified into the *update type, problem type* and *aggressive level* [22]. Algorithms of update type are straightforward. In this algorithm: (i) for correcting predicted answers no update is made (ii) instances with corresponding unit vector from weight vector are added (iii) most recent learning is used for updating the weight vector [22]. On the other hand, [23] proposes online algorithms that bring up to date weight vector using the multiplicative method. Weighed Majority, Winnow, and Exponentiated Gradient (EG) algorithms also use multiplicative updates. Multiplicative updates perform better than additive updates for the instances with many noisy components [22]. [24] proposed the p-norm algorithms that use both additive and multiplicative updates. Problem type algorithms follow question-answer approach. Although the *Perceptron* method was introduced for simply answering yes/no type questions, more complex answers are frequently required in real-world applications. For instance, the learner is often required to select an answer from a number of possible answers during multiclass categorization [25]. On the other hand, [25] proposed an aggressive level of perceptron. In this approach updates are conducted for correcting perceptron answers while input instances are quite closure to the decision boundary [25]. Some constraints such as communication in distributed learning, memory limitation, incremental updating in stream data, partial information arrival (e.g. due to corrupted, sanitization), etc. are some common problems for online learning algorithms [30]. Therefore, these constraints are required to be considered for online algorithms.

Offline Learning Algorithms. Offline learning algorithms are usually used for batch data processing, and do not designed for incremental learning. However, these algorithms can also be applied in real-time data analytics. In offline learning, the classifier needs to learn from a sequence of elements of the occurrence [26]. Then, the classifier predicts using guess and trial basis. Offline learning is used for quicker and less costly learning operations. Online learning and offline learning have been compared in [26] while illustrating the properties of these two approaches. This method of learning is used for regular and orderly incoming stream data. For example, if a system needs to authenticate the employees for accessing to a particular office using finger print, the classifier of the system is required to be trained using the stored finger prints previously taken from the user. Regression algorithm, instance-based algorithm, decision tree algorithm, Bayesian algorithms, etc. are some forms of algorithms introduced for offline learning.

Hybrid Learning Algorithms. In hybrid learning algorithms, both online and offline learning are combined together to improve performance in stream data analysis. For example, in order to accurate prediction, some real-time data analytics (e.g. Earthscope - a science project for tracking North America's geological evolution uses both history data and streaming data) requires both stream processing and batch processing of history data of similar event. In this case, combination of more than one online and/or offline learning algorithms are required. This learning approach is referred as hybrid learning. For instance, [27] proposes a new hybrid model for training the adaptive network based fuzzy inference system (ANFIS). This model combines one of the particle swarm optimization (PSO) algorithm with the recursive least square (LS) algorithm for training [27].

2.3   In Real-Time Response

Real-time response generation is the third building block in any real-time data analytics. After analysing the real time stream data, responses are generated to support decision-making. This section provides an overview on real-time response APIs that can be categorized as response access API and visualization API. We have found that there area couple of issues to handle with the Response Access API.

Response Access API. Responses are presented usually in different data formats such as XML, JSON, HTML, text, etc. Customized API development is often required for real-time response generation and access. A *sense and response* service architecture is presented in [28] in which a sense and response loop is always in execution state for real-time fraud detection in business process [28]. In this approach, after sensing and analyzing a real-time event data, an automatic response is generated for selecting the appropriate decision [28].

Real-Time Visualization API. Interactive visualizations link the computational processes with human analysis [7]. If all of the processes in different building blocks (i.e. processes in data collection and data analysis stage) are performed efficiently during real-time data analytics, a quick response can be generated based on this data analysis fora better and more informed decision.

3   Discussion and Future Challenges

One of the aims of this paper is to analyse the real-time data analytics algorithms from an architectural point of view. In line with this goal, this paper presented different building blocks of the real-time data analytics. In our observation, each of these building blocks has significant impact to ensure high performance for almost all kind of real-time analytical tasks. As shown in Fig. 1, real-time data analysis is performed in three phases including real-time data collection, real-time data analysis, and real-time response generation. One of the main challenges we have identified in real-time data collection involves data filtering (e.g. keyword based search, querying), data anonymization, and data correlation (e.g. pattern matching), which are not trivial problems. We also mentioned that the real-time data analysis can be generalized in three ways: online learning, offline learning, and/or hybrid learning. More efforts are required for increasing the efficiency of real-time machine learning algorithms. Thus improving the existing algorithms is one dimension of our possible future efforts. Additionally, we observed that real-time response requires Response Access API and/or Visualization API. A wide range of Response Access APIs and Visualization APIs are required to develop reactive data–centric large-scale mobile applications. Therefore, another line of direction for our future efforts includes developing the necessary APIs for accessing data from applications interface. Table 1 presents an overview and summary of our efforts related to the analysis of algorithms for real time stream data:

Table 1. Overview of real-time data analytics algorithms

Phases	Processes in each phases	Description	
Algorithms in Data Collection	Data Filtering	Input	Raw event's stream data
		Functions Performed	Exclude irrelevant event data from the stream
		Output	Filtered event stream data adjustable with processing rate
		Challenges	a) identifying appropriate irrelevant data for the query processing in real-time data analytics b)load shedding
	Data	Input	Filtered event stream data adjustable with processing rate
		Functions	Hide control parameters (e.g. source, timestamp,

Table 1. (*Continued*)

	Anonymizat-ion	Performed	route, identity, etc.) of event data
		Output	Anonymizedstream data
		Challenges	a)need anonymizing and de-anonymizing algorithm b)appropriate parameters selection for anonymizing c)preserving integrity of the event stream data without loss of critical data for analysis
	Data Correlation	Input	Anonymizedstream data
		Functions Performed	Correlates event stream data for data analysis
		Output	Sanitized and processed data for data analytics
		Challenges	a)identifying and joining anonymized data b)setting timestamp for data correlation
Algorithms in Real-time Data Analysis	Online/Offline /Hybrid learning	Input	Sanitized and processed data for data analytics
		Functions Performed	a) classification, b) pattern mining c) clustering d) create decision tree
		Output	Prediction as response for query processing in real-time data analytics
		Challenges	a) finding less time consuming and efficient classification, clustering, and pattern mining algorithms for stream data b) constraints such as communication in distributed learning, memory limitation, incremental updating in stream data, partial information arrival
Algorithms in Response Access	Response Access API	Input	Prediction as response for query processing in real-time data analytics
		Functions Performed	Generate response from decision tree
		Output	Response as HTML, XML,JSON or any machine readable format
		Challenges	a)authenticating response access request b)authorization of response request c)security of the response data d)need platform independent, portable and most understandable formatted response API e)need easily accessible and compatible response access API for the existing platforms and tools
	Visualization API	Input	Prediction as response for query processing in real-time data analytics
		Functions Performed	a)generate and visualize response from decision tree b) change& trend detection, event tracking
		Output	Graphical form of visualization from response
		Challenges	a)to deal with large size and high dimensionality of data b)rendering graphical view of large stream data within a very fractional timestamp

4   Conclusion

Real time data analytics can play an important role for developing smart solutions in sectors such as transportation, energy efficiency, and health care. However, the requirements for developing a framework to perform real-time analysis are expensive from a technology selection to algorithm development. In this paper, we present a qualitative study on real-time data analytics from an algorithmic perspective. The algorithms are classified based on the building blocks of real-time data analytics. Further, we summarize the real-time data analytic algorithms for understanding the processes, input/output, and existing challenges that are needed to be resolved. Therefore, the key contributions of this paper are two-folds (1) to classify the different real-time data analytics algorithms based on the architectural building blocks of real-time data analytics and (2) to identify the challenges of applying real-time data analytic algorithms.

References

1. Cha, S., Monica, W.: Developing a real-time data analytics framework using Hadoop. In: IEEE International Congress on BigData. IEEE (2015)
2. Singh, D., Reddy, C.K.: A survey on platforms for big data analytics. J. Big Data **2**, 8 (2015)
3. Yang, F., Tschetter, E., Léauté, X., Ray, N., Merlino, G., Ganguli, D.: Druid: a real-time analytical data store. In: Proceedings of the ACM SIGMOD International Conference on Management of Data, June 2014, pp. 157–168 (2014)
4. Morshed, S.J., Rana, J., Milrad, M.: Open source initiatives and frameworks addressing distributed real-time data analytics. In: 2016 IEEE International Parallel and Distributed Processing Symposium Workshops, Illinois, Chicago, USA (2016). doi:10.1109/IPDPSW. 2016.152
5. Aggarwal, C.C., Han, J., Wang, J., Yu, P.S.: On clustering massive data streams: a summarization paradigm. In: Aggarwal, C.C. (ed.) Data Streams: Models and Algorithms, vol. 31, pp. 9–38. Springer, New York (2007)
6. Faloutsos, C., Ranganathan, M., Manolopoulos, Y.: Fast subsequence matching in time-series databases. In: SIGMOD, pp. 419–429 (1994)
7. Keim, D.A., Krstajic, M., Rohrdantz, C., Schreck, T.: Real-time visual analytics for text streams. Computer **46**(7), 47–55 (2013)
8. Tripathy, B.K., Manusha, G.V., Mohisin, G.S.: An improved set-valued data anonymization algorithm and generation of FP-Tree. In: Venugopal, K.R., Patnaik, L.M. (eds.) ICIP 2012. CCIS, vol. 292, pp. 552–560. Springer, Heidelberg (2012)
9. Xie, J., Yang, J.: A survey of join processing in data streams. In: Aggarwal, C.C. (ed.) Data Streams: Models and Algorithms. Advances in Database Systems, vol. 31, pp. 209–236. Springer, New York (2007). ISBN: 10:0-387-28759-0
10. Babcock, B., Babu, S., Datar, M., Motwani, R., Widom, J.: Models and issues in data stream systems. In: ACM PODS Conference (2002)
11. Guha, S., Rastogi, R., Shim, K.: CURE: an efficient clustering algorithm for large databases. In: ACM SIGMOD Conference (1998)
12. Aggarwal, C., Procopiuc, C., Wolf, J., Yu, P., Park, J.-S.: Fast algorithms for projected clustering. In: ACM SIGMOD Conference (1999)

13. Aggarwal, C.C.: A survey of change diagnosis algorithms in evolving data streams. In: Models and Algorithms, pp. 85–102. IBM (2007)
14. Gaber, M.M., Zaslavsky, A., Krishnaswamy, S.: A survey of classification methods in data streams. In: Aggarwal, C.C. (ed.) Data Streams: Models and Algorithms, vol. 31, pp. 39–59. Springer, New York (2007)
15. Hastie, T., Tibshirani, R., Friedman, J.: The Elements of Statistical Learning: Data Mining, Inference, and Prediction. Springer, New York (2001)
16. Agrawal, R., Imielinski, T., Swami, A.: Mining association rules between sets of items in large databases. In: ACM SIGMOD Conference (1993)
17. Giannella, C., Han, J., Pei, J., Yan, X., Yu, P.: Mining frequent patterns in data streams at multiple time granularities. In: Proceedings of the NSF Workshop on Next Generation Data Mining (2002)
18. Han, J., Pei, J., Yin, Y.: Mining frequent patterns without candidate generation. In: Proceedings of the ACM SIGMOD Conference on Management of Data (2000)
19. Xifeng, Y., Han, J.: GSPAN: graph-based substructure pattern mining. In: Proceedings of the 2002 IEEE International Conference on Data Mining (ICDM 2002), p. 721 (2002)
20. Zaki, M.J.: Efficiently mining frequent trees in a forest. In: Proceedings of the Eighth ACM SIGKDD International Conference on Knowledge Discovery and Data Mining, KDD 2002, pp. 71–80 (2002)
21. Fiat, A., Woeginger, G.J.: Online Algorithms: The State of the Art. LNCS, vol. 1442. Springer, Heidelberg (1998)
22. Shalev-Shwartz, S.: Online Learning: Theory, Algorithms, and Applications, The Hebrew University of Jerusalem. Ph.D. thesis (2014)
23. Littlestone, N., Warmuth, M.: Relating data compression and learn ability. Unpublished Manuscript, November 1986
24. Ikonomovska, E., Mariano, Z.: Algorithmic techniques for processing data streams. In: Data Exchange, Information, and Streams, pp. 237–274 (2013)
25. Krauth, W., Mezard, M.: Learning algorithms with optimal stability in neural networks. J. Phys. A 20, 745 (1987)
26. Ben-David, S., Kushilevitz, E., Mansour, Y.: Online learning versus offline learning. Mach. Learn. 29, 45–63 (1997). Kluwer Academic Publishers, Netherlands
27. Shoorehdeli, M.A., Teshnehlab, M., Sedigh, A.K.: Novel hybrid learning algorithms for tuning ANFIS parameters using adaptive weighted PSO. In: IEEE International on Fuzzy Systems Conference, FUZZ-IEEE 2007, London, pp. 1–6 (2007)
28. Nguyen, T., Schiefer, J., Tjoa, M.A.: Sense & response service architecture (SARESA): an approach towards a real-time business intelligence solution and its use for a fraud detection application. In: Proceedings of DOLAP 2005, pp. 77–86. ACM, New York (2005)
29. Iyengar, V.S.: Transforming data to satisfy privacy constraints. In: Proceedings of KDD 2002, pp. 279–288. ACM, New York (2002)
30. Shamir, O.: Fundamental limits of online and distributed algorithms for statistical learning and estimation (2013). CoRR: abs/1311.3494

High-Dimensional Data Visualization Based on User Knowledge

Qiaolian Liu[1], Jianfei Zhao[1], Naiwang Guo[2], Ding Xiao[1], and Chuan Shi[1(✉)]

[1] School of Computer Science, Beijing University of Posts and Telecommunications,
Beijing, China
shichuan@bupt.edu.cn
[2] State Grid Shanghai Electric Power Research Institute, Shanghai, China
guonw@sh.sgcc.com.cn

Abstract. Due to the curse of the dimensionality, high-dimensional data visualization has always been a difficult and hot problem in the field of visualization. Some of the existing works mainly use dimensionality reduction methods to generate latent dimensions and visualize the transformed data. However, these latent dimensions often have no good interpretability with user knowledge. Therefore, this paper introduces a high-dimensional data visualization method based on user knowledge. This method can derive dimensions aligned with user knowledge to reorganize data, then it uses scatter-pie plot matrix, an extension of scatter plot matrix, to visualize the reorganized data. This method enables users to explore the relationship between the known and unknown data as well as the relationship between the unknown data and the derived dimensions. The effectiveness of the method is validated by the experiments.

Keywords: High-dimensional data · Visualization · TSVMs

1 Introduction

In science, engineering and biology, high-dimensional data often occur. Larger and larger variables bring us great challenges in data analysis. And people can only perceive 2D and 3D space. Therefore, due to the curse of dimensionality and the limited view space, high-dimensional data analysis has always been a difficult problem in the field of visualization.

There are usually two steps to do when we visualize the high-dimensional data. The first step we usually need to do is to transform the data, and the second is visualization. The most commonly used way when transforming the data is to transform the original data variables in a linear or non-linear way which is usually called Dimensionality Reduction (DR) [1], such as the well known Principal Components Analysis (PCA), Multidimensional Scaling (MDS) and Locally Linear Embedding (LLE). Those methods usually use the statistical properties and create latent dimensions. However, these latent dimensions are usually difficult to interpret with user knowledge. For better understanding and

© Springer International Publishing Switzerland 2016
Y. Tan and Y. Shi (Eds.): DMBD 2016, LNCS 9714, pp. 321–329, 2016.
DOI: 10.1007/978-3-319-40973-3_32

interpreting, a few works take the importance of user knowledge in exploring high-dimensional data into account. For example, an approach introduced by Gleiher [2] can generate projection functions meaningful to users. But it only considered the known data. Since user knowledge is limited, it is difficult for us to know all the observed data. And the widely used visualization techniques, such as the scatterplot matrix and parallel coordinates, cannot reflect user knowledge over different aspects of data.

To solve the limitations mentioned above, here we introduce an approach which integrates user limited knowledge to visualize and explore high-dimensional data. Our approach can derive dimensions that align with user knowledge and reorganize data. By providing a visualization method scatter-pie plot matrix, users can explore the reorganized data and discover new knowledge. We describe the main tasks of the process when visualizing and exploring the high-dimensional data with user limited knowledge. Then we use a dataset to demonstrate how our approach works. To make a summary, our method has the following features: (1) Derive new dimensions that align with user knowledge and reorganize the data, including the known and unknown data; (2) Discover the relationship between the known and unknown data as well as the relationship between the unknown data and the derived dimensions through scatter-pie plot matrix.

2 Methods

2.1 Motivation

We aim to visualize and explore high-dimensional data. However, for the curse of dimensionality and the limited view space, it is difficult for users to visualize and explore it. The traditional approaches usually mapped high-dimensional data into low-dimensional space by creating new latent dimensions using statistical methods. And these approaches usually called Dimensionality Reduction (DR). However, they usually ignore the importance of user knowledge in exploring data. Therefore, we expect to integrate user knowledge to derive dimensions for better understanding and interpreting the data. Although a few works considered about user prior knowledge, users usually cannot know all the observed data and they may be more interested in the unknown data in addition to the known data. Hence, we expect to take user known and unknown data into account when deriving dimensions that align with user knowledge. Then we can use the derived dimensions which align with user knowledge to reorganize the data, and by this way the view space will be saved and users can have a better understanding of the derived dimensions. Because of visualization is a more intuitive way to help user understand the data, it is an essential way for users to explore the data. Since users are more interested in the unknown data, we expect to visualize the data that can reflect the relationship between the known and unknown data as well as the relationship between unknown data and the derived dimensions. To solve the problem mentioned above, we derive two main tasks: *(1) Derive dimensions that align with user knowledge.* Considering about the user limited

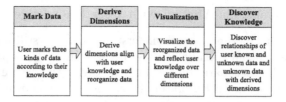

Fig. 1. Illustration of the pipeline when visual exploration of high-dimensional data.

prior knowledge, the unknown data are also taken into account. *(2) Visualize the reorganized data.* Since the data include both the known and unknown data, the view should reflect user knowledge over the data.

2.2   Main Framework

To solve the problem, our approach is designed to support the above tasks. Figure 1 is given as an illustration of the pipeline: (1) mark data, (2) derive dimensions, (3) visualization, (4) discover knowledge. To make it more concrete, here we provide an example to explain the workflow. For instance, the user who has a dataset of city livability data (see Table 1) can mark cities (Step 1) according to their knowledge. Cities belong to Europe, such as Rome, will be marked with Europe. Cities not belong to Europe, such as New York and Beijing, will be marked with non-Europe. However, cities such as Athens and Bogota are not familiar to user and user does not know whether they are belonged to Europe, so they are marked with nothing. Then our method which takes the known and unknown data into account enables user to derive dimension Europe-ness (Step 2) by integrating annotations user marked. Obviously, cities in Europe should be much more Europe-ness than other cities. And the derived dimensions are used to reorganize the data. When visualizing the reorganized data (Step 3), our design can reflect user knowledge over the different aspects of data. Finally, by exploring the reorganized data, user can discover (Step 4) the relationship between the known and unknown data as well as the relationship between the unknown data and the derived dimensions.

Next, we will introduce our method in two parts: firstly, derive dimensions that align with user knowledge to reorganize data. Secondly, visualize the reorganized data and explore the reorganized data to discover new knowledge.

Table 1. Sample data in city livability dataset

City	New York	Beijing	Mexico City	Rome	Paris	Tokyo	HongKong	Athens	Bogota	Cairo
Education indicators	1	3	2	1	1	1	1	2	3	4
Healthcare indicators	1	4	3	1	1	1	2	1	3	3
...	...	...	...	...	...	...	...	...	...	...

2.3   Derive Dimensions Aligned with User Knowledge

In order to make our method easy to understand, here we still use the example mentioned above, but our method can also be used in other dataset.

According to the user marks on the data, we divide the data into three kinds of types. One is user known European cities, one is user known non-European cities, and the last one is user unknown cities. And the value of European cities should be higher than those non-European cities. This reminds us the semi-supervised binary prediction problem. Therefore, we use the convention $\mathbf{y}$ denoted as the labeled vector, and vector $\mathbf{x}$ denoted as data objects. And data points labeled 1 means they are positive elements (e.g. European cities), -1 means they are negative elements (e.g. non-European cities), and 0 means they are unlabeled data (e.g. user unknown cities). Then we use projection function $f(\mathbf{x})$ denoted as the derived dimension and it aligns with user knowledge that European cities should have higher values than non-European cities.

We seek the projection function $f(\mathbf{x})$, and we usually think about the linear function $f(\mathbf{x}) = \mathbf{w} \cdot \mathbf{x} + b$. Since hyper-plane $\mathbf{w} \cdot \mathbf{x} + b = 0$ can separate the two classes and the distance $|\mathbf{w} \cdot \mathbf{x} + b|$ can present the correctness and certainty of data belonged to the class. And the positive sign of the label makes data which are far from the hyper-plane have high values that European cities are much more Europe-ness than non-European cities. Therefore, we use projection function $f(\mathbf{x}) = \mathbf{w} \cdot \mathbf{x} + b$ denoted as the derived dimension which meets that data in positive set have higher values than data in negative set.

Since Transductive Support Vector Machines (TSVMs) [3] has the following features, here we use TSVMs to solve the problem mentioned above. Firstly, it can generate projection function $f(\mathbf{x})$ aligned with user knowledge that data in positive set have higher values than data in negative set. Secondly, there are unlabeled data, such as the cities user unknown. Thirdly, since users expect to explore data they observed, they do not care about the unseen data. TSVMs takes the unlabeled data as a special test set, and focuses on the seen data and makes a transductive learning.

TSVMs is a transductive learning algorithm which introduced by Joachims. This method takes the unlabeled data as a special test set, and reduces classification error as far as possible. The basic ideas of the algorithm are shown as follows: given a set of sample data, including labeled data $(\boldsymbol{x_1}, y_1), \ldots, (\boldsymbol{x_n}, y_n)$, and unlabeled data $\boldsymbol{x_1^*}, \boldsymbol{x_2^*}, \ldots, \boldsymbol{x_k^*}$. Under the condition of linearly separable case, the learning process is shown in (1). This optimization problem can be solved by minimizing the L2 norm of $\mathbf{w}$ under the constraints and find the hyperplane $<\mathbf{w}, b>$ separates both training and test data with maximum margin and the label $y_1^*, \ldots, y_k^*$ of the test data.

$$\min_{y_1^*, \ldots, y_n^*, \mathbf{w}, b} \tfrac{1}{2}\|w\|^2$$
$$s.t.\ \forall_{i=1}^n : y_i[\boldsymbol{w} \cdot \boldsymbol{x}_i + b] \geq 1 \ and\ \forall_{j=1}^k : y_j^*[\boldsymbol{w} \cdot \boldsymbol{x}_j^* + b] \geq 1 \tag{1}$$

And under the conditions of non-linearly separable case, the learning process is shown in (2). It introduces slack variables ξ_i to allow errors occur and seeks the maximum margin and makes the errors minimum. C and C^* can be set to trade off margin size.

$$\min_{y_1^*,\ldots,y_n^*,w,b,\xi_1,\ldots,\xi_n,\xi_1^*,\xi_k^*} \frac{1}{2}\|w\|^2 + C\sum_{i=0}^{n}\xi_i + C^*\sum_{j=0}^{k}\xi_j^*$$
$$s.t. \ \forall_{i=1}^{n} : y_i[w\cdot x_i + b] \geq 1 - \xi_i \ and \ \forall_{i=1}^{n} : \xi_i > 0 \quad\quad (2)$$
$$\forall_{j=1}^{k} : y_i^*[w\cdot x_j^* + b] \geq 1 - \xi_j^* \ and \ \forall_{j=1}^{k} : \xi_j^* > 0$$

By solving the above optimization problem, we can get the projection function $f(\mathbf{x}) = \mathbf{w}\cdot\mathbf{x} + b$, which corresponding to the derived dimension that align with user knowledge. By this token, several dimensions can be derived to reorganize the data. In this paper, we use SVM^{light} [4] to solve the optimization problem.

2.4 Design of Scatter-Pie Plot Matrix

We expect our view can reflect user knowledge over different aspects of data, and explore the relationship between user known and unknown data as well as the relationship between the unknown data and new dimensions we derived. So scatter-pie plot matrix can meet our needs better. Scatter-pie plot matrix is an extension of scatter plot matrix and the pie chart view. It can present all the combinations of two dimensions.

Fig. 2. Illustration of Scatter-Pie when derive three dimensions. Each Scatter-Pie is divided into three parts to indicate user knowledge over these three dimensions. Special colors (red, green, blue) are filled when user knows this data object over this dimension, and gray is filled when user does not know this data object over this dimension. (Color figure online)

Scatter-Pie. Each scatter-pie in scatter-pie plot matrix represents a data object (see Fig. 2). Various parts of the scatter-pie stand for user knowledge over different dimensions, each part evenly and arranged in clockwise. Colors are used to encode user knowledge over different dimensions. Scatter-pie plot reflects the user knowledge over the different aspects of the data object. Before users derive one dimension, they will first mark their known data and unknown data. So if user knows the data object, special color will be used to show that user know this data object over this dimension. Figure 2 shows the scatter-pie plot of two data objects. The user defines three different dimensions, and uses three different colors to encode their knowledge over different dimensions. Users use this kind of color to fill the dimension when he/she knows the data object over the dimension. Red, green and blue are used in Fig. 2. If the user knows nothing about the data object over this dimension, gray is used to fill this part of the

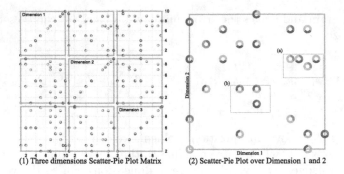

(1) Three dimensions Scatter-Pie Plot Matrix   (2) Scatter-Pie Plot over Dimension 1 and 2

Fig. 3. (1) Three dimensions Scatter-Pie Plot Matrix. (2) One panel in Scatter-Pie Plot Matrix. (Color figure online)

Fig. 4. The impact of labeled examples on correctness when deriving dimension North America-ness, Europe-ness and Olympics hosting-ness.

scatter-pie. This way of view reflects user knowledge over different aspects of data objects.

Scatter-Pie Plot Matrix. Figure 3(1) shows a scatter-pie plot matrix of three dimensions. Each panel in scatter-pie plot matrix is identified by pair-wise dimensions. And each data object is represented by scatter-pie. Figure 3(2) shows one panel in scatter-pie plot matrix. Data points in (a) which are very close to each other may have very similar characteristic over these two dimensions. And data points in (a) are located in the upper right of data points in (b), so they have high values over dimension 1. This way of view provides a lot of help for users to analyze the relationship between user known and unknown data as well as the relationship between the derived dimensions and the data.

3   Case Study

3.1   Dataset

The dataset we use in this paper is city livability data [5] which contains 140 cities from different countries and regions. Each city represents by 45 dimensions. Dimensions are measurements of different aspects of city, such as education indicators, healthcare indicators, crime rating. The sample data are shown in Table 1.

All the data are discrete, and up to 5. As shown in Table 1, the prevalence of violent crime in Mexico City is higher than New York and Beijing. And the healthcare indicators of Beijing are higher than other cities.

3.2   Evaluation

We expect to derive dimensions which align with user knowledge. Hence, we use correctness to ensure the effectiveness of our method. Correctness is defined as shown below: Correctness [2]: the elements in the positive set (denoted as P) should have higher values than elements in the negative set (denoted as N).

$$\forall_{i \in P} \forall_{j \in N} f(i) > f(j) \tag{3}$$

Therefore, cities belonged to positive set (e.g. European cities) are much more Europe-ness than cities belonged to negative set (e.g. non-European cities). Therefore, correctness is calculated as the percentage of times positive cases greater than the negative cases off the total comparison times.

The impact of labeled examples on correctness is shown as Fig. 4. When deriving dimension North America-ness, Europe-ness and Olympics hosting-ness, correctness rate is gradually increasing along with the increasing labeled examples. When the labeled examples increased from about 9 to 120, the correctness rate increased from about 0.7 to 0.9. And in the case of less labeled data (about 9 labeled data), the correctness rate is still above 0.7. It shows that our method can meet the user knowledge to a certain extent when deriving dimensions.

3.3   Visualization and Exploration

On the first step users mark three kinds of data, positive data (e.g. European cities) as 1, negative data (e.g. non-European cities) as −1, and unknown data as 0. And Europe-ness is derived by using our method. The other two dimensions of North America-ness and Olympics hosting-ness are derived by the same token. Then scatter-pie plot matrix is used to visualize the data over these three dimensions. And finally, by exploring the data, users can discover new knowledge through the view.

Exploring relationship between the derived dimensions and user known and unknown data. The scatter-pie plot over dimension Europe-ness and North America-ness is shown as Fig. 5. From Fig. 5(a), we can see that the value of city New York, Seattle, Houston and Washington which locate in continent North America is higher than other cities over North America-ness. And as shown in Fig. 5(b), the value of Berlin and Rome which locate in continent Europe is higher than other cities over Europe-ness. And this aligns with user knowledge. Milan and Paris are cites user unknown over the aspect whether they are European cities (shown as gray in the Scatter-Pie). And they are also very Europe-ness.

Exploring relationship between user known and unknown data. In Fig. 5(b), Milan, Berlin, Rome and Paris are very close to each other, so they are quite similar over the two dimensions. However, Berlin and Rome are known to user

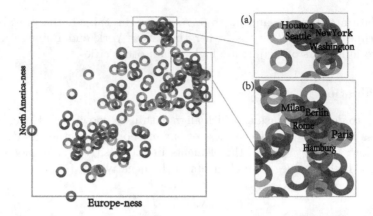

Fig. 5. Scatter-Pie Plot over dimension North America-ness and Europe-ness. Part of Scatter-Pie filled by color green represents user known North American or non-North American cities. Part of Scatter-Pie filled by color blue represents user known European or non-European cities. Part of Scatter-Pie filled by red represents user known Olympics hosting or non-Olympics hosting cities. Part of Scatter-Pie filled by color gray represents user unknown cities over this aspect of the data. (Color figure online)

over these two dimensions (shown as blue and green in the scatter-pie) and they are European cities and quite Europe-ness. Therefore, we think that Milan and Paris are also European cities to a large extent. And the facts show that they are European cities. Hence, our method provides a direction for users to know the two cities.

4   Conclusion

This paper presents an approach to explore high-dimensional data with user knowledge. It can derive dimensions that align with user knowledge to reorganize data and use scatter-pie plot matrix to visualize data. It enables users to discover the relationship between user known and unknown data as well as the relationship between user unknown data and the derived dimensions. Users are more concerned about their own oriented knowledge discovery process and do not have to waste more time to observe the characteristics of data they are not interested in. Because the users knowledge over this data may have certain errors, we hope considering the uncertainty of user knowledge and errors and analyze the effect of the error data on the data distribution in the future work. We temporarily do not provide a friendly interaction and unified operation mode to help users better analyze the data, but we hope to develop one. And friendly interactions such as zooming and filtering will be added to overcome the overlap of scatter-pies in the future work.

Acknowledgments. This work is supported in part by the National High-tech R&D Program (863 Program 2015AA050203), the National Natural Science Foundation of China (No. 61375058), and Co-construction Project of Beijing Municipal Commission of Education.

References

1. Wang, J.: Geometric Structure of High-Dimensional Data and Dimensionality Reduction. Springer, Heidelberg (2012)
2. Gleicher, M.: Explainers: expert explorations with crafted projections. IEEE Trans. Visual Comput. Graphics **19**(12), 2042–2051 (2013)
3. Joachims, T.: Transductive inference for text classification using support vector machines. In: ICML, pp. 200–209 (1999)
4. SVMlight. http://svmlight.joachims.org
5. City livability data. Buzzdata. Best City Contest. http://graphics.cs.wisc.edu/Vis/Explainers/data.html

A Data Mining and Visual Analytics Perspective on Sustainability-Oriented Infrastructure Planning

Dimitri N. Mavris, Michael Balchanos, WoongJe Sung, and Olivia J. Pinon[✉]

School of Aerospace Engineering, Georgia Institute of Technology,
270 Ferst Drive, Atlanta, GA 30332-0150, USA
dimitri.mavris@ae.gatech.edu, olivia.pinon@asdl.gatech.edu
http://www.asdl.gatech.edu

Abstract. The research presented in this paper focuses on developing a multi-scale, integrated environment that supports situational awareness, optimization, as well as forecasting and virtual experimentation at the campus level. One of the key features of this research is its ability to extend beyond the common data-driven load-forecasting exercise and integrate System-of-Systems (SoS) level predictive capabilities to enable the aforementioned functionalities. FORESIGHT, an interactive campus data browser designed to handle any visual analytics tasks on real-time data streams is presented.

Keywords: Sustainability · Infrastructure planning · Visual analytics · Data-driven modeling · Predictive modeling · Cyber-physical systems · Large-scale systems integration

1 Motivation

In a world where data is seen as a strategic asset, Big Data is a game changer. From an infrastructure standpoint, Big Data has the potential to help solve some of our most intractable environmental issues by helping us make better use of renewable energies, new modes of transportation, etc. By shedding a new light on the way we consume and live, Big Data can help us save energy and eventually inform and drive the development of more sustainable, energy-conscious environments [1]. When curated and mined with the proper data analytics techniques, these large amounts and varieties of data can lead to better utilization and optimization of generation assets, improved reliability, better integration of renewables, increased customer awareness and participation, and overall better planning and management of energy systems [1–3].

The research presented herein fits within the context of sustainability-oriented infrastructure and energy planning, and is in line with ongoing efforts led by academia and industry [4–8] to develop and apply cutting-edge data and visualization analytics to the energy sector. In particular, this effort builds on the idea similar to [9] that the data being streamed by sensors can inform every

© Springer International Publishing Switzerland 2016
Y. Tan and Y. Shi (Eds.): DMBD 2016, LNCS 9714, pp. 330–341, 2016.
DOI: 10.1007/978-3-319-40973-3_33

time horizon. Hence, this research, which is part of the Georgia Tech (GT) Smart Energy Campus initiative, focuses on developing a multi-scale, integrated environment that provides the following capabilities to the Georgia Tech campus community:

- Situational awareness about campus energy conditions and consumption levels, etc.
- Optimization of plant settings, etc.
- Forecasting and virtual experimentation to better understand the implications, in terms of campus energy consumption, of long term infrastructure decisions.

The initial steps in realizing the aforementioned integrated environment are detailed in [10]. The present paper focuses instead on introducing and discussing the steps taken towards enabling predictive capabilities and the assessment of energy-focused scenarios and practices. In particular, one of the remarkable features of this research is its ability to extend beyond the common data-driven load-forecasting exercise and integrate System-of-Systems (SoS) level predictive capabilities to enable optimization, forecasting and virtual experimentation.

The paper is structured as follows: Sect. 2 briefly introduces the approach implemented to support the development of the aforementioned capabilities. Then, Sects. 3 and 4 discuss the implementation of some of the core aspects of the approach. Finally, Sect. 5 presents some of the current functionalities of this integrated environment and ends with a discussion about the environment's envisioned capabilities.

2 Integrated Approach

A campus can be seen as a system-of-systems in which buildings, plants, modes of transportation, and energy delivery networks are designed to continuously respond to internal and external factors. While it is customary for such systems to be modeled using a physics-based approach, there are strong benefits in combining both physics-based and data-driven approaches. First, doing so enables a more accurate modeling of consumer behavior such as demand for electricity or cooling loads. Second, it ensures that the data-driven model can inform the development and execution of the physics-based model, model which usually requires more detailed information and a deeper level of understanding of the phenomenon or behavior being represented. Combining both approaches also allows one to alleviate the traditional limitations of data-driven approaches, i.e. the limited capability of a data-driven model to accurately capture and predict operation states that were not initially represented or contained within the original data set. The approach is broken down into five steps:

- Step 1: Data from Georgia Tech's existing metering infrastructure (both real time data streams and historical data) is imported, cleaned, and pre-processed to suit various data analysis purposes. Weather and building load profiles are then modeled by leveraging up-to-date machine learning algorithms and surrogate modeling techniques.

- Step 2: An integrated, System-of Systems (SoS) level modeling and simulation environment is developed following an object-oriented approach. This model allows for the evaluation of the total (SoS-level) campus energy consumption at the plants for a given demand (energy requirements) at the buildings level (systems-level).
- Step 3: An exploration of the combinatorial space of system-level operational settings is conducted in order to identify chiller settings (staging and temperature setpoints) that lead to minimum energy consumption on the chilled water (CW) network for a given combination of weather and building cooling demand levels.
- Step 4: The optimal chiller plant settings are then compared against historical settings and potential energy savings are identified and quantified.
- Step 5: A virtual test-bed called GT FORESIGHT is used to gain situational awareness about campus energy usage. Additional capabilities are under development to enable virtual experimentation and support sustainability-oriented infrastructure planning at the campus level.

3 Data-Driven Modeling

The Georgia Institute of Technology campus in Atlanta, GA accounts for about 200 buildings and multiple layers of energy distribution: electricity, chilled water, steam and natural gas networks. Data from more than 20,000 m or sensors distributed across the campus is stored in multiple data repositories for monitoring and management purposes. This data can be used not only for detection of anomalous events but also for prediction of future energy consumption, hence supporting energy usage optimization as well as sustainability-oriented infrastructure planning. In the particular context of this research, buildings need to be represented using a finite set of features for better integration with the predictive modeling capabilities discussed in Sect. 4. Given the large volume of data being collected and the high number of variables being captured (time stamp, location, type of sensor, etc.), feature extraction techniques are thus needed to reduce the number of features used to characterize buildings and facilitate model generalization. The approach taken to reduce the dimensionality of the building data is discussed in the following section.

3.1   Feature Extraction from Building Data

Many techniques have been discussed in the literature that are used to represent time series data [11,12]. Very often, the emphasis of these techniques is on reducing dimensionality by discretization in the time domain. In contrast to these techniques, the authors found that they could significantly reduce the dimensionality of the time series data and identify unique usage pattern for each building independently of seasonal usage variations by using a simple normalization technique. This technique exploits the daily periodicity of the building operation data, leading each measurement to be normalized by the corresponding daily mean value, as shown in Eq. 1:

$$\bar{Q} \equiv \frac{Q \times 24\,\text{hours}}{\int_{0:00}^{24:00} Q\,dt}. \tag{1}$$

where Q can be any measured quantity of interest.

Figure 1 illustrates the impact of the normalization on electricity consumption, where each plot is a two-dimensional histogram of the electric consumption (kW) for a specific building over a period of a week. These plots capture three years of historical electric consumption data measured at 15-min intervals. The brightness is representative of the frequency of the measured value at the time of the week the measurement was taken. Figure 1 compares both the original and normalized data for three different buildings. In particular, it shows that a unique usage pattern can be captured for each building, independently of the magnitude of the seasonal variation. Similarly, as shown in Fig. 2, unique usage patterns can be obtained for different types of buildings (residence halls, classroom-focused buildings, research-focused buildings, etc.). Hence, as expected, it clearly appears that the weekly and daily electricity consumption pattern of residence halls differ from that of other types of buildings. In terms of cooling loads, Fig. 2 also shows that there is a common pattern across very different types of buildings. Hence, implementing the aforementioned normalization technique significantly reduces the dimensionality of the sensor data by enabling decoupled modeling processes for (1) the usage pattern and (2) the magnitude of said usage.

The following section discusses the modeling of the cooling loads for faster integration into the predictive capabilities detailed in Sect. 4.

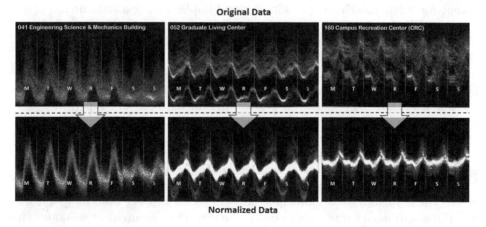

Fig. 1. Electricity consumption for three different buildings before and after normalization

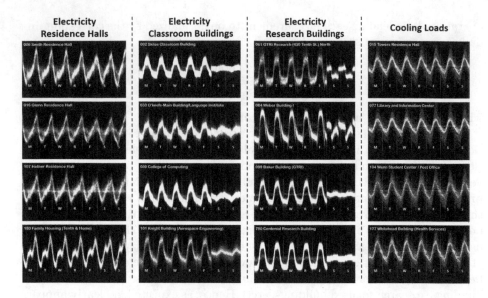

Fig. 2. Building signatures by building types

3.2   Cooling Load Modeling Using Neural Networks

The Georgia Tech campus has two main chilled water plants for campus-wide air-conditioning services, with each plant being composed of multiple chillers. The overall energy consumption of these plants is based on the chiller settings as well as the cooling loads of the individual buildings that are part of the chilled water network. Because the energy consumption of these chiller plants is significant except for a few months in the winter time, implementing a data-driven approach could help identify opportunities for campus-wide energy savings. Indeed, such an approach, when implemented at the chiller plant level, would allow for the identification of the chiller settings that minimize energy consumption and provide managers with a means to pro-actively address changes in cooling loads. Doing so in turn requires building a predictive model of upcoming cooling loads. Cooling loads are very sensitive to weather parameters such as temperature and humidity. The wet bulb temperature is a useful indicator, combining the effects of both dry bulb temperature and ambient humidity.

A neural network is trained using the data in order to capture the variability of the cooling loads in presence of weather and other factors. The neural net has a multi-layered structure with an input layer, two hidden layers, and an output layer. The input layer has four input nodes: one for the wet bulb temperature and three additional parameters to define the time the measurement was taken: a week of a year (0 to 52), a day of a week (0 to 6), and a minute of a day (0 to 1440). Each hidden layer has 15 hidden nodes whose activation function is the tangent sigmoid. The single output node is a linear unit to model each measurement of cooling loads. The weight training has been done for a batch of 75 % of the entire

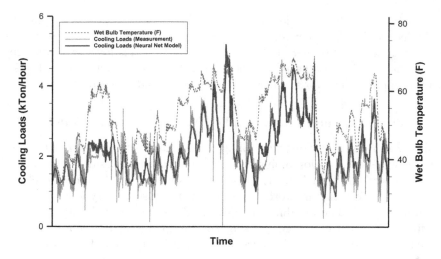

Fig. 3. Measured and modeled cooling loads (Color figure online)

data points using the Lavenberg-Marquardt algorithm [13] with the gradient calculated using the backprogation error [14]. During the training, the validation error for 15 % of the entire data points is monitored to prevent over-fitting. A detailed comparison of the neural net model with the actual measurements is shown in Fig. 3. It can be seen that the model properly captures the variation in cooling loads that are due to both weather effects and on-campus activities. More importantly, it indicates that including time information can be an effective means to model complicated socio-economic factors such as human activities and conditional changes in individual buildings.

4   Predictive Modeling Capabilities

A SoS-level energy usage forecasting and performance prediction model is built using a hybrid modeling approach that combines the strength of both data-driven and object-oriented modeling. In particular, this hybrid approach is thought to address some of the interaction effects and district-level integration challenges identified in the literature [4, 6] by providing a synthesis of a district-level object oriented environment that is composed of both data-driven system and component-level model blocks. In this model, the various modes of energy transfer are represented as discrete sets of energy layers [6]. Each layer includes the *source* side (e.g. generation of electricity, or chilled water), the *demand* side (e.g. electric loads and cooling on buildings), and the respective distribution networks and other energy flow control equipment [6, 15]. Some of the benefits of the layer-based modeling approach is the bottom-up, spiral-driven, layer-by-layer total system model implementation, as well as the scalability and transparency in correlating system responses to contributing effects. On the downside, energy layers that are not independent result in interaction effects that must be addressed in the district-level layer model. The proposed modeling approach is applied to the Chilled Water (CW) network for the following reasons: (1) the chiller water network is a major consumer of electric power, and (2) this layer exhibits significant inefficiencies in comparison to other energy layers, which in turn leads to potential opportunities for efficiency improvements and cost savings.

4.1   Overview of the Campus Chilled Water Network Model

A chilled water system for district cooling consists of three main areas: the chiller plant, the water distribution piping network, and the building side demand which receives the chilled water flow. The plant consists of parallel-connected electric chillers. The distribution network follows the primary-secondary loop piping layout paradigm [16]. The building side demand is represented through a cooling coil, effectively a heat-exchanger per single or "lumped" building representations. The selected baseline model involves a similar primary-secondary loop system with a total of six chillers in parallel arrangement, which provide a total capacity capable of serving a large number of connected buildings with varying cooling demands. As part of the primary loop, each chiller is linked to a fixed rate pump with a control valve. Additional pumps (variable speed drive) on the secondary loop are responsible for maintaining water flow to the buildings and the desired pressure differential at the loop endpoints. The chilled water network model has been implemented with the Modelica Buildings Library [17].

4.2   Chiller Plant Modeling

The chiller plant model block has been implemented as a condenser-evaporator combination, which calculates the power consumption per chiller, assuming a pre-selected supply water temperature. It is configured to provide a total of 12,250 tons of chilled water produced at full capacity by six chillers. Chiller reconfiguration is possible through input variables which determine the supply temperature and operating status per chiller. The plant simulation calculates the power consumed by each chiller and the total power for the entire plant, in response to maintaining the required supply temperature for the given campus heat load conditions. Power consumption calculations are based on the DOE-2 electric chiller modeling [18], as implemented by the Buildings library [17,19].

4.3   Campus Network and Building Side Modeling

Cooling demand for each building is determined by a number of factors: weather conditions, building usage profiles and occupancy levels, construction materials, glass area and the overall architectural building layout. Weather is the most influential factor, being the primary driver of seasonal trends in cooling load demand [20]. Effects of hydraulic settings on the cooling network may also affect chilled water distribution performance. As hydraulic/thermal interactions are hard to predict and capture, a data-driven modeling approach is preferred to build cooling demand prediction.

For energy sizing purposes, two main campus building districts are modeled as a "lumped" single building modeling block, effectively representing the same collective impact buildings that belong to the district. The east and west side building districts are implemented, with each block returning predicted profiles for the total equivalent heat load profile and building-side ΔT. The predicted profiles are calculated using the data-driven surrogate models discussed in Sect. 3.2. To maintain the hydraulic layer assumptions, pump models allow for flow rate control, applicable both for the primary loop and the condenser pump. A similar pump model with prescribed flow rates are used for the secondary loop pumps.

4.4   Model Calibration

To ensure reliable energy predictions, the chilled water network model has been calibrated against actual campus data. The individual chiller models are sourced by the Buildings Library and are based on product specifications and performance curves from manufacturer data for energy calculations. However, to improve model accuracy the chiller models have been calibrated against real campus data and tested to match actual plant performance responses. For completing the calibration, regression techniques were used to derive an equation-based model from measured performance data sets. Energy consumption predictions from the model have been compared to actual campus plant data for a week. Very close agreement of actual and predicted curves has been observed. The same steps have been followed for other time periods during different seasons [21], in order to ensure the prediction accuracy across all seasons.

4.5   Optimizing for Chiller Plant Efficiency

Part of the objectives behind the Smart Energy Campus initiative and the chilled water network model development, is to perform energy optimization and energy saving strategy testing for the chiller plant using model-based energy predictions. The difference ΔT between supply and return temperatures acts as a proxy metric for energy efficiency estimation and is the preferred energy efficiency indicator for both the plant and the buildings sides. Using expert feedback and other recent approaches [4,22], it is possible to improve plant efficiency by exploring alternative chiller configurations and planning operations. In particular, by leveraging predictive modeling capabilities and tradespace exploration methods, all feasible chiller configurations can be generated and sets of optimal chiller settings across a wide range of operating and weather conditions can be identified [23]. The optimal chiller setting identified do match the total available capacity with campus cooling demand, maintain the required flow rates through buildings, and lead to minimum power consumption at the chiller plant [23].

5   The FORESIGHT Predictive Campus Browser

FORESIGHT is an interactive, visual-analytics based campus data browser, designed as a front-end that supports real-time situational awareness and campus-level energy usage monitoring as well as model-based energy usage predictions, based on real time data streams. The combined capability allows for the user to navigate through time and campus location and observe past energy performance trends for any building of interest. Real-time measurements and historic data are queried from the data repositories, which include a database maintained by campus facilities. The data is sourced from sensor measurements and meter readings already installed across campus.

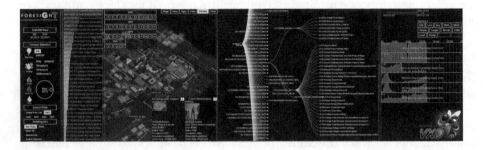

Fig. 4. Overview of the FORESIGHT environment

The list of sensors deployed across campus is grouped by buildings and sensor groups. This list can also be queried and visualized as an expanding tree diagram, hence allowing managers to quickly identify sensors related to specific buildings and most importantly, sensors that may be inoperative. An overview of the FORESIGHT browser (implemented in HTML by combining objects and routines implemented in WebGL, Javascript, PHP, SQL, and Python) is illustrated in Fig. 4. Beyond its role as a campus wide energy monitoring and diagnostic tool, the goal of the FORESIGHT browser is to provide a comprehensive prediction capability for campus-wide energy usage, that includes varying energy demand, accounts for total campus cooling load fluctuations, and utilizes weather forecast data. Based on weather forecasts and campus side cooling demand predictions, the browser calls the chilled water network model to simulate chiller operations. As illustrated in Fig. 5 the browser then projects the calculated energy consumption profiles for the assigned weather and demand profiles, for the given simulated time period. This capability is further illustrated and discussed through a case study which seeks to address the energy usage for a hot summer day period during the week of June 11th, 2015.

Assuming June 10th, 2015 as the starting date, weather data for the upcoming week (June 11th to 18th) are obtained through a NOAA's Digital Forecasting Database query. Dry Bulb temperature and Relative Humidity are shown in the top left of Fig. 5-(a). The corresponding cooling loads are then calculated by the pre-trained neural network-based modeler, as described in Sect. 3.2, and shown Fig. 5-(a) (*Cooling Loads for Sub-Network 1 and Sub-Network 2 time series*). Provided with chiller settings that match the actual campus chiller plant configuration, FORESIGHT then executes the campus-level chilled water plant sim-

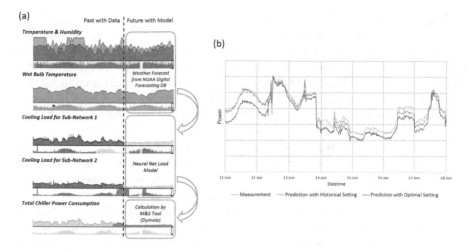

Fig. 5. Predicted chilled water plant energy profiles through FORESIGHT (Color figure online)

ulation, which in turn returns the predicted profile for the *Total Chiller Power Consumption*, as shown in Fig. 5-(a). Another benefit provided through FORE-SIGHT is the capability to identify cost savings generated by running the CW plant with optimum chiller settings (Fig. 5-(b)). To demonstrate this capability, an existing past operation that spans a one-week period in a particular summer time has been remodeled. The "optimal setting" has been obtained through a series of numerical experiments [23]. The reduction in power consumption due to the selection of the optimal chiller settings, as illustrated in Fig. 5-(b), can lead to significant hypothetical cost savings. As such, the environment developed within the context of this research can be leveraged to anticipate future energy usage and identify a cost-saving strategy that will continue to satisfy cooling demand.

6   Concluding Remarks and Future Steps

This paper discusses the steps undertaken to support both the short- and long-term planning of more sustainable, energy-conscious environments. In particular, the approach to develop a multi-scale, integrated environment that supports situational awareness, optimization, forecasting and virtual experimentation is presented. The core capabilities of this approach, which combines both data-driven modeling and predictive modeling, are discussed and further applied in the context of the GT campus. Ongoing efforts in characterizing buildings shows that using a simple normalization technique is sufficient to capture the unique usage patterns of different types of building. In addition, results obtained from implementing neural networks to model cooling loads suggest that including time information can be an effective means to capture human activities and conditional changes in individual buildings. Data analytics and NN-based surrogate modeling techniques are key to the development and integration of data-driven models into a SoS, district-level modeling architecture. Calibrated with real data, the district model provides accurate energy usage forecasting capabilities, under a broad range of weather fluctuations and various combinations of campus system configurations. The district model integrated environment is the main energy prediction engine under FORESIGHT, a campus browser for energy data analytics.

FORESIGHT is currently being extended to be used as a virtual test-bed to support both short- and long-term studies and decision making. Short-term studies could include enhancing campus readiness to upcoming peak load conditions or disruptions due to extreme and unusual weather conditions. Short- to medium-term planning could be looking at optimizing daily operations to minimize energy consumption. Finally, from a long-term decision making perspective, FORESIGHT would be able to assess the impact of infrastructure decisions (addition of a building, deployment of new energy technologies, increase in student population, etc.) on key environmental, economic, technical and social metrics of interest.

Acknowledgments. The authors would like to acknowledge the Aerospace Systems Design Laboratory (ASDL)'s Smart Campus team and extend their gratitude to the Georgia Tech Facilities group for their invaluable input and expertise.

References

1. Sungard: Big data - challenges an opportunities for the energy industry (2013)
2. Visweswariah, C., Gammons, C.B.: Preface - smart energy. IBM J. Res. Dev. **60**(1), 1–4 (2016)
3. Quitzau, A.: Transforming energy and utilities through big data and analytics, March 2014. http://www.slideshare.net/AndersQuitzauIbm/big-data-analyticsin-energy-utilities
4. Narayanan, S., Apte, M.G., Haves, P., Piette, M.A., Elliott, J.: Systems approach to energy efficient building operation: case studies and lessons learned in a university campus. In: ACEEE Summer Study on Energy Efficiency in Buildings, pp. 296–309 (2010)
5. Rowe, A., Berges, M., Bhatia, G., Goldman, E.: Sensor andrew: large-scale campus-wide sensing and actuation. IBM J. Res. Dev. **55**(1.2), 6.1–6.14 (2011). doi:10.1147/JRD.2010.2089662
6. Lee, S.H., Lee, J.-K.K., Augenbroe, G., Lee, J.-K.K., Zhao, F.: A design methodology for energy infrastructures at the campus scale. Comput. Aided Civil Infrastruct. Eng. **28**(10), 753–768 (2013). doi:10.1111/mice.12050
7. Pompey, P., Bondu, A., Goude, Y., Sinn, M.: Massive-scale simulation of electrical load in smart grids using generalized additive models. In: Antoniadis, A., Poggi, J.-M., Brossat, X. (eds.) Modeling and Stochastic Learning for Forecasting in High Dimensions, vol. 217, pp. 193–212. Springer, Heidelberg (2015). doi:10.1007/978-3-319-18732-7_11

8. IBM Research: Smarter Energy Research Institute (SERI). http://www.research.ibm.com/client-programs/seri/applications.shtml
9. Batty, M.: Big data, smart cities and city planning. Dialogues Hum. Geogr. **3**(3), 274–279 (2013)
10. Duncan, S., Balchanos, M., Sung, W., Kim, J., Li, Y., Issac, Y., Mavris, D., Coulon, A.: Towards a data calibrated, simulation-based campus energy analysis environment for situational awareness and future energy system planning. In: ASME 2014 8th International Conference on Energy Sustainability Co-located with the ASME 2014 12th International Conference on Fuel Cell Science, Engineering and Technology (2014). doi:10.1115/ES2014-6695
11. Laxman, S., Sastry, P.S.: A survey of temporal data mining. Sadhana **31**(2), 173–198 (2006). doi:10.1007/BF02719780
12. Tak-chung, F.: A review on time series data mining. Eng. Appl. Artif. Intell. **24**(1), 164–181 (2011)
13. Hagan, M.T., Menhaj, M.B.: Training feedforward networks with the Marquardt algorithm. IEEE Trans. Neural Networks **5**(6), 989–993 (1994)
14. Rumelhart, D.E., Hinton, G.E., Williams, R.J.: Learning representations by back-propagating errors. Nature **323**(9), 533–536 (1986)
15. Ali, M., Vukovic, V., Sahir, M.H., Fontanella, G.: Energy analysis of chilled water system configurations using simulation-based optimization. Energy Build. **59**, 111–122 (2013). doi:10.1016/j.enbuild.2012.12.011
16. Hubbard, R.: Energy impacts of chilled-water-piping configuration. HPAC Eng. **83**(11), 20 (2011)
17. Wetter, M., Zuo, W., Nouidui, T.S., Pang, X.: Modelica buildings library. J. Build. Perform. Simul. **7**(4), 253–270 (2014). doi:10.1080/19401493.2013.765506
18. Hydeman, M., Gillespie Jr., K.L.: Tools and techniques to calibrate electric chiller component models/discussion. ASHRAE Trans. **108**, 733 (2002)
19. Wetter, M., Zuo, W., Nouidui, T.S.: Recent developments of the Modelica buildings? Library for building energy and control systems brary. In: Modelica Conference, pp. 266–275 (2011)
20. Huang, W.Z., Zaheeruddin, M., Cho, S.H., Zhen, W., Zaheeruddin, M.: Dynamic simulation of energy management control functions for HVAC systems in buildings. Energy Convers. Manag. **47**(7–8), 926–943 (2006). doi:10.1016/j.enconman.2005.06.011
21. Browne, M.W., Bansal, P.K.: Different modelling strategies for in situ liquid chillers. Proc. Inst. Mech. Eng. Part A: J. Power Energ. **215**(3), 357–374 (2001). doi:10.1243/0957650011538587
22. Gao, D.-C., Wang, S., Sun, Y.: A fault-tolerant and energy efficient control strategy for primary secondary chilled water systems in buildings. Energy Build. **43**(12), 3646–3656 (2011). doi:10.1016/j.enbuild.2011.09.037
23. Balchanos, M.G., Kim, J., Duncan, S., Mavris, D.N.: Modeling and simulation-based analysis for large scale campus chilled water networks. In: AIAA Propulsion and Energy 2015, pp. 1–17 (2015)

Visual Interactive Approach for Mining Twitter's Networks

Youcef Abdelsadek[1]([✉]), Kamel Chelghoum[1], Francine Herrmann[1],
Imed Kacem[1], and Benoît Otjacques[2]

[1] Laboratoire de Conception, Optimisation et Modélisation des Systèmes,
LCOMS – EA 7306, Université de Lorraine, Metz, France
{youcef.abdelsadek,kamel.chelghoum,
francine.herrmann,imed.kacem}@univ-lorraine.fr
[2] e-Science Research Unit, Environmental Research and Innovation Department,
Luxembourg Institute of Science and Technology, Belvaux, Luxembourg
benoit.otjacques@list.lu

Abstract. Understanding the semantic behind relational data is very
challenging, especially, when it is tricky to provide efficient analysis at
scale. Furthermore, the complexity is also driven by the dynamical nature
of data. Indeed, the analysis given at a specific time point becomes unsus-
tainable even incorrect over time. In this paper, we rely on a visual interactive approach to handle Twitter's networks using *NLCOMS*. *NLCOMS*
provides multiple and coordinated views in order to grasp the underlying information. Finally, the applicability of the proposed approach is
assessed on real-world data of the ANR-Info-RSN project.

Keywords: Graph visualization · Interactive visualization · Community detection · Twitter's networks

1 Introduction

Nowadays, social networks like Twitter generates a large and complex quantity of data. The analysis of these data at their initial scale is very tricky even
impossible. Furthermore, additional meta-data can be added rendering them
more complex to analyse. Consequently, in order to provide an efficient data
analysis, in this context, one needs to pre-process, chooses the appropriate data
modelling structure and avoids analyst's cognitive charge overload. The latter is
very important and one possible way to manage it consists to provide a gradual
information acquisition. Additionally, even if the approach is overload-safe, an
inappropriate data structure might slowdown the analysis task. After, it comes
the visualization question, which is an important step in the knowledge acquisition process. What is the proper depiction which enhances the analysis task?
Answering this question might also lead to answer to the interactivity issue with
the provided interactions which improve the exploratory task.

   In this work, we use the modelling strength of graphs. The latter are well-
known to be suitable to model relational data where the nodes represent the

© Springer International Publishing Switzerland 2016
Y. Tan and Y. Shi (Eds.): DMBD 2016, LNCS 9714, pp. 342–349, 2016.
DOI: 10.1007/978-3-319-40973-3_34

entities which are interlinked by an edge whether a relationship exists between them. This rudimentary data structure combines, intuitiveness, efficiency and response time. As a concrete example, relationships among Twitter's users could be weighted with regard to their shared number of followers leading to an edge-weighted graph. In this context, it becomes straightforward to verify whether Twitter's users share common followers. Furthermore, the network topology and the edge-attribute might evolve over time. Considering our sample example, two Twitter's users could have not common follower, after a laps of time they could have many common followers and at a different time point they could get back to the initial status without any common follower. For an analyst knowing the causes of these abrupt status changes could be very helpful.

The remaining parts of this paper are structured as follow: In Sect. 2 the framework is introduced. Section 3 presents the used algorithm to detect the underlying communities. Section 4 describes the followed approach to handle Twitter's networks. In Sect. 5 the proposed approach is tested on real-world data of the ANR-Info-RSN project. Finally, Sect. 6 concludes this paper.

2 Framework Description

2.1 Graphs to Model Complex Systems

Let us define $G = (N, E, E^w)$ as a graph where N, E and E^w represent respectively the set of nodes of size v, the set of edges of size m and the edges weights. Graphs are very powerful for modelling relational data even for weighted relationships. Indeed, in this paper graphs are used to model a well-known relationship between Twitter's users which is the "re-tweet". Consequently, the nodes represent Twitter's users and a link exists between two nodes if they re-tweet each others. From there, an integer value is assigned to each edge $e^w \in E^w$ representing the re-tweet frequency.

2.2 Graph Representation Techniques

This section presents the various graph representations. Such representations can be divided into three major categories listed in the following:

1. **Node-link diagrams:** Node-link diagrams depict the nodes by circles whereas the relationship between two nodes is represented by a line. Figure 1a shows node-link diagram representation of a sample graph. In this context, one among the graph drawing algorithms [10] is the force-directed algorithm where nodes are as electrically charged particles which try to repulse each others while the edges keep them closer. The system becomes stable when the force reaches an equilibrium. This system is very efficient for producing nice drawings respecting the aesthetic criteria [16], like edge crossing minimization and edge length uniformity. In this paper, we use the force-directed algorithm implementation of [1], while allowing the algorithm parameters setting (i.e., the repulsive node charges, the link length, the gravity... etc.).

(a) Node-link diagram representation   (b) Matrix-based representation

Fig. 1. Graph representation techniques

2. **Matrix-based representation:** The matrix-based representation is a two dimensional array used for representing a graph. Row and columns depicts the nodes and the cells depict the edges. Figure 1b shows a matrix-based representation of the sample graph of Fig. 1a.
3. **Combination of depictions:** Obviously, the two above representations can be used both in multiple views [8]. But it can also be used in one view, by superposing node-link diagram on a matrix grid [15] or also by depicting the denser part of the graph by matrix representations [9].

Each representation has its strengths and drawbacks regarding the considered graph visual tasks [7,12]. Choosing a representation instead of another is crucial and has a great impact on the visualization efficiency. For example, with matrix-based representation it would be difficult to follow a path from a source node to a target node. Path detecting task is an important task in social networks to verify whether two nodes of the network communicate via intermediate nodes. In this paper we opt for a node-link diagram representation of networks.

3 Community Detection

In the described framework, the identification of the highly interconnected sub-networks, known as community detection [6,14] informs the analyst which are the Twitter's users groups that re-tweet each others most frequently. In order to detect such communities an improved version of the algorithm of [2] is considered, its main idea consists to use a collection of pairwise disjoint triangles as starting point for community detection. After, adjacent communities are successively compared (i.e., in terms of edge weights) allowing dominant communities to attract more members. An evaluation of this algorithm is showed in Fig. 2 on the LFR benchmark [11] where μ_t and μ_w are, respectively, the edge distribution and the edge weights distribution inside and outside communities. The other employed parameters are $v = 1000$, community size in [20, 100] and maximal degree up to 50. As similarity function the rand index (RI) of [17] is used. From Fig. 2a we can see that the optimality gap is about 5 % where a community structure exists within the network (i.e., $\mu_t < 0.5$).

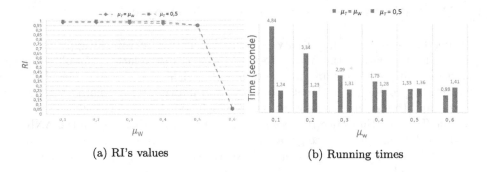

(a) RI's values   (b) Running times

Fig. 2. Evaluation on the LFR benchmark (Color figure online)

4 Approach

In order to handle the aforementioned Twitter's network, we rely on an interactive visualization approach [19]. To this end, an application is implemented to visualize and to interpret the network structure, the related information and the underlying communities, called *NLCOMS*, for (Node-Link and COMmunitieS). *NLCOMS* is user-oriented, providing interactions and data filters as illustrated in Fig. 3. Indeed, the analyst grasps the displayed information by interacting and exploring the network structure. Additionally, circle packing are used to layout the underlying communities, this also allows to display additional information related to each community as well as for each members within it. *NLCOMS* is driven by the visual information-Seeking Shneiderman's Mantara *"Overview First, Zoom and Filter, Then Details-on Demand"* [18]. A global view gives to the analyst a sight of the networks structure, after a zoom on the network or on the underlying communities is provided. Details appear when a selection occurs and effortless interactions are utilized avoiding pointless extra cognitive load. Besides, *NLCOMS* uses visual variable [5,13], like the node size, the node shape, the node position, the edge thickness and the lightness of the inner node colour to display additional information.

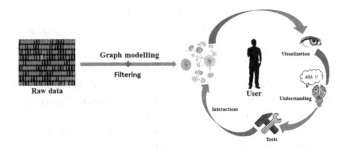

Fig. 3. Interactive visualization steps of *NLCOMS*

5   Real-World Data of the Info-RSN Project

In order to assess the applicability of the approach on real-world application, we consider the data of the ANR-Info-RSN project. In the latter, 17 millions of tweets are collected, these are tweeted from web articles (i.e., media). The objectives are to provide an explanation on how the information is shared through Twitter and to identify the network actors which contribute to the sharing phenomena. To reach this objectives, we have done pre-processing step on the ANR-Info-RSN database in order to get a graph model in which nodes are the persons who tweet and the edges represent a re-tweet, leading to a graph with about 4 millions of nodes and about 7 millions of edges. Additionally, tweets classification is done yielding to 24 tweet thematics (e.g., politic, sport, economy... etc.) and 31 media sources (e.g., le monde, le figaro, liberation... etc.). Furthermore, the date of publication is saved which is an important information if one wants to know the precedence in the sharing phenomena. Indeed, the analyst using *NLCOMS* can filter the tweets by the thematic, the media source and the date of publication which focuses the analysis task. Moreover, the "noise" (i.e., isolated nodes) can be filtered keeping for example the main connected component.

Besides, the node size, the node shape, the edge thickness, the lightness of the inner node colour and the node shape outline color represent, respectively, the number of followers, whether the person who tweets uses Twitter as reporter or as ordinary user, the number of re-tweets, the total number of tweets and the community node's membership. Moreover, interactive bar charts help the analyst to gather the communities characteristics. The bar charts give statistics about the thematic and the media source proportions within a selected community. In addition, donut charts encode for each member the tweets proportion with respect to a selected thematic (media source).

The details of the representative samples from the ANR-Info-RSN project database are presented in Table 1.

Table 1. The ANR-Info-RSN datasets characteristics

Data sets	Initial (v, m)	Without noise	Thematic	Media source
DS1	(1500, 1432)	(970, 989)	All	All
DS2	(3000, 3477)	(3000, 3477)	All	lefigaro.fr

In DS1 the network is sparse with star-like shape communities structure. From Fig. 4, the main actors can easily be distinguishable in the node-link diagram and the circle packing representation where the node size of Fig. 4b depicts the degree of a node. Additionally, Twitter's users with a bridge-like behaviour are observed, those link two communities. One would say that the centric Twitter's users emits the original tweet and the followers with the bridge-like Twitter's users propagate them. The combination of these representations enhances

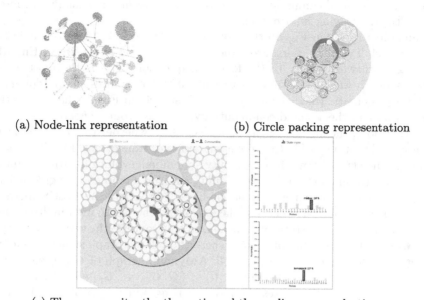

(a) Node-link representation   (b) Circle packing representation

(c) The community, the thematic and the media source selection

Fig. 4. DS1 of the ANR-Info-RSN project (Color figure online)

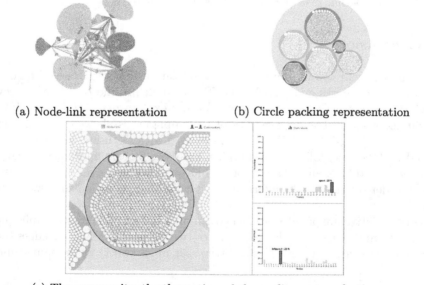

(a) Node-link representation   (b) Circle packing representation

(c) The community, the thematic and the media source selection

Fig. 5. DS2 of the ANR-Info-RSN project (Color figure online)

the understanding of community structure while grasping gradually and inter-
actively the underlying information.

Unlike in Fig. 4b, in Fig. 5b the circle size is proportional to the number of
tweets of each Twitter's users. From there, by decreasing circle size sorting, the
analyst can answer quickly to the following question; who is the most active
Twitter's user? And, if the most active member contributes in the dominant
community thematic (media source)? As an instance, in Fig. 5c the most active
Twitter's user in the selected community tweets only from "lefigaro.fr".

Furthermore, the analyst might want to confirm whether the observed Twitter's users roles at a specific time point sustain over time or not. In other words,
the analyst needs to follow the community's members evolution with new members joining/leaving the studied community and/or members changing behaviours (e.g., from simple followers to bridge-like). To this end, NLCOMS allows to
understand the information sharing phenomena in the whole with multiple time
steps instead of a unique static observation. In this context, the tweets network of
today will not be the same tomorrow, where the related graph structure evolves
over time, leading to dynamic graphs [4]. A dynamic graph of G can be seen as
a sequence of static graphs, denoted by $G_s = (G, G_1, \ldots, G_f)$ with f snapshots.
Additionally, NLCOMS utilizes the physical time and the axial time in order
to benefit from the advantages of both. The latter is used to explore the graph
structure historic by scrolling down and up. Moreover, NLCOMS maintains the
network layout that the analyst built up over time, so-called user *mental map* [3].
Generally, its preservation through the successive snapshots helps the analyst to
stay familiar with the network structure. This preservation avoids to disturb the
user from its original task (i.e., network structure analysis).

6   Conclusion

In this paper, we rely on an interactive visualization approach using NLCOMS
for Twitter's networks analysis. NLCOMS uses multiple and coordinated views
allowing user interactions and network structure exploratory with gradual information acquisition. The applicability of the approach is showed on real-world
data of the ANR-Info-RSN project. Several Twitter's users behaviours are
noticed with centric, followers and bridge-like users for the information sharing
phenomena. Additionally, the network structure evolution over time is considered, in order to analysis the information sharing phenomena on successive time
steps.

As perspective, we plan to consider community detection in multi-graphs (i.e.,
graphs with multiple edges). For example, re-tweet edges and mention edges (i.e.,
when a Twitter user cites another Twitter user in its tweet) at the same time.

Acknowledgements. We would like to thank the anonymous referees for their pertinent remarks which improved the presentation of this paper. This research has been
supported by the Agence Nationale de Recherche (ANR, France) during the Info-RSN
Project.

References

1. Data-Driven Documents. https://d3js.org/
2. Abdelsadek, Y., Chelghoum, K., Herrmann, F., Kacem, I., Otjacques, B.: Community detection algorithm based on weighted maximum triangle packing. In: Proceedings of International Conference on Computer and Industrial Engineering CIE45 (2015)
3. Archambault, D., Purchase, H.C.: The "map" in the mental map: experimental results in dynamic graph drawing. Int. J. Hum. Comput. Stud. **71**(11), 1044–1055 (2013)
4. Beck, F., Burch, M., Diehl, S., Weiskopf, D.: The state of the art in visualizing dynamic graphs. In: EuroVis STAR (2014)
5. Bertin, J.: Sémiologie graphique: les diagrammes, les réseaux, les cartes. Mouton, Paris (1967)
6. Clauset, A., Newman, M.E.J., Moore, C.: Finding community structure in very large networks. Phys. Rev. E **70**, 066111 (2004)
7. Ghoniem, M., Fekete, J., Castagliola, P.: A comparison of the readability of graphs using node-link and matrix-based representations. In: 10th IEEE Symposium on Information Visualization (InfoVis 2004), Austin, TX, USA, 10–12 October 2004, pp. 17–24 (2004)
8. Henry, N., Fekete, J.: Matrixexplorer: a dual-representation system to explore social networks. IEEE Trans. Vis. Comput. Graph. **12**(5), 677–684 (2006)
9. Henry, N., Fekete, J., McGuffin, M.J.: Nodetrix: a hybrid visualization of social networks. IEEE Trans. Vis. Comput. Graph. **13**(6), 1302–1309 (2007)
10. Kaufmann, M., Wagner, D.: Drawing Graphs: Methods and Models. Springer, New York (2001)
11. Lancichinetti, A., Fortunato, S.: Benchmarks for testing community detection algorithms on directed and weighted graphs with overlapping communities. Phys. Rev. E **80**(1), 016118 (2009)
12. Lee, B., Plaisant, C., Parr, C.S., Fekete, J., Henry, N.: Task taxonomy for graph visualization. In: Proceedings of the 2006 AVI Workshop on BEyond Time and Errors: Novel Evaluation Methods for Information Visualization, BELIV 2006, Venice, Italy, 23 May 2006, pp. 1–5 (2006)
13. Mackinlay, J.D.: Automating the design of graphical presentations of relational information. ACM Trans. Graph. **5**(2), 110–141 (1986)
14. Newman, M.: Modularity and community structure in networks. Proc. Nat. Acad. Sci. U.S.A. **103**(23), 8577–8582 (2006)
15. Otjacques, B., Feltz, F.: Representation of graphs on a matrix layout. In: 9th International Conference on Information Visualisation, IV 2005, London, UK, 6–8 July 2005, pp. 339–344 (2005)
16. Purchase, H.C.: Metrics for graph drawing aesthetics. J. Vis. Lang. Comput. **13**(5), 501–516 (2002)
17. Rand, W.: Objective criteria for the evaluation of clustering methods. J. Am. Stat. Assoc. **66**(336), 846–850 (1971)
18. Shneiderman, B.: The eyes have it: a task by data type taxonomy for information visualizations. In: Proceedings of the 1996 IEEE Symposium on Visual Languages, Boulder, CO, USA, 3–6 September 1996, pp. 336–343 (1996)
19. Spence, R.: Information Visualization: Design for Interaction, 2nd edn. Prentice-Hall Inc., Upper Saddle River (2007)

Privacy Policy

Key Indicators for Data Sharing - In Relation with Digital Services

Sheak Rashed Haider Noori[1], Md. Kamrul Hossain[1], and Juwel Rana[2,3(✉)]

[1] Daffodil International University, Dhaka, Bangladesh
drnoori@daffodilvarsity.edu.bd, Kamrul.ns@diu.edu.bd
[2] Telenor Group, Snaroyveien, 30 N-1360, Fornebu, Norway
juwel.rana@telenor.com
[3] Linnaeus University, Växjö, Sweden
juwel.rana@lnu.se

Abstract. Rapid growth of data intensive digital services are creating potential risks of violating consumer centric data privacy. Protection of data privacy is becoming one of the key challenges for most of the big data business entities. Due to thank of big data, recommendation and personalization are becoming very popular in digital space. However it is hard to find a well-defined boundary which illustrates privacy threat to consumers' in relation with improving already opted-in communication services.

In this paper, we initiated identifying key indicators for consumer configured privacy policy in relation with personalized services taking into consideration that "Privacy is a tool for balancing personalization". We survey user attitudes towards privacy and personalization and discovered key indicators for configuring privacy policy by analyzing survey data about privacy concern and data sharing attitude of the consumers. We found that consumers did not want to stop using social media based communication services due to privacy risks. Moreover, consumers have attitude of sharing their data, provided that appropriate personalization features are in place.

Keywords: Data sharing · Big data driven digital services

1 Introduction

Due to dynamic growth of data intensive communication services such as Facebook, Google+, and Twitter, there are potential risks of violating consumer-centric data privacy. In a way, protection of data privacy is becoming one of the key challenges for most of the big data business entities. For example in 2011, Facebook went through a privacy audit by the Irish data protection commissioner. Generally, it is hard to find a well-defined boundary or guidelines

---

J. Rana—The work has been carried out as part of an academic research project and does not necessarily represent Telenor views and positions.

© Springer International Publishing Switzerland 2016
Y. Tan and Y. Shi (Eds.): DMBD 2016, LNCS 9714, pp. 353–363, 2016.
DOI: 10.1007/978-3-319-40973-3_35

which illustrates privacy threat to consumers' in relation with improving or personalizing already opted-in communication services. Because, consumers usually receive less transparent information during the time of changing or adding new features for the services they already opted-in, and as a consequence of this, consumers usually have vague idea regarding the privacy configuration of most of the opted-in Web based communication services.

During the last few decades, telecom operators have been loyal in preserving and protecting personal data such as Communication Detail Records (CDR) from external privacy and security threads. Generally, the telecommunication industries have been providing good level of consumers' privacy. However, in some exceptional cases, telecom operators need to expose users' CDR to the legal government agencies.

However, apart from telecom industries, online communication service providers are also preserving huge amount of personal data of their consumers. Consumer-centric data have been used massively for recommendation, and personalization purposes [1–3]. In a way, today's users have more options in selecting communication services, and personalization is considered as an important feature for selecting such services.

According to Ramnath et al., personalization depends on two factors: 1. service providers' ability to acquire and process consumer-centric information, and 2. consumers' willingness to share information and use personalization services [4]. In this paper, we present key indicators for consumer-configured privacy policy that could motivate consumers for sharing information. This means consumer-specified simplification of today's privacy framework, taking into consideration that "Privacy is a tool for balancing personalization", that is not preventing consumers from being experienced to personalized services.

We collected survey data of more than 1192 internet subscribers from one of the fastest internet users growing Asian countries. Then, we discovered key indicators for configuring privacy policy by analyzing consumers collected survey data about privacy concern and data sharing attitude.

We have following hypotheses:

- Hypothesis 1: Consumers want personalization benefits from sharing their data
- Hypothesis 2: Consumers do not want to stop using social media due to privacy risks

The rest of the paper is structured as follows: Sect. 2 provides experimental design of the performed survey, Sect. 3 describes different steps for processing survey data. After that Sect. 4 discusses results and validation. Section 5 illustrates indicators for configuring privacy policy, then Sect. 6 describes related work. Finally, Sect. 7 concludes the paper.

2   Experimental Design

In order to test our hypothesis, an online survey has been conducted. We choose survey as a classic method for data collection, as it provides a unique opportunity to obtain detail insight of an experiment. We choose online survey since we can gather large numbers of feedback directly from the target group with a speed and efficiency while online data management systems can automatically convert the data into a useful state for analysis.

The survey was carried out in November 2014 over a four-weeks period, with 1150 participants between 18 and 55 years of age. The survey consisted of 40 primary questions with 22 demographic questions and 101 variables. All the variables can be found here [5]. In order to secure respondents' privacy, participation in the follow-up questions were tagged as optional. In addition to that, no email address was asked for submitting responses and cookies were not used in this whole process.

The survey process composed of a number of steps that were executed sequentially, from determining the research objectives to analyzing the data. The planning stage of the survey process was iterative. The research objectives, questionnaire, target population, sampling design, and implementation strategy were revised several times prior to implementing the survey.

The Survey Objective: At the first step of the survey process we determine the research objective by identifying a small set of key research questions to be answered by the survey. Eventually each question we linked to one or more variables collected in the data collection phase of the process.

The Target Population: In this step in the survey process we define the population to be studied for whom the study results will be applied and about which inferences will be made from the survey results. In this study, the target population is defined as "Persons living in a Asian country who are consumers of digital based services."

The Mode of Administration: Having specified the research objectives and defined the target population, the next step in the process was to determine the mode of administration for the survey. After thorough discussion and considering all the scenarios, the mode of administration of this survey was selected to be online. It is a feasible and cost-effective method to reach the target population and most importantly the target population is the internet users of a country in Asia which completely justifies this mode of administration. Online survey service provide "Survey Gizmo" (www.surveygizmo.com) was chosen over other services since it provides a helpful data analytics tool and gives the freedom of developing various types of questionnaires.

Developing the Questionnaire: In this step of the survey process we developed the questionnaire based on the research objectives. To get the idea about the users' attitude regarding data sharing, privacy, control and transparency, we classified the questionnaire into three broad categories supported by different scenarios considering demographic information, privacy attitude, and trust on communication service providers.

Sampling Approach: Having defined the target population, research objectives and the mode of administration, we specify the sampling design specification by describing the sampling frame and sample sizes to be used for the survey. To keep the margin of error 3 % which is reasonable with survey we took the sample size n = 1192. The method Random sampling is used for selecting the sample from the sampling frame. The sampling frame is simply the list of target population members from which the sample drawn. As mentioned previously, the frame chosen for sampling depends to a large extent on the mode of administration for the survey. For this survey, a logical frame is people who have access to digital services.

To minimize survey bias Random sampling is used for selecting the sample. We gave extra caution to ensure respondents are representative of the entire population to avoid Non-response bias. We ensure this by choosing the respondents who are consumers of internet based digital services of Asian region. To avoid response bias question wording and question order revised several times prior to implementation. Extra caution put not to influence of the interviewer. In our study we try to understand the user attitudes towards data sharing, privacy and personalization. The fact is population between the age 18 to 35 are the most common users of the internet based digital services.

Developing Data Collection and Data Processing Plans: Once the initial and basic design decisions were made, the data collection and data processing plans were developed. For this survey, the data collection plan is as follows.

3   Data Processing

The survey data collection is done over the time period of 3rd November 2014 to 1st December 2015. For performing the survey and collecting data, we took the benefits from Surveygizmo tool. The tool is specialized for performing survey study.

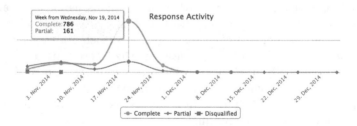

Fig. 1. Timeline of users participation in the survey. (Color figure online)

Among the responses collected through Surveygizmo, we found 1192 complete responses and 479 partially complete responses. Figure 1 shows time-line of users participation in the survey. The responses are collected in different ways such as email campaign, social media, hallway approach in both online and offline settings. Each of the settings have it is own campaign code for segmenting different groups of respondents for detailed study if necessary.

3.1 Data Cleaning

In the very first step of the data cleaning process, only the completed responses i.e., 1192 are considered. After that the completed responses are divided into two data-sets. One of the data-sets is prepared for users' privacy study and the other data-set is prepared for users' data sharing attitude study.

During the time of cleaning data-sets, we consider also response time as well as percentage of missing data. If a respondents response time is less than practically certain threshold, we eliminated those responses from the data sets. If a respondents ignore significant number of questions to be answered, we eliminated those responses.

For demographic and initial segmentation of the participants we prepared 22 variables. The variables are span from getting gender, age, education, occupation to smart device usage, internet usage, subscribed operators and so on. All the variable are divided into two major categories. One category is about privacy concerns so called attitude and the other is about data sharing so called Scenario variable. Details about these variables are given in [5].

4 Results and Validation

In hypothesis 1, we mentioned that "consumers want personalization benefits from sharing their data". From the list of attitude variables, it has already presented in V25 for the case of personalized services that 30.75 % respondents are extremely reluctant or reluctant to share Facebook Data. In V26, it is found that 27.73 % respondents are extremely disagreeing to share GPS data, while in V27, 24.02 % respondents are extremely disagreeing or disagreeing to share telecom infrastructure based location data. Figure 2 shows that users are more willing to share Facebook data rather than to receive non-interesting ads or campaigns. Moreover, Fig. 3 illustrates that smart-phone users are likely to share Facebook data and location data to receive personalized ads and coupons.

Thus the above numbers indicate that Smart-phone users are likely to share Facebook data, GPS data, and telecom-location data to receive personalized ads and coupons.

We also applied cross tabulation [6] between variable V25 from scenario variables and attitude variable V36. Scenario variable V25 is defined as *"If you give the app permission to see your Facebook Likes and read the information in your public Facebook profile (e.g., age and gender), the app could learn your interests and preferences and deliver ads of interest to you (e.g., ads for vegetarian restaurants offering discounts). How likely is it that you would accept sharing your Facebook Likes and public profile in exchange for receiving more personalized ads?"*. And the attitude variable V36 is defined as *"From the standpoint of personal privacy, please indicate to what extent you agree with each of the following statements: I am concerned that websites and mobile apps are collecting too much data about me."* The result from cross tabulation is shown in Table 1, which shows the variables are significantly ($p < 0.05$) associated. Even 46.5 % of

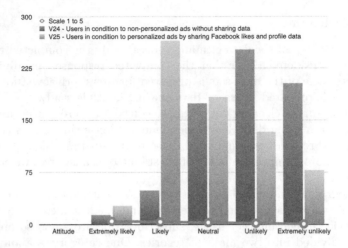

Fig. 2. Users are more willing to share Facebook data rather than to receive non-interesting ads or campaigns. (Color figure online)

conservative users, who are concerned about privacy are willing to share their data for personalization.

We also found that 48 % of concerned users are likely to share location data for personalized services. For sharing usage data, for example music playlist sharing, 68.4 % of concerned users are willing to share for better personalized music recommendation. However, the association between concerned users and location data is not high enough, while the association between concerned users and music play-list usage data is higher. Details statistical records are available in Tables 1 and 2 of appendix 2 [7]. All these statements validate hypothesis 1 - to be remarked that consumer wants personalized benefits in exchange of sharing data.

Table 1. Cross tabulation by attitude variable V36 and scenario variable V25.

		Scenario_V25			Total	Chi square
		Unlikely (Extremely Unlikely, Unlikely)	Neutral	Likely (Extremely likely, likely)		
Attitude_V36	Not Concern (Strongly disagree, disagree, neutral)	47 (44.3 %)	26 (24.5 %)	33 (31.1 %)	106	11.583** with 2 df
	Concern (Strongly agree, agree)	133 (28.5 %)	117 (25.1 %)	217 (46.5 %)	467	
	Total	180 (31.4 %)	143 (25.0 %)	250 (43.6 %)	573	

** indicate 5 % level of significance

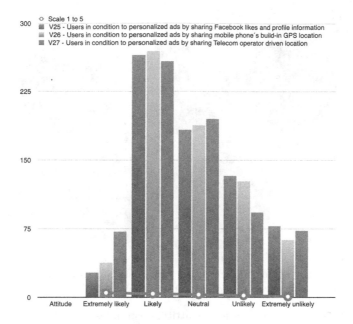

Fig. 3. Smart-phone users are likely to share Facebook data and location data to receive personalized ads and coupons. (Color figure online)

In the hypothesis 2, we mentioned that consumers do not want to restrict themselves using social media due to privacy risks. In the Fig. 4, it is found that respondents do not want to stop using social media services such as Google+, Facebook due to the fact that these services analyze the content of for better ads prediction. On average 80 % of the participants are not intending to make any interruption in using Facebook, Gmail or Yahoo services.

It has also observed that for streaming and e-commerce services such as Amazon, and Netflix on average 64 % of respondents do not willing to stop services due to privacy risk. Less than 10 % of participants think that they will be discontinued in using communication, social media or content recommending services due to privacy motive.

Cross tabulation is also applied to check the association between attitude variables V36 and V59. Attitude variable V36 defines as *"From the standpoint of personal privacy, please indicate to what extent you agree with each of the following statements: I am concerned that websites and mobile apps are collecting too much data about me."* and variable V59: *"Will you stop using Gmail or Yahoo Mail?"*

The results are presented in Table 2, which shows that there is association between these variables and the association is statistically significant ($p < 0.1$). Among the user who are concerned about their information, 83 % are not willing to stop using Gmail/Yahoo whereas only 3.1 % want to stop using Gmail/Yahoo

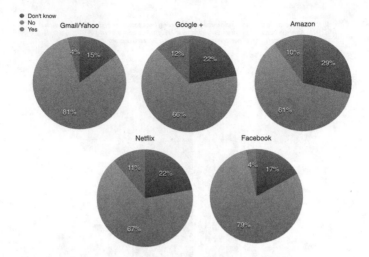

Fig. 4. Users are not willing to stop using major social media and communication services due to privacy concerns. (Color figure online)

Table 2. Cross tabulation by attitude variables V36 and V59.

		Attitude_V59			Total	Chi square
		No	Yes	Do not know		
Attitude_V36	Not Concern (Strongly disagree, disagree, neutral)	161 (76.3 %)	10 (4.7 %)	40 (19.0 %)	211	4.926* with df 2
	Concern (Strongly agree, agree)	595 (83.0 %)	22 (3.1 %)	100 (13.9 %)	717	
	Total	756 (81.5 %)	32 (3.4 %)	140 (15.1 %)	928	

* indicates 10 % level of significance

Mail due to privacy as well as 76.3 % of the not concern users are also not willing to stop.

All these numbers validates hypothesis 2 with the conclusion that respondents do not want to discard the using of communication or social media or content recommending services.

5   Key Indicators

By studying respondent's data, and data driven services, we found following indicators that could be vital configuring users' privacy policy for defining data sharing strategy:

Identifiable data: Users can be identified from the shared information. For example: age, gender, contact list, date of birth, credit card number. In the Attitude variable V53 defines as *"My contact list: I have sometimes stopped registering to a website or installing a mobile app because it wanted to collect"*, which can be applied for cross tabulation attitude variable V36. The results show

Table 3. Cross tabulation by attitude variable V36 and V53

		Attitude_V53		Total	Chi square
		Disagree	Agree		
Attitude_V36	Not Concern (Strongly disagree, disagree, neutral)	75 (39.1 %)	117 (60.9 %)	192	11.887***
	Concern (Strongly agree, agree)	168 (24.9 %)	507 (75.1 %)	675	
	Total	243 (28.0 %)	624 (72.0 %)	867	

*** indicate 1 % level of significance

more than 75 % of the users who are concerned about personal data are agree to stop registering a new digital service if the service or apps is required information regarding of the users' contact list. There is highly significant ($p < 0.01$) between personal data concern with sharing contact list for registering in a site or installing an apps. This implies that identifiable information is highly indicative factor for data sharing (Table 3).

Usage data: Users create huge amount of on-click usage data, communication logs, social media consumption data. More than 77 % and 61 % concern user and not concern user about personal risk would like to stop registering because of collecting browsing behavior respectively (Table 5 in Appendix 2).

Anonymized data: Users authorize for sharing their data with 3rd parties in a transactional and/or aggregated level without disclosing users' identity or actual content We found that 44.6 % of the users will stop registering in a site or installing apps because of sharing age and gender (Table 4 in Appendix 2).

Location data: Geo-location data can be collected from GPS. For example Location from Google Location API, GPS, Telecom services based location data, and so on. Half of the users would stop registering because of information regarding location (Table 6 in Appendix 2). There is no significant association between Concern about personal data and stopped registering due to location data collection, which indicates that if users get personalized offer from the provider, the likelihood of sharing location may be higher.

Streaming data: Where, when, and which song users' are listening or movies watching. For example Spotify data, Netflix data. Around 68.4 % of concerned users are willing to share their music playlist habit for better personalized music recommendation (Table 2 in Appendix 2), which shows that sharing of streaming services usage data could be done in case of personalized benefits. Next section discusses related work.

6   Related Work

In [8], Kenneally and Claffy introduced a reference framework which is a hybrid of policy and technical controls for data sharing that provides regulation on technical regulators and enables privacy-sensitive data sharing for data producers and consumers. To describe privacy risks and controls this framework serves as an analytic tool for assessing, a foundation for establishing privacy management controls and a template for developing operational solutions to balance privacy risk as well as utility rewards in data sharing.

An interpretative approach through repeated e-mail exchanges is adopted by [9] to investigate the social and psychological issues underlying consumers privacy concerns. This study indicate that the demand for active control over the disclosure or use of information showed the need for instruments that can allow consumers to take informed decisions in the exchanges with companies and trade appropriate benefits. [10] points out privacy preserving data integration and sharing challenges with some possible solution ideas.

According to [11], privacy in e-commerce is defined as the willingness to share information over the Internet that allows for the conclusion of purchases. They indicate that the presence of security features on an e-commerce site was important to consumers, and discuss how consumers security concerns may be addressed by similar technology protections as those of the business, such as encryption and authentication.

APEC privacy framework was intended as a means of improving the standard of information privacy protection throughout the APEC countries of the Asia-Pacific, [12] describes the Pathfinder projects as having "the goal of developing and implementing an accountable Cross-Border Privacy Rules system within APEC".

In [13] the authors proposed data sharing with privacy by a preserving data-set reconstruction based framework that can be regarded as "knowledge sanitization" approach, which is inspired by the inverse frequent set mining problem.

Toch et al., performed a survey study [14]. It provides users' attitude towards privacy and personalization, and analyzes the privacy risks associated. While use of personalization technique can give better user experience than the systems that do not use it, at the same time it raises new privacy concerns if privacy mechanisms are not provided. Users express uneasiness and personalized matter can expose potentially discomforting information to others. Culnan et al., provided fair procedures in place to protect individual privacy and giving control over the information that companies can build within a trust-based relationship with consumers' [15].

7   Conclusions and Future Works

In this paper, we presented potential key indicators that are considered to design flexible policy for data sharing in the context of Asia. This survey result revealed that individuals are willing to share personal data in exchange of personalization benefit. Appropriate privacy concern is considered as a factor that leads people to act more consciously to avoid risk of disclosing private information. However, intention to continue using digital services knowing the fact that these services might analyzes usage data for predicting personalized ads clarifies the sharing attitude from consumers' side.

References

1. Rana, J.: Improving Group Communication by Harnessing Information from Social Networks and Communication Services, ser. Licentiate thesis/Luleå University of Technology (2011). http://books.google.se/books?id=TLa7XwAACAAJ
2. Rana, J., Hallberg, J., Synnes, K., Kristiansson, J.: Harnessing the cloud for mobile social networking applications. Int. J. Grid High Perform. Comput. (IJGHPC) **2**(2), 1–11 (2010)
3. Synnes, K., Kranz, M., Rana, J., Schelén, O., Nilsson, M.: User-centric social interaction for digital cities. In: Creating Personal, Social, and Urban Awareness through Pervasive Computing, pp. 318–346 (2013)
4. Chellappa, R.K., Sin, R.G.: Personalization versus privacy: an empirical examination of the online consumers dilemma. Inf. Technol. Manag. **6**(2–3), 181–202 (2005)
5. Appendix 1 - defination of variables, 8 July 2015. https://www.dropbox.com/s/b4xzgfyper3kyms/Attitide_Scenario_Variables_Definition.pdf?dl=0
6. Michael, R.S.: Crosstabulation & chi square. Indiana University, Bloomington (2001). http://www.indiana.edu/~educy520/sec5982/week_12/chi_sq_summary011020.pdf. (Accessed on 15 April 2016)
7. Appendix 2 - association test using crosstabulation, 20 April 2016. https://www.dropbox.com/s/1ze7rv0klc9vi6c/Final_Results_Discussion.pdf?dl=0
8. Kenneally, E., Claffy, K.: Dialing privacy and utility: a proposed data-sharing framework to advance internet research. IEEE Secur. Priv. **8**(4), 31–39 (2010)
9. Olivero, N., Lunt, P.: Privacy versus willingness to disclose in e-commerce exchanges: the effect of risk awareness on the relative role of trust and control. J. Econ. Psychol. **25**(2), 243–262 (2004). http://EconPapers.repec.org/RePEc:eee:joepsy:v:25:y:2004:i:2:p:243-262
10. Clifton, C., Kantarcioğlu, M., Doan, A., Schadow, G., Vaidya, J., Elmagarmid, A., Suciu, D.: Privacy-preserving data integration and sharing. In: Proceedings of the 9th ACM SIGMOD Workshop on Research Issues in Data Mining and Knowledge Discovery, DMKD 2004, pp. 19–26. ACM, New York (2004). http://doi.acm.org/10.1145/1008694.1008698
11. Belanger, F., Hiller, J.S., Smith, A.J.: Trustworthiness in electronic commerce: the role of privacy, security, and site attributes. J. Strateg. Inf. Syst. **11**, 245–270 (2002)
12. Greenleaf, G.: Five years of the APEC privacy framework: failure or promise? Comput. Law Secur. Rev. **25**(1), 28–43 (2009). http://www.sciencedirect.com/science/article/pii/S0267364908001714
13. Chen, X., Orlowska, M., Li, X.: A new framework of privacy preserving data sharing. In: Proceedings of the IEEE ICDM Workshop on Privacy and Security Aspects of Data Mining Press, pp. 47–56 (2004)
14. Toch, E., Wang, Y., Cranor, L.F.: Personalization and privacy: a survey of privacy risks and remedies in personalization-based systems. User Model. User Adap. Inter. **22**(1–2), 203–220 (2012). http://dx.doi.org/10.1007/s11257-011-9110-z
15. Culnan, M.J., Armstrong, P.K.: Information privacy concerns, proceduralfairness, and impersonal trust: an empirical investigation. Organ. Sci. **10**(1), 104–115 (1999). http://dx.doi.org/10.1287/orsc.10.1.104

Efficient Probabilistic Methods for Proof of Possession in Clouds

Lukasz Krzywiecki, Krzysztof Majcher, and Wojciech Macyna[✉]

Department of Computer Science, Faculty of Fundamental Problems of Technology,
Wrocław University of Technology, Wrocław, Poland
{lukasz.krzywiecki,k.majcher,wojciech.macyna}@pwr.edu.pl

Abstract. Cloud computing is a new paradigm that has received the considerable attention in theory and practice quite recently. One of the applications of cloud computing is the storage of client's data on remote servers. While maintaining huge volumes of data, the cloud vendors may be tempted to cheat its clients by removing their data. Thus, to avoid such a situation, many proof of possession methods have been proposed. Usually they utilize complex cryptographic calculation which makes them not applicable to devices with limited resources. This paper proposes two novel methods of light-weight proof of possession. Instead of using the resource consuming cryptographic functions, these methods use only straightforward hash functions. In the first method, the client stores his data on one server in the cloud. The second approach addresses the scenario of data duplication between many independent servers.

Keywords: Cloud computing · Proof of possession · Hash function

1 Introduction

Cloud computing is a new paradigm that has received the considerable attention in theory and practice. Instead of building-up and maintaining the computer infrastructure, the customers may hold their hardware and software resources in the cloud. One of the applications of cloud computing is the storage of client's data on remote servers.

The number of data files outsourced to the cloud may grow for years. Despite the fact that many of them can be accessed very rarely, the customer should have a strong evidence that the cloud still possesses the data and the data are intact.

L. Krzywiecki—The paper is partially supported by the Polish National Science Centre, grant: DEC-2013/09/D/ST6/03927.

K. Majcher—The paper is partially supported by the Polish National Science Centre, grant: DEC-2013/09/D/ST6/03927.

W. Macyna—The paper is partially supported by the Department of Computer Science at Faculty of Fundamental Problems of Technology.

© Springer International Publishing Switzerland 2016
Y. Tan and Y. Shi (Eds.): DMBD 2016, LNCS 9714, pp. 364–372, 2016.
DOI: 10.1007/978-3-319-40973-3_36

The data stored in the cloud may be incorrect or incomplete due to the following reasons. First, the cloud provider may discard the data, which are rarely accessed by the user. Second, the cloud provider can store the data yet not in the fast storage as it is required by the contract with the customer, but in the second storage or offline. Besides, many security risks may exist in the cloud. It is clear that the client and the cloud's owner have contradicted interests as far as the data possession is concerned. The goal of the cloud's owner is to minimize the cost of the data possession. As a consequence, he can easily remove the data from the cloud without client's knowledge.

The Proof of Data Possession (PDP) is one of the verification methods which validates the correctness and completeness of the outsourced data on untrusted servers. The method should be efficient when the user must verify many data files periodically. The main assumption of PDP is that the client's file doesn't have to be downloaded from the server for verification. Many PDP methods base on the asymmetric cryptography. They require many exponentiation operations performed on the client's and server's side. Thus, they cannot be used on the devices with small computational power.

The aim of this work is to show that it is possible to build a practical system which doesn't require the advanced cryptography but bases on fast computing hash functions.

Our Contribution. In this work, we propose a strategy which forces the remote server to maintain the client's data as long as possible. We present an effective method for verification of the proof of possession. Our approach significantly differs from the methods proposed in the literature. Unlike other cryptographic protocols, it uses straightforward hash functions. Therefore, it can be used in such cases where complex calculations may not be performed. Despite its simplicity, we prove that our method guarantees a sufficient security level. Moreover, we show that the use of two independent remote servers increases the security of this approach.

The remainder of this paper is organised as follows. In the next section, we present the general PDP method. Then, we propose two PDP models. In the first model, the client stores all his data on one server. In the second one, the data are maintained in two independent clouds. Finally, we summarize the results of this work and draw conclusions.

2   General Method

In this section, we briefly recall the general Proof of Data Possession framework introduced in [1]. The PDP is a two party client-server protocol in which a client can check, whether or not, his files stored on a remote server are maintained unaltered. The process must be accomplished without downloading the entire file from the server.

The scheme includes three kind of procedures. In the preprocessing phase, the client uses function f to create metadata m for the file F. Generally, the metadata are kept locally while the original files are transferred to the remote server for a permanent storage. In the challenge phase, the client questions the server for a specific file F with a challenge c. In response, the server computes the proof of data possession of the file F by means of the original file and the received challenge c and sends the proof back to the client. After receiving the proof, the client validates it against the metadata stored in its local system to determine if the file F is really stored on the server.

Many papers propose cryptographic approaches to solve the PDP problems. The concept of PDP was introduced in [2]. In this approach, the file is divided into a set of blocks. With every block, a cryptographic tag is associated. To calculate the tag, an RSA number is used. This leads to the creation of long tags, challenge and response values and makes the approach complex and arithmetic heavy. In [3], the general approach from [2] was reused. The server stores tags that mix information on file blocks with the information that can be retrieved by the data owner. However, in comparison to [2], the size of the challenge and response data is drastically reduced. The approach consists of two schemes. The first scheme is based on pseudo-random functions and the second one on BLS signatures. To verify the first scheme, the secret key of the data owner is required. The security of the second scheme is proved under CDH assumption.

Many Internet Voting systems rely its security on other protocols i.e., SSL/TLS. A security vulnerability in lower-level protocol or a malware attack can lead to the following situation: a voting client does not talk directly to the election Bulletin Board (BB) (but with malicious server instead). Even if a digital signature s under the encrypted ballots cast so far is presented, it does not prove that the voting client talks directly to the election BB. The signature s could have been obtained by the malicious attacker at some distant time in the past and thus the presented view of BB does not correspond to its current state. When our protocol is performed (and reply is signed with BB's private key) it proves the current state of BB. So functionally it plays a role of a time-stamping server but we do not need any third-party to be involved in the process (which may increase overall security of the system).

3 Proposed Solutions

In this section, we present a problem analysis and main preliminaries for our solutions. After that, we propose two probabilistic consistency models of data in the clouds. In the first approach, the client stores all his data in one cloud. The second approach considers the data stored in two independent clouds which cannot exchange the data.

3.1 Preliminaries

The client holding its data in the cloud may be exposed to the unfair treatment from the cloud administrator. Since the cloud's owner wants to gain the highest possible profit from the data possession service, he may be tempted to remove the client's data when the cloud assesses that the probability of the detecting its foul play by the client is small.

Our solution bases on the "periodically request" technique. The client requests the server and the server is able to respond correctly only in case if it holds the client's data. In the first method, the client must have access to the pairs: challenge-respond. So, he must store it either in his own memory or on the external server. We show that algorithm works better, if the client can send a request which respond is unknown to him, but the server is not aware of this fact. In the second method, the client stores data on two servers and may compare responses for the same challenges from both servers.

For further studies we do the following assumptions:

- Time of data possession is divided into the equal periods.
- At the end of each time period the client sends a challenge to the cloud and the cost of data possession is calculated by the cloud.
- The cloud can hold a challenge sent by the client.

Below, we list the parameters used in the rest of the paper.

- w - the cost paid by the client for storing his data on the server in one time period.
- v - the cost paid by the client for one request.
- k - the fine paid by the server to the client in case of loosing his data.
- u - the cost incurred by the server for possessing the client's data in one time period.
- T - the number of time periods when the data was stored data in the cloud.
- $\mathcal{H}$ - the hash function defined by the signature: $\mathcal{H} : \{0,1\}^* \to \{0,1\}^d$ where d is a length of the output value.
- m - the number of client's files stored on the remote servers.

Apart from that, we formulate the following definitions:

Definition 1. By relating profit of the cloud we mean a difference between a profit of the cloud obtained during keeping client's data and a profit calculated after removing the data.

Definition 2. System is secure if the sum of the expected profit getting from every client of the cloud is negative.

3.2   Single-Server PDP Model

In this subsection, we present our first PDP method. We consider the case when the client's data are stored on one server.

The protocol works as follows. First, the client prepares a set Z_F consisting of n pairs: challenge-response defined as $Z_F = \{(c_i, r_i), i = 1, 2, ..., n\}$. Both, challenges and responses are generated by using the hash function $\mathcal{H}$. Hence: $c_i = \mathcal{H}(F, K_u)$ and $r_i = \mathcal{H}(F, c_i)$, where K_u is a secret key and F is the checked file. The creation of Z_F is carried out by the procedures: PrepareChallenge and

---

Algorithm 1. GenerateChallenge(input: b, F)

---

1 **if** $b=0$ **then**
2 $\quad\lfloor$ Returns a pair: $(c, \emptyset)$;

3 **if** $b=1$ **then**
4 $\quad\lfloor$ $Z_F \leftarrow Z_F \setminus \{(c,r)\}$;
5 $\quad\lfloor$ Returns a pair: (c,r);

Algorithm 2. Single PDP Protocol

---

1 $K_u \leftarrow Setup(\xi)$;
2 $\bar{c} \leftarrow PrepareChallenge(K_u)$;
3 $\bar{r} \leftarrow PrepareResonse(\bar{c})$;
4 At the end of each time period j the following loop is executed
5 **Loop**
6 $\quad$ Draw a number b from the set $\{0,1\}$ for a file F according to the distribution S;
7 $\quad$ $(c,r) \leftarrow GenerateChallenge(b, F)$;
8 $\quad$ Send the generated challenge c to the cloud C;
9 $\quad$ $r' \leftarrow CloudResponse(c, F, C)$;
10 $\quad$ **if** $b=1$ **then**
11 $\quad\quad\lfloor$ Verify(r, r');

PrepareResponse (see algorithm SinglePDPProtocol). We assume that c_i and r_i are much shorter than the file F for which they are produced. The set Z_F is kept on the client's computer. Then, the client estimates the probability p and fixes the distribution S as:

$$\mathbf{S} = \begin{cases} 1 \; with \, probability \; p \\ 0 \; with \, probability \; 1-p \end{cases} \tag{1}$$

At the end of each time period j, the client prepares a challenge c and sends it to the cloud by invoking **GenerateChallenge**. According to the distribution S, it may be a random challenge or a challenge from the set Z_F. In the first case, the client cannot check if he is cheated by the cloud. In the second case, the client receives a response r' from the cloud. If $r = r'$ it means that the verification is positive and the client is not cheated.

Security Analysis. We assume that the cloud knows the distribution S and the number n of elements in the set Z_F. Before we prove the security of the system, we present two lemmas.

Lemma 1. *The expected value of the relative profit of the cloud is:* $\frac{u}{p} - k$.

Proof. If the cloud removes the data and that fact is noted by the client after t time periods, its profit would be: $t(w + v) - k$. However, if the cloud possesses the client's data in the same time, its profit would be: $t(w + v - u)$. Thus, the cloud's relative profit is:

$$R(t) = t(w+v) - k - t(w+v-u) = tu - k \qquad (2)$$

The probability that the data removed by the cloud is discovered exactly after t time period is equal to:

$$P(t) = p(1-p)^{t-1} \qquad (3)$$

Hence, the expected value of the relative cloud's profit may be estimated as follows:

$$E = \Sigma_{t=1}^{\infty} P(t)R(t) = \Sigma_{t=1}^{\infty} p(1-p)^{t-1}(tu-k)$$
$$= pu\Sigma_{t=1}^{\infty} t(1-p)^{t-1} - pk\Sigma_{t=1}^{\infty}(1-p)^{t-1} \qquad (4)$$

After some calculations, the expected value of the relative cloud's profit is:

$$E = \frac{u}{p} - k \qquad (5)$$

Lemma 2. *The expected value of the number of time periods after which the client sent the last challenge from the set Z_F is:*

$$T = \frac{n}{p} - n \qquad (6)$$

Theorem 1. *If every client estimates p as $p = \frac{u}{k}$ and the time of storing data is $T < \frac{n}{p} - n$ then the system is secure.*

Proof. Let the parameters: k, u, w, v have the fixed values and $p > \frac{u}{k}$. By Lemma 1, we can conclude that until the client does not use every challenge from the set Z_F, the cloud's related profit is negative (if $p > \frac{u}{k}$ then $\frac{u}{p} - k < 0$). From Lemma 2, we know that for $p = \frac{u}{k}$, the expected time after which the client sent all challenges from Z_F is: $T = \frac{k*n}{u} - n$.

By proving the Theorem 1, we show that the cloud cannot cheat during the time given by the formula $T \leq \frac{k*n}{u} - n$, if it knows the client's distribution S and the number of challenges n. It is due to the fact that the cloud's related profit is negative and the cheating is not beneficial for the cloud.

3.3   Multi-server PDP Model

In this section, we consider the case when the client stores data on many independent servers. For simplicity, we assume that the client sends his data only to two independent clouds: C_1 and C_2.

The protocol works as follows. At the beginning, the client prepares the set Z_F and the probability p. This is made in the same manner as in the previous method. Then, the data are randomly distributed between the servers C_1 and C_2 using the procedure DataDistribution. Using the distribution we want to achieve the following property: the probability that the randomly chosen element stored in one cloud is also maintained in the second cloud is at least p. Lemma 3 proves that the distribution fulfils this property.

The verification of data possession is executed in the MultiPDP protocol as follows. After each time period j, the client sends a challenge to the first server. If the challenge is applied to the file which is stored on both servers, the client sends the same challenge to the second server. When the responses are different, it is the proof that at least one of the servers doesn't possess the data. In this case, the algorithm Verify() is used to estimate, which cloud has removed the data.

Algorithm 3. DataDistribution(input: p, m)

1 Divide the client's files into two subsets A and B containing $\frac{1}{2-p}m$ files;
2 Send A to C_1;
3 Send B to C_2;

Lemma 3. *If A and B are the subsets of the set D such that $|A|, |B| \geq \frac{1}{2-p}m$ then $\frac{|A \cap B|}{|A|} \geq p$*

Proof.

$$\frac{|A \cap B|}{|A|} = \frac{|A| + |B| - |A \cup B|}{|A|} \geq \frac{2 * \frac{1}{2-p}m - m}{\frac{1}{2-p}m} = p \qquad (7)$$

Security Analysis. In the security analysis we fix the following assumptions:

- the clouds know the probability p;
- the clouds are aware that the client distributed his data into two clouds and that the common files are challenged with the probability p.

Before we start the formal security analysis, let's note the obvious observation. The client doesn't need to use the elements from Z_F until he doesn't discover the foul play from the cloud. He may send the random challenge against the common files to both clouds. If he receives different responses from the clouds, it means that at least one of the clouds cheats.

Theorem 2. *If every client sets the probability p as $p = \frac{u}{k}$ then the system is secure.*

Proof. We know that the clouds C_1 and C_2 cannot determine the set $A \cap B$ on the basis of the request distribution. By Lemma 1, we see that for $p > \frac{u}{k}$, the expected value of the relative profit is negative. This prove that the system is secure.

Algorithm 4. Multi PDP protocol

---

1   $K_u \leftarrow Setup(\xi)$;
2   $\bar{c} \leftarrow PrepareChallenge(K_u)$;
3   $\bar{r} \leftarrow PrepareResonse(\bar{c})$;
4   Client's data is distributed according to the parameters: p and m defined above
5   $DataDistribution(p, m)$;
6   At the end of each time period j the following loop is executed
7   **Loop**
8   Send challenge c to the cloud C_1 about the randomly chosen file $F \in A$;
9      $r' \leftarrow CloudResponse(c, F, C_1)$;
10   **if** $F \in A \cap B$ **then**
11   Send a challenge c to C_2;
12        $r'' \leftarrow CloudResponse(c, F, C_2)$;
13   **if** $r' \neq r''$ **then**
14        $Verify()$;
15   **if** $F \notin A \cap B$ **then**
16   Send challenge c' to the cloud C_2 about the randomly chosen file $F' \in B \setminus A \cap B$;

The small disadvantage of this method is the growth of the cost of possession. It is due to the fact that the charge for the data files stored in two clouds (A and B) must be doubled. If we set $p = \frac{u}{k}$ then (according to Lemma 3) the common part $A \cap B$ is of size at most $\frac{pkm}{2k-u}$.

4   Conclusions

This study demonstrates the effective methods for checking the proof of possession in the clouds. Our methods drastically differ from the other approaches which mostly base on the cryptographic protocols. Although our methods use only straightforward hash functions, we prove their reliability.

In the Single Server PDP model, we show that when the client estimates the parameter p as $p = \frac{u}{k}$, he can store his data securely in the cloud over $\frac{n}{p} - n$ periods of time. The only possibility to force the cloud to further maintaining the data is to extend the set of stored pairs: challenge - response. Though, such an extension would increase the memory usage. In the Multi Server PDP model, when the client estimates the parameter p as $p = \frac{u}{k}$, the server must act fairly and the client can store his data without any time limits. However, the drawback of this solution lies in the growth of the data storing cost as some files have to be maintained on two servers.

Our methods may be particularly useful in the situations when the client's device has the limited computational power, and therefore, complex calculations are hard to execute. In this sense, it overpowers the other cryptographic approaches.

References

1. Deswarte, Y., Quisquater, J.J.: Remote integrity checking. In: Jajodia, S., Strous, L. (eds.) IICIS 2004. IFIP, vol. 140, pp. 1–11. Kluwer Academic Publishers, New York (2004)
2. Ateniese, G., Burns, R., Curtmola, R., Herring, J., Kissner, L., Peterson, Z., Song, D.: Provable data possession at untrusted stores. In: Proceedings of the 14th ACM Conference on Computer and Communications Security, CCS 2007, pp. 598–609. ACM, New York (2007)
3. Shacham, H., Waters, B.: Compact proofs of retrievability. In: Pieprzyk, J. (ed.) ASIACRYPT 2008. LNCS, vol. 5350, pp. 90–107. Springer, Heidelberg (2008)

Cloud-Based Storage Model with Strong User Privacy Assurance

Amir Rezapour[1], Wei Wu[2], and Hung-Min Sun[1(✉)]

[1] Department of Computer Science, National Tsing Hua University, Hsinchu, Taiwan
amir_rezapour@is.cs.nthu.edu.tw, hmsun@cs.nthu.edu.tw
[2] Fujian Provincial Key Laboratory of Network Security and Cryptology,
School of Mathematics and Computer Science,
Fujian Normal University, Fuzhou, China
weiwu@fjnu.edu.cn

Abstract. Cloud computing platforms require at least semi-trusted party as a host; we consider the problem of building a secure cloud storage service on top of a public cloud infrastructure where there is no link between the users' identity and the correspondent data. Furthermore the cloud provider does not required to be trusted by the customer.

Keywords: Cloud computing · Cloud storage · Secure storage · Data security · Data storage systems · Outsourcing

1 Introduction

In recent years, the concept of data outsourcing has become extremely popular. Based on a recent survey by Pew Research Center, experts anticipate that, in the next decade, cloud computing will become more dominant for end-users than desktop computing [4]. Data is moving from user-owned physical storages to dedicated online storage systems, e.g., Dropbox [1] and Google Drive [2]. By 2008, 69 % of all Internet users had either stored data online or had used a web-based software application [11]. In the opposite governments have frequently insist on that companies install backdoors in security solutions and build local servers to facilitate surveillance [13,14]. For data stored in the cloud, users are not aware when their data is being accessed by other parties. Privacy activists argue that consumers expect privacy in the cloud [10], while law enforcement agencies in United States, to which most cloud storage providers are subject, stipulate that "a person has no legitimate expectation of privacy in information he voluntarily turns over to third parties" [3]. Most of recent online storage service providers offer plenty of services and features followed in a very simple designs and do not offer privacy for their users.

Overview of Our Approach. In our model we have two database tables, *Users* and *Identification*. In the *Users* table we store the user's account information, and in the *Identification* table we store the *Identification Id*. During the signing up procedure, a user (Alice) generates and stores a random number

© Springer International Publishing Switzerland 2016
Y. Tan and Y. Shi (Eds.): DMBD 2016, LNCS 9714, pp. 373–378, 2016.
DOI: 10.1007/978-3-319-40973-3_37

R into *Identification* table using special steps in order to omit any relation between random number R and *Users* table. In the case that Alice installs special applications for accessing files, R can be installed in user applications in a secure way. In this study, we aim to introduce the concept of secure cloud-based storage in the context of cloud computing with regard to user privacy preserving.

2   Related Work

Research on cloud computing falls into two cases: cloud storage security and cloud computing security. Relative studies to the current issue can be found in the areas of "cloud storage" and "cloud privacy preserving". In Cryptographic cloud storage [12], the data processors are used to encrypt the user data. Thus, customers can be assured that the confidentiality of their data are protected, but still need to trust to the cloud provider. Ateniese et al. [5] first defined a model for provable data possession (PDP) for ensuring ownership of data files on untrusted storages. They utilize the RSA-based homomorphic linear authenticators for auditing outsourced data. However, among their two proposed schemes, the one with public auditability exposes the linear combination of sampled blocks to external auditors. When used directly, their protocol is not provably privacy preserving and thus may leak user data information to external auditors.

3   Attack Model

In this paper, attackers are classified into two types: Insider attacker(cloud providers), outsider attacker(the true intruders). The first type, possibly system administrator has higher probability to figure out the relation between files and owners. The second type of attackers has no special access to the information and records. Assuming all communications are encrypted, this attacker must be in possession of secret session key to access message flow between the user and cloud provider or should first spend some time to pass through the cloud providers' firewalls and other security mechanisms and then try to find some information in order to link the files to the users' accounts.

4   Proposed Scheme

4.1   Notation

Hash functions are compressing functions that take inputs of various sizes and return fixed-size outputs. Our construction relies on a one-way cryptographic hash function H.

Public − key cryptography uses asymmetric key algorithms (such as RSA)
Symmetric − key algorithms are a class of algorithms for cryptography.
$F(x_1|x_2,\ldots,|x_n)$. One way function that concatenates the inputs together.

E_{KS}. Symmetric-key algorithm Encryption scheme.

K_1, K_2, K_3 The secret keys of the secure communications respectively.

ParamGen. This algorithm outputs a system-wide parameter security parameter λ.

RandomGen. On the input of a Seed $S \in \{0,1\}^*$ and security parameter λ, This algorithm outputs a random number $R \in \{0,1\}^\lambda$. $H : \{0,1\}^* \rightarrow \{0,1\}^\lambda$.

4.2 Sign up and Setup Phase

In the sign up procedure, users are required to establish a secure communication several times. Set up procedure consists of three parts. We briefly explain how the algorithms work in a typical scenario:

1. Creating new *Identification Id*.
   (a) Both parties (Client and Server) establish a secure communication connection and share a session key K_1.
   (b) Server encrypts the security parameter λ, produced by *ParamGen*, and send λ to client.
   (c) Client is required to create a random number N'. She can chose one of the following methods:
      i. Invoking $RandomGen(S, \lambda)$ in order to generate a new random number.
      ii. Using $F(x_1|x_2|, \dots)$ and substitute $x_1, x_2, \dots$ with her information and salt parameter S to protect against dictionary attack.
   (d) Using session key, the client encrypts N' and sends the encrypted $E_{K1}(N')$ to the server.
   (e) Server decrypts the request using session key and inserts N' into *Identification* table.
2. Creating new user account.
   (a) Both parties establish a secure communication connection and share a session key K_2.
   (b) In this step, Client transfers her information by using session key K_2 to create a new account.
3. Activating the *Identification Id*.
   (a) Both parties establish a secure communication connection and share a session key K_3.
   (b) Using session key, once again the client encrypts N' and sends the encrypted $E_{K3}(N')$ to the server.
   (c) Server decrypts the massage to get N'. Then looks up N' in *Identification* table. If exists, the fact that somebody has inserted this value before is confirmed and sets the *In_Use* column to true.

In ideal case, user can insert several *Identification Ids* in the *Identification* table and skip the sign up part and follow the instructions. Besides, the cloud provider would easily accept any connection to insert a new random number in the *Identification* table. While each user has several *Identification Ids*, it becomes harder for cloud provider to make a link between user and her *Identification Ids*. On the other hand, user can use each *Identification Id* for a specific reason.

Another issue concerns a scenario where an intruder attempts to insert many *Identification Ids* in order to make resources unavailable. This problem can be solved by using either CAPTCHA [6] or anonymous e-cash [7].

The authentication with the cloud providers is by sending requests with valid *Identification Id*. The user is verified by the server if the following equation holds.

$$
\begin{aligned}
Identification_{ID} \in \{ &IdentificationId_1, \\
&IdentificationId_2, \dots \} \ \& \ In\_Use == True
\end{aligned}
\tag{1}
$$

Since the cloud provider has no information about the user's *Identification Id* and the corresponding user account, it will never realize that who is communicating with.

Although the communication between user and service provider is encrypted with appropriate cipher scheme, user is always required to encrypt the data with the user's own secret key before outsourcing the data to the cloud provider.

4.3   Basic Model

The *UsersData* table is divided in three columns, which are shown in Fig. 1. While file names may disclose user identifications, we use hash value or random number as naming policy and store the defined value in *File ID* column. The *DataStream* column contains the content of file. When a user attempts to store a new file, she is required to establish a secure communication and share a secret key k with cloud provider and encrypts her *Identification Id* using session key k and sends it to the server. Server uses Eq. (1) to verify the user's validity. If the equation holds true, then sends an acknowledge to the user that the user is verified and has the permission to send her data. Client uses generated random number as file name and send her file to server.

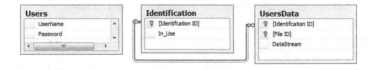

Fig. 1. Basic model database.

The client software is also required to map the generated *File ID* to the real file name in a local secure lookup table.

4.4   Security Analysis of Basic Model

Imagine that we have $\{n^m | m \geq 1\}$ files in the server with n users. Assuming that every user has at least one file in the server, and victim's data are in specific format known by attacker. If the attacker is given a chance to see these files, he will recognize the corresponding user. In the worst case where the number of files are less than the number of users, some of the users may not have any files in the server. As a result, the only thing that attacker cares is the number of users. Therefore we need to make a relation between *File ID* and *Identification Id* to resolve the above-mentioned problem. On the other hand, in cases where the attacker is an insider, even if user has several *Identification IDs*, the attacker/administrator can keep active *Identification IDs* in another table during the authentication part.

4.5   Improved Model

In the model, we eliminate the *Identification Id* from *UserData* table, and also we rename the *File ID* to simply *ID*. After generating a random number for *File ID*, the user invokes *F* function to concatenate *File ID* and *Identification Id*. We use the result of *F* as *ID* in *UserData* table. We follow the same steps in section C for storing and accessing the files.

4.6   Security Analysis of Improved Model

If he is insisting to find the desired data, he needs to decrypt the files one by one to find the first desired one. Even if he finds one of the victim's files, it does not mean that he can access the rest of the files.

5   Feasibility Analysis

To measure our protocol feasibility, we compare our approach to regular SSL connections. Comparing SSL with our approach, there is no significant difference in performance of login and exchange data parts with similar level of security.

6   Network Protocol

Using SSL connection will hide content of that information from an observer, but it might still leave the database operator (cloud provider). We resolve this problem by simply using proxy serves. Onion Routing is performed by dynamically building anonymous circuits within a network of onion routers as in Chaum Mixes [8]. A network of onion routers resists traffic analysis more effectively than any other deployed mechanisms for general internet communication [9,15].

7   Conclusion

This paper states the importance of protecting individual's privacy in the cloud computing and provides some privacy preserving techniques to be used in cloud storages. We showed that by simply omitting some relation between user entity and her properties, we can restrict the information leakage and hence protect uses' privacy without trusting cloud service provider.

Acknowledgments. This research was supported in part by the Ministry of Science and Technology, Taiwan, under the Grant MOST 104-3115-E-007-004.

References

1. Dropbox. https://www.dropbox.com
2. Google drive. https://www.google.com/drive/
3. Smith v. maryland (1979)
4. Anderson, J.Q., Rainie, H.: The Future of Cloud Computing. Pew Internet & American Life Project, Washington, DC (2010)
5. Ateniese, G., Burns, R., Curtmola, R., Herring, J., Kissner, L., Peterson, Z., Song, D.: Provable data possession at untrusted stores. In: Proceedings ofthe 14th ACM Conference on Computer and Communications Security, CCS 2007, pp. 598–609. ACM, New York (2007). http://doi.acm.org/10.1145/1315245.1315318
6. Baird, H.S., Popat, K.: Human interactive proofs and document image analysis. In: Lopresti, D.P., Hu, J., Kashi, R.S. (eds.) DAS 2002. LNCS, vol. 2423, pp. 507–518. Springer, Heidelberg (2002). http://dl.acm.org/citation.cfm?id=647798.736683
7. Camenisch, J.L., Hohenberger, S., Lysyanskaya, A.: Compact e-cash. In: Cramer, R. (ed.) EUROCRYPT 2005. LNCS, vol. 3494, pp. 302–321. Springer, Heidelberg (2005). http://dx.doi.org/10.1007/11426639_18
8. Chaum, D.L.: Untraceable electronic mail, return addresses, and digital-pseudonyms. Commun. ACM **24**(2), 84–90 (1981). http://doi.acm.org/10.1145/358549.358563
9. Goldschlag, D., Reed, M., Syverson, P.: Onion routing. Commun. ACM **42**(2), 39–41 (1999)
10. Gross, G.: Cloud computing may draw government action. InfoWorld (2008). http://www.infoworld.com/article/2653754/security/cloud-computing-may-draw-government-action.html
11. Horrigan, J.: Use of cloud computing applications and services. Pew Internet & American Life Project, Washington, D.C. (2008)
12. Kamara, S., Lauter, K.: Cryptographic cloud storage. In: Sion, R., Curtmola, R., Dietrich, S., Kiayias, A., Miret, J.M., Sako, K., Sebé, F. (eds.) RLCPS, WECSR, and WLC 2010. LNCS, vol. 6054, pp. 136–149. Springer, Heidelberg (2010). http://dl.acm.org/citation.cfm?id=1894863.1894876
13. Kinetz, E.: Google, skype targeted in india security crackdown. The Huffington Post (2011). http://www.huffingtonpost.com/2010/09/02/google-skype-targeted-in-_n_703198.html
14. Soghoian, C.: Caught in the cloud: privacy, encryption, and government back doors in the web 2.0 era. J. Telecomm. High Tech. L. **8**, 359 (2010)
15. Syverson, P.: Onion routing for resistance to traffic analysis. In: Proceedings of DARPA Information Survivability Conference and Exposition, vol. 2, pp. 108–110. IEEE (2003)

Social Media

The Role of Social Media in Innovation and Creativity: The Case of Chinese Social Media

Jiwat Ram[1(✉)], Siqi Liu[1], and Andy Koronois[2]

[1] International Business School, XJTLU, Suzhou, China
`jiwat.ram@gmail.com`
[2] School of Information Technology & Mathematical Sciences,
University of South Australia, Adelaide, Australia

Abstract. Social media has revolutionised our daily lives, both at individual and organisational levels. This presents an opportunity for businesses to drive growth and create value by tapping into the power of co-creation using social media. Despite its significance, little research exists on how social media could be used for innovations and creativity, and even moreso in the Chinese context with the mass penetration of social media. This study attempts to address this gap in knowledge by examining the role of social media in facilitating innovations in Chinese context. Given the exploratory nature of the research, we will conduct approximately 40 interviews with respondents such as marketing and communication managers from a wide range of industries including retail and service sectors. We will analyse data using Nvivo. The findings will provide guidelines to managers to put in place tailored strategies to optimise the benefits of social-media interactions for organisational growth.

Keywords: Social media · Innovation · Creativity · Social Networking Services (SNS) · Web 2.0 · Interactive content · Facebook · Twitter · Linkedin · Google+ · Weibo · Wechat

1 Introduction

There has never been a time when the role of social media in the modern context is so fundamental and diverse. As Facebook, Google+ and Twitter penetrate our lifestyles, residences, transportation systems and working environments wherever there are electronic devices, social media has moved society into cyber space [1]. Added to that is the emergence of new habits, friendships, and an information boom. Specifically, businesses adopt social media as a channel for building and distributing information and values. As a platform that engages millions of users in cyber space, allowing free voices and the rapid flow of information in diverse forms, it enables businesses to collaborate with customers in new and innovative ways [2; p. 36].

Businesses utilise social media for several different means including innovations and creativity. As Tierney and Drury [3] pointed out, social media has multiple uses many of which are in the composite measure of innovation and creativity. Innovation is a term that describes "introducing of something new" [4]. An innovation can be in

© Springer International Publishing Switzerland 2016
Y. Tan and Y. Shi (Eds.): DMBD 2016, LNCS 9714, pp. 381–390, 2016.
DOI: 10.1007/978-3-319-40973-3_38

terms of product, market, material and business models. For example, one of the major applications of innovation is in product design.

Because of the characteristics of social media in that it encourages self-generated content and sharing, companies could gather ideas from online communities and receive feedback conveniently [5]. The ideas generated by external contribution and used in internal design are called open-innovation [6; p. 24]. Besides product design, companies use social media for new marketing methods and customer relationship management [7]. Social media helps to form a virtual customer environment and creates online communities, which could enable companies to better interact with customers [8]. Not only could managers learn from customers' demands, but also they could enhance brand loyalty by various online marketing strategies. Loyal customers in return could serve as champions for the brands.

Social media is a perfect tool for internal management as well [9]. Employees could get to know each other in a cost-efficient way and enhance communications in the workplace. In this way, knowledge and experience in the enterprise context would be integrated actively. More recently, the term 'Organisational Social Media' has been used to describe the implementation of social media at an organisational level [10]. By doing this, various enterprise level activities will be supported, including relationship management, knowledge sharing, learning and creation. Other general uses of social media in innovation include disaster management [33], campaigns of social political organisations [11], special events [12], city marketing [13] and higher education [14].

As social media has gained huge proliferation in China in the past decade, the country has become the largest social media user in the world [15]. In 2014 alone, it is estimated that there were 560 million users in Q-zone—the largest Chinese SNS platform, and the estimated value of Q-zone at the end of 2012 was 11.24 billion, only second to Facebook, which has a value of 29.12 [16]. According to Chiu [17], the penetration rate of social media is 46 %, and netizens in China spend approximately 40 % of their online time in social media interactions.

The increase in the number of users and the type of platforms used for social media interactions has also led to new business practices in the Chinese business environment [17]. The issues surrounding internet supervision and the cultural context in China has brought about unique phenomena and business practices as well. For instance, the most eye-catching, self-created content is sometimes frivolous, rather than news-driven, and trends are sometimes manipulated through fraudulent accounts [18].

The use of social media in China, and globally, has resulted in a large number of studies with most of them focusing on theoretical analysis or conceptual frameworks. Some studies have conducted case analysis to summarise web-portal links and a variety of statistics to develop models of users' strategies. However, there is a paucity of empirical studies in the context of China and how social media is affecting the life and business environment in China. This study attempts to fill this gap in knowledge and investigates the role of social media in innovation and creativity in businesses in China. Specifically, we will examine the role of innovation and creativity in the creation of new business models, product designs, relationship management or marketing strategies. With this in mind, the study sets out to answer the following research questions:

What role does social media play in facilitating innovations and creativity in businesses in China? What type of innovations does it facilitate specifically?

This study is significant as it investigates an issue in an unexplored research area, and is expected to add to the body of knowledge on how social media can help in innovation and creativity. The findings will not only contribute towards theoretical development, but will also provide insights for managers and business owners about how to best leverage social media for growth of their enterprises. Moreso, the study will be significant in the Chinese context as little research exists in this area.

2 Literature Review

2.1 Social Media

Business-related usage of social media has seen a tremendous growth in the last decade. Social media is a type of Web 2.0 platform—an integrated platform where user-generated resource can be co-created, shared and amended *via* constantly developing software [19]. As Web 1.0 relies more on one-way communication, Web 2.0 emphasises the multi-channel interaction and user-oriented flow of information. Social media focuses on the social properties of the application of Web 2.0 technology. [20] define social media as "a group of Internet-based applications that build on the ideological and technological foundations of Web 2.0, and that allow the creation and exchange of User Generated Content" (p. 61). However, the concept of social media is often mixed up with Web 2.0 and user-generated content.

One of the prominent forms of social media is Social Networking Services (SNS), which embraces many specific functions such as maintaining and manipulating existing social networks. Simultaneously, the display of relationships and a public profile are key features of SNS [21].

2.1.1 Social Media in China

Since 2013 China has the world's largest social network market [22]. Chinese social network scene is characterised by a large amount of information exchange and government supervision [18]. Over three millions messages are posted on websites every day, in the form of BBS, blogs, communities and so on. Moreover, above 66 % of Chinese netizens are active users who convey their viewpoints via the internet frequently [23]. The leading network is Qzone, which has 645 million users and a valuation of 11,237 billion USD [23]. Another representation is Sina Weibo, a fast-growing website similar to Twitter, with 250 million registered accounts generating 90 million posts per day. The accounts in Weibo are categorised into three types of user accounts, in which a verified user account commonly denotes a famous figure in the public eye or a company in China [18].

A subdivisional graph of Chinese social media markets was made by Crampton [15], dividing social media into seven functional blocks. Besides crossovers, there is a significant difference between Chinese social media compared with its foreign counterparts.

2.1.2 Functions of Social Media

Moore [24; p. 50] argue that social media offers one prominent characteristic; its function is to realise multiple kinds of social activities started by anyone using applications or on the platform. The development of social media has effectively shaped the way people behave and think. Not only can people easily reach across distances and exchange opinions conveniently, but also they are the direct content-makers of the information online [25] Businesses no longer have the deciding rights over consumers regarding the information they want available to view, and have to passively become "observers" [20]. In order to equip corporations with the notion of the various forms of activities social media can generate, a honeycomb pattern of seven functional blocks has been raised [26]. These blocks are specific facets of user experience provided by different social media service: presence; relationships; identity; reputation; sharing; conversations; and groups. They are not mutually exclusive and each social media site could choose several facets of service.

2.2 Use of Social Media for Innovation and Creativity

Defined by Schumpeter [27; p. 47], innovation denotes "carrying out new combinations". This definition could be further specified into five subgroups: the introduction of a new product, process of production; new market; resource of supply or intermediate products; or new form of organisation. It is also a common belief that the innovation process is a collaboration and interaction between users, suppliers, companies and original designers. [28]. Cooper [35] has identified "strategy" and "power" to be the fundamental factors between organisation structure and the type of innovation. Past study [39] proved that innovation projects that rely on external resources outperform those on internal resources, especially in regards to development time and the required investment.

Due to the fact that innovation can take place in various ideological settings, past studies often categorise it into several subdivisions [4]. In terms of the areas where innovation influences, it could be separated into product and process innovation. In terms of the extent of changes accordant with innovation, it could be identified as radical or incremental. Another classification method is to divide it as a technological or an administrative innovation [36, 38, 40].

The study of utilisation of social media in innovation has been prevalent in the past decade. As Culnan [8] comment, the platform itself would not generate any revenue unless particular information is created and shared.

2.2.1 Customer Relationship Management and Virtual Customer Environment

One direct usage is the construction of online customer communities or say, virtual customer environment (VCE). Such VCE could be used to benefit several business sectors, including branding, sales, customer service and product development [8]. Once communities form, they serve as a champion for the brand, defending its reputation and resisting all negative information towards it. Busscher [41] discovered that customers tend to appeal to brands that offer campaigns with relevant eye-catching content, which show up on several platforms and have applications on media. Another study shows that customer loyalty is positively correlated to the rising amount of beneficial campaigns, popular relevant content and the appearance of brand names on various social media websites [37]. Based on this result, it is not difficult to understand why social media is a perfect choice for a brand to share technological-related, interesting content and to organise communities easily.

2.2.2 Open Innovations and Co-creation

Open innovation is a term initially defined by Chesbrough [6] as a concept that firms should explore both internally and externally to advance their technology and market. The definition was further improved to be "the use of purposive inflows and outflows of knowledge to accelerate internal innovation, and expand the markets for external use of innovation, as they look to advance their technology" [34; p. 1]. Past research has discovered a curvilineal relationship between search strategy and innovation performance [28].

Ståhlbröst [29] have drawn a conceptual framework for user recruitment and involvement in open-innovations, in which the four factors: content, platform, innovation process and community play vital roles. Social media has definitely enhanced open-innovation by its characteristics of speed, flexibility, reach and interactivity, as has been concluded in the study of [5]. They found that companies are using various internet-based tools to involve customers with their product design process. Because social media could easily carry dialogues in a cost-efficient way to global-wide users, companies can obtain user opinions and expertise [30]. Another study [31] states that social media helps with the implementation of ideas, rather than the acquisition of these.

2.2.3 Organisational Social Media

Organisational social media (OSM) is newly defined as technology that supports intra- and extra-organisational communication especially employees, management teams and external stakeholders [10]. It is a channel for a variety of activities that maintain relationships and interactions in the context of an organisation. Typical OSM includes SNS, Weichat and blogs. However, OSM differs from the general concept of social media in many aspects [32] Firstly, while the current revenue model of public social media aims to attract people to consume more time on the platform, it is obviously not the case in OSM. Secondly, the scale of OSM is not comparable to public size. As social media gains millions in audiences easily, OSM could mainly focus users within an organisational context, and maintain the real-life working circle. Furthermore, the feature of content in OSM is professional, while in the large public space it tends to be casual.

3 Methodology

Given the exploratory nature of the investigation, this study takes a qualitative approach to data collection and analysis. We will use an open-ended, semi-structured questionnaire for the interviews. The respondents are from industries including retail, such as food, clothing, travel, and service sectors including finance, IT, and media to name a few. The potential respondents are those who may be working as media communicators, marketing managers or process managers, as we expect them to have the knowledge of core business and the role of social media in facilitating innovations within their organisations. We plan to conduct approximately 40 interviews. Currently, based on our personal network, we have identified target respondents in an advertising agency, Top 500 financial institutions, city broadcast station, music company, and an international business school. We intend to extend our pool of potential respondents by using personal social networks as we enter into the data collection phase.

Interviews will be carried out either online or in a face-to-face environment and each interview is expected to last for approximately an hour. All the interviews will be conducted in the Chinese language so that subjects can convey their opinions in a comfortable way. The research questionnaire will be given or sent ahead of the interviews to the respondents, so that they feel better prepared for the interviews. The interviews will be digitally recorded, and written notes will also be taken of the respondents' answers during the interviews.

The recorded interviews will be then transcribed and translated into the English language. We will use content analysis employing Nvivo software to analyse the data. The use of Nvivo is expected to facilitate identification of underlying themes and critical issues through iterative coding and refinement procedure, and subsequent development of theory.

Initially, we will perform a detailed coding of the themes emerging from the data. We will do open coding to get an understanding of broad themes, and subsequently drill down and do further coding to extract new themes and sub-themes. Also we will analyse the linkages, patterns and connections among various themes and sub-themes. The patterns and inter-linkages emerging from the data will then be further analysed taking a comparing and contrasting approach by examining the perception of different types of respondents, such as the industry sectors, etc.

The analysis will focus on generating knowledge of how social media facilitates innovations and creativity within organisations. The findings will help us understand how information collected through social media interactions is channelled and leveraged into new ideas for product development, service improvements, business process improvements and development of new business strategies and models. We will also be able to generate an understanding of how organisations develop and build social media interactions and platforms that allow them to collect useful information and then transform information into knowledge in order to develop innovative solutions for growth of their business.

3.1 Questionnaire Development and Interviews

The authors have developed a semi-structured questionnaire. The questionnaire has four parts. The first part collects information on respondents' profile including position/title of interviewee, type of organisation, size of organisation, type of industry, and the major competitors of respondent's organisation.

The second part includes general questions such as: type of social media used by the respondents' organisation, its influence/impact on organisation, the business value created by the social media for the organisation and how it is used for building social capital. The third part of the questionnaire includes specific questions that seek to assess the impact of use of social media on innovation and ideas generation, co-creation and uniqueness for the use of social media for creativity in Chinese context.

The fourth part covers questions on the challenges and future applications of social media, and the recommendations and suggestion for the future use of social media for innovation and creativity. The data collection process has started and some interviews have been conducted.

4 Implications for Theory and Practice

The results of the study have several implications for theory and practice. From a theoretical perspective, firstly the study is a step towards development of a theoretical framework for understanding the innovation process facilitated by social media. Secondly, the study will identify the key elements of an innovation process ignited by social media. Thirdly, we will identify some of the issues that may be hindering the generation of innovations that otherwise could be facilitated by social media. Finally, we will provide some understanding of the platforms that may be more important for the generation of innovation through social media and hence open up opportunities for further exploration and set research direction.

Managerially, this study will provide guidelines to managers on how to leverage social media revolutions to their advantage. Secondly, the study will help managers put in place tailored strategies to optimise the benefits of social media for their organisational growth. Thirdly, the research findings will help managers prioritise their attention and focus on specific social media platforms that are compatible to their core business operations to create value for the business. Fourthly, the study will also provide some guidance to managers to decide the type of innovations they should try to achieve through social media platforms. Finally, the study will help managers in understanding the elements that inhibit innovations and creativity, which otherwise could be made possible from their social media platforms.

5 Limitations and Future Research Directions

The study has some limitations as well. First, being an exploratory study, the research will be collecting data from respondents representing a limited number of industries. Second, given the objective and the exploratory nature of the study, caution should be exercised in considering generalisation of the findings. Third, the study will come up with evidence of new processes and elements that generate innovations, with an aim to set the platform for further research.

The study is a significant milestone in social media research and sets out the direction of further research in a potentially unexplored area. Therefore, it opens up a number of opportunities for future research. Further research can be done by covering more industries and interviewing respondents including senior managers. More research is warranted in understanding how the innovation process facilitated by social media is different from the classical models of innovation process. Also further research could be conducted by taking a longitudinal approach to unravel the drivers and inhibitors of the innovation process facilitated by social media. The qualitative study could be followed up with quantitative cross-section survey-based studies to generalise the findings.

6 Conclusion

The onset of social media provides enormous opportunities to put in place strategies to create value from wide ranging and heterogeneous interactions in cyber space. One of the main applications is its usage in product development, customer relationships and marketing strategy. Our research explores business practices within the context of Chinese businesses. It aims to develop an initial preliminary understanding of how social media can facilitate innovations and creativity. Our study on the role of social media in driving innovations, especially the interaction between the properties of social media and innovation types, provides a unique perspective on social media research and innovation management. Moreover, it provides practical models for decision-makers who wish to utilise social media for furthering innovation success.

The study set the tone for future research on how to leverage the creation of online content. The findings will provide a research platform to look at existing co-creation models and develop a robust model of innovations through co-creation.

References

1. Barnes, N.G., Jacobsen, S.: Adoption of social media by fast-growing companies: innovation among the Inc. 500. J. Mark. Dev. Competitiveness 7(1) (2013)
2. Qualman, E.S.: How social media transforms the way we live and do business. Wiley, New York (2012)
3. Tierney, M.L., Drury, J.: Continuously improving innovation management through enterprise social media. J. Soc. Media Organ. 1(1), 1 (2013)
4. Gopalakrishnan, S., Damanpour, F.: A review of innovation research in economics, sociology and technology management. Omega 25(1), 15–28 (1997)
5. Sawhney, M., Verona, G., Prandelli, E.: Collaborating to create: the internet as a platform for customer engagement in product innovation. J. Interact. Mark. 19(4), 4–17 (2005)
6. Chesbrough, H.W.: Open Innovation: The New Imperative for Creating And Profiting from Technology. Harvard Business School Press, Boston (2003)
7. Habibi, M.R., Laroche, M., Richard, M.O.: Brand communities based in social media: how unique are they? evidence from two exemplary brand communities. Int. J. Inf. Manage. 34 (2), 123–132 (2014)
8. Culnan, M.J., McHugh, P.J., Zubillaga, J.I.: How large US companies can use Twitter and other social media to gain business value. MIS Quart Executive 9(4), 243–259 (2010)
9. Laroche, M., Habibi, M.R., Richard, M.O.: To be or not to be in social media: how brand loyalty is affected by social media? Int. J. Inf. Manage. 33(1), 76–82 (2013)

10. van Osch, W., Coursaris, C.K.: Organizational social media: a comprehensive framework and research agenda. In: 2013 46th Hawaii International Conference on System Sciences (HICSS), pp. 700–707 (2013)
11. Satti, M.M., Satti, M.M.: Establishing private social media networking platform for socio-political. IEEE Intell. Syst. **13**, 126–130 (2013). ISBN 978-1-4799-2569-8
12. Bukhari, I., Wojtalewicz, C., Vorvoreanu, M., Dietz, J.: Social media use for large event management: the application of social media analytic tools for the Super Bowl XLVI. In: Homeland Security (HST), Waltham, MA, pp. 24–29. IEEE (2012)
13. Zhou, L., Wang, T.: Social media: a new vehicle for city marketing in China. Cities **37**, 27–32 (2014)
14. Yadav, P.S., Srivastava, P.: A statistical analysis of impact of social networking media on higher education. In: 2013 2nd International Conference on Information Management in the Knowledge Economy (IMKE), pp. 9–13 (2013)
15. Crampton, T. China-social-media-evolution. http://www.thomascrampton.com/china/china-social-media-evolution/. Accessed Nov 2014 (2011)
16. Statista. Ranking of the most valuable social media brands worldwide as of 2012 (in billion U.S. dollars) (2012). http://www.statista.com/statistics/247752/most-valuable-social-media-brands-worldwide/. Accessed 5 Nov 2014
17. Chiu, C., Ip, C., Silverman, A.: Understanding social media in China (2012). http://www.mckinsey.com/insights/marketing_sales/understanding_social_media_in_china. Accessed 5 Nov 2014
18. Yu, L.L., Asur, S., Huberman, B.A.: Dynamics of Trends and Attention in Chinese Social Media (2013). arXiv preprint arXiv:1312.0649
19. O'Reilly, T.: What is Web 2.0: design patterns and business models for the next generation of software. Commun. Strat. **65**(1), 17–37 (2007)
20. Kaplan, A.M., Haenlein, M.: Users of the world, unite! the challenges and opportunities of social media. Bus. Horiz. **53**(1), 59–68 (2010)
21. Ellison, N.B.: Social network sites: definition, history, and scholarship. J. Comput. Mediated Commun. **13**(1), 210–230 (2007)
22. Thomas, C.: Social media in China: why and how (2011). www.thomascrampton.com/china/china-social-media/. Accessed Nov 2014
23. Statista. Social Networks in China (2014). http://www.statista.com/topics/1170/social-networks-in-china/. Accessed 1 Nov 2014
24. Moore, J.N., Hopkins, C.D., Raymond, M.A.: Utilization of relationship-oriented social media in the selling process: a comparison of consumer (B2C) and industrial (B2B) salespeople. J. Internet Commer. **12**(1), 48–75 (2013)
25. Agichtein, E., Castillo, C., Donato, D., Gionis, A., Mishne, G.: Finding high-quality content in social media. In: Proceedings of the 2008 International Conference on Web Search and Data Mining, pp. 183–194. ACM (2008)
26. Kietzmann, J., Hermkens, K., McCarthy, I., Silvestre, B.: Social media? get serious! understanding the functional building blocks of social media. Bus. Horiz. **54**, 241–251 (2011)
27. Schumpeter, J.A.: The theory of economic development: an inquiry into profits, capital, credit, interest, and the business cycle, vol. 55. Transaction Publishers, Piscataway (1934)
28. Laursen, K., Salter, A.: Open for innovation: the role of openness in explaining innovation performance among UK manufacturing firms. Strateg. Manag. J. **27**(2), 131–150 (2006)
29. Ståhlbröst, A., Betoni, M., Ebbesson, E., Lund, J., Følstad, A.: Social Media for User Innovation in Living Lab

30. Adetola, A., Li, S., Rieple, A., Níguez, T.-M.: Linking social media, intelligent agents and expert systems for formulating open innovation strategies for software development. In: Paper Presented at the WSEAS Proceedings of the 11th International Conference on E-Activities (2013)
31. Trott, P., Hartmann, D.: Why'open innovation'is old wine in new bottles. Int. J. Innov. Manage. 13(04), 715–736 (2009)
32. Graupner, S., Bartolini, C., Motahari, H., Erbes, J.: Evolving social media into productivity platforms. In: 2012 Annual SRII Global Conference (SRII), pp. 183–190 (2012)
33. Adam, N.R., Shafiq, B., Staffin, R.: Spatial computing and social media in the context of disaster management. IEEE Intell. Syst. 27(6), 90–96 (2012)
34. Chesbrough, H., Vanhaverbeke, W., West, J. (eds.): Open innovation: Researching a new paradigm. Oxford University Press, Oxford (2006)
35. Cooper, J.R.: A multidimensional approach to the adoption of innovation. Manag. Decis. 36 (8), 493–502 (1998)
36. Daft, R.L.: Bureaucratic versus non-bureaucratic structure and the process of innovation and change. JAI Press, Greenwich (1982)
37. Erdoğmuş, İ.E., Cicek, M.: The impact of social media marketing on brand loyalty. Procedia Soc. Behav. Sci. 58, 1353–1360 (2012)
38. Johannessen, J.A., Olsen, B., Lumpkin, G.T.: Innovation as newness: what is new, how new, and new to whom? Eur. J. Innov. Manag. 4(1), 20–31 (2001)
39. Mansfield, E.: Size of firm, market structure, and innovation. Eur. J. Polit. Econ., 556–576 (1963)
40. Walker, R.: Innovation type and diffusion: an empirical analysis of local government. Public Adm. 84(2), 311–335 (2006)
41. Busscher, N.: Social media: their role as marketing. IBA Bachelor Thesis Conference, University of Twente (2013)

Malay Word Stemmer to Stem Standard and Slang Word Patterns on Social Media

Mohamad Nizam Kassim[1](✉), Mohd Aizaini Maarof[2],
Anazida Zainal[2], and Amirudin Abdul Wahab[1]

[1] Strategic Research, CyberSecurity Malaysia,
The Mines Resort City, 43300 Seri Kembangan, Malaysia
{nizam,amirudin}@cybersecurity.my
[2] Faculty of Computing, Universiti Teknologi Malaysia,
81310 Skudai, Johor, Malaysia
{aizaini,anazida}@utm.my

Abstract. Word stemmer is a text preprocessing tool used in many artificial intelligence applications such as text mining, text categorization and information retrieval. It is used to stem derived words into their respective root words. Many researchers have proposed word stemmers for Malay language using various stemming approaches. Since the proliferation of social media, there are various word patterns have been used by social media users in which the existing word stemmers do not support in their stemming rules. These word patterns are slang words or informal conversation words which are used in daily conversation. Therefore, this paper proposes the new word stemmer for Malay language that able to stem standard and slang words. This paper also examines the differences between standard words and slang words. The experimental results show that the proposed word stemmer able to stem standard affixation and reduplication words and also stem slang affixation and reduplication words with better stemming accuracy.

Keywords: Malay word stemmer · Word stemming algorithm · Standard word · Slang word · Social media

1 Introduction

The advent of Web 2.0 technology creates social media platforms such as social networking, microblogging and video sharing that allow the internet users to create, publish and share their user-generated contents to other internet users without any editorial approval [13]. This scenario has led to information overloaded due to the amount of user generated contents that have been created on social media platform. In the context of Malay language, there are two types of written texts on social media i.e. formal and informal written text documents.

Formal text documents are written based on morphological structures of Malay language (standard words) whereas informal text documents are written based on colloquial speech communication (slang words). For instance, the standard affixation word of *'punyalah'* (belonging) in a formal text document could be written in the

© Springer International Publishing Switzerland 2016
Y. Tan and Y. Shi (Eds.): DMBD 2016, LNCS 9714, pp. 391–400, 2016.
DOI: 10.1007/978-3-319-40973-3_39

informal text documents such as *'punyelah'*, *'punyalaa'* and *'punyela'*. As a result, the existence of digital Malay text documents that may comprise of derived words (affixation and reduplication words) in the form of colloquial speech conversations on social media. These slang derived words are word pattern variations of affixation and reduplication words such as *mngambil* (slang affixation word for *mengambil*), *makanannye* (slang affixation word for *makanannya*), *kepunyeannye* (slang affixation word for *kepunyaannya*) and *burung2* (slang reduplication word for *burung-burung*). There are also slang derived words with special characters such as *k'jaan* (slang affixation word for *kerajaan*) and *di'lihat'kan* (slang affixation word for *dilihatkan*).

Unfortunately, the existing word stemmers for Malay language were developed only to stem standard derived words. Previous researchers only considered words patterns that can be found in formal Malay text documents [1–4, 6–12]. As a result, none of the existing Malay stemmers are able to stem slang affixation and reduplication words on social media. Therefore, it is desirable to develop the word stemmer that able to stem both standard and slang affixation and reduplication words on social media.

This paper is organized into five subsequent sections. Section 2 analyzes various word patterns in Malay language on social media. Section 3 discusses related works on the existing Malay word stemmers. Section 4 describes the proposed word stemmer that uses affixes removal method and dictionary lookup in order to remove standard and slang affixes from derived words. Section 5 discusses the experimental results and discussion where Facebook comments from Malaysiakini online news portal have been used to evaluate the proposed word stemmer for stemming standard and slang affixation and reduplication words. Finally, Sect. 6 concludes this paper with a summary.

2 Malay Word Patterns on Social Media

In Malay language, there are two types of derived words i.e. affixation and reduplication words based on standard morphological rules [5]. Affixation words are the derived word contains the prefixes (*ber+, di+, ke+*), suffixes (*+an, +kan*), confixes (per +an, di+i, peng+an), infixes (*+el+, +er+, +em+*), clitics (*+nya, +mu, +ku*) and particles (*+lah, +kah, +tah*) attached to the root words such as *memakan* (to eat), *makanan* (food) and *pemakanan* (nutrition). On the other hand, reduplication words reflect the plural forms of the root words where they may contain repeated root words or derived words with hyphen (-) such as *burung-burung* (birds), *makanan-makanan* (foods) and *surat-menyurat* (correspondence).

This paper analyzes word pattern variations of these standard derived words that exist on the social media by examining 3000 Facebook comments from Malaysiakini news portal as described in Table 1. The word analysis of these Facebook comments is essential for developing word normalization library for slang abbreviation, common words and root words and also developing numbers of word stemming rules for removing slang affixes. From the analysis, there are 126 distinct abbreviation words, 315 distinct common root words and possessive pronouns and 749 distinct root words. These words will be used as word library to normalize into standard root words using dictionary lookup method before and after word stemming as described by the following examples:

Table 1. Word patterns with special characters.

Word patterns	Slang word with corresponding standard word
1. Abbreviation	▪ Abbreviated words e.g. *org (orang), yg (yang), jgn (jangan)*
2. Common words	▪ Common root words e.g. *cume (cuma), tapi (tetapi), nak (hendak)* ▪ Possessive pronouns e.g. *dier (dia), hang (engkau), depa (mereka)*
3. Root words	▪ Slang root words e.g. *kene (kena), pompuan (perempuan), giler (gila)*
4. Affixation	▪ Standard Prefix + Slang Root Word e.g. *membace (membaca)* ▪ Slang Prefix + Standard Root Word e.g. *trmenung (termenung)* ▪ Standard Root Word + Slang Suffix e.g. *harapkn (harapkan)* ▪ Slang Root Word + Standard Suffix e.g. *besornya (besarnya)* ▪ Standard Prefix + Standard Root Word + Slang Suffix e.g. *perbuatannye (perbuatannya)*
5. Reduplication	▪ Slang Reduplication e.g. *kecik-kecik (kecil-kecil)* ▪ Root word + Number e.g. *benda2 (benda-benda)* ▪ Root word + Number + Suffix e.g. *kata2nye (kata-katanya)*

(a) *kl* (slang word) → *kuala lumpur* (with normalization)
(b) *bgmanapn* (slang word) → *bagaimanapun* (with normalization)
(c) *kpdnye* (slang word) → *kpd* (stemmed word) → *kepada* (with normalization)
(d) *kecik-kecik* (slang word) → *kecik* (stemmed word) → *kecil* (with normalization)

There are also 56 distinct slang affixes are used as prefixes (*br+, tr+png+, mng+*), suffixes (*+kn, +n*), confixes (*di+kn, png+n*), clitics (*+nye, +nyer, +2nye*) and particles (*+lahh, +laa, +lar*) in slang affixation and reduplication words as described by the following examples in Table 1. These distinct affixes will be used to develop word stemming rules for removing these slang affixes from slang affixation and reduplication on social media. It is important to note that this word library aims to normalize slang abbreviation, common words and root words and not slang derived words in order to minimize the size of word library. There are many word patterns variation from same derived word such as *permainannya* (his/her toys) could be written as *permainannye*, *prmainannye*, *permaennnye* and *permainnnya*. Word normalization of slang derived words before word stemming process seems impractical approach. Therefore, these slang derived words will first undergo word stemming process and then word normalization process in order to obtain the correct root words. Based on these word analysis in this section, word pattern variations on social media, particularly on slang affixation and reduplication words, require different word stemming approach from conventional word stemming approach in which based on morphological rules of Malay language.

3   Existing Malay Word Stemmers

The earliest research on word stemmer for Malay language was developed by Othman using rule-based affixes removal method for information retrieval [9]. Since then, there are many researchers have developed various word stemmers for Malay language using various stemming approaches i.e. rule application order [2, 6, 7, 11], rule frequency order [1, 3, 4], modified the rule frequency order [8] and other stemming approaches [10, 12]. These stemming approaches used by the existing word stemmers can be further categorized into four different affixes removal methods. These affixes removal methods are focused on removing prefixes, suffixes, confixes, infixes, clitics and particles from standard affixation and reduplication words. However, there is no single research in the previous research focus on removing prefixes, suffixes, confixes, infixes, clitics and particles from slang affixation and reduplication words. The comparison of affixes removal rules used in the existing word stemmers are as follows:

(a) There are six existing word stemmers [1, 2, 8, 9, 12] use affixes removal rules to stem standard affixation word with prefixes, suffixes, confixes, infixes, clitics and particles.
(b) There are three existing word stemmers [4, 6, 11] use affixes removal rules to stem standard affixation word with only prefixes, suffixes, clitics and particles while assuming that confixes are the combination of prefixes and suffixes.
(c) There is only one existing word stemmer [3] uses affixes removal rules to stem standard affixation word with prefixes, suffixes, confixes, clitics and particles while assuming that infixes are very rare in modern text documents.
(d) There is only one existing word stemmer [10] uses affixes removal rules to stem standard affixation word with prefixes, suffixes, infixes, clitics and particles and do have specific stemming rules to stem standard reduplication words while assuming that confixes are the combination of prefixes and suffixes.
(e) There is only one existing word stemmer [7] able to stem various standard reduplication words but do not has specific rules to stem affixation words.

It can be concluded that the existing word stemmers do not have specific word stemming rules to stem slang affixation and reduplication words because previous researchers focused on improving word stemmers to stem standard affixation words from stemming errors. The promising word stemming approach is modified rules application order (also known as rules frequency order) with background knowledge [8] due to the flexibility to rearrange various word stemming rules in order to find the best order of word stemming rules.

4 The Proposed Malay Word Stemmer

In general, the proposed word stemmer is aimed to stem standard and slang word patterns on social media platform. The proposed word stemmer was developed using Perl Programming v5.5 on MacBook Pro OS X El Capitan with 2.8 GHz Intel Core i7 processor and 8 GB 1600 MHz DDR3 memory. The stemming approach of the proposed word stemming is the combination of dictionary-lookup and rule application order based stemming rules with word normalization. The proposed word stemmer can be described as the following pseudo codes:

```
1   Input: Processing the Input
2   Accept the input text document.
3   Remove single and double quotes from the words.
4   Remove special character except URL, hashtag, hyphen
5     and numbers.
6   go to Step-1.
7
8   Output: Processing the Output
9   Root Words {stem1,stem2,stem3...stemn}.
10
11  Step-1: Checking the Word in The Document
12   IF i = 0, go to Output.
13   IF i = wordn, go to Step-2.
14
15  Step-2: Processing Root Words from Derived Words
16  Condition I
17   IF i = wordn is standard root word, accept the word.
18  go to Step-1.
19  Condition II
20   IF i = wordn is slang root word, normalize the word.
21  go to Step-1.
22
23  Step-3: Stemming Words Using Dictionary Lookup
24  Condition I
25   IF i = wordn is standard affixation, stem the word.
26   IF i = wordn is standard reduplication,
27     stem the word.
28  go to Step-1
29  Condition II
30   IF i = wordn is slang affixation word,
31     stem the word and normalize the word.
32   IF i = wordn is slang reduplication word,
33     stem the word and normalize the word.
34  go to Step-1.
35
36  Step-4: Stemming Words Using Affixes Removal Method
37  Condition I
38   IF i = wordn is standard affixation, stem the word.
39   IF i = wordn is standard reduplication,
40     stem the word.
41  go to Step-1
42  Condition II
43   IF i = wordn is slang affixation,
44     stem the word and normalize the word.
45   IF i = wordn is slang reduplication,
46     stem the word and normalize the word.
47  go to Step-1.
```

There are six important components in this proposed word stemmer. The first component aims to accept the text document and tokenize words from special

Table 2. Word pattern variations for Malay language on social media.

Original words	Tokenized words
1. Email	▪ abc@email.com → abc@email.com | not abc email com
2. Internet address	▪ http://www.xyz.com/index.html → http://www.xyz.com/index.html | not http www xyz com index html
3. Twitter	▪ hashtag : #abcd → #abcd | not abcd ▪ account : @xyz → @xyz | not xyz
4. Root words	▪ *M'sia* → *Msia* (shorthand for Malaysia) | not *M sia*
5. Affixation	▪ *K'jaan* → *Kjaan* [shorthand for *Kerajaan* (Government) | not *K jaan*
6. Reduplication	▪ *berwarna-warni* → *berwarna-warni* (colorful) | not *berwarna warni*

characters so that the original words are not lost once special characters are removed as described in Table 2. It is important to properly tokenize these words before normalizing and then stemming these words as described by the following examples:

(a) without proper word tokenization e.g. *k'jaan* (original word) → *k jaan* (without tokenization) → *k ja* (incorrect stemmed word)

(b) with proper word tokenization e.g. *k'jaan* (original word) → *kjaan* (with tokenization) → *kerajaan* (with normalization) → *raja* (correct stemmed word)

The word normalization is crucial in order to stem the word correctly if the word with special character is properly tokenized (e.g. *k'jaan* → *kjaan* → *kerajaan*→ *raja*). Otherwise, the word with special character will not be stemmed correctly (e.g. *k'jaan* → *k jaan* → *k ja*). The second component aims to check whether if there is a word to be stemmed and if there is no word in the text document, the final output will be generated. It is important to avoid the proposed word stemmer program to experience a *'program is not responding'* mode if there is no more word in the text document to be stemmed. The third component aims to differentiate standard root words from standard derived words by using Standard Root Word Dictionary that consists of 299 word entries so that only standard derived words will undergo word stemming process. It also identifies and normalizes slang common words and slang root words into standard common words and standard root words by using Slang Root Word Dictionary that consists of 1,190 word entries. Thus, only derived words will be considered as input to the fourth component and fifth component. These components are word stemming process whereby the fourth component aims to stem derived word by using dictionary lookup method and the fifth component aims to stem derived word by using affixes removal method. The use of two different stemming methods is to reduce stemming errors due to the complexity of addressing conflicting and multiple morphological rules in Malay language. The word stemming challenge arises when very similar affixation words are to be stemmed i.e., *memilih* (choosing), *memikir* (thinking) and *meminum* (drinking). The potential for stemming errors are described by the following examples in Table 3.

To address these stemming errors, the proposed word stemmer differentiates conflicting morphological rules during affix matching selection and spelling variations and exceptions by using rule-based affixes removal method and dictionary lookup method.

Table 3. Conflicting and multiple morphological rules in Malay language.

Scenario	Malay morphological rules
1. _memilih_ (choosing)	■ Correct: e.g. _pilih_ by removing the prefix (_mem+_) and inserting the character _p_ ■ Incorrect: e.g. _filih_ by removing the prefix (_mem+_) and inserting the character _f_ e.g. _milih_ by removing the prefix (_me+_) and inserting no character
2. _memikir_ (thinking)	■ Correct: e.g. _fikir_ by removing the prefix (_mem+_) and inserting the character _f_ ■ Incorrect: e.g. _pikir_ by removing the prefix (_mem+_) and inserting the character _p_ e.g. _mikir_ by removing the prefix (_me+_) and inserting no characters
3. _meminum_ (drinking)	■ Correct: e.g. _minum_ by removing the prefix (_me+_) inserting no characters ■ Incorrect: e.g. _finum_ by removing the prefix (_mem+_) and inserting the character _f_ e.g. _pinum_ by removing the prefix (_mem+_) and inserting the character _p_

Based on morphological study in Malay language, the combination of prefix (_mem+_) and root word with first letter _p_ to form affixation words (e.g. _memilih_) are more than combination of prefix (_mem+_) and root word with first letter _f_ and combination of prefix (_me+_) and root word with first letter _m_ to form affixation words. Thus, affixes removal method will be used to remove prefixes for combination of prefix (_mem+_) and root word with first letter _p_ while dictionary lookup method will be used to remove prefixes for combination of prefix (_mem+_) and root word with first letter _f_ and combination of prefix (_me+_) and root word with first letter _m_. These conflicting and multiple morphological rules may lead to overstemming or understemming errors if it is not addressed properly in the word stemming rules. Therefore, the fourth component uses two different dictionaries to stem specific derived words i.e. Standard Derivative Dictionary which consists of 2,065 word entries to stem specific standard derived words and Slang Derivative Dictionary which consists of 3950 word entries to stem specific slang derived words. On other hand, the fifth component uses two different affixes removal methods i.e. standard affixes removal rules which consists of 370 stemming rules to stem standard derived words and slang affixes removal rules which consists of 56 stemming rules to stem slang derived words. Once derived words are stemmed, if these stemmed words are slang root word, it will be normalized into standard root word by using Slang Root Word Dictionary. Lastly, the sixth component aims to generate the output of stemmed words.

5   Experimental Results and Discussion

In order to evaluate the proposed word stemmer, 3500 Facebook comments have been extracted from Malaysiakini online news portal from 01 December 2015 until 30 December 2015. These Facebook comments consist of 42,560 word occurrences or

7,345 unique words. These unique words were used as testing datasets to evaluate the proposed word stemmer. There are two experiments were conducted with specific conditions. The first experiment was to evaluate the proposed word stemmer with one stemming feature i.e. to stem standard derived word only which is similar to the existing word stemmers (Condition I). The second experiment was to evaluate the proposed word stemmer with two stemming features i.e. to stem both standard and slang derived words (Conditions I and II). The experimental results showed that the proposed word stemmer with two stemming features (Conditions I and II) performs better to stem standard and slang derived words against testing datasets as described in Table 4.

Table 4. Experimental results of the proposed word stemmer.

Experiment setup	Stemming accuracy	Stemming errors examples
Experiment I - Proposed word stemmer with one stemming feature against testing dataset (Condition I)	46.8 %	▪ Slang abbreviation (*jgn, kpd, dgn, pd*) ▪ Slang root words (*cume, kene, mase*) ▪ Slang affixation words (*berkate, berjln, jugakn, sudahlaa, layannye*) ▪ Slang reduplication words (*kata2nye, sepuas-puasnye, seluas2nya*) ▪ Other words (*ngam, sat, lepak, kantoi, cun, tibai, caya*)
Experiment II - Proposed word stemmer with two stemming features against testing dataset (Conditions I and II)	78.3 %	▪ Slang abbreviation (*dsai, spm, pj, pm*) ▪ Slang root words (*takadak, daegan, heran, mlam*) ▪ Slang affixation words (*beromabak, pngatahuan, memancut kan*) ▪ Slang reduplication words (*berulak-alik, mentri-menterinye*) ▪ Other words (*ngam, sat, lepak, kantoi, cun, tibai, caya*)

After analyzing the experimental results from two different experiments, the observation can be made as follows:

(a) Proposed word stemmer with one stemming feature (Condition I) is not able to normalize slang abbreviation and slang root words into standard words as described in Table 4. It also not able to stem slang affixation and reduplication words due to there are no such word stemming rules to stem these words.

(b) Proposed word stemmer with two stemming features (Conditions I and II) is able to normalize slang abbreviation and slang root words into standard words and also able stem slang affixation and reduplication words. However, there are stemming errors produced due to insufficient entries in Slang Root Word Dictionary, Slang Derivative Dictionary and insufficient rules in slang word stemming rules as described in Table 4.

To further discuss on stemming errors in Experiment II, there are three main root causes of these stemming errors i.e.

(a) Word normalization for slang abbreviation cannot be performed due to these abbreviations are referring to the specific person (*dsai – dato seri anwar ibrahim*), certificate (*spm – sijil pelajaran malaysia*), place (*pj – petaling jaya*) and position (*pm – perdana menteri*).
(b) Word normalization for slang root words cannot be performed due to these words are considered as misspelled words in colloquial speech communication such as *takadak (tiada), daegan (dengan), heran (hairan)* and *mlam (malam)*.
(c) Word stemming for slang affixation and reduplication words cannot be performed due to the slang root words are misspelled words in colloquial speech communication such as *beromabak (berombak), pngatahuan (pengetahuan), memancut kan (memancutkan)*.
(d) Word normalization for other words cannot be performed due to these words are other foreign colloquial speech communication such as *ngam (Cantonese language for good), sat (Kedah slang word for wait)* and *lepak (urban colloquial for hang-out)*

This study has shown promising results to further improve this proposed word stemmer in order to stem slang affixation and reduplication words on social media. The current limitation can be further improved by analyzing word pattern variations from large social media data.

6   Conclusion

This paper describes the proposed word stemmer that addresses the word stemming process for slang affixation and reduplication words on social media. However, there are limitations of this proposed word stemmer in addressing word pattern variations on social media as described in this paper. Our future work will focus on improving this proposed word stemmer that includes a misspelled word checker and a dictionary of popular colloquial speech communication used by Malaysian on social media in order to further reduce stemming errors.

Acknowledgments. The authors would like to thank the Editor-in-Chief and the anonymous reviewers of the manuscript for their valuable comments and suggestions. This research was funded by Universiti Teknologi Malaysia's Research University Grant PY/2014/02479.

References

1. Abdullah, M.T., Ahmad, F., Mahmod, R., Sembok, T.M.: Rules frequency order stemmer for Malay language. IJCSNS Int. J. Comput. Sci. Netw. Secur. **9**(2), 433–438 (2009)
2. Ahmad, F., Yusoff, M., Sembok, T.M.: Experiments with a stemming algorithm for Malay words. J. Am. Soc. Inf. Sci. **47**(12), 909–918 (1996)
3. Darwis, S.A., Abdullah, R., Idris, N.: Exhaustive affix stripping and a Malay word register to solve stemming errors and ambiguity problem in Malay stemmers. Malays. J. Comput. Sci. **25**, 196–209 (2012)
4. Fadzli, S.A., Norsalehen, A. K., Syarilla, I.A., Hasni, H., Dhalila, M.S.S.: Simple rules Malay stemmer. In: The International Conference on Informatics and Applications (ICIA 2012), pp. 28–35. The Society of Digital Information and Wireless Communication (2012)
5. Hassan, A.: Morfologi, vol. 13. PTS Professional, Kuala Lumpur (2006)
6. Idris, N., Syed, S.M.F.D.: Stemming for term conflation in Malay texts. In: International Conference on Artificial Intelligence (IC-AI 2001) (2001)
7. Kassim, M.N., Maarof, M.A., Zainal, A.: Enhanced rules application order approach to stem reduplication words in malay texts. In: Herawan, T., Ghazali, R., Deris, M.M. (eds.) SCDM 2014. AISC, vol. 287, pp. 657–665. Springer, Heidelberg (2014)
8. Leong, L.C., Basri, S., Alfred, R.: Enhancing Malay stemming algorithm with background knowledge. In: Anthony, P., Ishizuka, M., Lukose, D. (eds.) PRICAI 2012. LNCS, vol. 7458, pp. 753–758. Springer, Heidelberg (2012)
9. Othman, A.: Pengakar Perkataan Melayu untuk Sistem Capaian Dokumen. MSc thesis, Universiti Kebangsaan Malaysia, Bangi (1993)
10. Sankupellay, M., Valliappan, S.: Malay language stemmer. Sunway Acad. J. **3**, 147–153 (2006)
11. Tai, S.Y., Ong, C.S., Abdullah, N.A.: On designing an automated Malaysian stemmer for the Malay language. In: Proceedings of the Fifth International Workshop on Information Retrieval with Asian Languages, pp. 207–208. ACM (2000)
12. Yasukawa, M., Lim, H.T., Yokoo, H.: Stemming Malay text and its application in automatic text categorization. IEICE Trans. Inf. Syst. **92**(12), 2351–2359 (2009)
13. Van Dijck, J.: The Culture of Connectivity: A Critical History of Social Media. Oxford University Press, Oxford (2013)

Two-Phase Computing Model for Chinese Microblog Sentimental Analysis

Jianyong Duan[1(✉)], Chao Wang[1], Mei Zhang[1], and Hui Liu[2]

[1] College of Computer Science, North China University of Technology,
Beijing 100144, People's Republic of China
duanjy@hotmail.com
[2] Business Information Management School, Shanghai Institute of Foreign Trade,
Shanghai 201620, People's Republic of China

Abstract. The sentimental analysis of Chinese microblog is a crucial task for social network related applications, such as internet marketing, public opinion monitoring, etc. This paper proposes a two-phase computing model for microblog sentimental analysis, including topic classification for posts and topic sentimental analysis respectively. In the first phase, the Latent Dirichlet Allocation(LDA) model is employed into our model for topic classification. The topics of posts are scattered into the microblogs, it has some uncertainty. The LDA model can classify the fuzzy topics. In the second phase, sentimental dictionary and emotion knowledge are performed into our model for topic sentimental analysis. HowNet as the sentimental dictionary is used to the sentimental tendency analysis. The emotion knowledge mainly uses symbols in microblog. Besides of sentimental knowledge, the sliding window for sentimental analysis also introduced into the model as the modification at the sentence level. The experimental results show that this method achieves good performance.

Keywords: Sentimental analysis · Knowledge base · LDA model · Sliding window

1 Introduction

Microblog is a kind of social network, it is popular in our daily lives. The users post the short messages within 140 words. These posts record their lives, share their feelings and express their opinions. Those user's friends can immediately see these message, they can also forward, reply and make comments [7]. Sentimental analysis is an effective method for understanding these posts, it can mine users' viewpoints, emotional trends. However microblog is different from free text. The topics of its posts aren't always focus on fixed topics. Their lengthes of posts are short. Thus these posts have some characters [2]. Firstly the words of posts aren't standard, such as omitting subject-predicate or hidden topics. Secondly, the topics of posts are staggered for a continued period of time. It cannot clearly separate these posts as independent topics. Thirdly, the microblog language is

© Springer International Publishing Switzerland 2016
Y. Tan and Y. Shi (Eds.): DMBD 2016, LNCS 9714, pp. 401–408, 2016.
DOI: 10.1007/978-3-319-40973-3_40

colloquial and also contains some emotions, pictures and links. New language form of microblog leads to these differences, some text mining methods cannot be completely applied into these fields.

2 Related Work

Sentimental analysis extracts the users' emotion, viewpoint and tendency from their posts [4]. Early studies mainly focus on the formal texts, such as commercial products, film reviews. These texts contain full syntax and semantic information. The natural processing technologies can be easily performed and acquire good performances. With the rise of social networks, short messages produced by microblog increase rapidly. Aim to these short messages, sentimental analysis also combines machine learning methods and knowledge base [1]. Machine learning methods include Support Vector Machine (SVM), Maximum Expectation(ME), it views the sentimental analysis task as classification problem. Knowledge base mainly uses some sentimental dictionaries [9]. The sentimental words are divided into positive and negative emotional words. These polar words have important effect for the result of sentence analysis.

Due to the sparseness and divergence of topic semantics, the relations and references in the posts are not clear, they maybe hide in the topics [10]. And traditional emotional dictionary cannot satisfy the microblog analysis. So building more rich emotional dictionary will make sentiment analysis efficient.

3 Method

We propose two phase model for sentimental analysis of microblog. The first phase is topic classification by LDA model in Sect. 3.1. In the second phase, a kind of knowledge base, the extent sentimental knowledge from HowNet, is introduced into our model for sentimental analysis as Sect. 3.2. And then language processing method called as sliding window is used to improve the performance which is arranged in Sect. 3.3.

3.1 LDA Model for Topic Classification

The LDA is a kind of probability model which is generated by a document. It supposes that a document consists of some topics, and every topic consists of some words. It easily represents the document by its words with probability distribution. LDA model is suitable for the recognition of hidden topics in document [6].

LDA has three levels including document, topic and word levels. The documents set is represented as $D=\{d_1, d_2, ..., d_n\}$ and word set as $V=\{w_1, w_2, ..., w_n\}$, topic set as $T=\{t_1, t_2, ..., t_n\}$. The probability distribution of topics in document follows $\theta_d=\{\theta_1, \theta_2, ..., \theta_n\}$, and probability distribution of words in topic follows $\phi_t=\{\phi_1, \phi_2, ..., \phi_n\}$. And α is the probability of topic $p(t|d)$, and β is the probability of word $p(w|z)$. LDA model as Eq. 1.

$$p(w|d) = \sum_{t=1} p(w|t) \cdot p(t|d). \tag{1}$$

For document d, its words as $w_{d1}, w_{d2},...,w_{dn}$, their probability as following Eq. 2

$$p(w_{d1}, w_{d2}, ..., w_{dn})$$
$$= \prod_{i=1}^{dn} \sum_{z=1}^{D} p(w_i|z)p(z|d). \tag{2}$$

Two parameters should be estimated, such as θ and ϕ, Gibbs sampling method is adopted into our model. The generating process for a document is following process.

① Get the word distribution ϕ according to $\phi \sim Dir(\beta)$ by dirichlet distribution;
② Get the topic distribution θ according to $\theta \sim Dir(\alpha)$ by dirichlet distribution;
③ Get the word number V according to distribution $Possion(\xi)$;
④ Exact a topic z from every document which follows distribution θ;
⑤ Exact a word w and compute its possibility from topic z;
⑥Repeat ④-⑤ until all of the words are extracted.

3.2 Sentimental Dictionary Construction

Emotional word is one of the most important feature of sentimental analysis [8]. It generally refers to the subjective tendency and with positive and negative emotions. For example, there are a lot of words like "good", "happiness", "love", which have the strong emotional inclination, and some words like "sad", "hate", and "disgust" which are significantly negative. Constructing the emotional word dictionary is helpful for further sentimental analysis.

Sentimental Computing by HowNet. HowNet is a kind of reticular knowledge system by Chinese and English vocabulary. Its basic unit is sememe which cannot be separated and represents the smallest lexical semantics. Every word can be expressed by some HowNet sememe of concepts. It also provides Chinese sentimental word table [5]. But it doesn't include some network catch words and emotional signals, such as "帅爆 (handsome burst)" informal word and emotion in dictionary. In order to improve the performance of sentimental analysis, some social network catch words and signals should be added into the word table. The semantic similarity between words can be computed by its sememes, the distance between two sememes p_i and p_j is as Eq. 3.

$$Sim_p(p_i, p_j) = \frac{\alpha}{d + \alpha}. \tag{3}$$

where d is the distance in HowNet hierarchy. For two words s_1, s_2, they have t sememes, p_1, p_2,...,p_t, their similarity as Eq. 4.

$$Sim_s(S_1, S_2) = \frac{1}{t_1 t_2} \sum_{i=1}^{t_1} \sum_{j=1}^{t_2} \frac{1}{2^{(t_1-j+1)+(t_2-i+1)}} sim(p_{1i}, p_{2j}). \qquad (4)$$

For word w_1, it is composed of m sememes $S_1^1, S_2^1, ..., S_m^1$; and there are n sememes $S_1^2, S_2^2, ..., S_n^2$ for word w_2. Their semantic similarity is the computed by Eq. 5.

$$Sim_w(w_1, w_2) = \max_{i,j} Sim(S_i^1, S_j^2). \qquad (5)$$

The sentimental tendency of word is similarity comparison between benchmark word and target word. The benchmark words come from dictionary which is composed of positive and negative seed words. These benchmark words are ranked by descend order.

Suppose positive seed word set as P, negative seed word set as N in benchmark words, for a target word w, its similarity can be computed by Eq. 6.

$$o(w) = \frac{1}{K} \sum_{k=1}^{K} sim(w, P_k) - \frac{1}{L} \sum_{l=1}^{L} sim(w, N_l). \qquad (6)$$

where K, L are the numbers of P and N respectively. If $o(w) > 0$, the target word w is positive, or negative.

SO-PMI Based Sentimental Computing. HowNet is constructed by manual work, their pathes among sememes are subjective, it will lead to the inaccurate of sentimental calculation. In order to improve the accuracy of the algorithm, by setting a threshold, HowNet similarity results are compared with the threshold, thus the algorithm called SO-PMI(semantic orientation-pointwise mutual information) is introduced into this task as Eq. 7 and PMI as Eq. 8.

$$\begin{aligned} SO &- PMI(word) \\ &= \sum_{p \in P} PMI(w, p) - \sum_{n \in N} PMI(w, n) \cdot \end{aligned} \qquad (7)$$

$$PMI(w_1, w_2) = \log[\frac{P(w_1 \& w_2)}{P(w_1)P(w_2)}]. \qquad (8)$$

where p is the positive seed word, and n is negative seed word, w is the target word. $P(w_1)$ and $P(w_2)$ is the possibility of word w_1 and w_2 by independent way in the corpus, $P(w_1 \& w_2)$ is the co-occurrence of them. This method depends on the scale of corpus, thus the HITS value of Google is used to smooth the possibility of w.

3.3   Sentence Sentimental Computing Base on Sliding Window

For the text of posts, the written language uses informal sentences. The syntax and parse tools cannot be directly performed into sentence analysis. Especial for complex sentences, there are some words which are crucial for judging the sentimental polarity. They can transfer their emotions from positive to negative, as Table 1.

Table 1. Example of sentence sentimental polarity

Chinese	Translation	Polarity
①昨晚的电影好看啊	The movie looks good last night.	positive
②昨晚的电影不好看	The movie doesn't look good last night.	negative
③昨晚的电影不是特别难看啊	The movie doesn't look bad last night.	neutral

The emotion words sometimes show the obvious sentimental tendency. But we cannot simply judge by these positive and negative emotion words. A sliding window scoring algorithm is adopted into the sentence sentimental classification, as Eq. 9

$$Score(sentiment) = \sum (sen(word) \times H \times \prod_{i=1}^{l} t_i).\qquad(9)$$

where t_i is the coefficient of adverb, H is the negative coefficient for negative word every time. It sets a fixed window length. The algorithm slides its cursor from left to right word by word, some negative adverb, degree adverb and turn words are considered to adjust the scores.

4   Experimental Results

4.1   Data and Measures

We grabbed 4000 posts of the social network data by API tools which are provided by sina weibo, their domains including life, entertainment and news in 2015. These posts are preprocessed, including removing repetition and meaningless items, or some URL links and formatting symbols. Finally 3261 posts are manual tagged, as Table 2 shows.

These preprocessed posts are tagged by word segmentation and part-of-speech tool. Their sentimental results are measured by precision, recall, F-score and coverage. Their calculation formula as follow, The precision is the ratio between total posts and correct tagged posts, as Eq. 10 and the recall is the correct tagged posts in manual tagged posts, as Eq. 11.

$$Precision = \frac{N_{correct}}{N_{total}} \times 100\,\%.\qquad(10)$$

Table 2. Manual tagged results

Domain	Classifier number			Total number
	Positive	Neutral	Negative	
Life	598	241	139	978
Entertainment	475	306	364	1145
News	313	344	481	1138

$$Recall = \frac{N_{correct}}{N_{manual}} \times 100\%. \qquad (11)$$

Their related F-score measure as Eq. 12.

$$F_1 = \frac{precision \times recall}{precision + recall} \times 2. \qquad (12)$$

4.2 Results

We firstly classify the topics by LDA model, then compute their sentimental results by dictionary and sliding window method.

Parameter Setting. The manual tagged data is used to train the LDA model. The Kullback–Leibler(KL) divergence is used to measure the distance among topics. The topic number $|T|$ has influence for the KL-divergence, when $|T|=6$, the LDA model is most effective in our experiment, thus this value is used into out model.

Comparison Experiments. Two groups of contrast experiments are designed to verify the performance of our proposed method. The first group experiments are designed to check new constructed emotion dictionary. The combination of dictionary and LDA model is investigated by the second group of experiments.

Extended Sentimental Dictionary Results. The first comparison experiments are designed for HowNet based sentimental dictionary. The results as below Table 3 showed.

From the Table 3, we know that the dictionary combined sliding window method is more effective in precision, recall and F-score than HowNet method, especial for the negative posts.

The main reasons as follow. Firstly, our constructed dictionary collects more emotional words than HowNet itself, especially network emotional words. It facilitates the promotion of performance. Secondly, HowNet dictionary only contains the official words, our dictionary contains a large number of symbols that are

Table 3. General results on Precision, Recall and F-score

	Precision		Recall		F-score	
	Extend	HowNet	Extend	HowNet	Extend	HowNet
Positive	69.24%	65.37 %	63.65 %	58.34 %	66.33%	61.66%
Neutral	60.67 %	55.59 %	55.47%	49.28%	57.95%	52.25%
Negative	68.34%	61.68 %	61.93%	53.33%	64.98%	57.20%
Average	66.08%	60.88 %	60.35%	53.65%	-	-

used for the emotion expression. These signals are wildly used in social network. They are also a kind of important part of microblog language. In fact, Microblog has its own signal emotion library. These emotion signals express the positive or negative feelings. We use 67 emotion icons to support our model. Thirdly, our model adopts the sliding window method, it has advantage on the negative recognition than usual way which only concerns the number of negative words. Thus its determination on negative emotions are more accurate.

LDA and SVM Model Comparison. The second comparison experiment is between SVM-based method [3] and our LDA-based method. The SVM model uses frequent words as the input vector to cluster the topics and train the classifier. The experimental results as Table 4.

Table 4. General comparison between SVM and LDA model

	Precision		Recall		F-score		Coverage	
	LDA	SVM	LDA	SVM	LDA	SVM	LDA	SVM
T1	71.16%	66.24%	68.77%	63.94%	69.94%	65.07%	86.65%	80.82%
T2	74.24%	68.43%	70.54%	64.13%	72.34%	66.21%	87.06%	81.22%
T3	73.05%	67.83%	69.75%	62.34%	71.36%	64.97%	86.96%	79.63%
T4	69.47%	64.63%	64.41%	57.06%	66.84%	60.61%	80.42%	75.85%
T5	70.56%	65.14%	67.58%	59.38%	69.04%	62.13%	81.48%	76.48%
T6	68.96%	63.95%	63.58%	57.14%	66.16%	60.35%	79.84%	74.55%

From the Table 4, we know that the LDA model is better than SVM model in some measures, such as precision, recall, F-score and coverage. The LDA model is more superior than SVM model in identifying the hidden topics. Its advantages as following.

Firstly, microblog posts have more fragments and irregular expressions. It will lead to the higher dimensions of vector. The LDA model is more effectively in reducing the dimensions than SVM model. Secondly, SVM model heavily depends on the training samples. It needs large scales of samples to achieve good performance while LDA model can use less samples to acquire good results. Thirdly, SVM model doesn't work well on multiple classification problem. It is also difficult to combine the dictionary and sliding window.

5   Conclusion

This paper proposes the sentimental analysis for microblog. The LDA model is used to solve the problem of social network. It can effectively reduce the dimension and recognize the hidden topics to achieve topic clustering. The extend dictionary ensures the coverage of emotion expression including words and signals. The sliding window method can flexibly compute the sentence sentimental tendency. Future work will focus on the new feature learning and improve the LDA model.

Acknowledgment. The authors are grateful to the reviewers for reviewing this paper. This work is supported by the National Science Foundation of China (Grant No.61103112), Social Science Foundation of Beijing(Grant No.13SHC031), Ministry of Education of China (Project of Humanities and Social Sciences, Grant NO.13YJC740055) and Beijing Young talent plan(Grant No.CIT&TCD201404005)

References

1. Dong, L., Weiy, F., Liuy, S., Zhouy, M., Xu, K.: A statistical parsing framework for sentiment classification. In: ACL, pp. 265–308 (2015)
2. Feng, S., Kang, J.S., Kuznetsova, P., Choi, Y.: Connotation lexicon: a dash of sentiment beneath the surface meaning. In: ACL, pp. 1774–1784 (2015)
3. Jun-xia, C., Zhi-tang, L., Ming-guang, Z., Jin, X.: Novel topic detection method for microblog based on svm filtration. J. Commun. **34**(z2), 74–78 (2013)
4. Lazaridou, A., Titov, I.: A bayesian model for joint unsupervised induction of sentiment, aspect and discourse representations. In: ACL, pp. 1630–1639 (2015)
5. Lipenkova, J.: A system for fine-grained aspect-based sentiment analysis of Chinese. In: ACL, pp. 55–60 (2015)
6. Mohtarami, M., Lan, M., Tan, C.L.: Probabilistic sense sentiment similarity through hidden emotions. In: ACL, pp. 983–902 (2013)
7. Ramesh, A., Kumar, S.H., Foulds, J., Getoor, L.: Weakly supervised models of aspectsentiment for online course discussion forums. In: ACL. pp. 74–83 (2015)
8. Wang, L., Liu, K., Cao, Z., Zhao, J., de Melo, G.: Sentiment-aspect extraction based on restricted boltzmann machines. In: ACL, pp. 616–625 (2015)
9. Wang, Z., Lee, S.Y.M., Li, S., Zhou, G.: Emotion detection in code-switching texts via bilingual and sentimental information. In: ACL, pp. 763–768 (2015)
10. Xu, L., Liu, K., Lai, S., Chen, Y., Zhao, J.: Mining opinion words and opinion targets in a two-stage framework. In: ACL, pp. 1764–1773 (2013)

Local Community Detection
Based on Bridges Ideas

Xia Zhang$^{(\boxtimes)}$, Zhengyou Xia, and Jiandong Wang

Nanjing University of Aeronautics and Astronautics, Nanjing 210015, China
zhangxia58@163.com

Abstract. In complex network analysis, the local community detection problem is getting more and more attention. Because of the difficulty to get complete information of the network, such as the World Wide Web, the local community detection has been proposed by researcher. That is, we can detect a community from a certain source vertex with limited knowledge of an entire graph. The previous methods of local community detection now are more or less inadequate in some places. In this paper, We propose a method called W, which assumes that a "good" community is covered with a "bridge" to other communities, and through these "bridges" the community should have little overlap with the community to be found. The results of experiments show that whether in computer-generated random graph or in the real networks, our method can effectively solve the problem of the local community detection.

Keywords: Social network analysis · Local community detection · Bridge · Strange degree

1 Introduction

Community structure is a good way for researchers to analyze complex network, such as Social Networks [1], the Internet [2], the World Wide Web [3], the Paper Cited Network [4, 5] and Biological Networks [6]. These complex networks can be seen as graphs consisting of n vertices which are the entity of the network, and m edges which refer to the relationship between the vertices. The problems of community detection are according some limitations and information to find communities from these graphs. For example, people who have similar interests in daily life belong to one community. Then, community detection is to find these people.

The problem of finding communities in social networks has been studied for decades [14]. There are many approaches have been proposed to solve this problem [16]. For example, methods of global community detection based on global data such as graph partitioning [7], hierarchical clustering [8], partition clustering [9], spectral clustering [10]. However, most of those approaches require knowledge of the entire graph structure. This constraint is problematic for networks which are either too large or too dynamic to know completely, e.g. the WWW. [14] It may results in too much time complexity, due to traverse the entire graph. In some cases, we may not get complete information of the graph, just can get local information, or we just want to know some local information and the global community detection is not available.

© Springer International Publishing Switzerland 2016
Y. Tan and Y. Shi (Eds.): DMBD 2016, LNCS 9714, pp. 409–415, 2016.
DOI: 10.1007/978-3-319-40973-3_41

To solve these problems, local community detection has been proposed and only need to know information of partial vertices, such as these algorithms [12–15]. In the case of only local information is given, these methods can effectively solve the problem of local community detection. However, these methods also have some problems, more or less. For example, R-method [12] requires a pre-defined parameter K which is difficult to be got and changes with the different sizes of the communities. The restrictions of L method [14] are too strict to get a complete community.

In this paper, we present a new method called W, which assumes that a "good" community is covered with a "bridge" to other communities, and through these "bridges" the community should have little overlap with the community to be found. Based on some real network, we have done some experiments to compare the algorithm we proposed with algorithms proposed above. The results show that the algorithm we proposed is effective.

2 Our Algorithm

In order to facilitate the discussion later on the local community discovery algorithm described in general will be involved in some of the concepts do a brief introduction as well as the symbol of the relationship between these concepts can be found in Fig. 1. The community member of the starting node set is labeled by D. Set D and B C can be divided into two disjoint subsets. Community core members, is represented by C. Each node in the C satisfies the following $\Gamma(u) \subseteq D$: where $\Gamma(u)$ represents the Add v_0 node set of the node u. Community boundary member collection is labeled by B. Each node in the B has at least one of the adjacent domain nodes that are not within the collection D. Community adjacent node set is labeled by using S. Each node in the S does not belong to the D but has at least one of the adjacent domain nodes in the D. Unknown node set is labeled by using U, which is shown as Fig. 1.

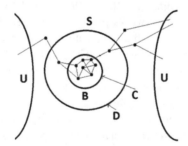

Fig. 1. Each subset of local community

Most of local community detection algorithm based on the community internal edge number and outside the community of the two indicators, average internal edge of larger number of usually indicates that the internal connection is denser and community structure is more significant. However, the larger number of external edges of the community is sometimes just because the current D collection has not yet captured the core of the community, which is particularly evident at the start node is located at the edge of the community. It is sometimes not accurate to use the external side of the evaluation of local communities.

By observing the community structure, we can think that when the community structure of D is obvious, the nodes in S set and the edge of D nodes are the "bridge", that is, the intersection of v_0 and D and $\Gamma(v_0)$ in S is very small. If it is a social network that represents the relationship between friends, then v_0's friends are often unfamiliar with the D and S. We define a new concept for the node in the s, as shown in the formula 1:

$$s(v) = \frac{|\Gamma(v) \cap U|}{d_v} \qquad (1)$$

Where d_v is the degree of the node v. $\Gamma(v)$ is the V of the adjacent domain of the node. Based on this, $1 - s(v)$ also indicates the degree of familiarity of node v. For a "good" community, we believe that the average number of internal edges should be larger, while the average of the nodes in the S should be small, the evaluation function W expressed the idea, which is defined as the formula 2.

$$W = \frac{1}{2} \times \frac{W_{in}}{W_{fam}} \qquad (2)$$

Where W_{in} represents the average internal number of nodes D, as shown in formula 3:

$$W_{in} = \frac{\sum_{u \in D} |\Gamma(u) \cap D|}{|D|} \qquad (3)$$

The average familiarity of each node in W_{fam} is defined as the formula 4:

$$W_{fam} = \frac{\sum_{v \in S} 1 - s(v)}{|S|} \qquad (4)$$

The time complexity of the algorithm is $O(k^2 d + k|S|d)$, where k is the average size of the local community. d is the average degree of nodes in the graph. $|S|$ is the average size of S set.

According to above discussion and analysis, our algorithm is as following Fig. 2.

3 Experiments and Discussion

In our experiments, we compare the results of different methods(R, M, L, G). We perform experiments with three datasets—a computer-generated graph and one real-world networks (the NCAA Football network).

Our W Algorithm

$C = \{ v_0 \}, W = 0$

Add v_0 of Add adjacent domain into S.

$B = \{ v_0 \}$

Do:

                    update **S Set**

  do

    Create a linear table Q to store the new node to join D.

According to the degree of node in ascending order

  For $v_j \in S$

      The gain of ΔW after adding D into W is calculated by v_j.

          if $\Delta W > 0$

      add v_j into D and Q

     $W = W + \Delta W$

    end if

  end for

  while Q is not NULL

do

    store nodes deleted from D by using linear table Q

  for $v_j \in D$

      calculate ΔW of W after v_j deleted from D

    if $\Delta W > 0$ and community is still connection by deleted v_j

      Delete v_j from D and store v_j into Q

       $W = W + \Delta W$

    end if

  end for

  while Q is not NULL

  while set D changed

  if D include v_0 return D

  else report v_0 Not belonging to any community.

  end if

End

Fig. 2. Our algorithm

3.1 Computer-Generated Graphs

First, we apply these algorithms to a set of computer-generated random graphs that have known community structure [11]. The graph consists of 128 vertices which are divided into 4 sets, and the degree of each vertex is 16. The number of edges in the sets is more than that between the sets, and assuming that every vertex has neighbors in the same sets a neighbor in the other sets.

In the computer-generated graphs, there are 32 vertices in each set of vertices, so we let the pre-defined k = 32, i.e. the algorithms add only 32 vertices into community C from start vertex or the quality metric is no longer increase. Then we compute the value of precision, recall and F-score about C. We use each vertex (128 vertices) as the start vertex to detect community, and then compute the average value of precision, recall and score. This experiment uses the LFR generation scheme, where the parameters are fixed to 10. Running results are shown in Figs. 3 and 4.

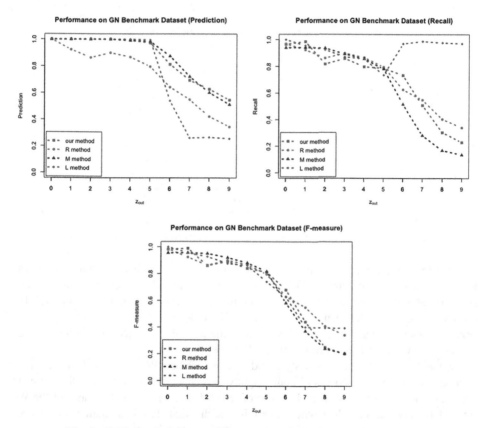

Fig. 3. Performance of community extraction algorithm in GN network

3.2 The NCAA Football Network

The dataset is collected from the competition schedule of 2006 NCAA Football Bowl Subdivision (formerly Division 1-A). There are 179 vertices (the lack of an outlier may be because the data changes) and 787 edges, the exist edge of each pair of vertices means there is a game between these two teams. In the network, there are 115

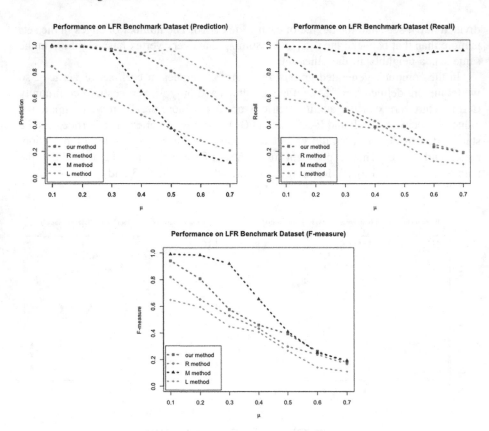

Fig. 4. Performance of community extraction algorithm on LFR data sets

universities divided into 11 conferences, there are more games between the two teams which are in a same conference. In addition, there are four independent schools, as well as the other vertices are not belong to any conferences, as we called them 'outliers'. In our experiments, we let every vertex which is belong to a conference (there are 179 −60 = 119 vertices) as the start vertex to detect the local community, and then compute the average value of precision, recall and F-score.

In the Table 1, we can obviously found that our method W is greater than the other method with the value of score, and it only slightly lower than the method L with the value of precision and the method M with the value of recall. However, the performance of the W method is very stable, unlike other algorithms in different data sets often performance differences, which makes our algorithm more suitable for use in engineering.

Table 1. Comparison with R, M, L algorithms based on NCAA Football Network

Algorithm	Precision	Recall	F-score
R	0.64	0.75	0.68
M	0.49	1.0	0.63
L	0.97	0.81	0.81
W	0.92	0.98	0.93

4   Conclusion

In this paper, We propose a method called W, which assumes that a "good" community is covered with a "bridge" to other communities, and through these "bridges" the community should have little overlap with the community to be found. We introduce the concept of familiarity and familiarity with the nodes in S. We believe that the average number of edges within the community, and the average number of nodes in the S collection are higher, the community is better. The results of experiments show that whether in computer-generated random graph or in the real networks, our method can effectively solve the problem of the local community detection. The performance of the W method is very stable, unlike other algorithms in different data sets often performance differences, which makes our algorithm more suitable for use in engineering.

References

1. Wasserman, S., Faust, K.: Social Network Analysis: Methods and Applications. Cambridge University Press, Cambridge (1994)
2. Faloutsos, M., Faloutsos, P., Faloutsos, C.: Comput. Commun. Rev. **29**, 251 (1999)
3. Albert, R., Jeong, H., Barabsi, A.L.: Diameter of the World-Wide Web. Nature **401**, 130–131 (1999)
4. Hopcroft, J., Khan, O., Kulis, B., Selman, B.: Natural communities in large linked networks. In: SIGKDD 2003, pp. 541–546 (2003)
5. Price, D.J.D.S.: Networks of scientific papers. Science **149**, 510–515 (1965)
6. Barabasi, A.L., Oltvai, Z.N.: Network biology: understanding the cell's functional organization. Nat. Rev. Genet. **5**, 101–113 (2004)
7. Kernighan, B.W., Lin, S.: An efficient heuristic procedure for partitioning graphs. Bell Syst. Tech. J. **49**(2), 291–307 (1970)
8. Zhu, J., Hastie, T.: Kernel logistic regression and the import vector machine. Adv. Neural Inf. Process. Syst. **14**, 1081–1088 (2001)
9. Fortunato, S.: Community detection in graphs. Phys. Rep. **486**(3/5), 75–174 (2010)
10. Ding, C., He, X.: A spectral method to separate disconnected and nearly-disconnected web graph components. In: Proceedings of the Seventh ACM SIGKDD International Conference on Knowledge Discovery and Data Mining. ACM (2001)
11. Girvan, M., Newman, M.: Community structure in social and biological networks. Proc. Natl. Acad. Sci. U.S.A. **99**(12), 7821–7826 (2002)
12. Clauset, A.: Finding local community structure in networks. Phys. Rev. E **72**(2), 026132 (2005)
13. Luo, F., Wang, J., Promislow, E.: Exploring local community structures in large networks. Web Intell. Agent Syst. **6**(4), 387–400 (2008)
14. Chen, J., Zaïane, O., Goebel, R.: Local community identification in social networks. In: International Conference on Advances in Social Network Analysis and Mining, ASONAM 2009, pp. 237–242. IEEE (2009)
15. Wu, Y., Huang, H., Hao, Z.: Local community detection using link similarity. J. Comput. Sci. Technol. **27**(6), 1261–1268 (2012)
16. Xia, Z., Bu, Z.: Community detection based on a semantic network. Knowl. Based Syst. **26**, 30–39 (2012)

Environment for Data Transfer Measurement

Sergey Khoruzhnikov[1], Vladimir Grudinin[1], Oleg Sadov[1],
Andrey Shevel[1,2], Stefanos Georgiou[1,3], and Arsen Kairkanov[1(✉)]

[1] ITMO University, St. Petersburg, Russian Federation
abkairkanov@corp.ifmo.ru
[2] National Research Centre "Kurchatov Institute", B.P. Konstantinov,
Petersburg Nuclear Physics Institute, Gatchina, Russian Federation
[3] Athens University of Economics and Business, Athens, Greece

Abstract. Measurement of the data transfer considered as often task when regular transfer over long distant network of large volume data is required. The data transfer over network depends on many conditions and parameters. Quite often measurements have to be repeated several times. The paper describes procedure how to implement appropriate measurements to store automatically all the parameters and messages during the data transfer. The saved history tracking permits to do detailed comparison of measurement results.

Keywords: Big data · Linux · Data transfer · Measurement · Internet

1 The Introduction

The large volume data is tightly connected to the big data [1]. The term "big data" have many aspects: store, analysis, transferring over data link, visualization, etc. In this paper authors are concentrating on procedure how to track data transfer. In some context the paper can be considered as part of research in SDN approach to the data transfer [2].

While performing a large data transfer many unexpected events may occur: data transfer rate could change, interruptions could appear, and further more. Usual desire in big data transfer over long distant network (Internet) is to increase the data transfer speed, increase the reliability, and so on. In order to achieve such a result, several quite reliable data transfer utilities [3] in Linux exist. However each specific case of data transfer might require specific parameter values, specific data transfer programs to achieve required results.

There are methods to decrease the time to transfer the data over network by compression the data just before transfer and uncompression immediately after. Such the approach requires additional assumptions: you have enough computing power to do compression and uncompression "on the fly" and you have precise knowledge that data might be compressed by significant factor. In reality many types of files are already heavily compressed and any attempts to compress them more will be resulted only in spending CPU time but no data volume decreasing. Anyway careful concrete analysis of balance between CPU time consumption and possible decrease data transfer time is very useful. Anyway to compare different data transfer possibilities it is very important to do many measurements and save all the detailed information about each measurement.

© Springer International Publishing Switzerland 2016
Y. Tan and Y. Shi (Eds.): DMBD 2016, LNCS 9714, pp. 416–421, 2016.
DOI: 10.1007/978-3-319-40973-3_42

2 Related Work

Different data transfer tools have different features and impact for the transfer e.g., total volume size, data type, files sizes, and etc. Popular Linux tools are discussed below in Sect. 3. Authors [4, 5] provided interesting information in big scale data transfer in general: WAN data links architecture and capacity, data transfer monitoring, protocols, reliability, analysis, discussions, etc. At the same time a little information how to carefully compare their results with data transfer performed in another time. In most cases authors just show results to illustrate their ideas but not intended to compare with other concrete data transfer results, for example, [6].

3 Popular Programs for Data Transfer

The number of data transfer programs is huge, may be thousands. Several most popular free of charge tools in Linux is planned to be discussed here.

openssh family [6–8] — well known data transfer utilities deliver strong authentication and a number of data encryption algorithms. Data compression before encryption to reduce the data volume to be transferred is possible as well. There are two openSSH flavors: patched SSH version [8] which can use increased size of buffers and SSH with Globus GSI authentication. No parallel data transfer streams.

bbcp [9] — utility for bulk data transfer. It is assumed that bbcp has been installed on both sides, i.e. transmitter, as client, and receiver as server. Utility bbcp has many features including the setting: TCP Window size, multi-stream transfer, I/O buffer size, resuming failed data transfer, authentication with ssh, other options dealing with many practical details.

bbftp [10] — utility for bulk data transfer. It implements its own transfer protocol, which is optimized for large files (significantly larger than 2 GB) and secure as it does not read the password in a file and encrypts the connection information. bbftp main features are: SSH and Grid Certificate authentication modules, multi-stream transfer, ability to tune I/O buffer size, restart failed data transfer, other useful practical features.

fdt [11] — Java based utility used for efficient data transfer. Since is written in Java, theoretically it can be executed in any platform. It can run as a SCP or client/server applications. Also, it's an asynchronous, flexible multithreaded system and is using the capabilities of Java NIO library. Features such as: support I/O buffer size tuning, restore files from buffers asynchronously, resume a file transfer session without any loss and when is necessary, and streams dataset continuously by using a managed pool of buffers through one or more TCP sockets.

gridFTP [12] is advanced transfer utility for globus security infrastructure (GSI) environment. The utility has many features: two security flavors: Globus GSI and SSH, the file with host aliases: each next data transfer stream will use next host aliases (useful for computer cluster), multi-stream transfer, ability to tune I/O buffer size, restart failed data transfer; other useful practical features.

Mentioned utilities are quite effective for data transfer from point of view of data link capacity usage.

More sophisticated tool FTS3 [13] is advanced tool for data transfer of large volume of the data over the network. FTS3 uses utility gridFTP to perform data transfer. In this tool in addition to useful data transfer features mentioned above there are a number of others: good data transfer history tracking (log), ability to use http, restful, CLI interfaces to control the process of the data transfer, get the information about data transfer status and more.

Each mentioned tool has specific features. It is not possible to tell which tool is most effective in concrete task of big data transfer before testing.

4   Measurement Procedures

4.1   Basic Requirements for Measurement

At first, the important measurement requirement is option to reproduce earlier obtained test results (so called history tracking data). In other words there is need to guarantee that concrete measurement can be repeated later on with exactly same parameters. Also for series of test runs is possible to compare different data transfer programs or equipment.

At second, one would need to remember that the measurement VM are running in Openstack cloud infrastructure. Among other things it is useful to remember that such parameters like TCP window must be set in VM and in host machine as well. Otherwise the changing parameters just in VM does not affect data transfer at all. A lot of advanced recommendations available elsewhere, for example, in [3] are describing cases where any Linux kernel parameters can be changed at any time. Such the reasons might prevent the achievement the maximum data transfer speed when you have no ability to change parameters in directory/proc (the root credentials are required) on host machines. Such the consideration might be applied to any cloud environment. Indeed no reason to expect that data transfer from one cloud environment to other cloud environment would be performed in most effective manner from the transfer speed point of view.

Each measurement run needs the measurement tracking: to write all the conditions during measurement. For example, start time, end time, all messages generated by the data transfer utility, system data. System data are quite important: used hardware (CPU, motherboard, network card, etc.), the values in directory/proc - about ½ thousand parameters might affect the data transfer over network, the kernel version, the list and versions of all Linux packages, etc. There is Linux sosreport [14] to do above job. Sosreport is a command in Linux flavor RHEL/CentOS which collects system configuration and diagnostic information of your Linux box like running kernel version, loaded modules, services and system configuration files. This command will normally complete within a few minutes. Once completed, sosreport will generate a compressed a file under/tmp folder. Different versions use different compression schemes (gz, bz2, or xz). The size of generated file might be around several MB.

Also important to save logs of CPU usage, swap usage, and other parameters during the data transfer for history tracking.

Another issue the state of the data link which is also needs to be watched and history saved during the transfer. Among useful tools to watch the state of the data link is probably most interesting pefrsonar. Perfsonar (cite from [15]) "provides a uniform interface that allows for the scheduling of measurements, storage of data in uniform formats, and scalable methods to retrieve data and generate visualizations. This extensible system can be modified to support new metrics, and there are endless possibilities for data presentation". There is whole network of deployed perfsonar servers (many perfsonar installations) in many distributed hosts which are interested for some communities. When the community members transfer the data each other the perfsonar network is used to find out data transfer bottleneck. Most of deployed perfsonar are dedicated to monitor high speed networks 10 and 100 Gbit. On less powerful data lines the desire to use perfsonar in quite intensive way might be stressful for data link capacity. The perfsonar is just tool to observe data links, but it can't replace own understanding what is going on in the data link.

All tracking data have to be written in special log directory. Presumably, this log directory needs to be saved for long time: often - years. Obviously the writing of all conditions must be done with special script or program to store all test conditions automatically.

4.2 Testbed and Tracking Data Architecture

It is used testbed developed for research in Software Defined Network in the Network Laboratory [16]. Usually for each measurement run we prepared two Virtual Machines (VM) in framework of Openstack.org. One VM was data transmitter and another one VM was used as receiver.

Each start of any measurement script is creating special log directory which has the name in form copydata<utility_name><host-where-utility-started><host-where-to-transfer><date-time>. The directory contains following files:

- result of command sosreport;
- output of command ping <to remote host>;
- result of traceroute <to remote host>;
- all messages of tested utility generated during measurement;
- any comments to the current measurement;
- special abstract for the test measurement consisting of following lines:
  - total volume of data transfer;
  - number of files;
  - the directory name where files to be transferred are;
  - average of file size;
  - standard deviation of file size;
  - transmitter VM hostname;
  - receiver VM hostname.

Such the detailed logs permit to find out what was going on in the measurement even any time in future. Example for the log directory is shown in Fig. 1.

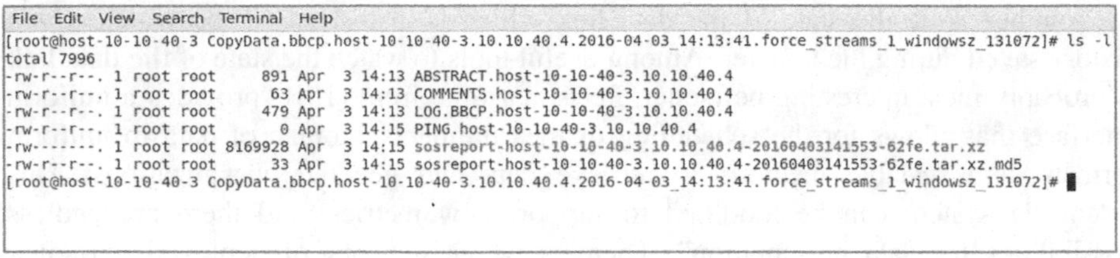

```
File  Edit  View  Search  Terminal  Help
[root@host-10-10-40-3 CopyData.bbcp.host-10-10-40-3.10.10.40.4.2016-04-03_14:13:41.force_streams_1_windowsz_131072]# ls -l
total 7996
-rw-r--r--. 1 root root     891 Apr  3 14:13 ABSTRACT.host-10-10-40-3.10.10.40.4
-rw-r--r--. 1 root root      63 Apr  3 14:13 COMMENTS.host-10-10-40-3.10.10.40.4
-rw-r--r--. 1 root root     479 Apr  3 14:13 LOG.BBCP.host-10-10-40-3.10.10.40.4
-rw-r--r--. 1 root root       0 Apr  3 14:15 PING.host-10-10-40-3.10.10.40.4
-rw-------. 1 root root 8169928 Apr  3 14:15 sosreport-host-10-10-40-3.10.10.40.4-20160403141553-62fe.tar.xz
-rw-r--r--. 1 root root      33 Apr  3 14:15 sosreport-host-10-10-40-3.10.10.40.4-20160403141553-62fe.tar.xz.md5
[root@host-10-10-40-3 CopyData.bbcp.host-10-10-40-3.10.10.40.4.2016-04-03_14:13:41.force_streams_1_windowsz_131072]# 
```

Fig. 1. Example of the log directory.

Also a range of scripts were used to produce graphics results of the measurements. Most of required scripts have been developed and available in https://github.com/itmo-infocom/BigData.

5 Conclusion

Authors developed the procedure to do measurements of data transfer speed and the set of scripts to store all tracking information. Specific feature of the procedure is ability to store all values in defined format. Detailed tracking information gives ability to compare the results of measurements which have been performed in different days and environments.

Acknowledgements. The research has been carried out with the financial support of the Ministry of Education and Science of the Russian Federation under grant agreement #14.575.21.0058.

References

1. ISO/IEC JTC 1 - Big Data. Preliminary report (2014). http://www.iso.org/iso/home/store/publication_item.htm?pid=PUB100361
2. Khoruzhnikov, S.E., Grudinin, V.A., Sadov, O.L., Shevel, A.Y., Kairkanov, A.B.: Transfer of large volume data over internet with parallel data links and SDN. In: Tan, Y., Shi, Y., Buarque, F., Gelbukh, A., Das, S., Engelbrecht, A. (eds.) ICSI-CCI 2015. LNCS, vol. 9142, pp. 463–471. Springer, Heidelberg (2015)
3. Data Transfer Tools. http://fasterdata.es.net/data-transfer-tools
4. NIST Big Data public working group. http://bigdatawg.nist.gov
5. Johnston, W.E., Dart, E., Ernst, M., Tierney, B.: Enabling high throughput in widely distributed data management and analysis systems: lessons from the LHC (2013). https://tnc2013.terena.org/getfile/402
6. OpenSSH. http://openssh.org
7. Ah Nam, H. et al: The practical obstacles of data transfer: why researchers still love scp. In: NDM 2013 Proceedings of the Third International Workshop on Network-Aware Data Management, Article No. 7 (2013). doi:10.1145/2534695.2534703
8. Patched OpenSSH. http://sourceforge.net/projects/hpnssh
9. BBCP – utility to transfer the data over network. http://www.slac.stanford.edu/~abh/bbcp

10. BBFTP – utility for bulk data transfer. http://doc.in2p3.fr/bbftp
11. Fast Data Transfer. http://monalisa.cern.ch/FDT
12. Grid/Globus data transfer tool. Client part is known as globus-url-copy. http://toolkit.globus.org/toolkit/data/gridftp
13. File Transfer Service. http://www.eu-emi.eu/products/-/asset_publisher/1gkD/content/fts3
14. Generate debug information for the system. http://linux.die.net/man/1/sosreport
15. Perfsonar. http://www.perfsonar.net
16. Laboratory of the Network Technology. http://sdn.ifmo.ru

Query Optimization and Processing Algorithm

Ant Colony-Based Approach
for Query Optimization

Hany A. Hanafy[(⊠)] and Ahmed M. Gadallah

Computer Science Department, ISSR, Cairo University, Giza, Egypt
hany_orfios@yahoo.com, ahmgad10@yahoo.com

Abstract. Many approaches have been proposed aiming to reduce the cost of join operations. Such join operations represent the key factor of the inquiry process to retrieve related information from different data tables in large relational databases. Yet, there is still a need for more intelligent query optimizing approaches to reduce the response time of query execution. This paper proposes an approach for reaching optimal query access plans for complex relational database queries including a set of join operations. The proposed approach is based on ant colony optimization technique to benefit from its ability of parallel search over several constructive computational threads which aims to reach an optimal query access plan. A comparative study shows the added value of the proposed approach.

Keywords: Query optimization · Ant colony · Logical optimizer · Query access plan

1 Introduction

Commonly, query optimizer represents a very important part of almost any database management system (DBMS). It is responsible for examining and assessing different alternatives of query access plans (QAPs) for a given query statement in order to choose the most efficient one [4]. The main objective of this work is to propose an efficient ant colony-based approach aiming to reach an optimal access plan of any given complex query for relational databases. The proposed approach concentrates mainly on the logical optimization phase. The results of the published models are not sufficiently available, but for the sake of comparisons, the results of our enhanced model have been compared with that generated by SQL Server 2012. Generally, ant colony optimization ACO represents one of widely applied evolutionary computing approaches in many domains [3]. Commonly, ACO is a class of optimization algorithms whose first member is called Ant System proposed by Colorni, Dorigo and Maniezzo [3]. The main underlying idea of such algorithms is loosely inspired by the behavior of real ants in simultaneous search. Such behavior represents a parallel search over several constructive computational threads based on local problem data and on a dynamic memory structure containing information on the quality of previously obtained result. Commonly, ACO algorithm has good potential for problem solving and recently has attracted great attention specifically for solving NP-Hard set of problems, [11]. One of the earliest best works for solving the traveler sales man problem (TSP) uses the Ant

© Springer International Publishing Switzerland 2016
Y. Tan and Y. Shi (Eds.): DMBD 2016, LNCS 9714, pp. 425–433, 2016.
DOI: 10.1007/978-3-319-40973-3_43

Colony System (ACS) which has the same architecture of Query Access Plan problem in both layout and objectives [5]. The authors of [7] applied ACS algorithm for solving TSP and claim that the ACS outperforms other nature-inspired algorithms such as simulated annealing and evolutionary computation.

The rest of this paper is organized as follows: Sect. 2 explains the optimization process. The query access plan problem is given in Sect. 3. Section 4 presents the proposed cost model. A discussion of the proposed approach for getting the optimal query access plan is given in Sect. 5. Section 6 illustrates the experimental results. The conclusion is given in Sect. 7. Finally, Sect. 8 presents the future work.

2   Optimization Process

Generally speaking, the selection of an optimal query access plan represents the main objective of the query logical optimizer. Such objective is achieved via a set of consequent steps. Firstly, it generates a set of candidate query access plans represented as join trees or query graphs. In each join tree, each relation is represented by a leaf node and each join operation is represented by an inner node [2]. Consequently, the logical optimizer starts evaluating each candidate query access plan respecting the total cost of the involved join operations. On the other hand, the physical optimizer focuses on reaching an optimal procedure to process join operations of the optimal query access tree [8]. The criterion of physical optimization is the input-output processing cost [1].

3   Query Access Plan Selection Problem

Commonly, the join operation between two relations is one of the most time consuming algebraic operations [6]. In consequent, the cost of complex query statements are affected mainly by the processing cost of the involved join operations. Such cost depends mainly on the execution sequence of the join operations between the involved relations in the given query statement which is called the query access plan (QAP). Therefore, selecting an optimal QAP is a combinatorial problem where the search space contains all candidate QAPs. Usually, each QAP is represented by a graph structure that can be mapped into a binary tree. So, the search space of the query optimization process includes a set of binary trees representing the candidate QAPs [6].

Recently, many previous works are concerned with algorithms of obtaining an optimal access plan of a complex query. Those algorithms are classified into four different groups: (a) Deterministic Algorithms, Every algorithm in this class builds a solution, systematically, in a deterministic way, either by applying a heuristic or by exhaustive search [12], (b) Randomized Algorithms, which aim to find the state of the solution that give the globally minimum cost. [13] (such as Iterative Improvement Algorithm [15], Simulated Annealing Algorithm (SA) [16], Two-Phase Optimization (2PO) [14], Toured Simulated Annealing [17], and Random Sampling [18]), (c) Genetic Algorithms, which imitate the biological evolution by using a randomized search strategy, while looking for good problem solutions. It starts basically with a random population and generates offspring by random crossover and mutation.

The members that survive the subsequent selection are considered the "fittest" ones, and the next generation relies on them. And the algorithm reaches its end when there is no further improvement and the solution is represented by the fittest member of the last population [12], and (d) Hybrid Algorithms, which combine the strategies of pure deterministic and pure randomized algorithms: solutions obtained by deterministic algorithms are used as starting points for randomized algorithms or as initial population members for genetic algorithms [6, 9].

In literature, reaching an optimal QAP requires achieving two consecutive operations. The first operation is concerned with constructing the QAPs search space including a set of binary trees. Each binary tree is equivalent to a candidate QAP derived from the complete query graph of the relations involved in the query statement. Rationally, the complexity of a query statement is proportional to the cardinality of its search space. Commonly, the cardinality of the search space of a query statement with n involved relations is (n-1)! [9]. Almost, left-deep tree structure is used to represent QAPs in the search space. It consists of different levels of internal nodes. The lowest level of those internal nodes is derived by joining any chosen couple of base relations. On the other hand, any other internal node is derived by joining two nodes, the right node is one of the base relations and the left one is the just lower internal node in the query tree [9]. Consequently, the second operation is concerned with evaluating each candidate QAP according to a specific cost function in order to select a QAP with the lowest cost.

4 The Cost Model of the Proposed Approach

Generally, to formulate a cost model for a QAP, we have to identify firstly the factors that affect the cost of a query. Those factors include: (a) The number of base relations, (b) the equivalent join tree, (c) the expected cardinality of each involved relation, and (d) the expected occurrence for each distinct value of the involved relations' attributes [2]. Some of these factors are known a priori such as the number of involved relations and the structure of the join tree. In contrary, other factors are not known before processing such as the expected cardinality of each relation [10], and the expected occurrence frequency for each distinct value of each attribute. Commonly, the expected cardinality, number of tuples, of each leaf relation lies between the expected lower and upper bounds of that relation cardinality. For simplicity, the average of lower and upper bounds for each relation is taken as its expected cardinality. If the relation is an intermediate node, the cardinality of this relation generated out of the join operation may depend on the number of distinct values for each joining attribute that belongs to both of the two intersected relations. Actually, the number of distinct values of each attribute is not explicitly given. So, to estimate the number of distinct values, a probability distribution for the distinct values of each attribute may be used. The probability of each distinct value for a specific attribute depends on the occurrence frequency of this attribute. Suppose that, a specific attribute has N distinct values and the distribution of the distinct attribute values is a uniform one. Consequently, the probability of the occurrence of any distinct value of this attribute equals (1/N). Generally, the proposed cost model is based on both of the expected occurrence of each distinct attribute value which has been assumed as a uniform distribution and the number of tuples of the intermediate relations. Commonly, the cost of join operations involved in a complex query having m relations can be estimated as follows.

Assuming that t_i represents an inner node in the join tree for each i in $[1, m-1]$ where m represents the involved number of relations in the join tree. Accordingly, the cost equation of any join tree equivalent to one of candidate QAP_j is given by Eq. (1):

$$\text{Cost}(QAP_j) = \sum_{i=1}^{m-1} n(t_i). \tag{1}$$

Where, $n(t_i)$ is the expected number of tuples in relation t_i which may be a leaf relation or an intermediate relation in the join tree corresponding to a candidate QAP_j.

On the other hand, the length of any intermediate relation t is $n(t)$, where the relation t represents the result of the join operation between the two involved relations (r, s). Such length can be computed using Eq. (2).

$$n(t) = (\text{Cartesian product of relations r and s}) * \text{selectivity factor}. \tag{2}$$

In other words, the expected length $n(t)$ can be given as shown in Eq. (3).

$$n(t) = \frac{n(r)*n(s)}{\prod_{c_j \in C} \min(v(c_j, r), v(c_j, s))}. \tag{3}$$

Where, $n(r)$ and $n(s)$ represent the count of tuples in relations r and s respectively, v (c_j, r) and $v(c_j, s)$ represent the number of distinct values of each joining attribute c_j in relations r and s respectively and c re-presents the set of joining attributes.

As an exceptional case, if there is no joining or common attributes between relations r and s then t will represent the Cartesian product of relations r and s. Consequently the join selectivity factor becomes equal to 1. Thus, Eq. (3) will be reduced to as depicted in Eq. (4).

$$n(t) = n(r) * n(s). \tag{4}$$

The estimated number of distinct values for each attribute A in the resulted relation t from a join operation between two relations r and s is given by Eq. (5).

$$V(A, t) = \begin{cases} V(A, r) : A \in r - s \\ V(A, s) : A \in s - r \\ \min(V(A, r), V(A, s)) : A \in r \, and \, A \in s \end{cases} \tag{5}$$

Where $V(A, r)$ and $V(A, s)$ are the estimated count of distinct values for attribute A in relations r and s respectively.

As depicted in Eq. (5), if an attribute A belongs to both relations r and s then the estimated number of its distinct values in the resulted relation t will be the minimum number of distinct values of attribute A in both r and s.

5 The Proposed Query Optimization Approach

The proposed query optimization approach aims to reach an optimal query access plan from all valid query access plans for a given query statement. It represents an ant colony-based optimization approach. Commonly, the collective and cooperative behavior of ACO emerging from the interaction of different search threads makes it effective in solving combinatorial optimization problems [3]. In fact, ACO algorithm uses a set of artificial ants (individuals) which cooperate to reach the solution of a given problem by exchanging information via pheromone deposited on graph edges. The ACO algorithm is employed to imitate the behavior of real ants and it can be represented as depicted in Algorithm 1.

```
Algorithm 1. Ant colony optimization.

Initialize
Loop
   Each ant is positioned on a starting node
   Loop
      Each ant applies a state transition rule to incrementally
          build a solution and a Local pheromone updating rule
   Until all ants have built a complete solution
   A global pheromone updating rule is applied
Until reach to optimal solution
End.
```

The proposed approach to estimate the optimal QAP by ACO has the following steps:

1. Compute the selectivity factor as shown in Eq. (6).

$$\eta_{ij} = \frac{1}{d_{ij}}. \tag{6}$$

Where, d_{ij} represents the number of tuples resulted from joining relations i and j.
2. Calculate the cardinality of the resulted relation from joining relations i and j using Eq. (7).

$$d_{ij} = \frac{n(i) * n(j)}{\pi_{C_r \in C} \min(V(C_r, i), V(C_r, j))} \tag{7}$$

Where $v(c_r, i)$ indicates the number of distinct values of attribute c_r in the relation i.
3. Compute the new pheromone value τ_{ij} of the inter node representing the result of joining relations i and j using Eq. (8).

$$\tau_{ij} = (1 - P) * \tau_{ij} + \sum_{k=1}^{m} \Delta\tau_{ij}^k. \tag{8}$$

Where, P indicates the evaporation rate, m is the number of ants and $\Delta\tau_{ij}^k$ represents the amount of pheromone change made by ant k.

4. Consequently, Eq. (9) is used to compute the quantity of pheromone $\Delta\tau_{ij}^k$ for a specific ant k.

$$\Delta\tau_{ij}^k = \begin{cases} Q/L_k & \text{if ant k uses edj}(i,j)\text{for} \\ & \text{relations } i,j \text{ in its tour} \\ 0 & \text{otherwise} \end{cases} \tag{9}$$

Where, Q is a constant, and L_k is the count of tuples (effort) of the joining tour constructed by ant k.

5. Finally, Eq. (10) is used to calculate the probability P_{ij}^k of joining relation j with relation i by ant k.

$$P_{ij}^k = \begin{cases} \dfrac{\tau_{ij}^{\alpha} * \eta_{ij}^{\beta}}{\sum_{C_{ij}\in N(_sP)} \tau_{ij}^{\alpha}\cdot\eta_{ij}^{\beta}} & \text{if } C_{ij} \in N(_sP) \\ 0 & \text{otherwise} \end{cases} \tag{10}$$

Where, $N(s^p)$ is the set of feasible access plan edge (i, L) where L is the entities not yet visited by ant k, and both parameters α and β control the relative importance of the pheromone versus the heuristic information η_{ij}.

6 Experimental Results

The results of the proposed approach are compared with that generated by SQL Server 2012. The proposed cost function is taken as a criterion for evaluation and comparison. The software tools that are used in this experiment are SQL Server 2012 enterprise edition, visual C#.net 2012. Northwind database is used in the case study which is a sample database in SQL Server that contains the sales data for a fictitious company that imports and exports food items around the world. The comparative criterion that is used in the evaluation is based on the formula that is used in the cost function. This criterion represents the cost of the selected QAP and which is computed using Eq. (1). The evaluation is based on the cost function as a comparative criterion. To generate an estimated optimal query access plan in SQL Server 2012, the output of the utility "Display Estimated Execution Plan" included in SQL Query Analyzer tool is used. Table 1 shows Northwind database relations with an index or identifier for each. The used join cases are given in Table 2. Table 3 includes the results of the used cases.

As shown in Table 2, it can be noted that in the cases 4, [6–10], 11, [14–17], 19, [20–23] and 25, the proposed query optimization approach has lower cost than SQL Server 2012 query optimizer. That is the relative cost of the proposed approach to SQL Server 2012 is between 0.38 (in case 4) and 1.03 (in case 5). While such relative cost in the cases 13, 18, 20 and 24 the proposed query optimizer has a very little increase than

Table 1. Index of relations

Relation id	Relation name	Relation id	Relation name	Relation id	Relation name
1	Categories	5	Employees	9	OrderDetails
2	Products	6	Orders	10	Territories
3	Suppliers	7	Shippers	11	EmployeeTerritories
4	Customers	8	Region		

Table 2. Comparison between the proposed optimizer and SQL Server optimizer

Case No.	No. of relations	Sequence of inserted relations in the corresponding case	Estimated path by SQL Server 2012	Cost of estimated path in SQL Server 2012	Estimated path by the proposed approach	Cost of estimated path in the proposed approach	Relative cost between the proposed approach and SQL Server 2012	Relative average cost of the proposed approach to SQL server 2012
1		5/9/6/2	6/5/9/2	9300	6/5/9/2	9300	1	
2		4/5/9/6	5/6/4/9	6600	4/6/5/9	6600	1	
3	4	1/9/6/2	1/2/9/6	8080	1/2/9/6	8080	1	88%
4		8/9/6/5	8/9/6/5	108000	5/6/9/8	41300	0.38	
5		5/4/6/7	7/6/5/4	2600	7/5/6/4	2670	1.03	
6		5/11/9/6/2	9/6/2/5/11	26285	6/5/9/2/11	23585	0.90	
7		4/5/9/6/2	6/5/4/9/2	10600	6/5/4/9/2	10600	1	
8		3/1/9/6/2	9/6/2/3/1	16000	2/1/3/9/6	8160	0.51	70%
9	5	4/7/9/6/2	9/6/2/4/7	16000	4/7/6/9/2	10000	0.63	
10		4/8/9/6/2	6/8/4/9/2	95400	6/4/9/2/8	45300	0.47	
11		4/5/11/9/6/2	6/9/2/4/5/11	30285	6/4/5/9/2/11	24885	0.82	
12		3/4/5/9/6/2	6/5/4/9/2/3	14600	6/5/4/9/2/3	14600	1	
13	6	3/4/1/9/6/2	1/2/3/9/6/4	12160	3/1/2/9/6/4	12350	1.01	90%
14		4/7/1/9/6/2	9/6/2/4/1/7	20000	6/4/7/9/2/1	14600	0.73	
15		3/4/8/9/6/2	9/6/2/4/3/8	52000	2/3/9/6/4/8	48080	0.92	
16		1/4/5/11/9/6/2	1/2/9/6/5/11/4	40650	6/4/9/2/1/5/11	31585	0.78	
17		3/4/5/11/9/6/2	9/6/2/4/3/5/11	34285	6/4/9/2/3/5/11	31585	0.92	
18	7	3/4/5/1/9/6/2	2/1/3/9/6/5/4	16160	1/3/2/9/6/5/4	16350	1.01	86%
19		3/4/7/1/9/6/2	9/6/2/4/3/1/7	24000	1/3/2/9/6/7/4	16350	0.68	
20		3/4/8/1/9/6/2	9/6/2/4/3/1/8	52000	2/1/9/6/3/4/8	52080	0.93	
21		1/4/5/11/9/6/2/3	2/1/3/9/6/5/11/	40730	4/5/6/9/2/1/3/11	33545	0.82	
22		3/4/5/11/9/6/2/7	6/9/2/4/3/5/11/	48570	4/5/6/9/2/3/7/11	33545	0.69	
23	8	3/1/5/11/9/6/2/7	6/9/2/3/5/11/1/	58855	2/3/1/9/6/7/5/11	30445	0.52	78%
24		3/4/7/1/9/6/2/5	6/7/5/4/9/2/1/3	19900	2/3/1/9/6/5/4/7	20160	1.01	
25		3/4/8/1/9/6/2/5	9/6/2/4/3/5/1/8	60000	2/3/1/9/6/5/4/8	52160	0.87	

SQL Server optimizer by just 0.01. Also, there are five cases namely 1, 2, 3, 7 and 12 have the same processing costs. On the other hand, the average of relative average cost of the proposed approach to SQL server 2012 equals 83 % which indicates a reduction in processing cost by around 17 %. Also from the results shown in Table 3, it can be noted that, the overall variability range of the proposed optimizer is lower than the overall variability range of SQL Server optimizer. On the other hand, it is clear that the overall mean cost of the proposed optimizer is lower than that in SQL Server 2012 optimizer, and the variability range of the proposed approach is lower than the variability range of SQL Server.

Table 3. Some statistical measurements extracted from the above results

No of relations	Mean		Median		Variability	
	The proposed approach	SQL Server 2012	The proposed approach	SQL Server 2012	The proposed approach	SQL Server 2012
4	13590	26916	8080	8080	2670:41300	2600:108000
5	19529	32857	10600	16000	8160:45300	10600:95400
6	22903	25809	14600	20000	12350:48080	12160:52000
7	29590	34219	31585	34285	16350:52080	16160:56000
8	33971	45611	33545	48570	20160:52160	19900:60000
Average	23916.6	33082.4	20160	24000	2670:52160	2600:108000

7 Conclusion

This paper proposes a novel ant colony-based approach for relational database query optimization. Therefore, the cost of processing join operations dominates the cost of other relational algebraic operations. Accordingly, the proposed query optimization approach emphasizes basically on how to determine the optimal query access plan respecting join operations. The proposed approach transforms each candidate query access plan into a right binary tree which is called a join tree. Therefore the search space of the optimization problem consists of different alternatives of join trees. In consequent, the more complexity of a query statement the more candidate query access plans in the search space of the query optimizer. Accordingly, the proposed approach is based on an evolutionary computing technique to reduce the cost of reaching an optimal query access plan.

An ant colony optimization technique is exploited as a random search procedure to determine the optimal join tree equivalent to the optimal access plan. For simplicity, the proposed approach adopts the complete graph type to represent a given query. The proposed approach is applied on many different cases to check its performance against SQL Server 2012 query optimizer. A comparative study has been presented between the results of the proposed approach and SQL SERVER 2012. The results shows a reduction in average in the processing cost of the obtained optimal query access plan of the proposed approach compared with the obtained one by SQL Server 2012 query optimizer.

8 Future Work

The proposed approach can be extended to consider the physical optimizer rather than the logical one. Also, it is worthy to study the relative effectiveness of using the constrained graph type rather than the unconstrained one used in the proposed approach.

References

1. Chaudhuri, S.: An Overview of Query Optimization in Relational Systems, pp. 34–43. ACM Press, New York (1998)
2. Dong, H., Liang, Y.: Genetic Algorithms for Large Join Query Optimization, pp. 1211–1218. ACM, New York (2007)
3. Hlaing, Z., Khine, A.: Solving traveling salesman problem by using improved ant colony optimization algorithm. Int. J. Inf. Educ. Technol. 1(5), 404–409 (2011)
4. Jin, L., Li, C.: Selectivity estimation for fuzzy string predicates in large data sets. In: Proceedings of the 31st VLD Conference, Trondheim, Norway, pp. 397–408 (2005)
5. Krynicki, K., Jean, J.: AntElements: an extensible and scalable ant colony optimization middleware. In: GECCO 2015, Madrid, Spain, 11–15 July 2015, pp. 1109–1116 (2015)
6. Mahmoud, F., Shaban, S., Abd El-Naby, H.: A proposed query optimizer based on genetic algorithms. Egypt. Comput. J. 37(1) 1–22 (2010)
7. Mavrovouniotis, M., Müller, F., Yang, S.: An ant colony optimization based memetic algorithm for the dynamic travelling salesman problem. In: GECCO 2015, pp. 49–56 (2015)
8. Mishra, P., Eich, M.H.: Join processing in relational databases. ACM Comput. Surv. 24, 63–113 (1992)
9. Steinbrunn, M., Moerkotte, G., Kemper, A.: Heuristic and randomized optimization for the join ordering problem. VLDB J. 6, 191–208 (1997)
10. Yu, P.S., Cornell, D.W.: Buffer management based on return on consumption in a multi-query environment. VLDB J. 2, 1–37 (1993)
11. Yu, X., Chen, W., Zhang, J.: A set-based comprehensive learning particle swarm optimization with decomposition for multiobjective traveling salesman problem. In: GECCO 2015, Madrid, Spain, 11– 15 July 2015, pp. 89–96 (2015)
12. Selinger, P.G., Astrahan, M.M., Chamberlin, D.D., Lorie, R.A., Price, T.G.: Access Path Selection in a Relational Database Management System. ACM Inc. (1979)
13. Favaretto, D., Moretti, E., Pellegrini, P.: An ant colony system approach for variants of the traveling salesman problem with time windows. J. Inf. Optim. Sci. 27(1), 35–54 (2006)
14. Ioannidis, Y.E., Kang, Y.C.: Randomized algorithms for optimizing large join queries. In: ACM (1990)
15. Swami, A.: Optimization of large join queries: combining heuristics and combinatorial techniques. In: ACM, SIGMOD Conference, pp. 367–376 (1989)
16. Ioannidis, Y.E., Wong, E.: Query optimization by simulated annealing. In: ACM, SIGMOD Conference, pp. 9–22 (1987)
17. Lanzelotte, R., Valduries, P., Zait, M.: On the effectiveness of optimization search strategies for parallel execution spaces. In: Proceedings of the Conference on Very Large Databases, pp. 493–504 (1993)
18. Galindo-Legaria, C., Pellenkoft, A., Kersten, M.: Fast, randomized join-order selection why use transformations? In: Proceedings of the 20th International Conference on Very Large Databases, pp. 85–95 (1994)

A Range Query Processing Algorithm Hiding Data Access Patterns in Outsourced Database Environment

Hyeong-Il Kim, Hyeong-Jin Kim, and Jae-Woo Chang$^{(\boxtimes)}$

Department of Computer Engineering,
Jeonbuk National University, Jeonju, South Korea
{melipion,yeon_hui4,jwchang}@jbnu.ac.kr

Abstract. Research on secure range query processing techniques in outsourced databases has been spotlighted with the development of cloud computing. The existing range query processing schemes can preserve the data privacy and the query privacy of a user. However, they fail to hide the data access patterns while processing a range query. So, in this paper we propose a secure range query processing algorithm which hides data access patterns. Our method filters unnecessary data using the encrypted index. We show from our performance analysis that the proposed range query processing algorithm can efficiently process a query while hiding the data access patterns.

Keywords: Database outsourcing · Database encryption · Encrypted index structure · Range query processing · Hiding data access patterns

1 Introduction

A database outsourcing has been spotlighted as a new paradigm for the database management. In the database outsourcing environment, a data owner can outsource his/her database and their managements to a cloud. By outsourcing the database, the data owner (DO) can flexibly utilize the resource of the cloud, thus reducing the management costs. The cloud not only stores the database, but also provides an authorized user with querying services on the outsourced database.

However, if the original database is outsourced to the cloud, the cloud or an attacker can abuse the private information stored in the database. For example, if a real estate agent outsources his/her original database to the cloud, the cloud or an attacker can sell the property information to the other agents. In addition, the private information of a user such as preference and disease can be revealed to the attacker. For example, if a user sends a query with his/her location information to enjoy location-based services, the attacker can find places where the user frequently visit.

Meanwhile, a range query is one of the most typical query types which is widely used as a baseline scheme in various fields. However, some privacy threat can occur when processing the range query. This is because the range information is closely related to the interest and preference of a user. Therefore, researches on the range query processing methods which preserve the data privacy and the query privacy have been

© Springer International Publishing Switzerland 2016
Y. Tan and Y. Shi (Eds.): DMBD 2016, LNCS 9714, pp. 434–446, 2016.
DOI: 10.1007/978-3-319-40973-3_44

performed. The existing secure range query processing schemes fall into two categories. First, the database transformation based schemes [1, 2] convert the original database before outsourcing. However, they are vulnerable to various attacks such as chosen plaintext attack. Second, the database encryption based schemes [3–8] encrypt the database before outsourcing. Therefore, they can preserve the data privacy and the query privacy from an attacker.

However, there is no work that hides the data access patterns during processing the range query. The data access patterns are the good source to derive the actual data items and the private information of a querying issuer. This is the critical problem because the data access patterns can be exposed even though the data and query are encrypted [9]. To hide the data access pattern from the cloud, some researches [3, 4] locate an encrypted index at the user side. However, the user who has the relatively low performance computing resources should retrieve the index for the query processing. To the best of knowledge, a scheme proposed in [10] is the only work that hides the data access patterns over the encrypted database. However, the scheme only supports kNN query processing and requires high computation cost.

To solve the problem, in this paper we propose a new range query processing algorithm on the encrypted database. Our method filters unnecessary data using the encrypted index. Our method preserves data privacy and query privacy. In addition, our method also conceals the data access patterns while supporting efficient query processing. Our key contributions can be summarized into three folds. (i) We present a framework for outsourcing both the encrypted database and the encrypted index. (ii) We propose a new range query processing algorithm using an encrypted index that conceals the data access patterns while supporting efficient query processing. (iii) We also present an extensive experimental evaluation of our scheme under the various parameter settings to verify the efficiency of our proposed scheme.

The rest of the paper is organized as follows. Section 2 introduces the existing secure range query processing algorithms. In Sect. 3, we describe the overall system architecture and present various secure protocols used for our proposed range query processing algorithm. Our proposed secure range query processing algorithm based on the encrypted index is presented in Sect. 4. Section 5 shows the performance analysis of our secure range query processing algorithm. Finally, we conclude the paper with some future research directions in Sect. 6.

2 Related Work

2.1 Secure Range Query Processing Schemes

The existing secure range query processing schemes can be categorized into two folds; database transformation based schemes and database encryption based schemes. Database transformation based schemes are as follows. M. Yiu et al. [1] proposed HSD* (hierarchical space division) scheme. HSD* transforms the database by converting the distribution of the data and inserting errors into the data by using secure hash function. H. Kim et al. [2] proposed a shear-based transformation scheme to prevent the information leakage caused by the data proximity. However, the cloud can know values of a transformed database in both schemes. By using that, an attacker can infer the original data values with some information such as data distribution.

Database encryption based schemes can solve the problem of the database transformation based schemes by encrypting the original data. M. Yiu et al. [1] proposed the cryptographic transformation (CRT) method which utilizes encrypted R-tree index. However, the CRT has a drawback that the most of the computation is performed at the user side rather than the cloud. In addition, data access pattern is not preserved as the user hierarchically requests the required R-tree nodes to the cloud. H. Hu et al. [3] proposed a method based on provably secure privacy homomorphism encryption scheme. However, in this scheme, a user must process a query together with the cloud because the user has an access to an encrypted index. Moreover, the scheme cannot hide the data access patterns. A scheme proposed by B. Hore et al. [4] partitions the data into a set of buckets and builds indices for buckets. However, this scheme forces a data owner to store and to search the indices locally, rather than at the cloud. P. Wang et al. [5] proposed a scheme which utilizes the encrypted version of R-tree. However, the scheme has a shortcoming that the data access patterns are revealed because the cloud returns a set of nodes which intersect the query range. B. Wang et al. [6] proposed an encrypted R-tree based range query processing scheme by using Point Predicate Encryption (PPE). However, as the authors mentioned in [6], the scheme reveals the values of each query to the cloud. In addition, the data access patterns are revealed to a cloud because all the identifiers of the data satisfying the query are returned by the cloud. R. Li et al. [7] proposed a range query processing algorithm that achieves index indistinguishability. For this, they devised a PB-tree whose node is represented using a Bloom filter. However, this scheme probabilistically leaks the data access patterns because retrieved nodes are revealed to the cloud. Most recently, Kim et al. [8] proposed a range query processing scheme using the Hilbert-curve order based index. The scheme can preserve the query privacy because a data group generated by the Hilbert-curve order is considered as a query processing unit. However, a user is in charge of index traversal during the query processing step.

2.2   Preliminaries

Paillier Crypto System. The Paillier cryptosystem [11] is an additive homomorphic and probabilistic asymmetric encryption scheme for public key cryptography. The public key pk for encryption is given by (N, g), where N is a product of two large prime numbers p and q, and g is in $\mathbf{Z}^*_{N^2}$. The secret key sk for decryption is given by (p, q). Let $E()$ denote the encryption function and $D()$ denote the decryption function. The Paillier crypto system has the following properties. (i) Homomorphic addition: The product of two ciphertexts $E(m_1)$ and $E(m_2)$ results in the encryption of the sum of their plaintexts m_1 and m_2; $E(m_1 + m_2) = E(m_1)*E(m_2) \bmod N^2$. (ii) Homomorphic multiplication: The bth power of ciphertext $E(m_1)$ results in the encryption of the product of b and m_1; $E(m_1*b) = E(m_1)^b \bmod N^2$. (iii) Semantic security: Encrypting the same plaintexts with the same public key results in distinct ciphertexts.

Adversarial Models. There are two main types of adversaries, *semi-honest* and *malicious* [12]. In our system, we assume that the clouds act as adversaries. In the *semi-honest* adversarial model, the clouds correctly follow the protocol specification, but try to use the intermediate data to learn more information that are not allowed to them. Meanwhile, in the *malicious* adversarial model, the clouds can arbitrarily deviate from the protocol specification, according to the adversary's instructions. In general, if a protocol has proven that it is secure against the *malicious* adversaries, the protocol ensures that no adversarial attack can succeed. However, protocols against malicious adversaries are too inefficient to be used in practice. However, protocols under the *semi-honest* adversaries are efficient in practice and can be used to design protocols against malicious adversaries. Therefore, by following the work done in [10], we also consider the semi-honest adversarial model in this paper.

3   System Architecture and Secure Protocols

3.1   System Architecture

Figure 1 shows the overall system architecture for our query processing scheme on the encrypted database. The system consists of four components: data owner (*DO*), authorized user (*AU*), and two clouds (C_A and C_B, respectively). The *DO* owns the original database (*T*) of n records. A record t_i ($1 \leq i \leq n$) consists of m attributes (or columns) and j^{th} attribute value of t_i is denoted by $t_{i,j}$. To provide the indexing on *T*, the *DO* partitions *T* by using kd-tree. If we retrieve the tree structure in hierarchical manner, the access pattern can be disclosed. So, we only consider the leaf nodes of the kd-tree and all the leaf nodes are retrieved once during the query processing. Let h denote the level of the constructed kd-tree and F be the fanout of each leaf node. The total number of leaf nodes is 2^{h-1}. From now on, a node means a leaf node. Each node is represented as the lower bound $lb_{z,j}$ and the upper bound $ub_{z,j}$ for $1 \leq z \leq 2^{h-1}$ and $1 \leq j \leq m$. Each node stores the identifiers (*id*) of data being located inside the node region.

To preserve the data privacy, the *DO* encrypts *T* attribute-wise using the public key (*pk*) of the Paillier cryptosystem [11] before outsourcing the database. So, the *DO* generates $E(t_{i,j})$ for $1 \leq i \leq n$ and $1 \leq j \leq m$. The *DO* also encrypts the kd-tree

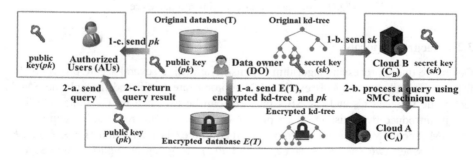

Fig. 1. The overall system architecture

nodes to support efficient query processing. The *lb* and the *ub* of each node are encrypted attribute-wise, so $E(lb_{z,j})$ and $E(ub_{z,j})$ are generated for $1 \leq z \leq 2^{h-1}$ and $1 \leq j \leq m$.

We assume that C_A and C_B are non-colluding and semi-honest (or honest-but-curious) clouds. So, they correctly perform the given protocols and do not exchange unpermitted data. However, they may try to obtain additional information from the intermediate data during executing their own protocol. This assumption is not new as mentioned in [10, 13] and has been used in the related problem domains (e.g., [14]). Especially, as most of the cloud services are provided by renowned IT companies, collusion between them which will damage their reputation is improbable [10].

To support range query processing over the encrypted database, a secure multiparty computation (SMC) is required between C_A and C_B. For this, the *DO* sends the encrypted database and a decryption key to different clouds. In particular, the *DO* outsources the encrypted database and its encrypted index to the C_A with *pk* while the *sk* is sent to the C_B. The encrypted index includes the region information of each node in cipher-text and the *ids* of data that are located inside the node in plain-text. The *DO* also sends *pk* to *AUs* to enable them to encrypt a query. At query time, an *AU* first encrypts a query attribute-wise. Then, the *AU* sends $E(q.lb_j)$ and $E(q.ub_j)$ for $1 \leq j \leq m$ to C_A. C_A processes the query with the help of C_B and returns a query result to the *AU*.

As an example, assume that an *AU* has 8 data in two-dimensional space (e.g., x-axis and y-axis) as depicted in Fig. 2. The data are partitioned into 4 nodes (e.g., node₁–node₄) for a kd-tree. The *DO* encrypts each data and the information of each node attribute-wise. For example, t_1 is encrypted as $E(t_1) = \{E(2), E(1)\}$.

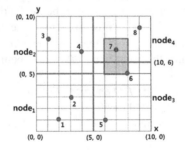

Fig. 2. An example in two-dimensional space

3.2   Secure Protocols

Our range query processing algorithm is constructed using several secure protocols. In this section, all the protocols except SBN protocol are performed through the SMC technique between C_A and C_B. SBN protocol can be executed by C_A alone. We first briefly introduce two existing secure protocols that we adopt from the literatures [10, 15]. SM (Secure Multiplication) protocol [10] computes the encryption of $a \times b$, i.e., $E(a \times b)$, when two encrypted data $E(a)$ and $E(b)$ are given as inputs. SBD (Secure Bit-Decomposition) protocol [15] computes the encryptions of binary representation of the encrypted input $E(a)$. The output is $[a] = < E(a_1), ..., E(a_l) >$ where a_1 and a_l denote the most and least significant bits of a, respectively. In this paper, we use symbol $[a]$ to denote the encryptions of binary representation. Meanwhile, we propose new secure protocols used for our range query processing algorithm.

SBN Protocol. SBN (Secure Bit-Not) protocol performs the bit-not operation when an encrypted bit $E(a)$ is given as input. The output of SBN $E(\sim a)$ is computed by $E(a)^{N-1} \times E(1)$. Note that "-1" is equivalent to "$N-1$" under Z_N.

SCMP Protocol. When $[u]$ and $[v]$ are given as inputs, SCMP (Secure Compare) protocol returns $E(1)$ if $u \leq v$, $E(0)$ otherwise. We devise SCMP by modifying SMIN [10] protocol which outputs $[min]$ between two inputs $[u]$ and $[v]$. The variables generated during SMIN can be categorized into two folds. One set of the variables include hints about what the minimum value is. Another set of the variables is used to securely extract the minimum value. Because we only need the information about whether u is smaller or not, we only compute the former (e.g., W, G, H, Φ, L, L'). The goal of designing SCMP is to make the returned value from C_B be exactly opposite for the same inputs, based on the functionality selected by C_A. SMIN can achieve this goal when two inputs have different values. However, if two values are the same, SMIN fails to attain the goal.

To solve this problem, we design SCMP as follows. First, C_A appends $E(0)$ to the least significant bits of $[u]$ and $E(1)$ to the least significant bits of $[v]$. This makes $u \leftarrow u \times 2$ and $v \leftarrow v \times 2+1$. When a value is greater than another, SCMP does not affect the large and small relationship between u and v. Only when two values are the same, SCMP makes u smaller than v. By doing so, SCMP can solve the security problem of SMIN that C_B can notice whether the input values are same or not. In SMIN, only if two inputs have the same values, $D(L')$ does not include 1 or 0.

Second, C_A randomly chooses one functionality between $F_0{:}u > v$ and $F_1{:}v > u$. The selected functionality is oblivious to C_B. Then, C_A computes $E(u_i \times v_i)$ using SM and W_i, depending on the selected functionality. In particular, if $F_0{:}u > v$ is selected, C_A computes $W_i = E(u_i) \times E(u_i \times v_i)^{N-1} = E(u_i \times (1-v_i))$. If $F_1{:}v > u$ is selected, C_A computes $W_i = E(v_i) \times E(v_i \times u_i)^{N-1} = E(v_i \times (1-u_i))$. For $F_0{:}u > v$, $W_i = E(1)$ when $u_i > v_i$, and $W_i = E(0)$ otherwise. Similarly, for $F_1{:}v > u$, $W_i = E(1)$ when $v_i > u_i$, and $W_i = E(0)$ otherwise.

Third, C_A performs bit-xor between $E(u_i)$ and $E(v_i)$ and stores the result into G_i. C_A computes $H_i = (H_{i-1})^{r_i} \times G_i$ and $\Phi_i = E(-1) \times H_i$ where $H_0 = E(0)$. Here, r_i is a random number in Z_N. Assume that j is the index of the first appearance of $E(1)$ in G_i. j means the first position where the minimum value between u and v can be determined.

Fourth, C_A computes $L_i = W_i \times \Phi_i^{r_i}$ where L_i involves the information about which value is smaller between u and v at j. C_A generates L' by permuting L by using a random permutation function π_1 and sends L' to C_B.

Fifth, C_B decrypts L' attribute-wise and checks whether there exists 0 in L_i' for $1 \leq i \leq l$. If so, C_B sets α as 1, and 0 otherwise. After encrypting α, C_B sends $E(\alpha)$ to C_A. Table 1 shows the values of $E(\alpha)$ returned by C_B for every case. The returned values are exactly opposite with the selected functionalities for every case, which coincides with the goal of the designing the SCMP protocol.

Table 1. Value of E(α) returned by C_B

		Selected functionality	
		$F_0: u > v$	$F_1: v > u$
Actual relationship between u and v	$u > v$	$E(1)$	$E(0)$
	$v > u$	$E(0)$	$E(1)$
	$u = v$	$E(0)$	$E(1)$

Finally, C_A performs $E(\alpha) \leftarrow SBN(E(\alpha))$ only when the selected functionality is F_0: $u > v$ and returns the $E(\alpha)$. So, the final $E(\alpha)$ is $E(1)$ when $u \leq v$, regardless of the selected functionality. Note that the only information decrypted during SCMP is L' which is seen by C_B. However, C_B cannot obtain additional information from L' because the selected functionality is oblivious to C_B. Therefore, SCMP is secure under the semi-honest model.

SRO Protocol. When the encryptions of binary representation of two ranges [$range_1$] and [$range_2$] are given as inputs, SRO (Secure Range Overlapping) protocol returns E (1) when $range_1$ overlaps $range_2$, $E(0)$ otherwise. Assuming that both $range_1$ and $range_2$ consist of [lb_j] and [ub_j], where $1 \leq j \leq m$, the two ranges overlap only if two following conditions are satisfied; (i) $E(range_1.lb_j) \leq E(range_2.ub_j)$, (ii) $E(range_2.lb_i) \leq E(range_1.ub_j)$, for $1 \leq j \leq m$. These conditions can be determined by using SCMP.

The overall procedure of SRO is as follows. C_A initializes $E(\alpha)$ as $E(1)$. C_A obtains $E(\alpha')$ by performing SCMP([$range_1.lb_j$], [$range_2.ub_j$]) and updates $E(\alpha)$ by executing SM($E(\alpha)$, $E(\alpha')$). C_A repeats this step for $1 \leq j \leq m$. Similarly, C_A computes $E(\alpha')$ by performing SCMP([$range_2.lb_j$], [$range_1.ub_j$]) and updates $E(\alpha)$ by executing SM($E(\alpha)$, $E(\alpha')$) for all attribute values. Only when all conditions are satisfied, the value of $E(\alpha)$ remains $E(1)$. Finally, C_B returns the final $E(\alpha)$. Note that no decryption is performed during SRO except performing SCMP and SM protocols. So, SRO is secure under the semi-honest model because the securities of both SCMP and SM have been verified.

SPE Protocol. When the encryptions of binary representation of a point [p] and [$range$] are given as inputs, SPE (Secure Point Enclosure) protocol returns $E(1)$ when p is inside the range or on a boundary of the range, $E(0)$ otherwise. The overall procedure of SPE is identical to SRO. This is because if a low bound and an upper bound of a range is the same, the range can be considered as a point. However, to make the relations between inputs clear, we also define SPE protocol. However, we omit the detailed explanation of SPE because it is similar to SRO.

4   Secure Range Query Processing Algorithm

In this section, we present our secure range query processing algorithm (SRange$_I$) using the kd-tree on the encrypted database. SRange$_I$ consists of two steps; encrypted kd-tree search step and result retrieval step. In the encrypted kd-tree search step, the algorithm filters out the data that are stored in the kd-tree nodes which does not overlaps the query range. In the result retrieval step, the algorithm refines the candidate results to find the actual query results.

4.1 Step 1: Encrypted kd-tree Search Step

To support efficient range query processing, we newly design the encrypted index search scheme. Our scheme does not reveal the retrieved nodes of the index for query processing while extracting data in the nodes which overlaps the query range. In this paper, we consider kd-tree as an index structure because it is suitable for indexing multi-dimensional data. However, we emphasize that our index search scheme can be applied to any other indices whose entities (e.g., nodes) store region information.

The procedure of the encrypted kd-tree search step is as follows. First, C_A computes $[q.lb_j]$ and $[q.ub_j]$ for $1 \leq j \leq m$ by using SBD. C_A also computes $[node_z.lb_j]$ and $[node_z.ub_j]$ for $1 \leq z \leq num_{node}$ and $1 \leq j \leq m$ by using SBD where num_{node} is the total number of kd-tree leaf nodes. Then, C_A securely finds nodes which overlap the query range by executing $E(\alpha_z) \leftarrow SRO([q], [node_z])$ for $1 \leq z \leq num_{node}$. Note that the nodes with $E(\alpha_z) = E(1)$ overlap the query range, but both C_A and C_B cannot know whether the value of each $E(\alpha_z)$ is $E(1)$. This is because Paillier encryption provides a semantic security. Second, C_A generates $E(\alpha')$ by permuting $E(\alpha)$ using a random permutation function π and sends $E(\alpha')$ to C_B. For example, SRO returns $E(\alpha) = \{E(0), E(0), E(1), E(1)\}$ in Fig. 2 as the query range overlaps the $node_3$ and $node_4$. Assuming that π permutes data in reverse way, C_A sends the $E(\alpha') = \{E(1), E(1), E(0), E(0)\}$ to C_B.

Third, upon receiving the $E(\alpha')$, C_B obtains α' by decrypting the $E(\alpha')$ and counts the number of α' with the value of 1. The number of $\alpha' = 1$ is stored into c. Here, c means the number of nodes that overlaps the query range. Fourth, C_B creates c number of node groups (e.g., NG). C_B assigns to each NG a node with $\alpha' = 1$ and $num_{node}/c-1$ nodes with $\alpha' = 0$. Then, C_B computes NG' by randomly shuffling the ids of nodes in each NG and sends NG' to C_A. For example, C_B can know that $node_1$ and $node_2$ overlap the query range because $\alpha' = \{1, 1, 0, 0\}$. However, C_B cannot correctly point out ids of the nodes because the values in α' were permutated by C_A. As two node groups are required, C_B assigns $node_1$ and $node_2$ to NG_1 and NG_2, respectively. In this example, $num_{node}/c-1$ is calculated as 1 because $num_{node} = 4$ and $c = 2$. So, C_B randomly assigns a node to each node group. Assume that C_B assigns $node_3$ to NG_1 and $node_4$ to NG_2. So, $NG_1 = \{1, 3\}$ and $NG_2 = \{2, 4\}$. Then, C_B randomly shuffles the ids of the nodes in each NG. The result can be like $NG_1' = \{1, 3\}$ and $NG_2' = \{4, 2\}$.

Fifth, C_A obtains NG^* by permuting the ids of nodes using π^{-1} in each NG'. In each NG^*, there exists only one node overlapping the query range. However, C_A cannot know the correct id of the node because the ids of the nodes are shuffled by C_B. Sixth, C_A gets access to one datum in each node (e.g., $node_z$) for each NG^* and performs $E(t'_{i,j}) \leftarrow SM (node_z.t_{s,j}, E(\alpha_z))$ for $1 \leq s \leq F$ and $1 \leq j \leq m$. Here, α_z is the outputs of SPE, corresponding to the $node_z$. The data in the nodes overlapping the query range is not affected by SM because the $E(\alpha_z)$ values of the nodes are $E(1)$. However, the data in other nodes become $E(0)$ by performing SM because the $E(\alpha_z)$ values of the nodes are $E(0)$. If a node has the less number of data than F, it performs SM by using $E(max)$, instead of using $node_z.t_{s,j}$, where $E(max)$ is the largest value in the domain. If the node does not overlap the query range, the result of SM becomes $E(0)$. If the node overlaps the query range, the result of SM becomes $E(max)$. However, it does not affect the query accuracy because the data is pruned in the later query processing step.

When C_A accesses one datum from every node in a NG^*, C_A performs a homomorphic addition such as $E(cand_{cnt,j}) \leftarrow \prod_{i=1}^{num} E(t'_{i,j})$, where num means the total number of nodes in the selected NG^*. By doing so, a datum in the node overlapping the query range is securely extracted without revealing the data access patterns. Finally, by repeating these steps, all the data in the nodes are safely stored into the $E(cand_{cnt,j})$. Here, cnt means the total number of data extracted during the index search. As an example, C_A obtains $NG_1^* = \{2, 4\}$ and $NG_2^* = \{1, 3\}$ by permuting $NG_1' = \{3, 1\}$ and $NG_2' = \{4, 2\}$ using π^{-1}. C_A accesses one datum in each node, for each NG^*, respectively. In particular, C_A accesses $E(t_3)$ in $node_2$, $E(t_7)$ in $node_4$ for NG_1^*. The results of SM using $E(t_3)$, e.g., $E(t'_1)$, are $E(0)$ for every attribute because the $E(\alpha)$ value of the corresponding node (e.g., $node_2$) is $E(0)$. However, the results of SM using $E(t_7)$, e.g., $E(t'_2)$, become $E(7)$ for both x and y dimensions. So, the results of the attribute-wise homomorphic addition of $E(t'_1)$ and $E(t'_2)$ are $E(7)$ and $E(7)$ for x and y dimension, respectively. Thus, one datum $E(t_7)$ in $node_4$ is securely extracted into E $(cand_1)$. Similarly, values of $E(t_8)$ can be securely extracted into $E(cand_2)$ by using E (t_4) and $E(t_8)$. In the same way, for NG_2^*, all the data in the $node_3$ (e.g., $E(t_5)$ and $E(t_6)$) are securely extracted into $E(cand_3)$ and $E(cand_4)$, respectively.

4.2   Step 2: Result Retrieval Step

The result retrieval step finds all the data inside the query region among the $E(cand)$ extracted in step 1. The procedure of the result retrieval step is as follows. First, C_A computes $[cand_{i,j}]$ for $1 \leq i \leq cnt$ and $1 \leq j \leq m$ by using SBD. Here, cnt is equal to $F \times$ (# of node groups). Second, C_A securely finds data inside the query range by executing $E(\alpha_i) \leftarrow SPE([cand_i], [q])$ for $1 \leq i \leq cnt$. Note that the data with $E(\alpha_i) = E$ (1) are included in the query range. However, both C_A and C_B cannot know whether the value of each $E(\alpha_i)$ is $E(1)$ because Paillier encryption provides a semantic security. For example, when $E(cand) = \{E(t_7), E(t_8), E(t_5), E(t_6)\}$ is given from the step 1, SPE returns $E(\alpha) = E(1)$ for $E(t_7)$ and $E(t_6)$, which are inside the query range. However, $E(\alpha) = E(0)$ is returned by SPE for $E(t_8)$ and $E(t_5)$ that are outside the query range.

Meanwhile, the data with $E(\alpha) = E(1)$ should be sent to the user. To minimize the computation cost at the user side, it is required to send decrypted results. However, if the cloud decrypts the results, the actual content of the data are revealed to the cloud. So, the algorithm returns the result as follows. Third, C_A computes $E(\gamma_{i,j}) = E(result_i) \times E(r_{i,j})$ for $1 \leq i \leq cnt$ and $1 \leq j \leq m$ by generating random values $r_{i,j}$. C_A generates $E(\alpha')$, $E(\gamma')$, and r' by permuting $E(\alpha)$, $E(\gamma)$, and r, using a random permutation function π_1. Then, C_A sends $E(\alpha')$ and $E(\gamma')$ to C_B, and r' to AU, respectively. Fourth, C_B decrypts $E(\alpha_i')$ and $E(\gamma'_{i,j})$ for $1 \leq i \leq cnt$ and $1 \leq j \leq m$. Then, C_B sends α' and γ' to AU. Meanwhile, C_B cannot know the exact ids corresponding to the final results because the α' and γ' are permuted by C_A. Finally, AU computes $\gamma'_{i,j} - r'_{i,j}$ for $1 \leq i \leq cnt$ and $1 \leq j \leq m$ only for the corresponding $\alpha_i = 1$.

5   Performance Analysis

There is no existing range query processing schemes that hides the data access patterns. So, in this section, we compare our $SRange_I$ with a baseline algorithm $SRange_B$. $SRange_B$ only performs result retrieval step by considering all the data without using an index. So, we can analyze the effect of the using the proposed index search scheme. We do the performance analysis of both schemes in terms of query processing time with different parameters. We used the Paillier cryptosystem to encrypt a database for both schemes. We implemented both schemes by using C ++. Experiments were performed on a Linux machine with an Intel Xeon E3-1220v3 4-Core 3.10 GHz and 32 GB RAM running Ubuntu 14.04.2. To examine the performance under various parameters, we randomly generated synthetic datasets by following [10]. We used the parameters shown in Table 2. We set the size of the range as 0.1 which means the relational portion of the range compared to the total domain size (i.e., l) in each dimension where $l = 12$.

Table 2. Experimental parameters

Parameters	Values	Default value
Total number of data (n)	2 k, 4 k, 6 k, 8 k, 10 k, 15 k, 20 k	6 k
Level of kd-tree (h)	5, 6, 7, 8, 9	7
# of attributes (columns) (m)	2, 3, 4, 5, 6	6
Encryption key size (K)	512, 1024	1024

Figure 3 shows the performance of $SRange_I$ for varying the level of kd-tree. Figure 3(a) shows the performance of $SRange_I$ for varying h and n for $K = 512$. Overall, as the n becomes larger, the query processing time increases. Meanwhile, when the n increases, the h that shows the best performance becomes larger. For example, $h = 6$ show the best performance when $n = 2$ k while $h = 8$ show the best performance when $n = 10$ k. For all cases, when the h is increased, the query processing time decreases for the smaller h while the query processing time increases for the larger h. This result comes from the following properties. As the h increases, the total number of leaf nodes grows and the more computation cost is required for SRO to find the relevant nodes. However, the number of data in a node becomes smaller as h increases. So, the less computation cost is required to execute SPE as h increases. Thus, there exists the trade-off between the computation time and the h. The trend is similar when $K = 1024$ as shown in Fig. 3(b). With the same parameter settings, the query processing time increases almost by a factor of 3 when K changes from 512 to 1024.

Figure 3(c) shows the performance of $SRange_I$ for varying h and m for $K = 512$. When h is increased, a similar trend is observed as shown in Fig. 3(a). However, as the m becomes larger, the query processing time linearly increases. This is because all the protocols including SRO and SPE should process additional data as the m increases. The trend is similar when K = 1024 as shown in Fig. 3(d). With the same parameter settings, the query processing time increases almost by a factor of 3 when K changes from 512 to 1024. Overall, because $SRange_I$ shows good performance when $h = 7$ in our parameter setting, we set the h as 7 in next performance evaluation.

444   H.-I. Kim et al.

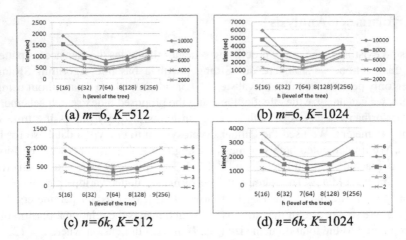

(a) *m*=6, *K*=512   (b) *m*=6, *K*=1024

(c) *n*=6k, *K*=512   (d) *n*=6k, *K*=1024

Fig. 3. Performance of SRange_I for varying *h* (Color figure online)

Figure 4(a) shows the performance of both schemes in logarithmic scale varying the *n* for m = 6 and *K* = 1024. Overall, as the *n* becomes larger, the query processing time linearly increases for both schemes. This is because, for SRange_I, the number of data stored in each node increases as the *n* grows. So, the computation costs of SPE linearly increase. In case of SRange_B, because the scheme considers all the data, the computation time is linearly increased as *n* increases. Overall, SRange_I shows much better performance than SRange_B because SRange_I filters irrelevant data by using the index. On average, SRange_I shows about 25 times better performance than SRange_B.

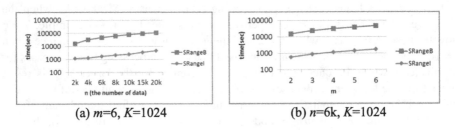

(a) *m*=6, *K*=1024   (b) *n*=6k, *K*=1024

Fig. 4. Comparison of SRange_I and SRange_B (Color figure online)

Meanwhile, Fig. 4(b) shows the performance of both schemes in logarithmic scale varying the *m* for *n* = 6 k and *K* = 1024. Overall, as the *m* becomes larger, the query processing time linearly increases for both schemes. This is because the more values need to be computed for both schemes as the *m* increases. However, on average, SRange_I shows about 27 times better performance than SRange_B.

6   Conclusion

With the popularity of the outsourced databases, researches on the range query processing methods over the encrypted database have been actively performed. However, there is no work that hides the data access patterns. To solve the problem, we proposed a secure range query processing algorithm. Our method preserves data privacy and query privacy, and conceals the data access patterns. To support efficient query processing, we used an encrypted index to filter out unnecessary data without revealing data access patterns. We showed from our performance analysis that our algorithm achieves efficient query processing performance. As a future work, we plan to expand our work to support other query types, such as Top-k and skyline queries.

Acknowledgements. This work was supported by the ICT R&D program of MSIP/IITP (IITP-2015-R0113-15-0005). This work was also supported by the Human Resource Training Program for Regional Innovation and Creativity through the Ministry of Education and National Research Foundation of Korea (NRF-2014H1C1A1065816).

References

1. Yiu, M.L., Ghinita, G., Jensen, C.S., Kalnis, P.: Enabling search services on outsourced private spatial data. VLDB J. **19**(3), 363–384 (2010)
2. Kim, H., Hossain, A., Chang, J.: A spatial transformation scheme supporting data privacy and query integrity for security of outsourced databases. Secur. Commun. Netw. **7**(10), 1498–1509 (2014)
3. Hu, H., Xu, J., Ren, C., Choi, B.: Processing private queries over untrusted data cloud through privacy homomorphism. In: Proceedings of the ICDE, pp. 601–612 (2011)
4. Hore, B., Mehrotra, S., Canim, M., Kantarcioglu, M.: Secure multidimensional range queries over outsourced data. VLDB J. **21**(3), 333–358 (2012)
5. Wang, P., Ravishankar, C.V.: Secure and efficient range queries on outsourced databases using R-trees. In: Proceedings of the ICDE, pp. 314–325 (2013)
6. Wang, B., Hou, Y., Li, M., Wang, H., Li, H.: Maple: scalable multi-dimensional range search over encrypted cloud data with tree-based index. In: Proceedings of the ASIACCS, pp. 111–122 (2014)
7. Rui, L., Liu, A.X., Wang, A.L., Bruhadeshwar, B.: Fast range query processing with strong privacy protection for cloud computing. VLDB Endowment **7**(14), 1953–1964 (2014)
8. Kim, H., Hong, S., Chang, J.: Hilbert curve-based cryptographic transformation scheme for spatial query processing on outsourced private data. Data Knowl. Eng. (2015). doi:10.1016/j.datak.2015.05.002
9. Islam, M.S., Kuzu, M., Kantarcioglu, M.: Access pattern disclosure on searchable encryption: ramification, attack and mitigation. In: Proceedings of the Network and Distributed System Security Symposium (2012)
10. Elmehdwi, Y., Samanthula, B.K., Jiang, W.: Secure k-nearest neighbor query over encrypted data in outsourced environments. In: Proceedings of the ICDE, pp. 664–675 (2014)
11. Paillier, P.: Public-Key cryptosystems based on composite degree residuosity classes. In: Stern, J. (ed.) EUROCRYPT 1999. LNCS, vol. 1592, pp. 223–238. Springer, Heidelberg (1999)

12. Carmit, H., Lindell, Y.: Efficient Secure Two-Party Protocols: Techniques and Constructions. Springer Science & Business Media, Heidelberg (2010)
13. Liu, A., Zheng, K., Li, L., Liu, G., Zhao, L., Zhou, X.: Efficient secure similarity computation on encrypted trajectory data. In: Proceedings of the ICDE, pp. 66–77 (2015)
14. Bugiel, S., Nürnberger, S., Sadeghi, A.-R., Schneider, T.: Twin clouds: secure cloud computing with low latency. In: De Decker, B., Lapon, J., Naessens, V., Uhl, A. (eds.) CMS 2011. LNCS, vol. 7025, pp. 32–44. Springer, Heidelberg (2011)
15. Samanthula, B.K., Chun, H., Jiang, W.: An efficient and probabilistic secure bit-decomposition. In: Proceedings of the ASIACCS, pp. 541–546 (2013)

Big Data

Big Data Tools: Haddop, MongoDB and Weka

Paula Catalina Jaraba Navas[✉], Yesid Camilo Guacaneme Parra,
and José Ignacio Rodríguez Molano

Facultad de Ingeniería,
Universidad Distrital Francisco José de Caldas, Bogotá, Colombia
{pcjaraban, ycguacanemep}@correo.udistrital.edu.co,
jirodriguez@udistrital.edu.co

Abstract. Big Data is a term that describes the exponential growth of all sorts of data –structured and non-structured– from different sources (data bases, social networks, the web, etc.) and which, as per their use, may become a benefit or an advantage for a company. This paper shows the current importance of Big Data, together with some of the algorithms that may be used with the purpose of reveling patterns, trends and data associations that may generate valuable information in real time, mentioning characteristics and applications of some of the tools currently used for data analysis so they may help to establish which is the most suitable technology to be implemented according to the needs or information required.

Keywords: Big data · Analysis tools · Hadoop · Mongodb · Weka

1 Introduction

Currently, the "data intelligence" talk is replacing that of "data science", and it is with this evolution in terms that everything related to Big Data begins to be valued, since it is no longer limited to the technology realm, but it becomes possible to recognize the value of all the available information and it is used to obtain great business profit for instance, since the companies may obtain a competitive advantage if they know how to suitably use the information they have [1].

Nowadays, with the advances in technology, a lot of digital data is created that has traits such as "massive, high dimensional, heterogeneous, complcx, unstructured, incomplete, noisy, and erroneous," which may change the way this data is analyzed [2], but it is also very important to take into account security, privacy, fault tolerance and quality of data [3] with the purpose of not getting ambiguous or abnormal data to analyze.

Since data has varied and complex characteristics, as mentioned above and as it will be further detailed, it becomes necessary to have tools in place that are able to analyze it efficiently, so valuable information is obtained in the right moment, tools this paper will describe in deeper detail as it is developed.

© Springer International Publishing Switzerland 2016
Y. Tan and Y. Shi (Eds.): DMBD 2016, LNCS 9714, pp. 449–456, 2016.
DOI: 10.1007/978-3-319-40973-3_45

2 Big Data

Starting with the development of internet and its adoption at a great scale by the late 1980s and early 1990s, the generation of data has grown exponentially, which makes increasingly greater the amount of data that needs to be managed and stored [4]. This brings with it the term Big Data, a concept that refers to all information that cannot be analyzed by means of everyday tools [5]. But Big Data does not refer just to great volume of data and complex analysis; it is also useful when the information is varied, meaning, coming from mobile devices, from different digital sensors, from automobiles, etc., and that needs to be rapidly processed or analyzed to obtain a response at the right moment.

When collecting data from different sources, it becomes necessary to divide them in three main groups: [6].

- Structured Data: Data that is formatted in order to clearly define aspects such as its length, for instance dates, numbers, etc. [7]. Generally, traditional databases and spreadsheets contain structured data.
- Semi-structured Data: Data that has been processed to a certain extent, meaning, data that does not correspond to a specific format but that its elements are separated by means of markers. An example of this sort of data are the ones that come from traditional web pages (HTML) [8].
- Non-structured Data: This sort of data lacks a format, since it is in the state it was collected, without undergoing any sort of processing; some examples of this type of data are the PDF, multimedia documents, and e-mail [9].

Big Data allows unblocking a great amount of information that may be useful and allows making narrow segmentation of something specific, thus having the most precise information of that which is being studied [10]. Once the importance of Big Data is established, some of the most significant benefits brought by the use of this tool will be mentioned: [11]

- It allows carrying out a detailed analysis on everything related to web browsing, in order to have greater visibility regarding the needs and the environment in which clients operate. This may be achieved by means of an analysis on the social networks to help us ascertain the role that the client plays in its social circle, or by means of an analysis on the browsing data, identifying the web sites visited and the searches done, obtaining a greater knowledge on the client and improving the company's business strategy.
- Provides to us the possibility of anticipating possible future problems by means of checking the veracity of the data in the face of inaccurate information.
- It is useful for improving processes that allow, for instance, to reduce risk when making decisions, reduce costs or possible losses because of fraud, analyzing the information in real time, among others.

Besides the aforementioned benefits, it is necessary to know that due to the vast amounts of data generated each instant, the necessary software and hardware for the adoption of Big Data become expensive, and that in most cases there is little collaboration for the implementation of this project; therefore it is necessary to be certain of the need of Big Data in a company.

3 Data Analysis

All data related to Big Data is generated second after second and come from different sources; it is precisely the great diversity of data types [12] what complicates the storage and analysis because of the integration of data with different structures, as it has been mentioned. Because of this, Big Data is divided in three main operations: storage, analytics (which will be discussed in depth below) and integration, through which solutions are posed so that in an efficient manner the dimensions of this tool can be scaled [13]. There are different techniques for Big Data Analysis; some of these tools are:

3.1 Data Mining

"This is a non-trivial process of valid, new, potentially useful and understandable identification of comprehensible patters that are hidden in data" [14] meaning, it is a tool for exploiting and analyzing data in an efficacious manner for the desired purposes. Big Data wouldn't be useful without this technique for data analysis, since it helps to summarize and simplify data in a way that may be recognized and then allows to collect specific information on the base of patters that this technique yields [15].

3.2 Association

Consists in finding relationships in data, that is, associating variables according to the similarities among them. But within the context of Big Data, the big challenge is to build association models that allow closing the gap among the different sources of heterogeneous data; for instance, the performance of browsers or recommendation systems would be significantly improved if complex "text-image-video" associations could be analyzed, such as the new on the web, comments on twitter and video clips [16].

3.3 Clustering

It is a type of data mining that divides in small groups the data out of which the similitude among them is unknown, with the purpose of finding similarities among the groups and evaluating the results obtained; for this, there are different techniques and algorithms [17].

With Big Data Analytics a greater analysis speed is achieved thanks to the new technologies that have been developed, which in its stead allows having the capability of analyzing greater amounts of data; besides, there are tools in place previously used in Business Intelligence, such as Data Warehouse and Data Mining, plus other more effective ones, such as Hadoop, MapReduce, among others, which will be discussed in depth below.

4 Tools for Data Analytics

The following section presents a number of tools that currently are trend in storage, management, and analysis of big amounts of data. This, with the purpose of having a clearer perspective when choosing the suitable tool that allows better use of resources and data.

4.1 Hadoop

Hadoop (HDFS) is a distributed file system designed to be executed from the hardware of a computer or information system [18, 19]. Among its characteristics:

- Hardware: Hadoop is made up of hundred or thousands of connected servers that store and execute the user's tasks; the possibility of failure is high, since if only one of the servers fails, the whole system fails. Therefore, the Hadoop platform always has a certain percentage of inactivity [19, 20].
- Transmission: The applications executed by means of Hadoop are not for general use, since it processes sets of data without contact with the user.
- Data: usually applications executed in this type of tool are of a great size; Hadoop adapts to support it with a great number of nodes that distribute data. This distribution brings as a benefit the increase on the bandwidth since the information is available in several nodes, it has a great performance in the access to data and its continuous presentation (streaming).
- Computation: An advantage Hadoop has regarding the other systems is that the processing of information takes place in the same place where it is store, which does not overcrowd the network since it does not have to transmit the data elsewhere to be processed.
- Portability: Hadoop, as many Open Source applications, was designed with ease of migration to different platforms.
- Accessibility: The access and browsing that Hadoop allows in its data group may be carried out in several ways. Some of them are: Java program interface and by means of a web server.

Applications where Hadoop is present: response in real time, whether for decision-making processes or immediate responses (fraud control, performance, etc.), aside from particular applications, such as research and development, behavioral analysis, marketing and sales, failure detection in machinery and the IoT universe.

4.2 MongoDB

MongoDB is a distributed NoSQL data manager of a documental sort, which means that it is a non-relational database. Data exchange in this manager is done by means of BSON, which is a text that uses a binary representation for data structuring and mapping. This manager is written in C++, may be executed from different operational systems; it is open-source code [21–23]. This data manager has the following characteristics:

- Flexible storage, since it is sustained by JSON and does not need to define prior schemes.
- Multiple indexes may be created starting on any attribute, which facilitates its use, since it is not necessary to define MapReduce or parallel processes.
- Queries are based on documents, and they have high performance for querying as well as updating.
- MongoDB has a high capability for growth, replication, and scalability. More than one of these properties may be obtained increasing the number of machines.
- Independent file storage support, for any size, based on GFS which is a storage specification implemented by all supported drivers.

MongoDB Application: It is suitable for making Internet applications that record a high amount of data, such as: data collection with sensors, social network maintenance infrastructures, statistics collection (reporting), among others. In general, MongoDB may be used for almost anything without so much rigidity [23].

4.3 Weka

It is a set of machine learning algorithms for data mining tasks. The algorithms can either be applied directly to a data set or called from its own Java code. WEKA is more than a program. It is a collection of interdependent programs in the same user interface, which is mainly made up by: data pre-processing, classification, regression, clustering, association rules and visualization, and it works for the development of machine learning schemes [24]. In recent years it has been used for agricultural data analysis; in some cases, for instance, to respond to whether a series of rules that model decision factors in cattle sacrificing may be found [25]. WEKA's basic characteristics are:

- Data pre-processing: As well as a native file format (ARFF), WEKA is compatible with several other formats (for instance, CSV, ASCII Matlab files), and database connectivity through JDBC.
- Classification: Classification is done with about 100 methods. Classifiers are divided in "Bayesian" methods, lazy methods (closest neighbor), rule-based methods (decision charts, OneR, Ripper), learning threes, learning based on diverse functions and methods. On the other hand, WEKA includes meta-classifiers, such as bagging, boosting, stacking, multiple instance classifiers, and interfaces implemented in Groovy and Jython.
- Clustering: unsupervised learning supported by several clustering schemes, such as EMbased Mixture model, k-means, and several hierarchy clustering algorithms.
- Selection attribute: The set of attributed used is essential for the performance classification. There are several selection criteria and search methods available.
- Data visualization: Data may be visually inspected representing attribute values against class, or against other attribute values. There are visualization-specialized tools for specific methods [26, 27].

Besides Hadoop, MongoDB and WEKA, there are other alternatives for the management of big data deposits, such as the case of the Appliances. An Appliance may be defined as the application whose purpose is managing, collecting, and analyzing big amounts of data; this hardware and software is designed solely to carry out these tasks. An example of this is the Oracle Big Data Appliance [28].

Why to choose MongoDB or Hadoop when both may fit without any issues in a typical Big Data problem? Depending on the characteristics of the project to be carried out tools could be chosen, but in some cases there is no need to choose between these two tools. How to use MongoDB and Hadoop together? The way they may be combined is using Hadoop for data processing and analysis, while MongoDB takes care of real-time operative data storage.

Other tools such as WEKA and the Appliance-type ones are much more specific and limited, which makes their selection to be done based on the solution requirements for a determined issue.

5 Conclusions

Big Data is a concept that for some time has been used in the IT world, one that every day, with the development of new technology, becomes stronger, since every moment the amount of data produced increases, becoming the most accurate tool for data research and business applications. This gives greater usability to Big Data as a whole with Data Mining, since it is necessary to store and analyze this huge amount of data, to translate them into information and knowledge so they generate a benefit.

According to what has been described about Big Data, an analysis on the viability of implementing this technology in a given company shall be carried out, because not all companies have the needed economic resources, infrastructure, and the necessary trained personnel for this project, besides the fact that not all companies need Big Data to be able to remain in the market. Moreover, most Big Data applications cannot be successfully implemented, because of the companies' privacy policies, because they do not easily allow access to their data.

Within the context of Big Data, real-time data processing is a very difficult task, since the size or complexity of Big Data exceeds the usual technical capabilities for data capture, management, and processing within the limits of reasonable cost and time. This data has brought forth new information architectures for intensive, real-time data processing, such as the open code Apache Hadoop, a project that is executed in high-performance clusters, which makes it necessary to be able to distinguish among the different alternatives available for data analysis.

References

1. Schroeck, M., Shockley, R., Smart, J., Morales, R., Tufano, P.: Analytics: the real-world use of big data. IBM Global Business Services, Saïd Business School, University of Oxford, pp. 1–20 (2012)
2. Boyd, D., Crawford, K.: Critical questions for big data. Inf. Commun. Soc. 15(5), 662–679 (2012)

3. Katal, A., Wazid, M., Goudar, R.: Big data: issues, challenges, tools and good practices. In: 2013 Sixth International Conference on Contemporary Computing, pp. 404–409 (2013)
4. Chen, H., Chiang, R., Storey, V.: Business intelligence and analytics: from big data to big impact. MIS Q. **36**(4), 1165–1188 (2012)
5. Jagadish, H., Gehrke, J., Labrinidis, A., Papakonstantinou, Y., Patel, J., Ramakrishnan, R., Shahabi, C.: Big data and its technical challenges. Commun. ACM **57**(7), 86–94 (2014)
6. Purcell, B.: The emergence of 'big data' technology and analytics. J. Technol. Res. **4**, 1–7 (2013)
7. Coronel, C., Morris, S., Rob, P.: Database Systems: Design, Implementation, and Management (2009)
8. Wu, X., Zhu, X., Wu, G., Ding, W.: Data mining with big data. IEEE Trans. Knowl. Data Eng. **26**(1), 97–107 (2014)
9. Demchenko, Y., De Laat, C., Membrey, P.: Defining architecture components of the big data ecosystem. In: 2014 International Conference on Collaboration Technologies and Systems, CTS 2014, pp. 104–112 (2014)
10. McKinsey & Company: Big data: The next frontier for innovation, competition, and productivity. McKinsey Glob. Inst., p. 156, June 2011
11. Desouza, K., Smith, K.: Big data for social innovation. Stanford Soc. Innov. Rev. **12**(3), 38–43 (2014)
12. Tsai, C., Lai, C., Chao, H., Vasilakos, A.: Big data analytics: a survey. J. Big Data **2**(1), 21 (2015)
13. Chen, M., Mao, S., Liu, Y.: Big data: a survey. Mob. Netw. Appl. **19**(2), 171–209 (2014)
14. Fayyad, U., Piatetsky-Shapiro, G., Smyth, P.: From data mining to knowledge discovery in databases. AI Mag. 37–54 (1996)
15. Bartere, M., Yenkar, V.: Review on data mining with big data. Int. J. Comput. Sci. Mob. Comput. **3**(4), 97–102 (2014)
16. Menandas, J., Joshi, J.: Data mining with parallel processing technique for complexity reduction and characterization of big data. Glob. J. Advanced Research **1**(1), 69–80 (2014)
17. Jain, K., Murty, M., Flynn, P.: Data clustering: a review. ACM Comput. Surv. **31**(3), 264–323 (1999)
18. Shvachko, K., Kuang, H., Radia, S., Chansler, R.: The hadoop distributed file system. In: 2010 IEEE 26th Symposium on Mass Storage Systems and Technologies, MSST2010 (2010)
19. Borthakur, D.: The hadoop distributed file system: Architecture and design. Hadoop Project Website, pp. 1–14 (2007)
20. Dittrich, J., Quian, J.: Efficient big data processing in hadoop mapreduce. In: Proceedings of the VLDB Endowment, vol. 5, no. 12, pp. 2014–2015 (2012)
21. MongoDB Inc 2008–2016. https://docs.mongodb.org/manual/introduction/
22. Boicea, A., Radulescu, F., Agapin, L.: MongoDB vs Oracle - database comparison. In: Proceedings of 3rd International Conference on Emerging. Intelligent Data and Web Technologies, EIDWT 2012, September 2012, pp. 330–335 (2012)
23. Gyorodi, C., Gyorodi, R., Pecherle, G., Olah, A.: A comparative study: MongoDB vs. MySQL. In: 13th International Conference on Engineering Modern Electric System (2015)
24. Hall, M., Frank, E., Holmes, G., Pfahringer, B., Reutemann, P., Witten, I.: The WEKA data mining software. ACM SIGKDD Explor. Newsl. **11**(1), 10 (2009)
25. Garner, S.: WEKA: the waikato environment for knowledge analysis. In: Proceedings of New Zealand Computer Science, pp. 57–64 (1995)

26. Bouckaert, R., Frank, E., Hall, M., Holmes, G., Pfahringer, B., Reutemann, P., Witten, I.: WEKA—experiences with a java open-source project. J. Mach. Learn. Res. **11**, 2533–2541 (2010)
27. Witten, I., Frank, E., Trigg, L., Hall, M., Holmes, G., Cunningham, S.: Weka: practical machine learning tools and techniques with java implementations. Seminar **99**, 192–196 (1999)
28. Oracle. Blogs.Oracle.Com

Big Data Meaning in the Architecture of IoT for Smart Cities

Christian David Gómez Romero, July Katherine Díaz Barriga[✉],
and José Ignacio Rodríguez Molano[✉]

Universidad Distrital Francisco José de Caldas, Bogotá, Colombia
dagoro06@gmail.com, julykdiazb@gmail.com,
jirodriguez@udistrital.edu.co

Abstract. Internet of Things (IoT) is the technology that allows making interconnections between devices and internet; its applications have been developed to give answer to society's needs and requirements. In the last years, communities have gotten interested into incorporate this and some other Information Technologies to the cities, to make of those Smart Cities. Currently, applications just reply to particular necessities but general structures of IoT are being developed to improve the Smart City functioning and there is where Big Data (Classification and analysis of information) takes an important place inside the architecture, because this area manages the complexity, quantity and the variety of data for the right working of systems and the acquisition of classified useful data in real time. This paper aims to explain the importance of Big Data as Information Technology (IT) to organize and direct correctly the information in complex systems as the involved in the development of the Smart Cities.

Keywords: Big Data · Architecture · Internet of Things (IoT) · Smart City

1 Introduction

The Internet of Things (IoT) is one of the leading technologies that is related o our daily life, given that it can encourage different relations between humans and devices. Focusing on the impact of this technology, the IoT looks for transforming traditional cities into Smart Cities, what means that proper use of technologies and tools can result in the correct management of the different areas that compose its structure [1].

The Internet of Everything's idea is to allow interconnections and the correct information flow that starts with recognition of data from labels or sensors incorporated in gadgets identifying networks to be connected in any moment and to interact with other devices [2, 3]. The applications developed around IoT are not just directed to an individual final user, those look for ensuring the vital lines of the Smart Cities, which means that guarantee the normal operation of the vital systems in the city [4] with services like the water and energy supply, fire alarms [5] and some specialized applications in other sectors like mobility with apps for parking place service to identify the nearest parking place [6] and traffic control.

Currently, the Internet of things is getting importance keeping in mind that business models have seen the need of using Information technologies to improve the different

© Springer International Publishing Switzerland 2016
Y. Tan and Y. Shi (Eds.): DMBD 2016, LNCS 9714, pp. 457–465, 2016.
DOI: 10.1007/978-3-319-40973-3_46

processes and make a better management of information, knowing that Big Data is a concept that applies to data sets of extreme size which are beyond the ability of being manipulated by manual techniques [7].

2   Methodology

Taking into account the research objective, authors have studied available data in order to identify the general architecture of the Internet of Things for the Smart Cities and which is the role of Big Data inside it. The present paper shows the importance of how information technologies contribute to the development of cities, then it is presented a conceptualization of IoT, Smart City and Big Data meaning. In the next sections, there are the general architecture of IoT for the Smart Cities, the importance of Big Data to manage information, its structure and which are the challenges in this area of development.

3   Conceptualization

3.1   Internet of Things (IoT)

IoT's concept was coined by Kevin Ashton in 1999 [8–10], when the viewpoint of a broader device to device communication became a reality [2]. The Internet of things is defined as a self-organizing system of unfettered devices which provide converged systems that improve processes' efficiency [11]. It also makes reference to the iden-tifiable physical objects connected to internet [12], which allow to establish many kinds of communication and sharing data with the use Information Technologies (IT), to offer a variety of services by interconnecting virtual and physical things based on the interoperability of Information and Communication Technologies (ICT) [13].

The Internet of things has some essential characteristics, given by the development of some applications that respond to specific needs. However, it follows the next objectives [14, 15] in search of getting "almost all connected":

Convergence. Given by the possibility to process anything (any kind of informa-tion – data, pictures, videos, etc.) with any device.
Communication. To be connected in any place and in any moment.
Connectivity. Means to be connected with any network in any path.
Content. From any context in anytime, without discrimination of content.
Computing. Accessible for anybody who knows how it works and without restrictions of time (anytime).
Collections. A large variety of service (any service) for any kind of business.

3.2   Smart City

An Smart City is defined as the place or city that aims to do a better use of public resources, for improving the city's performance and increase quality of general services for citizens, reducing the operational cost of public management [16]. Its objective is to achieve effectiveness and efficiency in the management of resources and to provide services to cover general and some specific needs of society [17].

3.3   IoT Development in Smart Cities

There is not exactly information about when the Internet of Things started to work for the Smart Cities, nevertheless, both concepts aim to make changes from the proper use of technologies. The Internet of Everything platforms for Smart Cities has been developed around public services like energy, water, air quality and transportation (traffic) among others [17, 18]. Its vision in cities is to improve the 'livability', under six principals which are: transportation choices, location and energy efficient, economic competitiveness, target federal funding, align federal polices, and funding and enhance exclusive characteristics from investment for communities [13].

3.4   Applications of IoT for Smart Cities

Different kinds of applications has been developed for Smart Cities, making use of Information and Communication Technologies in their programming technologies (ICT) [8], reason why the apps receive a classification not only by ICT usage but for their nature and the current trends, as it is shown in the Table 1 (adapted of [16, 26]), some of those applications are explained below.

Table 1. Classification of applications for Smart Cities

Application classification of IoT for a Smart City			
1	Smart lighting	6	Traffic control
2	Energy consumption	7	Smart parking
3	Noise monitoring	8	Structural health of buildings
4	Surveillance cameras	9	Smart buildings
5	Management's cost	10	Centralized and integrated system control

Smart lighting. Developed from the need of making an efficient usage of the public lighting resources [16], it is achieved with the use of sensors that point during the day the illumination requirements [20]. It is the way modern to reduce the energy consumption of the city, trying to get a system of adaptable street lighting [21].

Noise monitoring. It aims to detect different sources of noise through a tracking service and data analysis of measurements to identify points of contamination in determined areas, in real time [16].

Surveillance cameras. It was developed from the need of getting security's monitoring, in order to track questionable activities which can put in risk the integrity or users. This application has presented some problems inasmuch that people refuse to be monitored because of the violation of their privacy [22].

3.5   Big Data

Big Data is the term that describes a set of non-structured and complex data which come from sensors, social media, applications and devices that work with internet and require of last technologies to storage, manage, analyze and visualize the information.

Big Data Analysis (BDA) is a way to innovate the marketing since it primarily generates a global revolution in the use of mass media and devices, given that treatment of data is going to create support processes which allow the integration of intelligent systems [23], there upon BDA is implemented in order to deliver a better management of massive data in real time.

Nowadays, Big Data is enabling that great aspects of human life be studied as scientist and marketing area, given the volume of data generated daily and the analysis of its complexity [24]. Its challenge is in convert generated data in tools that allow to managers to solve problems acting rightly in decision making. [25].

4   IoT General Architecture for Smart Cities

The IoT pretends to interconnect devices to internet, following an information flow from some points without which IoT framework couldn't work in a Smart City:

Users. They are origin of informatics systems, thanks to their needs and information (first data), frameworks are developed to offer them final processed (new) data [26].
Devices. Those are the physical medium to give and get information, with which through touchable technologies it is possible to live connected and communicated.
Technologies. Used to read information and consolidate real data, those have many physical interfaces (sensors, labels, codes), and software to process data.
Storage. Given by the cloud (Cloud Computing) that is defined as unlimited storage, compute and network capabilities to integrate IoT devices and provide elastic runtime infrastructure for IoT systems [27], improving the accessibility to data [28].
Processing and classification. It is the link in which Big Data acts as an information manager that explore and extract useful data for users in almost realtime [28], because of the large amount of complex data originated from different sources that exceed the capabilities of traditional data processing technologies [29].
Applications' sectors. The applications of IoT for Smart Cities look for promoting the correct working of public systems, therefore those have been developed in the next areas: E-government, public services, health services, public safety, ITC business implementation, traffic mobility, smart building and among others.

4.1   IoT Architecture for Smart Cities

Figure 1 explains the cycle of information flow in the Internet of Things general structure for Smart Cities. The architecture is composed by the parts indicated above for the general framework, making of users the beginning and the end of the cycle and specifying the important elements of each component as explained before.

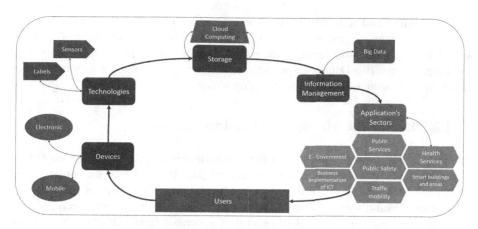

Fig. 1. Information flow in IoT architecture for Smart Cities.

4.2 Big Data Importance in the Sectors of Application

E-government. This field tries to attend the city's necessities through strategies of management of technologies and politics of procedure that guarantee the security of transactions among companies and users, aiming to avoid the generation of 'information island' effect and promoting the data security [15].

Public Services. The applications aim to get the optimization of traditional public services [16]. Some common services that use this kind of technology's platforms are: Energy supply [30], public lighting, traffic control, cameras of monitoring [16], natural gas [31] and water supply [18, 32], through the smart waste management [30]. Big Data is represented by all measurements taken to register the consumption of users and to make the correct charge for services to the users.

Public Safety. The development of systems for real-time monitoring look for responding to accidents [33] or disaster events [34]. This area organize security systems in order to improve life quality [12], providing methods of quick time response, protocols of security and facing users' discuss about data privacy.

Health Services. With services like Tele-HealthCare [35] Healthcare for elders [12] and eHealth [13], this is the most outstanding application field, because patients request privacy of personal and sensitive information [22]. Big data in this field pretends to avoid wrong diagnoses such as any action that put in risk patients' lives.

Business Implementation of ICT. The development of apps response to business demands from private and public sector, and seeks to integrate Information and Communication Technologies for companies for reducing costs [36]. Privacy of Data is the main challenge, because a loss of Big Data means huge losses for business.

Traffic Mobility. Applications like Smart Parking (to reduce time of search for parking place [37]) and Smart Traffic (to get access to urban mobility and transportation resources [33]) are developed to give answer to common traffic problems. This data requires of careful analysis to reduce accidents and traffic jams.

Smart Building and Areas. As one of the most innovative areas, applications aim to automate buildings for ensuring the physics security of buildings and users. Therefore, applications guarantee that buildings be insulated against noise [38], excess of lighting and other factors. Big Data is responsible of managing the points of factors that can affect the well-being of users or the building structure.

5 Big Data in the Management of Information

Big Data is taking greater impulse in the administration of information because, it is linked to cloud environments and to the correct data flow, to face the Smart City's challenges taking into account the massive data and the requirement of efficient systems (with velocity, variety, veracity, transference among other of Big Data) [24].

In the last years, the analysis of exact data generated links between the academy and the industry to find ways for reducing energy consumption, traffic problems and air contamination [39].

5.1 Big Data Structure

Big companies have the largest quantity of generated data, so those require a detailed analysis of information for future developments, reason why Big Data is composed by four V's characteristics (Volume: Processes on data generates more data (classified), therefore data need to be hold especially in a Smart City. [40], Velocity: Collecting and processing data in accelerated rhythms with the guarantee of the constant information flow, Variety: Accuracy of information with fundamental characteristics like quality of data and management of metadata, and value of data: Extraction of meaningful information of data sets, principally useful information for businesses [41]). [23, 25, 42] and three E's (Energy: requiere for the systems, exchange: of all kind of data, and empathy: compatibility among).

5.2 Information Transmission in Big Data

The data follow has some behaviors according to its variety and volume:

> **Structured:** Aligned data follow a specific pattern, then it is easier to manage information through the usage of basic languages of programming.
> **Semi-Structured:** Traditional techniques do not work for managing Big Data. It requires of defined rules which define dynamic processes for the tracking of data.
> **Non-Structured:** Its content does not have a specific pattern. The information is generated from text, videos, social media and others. [24]

6 Big Data Challenges in the Architecture

The IoT platforms aim to integrated Information Technologies like Big Data and Data Mining for improving the systems' performance [43]. Some challenges and difficulties of Big Data's role in the Smart Cities are shown below:

Principal worries: Data manipulation, storage availability, compatibility of systems, among others, attending to the autonomy and the adaptability of data for the development of applications [44] specially in a Smart Cites.

Security and monitoring: To enhance users' reliability, sensible data should be protected and restricted to private access [45].

Technological development: It looks for reducing the heterogeneity between operative systems and to face the energetic barriers of devices [46]. Emphasis is done in the idea that the IoT and the Smart City could not exist with reliable data [19].

Standardization: In order to avoid the wrong usage of critical information [4], the requirement is on the protection of sensible data and the use of it without authorization [45, 46] have block the manipulation of existent IoT's platforms.

Privacy: People does not feel entrusted with the idea of sharing personal data with the world, they believe in technology but not in its managers [3, 47].

7 Concluding Remarks

Big Data as the management of information is one of the most important Information Technologies applied to the IoT for the Smart Cities because without it, there were not be possible to generate value in information, given that platforms lack of velocity to process data, coverage to hold great volume of information and the ability of classifying the data according with their variety. This paper showed a proposal of a general architecture such as the important elements inside of Big Data structure to achieve success applications of IoT in the Smart Cities from a general review.

References

1. Borgia, E.: The Internet of Things vision: key features, applications and open issues. Comput. Commun. **54**, 1–31 (2014)
2. Efremov, S., Pilipenko, N., Voskov, L.: An integrated approach to common problems in the Internet of Things. Procedia Eng. **100**, 1215–1223 (2015)
3. Lee, I., Lee, K.: The Internet of Things (IoT): applications, investments, and challenges for enterprises. Bus. Horiz. **58**(4), 431–440 (2015)
4. Botta, A., de Donato, W., Persico, V., Pescapé, A.: Integration of cloud computing and Internet of Things: a survey. Futur. Gener. Comput. Syst. **56**, 684–700 (2015)
5. Tran, T., Ha, Q.P.: Dependable control systems with Internet of Things. ISA Trans. **59**, 303–313 (2015)
6. Erguler, I.: A potential weakness in RFID-based Internet-of-things systems. Pervasive Mob. Comput. **20**, 115–126 (2015)
7. Becker, D., Mcmullen, B., King, T.D.: Big data, big data quality problem. In: 2015 IEEE International Conference on Big Data, pp. 2644–2653 (2015)
8. Gubbi, J., Buyya, R., Marusic, S., Palaniswami, M.: Internet of Things (IoT): a vision, architectural elements, and future directions. Futur. Gener. Comput. Syst. **29**(7), 1645–1660 (2013)

9. Montenegro, C., Rodríguez, J., Marín, C.: Redes de Ingeniería Redes de Ingeniería Redes de Ingeniería, pp. 37–44 (2015)
10. Weber, R.H.: Internet of Things – need for a new legal environment? Comput. Law Secur. Rev. **25**(6), 522–527 (2009)
11. Basu, S., Tripathy, S., Chowdhury, A.R.: Design challenges and security issues in the Internet of Things. In: 2015 IEEE Region 10 Symposium, pp. 90–93 (2015)
12. Ma, J.: Internet of Things: technology evolution and challenges. In: IEEE Conference Publications (2014)
13. Jara, A.J., Sun, Y., Song, H., Bie, R., Genooud, D., Bocchi, Y.: Internet of Things for cultural heritage of Smart Cities and Smart Regions. In: 2015 IEEE 29th International Conference on Advanced Information Networking and Applications, pp. 668–675 (2015)
14. Burange, A.W., Misalkar, H.D.: Review of Internet of Things in development of Smart Cities with data management & privacy (2015)
15. Ganchev, I., O'Droma, M.: A generic IoT architecture for Smart Cities. In: 25th IET Irish Signals and System Conference 2014, China-Ireland International Conference on Information and Communications Technologies (ISSC 2014/CIICT 2014), pp. 196–199 (2014)
16. Zanella, A., Bui, N., Castellani, A., Vangelista, L., Zorzi, M.: Internet of Things for Smart Cities. IEEE Internet Things J. **1**(1), 22–32 (2014)
17. Hofer, S.: Smart Cities and the Internet of Things, pp. 485–494 (2014)
18. Lea, R., Blackstock, M.: Smart Cities. In: Proceedings of 2014 International Workshop on Web Intelligence and Smart Sensing, IWWISS 2014, pp. 1–2 (2014)
19. Weinberg, B., Milne, G., Andonova, Y., Hajjat, F.: IoT: convenience vs. privacy and secrecy. Bus. Horiz. **58**(6), 615–624 (2015)
20. Kumar, N.: Smart and intelligent energy efficient public illumination system with ubiquitous communication for Smart City. In: 2013 International Conference on Smart Structures and Systems, ICSSS 2013, pp. 152–157 (2013)
21. Vakali, A., Anthopoulos, L., Krco, S.: Smart Cities data streams integration: experimenting with IoT and social data flows. In: Proceedings of the 4th International Conference on Web Intelligence, Mining and Semantics (WIMS 2014), pp. 1–5 (2014)
22. Miorandi, D., Sicari, S., De Pellegrini, F., Chlamtac, I.: Internet of things: vision, applications and research challenges. Ad Hoc Netw. **10**(7), 1497–1516 (2012)
23. Zhou, K., Fu, C., Yang, S.: Big data driven smart energy management: from big data to big insights. Renew. Sustain. Energy Rev. **56**, 215–225 (2016)
24. Sharma, S.: Expanded cloud plumes hiding Big Data ecosystem. Futur. Gener. Comput. Syst. **59**, 63–92 (2016)
25. Xu, Z., Frankwick, G.L., Ramirez, E.: Effects of big data analytics and traditional marketing analytics on new product success: a knowledge fusion perspective. J. Bus. Res. **69**(5), 1562–1566 (2015)
26. Benazzouz, Y., Munilla, C.: Sharing user IoT devices in the cloud. In: 2014 IEEE World Forum Internet Things, 6–8 March 2014, pp. 373–374 (2014)
27. Nastic, S., Sehic, S., Le, D., Truong, H.L., Dustdar, S.: Provisioning software-defined IoT cloud systems. In: 2014 International Conference on Future Internet Things Cloud, pp. 288–295 (2014)
28. Díaz, J., Carlos, C., Candía, R., Usman, A.: Public management of IT: comparative case study between a developing and a developed. In: IEEE Conference Publications, pp. 1–8 (2015)
29. Amato, A., Di Martino, B., Venticinque, S.: Big data processing for pervasive environment in cloud computing. In: 2014 International Conference Intelligent Networking and Collaborative Systems, pp. 598–603 (2014)

30. Bonino, D., Alizo, M.T.D., Alapetite, A., Gilbert, T., Axling, M., Udsen, H., Soto, J.A.C., Spirito, M.: ALMANAC: Internet of Things for Smart Cities. In: 2015 3rd International Conference on Future Internet Things Cloud, pp. 309–316 (2015)
31. Suciu, G., Halunga, S., Vulpe, A., Suciu, V.: Generic platform for IoT and cloud computing interoperability study. In: International Symposium on Signals, Circuits and Systems, ISSCS 2013, pp. 1–4 (2013)
32. Skarmeta, A., Moreno, M.V., Garda, D.: SMARTIE project: secure IoT data management for Smart Cities, no. 609062, pp. 7–9 (2015)
33. Formisano, C., Pavia, D., Gurgen, L., Yonezawa, T., Galache, J.A., Doguchi, K., Matranga, I.: The advantages of IoT and cloud applied to Smart Cities. In: 2015 3rd International Conference on Future Internet Things Cloud, pp. 325–332 (2015)
34. Tao, C., Ling, X., Guofeng, S., Hongyong, Y., Quanyi, H.: Architecture for monitoring urban infrastructure and analysis method for a smart-safe city. In: 2014 6th International Conference on Measuring Technology and Mechatronics Automation, pp. 151–154 (2014)
35. Dijkman, R., Sprenkels, B., Peeters, T., Janssen, A.: Business models for the Internet of Things. Int. J. Inf. Manage. 35(6), 672–678 (2015)
36. Jia, X., Wang, J., He, Q.: IoT business models and extended technical requirements. In: IET International Conference on Communication Technology and Application (ICCTA 2011), vol. 1, pp. 622–625 (2011)
37. Mainetti, L., Patrono, L., Stefanizzi, M.L., Vergallo, R.: A smart parking system based on IoT protocols and emerging enabling technologies (2015)
38. Singh, N., Davar, S.: Noise pollution-sources, effects and control. J. Hum. Ecol. 16(3), 181–187 (2004)
39. Frizzo-Barker, J., Chow-White, P.A., Mozafari, M., Ha, D.: An empirical study of the rise of big data in business scholarship. Int. J. Inf. Manag. 36(3), 403–413 (2016)
40. Liu, J. Li, J., Li, W., Wu, J.: Rethinking big data: a review on the data quality and usage issues. ISPRS J. Photogramm. Remote Sens. (2015)
41. Bello-Orgaz, G., Jung, J.J., Camacho, D.: Social big data: recent achievements and new challenges. Inf. Fusion 28, 45–59 (2016)
42. Zhou, K., Yang, S.: Understanding household energy consumption behavior: the contribution of energy big data analytics. Renew. Sustain. Energy Rev. 56, 810–819 (2016)
43. Glova, J., Sabol, T., Vajda, V.: Business models for the Internet of Things environment. Procedia Econ. Financ. 15(14), 1122–1129 (2014)
44. Kyriazis, D., Varvarigou, T.: Smart, autonomous and reliable Internet of Things. Procedia Comput. Sci. 21, 442–448 (2013)
45. Henze, M., Hermerschmidt, L., Kerpen, D., Häußling, R., Rumpe, B., Wehrle, K.: A comprehensive approach to privacy in the cloud-based Internet of Things. Futur. Gener. Comput. Syst. 56, 701–718 (2015)
46. Yan, Z., Zhang, P., Vasilakos, A.V.: A survey on trust management for Internet of Things. J. Netw. Comput. Appl. 42, 120–134 (2014)
47. Weber, R.H.: Internet of things: privacy issues revisited. Comput. Law Secur. Rev. 31(5), 618–627 (2015)

Linear TV Recommender Through Big Data

Mikhail A. Baklanov[1]([✉]) and Olga E. Baklanova[2]([✉])

[1] Tomsk State University, Tomsk, Russia
baklanov.ma@gmail.com
[2] D. Serikbayev East-Kazakhstan State Technical University,
Ust-Kamenogorsk, Kazakhstan
OEBaklanova@mail.ru

Abstract. This paper contains development of methods of improving TV-watching experience using Machine Learning for Linear TV recommendations. TV is a shared device, so the recommendations based on taste of only one user, may not be sufficiently effective. This paper discusses how Data Mining viewing data to improve the effectiveness of the advisory system. The main idea is to get new insights about the users, thus creating new knowledge that can be used for more accurate recommendations. This paper describes the methods of data mining on watching TV subscribers, as well as measures the effectiveness of the use of derived hypotheses in existing approaches to building recommender systems. Usage of such recommender could completely transform the TV advertisement and creates a new synergy between e-Business and TV by defining who is in front of TV and what he likes. From the other hand Smart TV allows user to make an order right from his TV-set that dramatically improves conversion rates. Existing methods and new method effectiveness are compared with offered approach by analyzing real people content consumption during one year.

Keywords: Content recommenders · Linear TV · Smart TV · Machine learning · Data mining

1 Introduction

Traditional television is gradually losing ground. According to latest studies about 25 % of the total TV watching takes channel surfing. This routine is faced by 900 million pay -TV customers all over the world. One of the reasons of it is the outdated pattern of TV-watching that didn't changed for 50 years: a customer turn on the TV-channel, estimate is it good enough, and make a decision to stay, or to try another channel. This pattern worked perfectly when there were only 6–10 channels, but it takes too much time when there are hundreds of TV-channels. In the new paradigm of TV-watching in the first place is subjected to such characteristics of services as personal selection of content, interactivity and instant start view.

Is it possible to use Machine Learning and process Big Data, to make machines do this routine instead of human? Now there are several examples

© Springer International Publishing Switzerland 2016
Y. Tan and Y. Shi (Eds.): DMBD 2016, LNCS 9714, pp. 466–474, 2016.
DOI: 10.1007/978-3-319-40973-3_47

of successful usage of recommender systems in VOD services. The most famous case is recommender algorithm Cinematch made by Netflix. However, at present the best part of commercial recommenders use heuristic methods which impact in most cases insignificant for customers, thus it does not bring enough added to a product. Moreover, the usage of ordinary machine learning algorithms is complicated by the limitations of input devices, the novelty of TV-shows, patterns of content consumption and the fact that TV-set is not a personal device, it used by a whole family or household.

This paper aims to analyze customers requests for recommender systems and define the most effective methods for linear TV recommendations using machine learning.

2   Problem Formulations and Motivation

Developed recommendation system aims to improve user satisfaction of the passive consumption of video content on TVs with the delivery of content via broadband (OTT) and IPTV-network.

Development of recommendation systems always lies at the intersection of several areas of knowledge. The origins of recommendation systems are in the works for cognitive science [1], information retrieval [2], forecasting [3], as well as a reference to the management and modeling of consumer choice in marketing. Recommendation system took form as an independent area of the research in the mid-90s of the twentieth century, when the researchers focused on the problems associated with predicting user ratings. The most common problem with the issuance of the recommendations was to assess the problem of the ratings of various objects with which the user has not yet encountered. This assessment was usually based on the ratings that the user assigned to other objects. If we can assume which rating the user will put to this or that object, then we can decide what to recommend to the user.

Formalizing the problem:

Let U - number of users and S - the set of all objects that can be recommended (books, movies, restaurants etc.). Let h - a function that measures user satisfaction, i.e. the extent to which a subject s like user u. Thus, for each user $u \in U$ we want to select an object $s' \in S$ that would maximize user satisfaction. To put it more formally:

$$\forall c \in C, s' \in C = \arg\max_{u \in U} h(u, s). \tag{1}$$

Existing approaches to the recommenders can be divided into three large groups.

3   Important Existing Approaches

3.1   Method of Content Filtering (Item-Based)

Content Filtering (item-based) involves the creation of user profiles and objects. In order to take into account relevant recommendations of the object parameters corresponding user preferences. The recommendation system objects are described using keywords (tags), and create a profile that characterizes its attitude to certain objects.

In the item-based systems, the function of satisfaction $h(u, s)$ user u of a particular content item s is determined on the basis of information on user satisfaction with the content item $s_i \in S$, which are "similar" to s. For example, the recommendation system for films to recommend movies to the user u, the system tries to understand what is common between the films having the user previously praised highly. After that, the user will be recommended movies as much as possible similar to the ones that the user has given high marks.

In fact, content that the user consumes forms a profile in the form of a plurality of parameters characterizing the object s. As a parameter often, protrude keywords corresponding weights for each object. Thus, the problem arises of how to weigh these parameters. One of the most prominent ways to deter- mine the weights of keywords in information retrieval is TF-IDF [2] measure.

In addition to the heuristic, these is based mostly on information retrieval methods, other technology recommendations item-based and are widely used. Examples include the use of a naive Bayesian classifier, and various machine learning techniques, including clustering, decision trees and neural networks [4]. These techniques differ from information retrieval approaches in that they try to predict user satisfaction, based on a heuristic formula, like the cosine factor, rather than the model derived from data based on the use of mathematical statistics and machine learning.

3.2   Collaborative Filtration (User-Based)

Collaborative filtering uses a well-known group of users preferences to predict the unknown preference of another user. The basic assumption is that those who are equally evaluated objects of any kind in the past tend to give a similar assessment of other subjects in the future.

In contrast to the Item-based methods, User-based methods try to predict user satisfaction with an object on the basis of how other users rate this item. Those users u satisfaction of objects s $h(u, s)$ is calculated on the basis of users u_j which for any signs are similar to u. An important feature here is that the characteristics by which the user can be considered similar to the other users, may go beyond the system. For example, social networking profiles or demographic information obtained explicitly, can be the basis to assess the similarity of the new primary user of existing ones. This approach is often used to solve "cold" start problem.

While the above-described techniques used to calculate the similarity between users, Sarwar et al. [9] proposed to use the same technique, but to calculate the correlation between the objects and obtain the ratings of them.

3.3   Hybrid Recommendation Systems

Hybrid recommendation systems are a combination of content filtering and collaborative filtering. Some of recommendation systems use hybrid methods combining user-based and item-based methods that partially or completely neutralize some of the disadvantages of each approach. You can select the following ways of combining different approaches in hybrid systems of reference:

- the introduction of item-based and user-based methods separately and combining them received from assessment;
- the introduction of some item-based settings in the user-based approach;
- the introduction of some user-based settings in the item-based approach;
- the creation of a general model, which uses parameters of both approaches.

One way to build hybrid recommender system is the implementation of two independent item-based and user-based systems. Then there are two possible scenarios. In the first, we can combine the ratings received from each system using a linear combination of ratings [10] or the scheme described in [11]. The second scenario is to use only one of the systems depending on what herein will work better. For example, the system Daily Learner [12] selects recommender systems, which can give a recommendation to the lowest level of error.

The most popular approach to this category of hybrid recommender systems - a decrease of dimension for the group of content-based user profiles. For example, in [13] uses a latent semantic analysis (LSA), to create user profiles Collaborative representation, where the user profile is represented as a set of vectors, which leads to a significant improvement in performance compared to pure item-based approach.

Hybrid systems can also be supplemented by a variety of techniques, using a knowledge base in order to improve the quality of advice and solve some typical problems of recommender systems (new object, a cold start for the new user, and the like).

Several authors in the works [11,13,15] compared the performance of hybrid and pure item-based and user-based recommendation systems and show a definite advantage over the pure hybrid methods.

4   Big Data Processing to Improve Existing Approaches

The main purpose of the creating of the model is the answer to the question: how, using modern advanced machine learning technology, automate, or at least substantially improve the channel selection process? At the moment, there are examples of successful application of recommender systems in video on demand services. The most famous case - is Cinematch recommender from Netflix. However, at the moment most of the commercial recommender systems use heuristics that improve the process of searching for transmission only slightly. In addition, the use of standard algorithms of machine learning is complicated by the limitations associated with the input device, the novelty of television programs, patterns of content consumption and the fact that television is not a personal device, it is used by all household members.

The idea is to use data mining for finding useful insights that could help with recommendations. There are few major ways in improving recommenders accuracy. One of them is to segment single TV audience. TV is not a personal device; it is watched by household that in most cases consists of several household members with different tastes. Since many existing approaches specialized for one-person recommendations, it is possible to make them work for linear TV by adding auto-profiling feature. It is possible to use data mining methods for getting insights about how many household members use a TV and automatically determine who is in front of TV at the moment.

We took Total Broadcast rating (Rbr_s) as a distance measure for our clustering. For any household (u) is different and, in general, is calculated as follows:

$$Rbr_{su} = Q_{su} + P_{su}, \tag{2}$$

$$Q_{su} = Q_{su-1} + a_{su}l_{su} + \sum_{i=1}^{n}(b_{su}t_{isu} + c_{su}w_{isu}), \tag{3}$$

$$P_{su} = \sum_{j=1}^{m}(k_{jsu}tag_{jsu}), \tag{4}$$

where:

- $l_s \in \{-1, 0, 1\}$ and indicates the presence of a mark by the user that this transfer him like or dislike;
- t_i, $w_i \in \{0, 1, 2, n, ,\infty\}$ and denote, respectively, how many times were used pause and rewind within it (timeshift), and how many issues the user looked through this transfer to the end;
- a,b,c,k_j - the coefficients are calculated for each individual user on the basis of how great value to the user preferences;
- i - the number of an episode;
- j - the number of a parameter;
- tag_j - the value of parameters for TV-shows;
- s - the number of TV-show;
- n - the number of views made by user for all episodes of one TV-show;
- m - the number of parameters specific to a given TV-show;
- Q_s - the own rating of a given TV-show;
- P_s - the sum of the weights of all the parameters of the transfer multiplied by coefficients.

For each user (u) carry out clustering FOREL-like method of selecting the cluster centers based on the start time of viewing.

The new thing in this approach is to calculate k_j individually for each user by machine learning. System look through users actions and measure how important could be different factors for specific users. This approach allows simulating different tastes demonstrated by different users and creating TV-consuming model for each user to formalize how the user makes his choice.

5   Results and Discussion

As the representatives of the classical approach using collaborative filtering algorithms based on users and object-based. The study will take place on the data

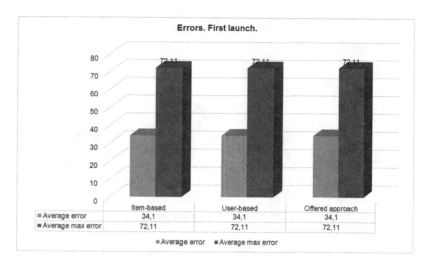

Fig. 1. Errors. The first launch. (Color figure online)

collected from more than 300,000 users of the Pay TV for 1 year of work. These data provide a history of decision-making by the user on which TV-show to watch, the order in which the channels have been submitted to it and user actions according these TV-shows.

As a measure of efficiency is considered the number of actions that are necessary for the user to find the most interesting programs for each method on average.

The most interesting programs here and further we consider the transfer, the user ultimately chose. We believe that the user has chosen the transfer, if it is:

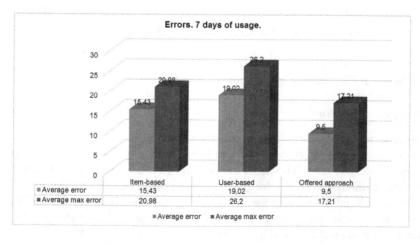

Fig. 2. Errors. The second launch. (Color figure online)

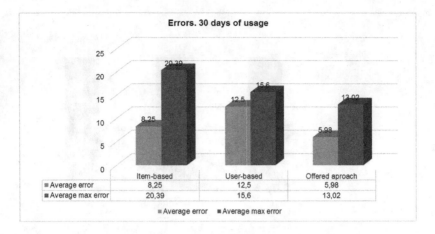

Fig. 3. Errors. The third launch. (Color figure online)

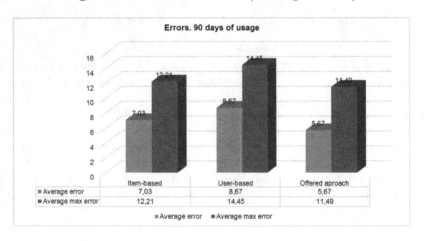

Fig. 4. Errors. The forth launch. (Color figure online)

- watched it for 5 min and looked through to the end (2 min);
- noted the transfer as a favorite;
- use a pause or rewind.

Users at any given time have access to 80 channels.

As a measure of effectiveness we use Error that means the number of action user needs to do to reach the most interesting TV-show, the less is better.

At first launch, due to the lack of any history all systems equally ineffective.

Data accumulated over the week, it enough that each of methods significantly reduces errors compared with random TV-shows ordering. As can be seen from the chart, the offered method provides delivery much closer to what the user wants to select, but the maximum error for users is still very large.

For thirty days, all the algorithms have shown significant progress, compared with 7 days. It is striking that the Item-Based approach, despite the significant decrease in the average error continues to send some people almost in the middle of the list.

The offered algorithm is slightly improved its results and, despite progress on the part of the other two, still shows the best results both in the middle and on the average maximum error.

6   Conclusion

The introduction of additional dimension that characterizes a user in terms of the way of how he make the choice instead of just measuring what items he or she prefers allowed to significantly improve results of recommender on the same dataset.

The usage of content recommenders allows improving TV digital information services and getting important insights about households watching TV. These insights could be helpful in E-business areas such as marketing costs reduction customer acquisition management. In addition, these insights could help to significantly improve quality of digital information services in linear TV recommendation system. That could be a good alternative to manual profile choice that used by many TV-providers who offers recommendations to their customers.

References

1. Rich, E.: User modeling via stereotypes. Cogn. Sci. **3**, 329–354 (1979)
2. Salton, G.: Automatic Text Processing. Addison-Wesley, Boston (1989)
3. Armstrong, J.S.: A Handbook for Researchers and Practitioners. Kluwer Academic, Norwell (2001)
4. Pazzani, M.: Learning and revising user profiles: the identification of interesting web sites. Mach. Learn. **27**, 313–331 (1997)
5. Goldberg, D., Nichols, D., Oki, B., Terry, D.: Using collaborative filtering to weave an information Tapestry. Comm. ACM. **35**(12), 61–70 (1992)
6. Breese, J., Heckerman, D., Kadie, C.: Empirical analysis of predictive algorithms for collaborative filtering. In: Proceedings 14th Conference Uncertainty in Artificial Intelligence (1998)
7. Jameson, A., Smyth, B.: Recommendation to groups. In: Brusilovsky, P., Kobsa, A., Nejdl, W. (eds.) Adaptive Web 2007. LNCS, vol. 4321, pp. 596–627. Springer, Heidelberg (2007)
8. Rana, C., Jain, S.: Building a book recommender system using time based content filtering. WSEAS Trans. Syst. Scopus **11**(2), 27–33 (2012)
9. Sarwar, B., Karypis, G., Konstan, J., Riedl, J.: Item-based collaborative filtering recommendation algorithms. In: Proceedings 10th International World Wide Web Conference (2001)
10. Claypool, M., Gokhale, A., Miranda, T., Murnikov, P., Netes, D., Sartin, M.: Combining content-based and collaborative filters in an online newspaper. In: Proceedings ACM SIGIR 99 Workshop Recommender Systems: Algorithms and Evaluation (1999)

11. Pazzani, M.: Framework for collaborative, content-based, and demographic filtering. In: Artificial Intelligence Review, pp. 393–408 (1999)
12. Billsus, D., Pazzani, M.: User modeling for adaptive news access. User Model. User-Adap. Inter. **10**(2–3), 147–180 (2000)
13. Soboroff, I., Nicholas, C.: Combining content and collaborationin text filtering. In: Proceedings of International Joint Conference on Artificial Intelligence Workshop: Machine Learning for Information Filtering (1999)
14. Zibriczky, D., Hidasi, B., Petres, Z., Tikk, D.: Personalized recommendation of linear content on interactive TV platforms: beating the cold start and noisy implicit user feedback. In: Proceedings of the International Workshop on TV and Multimedia Personalization (TVMMP), UMAP 2012, Montreal, Canada (2012)
15. Ricci, F., Rokach, L., Shapira, B., Kantor, P.B.: Recommender Systems Handbook. Springer, New York (2011)
16. Adomavicius, G., Tuzhilin, A.: Toward the next generation of recommender systems: a survey of the state-of-the-art and possible extensions. IEEE Trans. Knowl. Data Eng. **17**(6), 734–749 (2005)
17. Cremonesi, P., Modica, P., Pagano, R., Rabosio, E., Tanca, L.: Personalized and context-aware TV program recommendations based on implicit feedback. E-Commer. Web Technol. **239**, 57–68 (2016)
18. Turrin, R., Pagano, R., Cremonesi, P., Condorelli, A.: Time-based TV programs prediction. In: 1st Workshop on Recommender Systems for Television and Online Video at ACM RecSys (2014)
19. Puntheeranurak, S., Pitakpaisarnsin, P.: Time-aware recommender system using Nave Bayes classifier weighting technique. In: 2nd International Symposium on Computer, Communication, Control and Automation, pp. 266–269 (2013)
20. Robijt, S., Thys, S.: Towards personalized linear TV? a user-oriented approach. In: Proceedings of the ACM International Conference on Interactive Experiences for TV and Online Video, Brussels, Belgium (2015)

Data Models in NoSQL Databases
for Big Data Contexts

Maribel Yasmina Santos[✉] and Carlos Costa

ALGORITMI Research Centre, University of Minho, Guimarães, Portugal
maribel@dsi.uminho.pt, id6011@alunos.uminho.pt

Abstract. Data models are a central piece in information systems, being the relational data models very popular and extensively used. In Big Data, and due to the characteristics of the NoSQL databases, the data modeling task is seen in another perspective, as those databases are considered schema-free. Nevertheless, these databases also need data models that ensure the proper storage and querying of the data. Considering the vast amount of relational databases and the ever-increasing volume of data, the importance of data models in Big Data increases. In this work, a specific set of rules is proposed for the automatic transition between a traditional and a Big Data environment, considering two specific objectives: the identification of a columnar data model for HBase supporting operational needs and the identification of a tabular data model for Hive supporting analytical needs. The obtained results show the applicability of the proposed rules and their relevance for data modeling in Big Data environments.

Keywords: Data model · Big Data · Data warehousing · NoSQL databases

1 Introduction

Organizations are constantly being challenged in several areas, and the challenges emerge from the markets, stakeholders, information technologies, business needs, among others. In what concerns information technologies, the evolution in the capacity to collect, store and process data has started the need of developing new environments, using different technologies, which require a redesign of the organizations' information systems, and their business intelligence and analytics capabilities [1].

Data models are a central piece in information systems design and development, and their analytical capabilities, as they ensure that data needs are properly considered. In a traditional organizational environment, the relational data models are very popular and are defined following strict rules about the requirements these models should consider. However, when we move to an emergent context like the one represented by Big Data, and due to the characteristics of the NoSQL databases, the data modeling task changes of perspective, as those databases are schema-free. This means that the data model can change in runtime, due to the needs of data storage or analytical tasks. The models, in this context, are designed considering the queries that need to be answered [2]. Although schema-free, these databases do need data models that ensure the proper storage of the data and their search with specific queries.

© Springer International Publishing Switzerland 2016
Y. Tan and Y. Shi (Eds.): DMBD 2016, LNCS 9714, pp. 475–485, 2016.
DOI: 10.1007/978-3-319-40973-3_48

If we think on the vast amount of relational databases already implemented and foresee the need of transferring these databases to a columnar format, due to the ever-increasing volume of data, for instance, the importance of data models in Big Data increases. In contexts where we are expecting a fast transition from one environment to the other, the proposal of objective rules for this transition will benefit the users and will ensure proper data handling.

In this paper, a specific set of rules is proposed for a transition between a traditional organizational environment and a Big Data environment, considering two specific objectives: the identification of a columnar data model supporting operational needs and the identification of a tabular data model supporting analytical needs, both in Big Data contexts. While the first is suited to be implemented in a NoSQL database like HBase, the second is the basis for the data warehouse storage of Hive.

This paper is organized as follows. Section 2 presents related work. Section 3 describes the definitions and rules proposed for the automatic transformation of models. Section 4 uses a demonstration case to show the applicability of the proposed approach. Section 5 concludes with some remarks and guidelines for future work.

2 Related Work

In a Big Data context, where NoSQL databases are usually used, logical data models are schema-free, meaning that different rows in a table may have different data columns (less rigid structures) or that the defined schema may change on runtime [3]. In practical terms, those databases do have a data schema, but its definition follows a different approach. Instead of reflecting the relevant entities in a particular domain and the relationships between those entities, for instance, data schemas are defined having into consideration the queries that need to be answered, being data replicated as many times as needed, as long as the queries can be quickly answered. In this context, all queries that need to be answered must be known in advance [4], which could be a drawback if we consider analytical environments where data is available but the analytical needs depend on many different users and different contexts.

The work of [4] proposes an algorithm that automatically determines the most cost efficient data structure for a selected subset of NoSQL data stores, where cost efficiency is calculated based on the fees the developers need to pay in a cloud environment, which charges users based on the size of the stored data and the queries that need to be performed. This work uses the column-oriented data stores of Windows Azure Table and Amazon DynamoDB. The proposed approach starts from a predefined relational data schema and a set of queries, and performs automatic schema denormalization to find the optimal storage schema regarding a given query load. Also, mappings from the original queries to the newly created schemas are provided [4]. In this work, it is important to point out that queries must be known beforehand and that the proposed algorithm performs heavy denormalization, not optimizing the different number of generated data schemas.

Another work that proposes a heuristic-based approach for transforming a relational database into a columnar database, for HBase, is [3], and includes two phases. In the first one, three guidelines are used for transforming the relational database into the

HBase schema. In the second one, relationships between the two schemas are expressed and used to create a set of queries that transform the source relational data into the target representation. In the first phase, the authors recognize that business requirements and access/write patterns of the application are needed, and that this work is done by application experts, not proposing a semi-automatic or automatic process for dealing with the whole transformation.

The work of [5] recognizes that the design of big data warehouses differs considerable from traditional data warehouses, as their schema should be based on novel logical models that allow more flexibility than the relational model does. The authors propose a design methodology for the representation of a multidimensional schema at the logical level based on the key-value model. The proposed methodology is considered hybrid as integrates a data-driven approach design, using data repositories as main source of information, and a requirements-driven approach design, using information of the decision makers. In this case, the needs of decision makers are investigated, requiring additional information, besides input data models.

3 Data Schemas in Big Data Environments

With the advent of Big Data, the ability to collect, process and store data increases in a context where NoSQL databases are schema-free, allowing the storage of huge amounts of data without many concerns about the data structure. Those concerns emerge later on a schema-on-read approach, in which data is parsed, formatted and cleaned at runtime. Although having fewer concerns at the beginning of the collection phase, this adds several tasks latter when there is the need to develop specific applications to analyze the data. At some point, these schema-free repositories need to be transformed into some structured data model that allows data analysis by the users.

Considering that in a Big Data context there is the need to add structure to the data when analytical tasks need to be performed, this paper proposes a transformation process that leverages data modeling capabilities to the Big Data environment. The advantage of the proposed approach is that it considers all the business needs expressed in the operational data model that supports on-line transaction processing (OLTP) and uses that information for identifying useful data schemas in Big Data when analytical capabilities are needed. In this paper, a relational data model is used to automatically identify the appropriate data models in a NoSQL context, using the columnar data model of HBase and the tabular data model of Hive, here for a Big Data Warehouse context (BDW). In an operational context, those columnar data models allow data analysis in a real-time fashion, while the BDW allows analytical processes that run in a periodic fashion.

3.1 From an Operational Data Model to a Columnar Model

A column-oriented database in a NoSQL context is constituted by a set of tables defined row by row, but organized by groups of columns usually named column-families. This organization is followed by HBase and makes a vertical partitioning of the data. Each column-family may contain a variable number of columns and allows the lack of some columns between different rows of a same table [6]. Given this context, following are presented definitions and rules to formalize the transformation of a Relational Data Model to a Columnar Data Model.

Definition 1. A Relational Data Model, $RDM = (E, A, R)$, includes a set of entities $E = \{E^1, E^2, \ldots, E^n\}$, the corresponding attributes, $A = \{A^1, A^2, \ldots, A^n\}$, where A^1 is the set of attributes for entity E^1, $A^1 = \{A_1^1, A_2^1, \ldots, A_k^1\}$, and a set of relationships among entities $R = \{R_1^l(c_o|c_d), R_2^l(c_o|c_d), \ldots, R_m^l(c_o|c_d)\}$, where R_m^l express a relationship between E^m and E^l of cardinality c_o in the origin entity E^m and c_d in the destination entity E^l. Cardinalities can be of type $1 : n$, $m : n$ or $1 : 1$, with the optional 0 when needed.

Definition 2. A Columnar Data Model, $CDM = (T, CF)$, includes a set of tables $T = \{T^1, T^2, \ldots, T^n\}$, where each table integrates a key and a set of column-families, as $T^i = \{key^i, CF^1, \ldots, CF^m\}$. Each column-family integrates a set of columns representing the atomic values to be stored, $CF^j = \{C_j^1, \ldots, C_j^k\}$.

Rule CDM.1. Identification of Column-Families. The identification of column-families of a *CDM* follows a two-step approach:

Rule CDM.1.1. Identification of Descriptive Column-Families. Each entity only receiving cardinalities of 1 ($c_o = 1$ and $c_d = 1$) in the *RDM* corresponds to a descriptive column-family in the *CDM*, as this entity is used to complement the description of other entities (entity usually derived from the normal forms). The attributes of a descriptive column-family are constituted by the set of non-key attributes (excluding primary or foreign keys) present in the corresponding entities in the *RDM*.

Rule CDM.1.2. Identification of Analytical Column-Families. All entities present in the *RDM* and not identified by Rule CDM.1.1 as descriptive column-families, give origin to analytical column-families integrating the indicators or measures that can be analyzed considering the several descriptive column-families, as long as those entities have attributes of the relationships they are representing, which means that besides keys (primary or foreign), these entities need to integrate other attributes. The attributes of analytical column-families are constituted by the set of non-key attributes (excluding primary or foreign keys) present in the corresponding entities in the *RDM*.

Rule CDM.2. Identification of Tables. Two types of tables are proposed for a *CDM* supporting an operational system:

Rule CDM.2.1. Descriptive Tables. Descriptive tables are those tables that support specific data management tasks in an operational system. Correspond to the column-families identified by Rule CDM.1.1.

Rule CDM.2.2. Analytical Tables. For the identification of the set of analytical tables there is the need of identifying the data workflows present in the *RDM* and, from the set of data workflows, those that are able to represent all the data circulating in the *RDM*. For identifying the data workflows of a *RDM*, all entities receiving only cardinalities of 1 (used to identify the descriptive column-families by Rule CDM.1.1) start a data workflow following the *1:n* relationships associated to it, and all other *1:n* relationships that follows. The data workflow ends when a *n:1* relationship is found, meaning that it was possible to join a coherent piece of information that is related with each other and that was split in the *RDM* by the normalization forms. All identified workflows that are not fully contained by other workflows give origin to analytical tables.

Rule CDM.3. Integration of Column-Families into Tables. A specific table integrates a key, which is a very important component of a table in a *CDM*, and a set of column-families, which may vary depending on the type of table.

Rule CDM.3.1. Column-Families of Descriptive Tables. A descriptive table includes as a column-family, the column-family derived from the corresponding entity in the *RDM* (Rule CDM.1.1).

Rule CDM.3.2. Column-Families of Analytical Tables. An analytical table includes as column-families all the descriptive and analytical column-families associated with the entities included in the data workflow that gave origin to a specific table.

Rule CDM.4. Definition of the Tables' Key. A table's key should be able to assure an adequate performance throughout read and write access patterns from the application. The key represents a set of one or more attributes (concatenated) that have the potential to form a natural key that properly identifies each row in the *CDM*. This key must serve the applications' get, scan and put patterns, keeping them as short as possible, while maintaining the potential for adequate access patterns [6]. The order in which the attributes are concatenated plays a relevant role in the design of the key, since HBase stores keys in a sorted order [7].

To exemplify the proposed rules, let us consider a small example in which the *RDM* is represented by the relational data model depicted in Fig. 1.

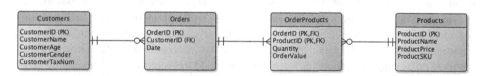

Fig. 1. Example of a *RDM* for orders

Taking into consideration the rules expressed for the transformation of a *RDM* into a *CDM*, the obtained model is depicted in Fig. 2, where the descriptive column-families *Customers$_{CF}$* and *Products$_{CF}$* (Rule CDM.1.1) are identified. By Rule CDM.1.2, the analytical column-families *Orders$_{CF}$* and *OrderProducts$_{CF}$* are identified. For tables, the tables of the *CDM* include as descriptive tables *Customer$_T$* and *Products$_T$* (Rule CDM.2.1). For analytical tables, two data workflows are identified, one starting in *Customers* and ending in *Products*, and the other starting in *Products* and ending in *Orders* (Rule CDM.2.2). However, as these workflows overlap, being one completely contained by the other, the contained one must be ignored.

This leads to the identification of one analytical table, here named as $Orders_T$. The integration of the column-families in the corresponding tables is achieved following Rule CDM.3. Rule CDM.4 must form a concatenated key obtained from the available attributes, as shown in Fig. 2. In the case of the customers' key, as well as in other keys, it might be needed to use the inverse of the key (with regard to the *CustomerTaxNum*), to avoid the creation of hot regions in the storage cluster.

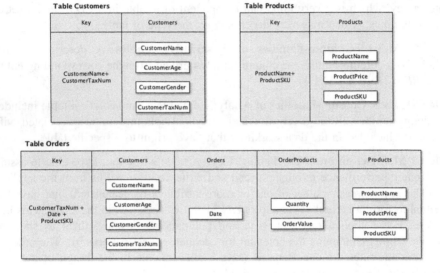

Fig. 2. Resulting *CDM* for orders

3.2   From a Columnar Model to a Tabular Data Model

In an analytical context for decision support, it is expected that the user could ask for aggregates based on the available data. In this work, it is proposed that the data warehouse model in the Big Data context, using Hive, be created based on the NoSQL columnar model (CDM). Hive [8] is a data storage mechanism in Big Data environments used as a data warehousing software that facilitates querying and managing large datasets that are in distributed storage [9]. Having the data in a distributed file system, Hive adds structure to the data and allows querying through the use of the HiveQL (Hive Query Language), a SQL-like language [10].

At this point, the *CDM* enables the derivation of a tabular data model that is formally defined as follows.

Definition 3. A Tabular Data Model, $TDM = (T, C)$, includes a set of tables $T = \{T^1, T^2, \ldots, T^n\}$, where each table integrates a set of columns, $T^i = \{C^1, \ldots, C^m\}$, storing the atomic values.

Rule TDM.1. Identification of Tables. All the analytical tables in a *CDM* give origin to tables in the *TDM*, as those will include the relevant data for data analysis and decision support.

Rule TDM.2. Identification of Columns. The identification of columns for each table identified by Rule TDM.1 follows a two-step approach.

Rule TDM.2.1. Identification of Descriptive Columns. The attributes that integrate the several descriptive column-families of the *CDM* give origin to descriptive columns of a table in the *TDM*.

Rule TDM.2.2. Identification of Analytical Columns. The attributes that integrate the several analytical column-families of the *CDM* give origin to analytical columns of a table in the *TDM*. As the *TDM* contains data that can be aggregated, the user can adopt different aggregation functions as SUM, MIN, MAX, AVG or COUNT to summarize the analytical columns.

Considering the example presented in previous subsection, one table is identified to be included in the TDM (Fig. 3), $Orders_T$ (Rule TDM.1). For $Orders_T$, the descriptive attributes *CustomerName, CustomerAge, CustomerGender, CustomerTaxNum, Date, ProductName, ProductPrice* and *ProductSKU* are identified as descriptive columns (Rule TDM.2.1), while *Quantity* and *OrderValue* are identified as analytical columns (Rule TDM.2.2). These analytical columns can now be manipulated in Hive, providing different analytical perspectives with different aggregations.

Table Orders

Customer Name	Customer Age	Customer Gender	Customer TaxNum	Date	Product Name	Product Price	Product SKU	Quantity	Order Value

Fig. 3. Resulting *TDM* for the orders

4 Demonstration Case

This section presents a more complete example of the model transformations proposed in this paper, for defining the data models in a Big Data environment taking into consideration an operational data model expressed in relational data model. The *RDM* used as starting point is presented in Fig. 4, from [11]. The model integrates eight entities, several attributes, and the relationships among the entities.

From this data model, we will start by the rules expressed in Sect. 3.1 for the identification of a columnar NoSQL data model. The descriptive column-families present in the diagram of Fig. 4 are $Hotels_{CF}$, $POIs_{CF}$, $Guests_{CF}$ and $Amenities_{CF}$ (Rule CDM.1.1) as these entities only receive relationships with cardinality of 1. All other entities in the model give origin to analytical column-families (Rule CDM.1.2), namely $Rooms_{CF}$ and $Reservations_{CF}$ (*HotelPOIs* and *RoomAmenities* are not identified as column-families as they do not integrate other attributes besides keys). The attributes of these column-families are the attributes of the corresponding entities in the *RDM*, excluding the keys, either primary (PK) or foreign (FK) keys. Regarding Rule CDM.2, the descriptive tables are $Hotels_T$, $POIs_T$, $Guests_T$ and $Amenities_T$ associated with the identified descriptive column-families (Rule CDM.2.1), while for the identification of the analytical tables there is the need of identifying the data workflows of the *RDM*

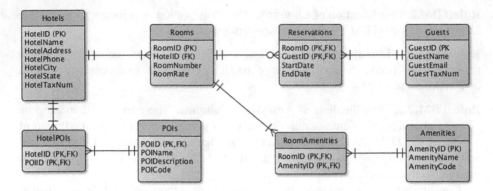

Fig. 4. *RDM* for the hotel's demonstration case (Adapted from: [11])

(Rule CDM.2.2). Starting by all entities only receiving relationships with cardinalities of 1, Fig. 5 presents the three identified data workflows, which lead to three analytical tables from now on named *Reservations$_T$*, *RoomAmenities$_T$* and *HotelPOIs$_T$*.

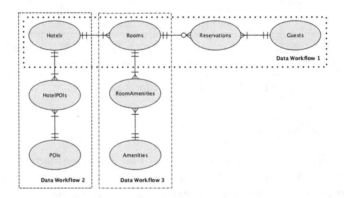

Fig. 5. Data Workflows for the *RDM*

Having identified the column-families and the several tables, it is now time to assign to each table its respective column-families. Each descriptive table integrates a column-family derived from its corresponding entity. For the analytical tables, *Reservations$_T$* integrates four column-families, *Hotels$_{CF}$*, *Rooms$_{CF}$*, *Reservations$_{CF}$* and *Guests$_{CF}$*, *RoomAmenities$_T$* integrates two column-families, *Rooms$_{CF}$* and *Amenities$_{CF}$*, and *HotelPOIs$_T$* also integrates two column-families, *Hotels$_{CF}$* and *POIs$_{CF}$*. Figure 6 depicts the identified *CDM* with the seven resulting tables.

Looking to the obtained model, and comparing it with the one presented in [11], it was possible to see that although both models present the same number of tables, seven, they are organized in a different way. Nevertheless, both are able to answer the same questions. At this point, it is important to mention that there are many possible ways to organize a columnar data schema [11]. In this paper, we presented one that was

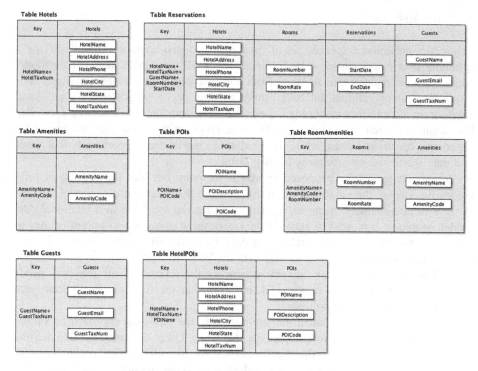

Fig. 6. *CDM* for the hotel's demonstration case

obtained through an automatic process that aims to help the users or data modelers in this task.

After the identification of the *CDM*, it is possible to proceed with the rules specified in Sect. 3.2 for the identification of a *TDM*. In this model, given the characteristics of Hive as a data warehouse for Big Data contexts, Rule TDM.1 allows the identification of the Hive tables based on the analytical tables of the *CDM*, which leads to the identification of *Reservations$_T$*, *RoomAmenities$_T$* and *HotelPOIs$_T$*. By Rule TDM.2, these tables will integrate several descriptive columns derived from the descriptive column-families *Hotels$_{CF}$*, *POIs$_{CF}$*, *Guests$_{CF}$* and *Amenities$_{CF}$* (Rule TDM.2.1) and analytical columns derived from the analytical column-families *Rooms$_{CF}$* and *Reservations$_{CF}$* (Rule TDM.2.2). For these analytical tables, Fig. 7 presents the obtained *TDM*.

Table RoomAmenities

Room Number	Room Rate	Amenity Name	Amenity Code

Table HotelPOIs

Hotel Name	Hotel Address	Hotel Phone	Hotel City	Hotel State	Hotel TaxNum	POI Name	POI Description	POI Code

Table Reservations

Hotel Name	Hotel Address	Hotel Phone	Hotel City	Hotel State	Hotel TaxNum	Room Number	Room Rate	Start Date	End Date	Guest Name	Guest Email	Guest TaxNum

Fig. 7. *TDM* for the hotel's demonstration case

5   Conclusions

This paper presented a specific set of rules in a two-step approach for identifying a columnar data model suited to be implemented in HBase, and a tabular data model prepared to be implemented in Hive. Both consider that there are organizational contexts where an operational database cannot continue to be supported by a relational database in a traditional technological environment, and that the transition for a Big Data context is needed. In this case, this work proposes the columnar data model for supporting operational tasks, while the tabular data model can support analytical needs in a data warehouse environment for Big Data.

As advantages of the proposed approach we point out that the process is fully automatic, guiding the identification of the tables of the columnar data model, as well as their column-families, using as input the information available in a relational data model. Moreover, a process to generate the key of these tables is also suggested, due to the importance of the key in searching for data. Using the information of the columnar data model, the transition for a tabular data model is also addressed in an automatic way. Besides these, it is an integrated process that considers all the data needs expressed in the relational data model, ensuring that the business needs that were initially modeled are still applicable.

As future work, it is planned the application of the proposed approach to a more complex scenario, in order to complement this work. Other data models, like the one supported by Cassandra, should also be considered, as well as other particular organizational needs that may be expressed in the relational data model used as input of the proposed process.

Acknowledgments. This work has been supported by COMPETE: POCI-01-0145-FEDER-007043 and FCT, *Fundação para a Ciência e Tecnologia*, within the Projects UID/CEC/00319/2013 (ALGORITMI) and MITP-TB/CS/0026/2013 (SusCity).

References

1. Chen, H., Chiang, R.H., Storey, V.C.: Business intelligence and analytics: from Big Data to Big Impact. MIS Q. **36**, 1165–1188 (2012)
2. Durham, E.-E., Rosen, A., Harrison, R.W., et al.: A model architecture for Big Data applications using relational databases. In: 2014 IEEE International Conference on Big Data (Big Data), pp. 9–16. IEEE (2014)
3. Li, C.: Transforming relational database into HBase: a case study. In: 2010 IEEE International Conference on Software Engineering and Service Sciences (ICSESS), pp. 683–687. IEEE (2010)
4. Vajk, T., Feher, P., Fekete, K., Charaf, H.: Denormalizing data into schema-free databases. In: 2013 IEEE 4th International Conference on Cognitive Infocommunications (CogInfoCom), pp. 747–752. IEEE (2013)
5. Di Tria, F., Lefons, E., Tangorra, F.: Design process for Big Data warehouses. In: 2014 International Conference on Data Science and Advanced Analytics (DSAA), pp. 512–518. IEEE (2014)

6. HBase: Apache HBase (2016). https://hbase.apache.org
7. Khurana, A.: Introduction to HBase schema design. White Paper, Cloudera (2012)
8. Hive: Apache Hive (2016). https://hive.apache.org
9. Thusoo, A., Sarma, J.S., Jain, N., Shao, Z., Chakka, P., Zhang, N., Antony, S., Liu, H., Murthy, R.: Hive-a petabyte scale data warehouse using hadoop. In: 2010 IEEE 26th International Conference on Data Engineering (ICDE), pp. 996–1005. IEEE (2010)
10. Capriolo, E., Wampler, D., Rutherglen, J.: Programming Hive. O'Reilly & Associates, Sebastopol (2012)
11. Hewitt, E.: Cassandra: The Definitive Guide. O'Reilly, Beijing (2011)

Probabilistic Mining in Large Transaction Databases

Hareendran S. Anand[1](✉) and S.S. Vinod Chandra[2]

[1] Department of Computer Science and Engineering,
Muthoot Institute of Technology and Science, Kochi, Kerala, India
anandhareendrans@mgits.ac.in
[2] Computer Center, University of Kerala, Trivandrum, Kerala, India

Abstract. In this era of big data analysis, mining results hold a very important role. So, the data scientists need to be accurate enough with the tools, methods and procedures while performing rule mining. The major issues faced by these scientists are incremental mining and the huge amount of time that is virtually required to finish the mining task. In this context, we propose a new rule mining algorithm which mines the database in a probabilistic approach for finding interesting relations. This paper also compares the new technique with the traditional Apriori, FP Growth and Eclat algorithms. The proposal has also been tested against the various modified approaches of these algorithms. The proposed algorithm finishes the task in O (n) in its best case analysis and in O (n log n) in its worst case analysis. The algorithm also considers less frequent high priority attributes for rule creation, thus makes sure the creation of valid mining rules. The major issue of traditional algorithms was the generation of invalid rules, longer running time and high memory utilizations. This could be remedied by this new proposal. The algorithm was tested against various datasets and the results were evaluated and compared with the traditional algorithm. The results showed a peak performance improvement.

Keywords: Probabilistic mining · Association rules · Rule mining · Apriori algorithm · Priority mining · Correlation mining

1 Introduction

Association rules are if-then statements, which help to uncover the vast relationship between seemingly unrelated data [1]. It uses a combination of statistical analysis, machine learning and database management to exhaustively explore the data to reveal the complex relationships that exists. This work aims to provide all such details for analysis through valid rule creation using a probabilistic mining approach. The process begins by scanning the transactional database. Along with the scanning the probabilities of each itemset is calculated and stored in a probabilistic array. Rules are created from this array during mining. There are some itemsets which may be less frequent but having a high impact in the database. All traditional algorithms prunes off such items in a very early stage. But the proposed algorithm provides an extra threshold for less frequent high priority itemsets thereby making them available for rule creation. The proposed algorithm is compared with the traditional mining algorithm like Apriori, FP growth,

© Springer International Publishing Switzerland 2016
Y. Tan and Y. Shi (Eds.): DMBD 2016, LNCS 9714, pp. 486–494, 2016.
DOI: 10.1007/978-3-319-40973-3_49

and variations of these traditional algorithms. The performance of the algorithm is evaluated asymptotically and the result obtained shows a peak improvement in the validity of rules created. The algorithm was further tested with real time transactional datasets and a comparison was drawn with the help of a trend analysis graph.

2 Literature Survey

Apriori algorithm put forward by Agrawal and Srikanth in 1993 was the most promising work in this area [2]. It quoted the various aspects of Apriori algorithm. Almost all association rule mining algorithms which were proposed after this holds the Apriori principle stated by Agrawal in some way or the other. There have been a lot of modified and advanced schemes proposed. Among them Zaki [3] introduced a new algorithm for fast discovery of association rules. The proposal was of great impact, but not all associated rules could be retrieved by this scheme. Association mining finds it application in various fields like rule mining in genomics [4], for finding synthetic data for testing market basket problem [5], for predictive analysis [6] etc. Apriori algorithm was also implemented using hash table technique [7, 8]. The new proposal was efficient but the time taken to complete the task was much higher. Hence while having a bulky dataset, the algorithm fails miserably. Kryszkiewicz and Rybinski [9] during 2000 proposed a new algorithm which mines very large databases based on association rules generation. But the time taken for mining was considerably large and it was not found to be efficient. In 1999, Kosters [10] proposed a method to extract clusters based on the Apriori algorithm. The method considers the highest possible order association rules. It was a combined algorithm based on both the Apriori algorithm and rough set theory (initially proposed by Lin [11]). Frequent pattern growth was another mining algorithm. Christian Borgelt in his work [12] explains how mining task is carried out in the FP tree. The memory utilization was not perfect and the system failed while handling large database. There was an enhancement to the FP growth algorithm. Malik [13] implemented an Enhanced FP Growth Algorithm, which was found to be more improved on mining results.

3 Probabilistic Mining

Associations thus found are used in various streams of human day to day activities. Market analysis, risk management, customer behavior, telecommunication, product and catalogue design, store layout and even in inventory management association rules play the vital role. These rules are created from transaction databases of tremendously high order.

Apriori Property: This property states that, if we have a superset of all the frequent item sets, then each item itself will be frequent. This is a thumb rule which is made used while calculating the frequent items from a database.

Correlation Threshold: This is a new term introduced in this paper for obtaining valid rules in less time complexity. This is actually a factor whose value lies between zero and one. This factor is required in order to maintain the flow of probability within the itemsets. Equation 1 shows how to find the correlation threshold C',

$$C' = [\alpha(P.\min) + \beta(P.\min * P.\max)]. \tag{1}$$

where P.min and P.max are the minimum and maximum probability of itemsets. The value of the probability is found out from the probabilistic array. While checking the formula, we have two constants α and β; these are termed as the correlation constants. The values of these constants are obtained by calculating the mean of probabilities. Normally the value of β; is initialized to the least probability of item set obtained from the initial probabilistic array. We should always check the condition that, $\alpha + \beta = 1$, in all situations (probabilistic property). There can also be a question regarding why minimum and maximum probabilities are used in finding correlation threshold. This can be justified, while mining frequent items our aim is to obtain those item sets which are very frequent. If we take the average of probability than minimum or maximum, then there are chances that even the most frequent items gets eliminated or the least frequent item to get included. By having the correlation factor, the algorithm's performance is also enhanced.

3.1   Derivation of Correlation Threshold Factor

By law of probability, if A1, A2, A3,...An be set of independent events, if P(Ai1Ai2... Aik) = P(Ai1)P(Ai2)...P(Aik) for any k, then we can say that the events A1, A2,... An are independent. In this work we make use of probabilistic array, if P1, P2,...Pn are the independent probability of the item sets A1, A2,... An, then by law of probability the chance that any two itemsets Ab and Ac appear in a single transaction can be given by Pbc. If both itemsets are independent then probability is Pb*Pc. For a total correlation it can be denoted by the minimum of Pb and Pc. i.e., Pb*Pc < Pbc < Pb. So, now to find the probability of occurrence of itemsets in single transaction, we need to make use of total correlation (Pb) and independent correlation (Pb*Pc). Let α be the total correlation coefficient and β be the non-total coefficient. Thus we can conclude the final equation as Pbc = α (Pb) + β (Pb * Pc).

Generalizing the equation we get, $C' = [\alpha(P.\min) + \beta(P.\min * P.\max)]$

3.2   Probabilistic Approach

The new proposal can be divided into two parts, first one is the frequent itemset generation and the second one is the rule creation phase. In the first phase of algorithm i.e. in the candidate itemset generation phase, threshold has to be found out for all strong associations in the database. The correlation threshold is a value between 0 and 1. The value 1, suggests that the variables are highly interlinked and the value close to zero mentions the dataset as highly independent. This correlation confirms the presence of all itemset appearing in traditional Apriori in proposed algorithm. The proposed algorithm is given in Algorithm 1.

Algorithm 1 Probabilistic Approach
___

Input: Database **D** with **n** elements

Output: Frequent item, **I** and Rule **S**

Data structure Used: Probabilistic Array, $PA_0[n]$

while (n!=NULL)

    Scan the database **D** and input the probability of the **n** elements into $PA_0[n]$

    for(i = 0; i < n; i++)

        Calculate correlation threshold C_i from $PA_0[n]$

        for (k = 0; k < n; k++)

            if ($C'_i = PA_i[k]$)

                update $PA_{i+1}[k]$

            for each frequent item set I of non empty array $PA_i[n]$

        if (Support(I)/Support($PA_i[n]$) > c'_i)

    generate rule s ➡(I-$PA_i[n]$)
___

Database, **D** is first scanned. Next step is to initialize the probabilistic array **PA[]**. If we have say, **n** elements in the database **D**, the array is initialized as, **PA[n]**. After performing the first round of scan we get the probability of all 1-itemset. It is then entered into the **PA[n]**. Next step is to find the correlation threshold straight from the probabilistic array. This is done by using the Eq. (1). The value thus calculated is taken as the minimum support threshold. All those items having a value less than the threshold is pruned off. This process is repeated and the 2-itemsets are generated similarly from the probabilistic array, **PA[n]** by finding new correlation threshold. Repeated database scan which was the drawback of Apriori is being avoided as the candidate itemset generation is done directly from the PA[n] and not by continuous scanning of **D**. Thus by scanning database once, the probabilistic array is filled and all the consecutive itemset generations are done from that array by checking the threshold.

Priority: In a database even the least frequent item can have a major impact in the rules generated. In all association algorithms such infrequent items are pruned off without much analysis. In this proposed work, the priority of all item sets is found and it is analyzed with the frequency. After this analysis, if the item set is still invalid it is eliminated or else it is considered for rule creation. For example, in case of serum analysis for myocardial infarction level of Troponins will be elevated. But in normal case its level in blood will be undetectable. All traditional mining algorithms prunes such items in the primary step itself, thus its level or presence may not be available in the final predicted rules. The maximum possible weight (W_{mp}): Let Y be a *p-itemset*, and X is a superset of Y with the *k-itemset* $(p < k)$. The maximum possible weight for any *k-itemset* containing Y is defined as

$$W_{mp}(Y,k) = \frac{1}{k} \left(\sum_{i,j \in y, j=1}^{n} w_j + \sum_{l=1}^{k-n} w_l \right) \tag{2}$$

In Eq. 2, the first part is the average weight for the p-itemsets and the second part is the average weight of the *(k-p)* maximum remaining itemsets.

Consider the following database in Table 1,

Table 1. Serum analysis database

Troponin	Myoglobin	Creatin	Sodium	Magnesium	Calcium	Sugar	UA
1	0	1	0	1	1	0	1
1	1	1	0	1	1	0	1
0	1	1	1	1	0	1	1
1	0	0	1	1	0	1	1
1	1	0	0	1	1	0	1
1	0	0	1	1	0	1	1
0	0	1	1	1	0	1	1
1	1	1	0	1	1	1	1
1	0	1	1	1	0	1	1
1	0	1	0	1	1	0	1
0	1	0	1	1	0	1	1
1	0	1	0	1	1	0	1

Table 1, provides the serum analysis report. The aim of our study is to find the most frequent occurrences of Troponins, Creatine Kinase and Myoglobin. These are the enzymes released during MI. If using the traditional scheme, it may provide the final frequent item list as <Na, Mg, BS, UA>. This has nothing to predict with the MI. Now let's look how the proposed system works, starting with the probabilistic array, we have Myoglobin with 5/11 and Mg, UA with 11/11. The initial threshold and the co relational constant β is fixed at 5/11. Now Itemset-2 is generated from the initial probabilistic array. From Eq. 1, we have the C1 = 44/121 = 0.3636. Now prune the itemsets whose threshold is below C1. Algorithm continues till the final frequent items are obtained. Figure 1 is the graph showing the comparison on the number of itemsets produced by the traditional algorithm to the proposed system.

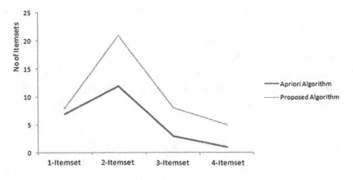

Fig. 1. Itemset generation comparison (Color figure online)

After the generation of Itemset-4, the proposed algorithm provides the mined results as <T, M, C, Mg>, <T, M, Mg, Ca>, <T, C, Mg, Ca>, <T, C, Mg, BS>, <Na, Mg, BS, UA>. Here the result has not pruned the presence of the most important enzymes that released during MI, thereby helping the diagnosis. Thus results affirm that even the least frequent but high priority itemset are included in rule formation making the results valid.

Generate Rule: This is the second step of the algorithm, here all those rules above the threshold T is calculated. Initially the rule set R is initialized to NULL. For each frequent item obtained, the ratio of frequent item to its supporting item sets are found out. If it is greater than the threshold, the rule is added to R. This process is continued until all the frequent items are visited for rule creation. The support count for each set for all combination needs to be found out using the support count Eq. 3 or 4.

$$\text{Threshold} = \text{SC (Individual Items)}/\text{SC (Rule ItemSet)} \tag{3}$$

$$\text{Threshold} = \text{SC (Individual Items)}/\text{SC (Conclusion ItemSet)} \tag{4}$$

3.3 Complexity Analysis

Time complexity of Apriori algorithm is the sum of time taken for generation of frequent items and time taken for rule generation. For n transactions with m itemsets, the time taken for frequent itemset generation is,

$$= \sum_{i=1}^{m} [(ni - (m+1)) + (\sum_{i=0}^{m-i} (ni - 1)) + 1] \tag{5}$$

Similarly for rule generation the time complexity calculated as,

$$
\begin{aligned}
&= c_1^k + c_2^k + \ldots + c_n^k \\
&= \sum_{k=1, j=c_k^m}^{k=m} [\sum_{i=1}^{i=j} C_i^j] \\
&= \sum_{k=1}^{k=m} m \sum_{i=1}^{i=j} C_i^j \\
&\cong O(n) \text{ as } n \to \infty
\end{aligned}
\tag{6}
$$

Thus total time complexity is the sum of (5) and (6),

$$\text{ie., } O(e^n) \text{ as } n \to \infty \tag{7}$$

The analysis part clearly describes that the algorithm works in the linear order, O(n) in the best case scenario, and even keeps the algorithm steady in O(n log n) in worst case scenarios, which is far better than the competitor algorithms of the same genre.

3.4   Discussions

The proposed algorithm was tested against the traditional algorithms like FP growth and Apriori. The results obtained are shown in the Table 2. The standard databases available on the internet are used for the testing purposes. (Databases are available on this link: http://fimi.ua.ac.be/data/). Time is represented in milliseconds.

Table 2. Comparision of runtime against various databases

Min. support	DB used	Apriori algo.	FP growth algo.	Proposed algo.
25 %	Chess	469	348	227
25 %	Accidents	42356	22588	16289
25 %	Mushroom	14432	4897	3189
25 %	Retail	7739	4230	3912
25 %	Webdocs	255650	225440	195230

A graphical trend comparison of the algorithms with increased size of itemsets and records is provided in the graph (Fig. 2).

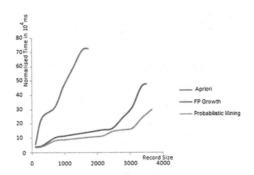

Fig. 2. Graphical comparison (Color figure online)

The algorithms work with relative time complexity when the size of dataset is small. As the size increases, we can see Apriori gets to an indefinite working loop. After a particular record size, the algorithm continuously delivers the last generated output, thereby creating an invalid rule. Even FP growth algorithm shows indefinite halt signs during the last stage of cycle (the flat part of the graph). The increase in sub-tree generation could be the major cause for this system halt while working with large record size. Probabilistic mining, on the other hand shows a very distinct performance improvement even with increases record size.

4   Conclusion

In this work a new association rule mining algorithm is put forward. It makes use of the priority model. From the priority model a probabilistic approach is used for frequent item mining and the rules are generated. The results are compared with the traditional mining algorithms like Apriori and FP growth. Algorithm was also tested by the datasets available in internet. Analysis of the algorithm in both time and space dimension was seen to be bound within O (n) and O (n log n), which is very much efficient than other mining algorithms. This proposal also helped to mine high priority non-frequent items for rule creation. Probabilistic mining could be extended to market basket analysis, single variable prediction and even to practical applications like fault tolerance, estimation predictions and so on. A scheme for employing very large vertical database mining could be seen as a future scope of this mining. Also, prioritizing itemsets depending on the cluster centers can also be considered as an enhancement for this method.

References

1. Boney, L., Tewfik, A.H., Hamdy, K.N.: Minimum association rule in large database. In: Third International Conference on Computing, pp. 12–16. IEEE Press (2006)
2. Agrawal, R., Srikant, R.: Fast algorithms for mining association rules. In. VLDB, pp. 487–499 (1994)
3. Zaki, M., Parthasarathy, S., Ogihara, M., Li. W.: New algorithms for fast discovery of association rules. In. Third International Conference on Knowledge Discovery and Data Mining, vol. 2, pp. 283–296 (1997)
4. Anandhavalli, M., Gautaman, K.: Association rule mining in genomics. Int. J. Comput. Theor. Eng. **1**, 1–13 (2007)
5. Cooper, C., Zito, M.: Realistic synthetic data for testing association rule mining algorithms for market basket databases. In: Kok, J.N., Koronacki, J., Lopez de Mantaras, R., Matwin, S., Mladenič, D., Skowron, A. (eds.) PKDD 2007. LNCS (LNAI), vol. 4702, pp. 398–405. Springer, Heidelberg (2007)
6. Varde, A.S., Takahashi, M., Rundensteiner, E.A., Ward, M.O., Maniruzzaman, M., Sisson, R.D.: Apriori algorithm and game of life for predictive analysis in materials science. Int. J. Knowl. Based Intell. Eng. Syst. **8**, 116–122 (2004)
7. Wu, H., Lu, Z., Pan, L., Xu, R., Jiang, W.: An improved apriori based algorithm for association rules mining. In. Proceedings of the Sixth International Conference on Fuzzy Systems and Knowledge Discovery, pp. 51–55 (2009)
8. Bodon, F.: A fast apriori implementation. In: Proceedings of the ICDM Workshop on Frequent Item-set Mining Implementation, vol. 9. IEEE Press (2003)
9. Kryszkiewicz, M., Rybiński, H.: Data mining in incomplete information systems from rough set perspective. In: Polkowski, L., Tsumoto, S., Lin, T.Y. (eds.) Rough Set Methods and Applications, vol. 56, pp. 567–580. Springer, Heidelberg (2000)
10. Kosters, W.A., Marchiori, E., Oerlemans, A.A.: Mining clusters with association rules. In: Hand, D.J., Kok, J.N., Berthold, M. (eds.) IDA 1999. LNCS, vol. 1642, pp. 39–50. Springer, Heidelberg (1999)

11. Lin, T.Y.: Rough set theory in very large databases. In: Symposium on Modeling, Analysis and Simulation, vol. 2, pp. 936–941 (1996)
12. Borgelt, C.: An implementation of FP growth algorithm. In: Proceedings of the Workshop on Open Source Mining Software. ACM Press (2005)
13. Malik, K., Raheja, N., Garg, P.: Enhance FP growth algorithm. Int. J. Comput. Eng. Manag. **12**, 54–57 (2011)

Computational Aspects of Pattern Recognition and Computer Vision

A First Attempt on Online Data Stream Classifier Using Context

Michał Woźniak[1]([envelope]) and Bogusław Cyganek[2,3]

[1] Faculty of Electronics, Department of Systems and Computer Networks, Wrocław University of Science and Technology, Wrocław, Poland
michal.wozniak@pwr.edu.pl
[2] AGH University of Science and Technology, Kraków, Poland
cyganek@agh.edu.pl
[3] ENGINE Center, Wrocław University of Science and Technology, Wrocław, Poland

Abstract. The big data is characterized by 4Vs (*volume, velocity, variety,* and *variability*). In this paper we focus on the *velocity*, but actually it usually comes together with *volume*. It means, that the crucial problem of the contemporary data analytics is to answer the question how to discover useful knowledge from fast incoming data. The paper presents an online data stream classification method, which adapts the classification with context to recognize incoming examples and additionally takes into consideration the memory and processing time limitations. The proposed method was evaluated on the real medical diagnosis task. The preliminary results of the experiments encourage us to continue works on the proposed approach.

Keywords: Data stream · Classification with context · Pattern classification

1 Introduction

The analysis of huge volumes and fast arriving data is recently the focus of intense research, because such methods could build a competitive advantage of a given company. One of the useful approach is the data stream classification, which is employed to solve problems related to discovery client preference changes, spam filtering, fraud detection, and medical diagnosis to enumerate only a few. Basically, there are two classifier design approaches:

- *"build and use"*, which firstly focuses on the training a model and then the trained classifier makes a decision,
- *"build, use, and improve"*, which firstly tries to build a model quickly and then, it uses the trained classifier to make a decision and tries to tune the model parameters continuously.

The first approach is very traditional and may be used only under the assumptions that data used for training and being recognized comes from the same distribution and the number of training examples ensures that model is trained well

© Springer International Publishing Switzerland 2016
Y. Tan and Y. Shi (Eds.): DMBD 2016, LNCS 9714, pp. 497–504, 2016.
DOI: 10.1007/978-3-319-40973-3_50

(i.e., it is not undertrained). Of course, for many practical tasks such assumption could be accepted, nevertheless, many contemporary problems do not allow to approve them and should take into consideration that the statistical dependencies describing the classification task as *prior* probabilities and conditional probability density functions could change. Additionally, we should respect the fact that data may come very fast, what causes that it is impossible to label arriving examples manually by a human expert, but each object should be labeled by a classifier. The first problem is called *concept drift* [1] and the efficient methods, which are able to deal with it, are still the focus of intense research, because appearance of this phenomena may potentially cause a significant accuracy deterioration of an exploiting classifier. Basically, the following approaches may be considered to deal with the above problem:

- detecting the drift and retraining the classifier,
- rebuilding the model frequently, and
- adopting the classification model to changes.

In this work, we focus on the data stream without the drift or where the changes are very slow, smooth, and not so significant. The proposed method will employ the model *build, use, and improve*, i.e., it could be used to classify incoming examples even in the case, if the classifier's model still requires training. Thus, we concentrate on the family of online learner algorithms that continuously update the classifier parameters, while processing the incoming data. Not all types of classifiers can act as online learners. Basically, they have to meet some basic requirements [2]: (i) each object is processed only once in the course of training; (ii) the memory and processing time are limited, and (iii) the training process could be paused at any time, and its accuracy should not be lower than that of a classifier trained on batch of data collected up to the given time.

In this research we adopt the online learning to the data stream classification, but proposed model also takes into consideration additional information about incoming objects. We assume, that each decision is not independent, but also could depend on the previous classification. This situation is typical for medical diagnosis, especially in the case of chronic disease diagnosis, as hypertension diagnosis and therapy planing, or considered in this work, human acid-base state recognition. For such diagnosis tasks not only the recent observations about patient are taken into consideration while decision is made, but a doctor should also consider a patient history as previous ordered therapies and diagnoses.

There are several works related to the recognition with context. The first work was published by Raviv in 1967 [3], who employed the Markov chain model to the character recognition. The "classification with context" has been promoted especially by Toussaint [4] and Harallick [5]. It has been widely applied to the several domains as image processing or medical diagnosis [6]. The main contribution of this work is the proposition of the novel data stream classifier with context, which makes a decision on the basis of a recent observations about the incoming object and additionally takes into consideration the previous classifications. According to the restrictions of data stream analytics tools, it will use the limited memory and computational time.

2 Probabilistic Model of On-line Data Stream Classification

As we mentioned before, in many pattern classification tasks there exist dependencies among patterns to be classified, e.g., for character recognition (especially in the case if we have a *prior* knowledge, that the incoming characters form words from a given language, then the probability of character appearance depends of previous recognized sign), image classification, and chronic disease diagnosis (where historical data plays the crucial role for high quality medical assessment), to name only a few.

The formalization of classification task requires successively classified objects are related one to another, but also could take into considerations the occurrence of external factors changing the character of these relationships. Let's illustrate this task using an example of medical diagnosis. The aim of this task is to classify the successive states of a patient. Each diagnosis could be the basis for the certain therapeutic procedure. Thus, we obtain the closed-loop system, in which the object under observation could be simultaneously subjected to control (treatment) dependent on the classification.

In this research we do not take into consideration the control, which could be recognized as the cause of the concept drift. As distinct from the traditional concept drift model, where drift appears randomly, in this case the drift has deterministic nature. In the future, we are going to extend the model by applying the methods related to so-called *recurrent concept drift* [7].

Let us present the mathematical model of the online classifier with context [4]. The online classification consists of the classification of a sequence of observations of the incoming objects. Let's $x_n \in \mathcal{X} \subseteq \mathbb{R}^d$ denotes the feature vector characterizing the nth object and $j_n \in \mathcal{M} = \{1, ..., M\}$ be its label. The probabilistic approach implies the assumption that x_n and j_n are the observed values of a pair of random variables $\mathbf{X}_n$ and $\mathbf{J}_n$. Let's model the interdependence between successive classifications as the first-order time-homogeneous Markov chain. Its probabilistic characteristics, i.e., the transition probabilities and initial probabilities are given by the following formulas, which describe the probability that a given object belongs to class j_n if the previous decision was j_{n-1}.

$$
\begin{aligned}
p_{j_n, j_{n-1}} &= P(\mathbf{J}_n = j_n | \mathbf{J}_{n-1} = j_{n-1}, \mathbf{J}_{n-2} = j_{n-2}, ..., \mathbf{J}_1 = j_1) \\
&= P(\mathbf{J}_n = j_n | \mathbf{J}_n = j_n) \quad j_n, j_{n-1}, j_{n-2}, ..., j_1 \in \mathcal{M} \quad (1)
\end{aligned}
$$

the transition probabilities form the transition matrix

$$
\mathbf{P} = \begin{bmatrix} p_{1,1} & p_{1,2} & \cdots & p_{1,M} \\ p_{2,1} & p_{2,2} & \cdots & p_{2,M} \\ \vdots & & \ddots & \vdots \\ p_{M,1} & p_{M,2} & \cdots & p_{M,M} \end{bmatrix} \quad (2)
$$

and initial probabilities

$$p_{j_1} = P(\mathbf{J}_1 = j_1), \quad j_1 \in \mathcal{M} \tag{3}$$

form the vector of initial probabilities

$$\mathbf{p} = \begin{bmatrix} p_1 \, p_2 \, \cdots \, p_M \end{bmatrix}^T \tag{4}$$

We also assume that the probability distributions of the random variables $\mathbf{X}_n$ and $\mathbf{J}_n$ exist and they are characterized by the conditional probability density functions (CPDFs)

$$f_i(x_n), \quad i \in \mathcal{M}, \ x_n \in \mathcal{X} \tag{5}$$

Additionally, the probability density functions $f(\overline{x}_n | \overline{j}_n)$ exists and the observed stream (sequence of observations) is conditionally independent, i.e.,

$$f_n(\overline{x}_n | \overline{j}_n) = \prod_{k=1}^{n} f(x_k | j_k) = \prod_{k=1}^{n} f_{j_k}(x_k) \tag{6}$$

where $\overline{x}_n = (x_1, x_2, ..., x_n)$ and $\overline{j}_n = (j_1, j_2, ..., j_n)$.

The optimal classifier Ψ^* makes a decision using the following formula[1]

$$\Psi^*(\overline{x}_n) = \arg\max_{k \in \mathcal{M}} p(k | \overline{x}_n) \tag{7}$$

where the *posterior* probability

$$p(j_n | \overline{x}_n) = \frac{p_{j_n} f_{j_n}(\overline{x}_n)}{\sum\limits_{k=1}^{M} p_k f_{j_n}(\overline{x}_n)} \tag{8}$$

could be calculated recursively

$$p_{j_n} f_{j_n}(\overline{x}_n) = f_{j_n}(x_n) \sum_{j_{n-1}=1}^{M} p_{j_n, j_{n-1}} p_{j_{n-1}} f(\overline{x}_{n-1} | j_{n-1}) \tag{9}$$

with the initial condition

$$p(j_1) f(x_1 | j_1) = p_{j_1} f_{j_1}(x_1) \tag{10}$$

3   Proposed Algorithm

Let's notice that the *posterior* probabilities using as the support functions could be calculated recurrently, but for this calculations a knowledge about the CPDFs is required. We propose the hybrid approach based mostly on non-parametric estimation, which could be used in the chosen *build, use and improve* model, but

---

[1] For so-called 0–1 loss function which returns 0 in the case of correct decision and 1 otherwise [8].

in the case of new examples come, it requires to store them, what may break the assumption about the memory limit. Because we have a limited memory at our disposal, we store only a fixed number of the training examples using for CPDF estimation and we update probability characteristics (transition and initial probabilities) continuously. Thus, the assumption about memory limitation is fulfilled. To ensure that the classification model is updated, we add the new incoming examples into training set only in the case, if their labels are available. It is consistent with the assumption that expert is not always available. In the future we can control which of the object should be labeled, e.g., using active learning paradigm [9] as proposed in the previous works of the author [10], where the decision about the labeling of an example is made on the basis of its distance from a classifier decision boundary. In the case, if new example is stored, the oldest example in the dataset is removed to ensure its fixed size of training set. Such a procedure allows us to continuously updating the training and keeping in the memory the examples which are most relevant to the recent concept. The detailed description of the method is presented in Algorithm 1. To calculate support functions we use the procedure inspired by the k_n−Nearest Neighbor as the CPDFs estimator [11], which pseudocode is presented in Algorithm 2. Such a method is not so computationally efficient, but for the fixed size of the training set its processing time is predicable, what fulfills the condition related to the processing time limitation.

4   Experiment

In order to study the performance of proposed algorithm and evaluate its usefulness to the computer-aided medical diagnosis, we carried out the computer experiments on real dataset included observation of the patients suffering from acid-base disorder. The human acid-base state (ABS) diagnosis task is related to disorders in produce and elimination of H^+ and CO_2 by organism. During the course of treatment, recognition of ABS is very important because pH stability of physiological fluids is required. The ABS disorder has a dynamic character and the current patient's state depends on symptoms, previously applied treatment and classification. The diagnosis of ABS as a pattern recognition task includes the five classes: breathing acidosis, metabolic acidosis, breathing alkalinity, metabolic alkalinity, normal state. The features contains the value of the gasometric examination of blood as pCO_2, concentration of HCO_3^+, pH and applied treatment (respiration treatment, pharmacological treatment, or no treatment). The dataset consists of the sequences of 78 patient observations (each sequence includes from 7 to 25 successive records). The whole dataset includes 1170 observations which came from the Medical Academy of Wroclaw. Results of experimental investigation are presented in Fig. 1.

The accuracy was evaluate not on the basis of a validation set, but we use the schema called "test-and-train" [12]. Basically, firstly the fixed number of the examples are used to build the first prototype of the classifier. Then each incoming object n is used to improve the model, which is evaluated on the next incoming example $n + 1$.

Algorithm 1. Online Context-Based Algorithm

Require: initial data stream
  $InitDS = \{(x_1, j_1), (x_2, j_2), ..., (x_n, j_n)\}$
  N maximum number of stored examples $N \geq n$
  {*training phase*}
  for $i := 1$ **to** M **do**
    $q_i \leftarrow$ number of examples from $InitDS$ which belong to class i
    for $j := 1$ **to** M **do**
      $q_{i,j} \leftarrow$ number of examples from $InitDS$ which belong to class i and appeared
      after object from class j, i.e., for a given k $j_k = i$ and $j_{k-1} = j$
    end for
  end for
  {*classification phase*}
  $j_p \leftarrow j_n;\ k \leftarrow 0$
  repeat
    $k \leftarrow k + 1$
    $x_k \leftarrow$ read new object from the data stream
    if $k == 1$ **then**
      for $i := 1$ **to** M **do**
        $F_i \leftarrow \frac{q_i}{n+k} \text{CPDF}(x_k, j_k)$
      end for
    else
      for $i := 1$ **to** M **do**
        $F_i^t \leftarrow CPDF(x_k, j_k) \sum_{j=1}^{M} \left(\frac{q_{i,j}}{q_i} F_i \right)$
      end for
      for $i := 1$ **to** M **do**
        $F_i \leftarrow F_i^t$
      end for
    end if
    $j_k \leftarrow \arg\max_{j \in \mathcal{M}} F_j$ {*returned label*}
    $j_p \leftarrow j_k$
    if j_k^* - the real label of x_k is known **then**
      $q_{j_k^*} \leftarrow q_{j_k^*} + 1;\ q_{j_{k^*}, j_p} \leftarrow q_{j_k^*, j_p} + 1$
      $n \leftarrow n + 1;\ InitDS \leftarrow InitDS \cup (x_k, j_k^*)$
      if $n > N$ **then**
        $n \leftarrow n - 1;\ InitDS \leftarrow InitDS \setminus (x_1, j_1)$
      end if
      reindex $InitDS;\ j_p \leftarrow j_k^*$
    end if
  until end of the data stream

As we can see, the methods which take into consideration context outperform the classifier which recognize objects independently. We can also observe, the methods have also the asymptotic characteristic. The accuracy of the proposed method a quite similar as the performance of the methods previously developer and applied to the problem of the ABS diagnosis [13], but we have to underline,

Algorithm 2. Support function based on k_n Nearest Neighbor estimator concept

---

Require: initial data stream
$InitDS = \{(x_1, j_1), (x_2, j_2), ..., (x_n, j_n)\}$
object x, class i

Ensure: $CPDF(x, i)$ - support function for x and class i

$$CPDF(x, i) \leftarrow \frac{[\sqrt{k_i}]}{dist(x, [\sqrt{k_i}] - nn)}$$

$\{dist(x, [\sqrt{k_i}] - nn)$ stands for distance between a given example x and $[\sqrt{k_i}]$th nearest neighbor and $[]$ means *entier*$\}$

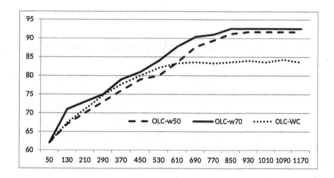

Fig. 1. Dependencies between the length of the data stream and accuracy for online classifier which does not take into consideration context (denoted as OLC-WC), and online context-based classifier with initial training set size 50 and 70 (denoted OLC-w50 and OLC-w70 respectively).

that the proposed approach does not requires so much memory, because only part of the data are stored. Of course we realize that the scope of the experiments was limited, but the preliminary results of the experiments encourage us to continue the work on the proposed methods in the future.

5 Final Remarks

The novel method of online classifier with context was presented in this work. Its performance seems to be very promising, therefore we would like to continue the work on the presented method. In the future we would like to include the method which will be able to take into consideration the model parameter change caused by the applied control. We are going to extend the model by applying the methods related to so-called *recurrent concept drift*. Additionally, we consider to retrain classifier using the batch mode, i.e., the model will be improved not object by object, by on the basis of collected data chunk, what could decrease the computational load of the algorithm. Finally, we are going to apply the classifier ensemble approach to the proposed method, e.g., by training new individual classifier on the basis of each incoming data chunk or to improve the models of the selected individuals in the classifier pool only.

Acknowlegements. This work was supported by EC under FP7, Coordination and Support Action, Grant Agreement Number 316097, ENGINE - European Research Centre of Network Intelligence for Innovation Enhancement (http://engine.pwr.wroc. pl/). This work was also supported by the Polish National Science Center under the grant no. DEC-2013/09/B/ST6/02264. All computer experiments were carried out using computer equipment sponsored by ENGINE project.

References

1. Widmer, G., Kubat, M.: Learning in the presence of concept drift and hidden contexts. Mach. Learn. **23**(1), 69–101 (1996)
2. Domingos, P., Hulten, G.: A general framework for mining massive data streams. J. Comput. Graph. Stat. **12**, 945–949 (2003)
3. Raviv, J.: Decision making in Markov chains applied to the problem of pattern recognition. IEEE Trans. Inf. Theor. **13**(4), 536–551 (1967)
4. Toussaint, G.T.: The use of context in pattern recognition. Pattern Recogn. **10**(3), 189–204 (1978)
5. Haralick, R.M.: Decision making in context. IEEE Trans. Pattern Anal. Mach. Intell. PAMI **5**(4), 417–428 (1983)
6. Żołnierek, A.: Pattern recognition algorithms for controlled Markov chains and their application to medical diagnosis. Pattern Recogn. Lett. **1**(5), 299–303 (1983)
7. Ramamurthy, S., Bhatnagar, R.: Tracking recurrent concept drift in streaming data using ensemble classifiers. In: Proceedings of the Sixth International Conference on Machine Learning and Applications, ICMLA 2007, Computer Society, pp. 404–409. IEEE, Washington, DC (2007)
8. Duda, R.O., Hart, P.E., Stork, D.G.: Pattern Classification, 2nd edn. Wiley, New York (2001)
9. Settles, B.: Active learning. Synth. Lect. Artif. Intell. Mach. Learn. **6**(1), 1–114 (2012)
10. Kurlej, B., Wozniak, M.: Active learning approach to concept drift problem. Log. J. IGPL **20**(3), 550–559 (2012)
11. Goldstein, M.: k_n-nearest neighbor classification. IEEE Trans. Inf. Theor. **18**(5), 627–630 (1972)
12. Bifet, A., Holmes, G., Pfahringer, B., Read, J., Kranen, P., Kremer, H., Jansen, T., Seidl, T.: MOA: a real-time analytics open source framework. In: Gunopulos, D., Hofmann, T., Malerba, D., Vazirgiannis, M. (eds.) ECML PKDD 2011, Part III. LNCS, vol. 6913, pp. 617–620. Springer, Heidelberg (2011)
13. Wozniak, M.: Proposition of common classifier construction for pattern recognition with context task. Knowl.-Based Syst. **19**(8), 617–624 (2006)

An Effective Semi-analytic Algorithm for Solving Helmholtz Equation in 1-D

Chunhui Zhu[1,2(✉)], Lijun Liu[1,2(✉)], Yanhui Liu[1,2], and Zhen Yu[1,2]

[1] Department of Electronic Science, Xiamen University,
Xiamen 361005, People's Republic of China
{zhuchhxd,liulijun}@xmu.edu.cn
[2] Department of Automation, Xiamen University,
Xiamen 361005, People's Republic of China

Abstract. An efficient and accurate algorithm for solving Helmholtz equation in 1-D is presented in this paper. The key point of this work is to derive the analytic form for the convolution of the Green's function and a complex exponential function with a finite support domain. A linear subtraction skill is introduced to improve the sampling efficiency. Therefore, the convolution of any function with the Green's function is given in a semi-analytic form, which can be computed in a fast way with the help of FFT or NUFFT.

Keywords: Helmholtz equation · Analytic convolution · FFT · NUFFT · Linear subtraction

1 Introduction

Helmholtz equation is often encountered in electromagnetics, seismology and acoustics. For example, in inverse problems such as electromagnetics and acoustics inversions, Helmholtz equation is usually needed to be solved in each iteration according to the updated parameters. Normally, tens to hundreds of iterations are required. Therefore, the effective solution of Helmholtz equation is very important to improve the efficiency of relative algorithms.

Traditionally, in order to use FFT, both the source term and the Green's function should be discretized. These discretizations will introduce errors into the final results. It is natural to improve the algorithms by using less discretizations and more analytic results. In this paper, we propose a novel algorithm for solving 1-D Helmholtz equation. The key point of the proposed algorithm is to achieve the convolution of any complex exponential function defined in a finite support domain with the Green's function analytically. Firstly, a linear subtraction skill is implemented to the source term, which separate it into a piecewise linear part

C. Zhu—This work is supported in part by the National Natural Science Foundation of China (NSFC) under Grants 61301008, 61304110 and 61301009, partly by the Fundamental Research Funds for the Central Universities under Grant 20720150014 and 20720160081.

© Springer International Publishing Switzerland 2016
Y. Tan and Y. Shi (Eds.): DMBD 2016, LNCS 9714, pp. 505–512, 2016.
DOI: 10.1007/978-3-319-40973-3_51

and a continuous part. The convolution of the piecewise linear part with the Green's function is derived analytically. The continuous part is decomposed into the summation of complex exponential functions by FFT or other numerical discrete Fourier transform method [9]. Then the convolution of the source term with the Green's function is given in a semi-analytic form. This semi-analytic form convolution can be computed by FFT or NUFFT. So the proposed method is high accurate due to the analytic convolution and can be computed in a fast way.

2   Problem Statement

This paper is concerned with the treatment of the Helmholtz equation in 1-D below

$$\nabla^2 f(x) + k_b^2 f(x) = -s(x) \tag{1}$$

where $s(x)$ represents the source term, whose support domain is finite. A typical method to solve the Helmholtz equation is to find its Green's function $g(x)$ in free space first, and then to obtain the solution by convolving $s(x)$ with the Green's function [5].

$$f(x) = \int_{-\infty}^{+\infty} g(x - x')s(x')dx' \tag{2}$$

For the 1-D case, the form of $g(x)$ is well known as $g(x) = -\frac{j}{2k_b}e^{-jk_b|x|}$. The computational complexity for direct numerical evaluation of the convolution is $O(N^2)$, where N is the number of the sampling points. Algorithms have been proposed based on FFT and convolution theorem [2] to accelerate this process, which have reduced the computational complexity to $O(N \log N)$ [8]. This work inherits this idea.

3   Green's Function in Spectral Domain

In this work, the forward and backward Fourier transform in the following forms are adopted as $F(u) = \int_{-\infty}^{+\infty} f(x)e^{-j2\pi ux}dx$ and $f(x) = \int_{-\infty}^{+\infty} F(u)e^{j2\pi ux}du$ where $F(u)$ is called the Fourier transform of $f(x)$. Generally, the Fourier transform of the Green's function [1], denoted as $G(u)$ are given as $G(u) = \frac{1}{4\pi^2 u^2 - k_b^2}$

Denote $u_0 = \frac{k_b}{2\pi}$, it is easy to notice that $G(u)$ has two singularities at $u = \pm u_0$. In this work we will use the following form of $G(u)$, which demonstrates the singularities exactly in an explicit form $G(u) = \mathscr{P}\frac{1}{4\pi^2 u^2 - k_b^2} + \frac{1}{4jk_b}[\delta(u-u_0)+\delta(u+u_0)]$.

where $\mathscr{P}$ means the principle value. For convenience, "$\xrightarrow{\mathscr{F}}$" is used to represent the forward Fourier transform in the rest of this work.

4 The Analytic Convolution

4.1 The Linear Subtraction Skill

When using Fourier transform, one property should be noticed. The spectral of a discontinuous function decreases very slow. When dealing with Fourier transform in discrete ways, a narrow band is preferred to reduce both the number of sampling points per wavelength and the bandwidth to be treated. Therefore, a linear subtraction skill is implement to the source term $s(x)$ first. This divide the source term into a piecewise linear function and a continuous function. The discretization is only required for the continuous function. The convolution of the piecewise linear function with the Green's function is derived analytically below.

Denote a linear function defined in $[x_1, x_2]$ as

$$f(x) = \begin{cases} ax + b, & x \in [x_1, x_2] \\ 0, & \text{else} \end{cases} \tag{3}$$

where a and b are constants. Then the convolution of $f(x)$ with $g(x)$ is

$$f(x) * g(x) = \frac{1}{2jk_b} \int_{x_1}^{x_2} (a\tau + b) e^{-jk_b|x-\tau|} d\tau \tag{4}$$

$$= \begin{cases} \int_{x_1}^{x} (a\tau + b) e^{-jk_b(x-\tau)} d\tau + \int_{x}^{x_2} (a\tau + b) e^{jk_b(x-\tau)} d\tau, & x_1 < x < x_2 \\ \int_{x_1}^{x_2} (a\tau + b) e^{jk_b(x-\tau)} d\tau, & x \leq x_1 \\ \int_{x_1}^{x_2} (a\tau + b) e^{-jk_b(x-\tau)} d\tau, & x \geq x_2 \end{cases} \tag{5}$$

This can be derived analytically as

$$f(x) * g(x) = \frac{a}{2\pi k_b^3} \{ -\pi \text{sgn}(x - x_2)[\sin(k_b(x - x_2)) - k_b(x - x_2)]$$

$$+ \pi \text{sgn}(x - x_1)[\sin(k_b(x - x_1)) - k_b(x - x_1)] \}$$

$$+ \frac{a}{k_b^2} \{ x_2 \text{sgn}(x - x_2) \sin^2(k_b \frac{x - x_2}{2}) - x_1 \text{sgn}(x - x_1) \sin^2(k_b \frac{x - x_1}{2}) \}$$

$$+ \frac{a}{2jk_b} \{ \frac{x_2 \sin(k_b(x_2 - x)) - x_1 \sin(k_b(x_1 - x))}{k_b} + \frac{\cos(k_b(x_2 - x)) - \cos(k_b(x_1 - x))}{k_b^2} \}$$

$$- \frac{b}{k_b^2} \{ \text{sgn}(x - x_1) \sin^2(k_b \frac{x - x_1}{2}) - \text{sgn}(x - x_2) \sin^2(k_b \frac{x - x_2}{2}) \}$$

$$+ \frac{b}{2jk_b^2} \{ \sin(k_b(x - x_1)) - \sin(k_b(x - x_2)) \} \tag{6}$$

where $\text{sgn}(x)$ is the Sign function.

4.2 The Analytic Convolution of a Complex Exponential Function Defined in a Finite Support Domain with the Green's Function

In this section, we will derive the convolution of a complex exponential function defined in a finite support domain $[p_0, p_1]$ with the Green's function. Denote the complex exponential function considered as $e_{[p_0, p_1]}^{j2\pi u_k x}$.

According to $G(u)$, it is easy to achieve the Fourier transform of $e^{j2\pi u_k x}_{[p_0,p_1]}$ as $F[e^{j2\pi u_k x}_{[p_0,p_1]}] = \frac{e^{j2\pi(u_k-u)p_1} - e^{j2\pi(u_k-u)p_0}}{j2\pi(u_k-u)}$, where $u_0 = k_b/(2\pi)$ as defined in Sect. 3. For convenience, denote $w = j2\pi u$ and $w_k = j2\pi u_k$.

According to the properties of Fourier transform, we can get the following Fourier transform pairs. The cumbersome derivations are omitted here.

$$
\begin{cases}
\frac{(2j\pi)^n}{2(n-1)!} x^{n-1}\mathrm{sgn}(x) \xrightarrow{\mathcal{F}} \frac{1}{u^n} \\
j\pi\mathrm{sgn}(x)e^{j2\pi u_0 x} \xrightarrow{\mathcal{F}} j\pi\mathrm{sgn}(x)e^{j2\pi u_0 x} \frac{1}{u-u_0} \\
j\pi\mathrm{sgn}(x)e^{-j2\pi u_0 x} \xrightarrow{\mathcal{F}} \frac{1}{u+u_0} \\
g(x) \xrightarrow{\mathcal{F}} G(u)
\end{cases}
\tag{7}
$$

and

$$
\begin{cases}
\frac{1}{2k_b}\sin(k_b|x|) \xrightarrow{\mathcal{F}} \frac{1}{w^2+k_b^2}, \\
\frac{1}{2}\mathrm{sgn}(x)\cos(k_b|x|) \xrightarrow{\mathcal{F}} \frac{1}{w^2+k_b^2} \\
\frac{1}{2}\mathrm{sgn}(x)e^{w_k x} \xrightarrow{\mathcal{F}} \frac{1}{w-w_k}
\end{cases}
\tag{8}
$$

$$
\begin{cases}
\frac{1}{2(w_k^2+k_b^2)}[(\frac{w_k}{jk_b} - \mathrm{sgn}(x))e^{-jk_b|x|}] \xrightarrow{\mathcal{F}} -\frac{Aw+B}{w^2+k_b^2} + \frac{1}{4jk_b}(\delta(u-u_0)+\delta(u+u_0))\frac{1}{w_k-w}, \\
\frac{1}{2(w_k^2+k_b^2)}\mathrm{sgn}(x)e^{w_k x} \xrightarrow{\mathcal{F}} -\frac{C}{w_k-w}
\end{cases}
\tag{9}
$$

and

$$
\begin{cases}
\frac{1}{w_k-w}\frac{1}{w^2+k_b^2} = \frac{Aw+B}{w^2+k_b^2} + \frac{C}{w_k-w} \\
A = C = \frac{1}{k_b^2+w_k^2}, \quad B = \frac{w_k}{k_b^2+w_k^2}
\end{cases}
\tag{10}
$$

From (8), (9) and (10) there is $h_1(x) \xrightarrow{\mathcal{F}} \frac{1}{w_k-w}G(u)$, where

$$
h_1(x) = \frac{1}{2(w_k^2+k_b^2)}\{[\frac{w_k}{jk_b} - \mathrm{sgn}(x)]e^{-jk_b|x|} + \mathrm{sgn}(x)e^{j2\pi u_k x}\}
\tag{11}
$$

From the convolution theorem and the shift properties of Fourier transform [2], the convolution of $e^{j2\pi u_k x}_{[p_0,p_1]}$ with the Green's function is

$$
\begin{aligned}
h_{u_k}(x) =& e^{j2\pi u_k p_1}h_1(x-p_1) - e^{j2\pi u_k p_0}h_1(x-p_0) \\
=& \frac{1}{w_k^2+k_b^2}\{[\frac{\pi u_k}{k_b} - \frac{\mathrm{sgn}(x-p_1)}{2}]e^{-jk_b|x-p_1|}e^{j2\pi u_k b} \\
& - [\frac{\pi u_k}{k_b} - \frac{\mathrm{sgn}(x-p_0)}{2}]e^{-jk_b|x-p_0|}e^{j2\pi u_k p_0}\} \\
& + \frac{1}{2(w_k^2+k_b^2)}\{[\mathrm{sgn}(x-p_1) - \mathrm{sgn}(x-p_0)]e^{j2\pi u_k x}\}
\end{aligned}
$$

5   A Novel Algorithm for Solving the Helmholtz Equation in 1-D

The object of this work is to solve the Helmholtz equation in 1-D by computing the convolution (2). A novel algorithm is demonstrated in this section base on Sects. 3 and 4 above. The algorithm can be described below.

Step (1). Divide the source term $s(x)$ into a continuous function $s_1(x)$ and a piecewise continuous function $s_2(x)$.

Step (2). Approximate the continuous function $s_1(x)$ with a linear summation of complex exponential functions $e^{j2\pi u_k x}$ as $J_1(x) \approx \sum_{k=-K/2}^{K/2-1} \beta_k e^{j2\pi u_k x}$, where $u_k = k\Delta u$, K and β_k are constants. Δu is the sampling interval in frequency domain. This approximation can be obtained through FFT or other numerical discrete Fourier transform method [6,9].

Step (3). Obtain the approximation of the convolution $f_1(x) = s_1(x) * g(x)$ as $f_1(x) = \sum_{k=-K/2}^{K/2-1} \beta_k h_{u_k}(x)$.

Step (4). Obtain the convolution $f_2(x) = s_2(x) * g(x)$ following (6).

Step (5). Add $f_1(x)$ and $f_2(x)$ together to achieve the computing results of convolution (2). Now let's discuss step (3) and step (4) in detail. Denote

$$
\begin{cases}
H_1(k) = \frac{1}{k_b^2 - 4\pi^2 u_k^2}, \ H_2(k) = \frac{\pi u_k}{k_b} H_1(k) \\
\gamma_k = \beta_k H_1(k), \tau_k = \beta_k H_2(k) \\
\tilde{h}(x) = \sum_{k=-K/2}^{K/2-1} \gamma_k e^{j2\pi u_k x}, \ \tilde{h}_1(x) = \sum_{k=-K/2}^{K/2-1} \tau_k e^{j2\pi u_k x}
\end{cases}
$$

then there is

$$
f_1(x) = \begin{cases}
[\frac{1}{2}\tilde{h}(p_1) + \tilde{h}_1(p_1)]e^{jk_b(x-p_1)} + [-\frac{1}{2}\tilde{h}(p_0) - \tilde{h}_1(p_0)]e^{jk_b(x-p_0)}, \\
\qquad\qquad\qquad\qquad\qquad\qquad\qquad\qquad\qquad\qquad\qquad x < p_0 \\
[\frac{1}{2}\tilde{h}(p_1) + \tilde{h}_1(p_1)]e^{jk_b(x-p_1)} + [\frac{1}{2}\tilde{h}(p_0) - \tilde{h}_1(p_0)]e^{-jk_b(x-p_0)} - \tilde{h}(x), \\
\qquad\qquad\qquad\qquad\qquad\qquad\qquad\qquad\qquad\qquad\qquad p_0 < x < p_1 \\
[-\frac{1}{2}\tilde{h}(p_1) + \tilde{h}_1(p_1)]e^{-jk_b(x-p_1)} + [\frac{1}{2}\tilde{h}(p_0) - \tilde{h}_1(p_0)]e^{-jk_b(x-p_0)}, \\
\qquad\qquad\qquad\qquad\qquad\qquad\qquad\qquad\qquad\qquad\qquad x > p_1
\end{cases}
\tag{12}
$$

In computing, x should be discretized into $\{x_n\}_{n=0}^{N-1}$. Denote N_1, N_2 and N_3 as the number of x_n in $(-\infty, p_0)$, (p_0, p_1) and $(p_1, +\infty)$, respectively. It can be detected that the most time consuming part is that for the N_2 points due to term $h(x)$ in (12). If x_n is uniform, then $\tilde{h}(x)$ can be computed through FFT with the complexity of $O((N_2 + K)\log(N_2 + K))$. If x_n is nonuniform, then $\tilde{h}(x)$ can be computed through NUFFT [3,4,7] with the complexity $O(N_2q^2) + O((N_2+mK)\log(N_2+mK))$, where $O(N_2q^2)$ is required only once for the same positions of sampling, q is related to the digits of the accuracy and m is the oversampling rate [3,4]. For the N_1 and N_3 points, which are outside the region of the support domain of the source, the computing complexity is only $O(K+N_1)$ and $O(K + N_3)$, respectively.

6   Numerical Examples

This part is going to numerically verify the proposed algorithm and demonstrate:
(1) The advantage of linear subtraction and (2) the comparison of the proposed
algorithm with traditional one in which the Green's function is discretized.

Example: In this example, we consider the solution for (1) with the source term
$s(x)$ in (13).

$$s(x) = \begin{cases} (\frac{x}{8})^2, & 0 < x < 4 \\ 0.5\sin(8\pi x - \frac{2}{3}\pi), & 4 \leq x < 8 \\ 4J_2(15x - 1), & 8 \leq x < 10 \\ 0, & else \end{cases} \tag{13}$$

$J_2(x)$ is the second order Bessel function of the first kind. First, $N = 512$ points
are uniformed sampled in $[0, 10]$ for x to get the approximations with a linear
summation of complex exponential functions $e^{j2\pi u_k x}$ for $s(x)$ and its continuous
part $s_1(x)$ with FFT at $u_k = k\Delta u$, where $k = -\frac{N}{2}, \cdots, \frac{N}{2} - 1$, $\Delta u = \frac{1}{T}$ and
$T = 10$. The results are shown in Figs. 1, 2 and 3. It is found from Fig. 1(a) and
(c) that the results without linear subtraction have less accuracy, which can be
detected obviously from the points marked by the red circles in Fig. 1(a). From
Fig. 1(b) and (d), we can also observe that linear subtraction helps to improve
the accuracy, and that the errors without linear subtraction are related with
the continuous property of the source term $s(x)$, while the errors with linear
subtraction are not. This verifies the correction of the proposed algorithm and
illustrates the advantage of linear subtraction.

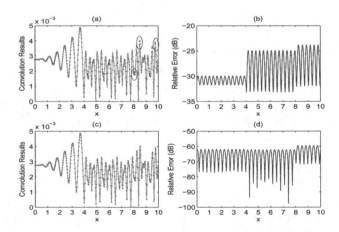

Fig. 1. Results by the proposed algorithm without and with linear subtraction. (a)
Solid and dotted lines are the results obtained by the proposed algorithm without
linear subtraction and accurate results, respectively; (b) Relative errors of the results
by the proposed algorithm without linear subtraction; (c) Solid and dotted lines are
the results obtained by the proposed algorithm with linear subtraction and accurate
results, respectively; (d) Relative errors of the results by the proposed algorithm with
linear subtraction. (Color figure online)

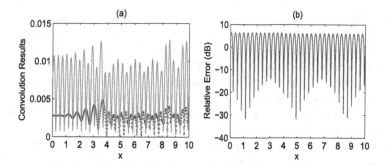

Fig. 2. Results by the algorithm in which the Green's function is discretized when the number of u is 521. (a) Solid and dotted lines are the results obtained by the algorithm in which the Green's function is discretized and accurate results, respectively; (b) Relative errors of the results by the algorithm in which the Green's function is discretized. (Color figure online)

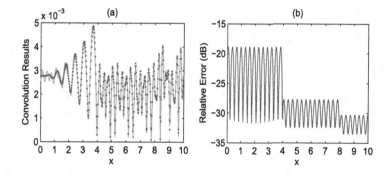

Fig. 3. Results by the algorithm in which the Green's function is discretized when the number of u is 52100. (a) Solid and dotted lines are the results obtained by the algorithm in which the Green's function is discretized and accurate results, respectively; (b) Relative errors of the results by the algorithm in which the Green's function is discretized. (Color figure online)

It is observed from Fig. 2 that with 512 sampled points of x and u, the results when the Green's function is discretized are far away from the real solution. It is due to the singularities of the Green's function in spectral domain at $\pm u_0$. In order to get reasonable results, more u is needed. Figure 3 shows the results when 51200 numbers of u are sampled. By comparing Fig. 3 with Fig. 1(d) and (b), we can see that the proposed algorithm get more than 40dB accuracy with only $\frac{1}{100}$ numbers of sampling points.

7   Conclusions

Helmholtz equation is one of the important differential equations in engineering. An effective algorithm is presented in this work to solve the 1-D Helmholtz equation. The main contributions of this work are: (1) use linear subtraction skill to reduce the number of sampling points in spectral domain; (2) derive the analytical result for the convolution of a piecewise linear function with the Green's function of 1-D Helmholtz equation; (3) develop the analytical convolution of a complex exponential function defined in a finite support domain with the Green's function of 1-D Helmholtz equation; (4) format the convolution results into a form that can be computed with the computational complexity of $O(N \log N)$, where N is proportional to the scale of the problem considered. Numerical example verified the proposed algorithm. It shows that with less computational abundance, this new algorithm can obtain much high accurate results than the algorithm in which the Green's function is discretized.

References

1. Chew, W.C.: Waves and Fields in Inhomogeneous Media, vol. 522. IEEE Press, New York (1995)
2. Chu, E.: Discrete and Continuous Fourier Transforms: Analysis, Applications and Fast Algorithms. CRC Press, Boca Raton (2012)
3. Greengard, L., Lee, J.Y.: Accelerating the nonuniform fast Fourier transform. SIAM Rev. **46**(3), 443–454 (2004)
4. Liu, Q., Nguyen, N.: An accurate algorithm for nonuniform fast fourier transforms (NUFFT's). IEEE Microw. Guided Wave Lett. **8**(1), 18–20 (1998)
5. Liu, Q.H., Lin, Y., Liu, J., Lee, J.H., Simsek, E.: A 3-D spectral integral method (SIM) for surface integral equations. IEEE Microw. Wirel. Compon. Lett. **19**(2), 62–64 (2009)
6. Liu, Y., Nie, Z., Liu, Q.H.: DIFFT: a fast and accurate algorithm for Fourier transform integrals of discontinuous functions. IEEE Microw. Wirel. Compon. Lett. **18**(11), 716–718 (2008)
7. Nguyen, N., Liu, Q.: The regular Fourier matrices and nonuniform fast fourier transforms. SIAM J. Sci. Comput. **21**, 283 (1999)
8. Yu, Z., Zhang, W., Liu, Q.: A mixed order stabilized bi-conjugate gradient FFT method for magnetodielectric objects. IEEE Trans. Antennas Propag. **62**(11), 5647–5655 (2014)
9. Zhu, C.H., Liu, Q.H., Shen, Y., Liu, L.: A high accuracy conformal method for evaluating the discontinuous Fourier transform. Prog. Electromagn. Res. **109**, 425–440 (2010)

Ensemble of One-Dimensional Classifiers for Hyperspectral Image Analysis

Paweł Ksieniewicz, Bartosz Krawczyk$^{(\boxtimes)}$, and Michał Woźniak

Department of Systems and Computer Networks, Wrocław University of Technology,
Wybrzeże Wyspiańskiego 27, 50-370 Wrocław, Poland
{pawel.ksieniewicz,bartosz.krawczyk,michal.wozniak}@pwr.edu.pl

Abstract. Remote sensing and hyperspectral data analysis are areas offering wide range of valuable practical applications. However, they generate massive and complex data that is very difficult to be analyzed by a human being. Therefore, methods for efficient data representation and data mining are of high interest to these fields. In this paper we introduce a novel pipeline for feature extraction and classification of hyperspectral images. To obtain a compressed representation we propose to extract a set of statistical-based properties from these images. This allows for embedding feature space into fourteen channels, obtaining a significant dimensionality reduction. These features are used as an input for the ensemble learning based on minimal-distance classifiers. We introduce a novel method for forming ensembles simple one dimensional classifiers. They are constructed independently on a low-dimensional representation - a single classifier for each extracted feature. Then a voting procedure is being used to obtain the final decision. Extensive experiments carried on a number of benchmarks images prove that using proposed feature extraction and ensemble of simple classifiers can offer a significant improvement in terms of classification accuracy when compared to state-of-the-art methods.

Keywords: Ensemble learning · Hyperspectral imaging · Computer vision · Feature extraction · Dimensionality reduction · Image classification

1   Introduction

Because we are living in big data century, therefore the efficient analytical tools which can analyze the huge volume of multidimensional data are still focus of intense research. One of the example of such a data is hyperspectral imaging, which is widely used in agriculture, mineralogy etc.

Hyperspectral image is a collection of high-resolution monochromatic pictures covering large spacial region for broad range of wavelengths. Structurally it is a three-dimensional matrix of reflectance. First two dimensions are standard lengths of a flat projection. The third is a spectral depth. Main idea of hyperspectral imaging is minimization of range covered by every band with maximization

© Springer International Publishing Switzerland 2016
Y. Tan and Y. Shi (Eds.): DMBD 2016, LNCS 9714, pp. 513–520, 2016.
DOI: 10.1007/978-3-319-40973-3_52

of band number. The current industrial standard, AVIRIS spectrometer, captures images with 224 channels in range $0.4 - 2.5\,\mu m$. A slice taken from hyperspectral cube provides us information of reflectance of the area for a given spectral band. Taking a vector alongside the spectral band axis provides us spectral signature, which carries information about reflectance of one particular pixel for every covered spectral band.

As we deal with multi-class and high-dimensional problem, we require a highly effective pattern classification system to be able to analyze such data [3].

In the remote sensing literature, many supervised and unsupervised classifiers have been developed to tackle the hyperspectral data classification problem [2]. Unsupervised classification algorithms have the advantage of not requiring labeled training samples, which limits the cost associated with the recognition process [11]. This comes at the price of highly limited class interpretability of results. Therefore, supervised [4] and semi-supervised [14] classification algorithms gained significant attention in remote sensing community. Recent advances in hyperspectral image mining focus on the following vital issues: (i) developing novel efficient image representations and low-dimensional embeddings [9], (ii) selecting the most information-rich spectral channels [8], (iii) target detection [12] and (iv) proposing accurate machine learning methods for segmentation and classification [6].

In this paper we propose a novel ensemble of simple classifiers based on low-dimensional feature extraction method. We extract statistical properties of hyperspectral image by calculating a set of 14 measures that are able to sufficiently describe the properties of a given scene. This allows us to significantly simplify the problem by an universal dimensionality reduction technique. Then a classifier committee is being constructed on the new feature space. We propose to form a pool of simple minimal-distance classifiers where each uses a single statistical feature extracted in the previous step. This way we obtain a set of highly independent base learners, each working in a simple one-dimensional space. A voting procedure is applied to combine their individual outputs and obtain a final decision. This method allows us to explore local properties of each feature, introduces a diversity among base classifiers and offers a highly parallel architecture for high-speed hypespectral image processing.

In the following sections we will present the details of the proposed feature extraction and classification framework and detailed results of experimental study to prove the effectiveness of our approach.

2   Low-Dimensional Feature Extraction for Hyperspectral Images

We propose a novel method for simultaneous feature extraction and low-dimensional embedding of hyperspectral images. It is based on the idea of creating a new representation, evolving from human color perception, preserving as much information as possible, with simple, time efficient computations.

We are interpreting the matrix of cone cells reacting on same wavelengths as a transformation, projecting three-dimensional input onto two-dimensional result. Hyperspectral imaging is there a discrete form of this three-dimensional input, which provides enough data to acquire other transformation functions. So created artificial cone cells matrixes will generate our statistical features.

New proposition is a significant extension of our previous proposal [5], introducing procedure of spatial blurring, normalization and histogram equalization. Also the extended set of statistical features is proposed.

The procedure run as follows. At the start, the class edges are recognized and calculated. Next, the collection of side information produced during first step, lets us to generate a filter for noisy bands of image. Next the features of filtered image are computed and, at the end, they are prepared for classification.

2.1 Noise Detection

A value denivelation in finite neighborhood of every pixel can be used to detect borders between non-texture areas of picture. A side effect of this method is the measurement of entropy ($\bar{H}$), calculated from amount of all values (ρ) divided by calculation of pixels per layer (ppl).

$$\bar{H} = \frac{\sum \rho}{ppl} \tag{1}$$

While every hyperspectral cube contains wavelengths with high noise ratio, adequate threshold to drain most of them would be a mean value of entropy. To separate hills of entropy changes we are using information about its dynamics. An vector of dynamics was made in a way analogous to edge detection, by calculating discrepancy between actual ($\bar{H}$) and next value ($\bar{H}'$) on the vector of entropy.

$$\bar{D}\bar{H} = |\bar{H} - \bar{H}'| \tag{2}$$

Mean dynamics filter was generated in an analogous way as the one for entropy. Concluding filter was the *blend* of mean entropy and mean dynamics filters.

2.2 Feature Computation

Filtering out the noise makes possible an effective usage of simple statistical operations like maximum or minimum, and improve the precision of average, mean, mode or median value. We have proposed a set of fourteen features: red/green/blue channels from pseudocolor HSV2RGB conversion, lowest/highest values in signature and their indexes, mean/median values of signature, difference between highest and lowest values in signature and distance between their indexes, and standard deviation/variance/mode of signature values.

2.3 Preparing Features for Classification

Some statistical features are giving us clear information, enough to distinguish classes in data, while some of them seems completely useless. To extract, boost and stabilize data coming from them, we have added three more steps of processing.

To stabilize information, we used the anisotropic diffusion [10]. Normalization paired with histogram equalization brought us more contrast and extraction of sparse values.

3   Ensemble of One-Dimensional Classifiers

The features described in the previous Section could be used as a direct input for any type of classifier. However, one should notice that they display two interesting properties: are informative on their own and are highly independent. These observations serve as a motivation for a more imaginative use of these features for forming an ensemble classifier.

We propose to construct a committee of simple learners, where each base model is constructed on a one-dimensional space consisting of a selected feature. This way we obtain an ensemble of 14 individual classifiers.

Let us now discuss the advantages of such an approach. By utilizing a single dimension we construct a simplified classifier working in a much more efficient space than when using all of hyperspectral bands. This alleviates the difficulty of the classification process and leads to simpler decision boundaries. Additionally, as our features are independent from each other the constructed pool displays a high diversity which translates into an efficient performance of the ensemble [13]. Each base classifier has a highly reduced complexity, while being mutually complementary to remaining learners. This way we are able to take advantage of new, informative features that are also robust to noise. This allows us to train base classifiers on a denoised, low-dimensional feature space which boost their performance. As such one-dimensional classifiers can be considered as weak learners then ensemble architecture should be able to improve their collective performance. Additionally, our proposal is characterized by a highly parallel structure that may contribute to the computational effectiveness.

One should note that there are no limitations on what type of base classifier and combination of individual outputs is being used. For this paper we propose to utilize minimal-distance nearest neighbor learner and combine them using a majority voting scheme.

4   Experimental Study

The aim of the experimental study was to examine the usefulness of the proposed ensemble learning algorithm for the task of hyperspectral image analysis.

4.1 Datasets

In experiments we are using hyperspectral imaging database provided by Group of the Computational Intelligence from *Universidad del Pais Vasco* (UPV/EHU)[1]. It consists of seven images described by ground truth maps.

- **Salinas** scene, collected by the AVIRIS sensor over Salinas Valley, California, with high spatial resolution (3.7-meter pixels). It includes vegetables, bare soils, and vineyard fields. Resolution 512 × 217, 224 bands, 16 classes.
- **Pavia University**, acquired by the ROSIS sensor during a flight campaign over Pavia, nothern Italy. Resolution 610 × 610, 103 bands, 9 classes.
- **Botswana**, acquired by the NASA EO-1 over the Okavango Delta, Botswana in 2001-2004. Resolution 256 × 1476, 242 bands, 14 classes.
- **Kennedy Space Center**, acquired by AVIRIS sensor over the Kennedy Space Center, Florida, on March 23, 1996. Resolution 614 × 512, 224 bands, 14 classes.

4.2 Set-Up

For the experiments we decided to compare our proposed ensemble (ODE-NN) with standard nearest neighbor classifier (NN) and three popular ensembles: Random Forests, Rotation Forest using decision trees and Rotation Forest using nearest neighbor classifiers. Details of parameters used for these classifiers are given in Table 1.

Table 1. Details of classifier parameters used in the experiments.

Algorithm	Parameters
NN	distance = Euclidean
Random Forest	no. of trees ∈ [10,30,50,···,210]
	no. of features in split ∈ [3,5,7,···,15]
	max. depth ∈ [3,5,7,9]
Rotation Forest	no. of classifiers ∈ [10,30,50,···,210]
	feature extraction = PCA
	no. of principal components uses = first 10 %
	base classifier = unpruned C5.0 or NN
ODE-NN	no. of classifiers = no. of extracted statistical features = 14
	base classifier = NN
	classifier combination = majority voting

We use a 5x2 fold CV combined F-test [1] for simultaneous training/testing and pairwise statistical analysis. It repeats two times five-fold cross-validation.

---

[1] http://www.ehu.eus/ccwintco/index.php?title=Hyperspectral_Remote_Sensing_Scenes.

The combined F-test is conducted by comparison of all versus all in order to check if differences in performance measures between two classifiers are statistically significant.

Parameters of classifiers were established using an internal 3 fold CV.

4.3   Experimental Results and Discussion

The results with the respect to accuracy are presented in Table 2.

Table 2. Results of the experimental results with the respect to the accuracy [%] and the statistical significance. Small numbers under the proposed method stand for indexes of classifiers from which it was statistically significantly better. The bolded results stands for the highest accuracy for a given dataset.

Dataset	NN[1]	Random Forest[2]	Rotation Forest[3]	Rotation Forest-NN[4]	ODE-NN
Salinas	69.34	73.45	74.45	74.18	**76.62**[1,2,3,4]
Pavia	86.46	95.64	97.03	97.18	**98.65**[1,2,3,4]
Botswana	91.42	**98.01**	97.15	97.43	95.29[1]
KSC	84.93	91.60	92.28	92.02	**94.15**[1,2,3,4]

Let us now take a look into the obtained results.

To no surprise the standard NN classifier fails to deliver satisfactory results for the task of hyperspectral image analysis. This can be explained by a high-dimensional nature of images, high number of pixels, lack of clear class borders and noise present in some of the channels. All of these factors deteriorates the performance of a minimal-distance classifier, proving numerous scientific reports on its lack of applicability in discussed pattern classification task.

The examined ensembles that are popular in the hyperspectral literature (Random Forest and Rotation Forest) are able to handle given pixel-based representation much more efficiently. This can be explained by their ability to reduce the dimensionality for each base classifier either by random feature drawing or using feature transformation and retaining a reduced number of principal components. Additionally, they are able to tackle the large number of training pixels by using bootstrap aggregation to reduce the size of training sets for each base learner. However, they are not robust to feature noise (common in hyperspectral domain) which may affect their performance [7]. What is interesting is the fact of good performance of Rotation Forest when used with NN classifiers. This shows the flexibility of this ensemble as it can be used not only with decision trees. For two datasets we are able to obtain a small gain in accuracy which shows the importance of selecting a proper base classifier for Rotation Forest.

The proposed ensemble of simple one-dimensional classifiers is able to outperform all of reference methods in a statistically significant way for three out of four datasets. This satisfactory performance can be contributed to several factors. First of all each base classifier is trained on the basis of only a single feature. This significantly simplifies its decision domain in comparison to reference methods (both decision forests are not able to achieve such high dimensionality reduction). Using one of 14 extracted statistical features guarantees that each base learner uses information-rich space efficiently describing properties of a given hyperspectral image. Additionally, extracted metric are robust to noise which allows to build noise-insensitive learners. By delegating a single classifier to each of the features independently we improve the diversity of our ensemble which directly contributes to its efficacy. By the proposed hybridization of efficient feature extraction approach with simple and diverse classifiers we are able to achieve very good recognition rates for complex and multi-class hyperspectral data.

5   Concluding Remarks

In this paper we have proposed a novel framework for efficient hyperspectral image analysis. It combined a low-dimensional feature extraction with an ensemble of simple and diverse minimal-distance classifiers.

We proposed to extract features from pixel-based image representation using a set of statistical properties of a given image. It allowed for a low-dimensional embedding of the original feature space, thus reducing he complexity of analyzed data. We showed how to compute 14 metrics from any hyperspectral image and process them to improve their discriminatory power. The proposed feature construction step allowed to alleviate the influence of noisy bands on the quality of hyperspectral data.

On the basis of these features we proposed to form an ensemble of classifiers. Each learner utilized a single feature to obtain a local specialization and diversity among pool members. This way we formed a set of simplified classifiers where each of them worked in the smallest possible new feature space. We showed that their voting-based combination may lead to a highly efficient classification. Additionally, the introduced architecture is highly parallel.

In the future we plan to investigate different base classifiers, combination methods and construct new base classifiers that maintain a trade-off between exploring combinations of features and very small dimensionality of their decision spaces.

Acknowledgment. This was supported in part by the statutory funds of Department of Systems and Computer Networks, Wrocław University of Technology and by the Polish National Science Center under the grant no. DEC-2013/09/B/ST6/02264.

All experiments were carried out using computer equipment sponsored by EC under FP7, Coordination and Support Action, Grant Agreement Number 316097, ENGINE - European Research Centre of Network Intelligence for Innovation Enhancement (http://engine.pwr.wroc.pl/).

References

1. Alpaydin, E.: Combined 5 x 2 cv F test for comparing supervised classification learning algorithms. Neural Comput. **11**(8), 1885–1892 (1999)
2. Ayerdi, B., Graña, M.: Hyperspectral image nonlinear unmixing and reconstruction by ELM regression ensemble. Neurocomputing **174**, 299–309 (2016)
3. Cyganek, B.: An analysis of the road signs classification based on the higher-order singular value decomposition of the deformable pattern tensors. In: Blanc-Talon, J., Bone, D., Philips, W., Popescu, D., Scheunders, P. (eds.) ACIVS 2010, Part II. LNCS, vol. 6475, pp. 191–202. Springer, Heidelberg (2010)
4. Hayes, M.H., Miller, S.N., Murphy, M.A.: High-resolution landcover classification using random forest. Remote Sens. Lett. **5**(2), 112–121 (2014)
5. Krawczyk, B., Ksieniewicz, P., Woźniak, M.: Hyperspectral image analysis based on color channels and ensemble classifier. In: Polycarpou, M., de Carvalho, A.C.P.L.F., Pan, J.-S., Woźniak, M., Quintian, H., Corchado, E. (eds.) HAIS 2014. LNCS, vol. 8480, pp. 274–284. Springer, Heidelberg (2014)
6. Ksieniewicz, P., Jankowski, D., Ayerdi, B., Jackowski, K., Graña, M., Woźniak, M.: A novel hyperspectral segmentation algorithm - concept and evaluation. Logic J. IGPL **23**(1), 105–120 (2015)
7. Lasota, T., Telec, Z., Trawiński, B., Trawiński, G.: Investigation of random subspace and random forest regression models using data with injected noise. In: Graña, M., Toro, C., Howlett, R.J., Jain, L.C. (eds.) KES 2012. LNCS, vol. 7828, pp. 1–10. Springer, Heidelberg (2013)
8. Li, S., Qiu, J., Yang, X., Liu, H., Wan, D., Zhu, Y.: A novel approach to hyperspectral band selection based on spectral shape similarity analysis and fast branch and bound search. Eng. Appl. AI **27**, 241–250 (2014)
9. Lin, D., Xu, X.: A novel method of feature extraction and fusion and its application in satellite images classification. Remote Sens. Lett. **6**(9), 687–696 (2015)
10. Perona, P., Malik, J.: Scale-space and edge detection using anisotropic diffusion. IEEE Trans. Pattern Anal. Mach. Intell. **12**(7), 629–639 (1990)
11. Wei, W., Zhang, Y., Tian, C.: Latent subclass learning-based unsupervised ensemble feature extraction method for hyperspectral image classification. Remote Sens. Lett. **6**(4), 257–266 (2015)
12. Willett, R.M., Duarte, M.F., Davenport, M.A., Baraniuk, R.G.: Sparsity and structure in hyperspectral imaging : sensing, reconstruction, and target detection. IEEE Signal Process. Mag. **31**(1), 116–126 (2014)
13. Woźniak, M., Graña, M., Corchado, E.: A survey of multiple classifier systems as hybrid systems. Inf. Fusion **16**, 3–17 (2014)
14. Yuan, Y., Lv, H., Lu, X.: Semi-supervised change detection method for multi–temporal hyperspectral images. Neurocomputing **148**, 363–375 (2015)

Industrial Internet of Things: An Architecture Prototype for Monitoring in Confined Spaces Using a Raspberry Pi

José Ignacio Rodríguez Molano[✉], Víctor Hugo Medina[✉],
and Javier Felipe Moncada Sánchez[✉]

Universidad Distrital Francisco José de Caldas, Bogotá, Colombia
jirodriguez@udistrital.edu.co,
victorhmedina@gmail.com, jfmoncadas@gmail.com

Abstract. This article contains an Internet description of things and its applications to the industry, the principles on which it is based, the elements and technologies available to achieve communication between people and objects and applications that have been developed in different areas and demonstrating the importance of the implementation of this current. Also there describes a monitoring prototype developed under the frame of the Internet of Things and implemented through the microcomputer Raspberry Pi, a cloud storage server and a mobile device.

Keywords: Industrial internet of things · Ubiquitous computing · M2M communications · Applications · Prototype · Monitoring · Raspberry Pi

1 Introduction

The industrial Internet of Things (IIoT) is connecting the machines between themselves with the physical world of the sensors, more and more omnipresent, there increasing the speed of the business and the development of the industrialist of exponential form.

The IIoT goes beyond the communication M2M, it is a question of the connectivity of the sensors, devices and machines across Internet. It comprises the connection of industrial networks and of services with different infrastructures of storage of information across the rendering of service of software and its autonomous control in the cloud.

Under the philosophy of ubiquitous communication and machine to machine communication, internet of things is defined as a set of technologies designed to allow the connection of heterogeneous objects trough different networks and communication methods; its main objective is to position intelligent devices in different locations to capture, store, and manage information to be accessible anywhere in the world for anyone.

2 What Is Internet of Things?

Internet of Things or IoT was proposed and developed by the laboratory network worldwide research in the field of internet of things, Auto-ID Labs, in 1999; IoT is a network based on radio frequency identification, linking objects by sensing devices and

© Springer International Publishing Switzerland 2016
Y. Tan and Y. Shi (Eds.): DMBD 2016, LNCS 9714, pp. 521–528, 2016.
DOI: 10.1007/978-3-319-40973-3_53

Internet [1]. Thus it is possible to characterize in real-time any type of electronic device and/or environmental element. Internet of Things as network can touch any object and body through middlemen links. This network has the means available to achieve data collection anytime and transfer information via communication networks for its processing through cloud computing or smart computing [1].

Tan and Wang [2] provide that the Internet of Things is the direct future of computing and communications. For its development is necessary the combination of different and innovative technologies as support; these technologies are defined like [3]:

- Wireless tracking and Technology.
- Technology sensors for detecting elements in the environment.
- Intelligent technologies such as intelligent materials and intelligent networks.
- Miniaturization technologies to reduce objects.

3 Characteristics of Internet of Things

Internet of Things is the result of new technologies and several complementary technical developments that provide capabilities that collectively help to bridge the gap between the virtual and physical world [4]. These capabilities include:

- Communication and cooperation: the objects have the ability to interface with the resources of the internet and even each other to make use of the data, services and update their status; in this measure, the wireless technologies such as GSM and UMTS, Wi-Fi, Bluetooth, ZigBee are highly relevant.
- Addressing capability: the objects in Internet of Things can be located and configured remotely.
- Identification: the objects can be uniquely identified through RFID technology (Radio Frequency Identification), NFC (Near Field Communication) and barcode scanning.
- Perception: the objects may collect information about its environment through sensors that can record this information, send it or react to this.
- Information processing: the smart objects have storage capacity and have a processor that allows you to interpret information.
- Location: the smart things have knowledge of their physical location or can be easily located. This is achieved with technologies such as GPS (Global Positioning System) or the mobile network.
- User Interfaces: the smart objects can properly communicate with people (either directly or indirectly, for example through a smartphone). Here are critical new interaction paradigms as tangible user interfaces, flexible displays based on polymers or methods of speech recognition, pictures or gestures.

4 Principles of Internet of Things

4.1 Ubiquitous Computing

Ubiquitous computing emerged in early 1990 by Mark Weiser. This concept is defined as a method for improving computer use effectively making it invisible to the user and is mainly characterized by the connection of things to computing [5]; thus the people it can focus solely on the task and not the tool [6].

Ubiquitous computing or UbiComp has two main objectives: (a) reduce the amount of attention that users invest in their devices and (b) create the necessary interfaces to access any information at any time and any place [7].

The concept of ubiquitous computing is a paradigm shift from a traditional view of computing. This new trend of information and communication technologies is based on miniaturization, thanks to that mobile devices and smart devices have become essential but invisible elements in the daily lives of anyone; such devices are equipped with sensors and communication systems which allow them to interact with the environment to collect information and then share it with someone, i.e. ubiquitous computing enables access to all kinds of information for anything anywhere. Currently the emphasis of studies related to ubiquitous computing refers to the practical uses that may develop within different social and work environments [8].

It is also possible to classify the application environment of UbiComp depending on the work being performed; There are four general classifications [7].

- Creative environments: generating ideas relating to products or projects, flexible connectivity for input and output devices necessary.
- Meeting Environments: support tools that enable the integration of persons providing the explanation of ideas and viewpoints (electric whiteboards, wireless projectors, etc.).
- Smart environments: gifted everyday spaces of intelligent tools for analysis and observation of the environment and automatically act according to certain preset parameters (dedicated to facilitate user operations).
- Environmental settings: settings are fully integrated with connected wireless networks and allow intelligently control the information required by the user friendly interface devices.

4.2 Machine to Machine Communications

Machine to Machine Communications (M2M) is the combination of information technology and communication with machines to provide a means to interact with each other using minimal human intervention, aiming to increase the comfort and safety of the end user [9].

This Machine to Machine communication refers to technologies that allow systems communicate with other devices of the same features through other devices such as sensors, which allow to capture and transmit event data through to a software application. Regardless of the type of machine or the type of data, information flows generally in the same way: from a machine through the network and conducted through a gateway to a system where it is processed.

Communication between systems and data transfer can be in two ways: uplink, to collect process information and downlink, for sending instructions, software updates, or to remotely control computers [4]. The basic elements that appear in all M2M environments are:

- System to be managed, which can be alarm mechanisms, control systems energy expenditure, information devices, weather stations, among others.
- M2M device connected to the computer terminal that provides communication with the server and handles the interaction with the elements to be monitored.
- Server, which is the computer that manages the sending and receiving of information systems.
- Communication network that handles data transmission either through wires or wirelessly.
- Applications that are responsible for collecting, storing and analyzing information collected by the devices and make the decisions necessary action.

4.3   Applications and Related Technologies

The most relevant technologies associated with the development of the Internet of Things and their applications are RFID (Radio-Frequency Identification), EPC (Electronic Product Code) and NFC (Near Field Communication).

Some applications are designed to perform best interaction and prospect the scope in an increasing field of the Internet of things, some these can be mentioned as follows:

- Medicine and healthcare
- Logistic Mobile Application
- Smart manufacturing
- Smart cities
- System for food quality
- Telecommunications.

5   Why Raspberry Pi?

The capture system is based on the Raspberry Pi which is equipped with different sensors capable of detecting changes in the environment and capture the information required by the user. Although there are different types of microcomputers and micro components that could be used in the construction of the base of the capture system, such as Arduino, Banana Pi, Pc Duino, UDOO, etc. The Raspberry Pi compared with Arduino has characteristics that make it a top plate in its functionality as it has hardware that allows: (1) fast data transfer, (2) ports for external hardware (easy connection), (3) internet via Ethernet or Wi-Fi cable and (4) video output (HDMI) and audio (mini-jack); in the market there microcomputers that have the same characteristics as the Raspberry (even improve certain aspects RAM) but these options have a higher purchase price to the Raspberry, positioning it as the best option for the authors to develop this capture system.

6 Prototype Architecture Based on Internet of Things and Using Raspberry Pi

Based on the principles mentioned above a prototype monitoring system is developed on the concepts of ubiquitous computing and M2M communication and implemented under the framework of the internet of things. The aim of this prototype is to capture images of a place and allow access to these real-time and remotely. A environment-object and object-object communication to achieve the proposed aim was established.

The communication environment-object of the system of vigilance allowed to monitor different environmental variables status changes were shown through images, for this there were in use four sensors that allowed determining the flow of people in a place, the gas presence in the atmosphere, surface stability and existence of contact between a person and the prototype. The reading of changes in the state of the sensors made by was processed in a micro-computer Raspberry Pi.

Object-object communication between the Raspberry Pi and a mobile device, in order to establish synchronization of images directly to the user across his Smartphone or tablet was established. This communication was achieved through the connection established between the Raspberry Pi and cloud storage server, Dropbox (It is possible to use any server that has within its service tools for application development or SDK); link possible by the ability of microcomputer connection wireless internet network.

The monitoring prototype has the following characteristics:

- Using sensor technologies: monitoring prototype uses different sensors for the detection of "weird" elements in the environment and initiate the capture and transmission of images. A sensor acts as a link between what happens in one place and so the user can see this place.
- Collection of data at any time: the prototype does not restrict capture of images and always be aware of every movement present at the place of installation of the system.
- Images transfer: it is possible transfer images within the communication network composed by the user (via a mobile device) and physical system (Raspberry Pi) by means of computing in the cloud (Dropbox).
- User interface: the prototype can communicate with the user through platforms known as personal email (Hotmail, Gmail, Outlook, etc.) or server storage (Dropbox, Amazon, Google Drive, etc.).
- Functional independence: under the guidance of ubiquitous computing reducing the users' attention on the device, the prototype works automatically and independently of the user, since their capture images and transfer functions are carried out only with the activation of a sensor and a wireless network.

- Communication with the mobile device: the system does not require direct intervention in the hardware or software to operate. The (image transfer) communication conducted under the principles of machine-machine communication in which the microcomputer Raspberry Pi and sensors represent the prototype and the mobile device is the terminal which enables communication with the user through a server and a communication network. Captured images are derived from one machine to another in the same way regardless of the sensor is in use.
- Total disposition of images: the system generates a communication network that allows the access to the user any place and consults at any time of the images captured thanks to the connection of the physical prototype (Raspberry Pi) with the servant online.

Prototype architecture is based on three levels. Each level represents a process to be carried out for that the system meets its objective which corresponds to the capture and synchronization information so that it can be used and/or accessed by the user.

The first level corresponding to External Level, so named because it is the level that is exposed to changes generated by exogenous factors to the system, can also be considered activators system functions (corresponding to some sensors that capture changes in the characteristics environment, each of these detects a specified type of modification of the environment), these activators to detect any alteration by wires send an electrical impulse which is directed to the Raspberry Pi.

After the pulse is generated if there isn't any process to transform it simply be lost, not triggered any reaction within the system, therefore the Intermediate Level is so important, because allow information flow using the internet and protocols for synchronization of information (SMTP and SSL) to the user which is the Target Level, where mobile devices that can be used to access this information is also included, thanks to the Raspberry Pi is possible to create a logic programming which converts the electrical signal into two types of data, it is possible to generate any reaction due to hardware that has the Raspberry Pi and various output devices that can be found (Figs. 1 and 2).

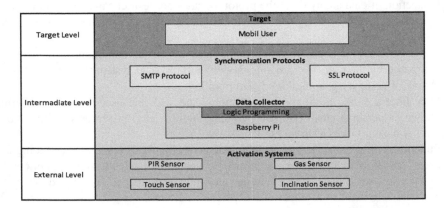

Fig. 1. Prototype architecture based on IoT. Source: Developed by the authors.

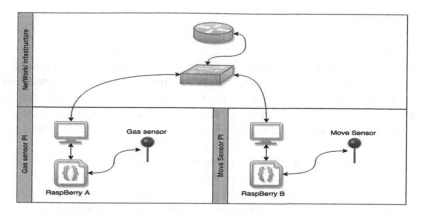

Fig. 2. Connection diagram prototype. Source: Developed by the authors.

When executing logic programming are generated procedures that allow the operation of the prototype, from the import of the libraries to capture images if some kind of alteration is detected; processes and the results obtained by executing logic programming are shown below.

6.1   Other Used Elements

- ADC0832 Analog-to-digital Converter Chip
- MQ-2 gas Sensor and Sensor of infrared movement
- 1 Keyes MQ-2 Sensor Gas plus Cable jumper mh
- 1 ADC0832 Analog-to-digital Converter Chip
- 1 Protoboard plus Cable.

The sensor of passive infrared movement or PIR is an electronic sensor that measures the changes in the levels of infrared radiation expressed by the objects that are located around him at a 6 m maximum distance. This sensor is named a debit because it does not express energy that could interfere in the movement detection, otherwise, it works to detect the energy expressed by other objects.

Every object expresses a small quantity of infrared radiation that temperature of the same one is determined by the level; the warmer the biggest object is it is the radiation level. The sensor PIR has the aptitude to detect the radiation differences in its coverage area and is activated when it detects some difference.

When the sensor detects some movement in the area, the digital exit transmits an electromagnetic pulse that is the sign of activation for the apprehension system (HIGH to 5 V) in the opposite case, when there is no movement detection no electromagnetic sign is expressed by which the system remains in rest (exit LOW).

7   Conclusions

The internet of things proposed to establish networks of communication between objects and people that allow bidirectional information flow with minimal intervention on the network. Communication networks focus on direct and global data transmission.

The developed prototype is a communication network which captures, processes and transfers data (images) to the user; this communication network established by connecting a capture subsystem and synchronization subsystem (private information storage server).

Communication between capture subsystem and the mobile device is established through the mobile application storage service Dropbox cloud, created on its website. Through programming language developed the communication link from the Raspberry Pi and Dropbox was created (there are also alternatives like Gmail and Amazon Virtual Private Cloud).

In developing an overall architecture for the analysis of environmental conditions is possible to apply this system to industrial (any process of production and marketing) and the everyday life, thus improving the conditions and ensuring better results in any activity undertaken by the availability of information.

References

1. Guo, L.G., Huang, Y.R., Cai, J., Qu, L.G.: Investigation of architecture, key technology and application strategy for the internet of things, vol. 2, pp. 1196–1199. IEEE Conference Publications (2011)
2. Tan, L., Wang, N.: Future internet: the internet of things, vol. 5, pp. V5–376–V5–380. IEEE Conference Publications (2010)
3. Ramirez, G.A.: Evaluación de introducción de internet de objetos en espacios de aprendizaje (2010)
4. Garcia, A.: El Internet de las Cosas y los nuevos riesgos para la privacidad (Tesis de maestria) (2012)
5. Liu, R., Wang, Y., Yang, H., Pan, W.: An evolutionary system development approach in a pervasive computing environment, pp. 194–199. IEEE Conference Publications (2004)
6. Liu, Y., Feng, L.: PCA: a reference architecture for pervasive computing, pp. 99–103. IEEE Conference Publications (2006)
7. Lupiana, D., O'Driscoll, C., Mtenzi, F.: Taxonomy for ubiquitous computing environments, pp. 469–475. IEEE Conference Publications (2009)
8. Sakamura, K., Koshizuka, N.: Ubiquitous computing technologies for ubiquitous learning, pp. 11–20. IEEE Conference Publications (2005)
9. Meddeb, M., Ben Alaya, M., Monteil, T., Dhraief, A., Drira, K.: M2M platform with autonomic device management service. Procedia Comput. Sci. 32, 1063–1070 (2014)

Efficient Multidimensional Pattern Recognition in Kernel Tensor Subspaces

Bogusław Cyganek[1,2(✉)] and Michał Woźniak[2]

[1] AGH University of Science and Technology,
Al. Mickiewicza 30, 30-059 Kraków, Poland
cyganek@agh.edu.pl
[2] Wrocław University of Technology,
Wybrzeże Wyspiańskiego 27, 50-370 Wrocław, Poland
Michal.Wozniak@pwr.wroc.pl

Abstract. In this paper we discuss algorithmically efficient methods of multidimensional patter recognition in kernel tensor subspaces. The kernel principal component analysis, which originally operates only on vector data, is joined with the tensor chordal kernel which opens a way of direct usage of the multidimensional signals, such as color video streams, seismic signals or hyperspectral images. We address the problem of efficient implementation of the eigendecomposition problem which is a core algorithm for both methods. For this the fixed point algorithm is employed. We show usefulness of this approach on the problem of visual pattern recognition and show speed-up ratio when using the proposed implementation.

Keywords: Kernel PCA · Chordal kernel · Tensor · Subspace classification

1 Introduction

Pattern recognition (PR) plays important role in information technologies. All recent achievements in search engines, automatic cars, smart phones, and many more draw from the latest developments in PR. However, majority of the "classical" PR methods operate in vector spaces, whereas todays data – such as video streams – are multidimensional [9, 10, 20, 21]. Therefore recent PR methods address this problem and try to process multidimensional data with available mathematical tools, such as tensor analysis [3, 8, 12, 19].

On the other hand, development of kernel methods opened new possibilities in PR domain. The main goal of this group of methods is to transform data into a usually higher dimensional space, called feature space, in which data classification is easier due to better separation of patterns from different classes [2]. All these lead to development of novel PR methods which are based on kernels, such as the kernel principal component analysis (KPCA) [15, 16], or support vector machines (SVM) [20, 21]. Nevertheless, most of the kernel methods are restricted to one-dimensional vector spaces, while processed data usually is of higher dimension. To deal with this problem, tensor and kernel based methods can be joined together to provide new quality, as will be shown. A tensor kernel was recently proposed by Signoretto *et al.* [17] based on

© Springer International Publishing Switzerland 2016
Y. Tan and Y. Shi (Eds.): DMBD 2016, LNCS 9714, pp. 529–537, 2016.
DOI: 10.1007/978-3-319-40973-3_54

subspace distances addressed in the work by Hamm and Lee [7]. They introduced so called *chordal kernel* to deal with tensors on Grassmann manifolds. It showed many interesting properties which verified in some recent works, such as the paper by Signoretto *et al.*, as well as the one by Cyganek *et al.* [4].

In this paper we study connection of two kernel methods: the KPCA and the chordal kernel for tensor patterns. KPCA is frequently used either for feature detection of prototype patterns or even directly to classification. However, this was only shown on vector input patterns. On the other hand, the chordal tensor allows application of KPCA to operate directly with tensor data. This opens new ways of processing these types of multidimensional signals of any dimension. However, what is a burden of the two methods, both are memory and time consuming. Therefore in this paper we focus mostly on providing a smooth connection of the two methods, as well as on their efficient implementation. Interestingly enough, they both rely on eigendecomposition algorithm. Therefore, for this task we propose to employ the fast fixed point algorithm, originally proposed by Bingham and Hyvärinen [1], then further exploited for signal processing, as presented in the work by Marot *et al.* [13].

2   Object Recognition with the Kernel Principal Component Analysis

The Principal Component Analysis (PCA) is the one of the well-known and frequently applied methods in data analysis and statistics [3, 16]. The main idea of PCA is to extract important information from a dataset $\{\mathbf{x}_i\}$ consisting of N exemplars of L-dimensional vectors $\mathbf{x}_i$. This is obtained by finding a transformation $\mathbf{T}$ of the input dataset into a new orthogonal space, in which each data point $\mathbf{x}_i$ can be represented as a linear combination of some coefficient and the orthogonal base vectors. These way the principal components are obtained which number does not exceed a number of the input data points. Moreover, the principal components are mutually uncorrelated random variables. Equivalently it can be shown that PCA maximizes the entropy of the principal components, which measures the amount of information conveyed by a random vector [11]. The above can be formulated as follows

$$\mathbf{y} = \mathbf{T}\bar{\mathbf{x}}, \tag{1}$$

where $\bar{\mathbf{x}}$ denotes a zero mean data, and $\mathbf{T}$ is the sought transformation which transforms $\bar{\mathbf{x}}$ into mutually uncorrelated variables $\mathbf{y}$. It can be shown that such transformation can be computed solving the following task

$$\mathbf{T}\Sigma_x\mathbf{T}^T = \Lambda. \tag{2}$$

where Σ_x is a covariance matrix of dataset $\{\mathbf{x}_i\}$ and Λ is a positive diagonal matrix. The above can be solved by computing eigenvectors of the positive symmetrical matrix Σ_x, i.e.

$$\lambda_j \mathbf{t}_j = \Sigma_x \mathbf{t}_j. \tag{3}$$

where $\mathbf{t}_j$ ($1 \leq j \leq N$) are eigenvectors and λ_j are eigenvalues of Σ_x.

The just outlined PCA method found dozens of applications, e.g. in data analysis and computer vision, to name a few [18]. PCA obtained sub-space can be used for pattern recognition, as will be discussed. However, it is a linear method which cannot cope with some nonlinear data dependencies. Nevertheless, it can be extended to nonlinear domain by a prior transformation of the input data into the so called feature space, which can be of arbitrary high dimensions [16]. This way, a Kernel PCA (KPCA) is obtained. Interestingly, in kernel based methods direct computations in the feature space are alleviated due to the so called kernel trick. It consists of such formulation of a problem which involves computation of only the inner products of vectors from the original domain. Moreover, as will be shown and which is the one of the main issues raised in this paper, the properly chosen kernel allows direct manipulation of the multidimensional data, represented in a tensor form, without necessity of transforming them into vectors, what usually leads to a loss of important information contained in neighboring relations of data points. Thus, Eq. (1) is transformed into

$$\mathbf{y}^{\Phi} = \mathbf{T}^{\Phi} \, \Phi(\bar{\mathbf{x}}). \tag{4}$$

where $\Phi : \mathcal{X} \to \mathcal{F}$ denotes a vector function which maps a point $\mathbf{x}$ from the input space X, into the $\Phi(\mathbf{x})$, which belongs to the inner product Hilbert feature space F.

Analogously to (2), a solution to (4), is obtained by eigendecomposition. However, instead of the correlation matrix Σ_x, the so called kernel matrix $\mathbf{K}$ needs to be eigendecomposed [16]. Elements k_{pq} of the $N \times N$ matrix $\mathbf{K}$ are defined as follows

$$k_{pq} = K(\mathbf{x}_p, \mathbf{x}_q) = \langle \Phi(\mathbf{x}_p), \Phi(\mathbf{x}_q) \rangle = \Phi^T(\mathbf{x}_p) \Phi(\mathbf{x}_q). \tag{5}$$

The eigendecomposition problem for KPCA can be represented as follows [15]

$$\varepsilon_j \mathbf{v}_j = \mathbf{K} \mathbf{v}_j, \tag{6}$$

where $\mathbf{v}_j$ ($1 \leq j \leq N$) are eigenvectors and ε_j are eigenvalues of $\mathbf{K}$. It is further assumed that the eigenvalues are normalized in accordance with the following formula [15, 16]

$$\varepsilon_j (\mathbf{v}_j \cdot \mathbf{v}_j) = 1, \tag{7}$$

which can be achieved simply by rearranging the above as follows

$$\tilde{\mathbf{v}}_j = \frac{\mathbf{v}_j}{\sqrt{\varepsilon_j}}. \tag{8}$$

In practice it means dividing each eigenvector by a square root of the corresponding eigenvalue.

However, in the standard linear PCA data had to be centered by subtraction of the mean value. Similarly, in (6) it is assumed that data is also centered but this time in the feature space, which is not that easy as subtraction of the mean of the original data [15]. Also, the empirical data vector, i.e. the kernel values of a test data and all training data, needs to be centralized, as will be discussed.

As alluded to previously, to remove the influence of any translation of the coordinate system, the kernel matrix needs to be centralized. This computation allows also pattern recognition with the first largest eigenvectors of the centralized kernel matrix. Center-adjusted kernel is computed directly from the kernel matrix, as follows

$$\hat{\mathbf{K}} = (\mathbf{I} - \mathbf{1}_N) \, \mathbf{K} \, (\mathbf{I} - \mathbf{1}_N). \tag{9}$$

where $\mathbf{1}_N$ denotes an $N \times N$ matrix of values $1/N$ and $\mathbf{I}$ denotes an identity matrix, i.e. with ones exclusively on its diagonal. Summarizing, at first the kernel matrix is computed. In our system this is done using the chordal kernel, as will be discussed in the next section. Then, the centralization (9) is performed. Finally, the eigenproblem (6) is solved resulting in a number of eigenvectors which correspond to a chosen number of important eigenvalues. Their choice is one of the parameters of the method. However, also automatic methods of eigenvalue selection exist [11]. The computed eigenvalues are used for pattern recognition, as described. It is worth noticing, that to solve the eigen-problem (6) the fast fixed point method can be used. Detailed algorithm of this method is described in [1, 13]. Savings can be significant especially for large number of patterns. Let us also observe, that the fast fixed point method is used twice in the propose system – once to compute eigendecompositions required to compute the chordal distance, and second time to solve (6). This is one of the novelties presented in this paper.

For a test object (tensor is our case) $\mathbf{x}$, at first the so called empirical feature vector needs to be computed [11, 16].

$$\mathbf{k}(\mathbf{x}) = [K(\mathbf{x}, \mathbf{x}_1), \quad K(\mathbf{x}, \mathbf{x}_2), \quad \ldots, \quad K(\mathbf{x}, \mathbf{x}_N)]^T. \tag{10}$$

Then its projection onto the space spanned by the eigendecomposition of $\mathbf{K}$ is computed to yield a number of initial principal components. However, what is frequently overlooked in literature is that, similarly to the kernel matrix, also the empirical feature vector needs to be centered. This can be done by the following formula

$$\hat{\mathbf{k}}(\mathbf{x}) = \big(\hat{\mathbf{k}}(\mathbf{x}) - \mathbf{1}'_N \mathbf{K} \big) (\mathbf{I} - \mathbf{1}_N), \tag{11}$$

where $\mathbf{1}'_N$ denotes an $1 \times N$ vector of values $1/N$, and K is the *not centralized* kernel matrix.

Finally the following projections can be computed

$$p_j = \langle \hat{\mathbf{k}}(\mathbf{x}), \mathbf{v}_j \rangle, \tag{12}$$

for $j \le M \le N$, where M denotes a chosen number of initial components. These can be used for pattern classification in the following scenarios:

1. Compute p_j for all training patterns and for the test one and find the class by the nearest-neighbor approach;
2. Compute a sum of squared projections and choose the smallest one;
3. Compute the spectral feature vector for each class and for the test one and find the class by the nearest-neighbor approach.

However, for a multidimensional patterns a vector based approach is insufficient since it does not utilize information contained in relative positions of values. In this respect, a kernel based approach allows us to avoid vectorization problem and usually the whole procedures leads to better results, as will be discussed. For tensor objects, elements of the kernel matrix $\mathbf{K}$ can be directly computed from the appropriately designed kernel function. In our experiments these are values computed as follows

$$k_{pq} = \mathbf{K}(X_p, X_q). \tag{13}$$

where X_p denote L-dimensional tensors. One of the possible kernels which directly operate on any dimensional tensor objects is the chordal kernel, discussed in the next section.

3 Chordal Kernels for Tensor Data

In this section we present only a short outline of the chordal kernel. More details can be found in publications [4, 17]. On the other hand, tensor methods are discussed for example in [3, 8].

Let us start with a definition of a tensor

$$\mathcal{A} \in \Re^{N_1 \times N_2 \times \ldots N_L}. \tag{14}$$

From the tensor $\mathcal{A}$ of dimension L, the so called flattening matrices $\mathbf{A}_{(j)}$ can be created

$$\mathbf{A}^{(j)} \in \Re^{N_j \times (N_1 N_2 \ldots N_{j-1} N_{j+1} \ldots N_L)}, \tag{15}$$

where $1 \leq j \leq L$ [3]. In the above, j denotes a row index of $\mathbf{A}^{(j)}$, while its column index is a product of all the rest L-1 indices of the tensor $\mathcal{A}$.

For two tensors $\mathcal{A}$ and $\mathcal{B}$, and their j-th flattened mode matrices $\mathbf{A}^{(j)}$ and $\mathbf{B}^{(j)}$, a chordal kernel is defined as follows [7, 17]

$$K^2(\mathcal{A}, \mathcal{B}) = \prod_{j=1}^{L} \exp\left(-\frac{1}{2\sigma^2} \left\| \mathbf{D}_{\mathbf{A},1}^{(j)} \mathbf{D}_{\mathbf{A},1}^{T(j)} - \mathbf{D}_{\mathbf{B},1}^{(j)} \mathbf{D}_{\mathbf{B},1}^{T(j)} \right\|_F^2\right), \tag{16}$$

where $\mathbf{D}_{\mathbf{A},1}^{(j)}$ and $\mathbf{D}_{\mathbf{B},1}^{(j)}$ are the matrices of the SVD decomposition of the corresponding j-th flattenings of the tensors A and B, respectively. For a $\mathbf{A}^{(j)}$ matrix, the corresponding $\mathbf{D}_{\mathbf{A},1}^{(j)}$ is computed from the following decomposition [6, 14]

$$\mathbf{A}^{(j)} = \mathbf{S}^{(j)}\mathbf{V}^{(j)}\mathbf{D}^{T(j)} = \begin{bmatrix} \mathbf{S}_{A,1}^{(j)} & \mathbf{S}_{A,2}^{(j)} \end{bmatrix} \begin{bmatrix} \mathbf{V}_{A,1}^{(j)} & \mathbf{0} \\ \mathbf{0} & \mathbf{0} \end{bmatrix} \begin{bmatrix} \mathbf{D}_{A,1}^{T(j)} \\ \mathbf{D}_{A,2}^{T(j)} \end{bmatrix}. \tag{17}$$

The same approach is used to compute $\mathbf{D}_{B,1}^{(j)}$. It is worth noticing, that columns of $\mathbf{D}_{A,1}^{(j)}$ and $\mathbf{S}_{A,1}^{(j)}$ constitute orthogonal bases for the ranges $R\left(\mathbf{A}^{T(j)}\right)$ and $R\left(\mathbf{A}^{(j)}\right)$, respectively.

Detailed algorithm of the chordal kernel is discussed in [4]. Its computation requires $2L$ SVD decompositions, which for large tensors are memory and time demanding. To mitigate this burden, in the presented system we used a faster computation of the limited number of leading components using the already mentioned fixed point method.

4 Experimental Results

The method presented in this paper was implemented in C ++ in the Microsoft Visual 2013. Experiments were run on a laptop computer with the Intel® Core™ i7-4800MQ CPU @2.7 GHz, 32 GB RAM, and the 64-bit Windows 7 operating system.

In the experiments the Georgia Tech Face Database [5] was tested since it is known to be difficult for many classification methods. It contains 50 color images of persons, each taken in 15 poses. In our approach, each color image is treated as a 3D tensor. This is a challenging task for classification due to high dimensionality of data, as well as because of high variations of the patterns. We conducted two types of experiments: The first to assess speed-up ratio due to the used fast decomposition methods; In the second step, the accuracy was measured.

In the first experiments X_p are chosen as 3D tensors of five exemplary images taken from the dataset. Examples are shown in Fig. 1. In all experiments the number of important components used for computation of the chordal tensor was set to the value giving best results which was obtained by experiments. Table 1 shows average computation times for the Jacobi and the fixed point method of eigendecomposition.

Fig. 1. Training images from the Georgia tech face database [5] used in experiments.

In the second experiments the accuracy of face recognition was measured. In this case the leave-one-out method was used in which for each class one image is taken out

Table 1. Timings when using the Jacobi and fast fixed point algorithms.

Tensor size	$3 \times 141 \times 196 \times 3$	$3 \times 181 \times 241 \times 3$	$5 \times 181 \times 241 \times 3$
Jacobi method	9.2	18.7	47.3
Fixed point	1.8	2.8	7.1

for testing while the other are used for training. The KPCA was set as described in previous sections. The features are computed as projections given by Eq. (12).

The features are then classified with the simple nearest-neighbor classifier. Then the minimal Euclidean distance is sought which indicates the output class. Results for two types of kernels, i.e. the tensor one and the simple exponential based on vector representation, are shown in Table 2. It is clear that the former leads to better results. However, in both cases these are not as good as for instance the ones obtained with the SVM classifiers, as presented in our previous work [4].

Table 2. Accuracy of the KPCA system.

Kernel	Accuracy
Chordal (tensor)	0.85
Exponent (vector)	0.78

However, what is an important aspect of the presented method is computation of the *vector features* in the form of projections (12) directly out any-dimensional tensor patterns. Such features can fit better for some processing methods, or to save on computational complexity, compared to the processing of the original multidimensional objects. This property will be further explored in our future research.

5 Conclusions

In this paper efficient connection of the kernel principal component analysis method joined with the tensor based kernels is proposed. The method allows processing of multidimensional signals without their breaking into vector representation. This frequently leads to better classification results due to retained information on mutual relations among feature components. However, both types of methods require significant memory and computational resources. Therefore, in this paper we employ an efficient eigendecomposition method which greatly shortens computation time, as was measured and presented. The other experiments show that application of the tensor kernel leads to better results as compared to simple vector based representations.

Since KPCA can be used for efficient generation of features, which can be trained with other type of classifier, such as SVM, in future research we will address this issue. Also, the method can be verified with other types of multidimensional signals, such as hyperspectral images.

Acknowledgments. This work was supported by the Polish National Science Center under the grant No. NCN DEC-2014/15/B/ST6/00609.

This work was also supported by EC under FP7, Coordination and Support Action, Grant Agreement Number 316097, ENGINE – European Research Centre of Network Intelligence for Innovation Enhancement (http://engine.pwr.wroc.pl/). All computer experiments were carried out using computer equipment sponsored by ENGINE project.

References

1. Bingham, E., Hyvärinen, A.: A fast fixed-point algorithm for independent component analysis of complex valued signals. Int. J. Neural Syst. **10**(1), 1483–1492 (2000). World Scientic Publishing Company
2. Cortes, C., Vapnik, V.: Support-vector networks. Mach. Learn. **20**, 273–297 (1995)
3. Cyganek, B.: Object Detection and Recognition in Digital Images: Theory and Practice. Wiley, London (2013)
4. Cyganek, B., Krawczyk, B., Woźniak, M.: Multidimensional data classification with chordal distance based kernel and support vector machines. Eng. Appl. Artif. Intell. **46**(Part A), 10–22 (2015). Elsevier
5. Georgia Tech Face Database (2013). http://www.anefian.com/research/face_reco.htm
6. Golub, G.H., van Loan, C.F.: Matrix Computations. Johns Hopkins Studies in the Mathematical Sciences. Johns Hopkins University Press, Baltimore (2013)
7. Hamm, J., Lee, D.: Grassmann discriminant analysis: a unifying view on subspace-based learning. In: Proceedings of the 25th International Conference on Machine Learning, pp. 376–383. ACM
8. Kolda, T.G., Bader, B.W.: Tensor decompositions and applications. SIAM Rev. **51**(3), 455–500 (2009)
9. Krawczyk, B., Schaefer, G.: A hybrid classifier committee for analysing asymmetry features in breast thermograms. Appl. Soft Comput. **20**, 112–118 (2014)
10. Krawczyk, B., Galar, M., Jelen, L., Herrera, F.: Evolutionary undersampling boosting for imbalanced classification of breast cancer malignancy. Appl. Soft Comput. **38**, 714–726 (2016)
11. Kung, S.Y.: Kernel Methods and Machine Learning. Cambridge University Press, Cambridge (2014)
12. De Lathauwer, L.: Signal processing based on multilinear algebra. Ph.D. dissertation, Katholieke Universiteit Leuven (1997)
13. Marot, J., Fossati, C., Bourennane, S.: About advances in tensor data denoising methods. EURASIP J. Adv. Signal Process. **1**, 1–12 (2008)
14. Meyer, C.D.: Matrix Analysis and Applied Linear Algebra Book and Solutions Manual. SIAM, Philadelphia (2001)
15. Schölkopf, B., Smola, A., Müller, K.-R.: Nonlinear component analysis as a kernel eigenvalue problem. Technical report No. 44, Max-Planck-Institut, pp. 1–18 (1996)
16. Schölkopf, B., Smola, A.J.: Learning with Kernels. MIT Press, Cambridge (2002)
17. Signoretto, M., De Lathauwer, L., Suykens, J.A.K.: A kernel-based framework to tensorial data analysis. Neural Netw. **24**, 861–874 (2011)
18. Turk, M.A., Pentland, A.P.: Face recognition using eigenfaces. In: IEEE Conference on Computer Vision and Pattern Recognition, pp. 586–590 (1991)
19. Vasilescu, M.A.O., Terzopoulos, D.: Multilinear analysis of image ensembles: tensorfaces. In: Heyden, A., Sparr, G., Nielsen, M., Johansen, P. (eds.) ECCV 2002, Part I. LNCS, vol. 2350, pp. 447–460. Springer, Heidelberg (2002)

20. Woźniak, M.: A hybrid decision tree training method using data streams. Knowl. Inf. Syst. **29**(2), 335–347 (2011)
21. Woźniak, M., Grana, M., Corchado, E.: A survey of multiple classifier systems as hybrid systems. Inf. Fusion **16**(1), 3–17 (2014)

Fingerprint Reference Point Detection Based on High Curvature Points

Krzysztof Wrobel, Rafal Doroz$^{(\boxtimes)}$, and Piotr Porwik

Institute of Computer Science, University of Silesia,
ul. Bedzinska 39, 41-200 Sosnowiec, Poland
{krzysztof.wrobel,rafal.doroz,piotr.porwik}@us.edu.pl
http://zsk.tech.us.edu.pl/
http://biometrics.us.edu.pl/

Abstract. The problem considered in this paper is associated with the image processing and the design of algorithm which allows selecting reference point on the fingerprint image. The reference point is used to align between the fingerprints in the fingerprint authentication systems faster than the conventional techniques. The reference point is the point with maximum curvature on the friction ridge, which is usually located in the central fingerprint area. Fingerprint homogeneous ridges are extracted from the image and then are processed by the IPAN99 algorithm which allows to detect curvatures of these lines.

The experimental results on datasets of FVC2000, FVC2002, FVC2004 and NIST, show the high efficiency and satisfactory accuracy of the proposed algorithm. Proposed solution allows detecting reference points more precisely than other algorithms.

Keywords: Biometrics · Fingerprint · Reference point · IPAN algorithm

1 Introduction

Nowadays, people require much higher information security. The traditional identification methods, such as password, magnetic card, PIN, and even personal signature are already insufficient and far from being able to meet today's environment. Biometrics is a personal identification technology based on an analysis of physiological or behavioral features of a given person [5,9,10]. In recent years, thanks to continuous technological development, a gradual increase of biometric techniques can be observed [2,14].

One of the most popular biometric techniques is fingerprint recognition. Fingerprint is a set of pattern of ridges, valleys (furrows) as well as characteristics that occur at minutiae points (ridge bifurcation or a ridge ending). These patterns are disclosed using inked impression on a paper or sensors (digital scanners). In police laboratories, to reveal difficult (latent) fingerprints magnetic powders, chemical baths and multi-impulse time resolved luminescence are also

© Springer International Publishing Switzerland 2016
Y. Tan and Y. Shi (Eds.): DMBD 2016, LNCS 9714, pp. 538–547, 2016.
DOI: 10.1007/978-3-319-40973-3_55

applied. Fingerprints may come from different places such as crime scenes, police stations, biometric systems and many others.

Fingerprint recognition technique is well known for many years and it is still developed and improved. Popularity of this method follows from their high efficiency, acceptability and applications in forensics. In practice, fingerprint analysis is a task from image processing domain because fingerprints traces are always converted to the digital images. Currently, fingerprint matching method can be classified into several categories [15]: minutiae based methods, where minutiae such as ridges endings and ridge bifurcations in two fingerprints are compare, ridge based methods where only ridges are matched, texture based methods in which the texture features of two fingerprints are matched, and neural network based methods. The state-of-the-art fingerprint minutiae based matching methods are the most popular because they have high reliability and acceptability in forensic sciences and automated fingerprint identification systems (AFIS) in many countries [3,15]. For these reasons minutiae based representation is also adapted in standard biometrics which is always concerned with the security its main interest is to reduce frauds and control access to the restricted areas. Standard biometric systems are comprised of a sensor for scanning a fingerprint and a processor which transform the scanning image to a digital form. Captured digital image is compared with fingerprints from database and then, the best match is determined. The match is generally used to allow or disallow access or is used for person identification or verification.

Image of fingerprint contains two important areas where so called the core and delta points (also referred to as singular points) are located. It should be noted that these points are always strongly stable and also scale invariant, so singular points are the most important global characteristics of a fingerprint.

The core point is defined as a region where the ridge curvature is highest and direction of ridge is changing rapidly [5]. The delta area is located as a triangular area where the ridges radiate outward in three directions [5]. The methods of point pattern matching become easier if the core point is known. Fingerprints are identified by examining and comparing the minutiae characteristics of two different fingerprint impressions to determine if these characteristics occupy the same relative area and position, and if their unit relationship to each other is in agreement. It means that some landmarks (here singular points) on the fingerprint image should be determined.

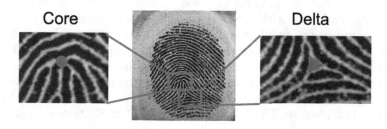

Fig. 1. Singular points in a fingerprint.

The magnified areas where characteristic singular landmarks occur on the fingerprint image were depicted in Fig. 1. Correct designation of singular points gives the some important profits - classification process can be shortened and fingerprint classification accuracy can be higher [3,12,15].

2 Related Work

There are several published studies on singular points detection in fingerprint images. In [5] the Authors proposed localization a convex core points as a reference point based on multiple resolution analysis of the differences of sine component integration between two defined regions of the orientation field. Unfortunately, in this method localization of core points on the edge of the image is not possible. The papers [12,13] present the method based on so-called identification masks. This method is sensitive to change the image resolution. Therefore, it has limited applications in case when finger scanners with different resolution are employed. The different approach to localization of the reference point has been proposed in [4]. In this method, the reference point localization is based on scale space analysis of the Poincare index and orientation variance. The main drawbacks of this method are its high computation cost, inability to handle a wide range of fingerprint types, and extreme sensitivity to noise. The authors of the paper [8] describe algorithm for detecting a convex core point as a unique reference point which can be appointed for all types of fingerprints. In order to detect robust core point candidates, a modified complex filter is proposed to detect the core points. This method has high effectiveness but it was checked by means of the one dataset only. Reference point detection describe also work [7]. The proposed method utilizes a discrete wavelet transform to extract the ridge information from a color image. So, this method is limited to color images only, which seems to be a too large limitation.

3 Proposed Method

The proposed method consists of three main stages. In the first stage the preparation of a digital image of a fingerprint for further stages of the analysis is done. Next, the process of extracting ridges in a digital fingerprint image is applied. Because we have a digital image, ridges can be interpreted as a chain of points (pixels). On the basis of the chain of pixels by means of the IPAN99 algorithm [1,3] the ridge and point with the greatest curvature in pointed out.

A fingerprint image, in which a reference point is determined, may be characterized by poor quality, low contrast and may be noised or blurred (Fig. 2a). This makes it difficult to extract the friction ridges necessary to determine such a point. For this reason, in the proposed method, the fingerprint image was subjected to a quality improvement process (Fig. 2b). The method described in [12] was used for this purpose. Then the operation of skeletonization was performed. It consists in the use of thinning algorithms that allow reducing the thickness of lines in the image. After thinning algorithm, the line thickness is equal to

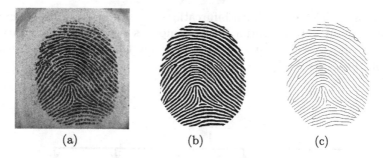

(a)   (b)   (c)

Fig. 2. Results of the preprocessing: (a) a low-quality fingerprint image, (b) the image after quality improvement, (c) the image after skeletonization.

one pixel, which facilitates creation of chains of points (Fig. 2c). It realizes the Pavlidis's thinning algorithm [11].

The thinned fingerprint image (Fig. 2c) is an input image for the next processing stages.

3.1 Extraction of the Ridges

The each ridge l of the thinned fingerprint image is described by chain of the points $C_l = (p_1, ..., p_n)$, where n is a number of points (pixels) belonging to a given line l. Analyzed points in chain are always adjacent points. In the first step, points of thinned fingerprint image are labeled according to the next principles:

- Label L0 - for points that do not belong to a ridges of fingerprint,
- Label L1 - for points that lie at the beginning or end of the ridge,
- Label L3 - for points that lie at the bifurcation of the ridge,
- Label L2 - for the remaining points.

The different type of labeled ridge's points are presented in Fig. 3.

L0	L0	L0	L0	L0	L0	L0	L0	L0	L0
L0	L0	L0	L0	L0	L0	L0	**L1**	L0	L0
L0	L0	L0	L0	L0	L0	L0	**L2**	L0	L0
L0	L0	L0	**L2**	**L2**	L0	**L2**	L0	L0	L0
L0	L0	**L2**	L0	L0	**L3**	L0	L0	L0	L0
L0	**L1**	L0	L0	L0	**L2**	L0	L0	L0	L0
L0	L0	L0	L0	L0	L0	**L2**	L0	L0	L0
L0	L0	L0	L0	L0	L0	L0	**L2**	L0	L0
L0	L0	L0	L0	L0	L0	L0	L0	**L1**	L0
L0	L0	L0	L0	L0	L0	L0	L0	L0	L0

Fig. 3. An example of a ridge points with marked labels.

Labels help to analyze the fingerprint textures and find appropriate points on ridges. Algorithm IPAN99 designates only curvature of homogeneous lines.

It means that complex ridges with bifurcations have to be separately analyzed. For example, if area of fingerprint image comprises the ridges configuration as in Fig. 4 then ridges will be divided into six single homogeneous lines, what is depicted in the same Fig. 4.

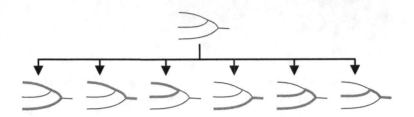

Fig. 4. Separation of ridges as homogeneous lines (without bifurcations).

Finally the set of chains $F = (C_1, ..., C_m)$ is formed, where m is a number of all separated homogeneous lines (ridges) which cover fingerprint image.

3.2   Determination of the Ridge Curvature

By means of the IPAN99 algorithm, the chains $C_l \in F$ of points are analyzed. Mentioned algorithm is well described in [1,3], therefore details of implementation were omitted here. By means of this algorithm the ridge curvature at a given point is calculated. Let p_i be an actually analyzed point of a given ridge l then between three selected points the triangle is inscribed (Fig. 5). Length of the triangle sides a and b is established on the basis of the conditions: $d_{min}^2 \leq a^2 \leq d_{max}^2$ and $d_{min}^2 \leq b^2 \leq d_{max}^2$, where: parameter $d_{min}(d_{max})$ specifying the minimum (maximum) length of triangle sides. The triangle side c is automatically established.

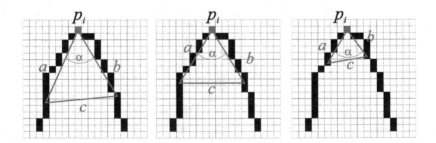

Fig. 5. Typical triangles inside the fingerprint ridges.

For every triangle the angle α is calculated as follows: $\alpha = arccos \frac{a^2+b^2-c^2}{2ab}$. Finally, for every chain $C_l \in F$ the set $G_l = \{\alpha_i^l, p_i^l(x_i, y_i)\}_{i=1}^n$, is formed, where α_i^l denotes curvature of the ridge l at the point coordinates $p_i^l(x_i, y_i)$. The greatest curvature of the ridge l can be found from the simple formula $\alpha_{min}^l = min\{\alpha_i^l \in G_l\}_{i=1}^n$. The same formula should be applied to the all homogeneous ridges m that form the fingerprint image. Then the greatest global curvature $\alpha_{min}(l)$ can be found from the formula $\alpha_{min}(l) = min\{\alpha_{min}^l\}_{l=1}^m$. The curvature $\alpha_{min}(l)$ occurs at the point $p_i^l(x_i, y_i)$ of the ridge l.

4   Experimental Results

Experiments carried out were compared with the police dactyloscopy expert. Expert's indications were treated as a reference values. It is worth noted that in practice the police expert always manually points out singular places on the fingerprint image. Using the proposed methodology we compared our approach with other results. During experiments the FVC2000[1], FVC2002[2], FVC2004[3] and NIST[4] databases were used to test the performance of the core point detection. Images in these datasets have various characteristics all of them were tested (Table 1).

Table 1. Baseline characteristics of the studied fingerprint images.

Database	Image size [px]	Resolution	Sensor type type	Number of fingerprints
FVC2000 DB4 SetB	240×320	500 dpi	Synthetic generator	80
FVC2000 DB2 SetB	256×364	500 dpi	Low-cost capacitive sensor	80
FVC2002 DB4 SetB	288×384	500 dpi	SFinGe v2.51	80
FVC2002 DB2 SetB	296×560	569 dpi	Optical sensor	80
FVC2000 DB1 SetB	300×300	500 dpi	Low-cost optical sensor	160
FVC2002 DB3 SetB			Capacitive sensor	
FVC2004 DB2 SetB	328×364	500 dpi	Optical Sensor	80
NIST	360×364	500 dpi	Unknown	115
FVC2002 DB1 SetB	388×374	500 dpi	Optical sensor	80
FVC2000 DB3 SetB	448×478	500 dpi	Optical sensor	80
FVC2004 DB1 SetB	640×480	500 dpi	Optical sensor	80

Previously mentioned parameters $d_{min}(d_{max})$ were selected based on a grid-search procedure. The detailed ranges of the tested values and best selected parameters are given in Table 2. In the remaining part of this paper, we only present results for the best obtained settings.

[1] http://bias.csr.unibo.it/fvc2000/databases.asp.
[2] http://bias.csr.unibo.it/fvc2002/databases.asp.
[3] http://bias.csr.unibo.it/fvc2004/databases.asp.
[4] http://www.nist.gov/itl/iad/ig/special_dbases.cfm.

Table 2. Details of optimization algorithm parameters used in the experiments.

Parameter	Initial range	Best value
d_{min}	From 1 to 50	17
d_{max}	From 1 to 50	19

The databases were separately tested. Accuracy coefficient was measured as the Euclidean distance between references values pointed out by fingerprint expert and values generated by proposed in this paper method. Simple example, where expert and our algorithm pointed out the reference points is presented in Fig. 6.

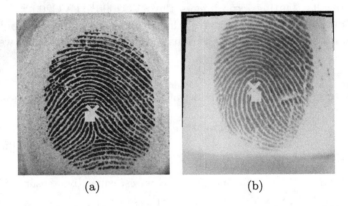

(a)   (b)

Fig. 6. Expert's (squares) and proposed approach (crosses) reference points location.

Our method was compared with three other algorithms. First of them is described in [13], whereas second is presented in [5] and third approach is presented in [6].

Table 3 shows that the highest reference point localization accuracy has a proposed approach. It is worth noted that all methods generate some errors compared to expert's reference values. Additionally, the results have been statistically evaluated by the paired t-Student test. Obtained results are sufficient to conclude that there are statistically significant differences between methods presented in Table 3. Computed the p-value statistic presents Table 4. Statistical analysis show that proposed in this paper reference point localization method gives statistically better results against other propositions. It shows Table 4. In practice, distance errors can be categorized, what is presented in Table 5. Figures 7 present the charts, where dependencies between reference point localization and accuracy are shown with respect to Table 5.

Table 3. Average difference (in pixels) between expert indications and various algorithms.

Database	Proposed method	Method 1 [13]	Method 2 [5]	Method 3 [6]
FVC2000 DB4 SetB	13.0 ± 13.83	20.60 ± 17.31	26.0 ± 22.30	26.9 ± 16.97
FVC2000 DB2 SetB	23.0 ± 23.72	34.3 ± 35.68	41.1 ± 22.30	42.7 ± 57.60
FVC2002 DB4 SetB	14.4 ± 9.36	22.2 ± 19.66	19.6 ± 18.50	29.8 ± 22.93
FVC2002 DB2 SetB	15.5 ± 17.56	32.4 ± 27.99	32.3 ± 41.30	25.2 ± 25.61
FVC2000 DB1 SetB	17.3 ± 16.39	23.4 ± 24.69	28.5 ± 18.60	36.3 ± 50.69
FVC2002 DB3 SetB				
FVC2004 DB2 SetB	13.7 ± 10.94	22.1 ± 24.49	26.6 ± 13.20	34.5 ± 51.51
NIST	11.6 ± 12.90	17.5 ± 20.06	22.9 ± 13.40	22.5 ± 42.51
FVC2002 DB1 SetB	13.2 ± 17.28	19.4 ± 13.71	27.8 ± 21.10	29.9 ± 45.27
FVC2000 DB3 SetB	24.4 ± 28.95	30.3 ± 21.61	31.7 ± 30.60	30.7 ± 43.89
FVC2004 DB1 SetB	8.3 ± 4.28	12.1 ± 4.61	14.8 ± 6.04	17.5 ± 11.77
Mean	**15.44**	**23.43**	**27.13**	**29.60**
Std	**4.96**	**6.97**	**7.25**	**7.19**

Table 4. Results of the t-paired Student test on the 95 % confidence interval in group of methods from Table 3.

	Comparison	p-value	95 % confidence interval	Comment
Proposed method	Method 1 [13]	0,0001	−10,64 to −5,34	Difference is statistically significant
	Method 2 [5]	0,0001	−14.78 to −8.60	Difference is statistically significant
	Method 3 [6]	0,0001	−17.72 to −10.60	Difference is statistically significant

Table 5. Errors in the reference point localization [8].

Type of error	Distance error	Error description
Accurate	Distance error is not larger than 10 pixels	The error that may be caused by human vision
Small	Distance error is between 10 pixels and 20 pixels	Error which may be caused by both human vision and algorithm
Significant	Distance error is between 20 pixels and 40 pixels	Error which may have negative effect on the subsequent processing steps, but it is still acceptable
Unaccepted	Distance error is larger than 40 pixels	Error is not accepted in fingerprint recognition systems

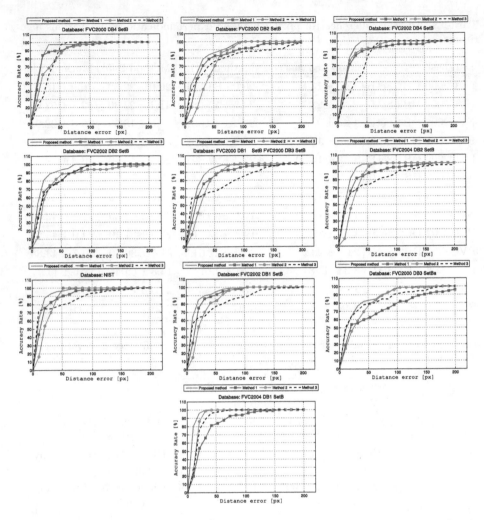

Fig. 7. Dependencies between localization error and accuracy of reference point localization for different database instances.

5   Conclusion

The proposed solution may be used in biometric systems with various types of scanners. The presented method has a high and stable accuracy of reference point localization on fingerprint images and is resistant to geometric transformations, such as rotation and translation of input fingerprint image. Besides the efficiency, our algorithm is quite easy to be implemented and can deal with large rotated fingerprint images. Experimental results on FVC datasets show advantage proposed solution over other algorithms. Experimental results demonstrate that the proposed method can consistently extract reference points with the high accuracy and consistency. Reference point can be used for alignment (translation and rotation) parameters in fingerprint matching.

References

1. Chetverikov D., Szabo Z., Detection of high curvature points in planner curves. In: 23rd Workshop of the Australian Pattern Recognition Group, pp. 175–184 (1999)
2. Doroz R., Porwik P., Wrobel K.: Signature recognition based on voting schemes. In: International Conference on Biometrics and Kansei Engineering (ICBAKE), Tokyo, Japan, pp. 53–57 (2013)
3. Doroz, R., Wrobel, K., Palys, M.: Detecting the reference point in fingerprint images with the use of the high curvature points. In: Nguyen, N.T., Trawiński, B., Kosala, R. (eds.) ACIIDS 2015. LNCS, vol. 9012, pp. 82–91. Springer, Heidelberg (2015)
4. Guo, J.M., Liu, Y.F., Chang, J.Y., Lee, J.D.: Fingerprint classification based on decision tree from singular points and orientation field. Expert Syst. Appl. **41**, 752–764 (2014)
5. Jain, A.K., Prabhakar, S., John, L., Pankanti, S.: Filter bank based fingerprint matching. IEEE Trans. Image Process. **9**(5), 846–859 (2000)
6. Kawagoe, M., Tojo, A.: Fingerprint pattern classification. Pattern Recogn. **17**(3), 295–303 (1984)
7. Khalil, M.S.: Reference point detection for camera-based fingerprint image based on wavelet transformation. BioMed. Eng. OnLine **14**, 1–23 (2015)
8. Le, H.T., Van, T.H.: Fingerprint reference point detection for image retrieval based on symmetry and variation. Pattern Recogn. **45**, 3360–3372 (2012)
9. Maltoni, D., Maio, D., Jain, A.K., Prabhakar, S.: Handbook of Fingerprint Recognition, 2nd edn. Springer, London (2009)
10. Marzec, M., Koprowski, R., Wrobel, Z.: Automatic method for detection of characteristic areas in thermal face images. Multimedia Tools Appl. **74**(12), 4351–4368 (2015)
11. Pavlidis, T.: A thinning algorithm for discrete binary images. Comput. Graph. Image Process. **13**, 142–157 (1980)
12. Porwik, P., Wieclaw, L.: A new approach to reference point location in fingerprint recognition. IEICE Int. J. Electron. Express. **1**(18), 575–581 (2004). Japan
13. Porwik, P., Wrobel, K.: The new algorithm of fingerprint reference point location based on identification masks. In: Kurzyński, M., Puchała, E., Wożniak, A. (eds.) CORES 2005. AISC, vol. 30, pp. 807–814. Springer, Heidelberg (2005)
14. Wrobel K., Doroz R., Palys M.: A method of lip print recognition based on sections comparison. In: International Conference on Biometrics and Kansei Engineering (ICBAKE), Tokyo, Japan, pp. 47–52 (2013)
15. Zhang, Q., Yin, Y., Yang, G.: Unmatched minutiae: useful information to boost fingerprint recognition. Neurocomputing **171**, 1401–1413 (2016)

Study of the Harmonic Distortion (THD) and Power Factor Oriented to the Luminaries Used in the Traffic Light System of Bogotá City, Colombia

Carlos Andres Parra Martinez[✉], Hugo Alejandro Serrato Vanegas[✉], and José Ignacio Rodriguez Molano[✉]

Universidad Distrital Francisco José de Caldas, Bogotá, Colombia
ingenieromartinez_electrico@hotmail.es,
hualseva@hotmail.com, jirodriguez@udistrital.edu.co

Abstract. In order to achieve a "healthy" power system, it is important to monitor existing values of electromagnetic interference, focusing on the quality of permanent technical products in relation to the phenomena present in the power grid. In this study harmonic distortion measurements are made in the voltage wave (THDv) and in the current wave (THDI) in order to determine the levels of harmonic distortion and power factor in the luminaries system that compose the current traffic light system (LED and halogen) in Bogota. Besides, this study contrasts the measurements found against the technical levels of THD both for voltage and for current, for each kind of luminaire recommended in the IEC 61000-3-2.

Keywords: Harmonic distortion · Power factor · Power quality · Traffic lights

1 Introduction

Bogota City (Colombia) has overflown any projections of expansion and growth. Since 1968, the Administrative Department of Planning hand other institutions have tried everything to project and legislate matters relating to the development of the capital [1]. Since then, the entity underwent several reforms in its functions, as well as in its organizational and administrative structure. In the same sense, in 2006, the Planning section was created and within this, the Department was transformed by the current District Planning Department, through which the public policies of the city articulate their dimensions: territorial, sectorial and expenditure, with the participation of different actors in search of an organized development that benefits everyone in the District [2].

The traffic light system of the capital is not as developed as it should be [3]. Therefore, it has become a real problem in mobility. For example, in 2008, the traffic light network was more than 30 years old and did not allow any programming on timing for the traffic lights according to traffic flow [4]; gradually, and in order to improve the mobility of vehicles during peak hours and reduce the waiting time of drivers and pedestrians at traffic lights, the District Secretariat for Mobility has been setting up an intelligent traffic light network [5].

© Springer International Publishing Switzerland 2016
Y. Tan and Y. Shi (Eds.): DMBD 2016, LNCS 9714, pp. 548–556, 2016.
DOI: 10.1007/978-3-319-40973-3_56

If the modernization process is successfully completed, as expected, there will be other technical and operational challenges for the implementation of an Intelligent Traffic System; especially, when equipment based on power electronics is wide spreading. With the rise of technological developments in the recent decades, this equipment has led to the use of electronic based loads, susceptible to electromagnetic interference, such as harmonic distortion, fast voltage fluctuations (flicker), transients, sags, swell and others [6].

2 Why a Study on Power Quality in Bogota's Traffic Light System

There are several sensors and control equipment that interact in the crossing signaling (traffic light). This equipment commonly uses power converters, essentially nonlinear loads, as well as new LED technology in traffic lights. Although LED technology is more efficient, it also brings disturbances to the power grid. This equates to an increase in operating costs, increased interconnections, a system susceptible of failures, reduced equipment life and erratic operation thereof, among many other implications (see harmonic distortion) [7].

These concerns must always be considered, because they will directly affect the welfare of mobility. Moreover, the generation of a sinusoidal voltage waveform, of amplitude and frequency as constant as possible or with a tolerable range regulation for the loads defines the loads design, transmission devices, protection, distribution, control, and insulation. In essence, it sets the benchmarks for design [8].

3 Electromagnetic Interferences in the Traffic Light System

Service continuity of electricity services is what has been traditionally defined as reliability, particularly: harmonics, transients, voltage fluctuations, and power factor [9].

3.1 Harmonic Distortion

Harmonics are mainly generated from non-linear loads such as transformers, electric engines, generators, arc furnaces, arc welders, DC converters, inverters, television sources, switch mode power supplies, high pressure discharge lamps, fluorescent lights, light-emitting diodes, laptops, mobile phone chargers, electronic products, and other similar loads coming from electronic equipment [10, 11].

The rate of total harmonic distortion:

$$\%THD_I = \frac{\sqrt{I_{2RMS}^2 + \cdots + I_{nRMS}^2}}{I_{1RMS}} \times 100. \tag{1}$$

The total harmonic distortion of the voltage wave is:

$$\%THD_V = \frac{\sqrt{V^2_{2\,RMS} + \cdots + V^2_{n\,RMS}}}{V_{1RMS}} \times 100. \tag{2}$$

The interest in measuring the THD is that power systems, including the traffic lights, are sensitive to non-linear loads and can present a number of undesirable effects, including overheating and damage to electrical conductors, premature failure of transformers, line voltage distortion in feeders, and branch circuits fed from high impedance sources (generators, transformers and high impedance regulators, primary feeders, etc.), unwanted shot of switches and relays, overheating and failure of capacitor banks for power factor correction, noise induction in lines (by magnetic or electromagnetic coupling between electric power circuits and communications), errors in measurement equipment, etc. [12].

3.2 Power Factor

Despite the relentless pursuit of power systems in the ideal condition of unity power factor, in practice, it is not possible to achieve given the harmonic content on the network, whereby we would have factor of real power that, as expected, is less than the ideal power factor.

$$fp' = \cos \theta' = \frac{P'}{|S|'} < fp = \cos \theta = \frac{P}{|S|} = \frac{P'}{V'.I'}. \tag{3}$$

With some mathematical basics, it is possible to associate the power factor THD of both voltage and current, as:

$$RPF = fp' = \cos \theta' = \frac{P'}{|S|'} = \frac{P'}{V'.I'} = \frac{P}{V_{1RMS}I_{1RMS}\sqrt{\left(1 + \frac{THD_V}{100}\right)^2}\sqrt{\left(1 + \frac{THD_I}{100}\right)^2}}. \tag{4}$$

4 Practical, Recommendations, Methodology, and Measures

It is necessary to make measurements of harmonic distortion on the voltage waveform (LDLT) and in the current wave (THDI), as well as the power factor (pf or PF), of all the luminaries types present in the traffic light system. To carry them out, the practical recommendations and requirements for harmonic control in electrical power systems, IEC 61000-3-2 will be followed.

Where, for each one of the luminaries: Green module halogen luminarie, LED Luminarie for pedestrian crossing SoBright type, LED Luminarie turn arrow SoBright type and full LED Luminaries SIMSA type, will account for measures with a digital meter model PF9811 of the 9800 series, produced by EVERFINE. As depicted in Fig. 1a and b, they have tolerances of 0–20 % THD, power factor of 0.9 to 1.0 and an error in the measurement of ±5 %; in a conventional power source, SOURCE, of 120 V in AC; those measures will be consequently characterized and tabulated.

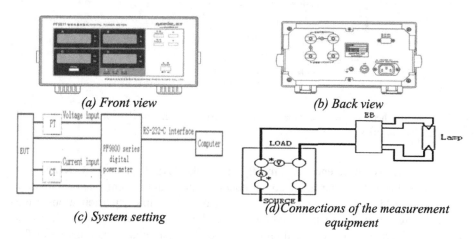

(a) Front view

(b) Back view

(c) System setting

(d) Connections of the measurement equipment

Fig. 1. Digital meter of harmonic distortion PF9811 EVERFINE [13].

The measuring equipment PDF Everfine 9811 uses the voltmeter and ammeter method, Fig. 1c, so that, Fig. 1d, the THD and power factor are measured by the method of voltmeter or power transformer (PT) and the ammeter or current transformer (CT).

5   Results

Once the connections in Fig. 1d, with the measuring equipment Everfine PF 9811 for the full SIMSA LED type, TRV-G08DR2R2 model; built for an input of 65–140 V AC; a nominal operating frequency of 50 or 60 Hz, and power of 14.5 W; with the first three columns characterizing the network, including the rating of the luminaries[1]:

The relation between the nominal voltage and the current ratio appears in Fig. 2; in order to identify the behavior of the average values of voltage and current, a trend line is added. For a linear approximation to the dispersion data (values measured for voltage and current), R2 is equal to 0.9694; to the full SIMSA LED luminaries is non-linear.

In Fig. 3a and b it is possible to see the harmonic distortion, both for voltage and current. In an ideal case, the relation between the harmonic distortion corresponding to the voltage wave and the current wave should be constant and as close to zero as possible.

On another hand, both values, in each dispersion, do not exceed 10 % of THD, so, it is possible to infer that (the luminaries) do not individually affect the power factor of

---

[1] All the values of voltage, current, and power are in RMS.

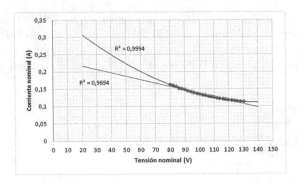

Fig. 2. Relation between the nominal current versus the nominal voltage for the full SIMSA LED luminaries

the load (if there is a difference, it is mostly due to the THD-I, of Table 1. Hence, the consideration that the first harmonic component of voltage and current is approximately 100 % of the RMS wave value, or what is the same, an incipient participation of the harmonics greater than 1 in the waveform distortion. Of course, the above happens without considering an important number of luminaries simultaneously active at the same point of common coupling (PCC).

Table 1. Features of the network and measures of the power factor and THD THD-V-I for the full LED type light SIMSA.

Voltage measured [V]	Nominal voltage [V]	Nominal current [A]	Nominal Capacity [W]	P.F.	THD-V [%]	THD-I [%]
98	98,5	0,136	13,44	0,998	2,4	6,2
102	102,2	0,132	13,53	0,998	2,2	6,2
106	106,3	0,128	13,66	0,998	2,4	6,2
110	110,1	0,125	13,80	0,998	2,4	5,9
114	114,1	0,122	13,93	0,997	2,4	6,0
118	118,0	0,119	14,08	0,997	2,4	6,3
122	122,3	0,116	14,25	0,997	2,5	5,9

There is a null input of the even harmonics for the first fifteen multiples of the fundamental frequency; as expected, the odd harmonics for the full SIMSA LED luminaries are the most critical, being prone to wave harmonic current pollution, predominantly with third order harmonics; this is understandable do to the use of AC/DC converters with low power in the luminaries (less than 100 W); however, it is important to highlight that the individual contribution of a single lamp in terms of generating harmonic contamination in the system is insignificant. Besides, a significant number of luminaries should be considered in simultaneous service to a same PCC.

The same procedure is followed for the LED luminaries with turning arrow SoBright, A10-G08THA117GC model with 84 LEDs; built for an input of 80–135 V AC;

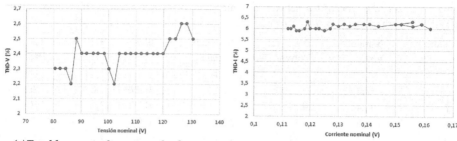

(a)*Total harmonic distortion of voltage vs. nominal voltage*

(b)*Total harmonic distortion vs. nominal current*

Fig. 3. Characterization of harmonic distortion for the full SIMSA LED luminaire

a nominal operating frequency of 50 or 60 Hz, and less than 15-W (using an AC/DC low power converter) power. The following measures were obtained (Table 2):

Table 2. Characterizing the network and measures of power factor and THD THD-V-I for the LED Luminaire with turn arrow SoBright type

Voltage measured [V]	Nominal voltage [V]	Nominal current [A]	Nominal Capacity [W]	P.F.	THD-V [%]	THD-I [%]
98	98,0	0,128	12,61	0,998	2,5	6,8
102	102,2	0,123	12,57	0,998	2,6	7,0
106	106,5	0,117	12,53	0,998	2,6	7,1
110	110,0	0,114	12,52	0,998	2,4	7,0
114	114,0	0,109	12,50	0,998	2,6	6,8
118	118,2	0,105	12,48	0,998	2,6	6,7
122	122,3	0,102	12,46	0,997	2,6	6,7

Once again, the same happens for the LED Luminaries with turn arrow SoBright type, the load is not linear, R^2 equals to 0.9981 for a polynomial trend line of degree two; the graph is omitted. The same happens for the relation between voltage and nominal current vs. harmonic distortion (the performance in comparative terms with the full SIMSA LED luminaries remains).

Likewise, for the LED Luminaries for pedestrian crossing SoBright type, model P10-G08THA120RC with 76 LEDs; built for an input of 80–135 V AC; a nominal operating frequency of 50 or 60 Hz, and less than 15 W (using AC/DC low power converter). The following measures were obtained (Table 3):

The type of no linear load, the power factor behavior, as well as the harmonic distortion for voltage and current are the same as before.

For the green module halogen luminaries, the load is linear. The following measures were obtained (Table 4):

Table 3. Characterization of the network and measures of power factor, THD-V and THD-I type LED luminaire for pedestrian SoBright

Voltage measured [V]	Nominal voltage [V]	Nominal current [A]	Nominal Capacity [W]	P.F.	THD-V [%]	THD-I [%]
98	98,2	0,130	12,85	0,999	2,6	5,6
102	102,4	0,125	12,83	0,998	2,5	5,7
106	106,3	0,120	12,82	0,998	2,5	5,7
110	110,3	0,116	12,83	0,998	2,5	5,8
114	114,2	0,112	12,83	0,998	2,4	5,7
118	118,3	0,108	12,83	0,998	2,5	5,6
122	122,2	0,105	12,84	0,998	2,5	5,3

Table 4. Characterizing the network and measures of power factor and THD THD-V-I for the green module halogen luminaire

Voltage measured [V]	Nominal voltage [V]	Nominal current [A]	Nominal Capacity [W]	P.F.	THD-V [%]	THD-I [%]
98	98,1	0,405	39,82	1	2,5	2,4
102	102,1	0,413	42,23	1	2,5	2,3
106	106,3	0,423	45,03	1	2,5	2,2
110	110,1	0,431	47,55	1	2,6	2,3
114	114,1	0,440	50,31	1	2,4	2,3
118	118,1	0,449	53,07	1	2,5	2,3
122	122,2	0,457	55,95	1	2,6	2,4

In fact, for being a green module halogen luminaire with linear load, it is expected that it does not "inject" an important number of interfering harmonics in to the network, where the percentages do not exceed 3 % of THD for voltage and nominal current. Generally, the performance of full LED luminaries SIMSA type, pedestrian and turn arrow SoBright type, has similar power consumption (about 13 W), but not greater THD-I compared to THD-V, The dominance of the third harmonic remains.

The consumption of the halogen luminaries is four times greater than that of the LED luminaries, thus, it is necessary to proceed with a technological change, and related issues (high THD when a significant number of LED lights are active simultaneously at the same PCC).

6   Conclusions

It is important to mitigate or eliminate (if possible) the harmful effects of electromagnetic interference on the power grid if what is expected is a major factor of power, with voltage stability, lower losses on the network, no resonance problems and amplification of electrical disturbances; which means a much lower load on the equipment, longer duration, as well as lower maintenance and replacement costs if the equipment is worn or damaged.

Taking into account that the IEC 61000-3-2 standard, classifies equipment into four classes (A, B, C, D) based on the following criteria: (1) Number of pieces of equipment in use, (2) Duration (number operating hours), (3) Simultaneous use (the same type of equipment used in the same period), (4) Energy consumption, (5) Harmonic spectrum, we can highlight the findings below.

Individually, the full LED luminary SIMSA type, as well as the LED Luminaries for pedestrians and with turn arrow SoBright are class A.

For the purpose of this study, the luminaires that are currently used in conventional crossings with traffic lights were selected. These luminaires are provided under the inter-administrative contract No. 20151131 signed on June 26th 2015 between Universidad Francisco José de Caldas and the District Secretariat for Mobility in Bogota. Before the results, it is important to point out that, although the control equipment and joint sensors affect the measurements of harmonics, they are out of the range of this study. For that reason, they are not taken into account; however, it is recommended that they are studied in future research works.

In addition, according to the CRISP -DM [CRISP -DM, 2000] method, in the process of data understanding, data preparation, modeling, evaluation and implementation [14], for luminaires variables rated voltage, rated current were considered, harmonic voltage, harmonic current, the total THD, power factor, hysteresis, voltage THD, current THD and among which the most relevant to the rated voltage, rated current and THD study.

For an equipment, luminary or bulb to be considered Class A, it must maintain limits on THD-I as follows: for the third harmonic of 2.30 %, for the fifth of 1.14 %, for the seventh of 0.77 %, for the ninth of 0.40 %, for the eleventh of 0.33 %, for the thirteenth of 0.21 %, and those contained between the fifteenth and the thirty-ninth harmonic of $0.15 \times 15/n$, where n equals the number of the harmonic.

In general, the behavior of LED luminaries, either for full SIMSA, with turn arrow, or pedestrian SoBright, shows similar power consumption (about 13 W), but not higher THD-I compared to THD-V; there is a predominance of the third harmonic. Also, for the LED and halogen luminaries, the dispersion does not exceed the 10 % of THD, then, reviewing (20), it follows that individual luminaries do not affect the power factor of the load; therefore, there is a clear consideration that the first harmonic component of voltage and current is about 100 % RMS value of the wave; which is to say that it has an insignificant participation in the harmonics that are greater than one in the wave distortion. Off course, this is without considering an important number of luminaries simultaneously connected to a single PCC.

References

1. Decreto 3133: Por el cual se reforma la organización administrativa del distrito especial de Bogotá (1968)
2. Acuerdo 256: Por el cual se dictan normas básicas sobre la estructura, organización, y funcionamiento de los organismos y las entidades de Bogotá D.C. y se expiden otra disposiciones (2006)
3. Mantenimiento correctivo y preventivo de los semáforos y redes eléctricas del sistema de semaforización de Bogotá D.C. y de las nuevas intersecciones que se vayan integrando al sistema (2014)
4. Vásquez, A.: Semaforización en Bogotá: Plan de choque, Bogotá (2008)
5. Chica, A.: Instalan red de semáforos inteligentes en Bogotá, 25 Junio 2013. http://caracol.com.co/radio/2003/05/26/bogota/1053900000_036217.html. Accessed 31 Oct 2015
6. Abreu, A.: Calidad de potencia eléctrica en redes de distribución, Maracaibo (2005)
7. Guerrero, R., Martínez, I.: Calidad de energía Factor de potencia y filtrado de armónicos. McGraw-Hill Educación, México (2012)
8. Baggini, A.: Handbook of Power Quality, p. 545. Wiley, West Sussex (2008)
9. Monzón, M.: Calidad de suministro eléctrico: Huecos de tensión, mitigación de sus efectos en las plantas industriales. Publicaciones Universidad Carlos III de Madrid, Madrid (2013)
10. Arrillaga, J., Bradkey, D.A., Bodger, P.S.: Power System Harmonic. Wiley, New York (1985)
11. Wadhwa, C.L.: Electrical Power Systems. New Age International, New Delhi (2014)
12. Ramírez, S., Cano, E.: Calidad del servicio de energía eléctrica. Publicaciones Universidad Nacional de Colombia, sede Manizales, Manizales (2006)
13. EVERFINE LTD.: User's Manual PF9800 Series: Power Digital Meter, 13 Noviembre 2015
14. Gallardo Aranciba, J.A.: Metodología para la Definición de Requisitos en proyectos de Data Mining ER-DM. Facultad de Informática, UPM, Madrid, España (2009)

Extraction of Dynamic Nonnegative Features from Multidimensional Nonstationary Signals

Rafał Zdunek$^{(\boxtimes)}$ and Michalina Kotyla

Department of Electronics, Wroclaw University of Technology,
Wybrzeze Wyspianskiego 27, 50-370 Wroclaw, Poland
`rafal.zdunek@pwr.edu.pl`

Abstract. In the paper, we study the problem of time-varying feature extraction from a long sequence of dynamic multidimensional observations. Imposing the nonnegativity constrains onto the estimated features, the problem can be represented by an on-line nonnegative matrix factorization (NMF) model. To update the nonnegative factors in such a model, we used various computational strategies, including the row-action projections (Kaczmarz algorithm), rank-one least square updates, and modified proximal gradient iterations. The numerical experiments, performed on the benchmarks of nonstationary spectral signals, demonstrated that the Kaczmarz algorithm appeared to be the most efficient, both with respect to the performance and the computational time.

Keywords: Dynamic feature extraction · On-line NMF · Row-action projections · Proximal gradients · Nonstationary signal processing

1 Introduction

In the era of big data, massive data are characterized by a large volume, a considerable variety, and often a high speed of their acquisition. Extraction and tracking of functional and relevant information from time-varying volumetric data is a challenging and also very important task with many real-world applications in computer vision, pattern recognition, machine learning, and signal processing [1–8]. Fast and efficient computational tools are needed to efficiently tackle such a problem.

The features extracted from nonnegative observations (such as images, spectra, matrices of probability, etc.), are usually easier in interpretation and contain more meaningful information if they are nonnegatively constrained. This assumption is satisfied if Nonnegative Matrix Factorization (NMF) [9,10] is applied to the observed data. It is an unsupervised learning technique that is commonly used in machine learning and data analysis for feature extraction and dimensionality reduction of nonnegative data. The fundamental version of NMF assumes a batch mode decomposition of a nonnegative matrix of observations into two lower-rank nonnegative matrices. The one represents nonnegative features, and the other contains coefficients of their nonnegative combinations.

© Springer International Publishing Switzerland 2016
Y. Tan and Y. Shi (Eds.): DMBD 2016, LNCS 9714, pp. 557–566, 2016.
DOI: 10.1007/978-3-319-40973-3_57

The batch-mode processing can be easily performed with many relatively simple computational strategies. However, it does not allow us to obtain time-varying features that change smoothly with time instances, and it is not computationally efficient if the observed data arrives sequentially. To overcome the first problem, the continues NMF model [11] can be used. The other problem can be tackled with Online NMF (ONMF) [12], which has a wide area of applications. Wang *et al.* [13] applied it to document clustering. Lefevre *et al.* [14] analyzed spectrograms with a special version of ONMF that minimizes the Itakura-Saito distance. Another important application is blind separation of moving sources.

ONMF is particularly useful for processing streaming data. With reference to the basic NMF model, it allows us to substantially reduce a computational complexity both in time and memory. Furthermore, it gives us a possibility of updating the feature vectors over the time. When the basic model of NMF is applied to the magnitude spectrogram of an audio signal, it estimates the feature vectors that represent frequency profiles, common for the whole set of observed signals. ONMF extracts time-varying frequency profiles that are most suitable for analyzing nonstationary stochastic signals.

The factors in ONMF can be estimated with various optimization algorithms. Example include the geometry-based algorithms [15] or stochastic approximation algorithms [16]. In the paper [17], a new observed datum is modeled by a hyperplane in the space of the feature vectors. To update a solution, the row-action projections from the Kaczmarz's algorithm [18] was used. The algorithm have played an important role in developing Computerized Tomography (CT), and currently it has a wide area of applications.

Motivated by the results obtained in [17], we further develop such an algorithmic approach by proposing new updating rules. One of them assumes the projected rank-one least square update of the feature vectors by using the Sherman-Morrison formula. This rule is simple to implement, however, it does not satisfy the Karush-Kuhn-Tucker (KKT) optimality conditions for updating nonnegative solutions. To relax this problem, we use the proximal gradient approximations that have already found a number of successful applications in signal and image processing, including the basic NMF model [19].

The paper is organized as follows: Sect. 2 discusses the dynamic and ONMF model. The optimization algorithms for estimating the factors in the discussed models are presented in Sect. 3. The experiments carried out for nonstationary signals are described in Sect. 4. Finally, the conclusions are drawn in Sect. 5.

2   Model

The basic model of NMF assumes an approximate decomposition of the nonnegative input matrix $\boldsymbol{Y} = [y_{it}] \in \mathbb{R}_+^{I \times T}$ into the lower-rank nonnegative matrices $\boldsymbol{A} = [a_{ij}] \in \mathbb{R}_+^{I \times J}$ and $\boldsymbol{X} = [x_{jt}] \in \mathbb{R}_+^{J \times T}$, given the lower rank J, and possibly some prior knowledge on the matrices $\boldsymbol{A}$ or $\boldsymbol{X}$. Usually: $J << \min\{I, T\}$. Thus: $\boldsymbol{Y} \cong \boldsymbol{A}\boldsymbol{X} \in \mathbb{R}_+^{I \times T}$.

The factors $\boldsymbol{A}$ and $\boldsymbol{X}$ are typically estimated from $\boldsymbol{Y}$ by using the following alternating optimization scheme: For $s = 1, 2, \ldots, \mathbf{do}$:

$$\boldsymbol{X}^{(s)} = \arg\min_{\mathbf{X} \geq 0} \Psi(\boldsymbol{Y} \| \boldsymbol{A}^{(s-1)} \boldsymbol{X}), \tag{1}$$

$$\boldsymbol{A}^{(s)} = \arg\min_{\mathbf{A} \geq 0} \Psi(\boldsymbol{Y} \| \boldsymbol{A} \boldsymbol{X}^{(s)}), \tag{2}$$

where $\Psi(\boldsymbol{Y} \| \boldsymbol{A}\boldsymbol{X})$ is an assumed objective function that measures disimilarity between the observed data in $\boldsymbol{Y}$ and the model $\boldsymbol{A}\boldsymbol{X}$.

Most NMF algorithms perform a batch-mode processing, i.e. the whole matrix $\boldsymbol{Y}$ should be accessible to update the solution to the problems (1) and (2). However, this approach is not computationally efficient if the data arrive sequentially (streaming data). If the number of observed samples in the batch-mode processing is small, the amount of relevant information might not be sufficient to train the model well. On the contrary, the training might be computationally demanding or even intractable. These difficulties can be overcome if the ONMF model is used. It assumes a sequential-mode processing, where at a time instant t, we observe the sample $\boldsymbol{y}_t \in \mathbb{R}_+^I$ that represents I signals or realizations of I random variables. Starting from a given time instant, all the subsequent samples $\{\boldsymbol{y}_t\}$ are gathered sequentially. Let the samples observed in the past form the matrix $\boldsymbol{Y}_{(t-1)} = [\boldsymbol{y}_1, \boldsymbol{y}_2, \ldots, \boldsymbol{y}_{t-1}] \in \mathbb{R}_+^{I \times (t-1)}$. Thus, the ONMF model has the following form:

$$\boldsymbol{Y} = \left[\boldsymbol{Y}_{(t-1)}, \boldsymbol{y}_t \right] \cong \boldsymbol{A} \left[\boldsymbol{X}_{(t-1)}, \boldsymbol{x}_t \right]. \tag{3}$$

The total number of recorded samples can be very large or even unlimited - we observe a slowly-varying process. However, we assume that at the moment of starting the sequential data processing, the observed history is not very long, i.e. the number $(t - 1)$ is rather small but $\min\{t - 1, I\} \gg J$. As a result, an initial approximation for $\boldsymbol{A}$ and $\boldsymbol{X}_{(t-1)} \in \mathbb{R}_+^{J \times (t-1)}$ can be easily obtained by applying the standard NMF model to $\boldsymbol{Y}_{(t-1)}$. Having $\boldsymbol{A}$, $\boldsymbol{X}_{(t-1)}$, and a new sample $\boldsymbol{y}_t$, the corresponding vector $\boldsymbol{x}_t$ can be readily calculated, and then it will be used to update the factor $\boldsymbol{A}$.

Note that the matrix $\boldsymbol{A}$ is updated sequentially, hence it can be represented by $\boldsymbol{A}_{(t)}$ for each t. Hence, the model (3) can be regarded as:

$$\forall t : \boldsymbol{y}_t = \boldsymbol{A}_{(t)} \boldsymbol{x}_t \tag{4}$$

or in the the the continuous-time representation as:

$$\boldsymbol{y}(t) = \boldsymbol{A}(t)\boldsymbol{x}(t). \tag{5}$$

It resembles the continuous NMF which was given in [11] but in our approach, we use different computational methods to update the time-varying factors.

3   Algorithms

Assuming the residual error is normally distributed with a zero-mean, the objective function can be expressed by the squared Euclidean distance: $\Psi(\boldsymbol{Y}\|\boldsymbol{A}\boldsymbol{X}) = \frac{1}{2}\|\boldsymbol{Y}-\boldsymbol{A}\boldsymbol{X}\|_F^2$. The problem (1) can be split into T independent LS subproblems. Considering the same assumption in estimation of $\boldsymbol{x}_t$ from (4), we have:

$$\boldsymbol{x}_t = \arg\min_{\mathbf{x}} \frac{1}{2}\|\boldsymbol{y}_t - \boldsymbol{A}_{(t)}\boldsymbol{x}\|_2^2, \quad \text{s.t.} \quad \boldsymbol{x} \geq \boldsymbol{0}. \tag{6}$$

When a new sample $\boldsymbol{y}_t$ arrives, the corresponding encoding vector $\boldsymbol{x}_t$ can be updated by applying any nonnegative least squares (NNLS) solver [10] to the problem (6). In the experiments, we used the active-set method.

A more challenging problem is to update $\boldsymbol{A}_{(t)}$ with only one pair of vectors $\{\boldsymbol{y}_t, \boldsymbol{x}_t\}$. Replacing $\boldsymbol{A}$ with $\boldsymbol{A}_{(t)}$ in (3), and applying the transpose operator, we get:

$$\begin{bmatrix} \boldsymbol{X}_{(t-1)}^T \\ \boldsymbol{x}_t^T \end{bmatrix} \boldsymbol{A}_{(t)}^T = \begin{bmatrix} \boldsymbol{Y}_{(t-1)}^T \\ \boldsymbol{y}_t^T \end{bmatrix}. \tag{7}$$

In an geometric approach, each row of (7) determines one hyperplane in $\mathbb{R}^J$, and the pair $\{\boldsymbol{y}_t, \boldsymbol{x}_t\}$ adds a new hyperplane to the overdetermined system of $t-1$ linear equations. The matrix $\boldsymbol{A}_{(t)}$ should be updated only with this new hyperplane. In what follows, we consider various computational strategies to tackle this problem.

3.1   Row-Action Projections

Let $\underline{\boldsymbol{a}}_i^{(t)} \in \mathbb{R}^{1\times J}$ be the i-th row of $\boldsymbol{A}_{(t)}$. Note that the system (7) can be rewritten as: $\begin{bmatrix} \boldsymbol{X}_{(t-1)}^T \\ \boldsymbol{x}_t^T \end{bmatrix} \left(\underline{\boldsymbol{a}}_i^{(t)}\right)^T = \begin{bmatrix} [y_{i,1:t-1}]^T \\ y_{it} \end{bmatrix}$ for $i = 1,\ldots,I$. To update the solution $\underline{\boldsymbol{a}}_i^{(t)}$ with the last equation in (7), the previous approximate $\underline{\boldsymbol{a}}_i^{(t-1)}$ can be mapped onto the hyperplane determined by the normal vector $\boldsymbol{x}_t$ in $\mathbb{R}_+^J$. The affine mapping is given by $P^{(t)} : \mathbb{R}^J \to \mathbb{R}^J$:

$$P^{(t)}\left((\underline{\boldsymbol{a}}_i^{(t-1)})^T\right) = \left(\underline{\boldsymbol{a}}_i^{(t-1)}\right)^T + \frac{y_{it} - \underline{\boldsymbol{a}}_i^{(t-1)}\boldsymbol{x}_t}{\|\boldsymbol{x}_t\|_2^2}\boldsymbol{x}_t. \tag{8}$$

To enforce the nonnegativity, the point $P^{(t)}\left((\underline{\boldsymbol{a}}_i^{(t-1)})^T\right)$ is projected onto the nonnegative orthant $\mathbb{R}_+^J$, which leads to the updating rule:

$$\left(\underline{\boldsymbol{a}}_i^{(t)}\right)^T = P_\Omega\left(P^{(t)}\left((\underline{\boldsymbol{a}}_i^{(t-1)})^T\right)\right) \in \mathbb{R}_+^J, \tag{9}$$

where $P_\Omega(\xi) = \max\{0, \xi\}$.

Note that the mapping (8) is independent on i. Hence, it can be simultaneously applied to all the rows of $\boldsymbol{A}_{(t)}$:

$$\boldsymbol{A}_{(t)} = P_\Omega \left(\boldsymbol{A}_{(t-1)} + \frac{\boldsymbol{y}_t - \boldsymbol{A}_{(t-1)}\boldsymbol{x}_t}{||\boldsymbol{x}_t||_2^2} \boldsymbol{x}_t^T \right). \tag{10}$$

Let $\bar{\boldsymbol{A}}$ be the matrix of features that are estimated from initial samples using any standard NMF algorithm. The update for $\boldsymbol{A}_{(t)}$ can therefore be expressed by the recurrence formula:

$$\boldsymbol{A}_{(t)} = P_\Omega P^{(t)} P_\Omega P^{(t-1)} \ldots P_\Omega P^{(1)} (\bar{\boldsymbol{A}}). \tag{11}$$

If $\Omega = \mathbb{R}^{I \times J}$, $\forall t : \boldsymbol{X}_{(t-1)} = \boldsymbol{X}$, $\underline{\boldsymbol{y}}_t^T \in R(\boldsymbol{X}_{(t-1)}^T)$, then according to [20], $\lim_{t \to \infty} \boldsymbol{A}_{(t)}^T = P_N(\bar{\boldsymbol{A}}^T) + \boldsymbol{G}\underline{\boldsymbol{y}}_t^T$, where $R(\boldsymbol{Z})$ is the range of $\boldsymbol{Z}$, $P_N(\cdot)$ is the orthogonal projection onto the nullspace of $\boldsymbol{X}^T$, and $\boldsymbol{G}$ is the pseudoinverse of $\boldsymbol{X}^T$. Hence, if the system (7) is consistent and $P_N(\bar{\boldsymbol{A}}^T) = \emptyset$, the approximations in (11) are convergent to a LS solution. In our case, $\Omega = \mathbb{R}_+^{I \times J}$. One can suppose that such approximations lead to a NNLS solution according to the KKT condition (nested projections onto the nonnegative orthant), but further research is needed to explain this supposition.

Regarding elementary multiplication operations, a computational complexity of (10) for each t can be estimated as $O(IJ)$.

3.2   Rank-One Least Squares

One of the most known computational strategies for solving NMF problems is the Alternating Least Squares (ALS) algorithm [10]. Below we propose the modified ALS in which one factor is only rank-one updated. To estimate $\boldsymbol{A}_{(t)}$, the system (7) is transformed to the normal equations:

$$(\boldsymbol{X}_{(t-1)}\boldsymbol{X}_{(t-1)}^T + \boldsymbol{x}_t\boldsymbol{x}_t^T)\boldsymbol{A}_{(t)}^T = \boldsymbol{X}_{(t-1)}\boldsymbol{Y}_{(t-1)}^T + \boldsymbol{x}_t\boldsymbol{y}_t^T. \tag{12}$$

Let $\boldsymbol{M}_{(t-1)} = \boldsymbol{X}_{(t-1)}\boldsymbol{X}_{(t-1)}^T$ and $\boldsymbol{N}_{(t-1)} = \boldsymbol{X}_{(t-1)}\boldsymbol{Y}_{(t-1)}^T$. Since $\forall t \geq 1$: $\boldsymbol{M}_{(t-1)} = \boldsymbol{M}_{(t-2)} + \boldsymbol{x}_{t-1}\boldsymbol{x}_{t-1}^T$ and $\boldsymbol{N}_{(t-1)} = \boldsymbol{N}_{(t-1)} + \boldsymbol{x}_{t-1}\boldsymbol{y}_{t-1}^T$, it is therefore obvious that it can be expressed by:

$$\boldsymbol{M}_{(t)}\boldsymbol{A}_{(t)}^T = \boldsymbol{N}_{(t)}. \tag{13}$$

Considering $\boldsymbol{M}_{(t)} = \boldsymbol{M}_{(t)}^T$, the update for $\boldsymbol{A}_{(t)}$ can be expressed by: $\boldsymbol{A}_{(t)} = \boldsymbol{N}_{(t)}^T \boldsymbol{M}_{(t)}^{-1}$. Because $\text{rank}(\boldsymbol{x}_t\boldsymbol{x}_t^T) = 1$, the inverse to $\boldsymbol{M}_{(t)}$ can be computed by applying the Sherman-Morrison formula:

$$\boldsymbol{A}_{(t)} = \boldsymbol{N}_{(t)}^T \left(\boldsymbol{M}_{(t-1)}^{-1} - \frac{\boldsymbol{w}_t\boldsymbol{w}_t^T}{1 + \boldsymbol{x}_t^T\boldsymbol{w}_t} \right), \tag{14}$$

where $\boldsymbol{w}_t = \boldsymbol{M}_{(t-1)}^{-1}\boldsymbol{x}_t$. The inverse to $\boldsymbol{M}_{(t)}$ is updated according to the rule: $\boldsymbol{M}_{(t)}^{-1} = \boldsymbol{M}_{(t-1)}^{-1} - \frac{\boldsymbol{w}_t\boldsymbol{w}_t^T}{1 + \boldsymbol{x}_t^T\boldsymbol{w}_t}$. To enforce the nonnegativity, a simple projection onto the nonnegative orthant is imposed: $\boldsymbol{A}_{(t)} \leftarrow P_\Omega(\boldsymbol{A}_{(t)})$. Unfortunately, it does not guarantee the update satisfies the KKT optimality conditions.

The computational complexity of the updating rule (14) can be approximated by $O(IJ + J^2)$, which leads to $O(IJ)$ for $I >> J$.

3.3 Proximal Gradients

We assumed the objective function $\Psi(\boldsymbol{Y}\|\boldsymbol{AX})$ is differentiable and convex with respect to $\boldsymbol{A}$ or $\boldsymbol{X}$ (but not jointly). Let

$$F(\boldsymbol{A}, \hat{\boldsymbol{A}}_{(t-1)}) = \Psi(\boldsymbol{Y}\|\hat{\boldsymbol{A}}_{(t-1)}\boldsymbol{X}_{(t)}) + \langle \boldsymbol{G}(\hat{\boldsymbol{A}}_{(t-1)}), \boldsymbol{A} - \hat{\boldsymbol{A}}_{(t-1)}\rangle + \frac{\hat{L}_A}{2}\|\boldsymbol{A} - \hat{\boldsymbol{A}}_{(t-1)}\|_F^2$$

be the majorization function for $\Psi(\boldsymbol{Y}\|\boldsymbol{AX}_{(t)})$, where $\boldsymbol{G}(\boldsymbol{A}) = \nabla_{\boldsymbol{A}}\Psi(\boldsymbol{Y}\|\boldsymbol{AX}_{(t)})$ and $\hat{L}_A$ is upper bounded by the the Lipschitz constant L_A of $\Psi(\boldsymbol{Y}\|\boldsymbol{AX}_{(t)})$. For the Euclidean function, $L_A = \|\boldsymbol{X}_{(t)}\boldsymbol{X}_{(t)}^T\|_2$. The problem (2) can be reformulated as:

$$\boldsymbol{A}_{(t)} = \arg\min_{\boldsymbol{A}} \left\{ F(\boldsymbol{A}, \hat{\boldsymbol{A}}_{(t-1)}) + h(\boldsymbol{A}) \right\} = \mathrm{prox}_h(\hat{\boldsymbol{A}}_{(t-1)}), \qquad (15)$$

where $\mathrm{prox}_h(\hat{\boldsymbol{A}}_{(t-1)})$ is the proximal mapping of the convex but unnecessarily differentiable function $h(\cdot)$ at $\hat{\boldsymbol{A}}_{(t-1)}$. To enforce the nonnegativity, let $h(\boldsymbol{A}) = I_\Omega(\boldsymbol{A})$ be an indicator function on the set Ω. The solution to (15) is therefore given by the updating rule:

$$\boldsymbol{A}_{(t)} = P_\Omega\left(\hat{\boldsymbol{A}}_{(t-1)} - L_A^{-1}\boldsymbol{G}(\hat{\boldsymbol{A}}_{(t-1)})\right). \qquad (16)$$

To accelerate the convergence, the approximation $\hat{\boldsymbol{A}}_{(t-1)}$ is computed by the Nesterov's extrapolation rule [19]: $\hat{\boldsymbol{A}}_{(t-1)} = \boldsymbol{A}_{(t-1)} + \beta_t(\boldsymbol{A}_{(t-1)} - \boldsymbol{A}_{(t-2)})$, where $\beta_t = \frac{\gamma_{t-1}-1}{\gamma_t}$, and γ_t is a positive root to $(\gamma_t)^2 - \gamma_t - (\gamma_{t-1})^2 = 0$.

For the Euclidean function: $\boldsymbol{G}(\boldsymbol{A}) = \boldsymbol{AXX}^T - \boldsymbol{YX}^T$. Considering the model (7) and the Eq. (12), the gradient $\boldsymbol{G}(\boldsymbol{A}_{(t)})$ can be expressed by:

$$\boldsymbol{G}(\boldsymbol{A}_{(t)}) = \boldsymbol{A}_{(t)}\left(\boldsymbol{M}_{(t-1)} + \boldsymbol{x}_t\boldsymbol{x}_t^T\right) - \boldsymbol{N}_{(t-1)} - \boldsymbol{y}_t\boldsymbol{x}_t^T = \boldsymbol{A}_{(t)}\boldsymbol{M}_{(t)} - \boldsymbol{N}_{(t)}. (17)$$

Hence, it can be updated for each t with only two rank-one matrices. Regarding the matrix-matrix product $\boldsymbol{A}_{(t)}\boldsymbol{M}_{(t)}$, the computational complexity of the gradient amounts to $O(IJ^2)$. This version of the Proximal Gradient (PG) method will be referred to as PG-ONMF.

The gradient updating rule (17) can be further rewritten to the form:

$$\boldsymbol{G}_{(t)} = \boldsymbol{G}_{(t-1)} - \boldsymbol{r}_t\boldsymbol{x}_t^T, \qquad (18)$$

where $\boldsymbol{r}_t = \boldsymbol{y}_t - \hat{\boldsymbol{A}}_{(t-1)}\boldsymbol{x}_t$ is a residual vector. Moreover, the Lipschitz constant L_A can be also dynamically updated by the approximate Frobenious-based rule:

$$L_{(t)} = \sqrt{L_{(t-1)} + 2\sum_{k,l} m_{kl}^{(t-1)}x_{kt}^{(t-1)}x_{lt}^{(t-1)} + \sum_{k,l}(x_{kt}^{(t-1)}x_{lt}^{(t-1)})^2}, \qquad (19)$$

where $\boldsymbol{M}_{(t-1)} = [m_{kl}^{(t-1)}]$, $\boldsymbol{X}_{(t-1)} = [x_{k,t-1}^{(t-1)}]$, and $L_{(t-1)} = \|\boldsymbol{X}_{(t-1)} \boldsymbol{X}_{(t-1)}^T\|_F^2$. The update rules (18) and (19), combined with (16) will be denoted by MPG-ONMF.

4   Experiments

The proposed algorithms have been tested on the benchmark of original signals, selected from the dataset $AC10\_art\_spectr\_noi$ that is distributed with the *NMFLAB for Signal Processing* [10]. It is a Matlab toolbox designed for testing NMF algorithms. We selected 8 spectral signals, from which 4 pairs of the signals were created. Four time-varying features are obtained by interpolating the signals in each pair. This approach aims to simulate slowly-varying nonstationary spectral signals or other nonstationary multidimensional streaming data, which can be found in many spectroscopic techniques. For example, the Raman spectra of the specimen whose properties change with time or temperature. The time-varying features that are used in the experiments are illustrated in Fig. 1. Their spectral resolution is limited to 200 bands, i.e. $I = 200$. The discussed algorithms are designed for processing an unlimited number of streaming samples. However, to evaluate the quality of the estimates versus time and their computational complexity, we analyze the sampled signals with $T = 10^4, 10^5, 10^6$.

The time-varying linear mixtures $\boldsymbol{Y} \in \mathbb{R}^{I \times T}$ are created according to the model (4). The entries of the mixing matrix $\boldsymbol{X} \in \mathbb{R}_+^{4 \times T}$ were generated randomly

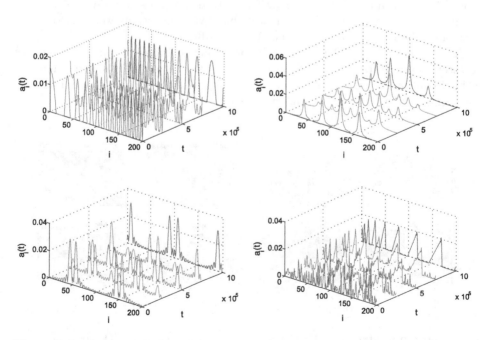

Fig. 1. Four time-varying spectral features $\{a_{ijt}\}$, where: t - time instant, i - wavelength index, $j = 1, \ldots, 4$ - index of the feature.

Table 1. Runtime [in s] and mean-SIR values [dB] for estimating the whole time-window features in A and the factor X. The number of observed samples is T. We cannot apply MUE to $T = 10^7$ due to the RAM demand exceeds the limit of 512GB.

Algorithm	$T = 10^5$			$T = 10^6$			$T = 10^7$		
	SIR_A	SIR_X	Time	SIR_A	SIR_X	Time	SIR_A	SIR_X	Time
MUE	7.2	4.89	439.7	2.02	5.03	4443	–	–	–
RO-LS	5.48	9.75	93.1	5.46	9.8	880.2	5.5	9.9	10639
PG-ONMF	5.48	9.81	109.8	5.48	9.88	1057	5.5	9.96	12303
MPG-ONMF	16.94	27.02	107.8	16.94	27.19	1043	16.98	28.48	12237
RAP-ONMF	17.03	28.18	82.6	17.03	28.1	753.2	17.1	29.6	9076

from a normal distribution $\mathcal{N}(0,1)$, and then the negative entries are replaced with a zero-value. The columns with all-zero entries were removed.

To estimate the matrices A and X from Y we used the following algorithms: MUE – the standard Lee-Seung algorithm [9] for minimizing the Euclidean distance, RO-LS – rank-one least-squares (see Sect. 3.2), PG-ONMF – proximal gradient ONMF (see Sect. 3.3), MPG-ONMF – modified proximal gradient ONMF (see Sect. 3.3), and RAP-ONMF – row-action projection ONMF (see Sect. 3.1). All the tested algorithms were initialized by the same random initializer generated from an uniform distribution. To analyze the efficiency of the discussed methods, 10 Monte Carlo (MC) runs of the NMF algorithms were performed, each time the initial matrices A and X were different.

The performance of the discussed algorithms was evaluated with the Signal-to-Interference Ratio (SIR) [10] between the estimates and the true signals. Table 1 contains the mean-SIR values and the runtime [in seconds] for estimating the time-varying features (the matrices $A_{(t)}$) and the mixing matrix X.

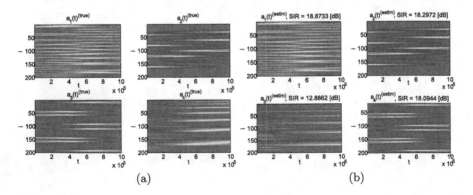

Fig. 2. 2D representations of four time-varying features $\{a_1(t), a_2(t), a_3(t), a_4(t)\} \in \mathbb{R}^I$: (a) original; (b) estimated with RAP-ONMF (SIR values included in the titles)

Figure 2 illustrates 2D representations of four time-varying features $a_1(t)$, $a_2(t)$, $a_3(t)$, $a_4(t) \in \mathbb{R}^I$, estimated by RAP-ONMF.

5 Conclusions

In this paper, we analyze a few computational strategies based on the on-line NMF model for extracting time-varying nonnegative features from multidimensional streaming data. The proposed ONMF algorithms are tested on the synthetic data that simulate a time-varying linear mixture of nonstationary spectral signals. The results demonstrate that the best performance can be obtained by RAP-ONMF (see Fig. 2 and Table 1). The second best algorithm is MPG-ONMF. Unfortunately, RO-LS and PG-ONMF give much worse results. The difference between PG-ONMF and MPG-ONMF may result from the way of computing the Lipschitz constant. To save time, this parameter in PG-ONMF is set to the initial constant value for all time instances, whereas it changes adaptively in MPG-ONMF. RO-LS does not assure a monotonic convergence, and this fact may also strongly affect the performance. RAP-ONMF has the lowest computational complexity, and this statement is also confirmed by the runtime shown in Table 1.

Summing up, we proposed efficient algorithms for extracting time-varying nonnegative features from multidimensional streaming data. Further research is needed to deeply analyze the numerical properties of RAP-ONMF.

Acknowledgments. This work was partially supported by the grant 2015/17/B/ST6/01865 funded by National Science Center (NCN) in Poland. Calculations have been carried out in Wroclaw Centre for Networking and Supercomputing, grant no. 127.

References

1. Gray, M.S., Movellan, J.R., Sejnowski, T.J.: Dynamic features for visual speechreading: a systematic comparison. In: Mozer, M.C., Jordan, M.I., Petsche, T. (eds.) Advances in Neural Information Processing Systems (NIPS), vol. 9, pp. 751–757. Morgan-Kaufmann, San Fransisco (1997)
2. Nash, J.M., Carter, J.N., Nixon, M.S.: Dynamic feature extraction via the velocity Hough transform. Pattern Recogn. Lett. **18**(10), 1035–1047 (1997)
3. Puentes, J., Roux, C., Garreau, M., Coatrieux, J.L.: Dynamic feature extraction of coronary artery motion using DSA image sequences. IEEE Trans. Med. Imaging **17**(6), 857–871 (1998)
4. Caban, J., Joshi, A., Rheingans, P.: Texture-based feature tracking for effective time-varying data visualization. IEEE Trans. Visual Comput. Graph. **13**(6), 1472–1479 (2007)
5. Daza-Santacoloma, G., Arias-Londono, J.D., Godino-Llorente, J.I., Saenz-Lechon, N., Osma-Ruiz, V., Castellanos-Dominguez, G.: Dynamic feature extraction: an application to voice pathology detection. Intell. Autom. Soft Comput. **15**(4), 667–682 (2009)

6. Nguyen, K.T., Ropinski, T.: Feature tracking in time-varying volumetric data through scale invariant feature transform. In: Unger, J., Ropinski, T. (eds.) Proceedings of the SIGRAD 2013, Norrkping, Sweden, 13–14 June 2013, pp. 11–16. Linkping University Electronic Press (2013)
7. Bharath, R.R., Thanigaivel, K., Alfahath, A., Prasanth, T.: Feature extraction based dynamic recommendation for analogous users. Int. J. Comput. Sci. Inf. Technol. **5**(2), 1358–1362 (2014)
8. Strubell, E., Vilnis, L., Silverstein, K., McCallum, A.: Learning dynamic feature selection for fast sequential prediction. In: Proceedings of the 53rd Annual Meeting of the Association for Computational Linguistics and 7th International Joint Conference on Natural Language Processing, Beijing, China, 26–31 July 2015, pp. 146–155 (2015)
9. Lee, D.D., Seung, H.S.: Learning the parts of objects by non-negative matrix factorization. Nature **401**, 788–791 (1999)
10. Cichocki, A., Zdunek, R., Phan, A.H., Amari, S.I.: Nonnegative Matrix and Tensor Factorizations: Applications to Exploratory Multi-way Data Analysis and Blind Source Separation. Wiley, Chichester (2009)
11. Omlor, L., Slotine, J.J.E.: Continuous non-negative matrix factorization for time-dependent data. In: Proceedings of the EUSIPCO 2009, pp. 1928–1932 (2009)
12. Cao, B., Shen, D., Sun, J.T., Wang, X., Yang, Q., Chen, Z.: Detect and track latent factors with online nonnegative matrix factorization. In: Proceedings of the International Joint Conference on Artificial Intelligence (IJCAI), Hyderabad, India, 6–12 January 2007, pp. 2689–2694 (2007)
13. Wang, F., Tan, C., Konig, A.C., Li, P.: Efficient document clustering via online nonnegative matrix factorizations. In: Proceedings of the 11th SIAM Conference on Data Mining, pp. 908–919. SIAM/Omnipress (2011)
14. Lefevre, A., Bach, F., Fvotte, C.: Online algorithms for nonnegative matrix factorization with the Itakura-Saito divergence. In: 2011 IEEE Workshop on Applications of Signal Processing to Audio and Acoustics (WASPAA), pp. 313–316. IEEE (2011)
15. Zhou, G., Yang, Z., Xie, S., Yang, J.M.: Online blind source separation using incremental nonnegative matrix factorization with volume constraint. IEEE Trans. Neural Netw. **22**(4), 550–560 (2011)
16. Mairal, J., Bach, F., Ponce, J., Sapiro, G.: Online learning for matrix factorization and sparse coding. J. Mach. Learn. Res. **11**, 19–60 (2010)
17. Zdunek, R.: Row-action projections for nonnegative matrix factorization. In: Wermter, S., Weber, C., Duch, W., Honkela, T., Koprinkova-Hristova, P., Magg, S., Palm, G., Villa, A.E.P. (eds.) ICANN 2014. LNCS, vol. 8681, pp. 299–306. Springer, Heidelberg (2014)
18. Kaczmarz, S.: Angenaherte Auflosung von Systemen linearer Gleichungen. Bulletin de lAcademie Polonaise des Sciences et Lettres **A35**, 355–357 (1937)
19. Zdunek, R., He, Z.: Nesterov's iterations for NMF-based supervised classification of texture patterns. In: Theis, F., Cichocki, A., Yeredor, A., Zibulevsky, M. (eds.) LVA/ICA 2012. LNCS, vol. 7191, pp. 478–485. Springer, Heidelberg (2012)
20. Tanabe, K.: Projection method for solving a singular system of linear equations and its applications. Numer. Math. **17**, 203–214 (1971)

Author Index

Printed in the United States
by Bookmasters

Printed in the United States
By Bookmasters